PART FOUR Using Punctuation and Mechanics 417
■ ■ ■ ■ ■ ■ ■

PART SEVEN Writing When English Is Not Your First Language 837
■ ■ ■ ■ ■ ■ ■

PART THREE Understanding Grammar and Writing Correct Sentences 285
■ ■ ■ ■ ■ ■ ■ ■

■ ■ ■ ■ ■ ■ ■

Simon & Schuster
Handbook for Writers

NINTH EDITION

LYNN QUITMAN TROYKA

DOUGLAS HESSE

Upper Saddle River, NJ 07458

Library of Congress Cataloging-in-Publication Data
Troyka, Lynn Quitman
  Simon & Schuster handbook for writers / Lynn Quitman Troyka, Douglas Hesse. — 9th ed.
    p. cm.
  Includes index.
  ISBN-10: 0-13-602860-8
  ISBN-13: 978-0-13-602860-4
  1. English language—Rhetoric—Handbooks, manuals, etc. 2. English language—
Grammar—Handbooks, manuals, etc. 3. Report writing—Handbooks, manuals, etc.
I. Hesse, Douglas Dean. II. Title. III. Title: Simon and Schuster handbook for writers.
IV. Title: Handbook for writers.
  PE1408.T696 2009
  808'.042—dc22

                                                           2008037198

VP/Editorial Director: Leah Jewell
Editor in Chief: Craig Campanella
Executive Editor: Kevin Molloy
Project Manager, Editorial: Jessica A. Kupetz
Editorial Assistant: David Nitti
VP/Director of Marketing: Tim Stookesbury
Executive Marketing Manager:
  Megan Galvin-Fak
Senior Marketing Manager: Susan E. Stoudt
Marketing Assistant: Sara Fry
Text Permissions Specialist: Jane Scelta
Development Editor in Chief: Rochelle Diogenes
Development Editor: Paul Sarkis
Permissions Assistant: Peggy Davis
Senior Operations Specialist: Sherry Lewis
Manager, Image Rights and Permissions:
  Zina Arabia

Manager, Visual Research: Beth Brenzel
Image Permissions Coordinator:
  Ang'John Ferreri
Image Researcher: Beth Brenzel
Senior Art Director: Nancy Wells
Art Director: Anne Nieglos
Interior and Cover Designer: Anne DeMarinis
Cover Art:"Mulberry Tree" 1889 by Vincent Van
  Gogh © The Gallery Collection/Corbis
Full-Service Project Management: Karen Berry,
  Pine Tree Composition, Inc.
Copyeditor: Steve Hopkins
Composition: Pine Tree Composition, Inc.
Printer/Binder: Courier Companies
Cover Printer: Phoenix Color Corporation
Text Font: 10/12 Adobe Garamond

Microsoft® and Windows® are registered trademarks of the Microsoft Corporation in the USA and other countries. Screen shots and icons are reprinted with permission from the Microsoft Corporation.

This book is not sponsored or endorsed by or affiliated with the Microsoft Corporation.

For permission to use copyrighted material, grateful acknowledgment is made to the copyright holders on pages 907–911, which are considered an extension of this copyright page.

Pearson Education Ltd., London
Pearson Education Singapore, Pte. Ltd
Pearson Education Canada, Inc.
Pearson Education–Japan
Pearson Education Australia PTY, Limited

Pearson Education North Asia, Ltd., Hong Kong
Pearson Educación de Mexico, S.A. de C.V.
Pearson Education Malaysia, Pte. Ltd.
Pearson Education, Upper Saddle River,
  New Jersey

Prentice Hall
is an imprint of

PEARSON

www.pearsonhighered.com

10 9 8 7 6 5 4 3 2

                                            ISBN-13:
                                      978-0-13-602860-4

                                            ISBN-10:
                                       0-13-602860-8

Why Do You Need This New Edition?

The *Simon & Schuster Handbook for Writers* has been revised to provide more useful instruction and examples for writing students and instructors. Some of the helpful features that you'll find only in the new edition are:

❶ **The most up-to-date coverage of documentation styles:** this ninth edition features the most current standards for MLA and APA documentation, which you'll need in first-year composition as well as in many courses in your field of study.

❷ **New and revised Quick Reference boxes** highlight the most important must-have concepts for easy use. These are key to finding the information you need in the handbook.

❸ **New** Chapters 2 and 7, **"Essential Processes for Academic Writing"** and **"Strategies for Writing Typical Kinds of College Papers,"** give not only general

writing advice but also specific strategies for producing the most common types of academic writing in first-year composition and other courses. (This makes the ninth edition a great resource for any class, not just first-year composition.)

❹ **New** Chapters 43 and 44, **"Business and Professional Writing"** and **"Writing for the Public,"** are great resources for writing outside of your classroom, whether you are creating **resumés, cover letters**, or **personal Web sites**.

❺ The book's **exercises**, which are popular as assignments for many instructors, have been thoroughly revised.

❻ **Coverage and support for writing with new media** includes making oral presentations and using multimedia, document and visual design, and using audio and video.

❼ A **new** Chapter 8, **"Style and Tone in Writing,"** illustrates the importance of *how* you say something in addition to *what* you say.

HOW TO USE THE SIMON & SCHUSTER HANDBOOK FOR WRITERS

The *Simon & Schuster Handbook for Writers* is designed to help you find what you need to become a better writer. You will find many features intended to highlight key concepts and develop your skills. We are confident that you will find the *Simon & Schuster Handbook for Writers* to be a useful tool for you throughout college and beyond.

- **The detailed Overview of Contents** starting on the inside front cover lists all parts and chapters in the book. Locate the specific topic you need to reference and then turn to the page indicated.
- **MyCompLab®**
- A list of **supplementary material** available with this book can be found in the Preface.
- **Quick Reference boxes**, found throughout the text, highlight some of the most important issues that will come up as you write. You will also find them listed by subject in the Index.
- **Documentation Source Maps** are designed to clearly illustrate the process for citing different types of sources. Annotated replications of original sources are presented along with step-by-step guidelines. Color is used carefully to help students see where information is pulled from a source and then where it is placed in a citation.
- **The Terms Glossary** is an easy way to find the definitions for common writing-related terms. Words and phrases called out in SMALL CAPITAL LETTERS throughout the book can be found in the Terms Glossary.
- **The Index** provides quick and convenient navigation by topic, covering virtually everything in the book. Quick Reference boxes are also listed in the Index according to the topic they refer to.
- **The one-of-a-kind Quick Card** at the end of the book puts some of the most useful information on research and documentation in a portable format. Take the card to class, to the writing lab, or to the library for easy access to invaluable information.
- **A list of Proofreading Marks and Response Symbols** is provided on the inside back cover. Consult this list if your instructor uses revision and proofreading symbols when commenting on your writing.

The sample composite page to the right illustrates features that help you navigate the *Simon & Schuster Handbook for Writers*.

Quick Reference 15.7 ■ ■ ■ ■ ■ ■ ■

Forms of the verbs *do* and *have*

SIMPLE FORM	do	have
-S FORM	does	has
PAST TENSE	did	had
PRESENT PARTICIPLE	doing	having
PAST PARTICIPLE	done	had

Quick Reference boxes high- light key information.

🔴 **Alert:** In SMALL CAPS ACADEMIC WRITING, always use the standard forms for *be, do,* and *have,* as shown in Quick References 15.6 and 15.7.

The gym **is** [not *be*] a busy place.
The gym **is** [not *be*] filling with spectators. ●

Alerts call attention to important rules and best practices.

End of Alert

🔵 **ESOL Tip:** When *be, do,* and *have* function as auxiliary verbs, change their form to agree with a third-person singular subject—and don't add *-s* to the main verb.

NO   **Does** the library **closes** at 6:00?
YES   **Does** the library **close** at 6:00? ●

ESOL icons call out infor- mation of particular use for multilingual students.

End of ESOL Tip

EXERCISE 15-4   Using the auxiliary verbs in the list below, fill in the blanks in the following passage. Use each auxiliary word only once, even if a listed word can fit into more than one blank. For help, consult 15e.

are   have   may   will   might   can   has

EXAMPLE   Completing a marathon <u>can</u> be the highlight of a runner's life.

(1) The marathon _____ been a challenging and important athletic event since the 19th century. (2) Athletes who _____ training for a marathon _____ use one of the many online training guides. (3) Run- ning with a partner or friend _____ boost confidence and motivation.

Exercises for practice and skill building are offered throughout the text.

Indicates new section of a chapter

15f   What are intransitive and transitive verbs?

A verb is **intransitive** when an OBJECT isn't required to complete the verb's meaning: *I sing.* A verb is **transitive** when an object is necessary to complete the verb's meaning: *I need a guitar.* Many verbs have both transitive and intran- sitive meanings. Some verbs are only transitive: *need, have, like, owe, remember.* Only transitive verbs function in the PASSIVE VOICE. Dictionaries label verbs as transitive (*vt*) or intransitive (*vi*).

Small capitals call out Glossary key terms; these terms are also discussed in depth elsewhere in the text.

For more help with your writing, grammar, and research, go to **www.mycomplab.com**

mycomp lab ▌

A wealth of writing resources is available through MyCompLab.

ESSENTIAL FEATURES OF THE *SIMON & SCHUSTER* HANDBOOK FOR WRITERS

The *Simon & Schuster Handbook for Writers* is an indispensable tool for your composition course, but you'll find that it is full of information that you'll need for writing throughout college and beyond.

College writing. New Chapters 2 and 7, "Essential Processes for Academic Writing" and "Strategies for Writing Typical Kinds of College Papers," guide you not only through the writing process but also offer specific instruction for the most common types of academic writing in any of your college courses.

7e.3 Lab reports and empirical studies

A **lab report** is a specific and formal way of presenting and discussing the results of experiments or laboratory measurements, in fields such as chemistry, biology, physics, engineering, and other sciences. Lab experiments are one kind of **empirical research**, a name that generally refers to attempts to measure something (from physical substances to behaviors) in order to prove or disprove a theory or hypothesis. Disciplines other than the sciences use experiments, too; among them are psychology and other social sciences, some areas of education (for example, "Does this teaching strategy work better than that teaching strategy?"), economics, and so on. However, those disciplines also use sources like surveys or very specific observations to collect data. Both lab reports and other kinds of empirical research studies tend to have the same standard elements.

Important Sections of Lab Reports and Similar Empirical Studies

* **Introduction.** State your purpose, present background materials (for example, a review of previous studies), and your hypothesis.

Writing outside the classroom. New Chapters 43 and 44, "Business and Professional Writing" and "Writing for the Public," give you essential guidance for resumés and cover letters, memos, and reports.

Quick Reference 43.4

Guidelines for writing a resumé

* Place your name, address, e-mail address, and telephone number at the top. If you have a professional Web site or online PORTFOLIO (Chapter 47), include the URL.

* Make sure you have a professional e-mail address. No employer will be impressed by beermaster@gmail.com or daddyslittlegirl@hotmail.com.

* Make it easy to read. Label the sections clearly, and target the resumé to the position you want. Help employers see your most significant attributes as quickly and as easily as possible.

* Adjust your resumé to fit your PURPOSE. For example, if you're applying for a job as a computer programmer, you'll want to emphasize different facts than you would if you're applying for a job selling computers in an electronics store.

* Use headings to separate blocks of information. Include the following headings, as appropriate: Position Desired or Career Objective; Educa-

continued >>

Documentation chapters. Chapters 36–38 present everything you'll need throughout college when writing any research paper. MLA documentation reflects the anticipated 2009 updates to MLA style as outlined in the third edition of the *MLA Style Manual and Guide to Scholarly Publishing.* APA documentation, used in

39. Online Version of a Print Magazine Article—MLA
The example below is for the online version of the same article cited in 25, above. In addition to the print information, include the date you accessed the online version. (If the page numbers from the print version are available, include them, too, before the access date.)

Fallows, James. "The $1.4 Trillion Question." *The Atlantic.com.* Atlantic Monthly Group, Jan.-Feb. 2008. Web. 2 May 2008.

If the article is unsigned, begin with the title.

"Too Smart to Marry." *The Atlantic.com.* Atlantic Monthly Group, 14 Apr. 2005. Web. 7 Mar. 2005.

40. Online Version of a Print Journal Article—MLA
Hoge, Charles W., et al. "Mild Traumatic Brain Injury in U.S. Soldiers Returning from Iraq." *New England Journal of Medicine* 358.5 (31 Jan. 2008): 453-63. Web. 10 Sept. 2008.

the social sciences, reflects the latest (2007) guidelines for electronic sources. CSE documentation, for science and engineering, is completely updated to reflect the latest (2006) guidelines.

Writing with new media. Chapter 42, "Making Presentations and Using Multimedia," explains how and why to use tools like PowerPoint for presentations, and Chapter 46, "Multimodal Texts and Writing for the Web," teaches you how to create Web sites and other digital texts that incorporate not only images but also sound and video.

Extensive help for speakers of other languages. Part 7 is devoted to presenting English to nonnative speakers of English. Going beyond just the basics of grammar, this part of the book will help you understand what your instructors expect from your writing as well as giving you specific help with understanding the many rules of the English language.

MyCompLab. The new MyCompLab uniquely integrates proven resources and new assessment tools with a student's own writing. This seamless and flexible application, built for writers by writers, will help instructors and students accomplish everyday composition tasks more easily and effectively.

To David, the love of my life

LYNN QUITMAN TROYKA

To Don and Coral Hesse

DOUG HESSE

Personal Message to Students

FROM LYNN QUITMAN TROYKA AND DOUG HESSE

As writers, many of you have much in common with both of us. Sure, we've been at it longer, so we've had more practice, and most rules have become cemented in our heads. However, we share with you a common goal: to put ideas into words worthy of someone else's reading time.

We also share the constant desire to become better writers. Given our extensive teaching experience, this probably sounds odd. However, writing is a lifelong enterprise. Just as we did, you'll write not only in composition classes, but also in other courses throughout college. Writing will likely be an important part of your career, of your role as a public citizen, and even of your personal life. It has certainly been central to ours. Whenever we get stuck in an unfamiliar writing situation or while learning new writing technology, we rummage through strategies we've developed over time. We talk to friends and colleagues, in person, by phone, and by e-mail, and they consult us, too.

We offer this book to you, then, as our partners in the process of writing. We hope that its pages help you give voice to your thoughts—now and years from now. We trust you'll find our advice useful in the wide range of writing situations you're bound to encounter in college and in life. You're always welcome to write us at <troykalq@nyc.rr.com> or <ddhesse@du.edu> to share your reactions to this book and your experiences as writers. We promise to answer.

Each of us would like to end this message with a personal story.

From Doug: I first glimpsed the power of writing in high school, when I wrote sappy—but apparently successful—love poems. Still, when I went to college, I was surprised to discover all I didn't know about writing. Fortunately, I had good teachers and developed lots of patience. I needed it. I continue to learn from my colleagues, my students, and my co-author, Lynn.

From Lynn: When I was an undergraduate, handbooks for writers weren't common. Questions about writing nagged at me. One day, browsing in the library, I found an incorrectly shelved, dust-covered book whose title included the words *handbook* and *writing.* I read it hungrily and kept checking it out from the library. Back then, I could never have imagined that someday I might write such a book myself. Now that we've completed the ninth edition of the *Simon & Schuster Handbook for Writers,* I'm amazed that I ever had the nerve to begin. This proves to me—and I hope to you—that anyone can write. Students don't always believe that. I hope you will.

With cordial regards,

Lynn Quitman Troyka   *Doug Hesse*

Writing Situations and Processes

Understanding College and Other Writing Situations

1a What is the current scene for writers in college and beyond?

Writing well improves your success in college. That plain fact has been true for decades. However, writing plays an equally key role in your career and your life beyond the classroom. We wrote this book to help you achieve success in all of these settings. As writers and writing teachers, we find it fascinating—and heartening—to witness the current explosion of writing. You might be among the millions of people who regularly compose e-mails and text messages, keep journals or **blogs**, craft stories or poems, create Web sites, or use FaceBook or MySpace to connect with others—all without anyone asking you to do so. Ordinary people write about their favorite television programs, analyze politics, or simply share their experiences and thoughts. The Internet and wireless devices have made it easier for people to share writing, and digital technologies allow them to mix words, images, sounds, and videos. We live in an age when people do more writing than they have at any other time in history.

If you're someone who chooses to write out of personal interest, we offer this book to help you stretch into new types of writing. If you don't very much like to write, we hope that you might discover the satisfaction of putting your thoughts into words—and we hope this book helps ease your way. We've composed these pages because we repeatedly see in our classes that everyone can make the concentrated effort needed to become an effective writer. Certainly, if you spend time and energy working on your writing skills, your efforts can bring you academic, professional, and personal rewards.

Probably your most immediate interest in using this book is the writing you'll do in college. As a student, you can expect to write in almost every course, not just in English or first-year writing. Chapter 2 of this book explains general processes that are useful for most academic writing. Chapter 7 focuses on common types of college papers, while Chapters 39 to 41 give advice for writing in different disciplines.

Writing is also vital in your career. A survey of business leaders by the National Commission on Writing found that "most professional employees are expected to write" and that "individual opportunity in the United States depends critically on

Figure 1.1 Different varieties and styles of writing

the ability to present one's thoughts coherently, cogently, and persuasively on paper" (*Writing: A Ticket to Work . . . or a Ticket Out?* College Board, 2004). Recent studies of people in a variety of jobs and professions find that they spend an average of 30 percent of each day writing. We explain business writing in Chapter 43.

1b What is a writing situation?

Think of the following situations: writing a text message to a friend; a research paper for a history class; a job application letter; a Web site for a museum. These situations result in texts widely different in length, format, content, organization, style, and so on. A **writing situation** is the combination of several elements: your topic, your purpose, your audience, your role as a writer, and your context and special requirements.

Quick Reference 1.1

Elements of a writing situation

- **Topic:** What subject will you be writing about?
- **Purpose:** What should the writing accomplish? (see 1c)
- **Audience:** Who are your main readers? (see 1d)
- **Role:** How do you want your audience to perceive you?
- **Context and Special Requirements:** When and how will your writing be read? Do you have requirements such as length, type of writing, format, or due dates?

We explain the important concepts of **purpose** and **audience** in sections 1c and 1d, but first we'll define some other elements of the writing situation. You'll often be assigned a topic, the subject you need to write about and, perhaps, the sources (7b) that you'll need to use. Topics can be very general ("Write about poverty") or very specific ("Analyze the factors that led to James Ferguson's poverty"); you'll be more successful if you narrow broad topics (2b.3).

It may surprise you to learn that you can take on different **roles** (personalities or identities) for different writing situations. For example, suppose you're trying to persuade readers to save energy. You might emphasize your concerns as a prospective parent who is personally worried about the future, or you might instead present yourself as an objective and impersonal analyst.

The **context** of your purpose and audience can affect the writing situation. Context refers to the circumstances in which your readers will encounter your writing. For example, persuading people to buy fuel-efficient cars when gas costs $1 per gallon is very different from when it costs well over $4. Informing college students about child-care options when your message will appear on a poster in the student center is different from when that message appears in the campus newspaper.

Special requirements are practical matters such as how much time you're given to complete the assignment and the required length of your writing. For example, your reading audience expects more from an assignment that you had a week to complete than from one due overnight. In the second case, your readers realize you had to write in relative haste, though no one ever accepts sloppy or careless work. Your audience expects most from assignments that call for reading or other research, so be sure to build enough time for that process early into your schedule.

Understanding a writing situation guides your writing process and shapes your final draft. A writing process that might be effective in one situation might

not be appropriate for another, and the final drafts would have different characteristics. For example, consider the following task: "In a five-page paper for a political science course, describe government restrictions on cigarette advertising."
Your INFORMATIVE* purpose would require careful research and an objective, serious style, complete with a list of works cited or references. In contrast, if you were
asked to write a 300-word newspaper editorial arguing that "Smoking should (or
should not) be banned in all public places," your writing would reflect your
PERSUASIVE purpose for a public audience, explain positions more quickly, probably have a more energetic style, and include no list of references. Consider other
examples. Writing a history paper in the short, informal style of a text message definitely won't impress a professor. Similarly, texting your friends in long paragraphs
will make them impatient (and perhaps wonder who's using your cell phone).

   As the above examples show, your writing situation also helps determine
the tone of your writing. Tone refers to the attitude conveyed in writing, mostly
by the writer's word choice. A tone can be formal, informal, laid back, pompous,
sarcastic, concerned, judgmental, sympathetic, and so on. The tone you use
greatly affects your readers' sense of the ROLE you've chosen. If you want to
come across as a serious, thoughtful writer in an academic situation, but your
tone is sarcastic and biting, your readers won't take you seriously. We discuss
tone at greater length in section 17d.

EXERCISE 1-1   Either in a class discussion or in a short paper, explain how
these different situations would result in different kinds of writing: a résumé and
cover letter, a research paper for a sociology course, an e-mail to a friend about
that sociology paper, a poster for an upcoming concert, a newspaper editorial.

1c What does "purpose" mean for writing?

A writer's purpose motivates what and how he or she writes. Quick Reference
1.2 lists four major purposes for writing.

1c.1 What is expressive writing?

Expressive writing is writing to express your personal thoughts, feelings, and
opinions. Some expressive writing is for the writer's eyes only, such as that in diaries, personal journals, or exploratory drafts. Other people, however, express
themselves in e-mails to friends and colleagues or in blogs for all the world to
see. A crucial reason for much of this kind of writing is simply for people to make
connections with others. Social networking sites like Facebook, for example, do
impart information and, occasionally, try to persuade others; however, their
main purpose is to establish and deepen human contact. This purpose, which

---

*Words printed in SMALL CAPITAL LETTERS are discussed elsewhere in the text and are de-
fined in the Terms Glossary at the back of this book.

> **Quick Reference 1.2**   ■ ■ ■ ■ ■ ■ ■
>
> ### Purposes for writing
>
> - To express yourself or build connections with others
> - To inform a reader
> - To persuade a reader
> - To create a literary work
>
> In this handbook, we concentrate on two major purposes for most forms of college writing: to **inform** and to **persuade**. The two remaining purposes listed above are important for contributing to human thought and culture, but they relate less to what most college writing involves.

is as old as personal letter writing, has been invigorated by digital communication. For example, Figure 1.2 is part of a blog kept by Doug's friend, Dan.

Still other expressive writing is just to blow off steam. Writing that "Congressman Miller is a total idiot" might make an author feel good, but simply expressing that belief won't change many minds. Finally, some expressive writing for public audiences falls into the category of literary writing. The excerpt here comes from a memoir intended for public reading.

> For much of her life my mother longed, passionately longed, for a decent house. One with a yard that did not have to be cleared with an ax. One with a roof that kept out the rain. One with a floor that you could not fall through. She longed for a beautiful house of wood or stone. Or of red brick, like the houses her many sisters and their husbands had. When I was thirteen she found such a house. Green-shuttered, white-walled. Breezy. With a lawn and a hedge and giant pecan trees. A porch swing. There her gardens flourished in spite of the shade, as did her youngest daughter, for whom she sacrificed her life doing hard labor in someone else's house, in order to afford peace and prettiness for her child, to whose grateful embrace she returned each night.
>
> —Alice Walker, "My Mother's Blue Bowl"

1c.2 What is informative writing?

Informative writing seeks to give information to readers and usually to explain it. Another name for this type of writing is expository writing because it expounds on—sets forth in detail—observations, ideas, facts, scientific data, and statistics. You can find informative writing in textbooks, encyclopedias, technical and business reports, manuals, nonfiction books, newspapers, and many magazines.

The essential goal of informative writing is to educate your readers about something. Like all good educators, therefore, you want to present your infor-

Figure 1.2 A blog written for friends

mation clearly, accurately, completely, and fairly. In Chapter 3 of this handbook, we show you many strategies that writers use for informative writing. These strategies can help you deliver your message, but above all, your success depends on whether your readers can verify your information as accurate. Quick Reference 1.3 gives you a checklist to assess your informative writing. But first, here's a paragraph written to inform.

> "Diamonds in the rough" are usually round and greasy looking. But dia-
> mond miners are in no need of dark glasses to shield them from the dazzling
> brilliance of the mines for quite another reason: even in a diamond pipe,
> there is only one part diamond per 14 million parts of worthless rock.

Approximately 46,000 pounds of earth must be mined and sifted to produce the half-carat gem you might be wearing. No wonder diamonds are expensive!

—Richard B. Manchester, "Diamonds"

As informative writing, this paragraph works because it focuses clearly on its TOPIC (diamonds in the rough), presents facts that can be verified (who, what, when, where), and is written in a reasonable tone.

Quick Reference 1.3 ■ ■ ■ ■ ■ ■ ■

Informative writing

- Is its information clear?
- Does it present facts, ideas, and observations that can be verified?
- Does its information seem complete and accurate?
- Is the writer's TONE reasonable and free of distortions? (8d)

1c.3 What is persuasive writing?

Persuasive writing, also called *argumentative* writing, seeks to persuade readers to support a particular opinion. When you write to persuade, you deal with debatable topics—those that people can consider from more than one point of view. Your goal is to change your readers' minds—or at least to bring your readers' opinions closer to your point of view. To succeed, you want to evoke a reaction in your audience so that they think beyond their present position (for example, reasoning why free speech needs to be preserved) or take action (for example, register to vote). Examples of persuasive writing include newspaper editorials, letters to the editor, opinion essays in magazines, reviews, sermons, advertising, fund-raising letters, books that argue a point of view, business proposals, and so on. Chapter 5 of this handbook discusses many different ways to write effective arguments.

In general terms, persuasive writing means you need to move beyond merely stating your opinion. You need to give the basis for that opinion. You support your opinion by using specific, illustrative details to back up your **generalizations**, which are usually very broad statements. The first sentences of sections 1c.1, 1c.2, and 1c.3 in this chapter are examples of generalizations.

Quick Reference 1.4 gives you a checklist to assess your persuasive writing. But first, here's a short passage written to persuade.

Our nation's economic and democratic future depends on preparing more students to succeed in college, work and life. We must engage all students in meaningful and rigorous academic work in high school and prepare more of them to succeed in college.

Connecting studies to real-world issues through learning communities is a proven way to get students engaged and motivated. But there is a difference between providing students with good learning environments that include fellow students with similar interests and narrowing students' options by tracking especially less-advantaged students into career-oriented paths in high school.

The fact is that many of the well-paying jobs that today's ninth graders might have 10 years from now do not yet exist—and the technical demands of all jobs are changing so rapidly that narrowing one's academic focus too early won't prepare one well for college and will diminish rather than enhance one's employability over the long term.

The key to success in the global economy is having the broad capacities and knowledge developed by a solid liberal education. In an economy fueled by innovation, these capabilities have, in fact, become America's most valuable economic asset.

> —Debra Humphreys, "Give Students Broad
> Education, Not Narrow Vocational Tracks"

As persuasive writing, this passage works because it provides factual information on school and work; it expresses a point of view that resides in sound reasoning (American schools should emphasize broad general education and not narrow vocational tracks); it offers evidence (a logical line of reasoning); and it tries to get the reader to agree with the point of view.

Quick Reference 1.4 ■ ■ ■ ■ ■ ■ ■

Persuasive writing

- Does it present a point of view about which opinions vary?
- Does it support its point of view with specifics?
- Does it provide sound reasoning and logic?
- Are the parts of its argument clear?
- Does it intend to evoke a reaction from the reader?

EXERCISE 1-2 For each paragraph, decide if the dominant purpose is informative, persuasive, or expressive. Then, use the information in section 1c to explain your answers.

A. Trees are living archives, carrying within their structure a record not only of their age but also of precipitation and temperature for each year in which a ring was formed. The record might also include the marks of forest fires, early frosts and, incorporated into the wood itself, chemical elements the tree removed from its environment. Thus, if we only knew how to unlock its secrets, a tree could tell us a great deal about what was happening in its neighborhood from the time of its beginning. Trees can tell us what was happening before written records became available. They also have a great deal to tell us about our future. The records of past climate that they contain can help us to understand the natural forces that produce our weather, and this, in turn, can help us plan.

—James S. Trefil, "Concentric Clues from Growth Rings Unlock the Past"

B.   Actual physical location threatens to evaporate everywhere we look. Information, we are everywhere taught, has annihilated distances. Surgeons can cut you open from a thousand miles away. Facsimile Las Vegas casinos deliver Rome and New York on the same daily walk. You don't have to go to the office to go to the office. You can shop in your kitchen and go to school in your living room. And, sadly enough, when you actually do go out shopping, one mall seems much like another. For what actually matters, physicality doesn't matter anymore. Even with money; now, we are told, information about money is more important than the actual green.

—Richard Lanham, *The Economics of Attention*

C.   Although Littleman, my eleven-year-old poodle, has never been separated from his thirteen-year-old mother, Simone, they are remarkably different. Simone weighs in at about five kilograms with very delicate, sophisticated features and coarse, curly hair. Slightly shorter, Littleman tops the scale at no more than three kilograms and is quite handsome with his teddy-bear features and soft wavy hair. Simone was the first dog in the family and is a pedigreed poodle. In many ways she is the picture of a thoroughbred, with her snobby attitude and nonchalant manners. On the other hand, Littleman came into the family a year later with four other puppies of pure breeding, but they were never registered. Unlike his mother, Littleman is very friendly, almost to the point of being pesty at times.

—Linda Neal, student

EXERCISE 1-3   Consulting section 1c, write on each of these topics twice, once to inform and once to persuade your reader: diets, tastes in music, reality television, part-time jobs, road rage. Be prepared to discuss how your two treatments of each topic differ.

1d   What does "audience" mean for writing?

Your **audience** consists of everyone who will read your writing, but it especially refers to readers to whom you're most directly aiming your words. For example, anyone can read an issue of *The New England Journal of Medicine* (or at least try), but that publication is aimed at doctors and medical researchers. Thinking about audience means figuring out how to reach your audience in various kinds of situations. For example, papers that you write for a history course differ in form and style from lab reports that you write in biology, and both differ from memos that you write on the job, letters that you write to a newspaper editor, or e-mails that you write to a friend. Effective writers know they need to adjust their writing for different tasks and audiences.

After college, your audiences are likely to be readers of your business, professional, and public writing (Chapters 43–44). In college, you'll surely address a mix of audience types that expect to read ACADEMIC WRITING. Here's a list of categories of those audiences, each of which is detailed in the section listed in parentheses.

- General educated audiences (1d.1)
- Specialist audiences (1d.2)
- Your instructor (who represents your general or specialized readers) (1d.3)
- Your peers (classmates, co-workers, friends, or others like yourself) (6a)

The more specifics you understand about each of your audiences, the better your chances of communicating with them successfully.

ESOL Tips: (1) If you do not share a cultural background with your readers, it may be difficult for you to estimate how much your readers know about your topic. Discussing your topic with friends or classmates might help you decide what background information you need to include in your paper.

(2) As someone from a non-US culture, you might be surprised—even offended—by the directness with which people speak and write in the United States. If so, we hope you'll read our open letter—it introduces Part Seven of this handbook—to multilingual students about honoring their cultures. You may come from a written-language tradition that expects elaborate, formal, or ceremonial language; that reserves the central point of an academic essay for the middle; that requires tactful, indirect discussions (at least in comparison with the US style); and, in some cultures, that accommodates digressions that might, or might not, lead back to the main point. In contrast, US writers and readers expect language and style that are very direct, straightforward, and without embellishment (as compared with the styles of many other cultures). US college instructors expect essays in academic writing to contain a thesis statement (usually at the end of the introductory paragraph). They further expect your writing to contain an organized presentation of information that moves tightly from one paragraph to the next, with generalizations that you always back up with strong supporting details, and with an ending paragraph that presents a logical conclusion to your discussion. Also, for writing in the United States, you need to use so-called edited American English. This means following the rules used by educated speakers. In reality, the United States has a rich mixture of grammar systems, but academic

writing nevertheless requires edited American English. If you want to hear these forms spoken, listen to the anchors of television and radio news programs. You also need to choose words for your writing that are accurate in meaning and spelled correctly. ●

To analyze your audience, you might ask yourself whatever questions in Quick Reference 1.5 you think will be useful in each situation.

Quick Reference 1.5 ■ ■ ■ ■ ■ ■ ■

Ways to analyze your audience

WHAT SETTING ARE THEY READING IN?

- Academic setting? Specifically, what subject?
- Workplace setting? Specifically, what business area?
- Public setting? Specifically, what form of communication? (newspaper? blog? poster?)

WHO ARE THEY?

- Age, gender, economic situation
- Ethnic backgrounds, political philosophies, religious beliefs
- Roles (student, parent, voter, wage earner, property owner, veteran, and others)
- Interests, hobbies

WHAT DO THEY KNOW?

- General level of education
- Specific level of knowledge about topic: Do they know less than you about the subject? as much as you about the subject? more than you about the subject?
- Beliefs: Is the audience likely to agree with your point of view? disagree with your point of view? have no opinion about the topic?
- Interests: Is the audience eager to read about the topic? open to the topic? resistant to or not interested in the topic?

WHAT IS THEIR RELATIONSHIP TO YOU?

- Distance and formality: Do you know each other personally or not? Does your audience consist of friends, family, or close peers, or are they more remote?
- Authority: Does your reader have the authority to judge or evaluate you (a supervisor at work, a teacher). Do you have the authority to evaluate your reader, or does this not apply?

1d.1   What is a general educated audience?

A **general educated audience** is composed of experienced readers who regularly read newspapers, magazines, and books, not only because they have to but because they want to. These readers typically have a general knowledge of many subjects and are likely to understand something about your topic. If your writing contains too many technical details or unusual references, your writing may confuse and alienate these readers. Consequently, for general educated readers you need to avoid using specialized terms without plainly defining them, or referring to uncommon information without explaining it.

General educated readers usually approach a piece of writing expecting to become interested in it, to learn about a new topic, to add to their store of knowledge about a subject, or to see a subject from a perspective other than their own. As a writer, work to fulfill those expectations. While some readers aren't particularly knowledgeable or open to new ideas, your goal in most writing that's not intended for specialized audiences needs to be targeting a general audience, as defined above.

1d.2   What is a specialist audience?

A **specialist audience** is composed of readers who have a thorough knowledge of specific subjects or who are particularly committed to certain interests or viewpoints. Many people are experts in their occupational fields, and some become experts in areas that simply interest them, such as astronomy or raising orchids. People from a particular group background (for example, Democrats, Republicans, Catholics, or military veterans) are knowledgeable in those areas.

Specialist readers may also share certain assumptions and beliefs. For example, suppose you're writing for an audience of immigrants to the United States who feel strongly about keeping their cultural traditions alive. You can surely assume your readers know those traditions well, so you won't need to describe and explain the basics. Similarly, if you intend to argue that immigrants should abandon their cultural traditions in favor of US practices, you'll want to write respectfully about their beliefs. Whenever you introduce a concept that might be new to a specialist audience, explain the concept thoroughly rather than assuming the audience will understand it right away.

Examples of specialized audiences include:

- Members of specific academic disciplines (chemistry, political science, art history)
- People in specific professions (finance, education, engineering)
- People with common interests or hobbies (fans of certain television shows, of cooking, of NASCAR)

- People with common political beliefs (conservatives, liberals, independents) or views (on health care, the environment, immigration)
- People with common experiences (veterans, single parents, athletes)

1d.3 What is my instructor's role as audience?

As your audience, your instructor functions in three ways. First, your instructor assumes the role of your target audience by reading and responding to your writing as though he or she is one of your intended general or specific readers. Second, your instructor acts as a coach who is dedicated to helping improve your writing. Third, your instructor evaluates your final drafts.

Although instructors know that few students are experienced writers or experts on the subjects they write about, they expect your writing to reflect your having taken the time to learn something worthwhile about a topic and then to write about it clearly. They can recognize a minimal effort almost immediately.

Instructors are also people whose professional lives center on intellectual endeavors. Therefore, you need to write about topics that contain intellectual interest, and discuss them according to the expectations for academic writing.

Figure 1.3 Examples of specialized audience publications

Don't assume that your instructor can mentally fill in what you leave out of your writing. Indeed, you might think that it's wrong, even insulting to your instructor, if you extend your discussion beyond simple statements. Instructors—indeed, all readers—can't be mind readers, and they expect students' writing to fully explore their chosen topic. If you think you might be saying too little, ask your peers to read your writing and tell you if you've developed your topic sufficiently.

1e   What should I know about writing in a digital age?

Computers are important tools for creating documents, finding resources, managing work, and communicating with others. Almost all writing projects, whether in college or beyond, require them. Although some instructors make allowances for students with no access to a computer, they clearly prefer word-processed final drafts. If you don't own a computer or live with someone who does, you can usually get access to one on most college campuses (often in libraries and student centers), in public libraries, or in Internet cafés.

1e.1   Creating documents

A computer's word-processing software (for example, Microsoft Word or OpenOffice) offers invaluable help at various stages of the WRITING PROCESS. Word processing allows you easily to add, delete, revise, or move around material, even from one document to another. Some writers prefer to print their drafts to revise or edit them by hand and then enter the changes in the computer; other writers do almost all their revising and editing on the screen.

Word processing also allows you to make quick format changes. You can easily shift between single-spacing and double-spacing or put a WORKS CITED page into the correct DOCUMENTATION STYLE (Chapters 36–38). The toolbars typically found at the top of word-processing windows contain numerous formatting options, and exploring how they work can save you time in the long run. At the very least, learn how to set line spacing, margins, and indentations; how to use header and footer options to insert page numbers automatically; how to create footnotes; and how to check spelling and grammar. However, the special aids for writers that are built into word-processing software have limitations.

- **Spell-check tools** alert you when words don't match the dictionary in the software. These programs can be a big help for spotting a misspelled word or a typo, but they won't call your attention to your having typed *form* when you intended to type *from*. Therefore, always remember to read your work carefully after you use a spell-checker.
- **Thesaurus tools** suggest SYNONYMS for words. They can't, however, tell you which ones fit well into your particular sentences. Whenever a suggested

synonym is unfamiliar, look it up in your dictionary to be sure that it doesn't distort your communication. For example, a synonym for *friend* is *acquaintance,* but these words have different senses.

- **Grammar-** or **style-check tools** check your writing against the software's strict interpretations of rules of grammar, word use, punctuation, and other conventions. Can you always rely on those standards? No. While a tool can call attention to a possible error, the decision to change the usage is yours. Consult this handbook when you're not sure whether you need to deviate from the program's suggestions.

1e.2   Finding resources

In addition to helping you produce and revise writing, computers can help you find SOURCES. Nearly all library catalogs and databases are now searchable electronically, both from within the library and remotely through the Internet. Catalogs and databases are large collections of references that experts have gathered and organized. Some of those references exist only in print, but increasingly, they're also available online. Many workplaces also subscribe to database and information services that are useful in their business. Chapter 34 explains how to use catalogs and databases.

Sources on the World Wide Web, which you find using search engines like Google and Yahoo, usually aren't in databases that experts have compiled. Chapter 34 explains how to use the Web—and how to avoid misusing it. Remember that anyone can post anything online and that some of what you find is plain wrong.

Online sources present particular challenges to writers, including the possibility of **plagiarism**, a serious academic offense that occurs when you repre-

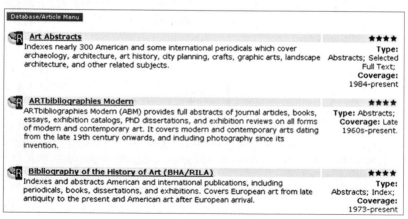

Figure 1.4 A library database

sent someone else's wording or ideas as your own. Chapter 35 describes effective and ethical ways of using sources and avoiding plagiarism.

1e.3 Managing your work

Computers allow you to save drafts of your papers and organize your work. For example, you might create a separate folder for each document you write and keep all notes, drafts, and ideas related to that project in the folder. Figure 1.5 shows how one student has started a folder for all the projects in her writing course. In

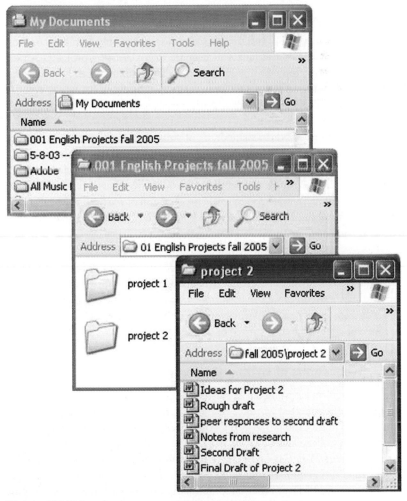

Figure 1.5 Using the computer to manage writing projects

the subfolder for project 2, she has ideas, notes, peer comments, and drafts. She created this folder in the "My Documents" directory in Microsoft Windows.

Computers and associated technologies also allow you to store vast quantities of your own writing and research, in forms even more portable than laptops. Storage devices such as flash drives (often called thumb, jump, or keychain drives) allow you cheaply to store hundreds or thousands of megabytes of information, in something small enough to keep in your pocket. Not only can you potentially keep every word you ever write (as a lifelong portfolio), but you can store photos and other images that you might need for a certain writing project, and you can download vast quantities of source materials from databases.

1e.4   Communicating with others

E-mail, instant messaging, and similar technologies not only help you communicate with friends but also help you prepare formal writing projects. For example, discussing a topic online with others can generate ideas. Some college instructors organize such discussions in Web-based programs such as WebCT or Blackboard. People in all walks of life often exchange ideas on discussion boards, listservs, and blogs.

Computers allow you to share drafts of your work without physically meeting with others. You can send a draft as an e-mail attachment or save it on a community server or Web site such as Google Docs. That way, classmates or colleagues—or even instructors or supervisors—have access to it and can offer suggestions for revision. If you're working on a collaborative project, the ability to share drafts and to discuss revisions online has many advantages. Chapter 6 explains how to work effectively with others.

⏺ **Alert:** College instructors vary in terms of the amount of input they want students to receive outside of class. A few teachers may not want you to have anyone (not a friend or family member or classmate or tutor) give you advice or feedback. Clarify each instructor's rules about such matters. Pleading ignorance of a law is rarely a sufficient defense. ●

1f   What forms of writing do computers enable?

For decades, formal writing has consisted of essays and reports containing only paragraphs of connected words. These forms will always remain essential, and you need to master them. However, computers enable different kinds of writing, both in college and beyond. You can place photographs or illustrations into documents. You can easily create tables and graphs, and you can use different fonts and graphic elements. As a result, writers can more easily produce brochures, pamphlets, or other documents that, in the past, required a graphic artist (see Chapter 45).

Other forms of writing, such as Web pages and blogs, are designed specifically to appear on computers rather than on paper. Sometimes they contain audio or video files, or they contain links to other documents and Web sites. The Web site of the Smithsonian Institution, shown in Figure 1.6, incorporates several images to create a pleasing effect, and it has links to many other pages. Some writing situations may call for you to make a Web page rather than write a traditional paper.

Blogs (short for We**b logs**) allow a writer to post messages that anyone can read on the Internet. Some people create blogs to serve as a diary of their daily experiences, while others write about professions or other matters of interest. Blogs can be very personal, such as those written for an audience of friends and family. They can also be relatively more formal or journalistic. Other blogs have taken on a national readership, as is the case with particular news, political, and author blogs.

A **wiki** is a Web site that allows multiple readers to change its content. Several people can work on the same document from remote places around the globe. Figure 1.7 is an image from Wikipedia, an online encyclopedia. Keep in mind that any Internet user can post an article to Wikipedia, and anyone can revise an article already posted there. You always need to question the accuracy of a wiki article. It can contain incorrect information. Always ask your instructor whether he or she will permit you to use it as a source for scholarly research. Also try to confirm all information you find in Wikipedia in other reliable sources. For more information on using and citing Wikipedia and other Web resources, see Chapters 36–38.

Figure 1.6 Images add interest to a Web site

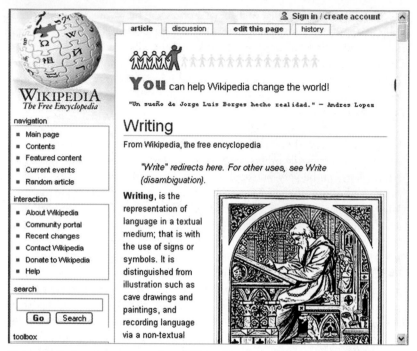

Figure 1.7 A screen capture from Wikipedia

A **digital portfolio** is a collection of several of your own texts in electronic format that you've chosen to represent the range of your skills and abilities. Unlike regular paper portfolios, digital versions contain links between—and within—individual texts; they can be modified and shared easily and cheaply; and they can be put online for public reading. Figure 1.8 shows the opening screen of one student's digital portfolio for a first semester writing course. Note that all the titles function as links to the papers themselves.

Presentations, using software such as PowerPoint, allow you to create visuals to accompany your oral remarks. PowerPoint slides can incorporate both words and images, as well as sounds and video clips. Chapter 42 provides more advice on creating presentations.

Podcasts are sound files that can be shared over the Internet. Their name derives from Apple's familiar iPod player. You can download podcasts to a computer or portable device for listening anywhere. What do podcasts have to do with writing? A good number of podcasts are miniature essays or commentaries that their writers have carefully polished and then read, as a script. Podcasts are the oral form of blogs. Figure 1.9 shows one of many podcast directories available on the Internet.

People who click on the button "listen" or "subscribe" get to the listed podcasts; the directory on the right shows other topic categories.

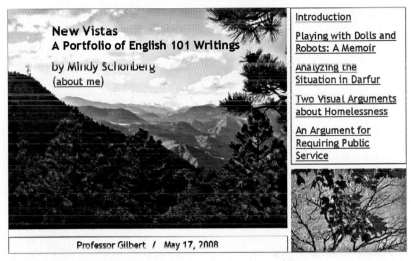

Figure 1.8 Opening screen of a student's digital portfolio

Figure 1.9 A screen capture of a podcast directory

Videos are motion image files or clips. People increasingly convey some ideas or information through short videos filmed with a camera, edited with computer software, and uploaded to the Internet. Video clips may enhance some presentations. Web sites like YouTube.com demonstrate the ease with which people can produce and upload videos, some of them amazingly good, many of them plain awful. Mainstream professional, educational, and commercial Web sites also frequently contain videos. Some blogs actually take the form of video logs or "vlogs."

What is a discussion of videos doing in a handbook of writing? Similar to podcasts, effective videos are often built around carefully written and narrated scripts, which may contain titles or captions. We discuss visuals in multimedia in Chapter 42. Always check with instructors before integrating audio or visual elements into your writing. And don't worry if your knowledge about producing any of these types of writing is limited. Instructors who require such projects can tell you how to proceed.

1g　What resources can help me with writing?

Every writer needs access to four essential resources: a dictionary, a thesaurus, a handbook for writers, and a library. The first three are each generally available in electronic form as well as in traditional print, although you may find the book versions more convenient. A **dictionary** is indispensable. Most college bookstores offer a variety of hardback "college dictionaries." Before buying one, browse through a few definitions, check the format and accessories (information in the front and back), and choose the book you like best. Keeping a lightweight paperback abridged dictionary in your book bag can be very handy for checking unknown words on the spot. Also, many dictionaries and other reference books can be downloaded onto a **personal digital assistant (PDA)** for even greater portability.

Unabridged dictionaries list all recognized words in standard use in English. Being comprehensive, they're usually oversized, so the reference section of every library usually stocks one in its reference section. Some college libraries may also maintain an unabridged dictionary online for their students.

Another valuable resource for writers is a **thesaurus**, which is a collection of *synonyms*. The alphabetically arranged ones are the easiest to use. Be sure you check for this feature since some thesauruses are not organized alphabetically. *Roget's 21st Century Thesaurus* is an excellent volume arranged alphabetically.

A **handbook for writers** is also vital for you to own. A handbook—such as the one you're reading—gives you detailed information about rules of grammar and punctuation and about other writing conventions. (Note that this handbook also exists in an online version that can be accessed through a code you received if you bought the book new.) It also offers extensive advice about how to write successfully, whether for college, business, or the public. It shows you step by step how to write and document research papers. Some handbooks, including this one, contain guidance on how to write for a variety of courses other than English. This resource is an invaluable writing tool in courses other than English, as well as in your career after college, and it will serve you well for years.

College libraries, sometimes called *learning resource centers,* are essential for writers. Libraries are fully stocked with all manner of reference books, circulating books, resources for online access, and more. Some resources are available online, in "full text versions," through the library's Web site. It's helpful to know what resources are available at your library so that you can dive right in when you need to get information. Chapter 34 provides extensive advice on using the library.

Finally, you need two other, less tangible resources as a writer: time and confidence. We know that people live incredibly busy lives, juggling work, school, and personal responsibilities. While it may seem obvious (or insensitive) to say that you need time to write effectively, we're simply encouraging you to create and protect time for yourself as a writer. It helps to think of writing as a series of several processes, and you'll need time to pursue them. Confidence may seem just as elusive, especially when you face challenging new writing situations. It might help to remember that countless people like you are steadily developing their writing skills each day. We see them in our classes all the time. We have confidence that your efforts will also bring rewards.

For more help with your
writing, grammar, and research,
go to **www.mycomplab.com**

2

Essential Processes
for Academic Writing

2a   What processes do academic writers use?

Many people think that professional writers can sit down at their computers, think of ideas, and magically produce a finished draft, word by perfect word. Experienced writers know better. They know that writing is a process, a series of activities that starts the moment they begin thinking about a subject and ends with proofreading the final draft. Experienced writers also know that good writing is rewriting, again and yet again. Their drafts are filled with additions, deletions, rewordings, and rearrangements.

> ~~Chapter One discusses what writing is. This chapter explains~~ ~~how writing happens.~~ Many people think that professional writers can sit down at their computers, think of ideas, and ^magically^ produce a finished draft, word by perfect word. Experienced writers know better. They know that writing is a process. ~~The writing process is~~ a series of activities that starts the moment ^they begin^ thinking about a subject ~~begins~~ and ends with the ^proofreading^ final draft. Experienced writers also know that good writing is rewriting, again and yet again. *Their drafts are filled with additions, deletions, rewordings, and rearrangements.*

Figure 2.1 Draft and revision of Lynn Troyka's first paragraph in Chapter 2

For example, see in Figure 2.1 how Lynn revised the paragraph you just read. Lynn didn't make all the changes at the same time, even though it looks that way on the example. She went through the paragraph four times before she was satisfied with it. Notice that she deleted two sentences, combined two sentences, added a sentence at the end, and changed wording throughout. For another example, see Figure 2.2 on page 26, an image of revisions Doug made in the opening of Chapter 1.

Writing is an ongoing process of considering alternatives and making choices. Knowing and practicing a few general processes will help you with almost every writing situation in college and beyond. Different assignments may emphasize some techniques more than others, and we'll discuss them in Chapter 7. Here, however, we focus on processes that are essential for nearly all writing.

In this chapter, we discuss each part of the writing process separately. In real life, the steps overlap. They loop back and forth, which is why writing is called a recursive process. Quick Reference 2.1 lists the steps.

Do you like, as we do, to visualize a process? If so, see the drawing in Figure 2.3 on page 27. The arrows show movement. You might move back before going ahead (perhaps as you revise, you realize you need to plan some more); or you might skip a step and come back to it later (perhaps in the middle of revising, you jump into editing for a few minutes because a punctuation or grammar rule affects how you express your point); and so on.

As you work with the writing process, allow yourself to move freely through each step to see what's involved. Notice what works best for you. As you de-

Steps in the writing process

- **Planning** means discovering and compiling ideas for your writing.
- **Shaping** means organizing your material.
- **Drafting** means writing your material into sentences and paragraphs.
- **Revising** means evaluating your draft and then rewriting it by adding, deleting, rewording, and rearranging.
- **Editing** means checking for correct grammar, spelling, punctuation, and mechanics.
- **Proofreading** means reading your final copy to eliminate typing or handwriting errors.

velop a sense of your preferred writing methods, adapt the process to fit each writing situation. No single way exists for applying the writing process.

Our personal advice from one writer to another is this: Most writers struggle some of the time with ideas that are difficult to express, sentences that won't take shape, and words that aren't precise. Be patient with yourself. Don't get discouraged. The more you write, the easier it will become—though writing never happens magically.

2b How do I begin a college writing project?

Begin every writing assignment by carefully analyzing the writing situation you're given. Some assignments are very specific. For example, here's an assignment that leaves no room for choice: "In a 500-word article for an audience of seventh graders, explain how oxygen is absorbed in the lungs." Students need to do precisely what's asked, taking care not to wander off the topic. More often, however, writing-class assignments aren't nearly as specific as that one. Often, you'll be ex pected to select your own topic (2b.1) or even your own purpose and audience.

2b.1 Selecting your own topic or purpose

If you have to choose a topic, don't rush. Take time to think through your ideas. Avoid getting so deeply committed to one topic that you cannot change to a more suitable topic in the time allotted.

Not all topics are suitable for ACADEMIC WRITING. Your topic needs to have ideas and issues meaty enough to demonstrate your thinking and writing abilities. Think through potential topics by breaking each one down into its logical

1A WHAT IS THE CURRENT SCENE FOR WRITERS IN COLLEGE

AND BEYOND?

Writing well is ~~important to~~ *improves your* college success. That plain fact has been true for decades. But

writing plays an equally key role in your career and life beyond classrooms. ~~In this book, we'd~~ *We wrote this book*

~~like~~ to help you achieve success in those many roles.

~~We live in an age when~~ *Today, more* people do more writing than they have at any other time in history. The

Internet and wireless devices have made it easier for people to share writing, ~~both formally and~~

~~informally,~~ *them* and digital technologies allow us to mix words, images, sounds, and videos. As

writers and writing teachers, ~~then,~~ we find it fascinating—and heartening—to witness the explosion of writing that *current*

people choose to do on their own. You might be among the millions of people who regularly write e-mails and text

messages, keep journals, craft stories or poems, create Web sites, use FaceBook to connect with others, or write

~~blogs~~ (Web logs)—all without anyone asking you to do so. Ordinary people write about their

favorite television programs, analyze politics, or simply share their experiences and thoughts.

If you're someone who chooses to write out of personal interest, we respect you and offer
new
this book to help you stretch into ~~less familiar~~ types of writing. If ~~you're someone who doesn't~~ *you don't*

very much like to write, we hope that you might explore the satisfaction of putting your

thoughts into words—and we hope this book helps ease your way. We've composed these pages

because we repeatedly see in our classes that everyone can make the concentrated effort needed

to become an effective writer. Certainly, if you spend ~~some~~ time and energy improving your

writing skills, your efforts will bring you academic, professional, and personal rewards.

As a student, you can expect to write in a variety of courses across the curriculum, not just
academic
in English. Chapter 2 of this book will explain general processes that are useful for most writing.

or first year writing.

2

Probably ~~not~~ your most immediate ~~interest~~ is the writing you'll do in college.

Figure 2.2 Doug's revisions of Chapter 1

subsections. Then, make sure you can supply sufficiently specific details to
back up each general statement. Conversely, make sure you aren't bogged down
with so many details you can't figure out what GENERALIZATIONS they support.

Work toward balance by finding a middle ground. Beware of topics so broad
that they lead to well-meaning but vague generalizations (for example, "Educa-

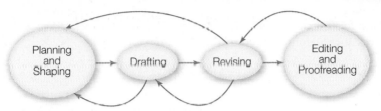

Figure 2.3 Visualizing the writing process

tion is necessary for success"). Also, beware of topics so narrow that they lead nowhere after a few sentences (for example, "Jessica Max attends Tower College").

Suppose your assignment doesn't indicate a writing purpose—for example, "Write an essay on smoking." Here, you're expected to choose a purpose and think about what you intend to write on the topic. Will you try to explain to a general educated audience why people smoke? Will you try to persuade a specialized audience of smoking parents to quit? Will you summarize the current literature on the costs of smoking in order to inform an audience of economists? Considering different audiences and purposes can help you find a topic angle that engages you.

Most instructors put each assignment in writing, in a handout, on a Web site, or perhaps on the board. But some instructors give assignments orally during class, expecting you to write them down. Try to record every word. Don't hesitate to ask questions if you don't catch all the words or if something isn't clear—and be sure to write down the answers because they often tend to slip from memory. Listen, too, to questions other students ask.

In the rest of this chapter, we present the writing processes of two college students, Sara Cardini and Alex Garcia, as they plan and shape their material. You'll see Cardini's essay evolving through three separate, complete drafts. Later, in Chapter 5, you'll see how Garcia's essay developed. To start, here are the written assignments each student received.

Sara Cardini received this assignment:

Addressing an educated audience, write an essay of 900 to 1,300 words discussing something you learned outside of a classroom. Your writing purpose can be informative or persuasive. Expect to write three drafts. (1) Your first draft, typed double-spaced, is due two classes from today. (2) Your clean second draft, typed double-spaced, without notes or comments, is due two classes later. Clip to it your first draft showing all notes you made to yourself or from comments your peer-response group made; you can handwrite notes and comments. I'll read your second draft as an "essay in progress" and will make comments to help you toward a third

continued >>

(and final) draft. (3) The third draft, typed double-spaced, is due one week after I return your second draft with my comments.

Alex Garcia was given this assignment:

Write an essay of 1,000 to 1,500 words that argues for a particular action on an issue that interests you. Your final draft is due in two weeks.

Cardini's first step was to analyze her writing situation (see Quick Reference 1.1). She looked at the very general topic—explain to an educated audience something you learned outside of a classroom—and she saw that she needed to narrow it considerably. She tentatively decided her purpose would be informative, though she thought she might have to switch to a persuasive purpose as she went along. She knew that she would share her first draft with her peer-response group to help her toward her second draft. She also understood that her instructor would be her final audience. She was aware of the requirements for time and length.

Garcia also read his assignment and analyzed his writing situation. Because the topic was very broad, he knew he would have to spend a good deal of time deciding what he wanted to write about. On the other hand, he understood that his assigned purpose was persuasive. The audience was not specified; he knew that his instructor would be the main audience, but he also decided to write in a way that would address a broader public audience. He kept in mind the requirements for time and length.

2b.2   Broadening a narrow topic

You know a topic is too narrow when you realize there's little to say after a few sentences. When faced with a too-narrow topic, think about underlying concepts. For example, suppose you want to write about Oprah Winfrey. If you chose "Oprah Winfrey's television show debuted in 1986," you'd be working with a single fact rather than a topic. To expand beyond such a narrow thought, you could think about the general area that your fact fits into—say, the impact of television shows on American culture. Although that is too broad to be a useful topic, you're headed in the right direction. Next, you might think of a topic that relates to Oprah's influence, such as "What impact has Oprah Winfrey's television show had on American culture since she began broadcasting in 1986?" Depending on your WRITING SITUATION (1b), you might need to narrow your idea further by focusing on Oprah's impact in a single area, such as how her book club influenced publishing and reading habits, how her guests and topics brought certain issues to national visibility, or how the style of her show affected other talk shows.

2b.3 Narrowing a broad topic

Narrowing a broad topic calls for you to break the topic down into subtopics. Most broad subjects can be broken down in hundreds of ways, but you need not think of all of them. Settle on a topic that interests you, one narrowed enough—but not too much—from a broad topic. For example, if you're assigned "relationships" as the topic for a 1,000-word essay, you'd be too broad if you chose "What kinds of relationships are there?" You'd be too narrow if you came up with "Alexandra and Gavin have dated for two years." You'd probably be on target with a subtopic such as "In successful relationships, people learn to accept each other's faults." You could use 1,000 words to explain and give concrete examples of typical faults and discuss various reasons why accepting them is important. Here are two more examples.

SUBJECT	*music*
WRITING SITUATION	freshman composition class
	informative purpose
	instructor as audience
	500 words; one week
POSSIBLE TOPICS	"How music affects moods"
	"The main characteristics of country music"
	"The types of songs in Disney animations"
SUBJECT	*cities*
WRITING SITUATION	sociology course
	persuasive purpose
	peers and then instructor as audience
	950 to 1,000 words; ten days
POSSIBLE TOPICS	"The importance of public transportation"
	"Discomforts of city living"
	"How open spaces enhance the quality of city life"

Sara Cardini, the student whose essay appears in this chapter, knew that her very general assigned topic—"Explain to an educated audience something you learned outside of a classroom"—was too broad. To narrow it, she used the following structured techniques for discovering and compiling ideas: browsing her journal (2c.1), FREEWRITING (2.c2), and MAPPING (2.c4). They helped her decide that she wanted to discuss how she learned about a culture other than her own. She realized that even her narrower topic "Japanese culture" would still be too broad. She considered "Japanese music" or "Japanese schools." In the end, she chose "Japanese videos" and, even more specifically, a kind of Japanese animation called "anime" (commonly pronounced AN-a-may). Extensive experience had taught her about the topic, and she could think of both generalizations and specific details to use in her essay. In addition, Cardini knew that if she needed to do research, she could find sources in books and magazines and on the Internet.

Alex Garcia also needed to narrow his topic to suit a 1,000- to 1,500-word essay. To explore several possible topics, he used BRAINSTORMING (2c.3). Once he had chosen a topic (whether buying organic food was worthwhile), he used the "journalist's questions" (2.c4) to compile more ideas and then a subject tree (2e) to check whether he was ready to begin drafting.

2c   How can I come up with ideas and information?

If you've ever felt you'll never think of anything to write about, don't despair. Instead, use structured techniques, sometimes called *prewriting strategies* or *invention techniques,* for discovering and compiling ideas. Professional writers use them to uncover hidden resources in their minds. For a list of the techniques, see Quick Reference 2.2.

Try out each one. Experiment to find out which techniques suit your style of thinking. Even if one technique produces good ideas, try another to see what additional possibilities might turn up.

Save all of the ideas you generate as you explore possible topics. You never know when something you have initially rejected might become useful from another point of view. Computers make it easy to keep a folder labeled, for example, "explorations," in which you can store your ideas.

Quick Reference 2.2   ■ ■ ■ ■ ■ ■ ■

Ways to discover and compile ideas for writing

- Keep an idea log and a journal (see 2c.1).
- Freewrite (see 2c.2).
- Brainstorm (see 2c.3).
- Ask the "journalist's questions" (see 2c.4).
- Map (see 2c.5).
- Talk it over (see 2c.6).
- Read, browse, or search (see 2c.7).
- Incubate (see 2c.8).

⊕ **ESOL Tip:** The structured techniques discussed here aim to let your ideas flow out of you without your judging them right away. If it's difficult for you to implement these techniques using English, consider doing several in your primary language. Then, choose one that seems to have potential for your writing and do it over again in English. ●

2c.1 Using an idea log or journal

As you develop the habits of mind and behavior of a writer, your ease with writing will grow. One such habit is keeping an idea log. Professional writers are always on the lookout for ideas to write about and details to develop their ideas. They listen, watch, talk with people, and generally keep an open mind. Because they know that good ideas can evaporate as quickly as they spring to mind, they're always ready to jot down their thoughts and observations. Some carry a pocket-size notepad, while others use a personal digital assistant (PDA) or a laptop. If you use an idea log throughout your college years, you'll see your powers of observation increase dramatically.

Additionally, many professional writers keep a daily writing **journal**. Doing this will allow you to have a conversation in writing with yourself. Your audience is you, so the content and tone can be as personal and informal as you wish. Even fifteen minutes a day can be enough. If you don't have that chunk of time, write in your journal before you go to bed, between classes, or on a bus. Some people find that the feel of pen on paper, perhaps in a bound blank journal, is important to this kind of writing. Others keep journals in computer files or online as BLOGS (short for "Web logs"). For examples of blogs (or to start one of your own), go to http://www.blogger.com.

Unlike a diary, a journal isn't a record of what you do each day. A journal is for your thoughts from your reading, your observations, even your dreams. You can respond to quotations, react to movies or plays, or reflect on your opinions, beliefs, and tastes. Keeping a journal can help you in three ways. First, writing every day gives you the habit of productivity; the more you write and the more you feel words pouring out of you onto paper, the more easily you'll write in all situations. Second, a journal instills the practice of close observation and discovery, two habits of mind that good writers cultivate. Third, a journal is an excellent source of ideas for assignments.

Figure 2.4 shows an excerpt of a journal entry Sara Cardini had made before she got the assignment to write about something she had learned outside the classroom. Even though she hadn't thought of her entry as a potential subject for a later essay, when she read through her journal for ideas, she realized that one of her great interests had started beyond classroom walls.

2c.2 Freewriting

Freewriting is writing nonstop. You write down whatever comes into your mind without stopping to wonder whether the ideas are good or the spelling is correct. When you freewrite, don't do anything to interrupt the flow. Don't censor any thoughts or flashes of insight. Don't go back and review. Don't delete.

> My first visit to an anime club. I see they spend all their time talking about Japan, eating Japanese food, and watching Japanese cartoons. Adults watching cartoons must be a bunch of nerds. But they say these are not like the cartoons made in the US. Better than The Lion King?! But I have gotten hooked on Sailor Moon. I see that fans of anime come from many different backgrounds, races, and ethnicities and watch anime for many different reasons. You can choose robots or samurai, romance, or comedy. There seems to be an anime for everyone. The experience sure opened my eyes.

Figure 2.4 Excerpt from Sara Cardini's journal

Freewriting helps get you used to the "feel" of your fingers rapidly hitting computer keys or your pen moving across paper. Freewriting works best if you set a goal—perhaps writing for fifteen minutes or filling one or two pages. Keep going until you reach that goal, even if you have to write one word repeatedly until a new word comes to mind. Some days when you read over your freewriting, it might seem mindless, but other days your interesting ideas may startle you.

In **focused freewriting**, you write from a specific starting point—a sentence from your general freewriting, an idea, a quotation, or anything else you choose. Except for this initial focal point, focused freewriting is the same as regular freewriting. Write until you meet your time or page limit, and don't censor yourself. If you go off the topic, that's fine: See where your thoughts take you. Just keep moving forward.

Like a journal, freewriting is a good source of ideas and details. When Sara Cardini thought her growing interest in Japanese animation might qualify for her assignment, she explored the topic through focused freewriting on watching anime (Figure 2.5).

2c.3 Brainstorming

Brainstorming means listing everything you can think of about a topic. Let your mind roam freely, generating quantities of ideas. Write words, phrases, or sentence fragments—whatever comes to you. If you run out of ideas, ask yourself exploratory questions, such as *What is it? What is it the same as? How is it different? Why or how does it happen? How is it done? What causes it or results*

> *In watching anime, my eyes were opened to a world I would never have known otherwise. I learned not to be so judgmental about animation (which I always thought was for kids). While anime seemed strange and confusing to me at first, before long I realized the importance of studying art from another country. The more I watched and understood anime, the less strange it seemed, and the more I realized that I had just been judging from my limited American point of view. Somewhere in Japan, there is probably some college student who is learning about America from our movies. Now, if the Japanese student and I ever meet, we will be closer to understanding each other*

Figure 2.5 Excerpt from Sara Cardini's freewriting

from it? What does it look, smell, sound, feel, or taste like? Who benefits from it? Who loses?

After you've compiled a list, go to step two. Look for patterns, ways to group the ideas into categories. You'll probably find several categories. Set aside any items that don't fit into a group. If a category interests you but has only a few items, brainstorm that category alone.

You can brainstorm in one concentrated session or over several days, depending on how much time you have for an assignment. Brainstorming with other writers can be especially fruitful: One person's ideas bounce off the next person's, and collectively more ideas come to mind. Chapter 6 explains strategies for working with others.

When brainstorming or freewriting on a computer, try "invisible writing." Temporarily darken your computer monitor. A blank screen can help you focus on getting the words out without the temptation to stop and criticize, but the computer will still be recording your words. When you can write no more, turn on the monitor to see what you have.

Brainstorming was a technique Alex Garcia used to find his topic about the benefits of organic foods. Brainstorming helped him think through several topics and generate some ideas about the one that most appealed to him (Figure 2.6).

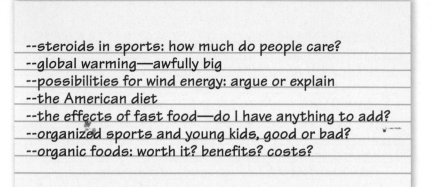

--steroids in sports: how much do people care?
--global warming—awfully big
--possibilities for wind energy: argue or explain
--the American diet
--the effects of fast food—do I have anything to add?
--organized sports and young kids, good or bad?
--organic foods: worth it? benefits? costs?

Figure 2.6 Alex Garcia's brainstorming

EXERCISE 2-1   Here's a list brainstormed for a writing assignment. The topic was "Ways to promote a new movie." Working individually or in a peer-response group, look over the list and group the ideas. You'll find that some ideas don't fit into a group. Then, add any other ideas you have to the list.

coming attractions	suspense
TV ads	book the movie was based on
provocative	locations
movie reviews	Internet trailers
how movie was made	adventure
sneak previews	newspaper ads
word of mouth	stars
director	dialogue
topical subject	excitement
special effects	photography

2c.4 The "journalist's questions"

When journalists report a story, they gather and write about information by asking who did what, when it happened, where it happened, and why and how it happened. The same questions come in handy for writers exploring a topic. The **journalist's questions** are *Who? What? When? Where? Why?* and *How?*

Alex Garcia used the journalist's questions to expand his thinking on the value of eating organic foods. His answers, listed below, showed him that he had enough material for a good essay.

WHO?   **Who** benefits from buying or selling organic food?

WHAT?   **What** kinds of organic foods are available?

WHEN?	**When** did the practice of growing organic foods begin?
WHERE?	**Where** can I find evidence if organic foods are healthier?
WHY?	**Why** do some people doubt the value of organic foods?
HOW?	**How** exactly should someone evaluate the evidence?

2c.5   Mapping

Mapping, also called *clustering*, is a visual form of brainstorming. Some writers find that they begin to think more creatively if they can actually see ways that their ideas connect. Other writers use mapping to help them check the logical relationships between ideas.

To map, write your topic in the middle of a sheet of paper and draw a circle around it. Now, moving out from the center, use lines and circles to show ideas that are subtopics of the topic in the center circle. Continue to subdivide and add details. At any time, you can move to a blank space on your map and start a new subtopic. Try to keep going without censoring yourself.

Sara Cardini used mapping to prompt herself to discover ideas about Japanese animation. When she finished, she was satisfied that she'd have enough to say in her essay. Figure 2.7 shows part of Sara Cardini's clustering for the second paragraph of her essay about Japanese anime.

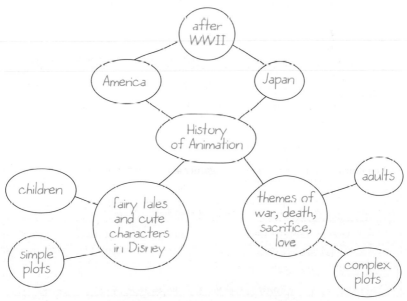

Figure 2.7 Part of Sara Cardini's mapping for her essay on anime

2c.6 Talking it over

Talking it over is based on the notion that two heads are better than one. When you discuss a topic with someone interested in listening and making suggestions, you often think of new ideas. You can even play roles, having other people pretend they disagree with you or are confused. Answering their questions or challenges can spur new thinking.

People you trust can serve as "sounding boards" and tell you if your ideas are complete and reasonable. If your instructor sets up PEER-RESPONSE GROUPS in your class, you might ask the other members to serve as sounding boards. Otherwise, talk with a good friend or another adult.

Chatting, in the traditional sense, means talking face to face. In a more recent sense, however, chatting also refers to instant messaging, e-mailing, text messaging, or using discussion features in course software like Blackboard. Exchanging ideas online not only stimulates your thinking but also acts as a writing warm-up. Figure 2.8 is an excerpt from instant messaging. Chapter 6 provides more advice on working with others.

2c.7 Reading and Browsing

Reading newspapers, magazines, and books can provide a constant source of ideas. While it might sound old-fashioned, academic writers do this all the time. Spending time in the PERIODICALS or new books section of a library or browsing a good bookstore can alert you to fresh topics. Just looking at magazine covers, images, or a table of contents is often productive. If browsing generates a topic, systematic searches will yield more information (Chapter 34).

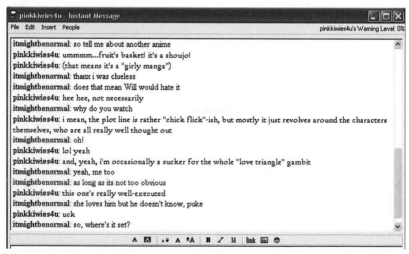

Figure 2.8 Instant messaging screen capture

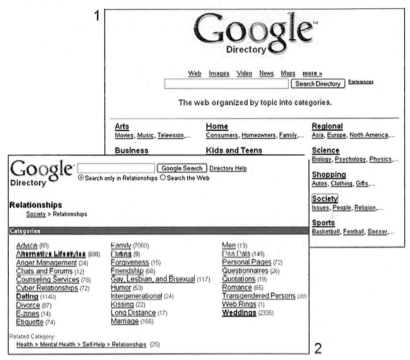

Figure 2.9 Screen shot of Google directory

Of course, **Internet searches** also help you find topics and locate specific information. Chapter 32 provides extensive guidelines for searching the WORLD WIDE WEB. Briefly, however, access the Yahoo! directory at http://dir.yahoo.com or the Google directory at http://www.google.com/dirhp. You'll see a screen that lists broad subject areas.

On the Google directory, click on the broad subject "Society" to see a number of slightly more specific topics, including one on "Relationships." Note that each of them would be much too broad to write about. However, if you keep clicking on topic headings, you'll move to more and more specific subjects. Under "Relationships," you'll find a heading for "Long Distance Relationships," which might be an idea for writing. Browsing through the layers of topics can help you think of several ideas for your writing. If you know a general topic area, you can type it in the search window of the program and then click on more specific subcategories. Figure 2.9 illustrates this process.

EXERCISE 2-2   Go to http://www.google.com/dirhp or http://dir.yahoo.com. Choose one of the headings on the directory. Continue to click on topics under that heading to create a path to a specific possible topic. Be ready to explain the path you used, what you found, and what you think the strengths and weaknesses of the topics you identified would be. Finally, go back to the opening page and repeat the process with a different heading.

● **EXERCISE 2-3**   Explore some of the following topics by typing them into
● the search window of a search engine. Be ready to explain the sequence of top-
● ics you discover.

1. global warming   3. weightlifting   5. disability
2. sustainability   4. world music

2c.8 Incubation

Incubation refers to giving your ideas time to grow and develop. This technique works especially well when you need to step back and evaluate what you've discovered and compiled for your writing. For example, you might not see how your material can be pulled together at first, but if you let it incubate, you might discover connections you didn't see originally. Conversely, if some parts of your essay seem too thin in content, incubation gives you distance from your material so that you can decide what works. Ideally, incubate your ideas overnight or for a couple of days; but even a few hours can help.

If you don't have the luxury of a lengthy incubation period, some strategies may help you jump-start it. One method is to turn your attention to something entirely unrelated to your writing. Concentrate hard on that other matter so that you give your conscious mind over to it totally. After a while, relax and guide your mind back to your writing. Often, you'll see what you've discovered and compiled for writing in a different way.

● **EXERCISE 2-4**   Try each structured technique for discovering and compil-
● ing ideas discussed in 2c.1 through 2c.8. Use your own topics or select from the
● suggestions below.

1. Professions and job prospects   4. Advertisements on television
2. An important personal decision   5. What you want in a life partner
3. Professional sports

2d What is a thesis statement?

A **thesis statement** is the central message of an essay. The thesis statement presents the TOPIC of your essay, your particular focus on that topic, and your PURPOSE for writing about that topic. As a writer, you want to write a thesis statement with great care so that it prepares your readers for what follows. Quick Reference 2.3 lists the basic requirements for a thesis statement.

Quick Reference 2.3

■ ■ ■ ■ ■ ■ ■

Basic requirements for a thesis statement

• It states the essay's subject—the topic that you discuss.
• It conveys the essay's purpose—either informative or persuasive.
• It indicates your focus—the assertion that presents your point of view.
• It uses specific language, not vague words.
• It may briefly state the major subdivisions of the essay's topic.

Some instructors add to these basic requirements for a thesis statement. You might, for example, be asked to put your thesis statement at the end of your introductory paragraph (as in the final draft of Sara Cardini's essay, in section 21.3). Some instructors require that the thesis statement be contained in one sentence; other instructors permit two sentences if the topic is complex. All requirements, basic and additional, are designed to help you develop a thesis statement that will guide the writing of your essay and help you communicate clearly with your reader. By the way, never confuse the role of a thesis statement with the role of an essay's title (21.3).

ESOL Tip: A thesis statement, especially in the introductory paragraph, is commonly found in the ACADEMIC WRITING of North American and some other cultures. Readers and writers from some cultures prefer not to state their main idea so bluntly at the beginning of a piece of writing. Because US readers of academic writing generally expect such a statement, using one will probably help your readers better understand your writing. ●

Most writers find that their thesis statement changes somewhat with each successive draft of an essay, so you shouldn't feel locked into your first thesis draft. Still, when you revise its language, be sure to stick to the essential idea you want to communicate. A thesis statement is a guide; it helps you stay on the topic and develop your ideas. To start, make an **assertion**—a sentence stating your topic and the point you want to make about it. This assertion focuses your thinking as you develop a preliminary thesis statement. Next, move toward a final thesis statement that most accurately reflects the content of your essay.

Following is the evolution of Sara Cardini's thesis statement from a simple assertion to the final version in her essay on anime. The final version fulfills all the requirements described in Quick Reference 2.3.

> **NO** I think Japanese animation is interesting. [This assertion is a start, but simply proclaiming something "interesting" is dull.]

NO   Most people think cartoons are simple entertainments for kids, but there are exceptions to that rule. [This statement draws readers in by promising to show them how their expectations may be inadequate, but it's very broad.]

NO   Anime films are sophisticated Japanese cartoons. [This statement is closer to a thesis statement because it's more specific. It promises to show that anime is sophisticated. However, the concept that anime contrasts with American cartoons is an important part of Sara's paper, and that concept is missing here.]

NO   The purpose of this paper is to explain Japanese anime and how anime films differ from American cartoons. [This version clearly states a main point of the paper, but it's inappropriate because it blandly announces what the writer is going to do.]

YES   Anime has traditions and features that distinguish it from American cartoons and make it sophisticated enough to appeal to adults. [The final version serves as Cardini's thesis statement by effectively conveying the main ideas and point of her essay.]

THESIS STATEMENTS FOR INFORMATIVE ESSAYS

For essays with an informative purpose (1c.2), here are more examples of thesis statements for 900- to 1,300-word essays. The NO versions are assertions or preliminary thesis statements. The YES versions are good because they fulfill the requirements in Quick Reference 2.3.

TOPIC   *Reality television*

NO   There are many kinds of reality television shows.

YES   A common feature of reality television shows is a villain, a contestant that viewers love to hate.

TOPIC   *Women artists*

NO   Paintings by women are getting more attention.

YES   During the past ten years, the works of the artists Mary Cassatt and Rosa Bonheur have finally gained widespread critical acclaim.

THESIS STATEMENTS FOR PERSUASIVE ESSAYS

For essays written with a persuasive purpose (1c.3), here are examples of thesis statements written for 900- to 1,300-word essays. Again, the NO versions are assertions or preliminary thesis statements. The YES versions fulfill the requirements in Quick Reference 2.3.

TOPIC   *Public transportation*

NO   Public transportation has many advantages.

YES   Investing in public transportation pays strong benefits in environmental quality, economic development, and social interactions.

TOPIC   *Deceptive advertising*

NO   Deceptive advertising can cause many problems for consumers.

YES   Deceptive advertising costs consumers not only their money but also their health.

EXERCISE 2-6   Each set of sentences below offers several versions of a thesis statement. Within each set, the thesis statements progress from weak to strong. The fourth thesis statement in each set is the best. Referring to requirements listed in Quick Reference 2.3, work individually or with a group to explain why the first three choices in each set are weak and the last is best.

A. 1. Advertising is complex.
    2. Magazine advertisements appeal to readers.
    3. Magazine advertisements must be creative and appealing to all readers.
    4. To appeal to readers, magazine advertisements must skillfully use language, color, and design.

B. 1. Soccer is a widely played sport.
    2. Playing soccer is fun.
    3. Soccer requires various skills.
    4. Playing soccer for fun and exercise requires agility, stamina, and teamwork.

C. 1. *Hamlet* is a play about revenge.
    2. Hamlet must avenge his father's murder.
    3. Some characters in the play *Hamlet* want revenge.
    4. In the play *Hamlet*, Hamlet, Fortinbras, and Laertes all seek revenge.

D. 1. We should pay attention to the environment.
    2. We should worry about air pollution.
    3. Automobile emissions cause air pollution.
    4. Congress should raise emissions standards for passenger cars and SUVs.

E. 1. Cell phones are popular.
    2. People use cell phones in many situations.
    3. The increased use of cell phones causes problems.
    4. Using cell phones while driving should be illegal.

EXERCISE 2-7   Here are writing assignments, narrowed topics, and tentative thesis statements. Alone or with a peer-response group, evaluate each thesis statement according to the basic requirements in Quick Reference 2.3.

1. **Marketing assignment:** 700- to 800-word persuasive report on a local restaurant. *Audience:* the instructor and the restaurant's owner. *Topic:* increasing business. *Thesis:* The restaurant could attract more students if it changed its menu and redesigned its interior.

2. **Theater assignment:** 300- to 500-word review of a performance. *Audience:* the instructor and other students in the class. *Topic:* a touring production of the musical *Wicked. Thesis:* The recent performance of *Wicked* was very interesting.

3. **Biology assignment:** 800- to 1,000-word informative report about DNA sequencing. *Audience:* the instructor and visiting students and instructors attending a seminar at the state college. *Topic:* people paying to learn their own genetic code. *Thesis:* Scientists should oppose individual DNA tests.

4. **Journalism assignment:** 200- to 300-word article about campus diversity. *Audience:* the instructor, the student body, and the college administration. *Topic:* international students. *Thesis:* There are 279 international students this year at Orwell College.

5. **Nursing assignment:** 400- to 500-word persuasive report about technology changes in nursing. *Audience:* nursing students and professionals. *Topic:* using handheld computers to track patient information. *Thesis:* Hospitals should train nurses more effectively to use handheld computers to enter patient data.

2e How do I plan and organize my ideas?

After you've generated ideas and information, you need to decide the best way to organize it. A plan helps you start drafting. Like a story, an essay needs a beginning, a middle, and an end: a shape. The essay's introduction sets the stage; the essay's body paragraphs provide the substance of your message in a sequence that makes sense; the concluding paragraph ends the essay logically. Each paragraph's length in an informative essay needs to be in proportion to its function. Introductory and concluding paragraphs are usually shorter than body paragraphs. Body paragraphs need to be approximately equal to each other in length. If one body paragraph becomes overly long in relation to the others, consider breaking it into two paragraphs. (We discuss paragraph writing in Chapter 3.) The major elements in an informative essay are listed in Quick Reference 2.4. (For the major elements in a persuasive essay using classical argument, see Quick Reference 5.1 in 5e.)

Shaping an essay takes place on two levels. One is grouping individual ideas or pieces of information into paragraphs. The other is arranging those paragraphs into the best possible order and relationship to each other.

To group your information, look for topics that are related to each other and, within them, search for layers of generality. Which ideas or information can fit under which topics? For example, suppose you're writing a paper about

---

Quick Reference 2.4 ■ ■ ■ ■ ■ ■ ■

Elements in an informative essay

1. **Introductory paragraph:** Leads into the topic of the essay and tries to capture the reader's interest (see 3c).

2. **Thesis statement:** States the central message of the writing. The thesis statement usually appears at the end of the introductory paragraph (2d).

3. **Background information:** Provides a context for understanding the points that a writer wants to make. You can integrate background information into the introductory paragraph. More complex information may require a separate paragraph of information (as in the second paragraph in Sara Cardini's essay, in section 2I).

4. **Points of discussion:** Supports the essay's thesis statement. They're the essential content of the body paragraphs in an essay (3d). Each point of discussion consists of a general statement backed up by specific details.

5. **Concluding paragraph:** Ends the essay smoothly, flowing logically from the rest of the essay (3k).

---

why the *Wizard of Oz* remains a popular movie. Among the ideas that you've brainstormed are the following:

The settings are spectacular.

Dorothy is a good mixture of innocence and determination.

The munchkin village is imaginative.

The Scarecrow is funny.

Oz appears magical at the end of the poppy field.

The Cowardly Lion is different from our expectations.

The Haunted Forest is truly creepy.

The characters are interesting.

Although the list seems somewhat random, you can see that several of the ideas are about characters, and several are about the setting. You can group the ideas under those generalizations, and you can generate even more specific ideas about each one. For example, more specific details about Dorothy's innocence could include the way she sings "Over the Rainbow," and specific examples of her determination could include her efforts to stay awake in the poppy field. Keep in mind that what separates most good writing from bad is the writer's ability to move back and forth between general statements and specific details.

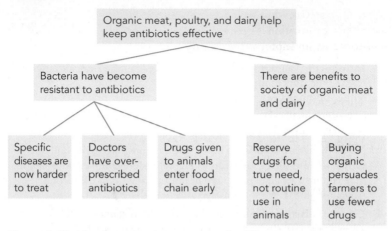

Figure 2.10 Alex Garcia's subject tree for the fifth paragraph in his essay

A **subject tree** shows you visually whether you have sufficient content, at varying levels of generality or specificity, to start a first draft of your writing. A subject tree also visually demonstrates whether you have a good balance of general ideas and specific details. If what you have are mostly general ideas—or, the other way around, mostly specific details—go back to techniques for discovering and compiling ideas (2c) so that you can come up with the sorts of materials that are missing. Alex Garcia created a subject tree, shown in Figure 2.10, using software tools to help him shape the fifth paragraph in his essay (5n).

Once you've sorted your ideas and information into groups organized by generalizations, you're ready to shape your work at another level. You need to figure out the best order for the sections and paragraphs that you've planned. Of course, like all elements of the writing process, organizing is recursive. Although an initial plan might change considerably as you revise your work, a plan is still helpful for writing your first draft.

2f What is outlining?

An **outline** lays out the relationships among ideas in a piece of writing. Outlines can lead writers to see how well their writing is organized. Many instructors require outlines either before or with an essay.

Some writers like to outline; others don't. If you don't, but you're required to write one, tackle the job with an open mind. You may be pleasantly surprised at what the rigor of outline writing does to your perception of your essay.

An outline can be *informal* or *formal.* Try outlining at various steps of the WRITING PROCESS: before drafting, to arrange ideas; while you draft, to keep track of your material; while you revise, to check the logical flow of thought or to reveal what information is missing, repeated, or off the topic; or in whatever other ways you find helpful.

INFORMAL OUTLINES

An **informal outline** is a working plan that lays out the major points of an essay. Because it's informal, it doesn't need to use the numbering and lettering conventions of a formal outline. Complete sentences aren't required; words and phrases are acceptable. Sara Cardini used an informal outline for planning her essay. Here is part of an informal outline for the third paragraph of her essay.

Sara Cardini's Informal Outline

Thesis statement: Anime has traditions and features that distinguish it from American cartoons and make it sophisticated enough to appeal to adults.

> qualities of anime
>
> > quick movements
> >
> > jazz and rock music
> >
> > large eyes for characters
> >
> > complicated drawings
> >
> > *Samurai X* as an example

FORMAL OUTLINES

A traditional **formal outline** follows long-established conventions for using numbers and letters to show relationships among ideas. MLA STYLE (see Chapter 36) doesn't officially endorse using an outline or, indeed, any one outline style. However, many instructors do assign outlines, and they prefer the traditional format shown here. Some instructors prefer a less traditional format for a formal outline, one which includes the content of the introductory and the concluding paragraphs. An example of such an outline appears in section 36e, written by a student whose instructor required that format for an MLA-style research paper. Either of these styles of formal outline—the traditional or the less traditional—can be a sentence outline, composed entirely of complete sentences, or a topic outline, composed only of words and phrases. So that you can compare the two styles of outlines, both examples below outline the third paragraph of Sara Cardini's essay on Japanese anime. Never mix the two styles in one outline.

Writers who use formal outlines say that a sentence outline brings them closer to drafting than a topic outline does. This makes sense because topic outlines contain less information. But you have to find out which type works better for you.

Topic Outline

Thesis statement: Anime has traditions and features that distinguish it from American cartoons and make it sophisticated enough to appeal to adults.

  I. Anime qualities

    A. Quick images

    B. Jazz and rock soundtracks

    C. Character eyes and features

    D. Colorful, complicated art

      1. *Samurai X* as example

      2. *Samurai X* about nineteenth-century warrior

      3. *Samurai X* art like old Japanese prints

Sentence Outline

Thesis statement: Anime has traditions and features that distinguish it from American cartoons and make it sophisticated enough to appeal to adults.

  I. Complex plots are but one of the distinctive features of anime.

    A. Anime images move quickly, with a style often more frantic than in American cartoons.

    B. Their soundtracks frequently use jazz and rock music rather than symphonic music.

    C. Most striking are the large eyes and sharp features of the characters.

    D. The drawing is more colorful, more complicated, and often more abstract than that in most American cartoons.

      1. A TV series called *Samurai X* is one of the most popular anime series with both American and Japanese audiences.

      2. *Samurai X* is set in the nineteenth century and tells the story of one warrior's life.

      3. *Samurai X* art is drawn beautifully to look both like older Japanese art prints and like more contemporary movies such as *Crouching Tiger, Hidden Dragon.*

EXERCISE 2-8   Here is a sentence outline. Individually or with your peer-response group, revise it into a topic outline. Then, be ready to explain why you prefer using a topic outline or a sentence outline as a guide to writing.

Thesis statement: Taxpayers should demand more investment in public transportation.

I. The current level of public transportation is inadequate everywhere.
  A. Cities need the ability to move lots of residents.
    1. Increased population in large cities causes transportation pressures.
    2. Some cities have responded well.
    3. Most cities have responded poorly.
  B. People need to move easily and cheaply between cities and towns.
    1. Cars are the only way to reach many cities and towns.
    2. It is easier and less expensive to travel in Europe.
II. The lack of public transportation causes many problems.
  A. Driving individual cars increases pollution.
  B. Space for building new roads and highways is limited.
  C. Congestion on city streets limits productivity.
  D. Many people aren't able to drive themselves.
    1. Young or elderly people may not drive.
    2. Many people cannot afford cars.
III. Improving public transportation is possible.
  A. Cities can expand bus services and light rail services.
  B. The United States can develop a wider national rail service.
  C. Although improvements are costly, we can afford them.
    1. We can reallocate money from building new roads.
    2. Building and running transportation creates jobs and adds to our tax base.
    3. Individual savings will offset any tax increases.

2g What can help me write a first draft?

Drafting means you get ideas onto paper or into the computer, in sentences and paragraphs. In everyday conversation, people use the word *writing* to talk about drafting, but writing is too broad a term here. The word *drafting* more accurately describes what you do when you write your first attempt—your first *draft*—to generate words.

A **first draft** is the initial version of a piece of writing. Before you begin a first draft, seek out places and times of the day that encourage you to write. You might write best in a quiet corner of the library, or at 4:30 a.m. at the kitchen table before anyone else is awake, or outside alone with nature, or with a steady flow of people walking by. Most experienced writers find they concentrate best when they're alone and won't be interrupted. But individuals differ, and you may prefer background noise—a crowded cafeteria, with the low hum of conversation at the next table or in the next room, for example.

A caution: Don't mislead yourself. You might consider yourself great at multitasking, but academic writing generally demands a higher level of concentration than other tasks. You can't produce a useful first draft while talking to friends and stopping only now and then to jot down a sentence. You won't draft smoothly while watching television or being constantly interrupted.

Finally, resist delaying tactics. While you certainly need a computer or a pad of paper and a pencil, you don't need fifteen perfectly sharpened pencils neatly lined up on your desk.

Quick Reference 2.5 offers suggestions for ways to move from planning and shaping into drafting. Experiment to see what works best for you. And be ready to adjust what works according to each WRITING SITUATION.

Quick Reference 2.5   ■ ■ ■ ■ ■ ■ ■

Ways to start drafting

- **Write a discovery draft.** Put aside all your notes from planning and shaping, and write a discovery draft. This means using FOCUSED FREEWRITING to get ideas on paper or onto your computer screen so that you can make connections that spring to mind as you write. Your discovery draft can serve as a first draft or as one more part of your notes when you write a more structured first draft.

- **Work from your notes.** Sort your notes from planning and shaping into groups of subtopics. When you start writing, you can systematically concentrate on each subtopic without having to search repeatedly through your pile of notes. Arrange the subtopics in what seems to be a sensible sequence, knowing you can always go back later and resequence the subtopics. Now, write a first draft by working through your notes on each subtopic. Draft either the entire essay or chunks of a few paragraphs at one time.

- **Use a combination of approaches.** When you know the shape of your material, write according to that structure. When you feel "stuck" and don't know what to say next, switch to writing as you would for a discovery draft.

Now, dive in. Using the planning and shaping you've done as a basis, start writing. The direction of drafting is forward: Keep pressing ahead. If you wonder about the spelling of a word or a point of grammar, don't stop. Use a symbol or other signal to alert you to revisit the question later. Use whatever you like: boldface, underlining, a question mark before and after, an asterisk, or all capital letters. If the exact word you want escapes you while you're drafting, substitute an easy synonym and mark it to go back to later. If you question your sentence style or the order in which you present supporting details, boldface or underline the passage or insert a symbol or the word *Style?* or *Order?* nearby so that you can return to it later. If you begin to run out of ideas, reread what you have written—not to start revising prematurely, but only to propel yourself to keep moving ahead with your first draft. Once you finish your draft, search for marks that you've used to alert yourself to reconsider something. If it's a word, you can use the "Edit > Find" function on your word processing program toolbar.

When drafting on the computer, use your "Save" function often to protect your work, at least every five minutes. (This can be set up as an automatic function.) To prevent losing what you've written, back up your files diligently. Also, print your work regularly—very definitely at the end of each work session—so that you always have a hard copy in case your computer develops problems. Instructors hear so many versions of "I had computer problems" that they've often stopped sorting out which reports are fake and which are real.

A first draft is a preliminary or *rough draft*. Its purpose is to get your ideas onto disk or into computer memory or on paper. Never are first drafts meant to be perfect.

2h   How can I overcome writer's block?

If you're afraid or otherwise feel unable to start writing, perhaps you're being stopped by **writer's block**. You want to get started but somehow can't. Often, writer's block occurs because the writer harbors a fear of being wrong. To overcome that fear, or any other cause of your block, first admit it to yourself. Face it honestly so that you can understand whatever is holding you back. Writer's block can strike professional as well as student writers, and a variety of techniques to overcome it have become popular.

The most common cause of writer's block involves a writer's belief in myths about writing.

MYTH	Writers are born, not made.
TRUTH	Everyone can write. Writers don't expect to "get it right" the first time. Being a good writer means being a patient rewriter.
MYTH	Writers have to be "in the mood" to write.
TRUTH	If writers always waited for "the mood" to occur, few would write at all. News reporters and other professional writers have deadlines to meet, whether or not they're in the mood to write.
MYTH	Writers have to be really good at grammar and spelling.
TRUTH	Writers don't let spelling and grammar block them. They write, and when they hear that quiet inner voice saying that a word or sentence isn't quite right, they mark the spot with a symbol or word in all capitals. After they're finished drafting,

they return to those spots and work on them, perhaps using this handbook or a dictionary or thesaurus to check themselves.

MYTH   Writers don't have to revise.

TRUTH   Writers expect to revise—several times. Once words are on paper, writers can see what readers will see. This "revision" helps writers revise.

MYTH   Writing can be done at the last minute.

TRUTH   Drafting and revising take time. Ideas don't leap onto paper in final, polished form.

Quick Reference 2.6 lists reliable strategies writers have developed to overcome writer's block. If you feel blocked, experiment to discover which works best for you. Also, add your own ideas about how to get started. As you use the list in Quick Reference 2.6, suspend judgment of your writing. Let things flow. Don't find fault with what you're keyboarding or writing. Your goal is to get yourself under way. You can evaluate and improve your writing when you're revising it. According to research, premature revision stops many writers cold—and leads to writer's block. Your reward for waiting to revise until after you finish your first draft is the comfort of having a springboard for the revision work in front of you.

Quick Reference 2.6   ■ ■ ■ ■ ■ ■ ■

Ways to overcome writer's block

- **Check that one of the myths about writing discussed in section 2h, or one of your own, isn't stopping you.**
- **Avoid staring at a blank page.** Relax and move your hand across the keyboard or page. Write words, scribble, or draw while you think about your topic. The physical act of getting anything on paper can stir up ideas and lead you to begin drafting.
- **Visualize yourself writing.** Many professional writers say that they write more easily if they first picture themselves doing it. Before getting out of bed in the morning or while waiting for a bus or walking to classes, mentally construct a visual image of yourself in the place where you usually write, with the materials you need, busy at work.
- **Picture an image or a scene, or imagine a sound that relates to your topic.** Start writing by describing what you see or hear.

continued >>

Quick Reference 2.6   (continued)

- **Write about your topic in a letter or e-mail to a friend.** This technique helps you relax and makes drafting nothing more than a chat on paper with someone you feel comfortable with.
- **Write a draft to a different audience.** If it feels intimidating writing for your instructor, imagine you're writing for a roommate or parent or someone much younger.
- **Try writing your material as if you were someone else.** When they take on a role, many writers feel less inhibited about writing. Pretend you're an expert, for example, and imagine that everyone wants to know what you think.
- **Start by writing the middle of your essay.** Skip the introduction and begin with a body paragraph, and write from the center of your essay out, instead of from beginning to end.
- **Use FREEWRITING or FOCUSED FREEWRITING.**
- **Change your method of writing.** If you usually use a computer, try writing by hand. When you write by hand, switch between pencil and pen or ink colors and treat yourself to good-quality paper so that you can enjoy the pleasure of writing on smooth, strong paper. Often that pleasure propels you to keep going.
- **Switch temporarily to writing about a topic that you care about passionately.** Write freely about that topic. Once writing starts to pour out of you, you can often use the momentum to switch back to the topic of your assignment.

2i How do I revise?

Revising is rewriting. When you see the word *revision,* break it down to *re-vision,* which means "to see again with fresh eyes." To revise, you evaluate, change, and reevaluate your draft to figure out ways to improve it. To do this, you need to read your writing honestly, without losing confidence or becoming defensive. After all, what's on the page is ink, not ego. As you work, look at whatever you change and evaluate the revision first on its own and then in the context of the surrounding material. Continue until you're satisfied that your essay is the best you can make it, in light of your specific WRITING SITUATION.

Whenever possible within your time frame, distance yourself from each draft. The best way is to leave a chunk of time between finishing a first draft and starting to revise. Doing so helps you develop an objective sense of your work. Student writers often want to hold on to their every word, especially if they had trouble getting started on a first draft. Resist such a feeling vigorously. Put away your draft and allow the rosy glow of authorial pride to dim a bit. The classical writer Horace recommended waiting nine years before revising! You might try to wait a few hours or even thirty minutes. Better yet, take a day or two before going back to look at your work with fresh eyes.

Also, as you're revising, don't start EDITING too soon. Editing comes after revising. Research shows that premature editing distracts writers from dealing with the larger issues that revision involves.

2i.1 Goals and activities during revision

Your goal during revision is to improve your draft at three levels: content, organization, and ideas.

To revise successfully, you need to understand that writing is revising. The myth that good writers never have to revise is nonsense. Final drafts evolve from first drafts. Here's how to prepare your mind for revising:

- Shift mentally from suspending judgment (during idea gathering and drafting) to making judgments. Read your draft objectively with "a cold eye" to evaluate it.

- Decide whether to write an entirely new draft or to revise the one you have. Be critical as you evaluate your first draft, but don't be overly harsh. Many early drafts provide sufficient raw material for revision to get under way.

- Be systematic. Don't evaluate at random. Most writers work best when they concentrate on each element sequentially. Start with your draft's overall organization; next, move to its paragraphs, then to its sentences, and finally to its word choice. If you need practice in being systematic, try using a revision checklist, either one supplied by your instructor or the one in this handbook.

You can engage in the activities of revision, listed in Quick Reference 2.7, by hand or on the computer, which allows you to make both large and small changes easily. Use "Cut" and "Paste" to reorder sentences or rearrange paragraphs. For example, you might decide to split up a paragraph, join two paragraphs, or otherwise shuffle them. Similarly, you might reorder the sequence of some sentences or interchange sentences between paragraphs. Sometimes, these experiments won't yield anything useful, but they might reveal a few surprises that help you "re-vision" your work.

As you try various revisions, use the "Save As" function on your computer to save drafts under slightly different names, such as "Animation Draft 1," "Animation Draft 2," and so on. By saving several drafts of your paper, you can al-

Quick Reference 2.7 ■ ■ ■ ■ ■ ■ ■

Major activities during revision

- **Add:** Insert needed words, sentences, paragraphs, or ideas. If your additions require new content, return to the structured techniques shown in section 2b.

- **Cut:** Get rid of whatever goes off the topic or repeats what has already been said.

- **Replace:** As needed, substitute new words, sentences, and paragraphs for what you have cut.

- **Move:** Change the sequence of paragraphs if the material isn't presented in logical order. Move sentences within paragraphs or to other paragraphs when your PARAGRAPH ARRANGEMENT does not allow the material to flow.

ways return to earlier versions if you later decide you prefer something in one of them. If you want to drop material, resist deleting it instantly. As handbook authors, we save almost everything. Doug, for instance, typically keeps a file named "Junk" for just this purpose. Lynn names her folder of discarded drafts of sentences, paragraphs, and whole essays "Discarded Stuff."

Beware of two temptations when writing with the computer. Because you can rearrange and otherwise revise endlessly, you may need to set limits, or you'll never finish the assignment. The opposite seduction is also possible: A neatly printed page may look like a final draft, but it definitely isn't one.

2i.2 The role of a thesis statement in revision

The THESIS STATEMENT of your essay has great organizing power because it controls and limits what your essay can cover. Therefore, as you revise, keep checking the accuracy of your thesis statement. Use the thesis statement's controlling power to bring it and your essay into line with each other. Adjust your thesis if necessary, for example, if revisions have resulted in more interesting or effective ideas—or have even changed your position. When your essay is finished, the thesis statement and what you say in your essay need to match. If they don't, you need to revise either the thesis statement or the essay—or sometimes both.

Every writer's experience with revising a thesis statement varies from essay to essay. Sara Cardini, the student you met earlier in this chapter as she did her planning and shaping, wrote several versions of her thesis statement (shown in 2d) for her drafts. You can read Cardini's three complete drafts, along with comments, at the end of this chapter.

2i.3   The role of a title in revision

Your **title** can also show you what needs revising because it clarifies the overall point of the essay. An effective title sets you on your course and tells your readers what to expect. Some writers like to begin their first drafts with a title at the top of the page to focus their thinking. Then, as they revise drafts, they revise the title. If, however, no title springs to mind, don't be concerned. Often, a good title doesn't surface until after drafting, revising, and even editing. Whatever you do, never tack on a title as an afterthought right before handing in your essay. A suitable title is essential for readers to think about as they begin focusing on your essay.

Titles can be direct or indirect. A **direct title** tells exactly what the essay will be about—for example, "The Characteristics of Japanese Animation." A direct title contains key words under which the essay could be cataloged in a library or an online database. A direct title shouldn't be too broad. For example, Cardini's first and second drafts of a title were "Japanese Videos" and "Japanese Anime" (2l.1 and 2l.2). By her final draft, Cardini had revised the title to "The Appeal of Japanese Animation for Adults" (2l.3). Conversely, a direct title should not be too narrow. "The Graphics of Anime" is too narrow a title for Cardini's essay, given what she discusses in it.

An **indirect title** only hints at the essay's topic. It tries to catch the reader's interest by presenting a puzzle that can be solved by reading the essay. When writing an indirect title, you don't want to be overly obscure or too cute. For example, a satisfactory indirect title for Cardini's final draft might be "More Than Simple Cartoons?" In contrast, the indirect title "Imagining That Walt Disney Had Been Japanese" wouldn't work because it's only remotely related to the point of the essay. Also, "Thanks, *Sailor Moon*" would probably be seen as overly cute for academic writing.

Alert: When you write the title at the top of the page or on a title page, never enclose it in quotation marks or underline it. Let your title stand on its own, without decoration. Where you place it will depend on which DOCUMENTATION STYLE you're using. ●

Whether direct or indirect, your essay title stands on its own. Never does the first sentence of an essay refer to the essay's title. For example, Cardini's essay, titled "The Appeal of Japanese Animation for Adults," would suffer a major blow if the first sentence were "It certainly does have appeals" or "I am the proof." Rather, the first sentence starts the flow of the essay's content.

2i.4   The role of unity and coherence

Chapter 3 shows you many techniques for achieving unity and coherence in an essay, but here we need to preview those concepts because they're central concerns as you revise.

An essay has **unity** when all of its parts relate to the THESIS STATEMENT and to one another. Does each paragraph—especially each body paragraph—contain examples, reasons, facts, and details that relate directly to your thesis and contribute to your writing situation? As you revise, do you notice that anything in the essay is off the topic? An essay achieves **coherence** through closely built relationships among ideas and details that are built on word choice, use of TRANSITIONAL EXPRESSIONS, clear use of PRONOUNS, and effective PARALLELISM.

2i.5 Using a revision checklist

A revision checklist can focus your attention as you evaluate and revise your writing. Use such a checklist, either one provided by your instructor or one that you compile on your own, based on Quick Reference 2.8.

Quick Reference 2.8 ■ ■ ■ ■ ■ ■ ■

Revision

Your goal is to answer *yes* to each question on the following list. If you answer *no,* you need to revise your writing accordingly. The section numbers in parentheses tell you where to look in this handbook for help.

1. Is your essay topic suitable and sufficiently narrow? (2b.3)
2. Does your thesis statement communicate your topic, focus, and purpose? (2d, Quick Reference 2.3)
3. Does your essay show that you are aware of your audience? (Quick Reference 1.5)
4. Have you checked for places where your reader would be confused or need more information?
5. Have you checked for places where a skeptical reader would object to your argument or not be convinced?
6. Is your essay arranged effectively?
7. Have you checked for material that strays off the topic?
8. Does your introduction prepare your reader for the rest of the essay? (3c)
9. Do your body paragraphs express main ideas in topic sentences as needed? (3e) Are your main ideas clearly related to your thesis statement? (2d)
10. Do you provide specific, concrete support for each main idea? (3f)
11. Do you use transitions and other techniques to connect ideas within and between paragraphs? (3j)
12. Does your conclusion give your essay a sense of completion?

ESOL Tip: If you'd like information about issues of English grammar that often affect multilingual students, consult Part Seven in this handbook. Topics include those related to culture and education, as well as linguistic concerns, such as ARTICLES (Chapter 51); WORD ORDER (Chapter 52); PREPOSITIONS (Chapter 53); VERBALS (Chapter 54); and MODAL AUXILIARY VERBS (Chapter 55).

2j   How do I edit?

Editing means checking the sentence-level wording and the technical correctness of your writing. You carefully examine your writing for correct grammar, spelling, punctuation, capitalization, and use of numbers, italics, and abbreviations. You see if you can improve the style of your sentences. Some people use the terms *editing* and *revising* interchangeably, but these terms refer to very different steps in the writing process. Revising refers to making changes that affect the content, meaning, and organization of a paper. In contrast, editing involves fine-tuning the surface features of your writing.

Editing is crucial. No matter how much attention you've paid to planning, shaping, drafting, and revising, you need to edit carefully. Slapdash editing distracts and annoys your reader; lowers that reader's opinion of you and what you say in your essay; and, in a college assignment, usually earns a lower grade.

Our best advice to you about editing is this: Don't rush. Editing takes time. Inexperienced writers sometimes rush editing, eager to "get it over with." Resist any impulse to hurry. Be systematic and patient. Checking grammar and punctuation takes your full concentration, along with time to look up and apply the rules in this handbook.

When do you know you've finished revising and are ready to edit? Ask yourself, "Is there anything else I can do to improve the content, organization, and development of this draft?" If the answer is no, you're ready to edit.

Word-processing programs include editing tools such as a spell-checker, style-checker, thesaurus, and readability analyzer. However, as we explained in Chapter 1, each of these tools has shortcomings serious enough to create new errors. Yet, if you use the tools intelligently, with their shortcomings in mind, they can be useful.

Whenever possible, edit on a paper copy of your writing. It's much easier to spot editing errors on a printed page than on a computer screen. Double-space your paper before printing it for revising or editing. The extra space gives you room to write your changes clearly so that you can read them easily later. After you finish editing, you can transfer your corrections to the computer. If you must edit onscreen, highlight every two or three sentences and read each slowly. By working in small segments, you reduce the tendency to read too quickly and miss errors.

Using an editing checklist—either one provided by your instructor or one based on Quick Reference 2.9 that you tailor to your particular needs—can help you find errors by moving through editing systematically. A time-saving method for editing is to create a personal list of common errors you tend to make repeatedly. For example, if the difference between *its* and *it's* always escapes you, or if you tend to misuse the colon, using your personal list of common errors while you edit can remind you to look carefully for those problems.

Quick Reference 2.9 ■ ■ ■ ■ ■ ■ ■

Editing

Your goal is to answer *yes* to each question below. If you answer *no,* you need to edit. The numbers in parentheses tell you which chapters in this handbook to go to for more information.

1. Are your sentences concise? (Chapter 11)
2. Are your sentences interesting? Do you use parallelism, variety, and emphasis correctly and to increase the impact of your writing? (Chapters 9–10)
3. Have you used exact words? (Chapter 12)
4. Is your usage correct and your language appropriate? (Chapter 13)
5. Have you avoided sexist or stereotypical language? (Chapter 12)
6. Is your grammar correct? (Chapters 14–22)
7. Is your spelling correct? (Chapter 31)
8. Have you used commas correctly? (Chapter 24)
9. Have you used all other punctuation correctly? (Chapters 23 and 25–29)
10. Have you used capital letters, italics, abbreviations, and numbers correctly? (Chapter 30)
11. Have you used the appropriate citation and documentation formats? (Chapters 36–38)

2k   How do I proofread?

To **proofread**, check your final draft for accuracy and neatness before handing it in. In contrast to editing, which is a check for technical correctness, proofreading is a check for typographical accuracy. This is your last chance to catch typing (or handwriting) errors and to make sure that you hand in a clean transcription of your final draft. You don't want all your hard efforts drafting, revising, and editing to be undercut by your not taking this final step.

When proofreading, read your work carefully line by line, looking for typing errors such as "form" vs. "from," letters or words accidentally omitted, words typed twice in a row, wrong indents to start each paragraph, and similar typos or slips. Then, print out a complete fresh copy. Reprinting just one page is often difficult because of reflowing text. Never expect your instructor to make allowances for handwritten corrections.

Some techniques for proofreading include: (1) using a ruler under each line as you read it to prevent yourself from looking beyond that line; (2) reading backwards, sentence by sentence, to prevent yourself from being distracted by the content of the paper; and (3) proofreading your final draft aloud, to yourself or to a friend, so that you can hear errors that have slipped past your eyes. As with revising and editing, whenever possible, print and proofread a double-spaced paper copy of your writing. Again, it's much easier to spot errors on a printed page than onscreen. If you must proofread onscreen, highlight every two or three sentences and read each slowly. Enlarging the type onscreen is another helpful trick to help you focus word by word.

21 A student essay in three drafts

The following sections observe Sara Cardini, a student, planning to write on the topic of Japanese animation. Elsewhere in this chapter, you'll find her writing assignment (2b), how she used an entry in her journal (2c.1), mapped her ideas (2c.5), wrote her thesis statement (2d), and outlined (2f).

21.1 The first draft of a student essay

Here's Cardini's first draft showing her own notes to herself about revisions to make in the second draft. The notes resulted from comments from other students in her peer-response group (6c) and from her personal rereading of her draft.

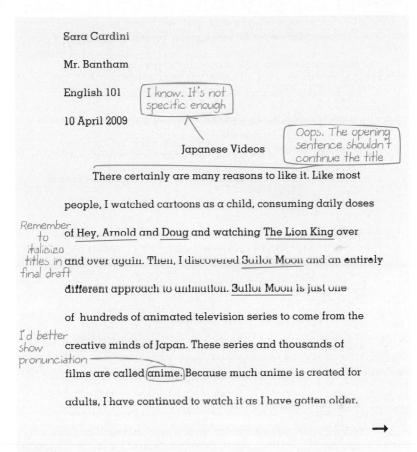

Sara Cardini

Mr. Bantham

English 101   *I know. It's not specific enough*

10 April 2009

Japanese Videos   *Oops. The opening sentence shouldn't continue the title*

There certainly are many reasons to like it. Like most

people, I watched cartoons as a child, consuming daily doses

Remember to italicize titles in final draft

of Hey, Arnold and Doug and watching The Lion King over

and over again. Then, I discovered Sailor Moon and an entirely

different approach to animation. Sailor Moon is just one

of hundreds of animated television series to come from the

I'd better show pronunciation

creative minds of Japan. These series and thousands of

films are called anime. Because much anime is created for

adults, I have continued to watch it as I have gotten older.

→

Figure 2.11 Sara Cardini's first draft, with notes

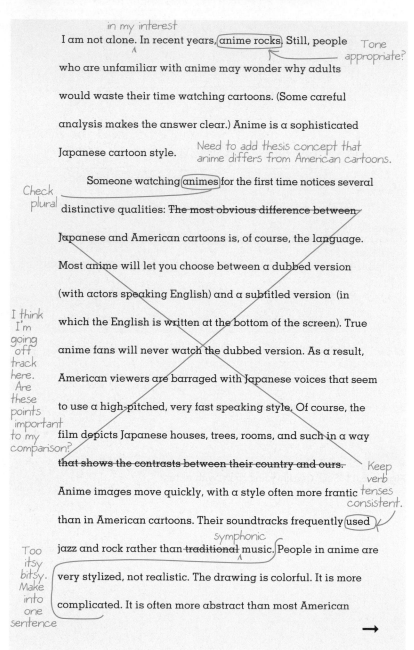

I am not alone. In recent years, ~~anime rocks~~ *in my interest* Still, people who are unfamiliar with anime may wonder why adults would waste their time watching cartoons. (Some careful analysis makes the answer clear.) Anime is a sophisticated Japanese cartoon style.

Tone appropriate?

Need to add thesis concept that anime differs from American cartoons.

Someone watching ~~animes~~ for the first time notices several distinctive qualities: ~~The most obvious difference between Japanese and American cartoons is, of course, the language. Most anime will let you choose between a dubbed version (with actors speaking English) and a subtitled version (in which the English is written at the bottom of the screen). True anime fans will never watch the dubbed version. As a result, American viewers are barraged with Japanese voices that seem to use a high-pitched, very fast speaking style. Of course, the film depicts Japanese houses, trees, rooms, and such in a way that shows the contrasts between their country and ours.~~

Check plural

I think I'm going off track here. Are these points important to my comparison?

Keep verb tenses consistent.

Anime images move quickly, with a style often more frantic than in American cartoons. Their soundtracks frequently ~~used~~ jazz and rock rather than ~~traditional~~ *symphonic* music. People in anime are very stylized, not realistic. The drawing is colorful. It is more complicated. It is often more abstract than most American

Too itsy bitsy. Make into one sentence

→

Figure 2.11 continued

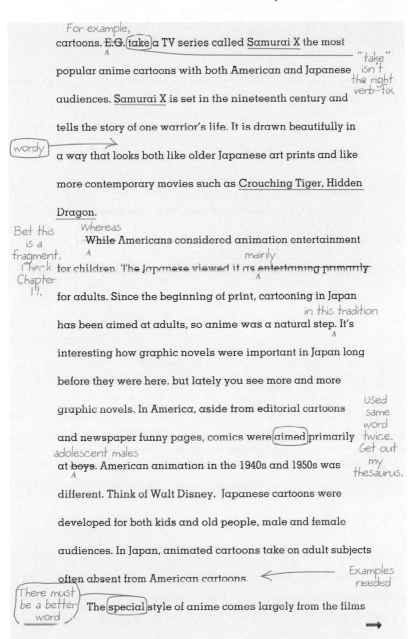

For example,

cartoons. ~~E.G.~~ (take) a TV series called <u>Samurai X</u> the most

popular anime cartoons with both American and Japanese

audiences. <u>Samurai X</u> is set in the nineteenth century and

"take" isn't the right verb—fix

tells the story of one warrior's life. It is drawn beautifully in

wordy

a way that looks both like older Japanese art prints and like

more contemporary movies such as <u>Crouching Tiger, Hidden</u>

<u>Dragon.</u>

Bet this is a fragment. Check Chapter 19.

Whereas

~~While~~ Americans considered animation entertainment

for children ~~The Japanese viewed it as entertaining primarily~~

mainly

for adults. Since the beginning of print, cartooning in Japan

has been aimed at adults, so anime was a natural step. It's

in this tradition

interesting how graphic novels were important in Japan long

before they were here, but lately you see more and more

graphic novels. In America, aside from editorial cartoons

and newspaper funny pages, comics were (aimed) primarily

adolescent males

at ~~boys.~~ American animation in the 1940s and 1950s was

Used same word twice. Get out my thesaurus.

different. Think of Walt Disney. Japanese cartoons were

developed for both kids and old people, male and female

audiences. In Japan, animated cartoons take on adult subjects

often absent from American cartoons. ← *Examples needed*

There must be a better word

The (special) style of anime comes largely from the films

Figure 2.11 continued

being produced for [narrow] audiences. The animators were   *Right word?*

creating works only for a Japanese market, at least until

quite recently. Therefore, they did not take into account the

traditions of other cultures. Indeed, US animation was

produced for an international audience, which called for

recognizable themes that came out of familiar European

traditions. For ~~rookie~~ *uninitiated* viewers then, anime provides a crash

course in ~~a~~ *an Eastern* culture quite different from their own. Nearly

all serious anime fans own guides that explain such things   *Add more detail here*

as Japanese social hierarchies. For instance, several anime

feature a *hagoromo* or feathered cloak worn by a mythological

figure known as the *tennyo*. Knowing that this figure has a

certain *symbolic* meaning for a Japanese viewer and is not just a

random decoration or character adds to the depth of a scene

in which it appears. Decoding some of these cultural

references is undoubtedly some of the fun and challenge for

the true *otakon*, or anime fan.

　　Japanese television has many daily animated series

that vary in terms of sophistication and audience. Some of

these have extremtly ~~complicated~~ *complex* scripts, while others are

bad by nearly any standard. Several of these television series

→

Figure 2.11 continued

[Add examples] now appear in the United States. A wide range of anime

feature films is readily available on DVD, and many have

even found their way into American theaters. For instance,

Akira is a film about life thirty years after a nuclear war.

Probably the most famous theatrical anime in the United   *Better look at this sentence again!*

States is Spirited Away. Directed by Hayao Miyasaki, in

which a young girl, Chihiro, is able to free her parents from

a spell after many magical adventures. The movie will become   *probably*

a ~~probably~~ classic. Anime appears in all kinds of types and

~~genres, from childish works like Pokémon to dark science~~

fiction like Ghost in the Shell.   *I think I should move this up as the topic sentence for this paragraph.*

Best word?   One reason (grown-ups) enjoy anime is because they

(missed) a form they loved as children. Anime gives them   *of design, creativity, sophistication and content*

Verb tense ok?   animated art but adds an adult level. While there have

been a few American cartoons aimed at adults (The Simpsons,

South Park), the animation is less detailed and the tone is

usually satiric. There is no such barrier in anime.

By studying anime, I also learned more about Japan.

I met people who took Japanese language classes and had

traveled to cities such as Tokyo and Osaka. I found out about

Japanese popular culture and how much fashion, music, etc.,

→

Figure 2.11 continued

the Japanese borrow from Americans and how much we

borrow from them. I discovered that while the Japanese are

very different in some traditions, they are very much like us

in terms of their love of movies, TV, and music. For the first

time, I became very interested in how people in another *Does this para relate directly to my thesis?*

country live. Now I am considering traveling to Japan

As Americans come to embrace anime, the form may

change. Some fans fear that the art of anime will be ~~wasted~~ *watered down*

in the bid for popularity and profits. Others celebrate the

combination of styles as some American animators borrow

from the Japanese. In this essay I have explained Japanese

animation. ← *I shoudn't declare what I have done. My ending needs work.*

Figure 2.11 continued

21.2 The second draft of a student essay

For her second draft, Cardini revised by working systematically through the notes she had written on the draft. The notes came from her own thinking as well as from the comments of the peer-response group with which she had shared her paper.

From the assignment (2b), Cardini knew that her instructor would consider this second draft an "essay in progress." Her instructor's responses would help her write a final draft. She expected two types of comments: questions to help her clarify and expand on some of her ideas, and references to some of this handbook's section codes (designated by number-letter combinations) to point out errors. Here is her second draft.

Sara Cardini

Mr. Bantham

English 101

14 April 2005

Japanese Anime

Think about the title as you clarify the overall point of your essay.

What might be an attention-catching opening line?

Like most people, I watched cartoons as a child, consuming daily doses of *Hey, Arnold* and *Doug* and watching *The Lion King* over and over again. Then, I discovered *Sailor*

When?

Moon and an entirely different approach to animation. *Sailor Moon* is just one of hundreds of animated television series to come from the creative minds of Japan. These series and thousands of films are called anime (commonly pronounced AN-ah-may). Because much anime is created for adults, I have continued to watch it as I have gotten older. I am not

What personal background do you have in this area?

For comma use, see 24c

alone in my interest. In recent years, anime has become hugely popular in the United States. Still, people who are unfamiliar with anime may wonder why adults waste their time watching cartoons. (Some careful analysis makes the answer clear.) The purpose of this paper is to

If this sentence is necessary, why put it in parentheses?

→

Figure 2.12 Sara Cardini's second draft, with her instructor's responses.

Indicate the purpose of your paper without announcing it.

explain Japanese anime and how it differs from the style of American cartoons.

Should this para come after the background information?

Think about a stronger link between paragraphs.

Someone watching anime for the first time notices several distinctive qualities. Anime images move quickly, with a style often more frantic than in American cartoons. Their soundtracks frequently use jazz and rock rather

Interesting, but I'd like to know more detail

than symphonic music. People in anime are very stylized, not realistic. The drawing is more colorful, more complicated, and often more abstract than in most American cartoons. For example, a TV series called *Samurai X* is one of the most popular anime cartoons with both American and Japanese

Since this para gives background information, does it belong here?

audiences. *Samurai X* is set in the nineteenth century and tells the story of one warrior's life. ←

Why is it popular?

Whereas Americans considered animation entertainment for children, the Japanese viewed it as mainly for adults. Since the beginning of print, cartooning in Japan has targeted adults,

This para needs a stronger topic sentence.

so anime was a natural step in this tradition. It's interesting how graphic novels were important in Japan long before they

Off topic?

were here, but lately you see more and more graphic novels.

→

Figure 2.12 continued

In the United States, aside from editorial cartoons and newspaper funny pages, comics were aimed primarily at [*From what?*] adolescent males. American animation in the 1940s and [*A little more guidance, please.*] 1950s was (different.) Think of Walt Disney. Japanese cartoons [*Off topic?*] were developed for both kids and old people, male and female audiences. In Japan, animated cartoons take on adult subjects often absent from American cartoons. These subjects include war, death, sacrifice, love, Japan's historical past and future, and even occasionally sex and violence. [*A link to the next para would be welcome here.*]

The unique style of anime comes largely from the [*Right word?*] films being produced for (narrow) audiences. The animators were creating works only for a Japanese market, at least until quite recently. Therefore, (it) did not take into account [*What does it refer to? See 16p*] the traditions of other cultures. (Indeed,) American animation [*Right word?*] was produced for an international audience, which called for recognizable themes that came out of familiar European traditions. For uninitiated viewers, then, anime provides a crash course in an Eastern culture quite different from their own. Nearly all serious anime fans own guides that explain such

→

Figure 2.12 continued

things as Japanese social hierarchies, clothing, dining habits,

traditions, rituals, and mythology. For instance, several anime *See next page.*

feature a *hagoromo*, or feathered cloak, worn by a mythological

figure known as the *tennyo*. Knowing that this figure has a

symbolic meaning for a Japanese viewer and is not just a

random decoration or character adds to the depth of a scene

in which it appears. Decoding some of these cultural references

Excellent point! is undoubetedly some of the fun and challenge for the true

otakon, or anime fan.

Anime appears in all kinds of types and genres, from

Do you really mean childish? childish works like *Pokémon* to dark science fiction like *Ghost*

in the Shell. Japanese televison has many daily animated series

that vary in terms of sophistication and audience. Some of *Meaning what?*

these have extremely complex scripts, while others are bad

by nearly any standard. Several of these television series

now appear in the United States, with some of the best known

including *Inuyasha* and *Evangelion*. A wide range of anime

feature films are readily available on DVD, and many have

even found their way into American theaters.

→

Figure 2.12 continued

See previous page.

For instance, *Akira* is a film about life thirty years after a

More detail would make this vivid.

nuclear war. Probably the most famous theatrical anime

video in the United States is *Spirited Away*, directed by

Hayao Miyasaki, in which a young girl, Chihiro, is able to

free her parents from a spell after many magical adventures.

The movie will probably become a classic.

One reason American adults enjoy anime is because

they miss a form they loved as children. Anime gives them

animated art but adds an adult level of design, creativity,

sophistication, and content. While there have been a few

American cartoons aimed at adults (*The Simpsons*, *South Park*).

the animation is less detailed and the tone is usually satiric.

There are no such barriers in anime.

Interesting concluding thoughts

As Americans come to embrace anime, the form may

Bringing in your voice again makes for an effective ending.

change. Some fans fear that the art of anime will be watered

down in the bid for popularity and profits. Others celebrate

the combination of styles as some American animators

borrow from the Japanese. In this essay I have proved that

anime deserves our attention.

But avoid making an absolute claim like this.

Figure 2.12 continued

Dear Sara,
   You've done yourself proud. And you've inspired me to look up the fascinating subject of Japanese anime.
   As you revise for your final draft, I'd urge you to acquire a little more personal voice. Think about how you feel on this subject and put that in words. Also, think about my questions and the codes that refer you to sections of the Troyka handbook. I will enjoy reading your final draft.

RB

21.3 A student's final draft

For her final draft, Cardini worked systematically through her second draft with an eye on her instructor's responses. Also, she revised in places where her instructor hadn't commented. As another check, Cardini referred to the revision checklist (Quick Reference 2.8).

Next, to edit her final draft, Cardini looked up the handbook codes (number-letter combinations) her instructor wrote on her second draft. She also consulted the editing checklist (Quick Reference 2.9). Then, before she started to proofread, she took a break from writing so she could refresh her ability to see typing errors. Distance from her work, she knew, would also help her see it more objectively.

Cardini's final draft appears on the following pages with notes in the margins to point out elements that help the essay succeed. These notes are for you only; don't write any notes on your final drafts.

Sara Cardini's final draft

Sara Cardini

Mr. Bantham

English 101

13 April 2008

Header at top right has name and page number

Includes name, course information, and date; double-spaced and flush left

The Appeal of Japanese Animation for Adults

Centers title

I confess that I am an animation addict. Like most people, I watched cartoons as a child, consuming daily doses of *Hey, Arnold* and *Doug* and watching *The Lion King* over and over again. Then in junior high, just about the time I was getting tired of cartoons, I discovered *Sailor Moon* and an entirely different approach to animation. *Sailor Moon* is just one of hundreds of animated television series to come from the creative minds of Japan. These series and thousands of films are called *anime* (commonly pronounced AN-ah-may). Because much anime is created for adults, I have continued to watch it as I have gotten older. In fact, my interest has grown so strong that I have studied Japanese, have attended anime conferences, and am now studying filmmaking. I am not alone in my interest. In recent years, anime has become hugely popular in the United States. Still, people who are unfamiliar with anime may wonder why adults would waste their time watching cartoons. Some careful analysis makes the answer clear. Anime has traditions and features that distinguish it from American cartoons and make it sophisticated enough to appeal to adults.

Includes attention-getting first line

Provides her credentials on this topic

Introduces a question

Offers a thesis

Animation developed differently in Japan and America after World War II. Whereas Americans considered animation

Provides background on topic

(Proportions shown in this paper are adjusted to fit space limitations of this book. Follow actual dimensions given in this book and your instructor's directions.)

Cardini 2

entertainment for children, the Japanese viewed it as mainly

Uses comparison and contrast to develop paragraph

for adults. Since the beginning of print, cartooning in Japan has targeted adults, so anime was a natural step in this tradition. In America, aside from editorial cartoons and newspaper funny pages, comics were aimed primarily at adolescent males. Therefore, American animation in the 1940s and 1950s was different from the type developed in Japan. The early work of Walt Disney, for example, came from fairy tales, or it featured cute animal characters. In Japan, animated cartoons take on adult subjects often absent from American cartoons. These subjects include war, death, sacrifice, love, Japan's historical past and future, and even occasionally sex and violence. The plot lines are often extremely complex. Stories that would be kept simple in a Disney film to avoid viewer confusion have no such restrictions in Japan.

Uses specific details to explain anime

Complex plots are but one of the distinctive features of anime. Anime images move quickly, with a style often more frantic than in American cartoons. Their soundtracks frequently use jazz and rock rather than symphonic music. However, perhaps most striking are the large eyes and sharp

Provides a concrete example

features of the characters. People in anime are very stylized, not realistic. The drawing is more colorful, more complicated, and often more abstract than most American cartoons. For example, a TV series called *Samurai X* is one of the most popular anime cartoons with both American and Japanese audiences. *Samurai X* is set in the nineteenth century and tells the story of one warrior's life. It is drawn beautifully in a way that looks both like older Japanese art prints and like more contemporary movies such as *Crouching Tiger, Hidden Dragon*.

continued >>

Cardini 3

The unique style of anime comes largely from the films being produced for specific audiences. The animators were creating works only for a Japanese market, at least until quite recently. Therefore, they did not take into account the traditions of other cultures. In contrast, American animation was produced for an international audience, which called for recognizable themes that came out of familiar European traditions. For uninitiated viewers, then, anime provides a crash course in an Eastern culture quite different from their own. Nearly all serious anime fans own guides that explain such things as Japanese social hierarchies, clothing, dining habits, traditions, rituals, and mythology. To cite one small example, several anime feature a *hagoromo*, or feathered cloak, worn by a mythological figure known as the *tennyo*. Knowing that this figure has a symbolic meaning for a Japanese viewer and is not just a random decoration or character adds to the depth of a scene in which it appears. Decoding some of these cultural references is undoubtedly some of the fun and challenge for the true *otakon*, or anime fan.

Uses cause and effect to explain differences

Cites a very specific example

Anime appears in all kinds of types and genres, from children's works like *Pokémon* to dark science fiction like *Ghost in the Shell*. Japanese television has many daily animated series that vary in terms of sophistication and audience. Some of these have extremely complex scripts, while others are painfully simplistic. Several of these television series now appear in America, with some of the best known including *Inuyasha* and *Evangelion*. A wide range of anime feature films are readily available on DVD in

Uses classification to explain types

Provides specific titles as examples

continued >>

Cardini 4

Focuses at length on one prominent example

America, and many have even found their way into theaters. For example, *Akira* is a film about life thirty years after a nuclear war. A misfit boy, Tetsuo, accidentally discovers the government experiments that led to that war and then learns that scientists are starting similar experiments once again. Probably the most famous theatrical anime films in the United States are *Howl's Moving Castle* and *Spirited Away*. In the last one, directed by Hayao Miyasaki, a young girl, Chihiro, is able to free her parents from a spell after many magical adventures. The movie will probably become a classic.

States a reason in the topic sentence

One reason American adults enjoy anime is because they miss a form they loved as children. Anime gives them animated art but adds an adult level of design, creativity, sophistication, and content. While there have been a few

Contrasts American cartoons with anime

American cartoons aimed at adults (*The Simpsons*, *South Park*), the animation is not very detailed and the tone is usually satiric. There are no such barriers in anime.

Speculates about the future in concluding strategy

As Americans come to embrace anime, the form may change. Some fans fear that the art of anime will be watered down in the bid for popularity and profits. Others celebrate the combination of styles as some American animators borrow from the Japanese. As an animation addict, I welcome more

Uses final comment to return to her opening idea

American animation for adults. Still, I would be disappointed if the distinctive qualities of anime disappeared. I fervently hope the Japanese animators will maintain their exotic creativity.

3 ■ ■ ■ ■ ■ ■

Writing Paragraphs, Shaping Essays

3a How do I shape essays?

A good essay has an effective beginning, middle, and end. The key word is *effective*. Beginnings interest your reader and create expectations for the rest of the essay, usually through a THESIS STATEMENT, your main point. Middles explain or provide arguments for the thesis, usually through a series of statements and supporting details or evidence. Writers organize their main ideas to build a logical and engaging sequence. What separates most good writing from bad is the writer's ability to move back and forth between main ideas and specific details. Endings provide closure. They make readers feel that the writing achieved its purpose and that the writer had a skilled sense of his or her audience to the very end. One key to shaping essays is understanding how paragraphs work.

3b How do paragraphs work?

A **paragraph** is a group of sentences that work together to develop a unit of thought. Paragraphing permits writers to divide material into manageable parts. When a group of paragraphs works together in logical sequence, the result is a complete essay or other whole piece of writing.

Paragraphs function differently in different types of writing. In many academic papers, each paragraph is a logical unit that develops a single idea, often expressed as a topic sentence (3e), with each topic sentence contributing to the paper's thesis. In such writings, you might think of individual paragraphs as bricks that form a wall, or as rooms that together form a building. In writings that tell a story or explain a process, there are often few topic sentences. In newspaper or journalistic writings, paragraph breaks frequently occur more for dramatic effect than for logic.

To signal the start of a new paragraph, indent the first line about one-half inch. Skip no extra lines between paragraphs. Business writing (Chapter 43) is an exception: It calls for BLOCK STYLE for paragraphs, which means you do not indent the first line but rather leave a double space between paragraphs.

We explain later in this chapter the rich variety of paragraph arrangements (3h) and rhetorical patterns (3i) at your disposal for writing paragraphs. But first, let's look at characteristics of paragraphs in general. We start by discussing introductory paragraphs (3c); then, body paragraphs (3d through 3i); and last, concluding paragraphs (3k).

3c   How can I write effective introductory paragraphs?

An **introductory paragraph** leads the reader to sense what's ahead. It sets the stage. It also, if possible, attempts to arouse a reader's interest in the topic.

A THESIS STATEMENT can be an important component in an introduction. Many instructors require students to place the thesis statement at the end of the opening paragraph. Doing so disciplines students to state early the central point of the essay. If an introduction points in one direction, and the rest of the essay goes off in another, the essay isn't communicating a clear message. Professional writers don't necessarily include a thesis statement in their introductory paragraphs. Most have the skill to maintain a line of thought without overtly stating a main idea. Introductory paragraphs, as well as concluding paragraphs (3k), are often shorter than body paragraphs (3d).

Be careful not to tack on a sloppy introduction at the last minute. The introductory paragraph plays too important a role to be tossed off with merely a few shallow lines. That doesn't mean you have to write an introduction first; you might put down ideas and a thesis to start, then return during the revision process to write an effective, polished introduction. For a list of specific strategies to use and pitfalls to avoid for introductory paragraphs, see Quick Reference 3.1.

Quick Reference 3.1   ■ ■ ■ ■ ■ ■ ■

Introductory paragraphs

STRATEGIES TO USE

- Providing relevant background information
- Relating briefly an interesting story or anecdote
- Giving one or more pertinent—perhaps surprising—statistics
- Asking one or more provocative questions
- Using an appropriate quotation
- Defining a KEY TERM
- Presenting one or more brief examples (3i)
- Drawing an ANALOGY (3i)

continued >>

| Quick Reference 3.1 | (continued) |

STRATEGIES TO AVOID

- Don't write statements about your purpose, such as "I am going to discuss the causes of falling oil prices."
- Don't apologize, as in "I am not sure this is right, but this is my opinion."
- Don't use overworked expressions, such as "Haste makes waste, as I recently discovered" or "Love is grand" or "According to Webster's dictionary."

Always integrate an introductory device into the paragraph so that it leads smoothly into the thesis statement. Some examples follow. In this chapter, each example paragraph has a number to its left for your easy reference. Here's an introductory paragraph that uses two brief examples to lead into the thesis statement at the end of the paragraph.

1 On seeing another child fall and hurt himself, Hope, just nine months old, stared, tears welling up in her eyes, and crawled to her mother to be comforted—as though she had been hurt, not her friend. When 15-month-old Michael saw his friend Paul crying, Michael fetched his own teddy bear and offered it to Paul; when that didn't stop Paul's tears, Michael brought Paul's security blanket from another room. Such small acts of sympathy and caring, observed in scientific studies, are leading researchers to trace the roots of empathy—the ability to share another's emotions—to infancy, contradicting a long-standing assumption that infants and toddlers were incapable of these feelings.

—Daniel Goleman, "Researchers Trace Empathy's Roots to Infancy"

In paragraph 2, the opening quotation sets up a dramatic contrast with the thesis statement.

2 "Alone one is never lonely," says May Sarton in her essay "The Rewards of Living a Solitary Life." Most people, however, don't share Sarton's opinion: They're terrified of living alone. They're used to living with others—children with parents, roommates with roommates, friends with friends, spouses with spouses. When the statistics catch up with them, therefore, they're rarely prepared. Chances are high that most adult men and women will need to know how to live alone, briefly or longer, at some time in their lives.

—Tara Foster, student

In paragraph 3, the writer asks a direct question, and next puts the reader in a dramatic situation to arouse interest in the topic.

3

What should you do? You're out riding your bike, playing golf, or in the middle of a long run when you look up and suddenly see a jagged streak of light shoot across the sky, followed by a deafening clap of thunder. Unfortunately, most outdoor exercisers don't know whether to stay put or make a dash for shelter when a thunderstorm approaches, and sometimes the consequences are tragic.

—Gerald Secor Couzens, "If Lightning Strikes"

EXERCISE 3-1   Write an introduction for each of the three essays informally outlined below. Then, for more practice, write one alternative introduction for each. If you have a peer-response group, share the various written introductions and decide which are most effective. For help, see section 3b.

1. Play at school

   Thesis statement: School recesses today differ tremendously from recess a generation ago.

   Body paragraph 1: types of recess activities thirty years ago

   Body paragraph 2: types of games now, including ultimate frisbee

   Body paragraph 3: other activities, including climbing walls and free running

2. Cell phones

   Thesis statement: Cell phones have changed how some people behave in public.

   Body paragraph 1: driving

   Body paragraph 2: restaurants

   Body paragraph 3: movies and concerts

   Body paragraph 4: sidewalks, parks, and other casual spaces

3. Identity theft

   Thesis statement: Taking some simple precautions can reduce the danger of identity theft.

   Body paragraph 1: discarding junk mail

   Body paragraph 2: watching store purchases

   Body paragraph 3: internet security

3d   What are body paragraphs?

In most academic writing, each **body paragraph**, the several paragraphs between an introductory paragraph (3c) and a concluding paragraph (3k), consists of a main idea and support for that idea. To be effective, a body paragraph needs three characteristics: development (3f), unity (3g), and coherence (3g). Quick Reference 3.2 gives an overview of all three characteristics.

Quick Reference 3.2   ■ ■ ■ ■ ■ ■ ■

Characteristics of effective body paragraphs

- **Development:** Have you included detailed and sufficient support for the main idea of the paragraph? (3f)

- **Unity:** Have you made a clear connection between the main idea of the paragraph and the sentences that support, develop, or illustrate the main idea? (3g)

- **Coherence:** Have you progressed from one sentence to the next in the paragraph smoothly and logically? (3g)

Paragraph 4 is an example of an effective body paragraph.

4   The Miss Plastic Surgery contest, trumpeted by Chinese promoters as "the world's first pageant for artificial beauties," shows the power of cosmetic surgery in a country that has swung from one extreme to another when it comes to the feminine ideal. In the 10th century, Emperor Li Yu ordered his consort to bind her feet; women practiced the painful ritual for more than 900 years in the belief that small feet were more alluring. In contrast, at the height of the Cultural Revolution in the 1960s and 1970s, Maoist officials condemned any form of personal grooming or beautification as "unrevolutionary" and regularly beat women for owning hairbrushes, wearing blush, or painting their nails.

    —Abigail Haworth, "Nothing About These Women Is Real"

Paragraph 4 has UNITY (3g) in that the main idea—the feminine ideal in China has swung from one extreme to another—stated in the TOPIC SENTENCE (3e) is supported by detailed examples. It has COHERENCE (3g) in that the content of every sentence ties into the content of the other sentences. Also, the paragraph *coheres*—sticks together—because of the use of transitional phrases ("In the 10th century" and "In contrast," for example). It has PARAGRAPH DEVELOPMENT (3f) in that the details provide support for the main idea.

3e   What are topic sentences?

A **topic sentence** contains the main idea of a paragraph and controls its content. Often, the topic sentence comes at the beginning of a paragraph, though not always. Professional essay writers, because they have the skill to carry the reader along without explicit signposts, sometimes decide not to use topic sentences. However, instructors often require students to use topic sentences. As apprentice writers, students might have more difficulty writing unified paragraphs.

TOPIC SENTENCE STARTING A PARAGRAPH

In ACADEMIC WRITING, most paragraphs begin with a topic sentence so that readers know immediately what to expect. Paragraph 5 is an example.

5   Music patronage was at a turning point when Mozart went to Vienna in the last part of the eighteenth century. Many patrons of music continued to be wealthy aristocrats. Haydn's entire career was funded by a rich prince. Mozart's father and, for a time, Mozart himself were in the employ of another prince. But when Mozart went to Vienna in 1781, he contrived to make a living from a variety of sources. In addition to performances at aristocratic houses and commissions for particular works, Mozart gave piano and composition lessons, put on operas, and gave many public concerts of his own music.

    —Jeremy Yudkin, "Composers and Patrons in the Classic Era"

Sometimes, a topic sentence both starts a paragraph and, in different wording, ends the paragraph. Paragraph 6 is an example.

6   Modern science cannot explain why the laws of physics are exactly balanced for animal life to exist. For example, if the big bang had been one-part-in-a-billion more powerful, it would have rushed out too fast for the galaxies to form and for life to begin. If the strong nuclear force were decreased by two percent, atomic nuclei wouldn't hold together. Hydrogen would be the only atom in the universe. If the gravitational force were decreased, stars (including the sun) would not ignite. There are just three of more than 200 physical parameter within the solar system and universe so exact that they cannot be random. Indeed, the lack of a scientific explanation has allowed these facts to be hijacked as a defense of intelligent design.

    —Robert Lanza, "A New Theory of the Universe"

TOPIC SENTENCE ENDING A PARAGRAPH

Some paragraphs give supporting details first and wait to state the topic sentence at the paragraph's end. This approach is particularly effective for building suspense or for creating a bit of drama. Paragraph 7 is an example.

7   Once the Romans had left, the political situation in Britain deteriorated rapidly. Softened by their dependence on the Roman legions, the Romanized Britons were ill equipped to defend themselves from renewed attacks by the Picts in the north. Then, even as the Britons were trying to cope with their fiercer northern neighbors, a much more calamitous series of events took place: waves of Germanic-speaking people from the Continent began to invade the island. The "English" were coming to England.

    —C. M. Millward, "The Arrival of the English"

TOPIC SENTENCE IMPLIED, NOT STATED

Some paragraphs are a unified whole even without a single sentence that readers can point to as the topic sentence. Yet, most readers can catch the main idea anyway. Paragraph 8 is an example. What do you think might be a straightforward topic sentence for it?

8 It is easy to identify with the quest for a secret document, somewhat harder to do so with a heroine whose goal is identifying and understanding the element radium, which is why in dramatic biography writers and directors end up reverting to fiction. To be effective, the dramatic elements must, and finally will, take precedence over any "real" biographical facts. We viewers do not care—if we wanted to know about the element radium, we would read a book on the element radium. When we go to the movies to see *The Story of Marie Curie* we want to find out how her little dog Skipper died.

—David Mamet, *Three Uses of the Knife: On the Nature and Purpose of Drama*

EXERCISE 3-2   Working individually or with a group, identify the topic sentences in the following paragraphs. If the topic sentence is implied, write the point the paragraph conveys. For help, consult section 3e.

A.   **9** A good college program should stress the development of high-level reading, writing, and mathematical skills and should provide you with a broad historical, social, and cultural perspective, no matter what subject you choose as your major. The program should teach you not only the most current knowledge in your field but also—just as important—prepare you to keep learning throughout your life. After all, you'll probably change jobs, and possibly even careers, at least six times, and you'll have other responsibilities, too—perhaps as a spouse and as a parent and certainly as a member of a community whose bounds extend beyond the workplace.

—Frank T. Rhodes, "Let the Student Decide"

B.   **10** The once majestic oak tree crashes to the ground amid the destructive flames, as its panic-stricken inhabitants attempt to flee the fiery tomb. Undergrowth that formerly flourished smolders in ashes. A family of deer darts furiously from one wall of flame to the other, without an emergency exit. On the outskirts of the inferno, firefighters try desperately to stop the destruction. Somewhere at the source of this chaos lies a former campsite containing the cause of this destruction—an untended campfire. This scene is one of many that illustrate how human apathy and carelessness destroy nature.

—Anne Bryson, student

C.   Rudeness isn't a distinctive quality of our own time. People today would be shocked by how rudely our ancestors behaved. In the colonial period, a French traveler marveled that "Virginians don't use napkins, but they wear silk cravats, and instead of carrying white handkerchiefs, they blow their noses either with their fingers or with a silk handkerchief that also serves as a cravat, a napkin, and so on." In the 19th century, up **11** to about the 1830s, even very distinguished people routinely put their knives in their mouths. And when people went to the theater, they would not just applaud politely—they would chant, jeer, and shout. So, the notion that there's been a downhill slide in manners ever since time began is just not so.

—"Horizons," *U.S. News & World Report*

3f How can I develop my body paragraphs?

You develop a **body paragraph** by supplying detailed support for the main idea of the paragraph communicated by your TOPIC SENTENCE (3e), whether stated or implied. **Paragraph development** is not merely a repetition, using other words, of the main idea. When this happens, you're merely going around in circles. We've deliberately manipulated paragraph 4 above to create paragraph 12. It is an example of a poorly developed paragraph. It goes nowhere; rather, it restates one idea three times in different words.

> **NO** The Miss Plastic Surgery contest, trumpeted by Chinese promoters as "the world's first pageant for artificial beauties," shows **12** the power of cosmetic surgery in a country that has swung from one extreme to another when it comes to the feminine ideal. In past decades, China did not promote personal grooming. Beautification is a recent development.

To check whether you are providing sufficient detail in a body paragraph, use the RENNS Test. Each letter in the made-up word *RENNS* cues you to remember a different kind of supporting detail at your disposal, as listed in Quick Reference 3.3.

Use the RENNS Test to check the quality of your paragraph development. Of course, not every paragraph needs all five kinds of RENNS details, nor do the supporting details need to occur in the order of the letters in *RENNS*. Paragraph 13 contains three of the five types of RENNS details. Identify the topic sentence and as many RENNS as you can before reading the analysis that follows the paragraph.

> U.S. shores are also being inundated by waves of plastic debris. On the sands of the Texas Gulf Coast one day last September, volunteers collected **13** 307 tons of litter, two-thirds of which was plastic, including 31,733 bags, 30,295 bottles, and 15,631 six-pack yokes. Plastic trash is being found far out to sea. On a four-day trip from Maryland to Florida that ranged 100 miles

offshore, John Hardy, an Oregon State University marine biologist, spotted "Styrofoam and other plastic on the surface, most of the whole cruise."

—"The Dirty Seas," *Time*

Quick Reference 3.3 ■ ■ ■ ▨ ■ ▨ ■

The RENNS Test: Checking for supporting details

R = Reasons provide support.

Jules Verne, a nineteenth-century writer of science fiction, amazes readers today **because he imagined inventions impossible to develop until recent years**.

E = Examples provide support.

For example, he predicted submarines and moon rockets.

N = Names provide support.

He forecast that the moon rockets would take off from an area in the **state of Florida**.

N = Numbers provide support.

Specifically, he declared as the point of departure **27 degrees North Latitude and 5 degrees West Longitude**.

S = Senses—sight, sound, smell, taste, touch—provide support.

Today, space vehicles are **heard blasting off** from Cape Kennedy, only eighty miles from the site Verne chose.

In paragraph 13, the first sentence serves as the topic sentence. Supporting details for that main idea include examples, names, and numbers. The writer provides examples of the kinds of litter found washed up on the beach and floating offshore. The writer names many specific things: Texas Gulf Coast, September, bags, bottles, six-pack yokes, Maryland, Florida, John Hardy, Oregon State University, marine biologist, and Styrofoam. And the writer uses specific numbers to describe the volume of litter collected (307 tons), to give counts of specific items (such as 31,733 bags), and to tell how far from shore (100 miles) the litter had traveled.

EXERCISE 3-3 Working individually or with a peer-response group, look again at the paragraphs in Exercise 3-2. Identify the RENNS in each paragraph. For help, consult 3f.

3g How can I create unity and coherence in paragraphs?

A paragraph has **unity** when the connection between the main idea and its supporting sentences is clear. A paragraph has **coherence** when its sentences relate to each other not only in content but also in choice of words and grammatical structures. Unity emphasizes meaning; coherence emphasizes structure.

Unity is ruined when any sentence in a paragraph "goes off the topic," which means its content doesn't relate to the main idea or to the other sentences in the paragraph. To show you broken unity, in paragraph 14 we've deliberately inserted two sentences (the fourth and the next to last) that go off the topic and ruin a perfectly good paragraph, shown as paragraph 15. (Neither a personal complaint about stress nor hormones produced by men and women during exercise belong in a paragraph defining different kinds of stress.)

NO

14

Stress has long been the subject of psychological and physiological speculation. In fact, more often than not, the word itself is ill defined and overused, meaning different things to different people. Emotional stress, for example, can come about as the result of a family argument or the death of a loved one. Everyone says, "Don't get stressed," but I have no idea how to do that. Environmental stress, such as exposure to excessive heat or cold, is an entirely different phenomenon. Physiologic stress has been described as the outpouring of the steroid hormones from the adrenal glands. During exercise, such as weightlifting, males and females produce different hormones. Whatever its guise, a lack of a firm definition of stress has seriously impeded past research.

YES

15

Stress has long been the subject of psychological and physiological speculation. In fact, more often than not, the word itself is ill defined and overused, meaning different things to different people. Emotional stress, for example, can come about as the result of a family argument or the death of a loved one. Environmental stress, such as exposure to excessive heat or cold, is an entirely different phenomenon. Physiologic stress has been described as the outpouring of the steroid hormones from the adrenal glands. Whatever its guise, a lack of a firm definition of stress has seriously impeded past research.

—Herbert Benson, MD, *The Relaxation Response*

In a coherent paragraph, the sentences follow naturally from one to the next. Techniques for achieving coherence are listed in Quick Reference 3.4; refer to the sections shown in parentheses for complete explanations.

Techniques for achieving coherence

- Using appropriate transitional expressions (3g.1)
- Using pronouns when possible (3g.2)
- Using deliberate repetition of a key word (3g.3)
- Using parallel structures (3g.4)
- Using coherence techniques to create connections among paragraphs (3g.5)

3g.1 Using transitional expressions for coherence

Transitional expressions are words and phrases that signal connections among ideas.

Transitions are bridges that lead your reader along your line of thought. They offer cues about what follows. Commonly used transitional expressions are listed in Quick Reference 3.5.

Transitional expressions and the relationships they signal

ADDITION	also, in addition, too, moreover, and, besides, furthermore, equally important, then, finally
EXAMPLE	for example, for instance, thus, as an illustration, namely, specifically
CONTRAST	but, yet, however, nevertheless, nonetheless, conversely, in contrast, still, at the same time, on the one hand, on the other hand
COMPARISON	similarly, likewise, in the same way
CONCESSION	of course, to be sure, certainly, granted
RESULT	therefore, thus, as a result, so, accordingly, consequently
SUMMARY	hence, in short, in brief, in summary, in conclusion, finally
TIME	first, second, third, next, then, finally, afterward, before, soon, later, meanwhile, subsequently, immediately, eventually, currently
PLACE	in the front, in the foreground, in the back, in the background, at the side, adjacent, nearby, in the distance, here, there

🔔 **Alert:** In ACADEMIC WRITING, set off a transitional expression with a comma, unless the expression is one short word (24c and 24g). ●

Vary your choices of transitional words. For example, instead of always using *for example,* try *for instance.* Also, when choosing a transitional word, make sure it correctly says what you mean. For instance, don't use *however* in the sense of *on the other hand* if you mean *therefore* in the sense of *as a result.* The three brief examples below demonstrate how to use transitional expressions for each context.

COHERENCE BY ADDITION

Woodpeckers use their beaks to find food and to chisel out nests. *In addition,* they claim their territory and signal their desire to mate by using their beaks to drum on trees.

COHERENCE BY CONTRAST

Most birds communicate by singing. Woodpeckers, *however,* communicate by the duration and rhythm of the drumming of their beaks.

COHERENCE BY RESULT

The woodpecker's strong beak enables it to communicate by drumming on dry branches and tree trunks. *As a result,* woodpeckers can communicate across greater distances than songbirds can.

Paragraph 16 demonstrates how transitional expressions (shown in **bold**) enhance a paragraph's COHERENCE. The TOPIC SENTENCE is the final sentence.

16   Before the days of television, people were entertained by exciting radio shows such as *Superman, Batman,* and "War of the Worlds." **Of course**, the listener was required to pay careful attention to the story if all details were to be comprehended. **Better yet**, while listening to the stories, listeners would form their own images of the actions taking place. When the broadcaster would give brief descriptions of the Martian space ships invading earth, **for example**, every member of the audience would imagine a different space ship. **In contrast**, television's version of "War of the Worlds" will not stir the imagination at all, for everyone can clearly see the actions taking place. All viewers see the same space ship with the same features. Each aspect is clearly defined, and **therefore**, no one will imagine anything different from what is seen. **Thus**, television can't be considered an effective tool for stimulating the imagination.

—Tom Paradis, "A Child's Other World"

3g.2 Using pronouns for coherence

Pronouns—words that refer to nouns or other pronouns—allow readers to follow your train of thought from one sentence to the next without boring repetition. Without pronouns, you would have to repeat nouns over and over. For example, this sentence uses no pronouns and therefore has needless repetition: *The woodpecker scratched the woodpecker's head with the woodpecker's foot.* In contrast, with pronouns the sentence can be *The woodpecker scratched its head with its foot.* Paragraph 17 illustrates how pronouns (shown in **bold**) contribute to COHERENCE.

17 After Gary Hanson, now 56, got laid off from **his** corporate position in 2003, **he, his** wife, Susan, and **his** son, John, now 54 and 27, respectively, wanted to do a spot of cleaning. Though **they** are hard at work, **they** are not scrubbing floors or washing windows. **They** are running **their** very own house-cleaning franchise, *The Maids Home Services,* which **they** opened in February.

—Sara Wilson, "Clean House: Getting Laid Off from His Corporate Job Gave This Franchisee a Fresh Start"

3g.3 Using deliberate repetition for coherence

A key word or phrase is central to the main idea of the paragraph. **Repetition** of key words or phrases is a useful way to achieve COHERENCE in a paragraph. The word or phrase usually appears first in the paragraph's TOPIC SENTENCE (3e) and then again throughout the paragraph. The idea of repetition is to keep a concept in front of the reader. Use this technique sparingly to avoid being monotonous. Paragraph 18 contains repeated words and phrases (shown in **bold**) closely tied to the concept of anthropology that make the paragraph more coherent.

18 **Anthropology**, broadly defined, is the study of **humanity**, from its evolutionary origins millions of years ago to its present great numbers and worldwide diversity. Many other disciplines, of course, share with **anthropology** a focus on one aspect or another of **humanity**. Like sociology, economics, political science, psychology, and other behavioral and social sciences, **anthropology** is concerned with the way people organize their lives and relate to one another in interacting, interconnected groups—societies—that share basic beliefs and practices. **Like** economists, **anthropologists are interested in** society's material foundations—in how people produce and distribute food and other valued goods. **Like** sociologists, **anthropologists are interested in** the way people structure their relations in society—in families, at work, in institutions. **Like** political scientists, **anthropologists are interested in** power and authority: who has them and how they are allocated. And, **like** psychologists, **anthropologists are interested in** individual development and the interaction between society and individual people.

—Nancy Bonvillain, "The Study of Humanity"

3g.4   Using parallel structures for coherence

Parallel structures are created when grammatically equivalent forms are used in series, usually of three or more items, but sometimes only two (see PARALLELISM, Chapter 18). Using parallel structures helps to give a paragraph coherence. The repeated parallel structures reinforce connections among ideas, and they add both tempo and sound to the sentence. Look back to paragraph 18 and the succession of sentences that begin with the word *like*.

In paragraph 19, the authors use several parallel structures (shown in **bold**): a parallel series of words (*the sacred, the secular, the scientific*); parallel phrases (*sometimes smiled at, sometimes frowned upon*); and six parallel clauses (the first being *banish danger with a gesture*).

19 Superstitions are **sometimes smiled at** and **sometimes frowned upon** as observances characteristic of **the old-fashioned, the unenlightened,** children, peasants, servants, immigrants, foreigners, or backwoods people. Nevertheless, they give all of us ways of moving back and forth among the different worlds in which we live—**the sacred, the secular,** and **the scientific.** They allow us to keep a private world also, where, smiling a little, we can **banish danger with a gesture** and **summon luck with a rhyme, make the sun shine in spite of storm clouds, force the stranger to do our bidding, keep an enemy at bay,** and **straighten the paths of those we love.**

—Margaret Mead and Rhoda Metraux, "New Superstitions for Old"

3g.5   Creating coherence among paragraphs

The same techniques for achieving COHERENCE in a paragraph apply to showing connections among paragraphs in a piece of writing. All four techniques help: transitional expressions (3g.1), pronouns (3g.2), deliberate repetition (3g.3), and parallel structures (3g.4).

Example 20 shows two short paragraphs and the start of a third. The writer achieves coherence among the paragraphs by repeating the key word *gratitude* and the related words *grateful, thankful,* and *thank* and by using them as a transition into the next paragraph. The writer also uses PARALLELISM within the paragraphs in this example.

20 To me, gratitude and inner peace go hand in hand. The more genuinely grateful I feel for the gift of my life, the more peaceful I feel. Gratitude, then, is worthy of a little practice.

If you're anything like me, you probably have many people to be thankful for: friends, family members, people from your past, teachers, gurus, people from work, someone who gave you a break, as well as countless others. You may want to thank a higher power for the gift of life itself, or for the beauty of nature.

As you think of people to be grateful for, remember that it can be anyone—someone who held a door open for you, or a physician who saved your life. . . .

EXERCISE 3-4 Working individually or with a peer-response group, locate the coherence techniques in each paragraph. Look for transitional expressions, pronouns, deliberate repetition, and parallel structures. For help, consult 3g.

A.   Kathy sat with her legs dangling over the edge of the side of the hood. The band of her earphones held back strands of straight copper hair that had come loose from two thick braids that hung down her back. She swayed with the music that only she could hear. Her shoulders raised, making circles in the warm air. Her arms reached out to her side; her open hands reached for the air; her closed hands brought the air back to her. Her arms reached over her head; her opened hands reached for a cloud; her closed hands brought the cloud back to her. Her head moved from side to side; her eyes opened and closed to the tempo of the tunes. Kathy was motion.

—Claire Burke, student

B.   Newton's law may have wider application than just the physical world. In the social world, racism, once set into motion, will remain in motion unless acted upon by an outside force. The collective "we" must be the outside force. We must fight racism through education. We must make sure every school has the resources to do its job. We must present to our children a culturally diverse curriculum that reflects our pluralistic society. This can help students understand that prejudice is learned through contact with prejudiced people, rather than with the people toward whom the prejudice is directed.

—Randolph H. Manning, "Fighting Racism with Inclusion"

C.   The snow geese are first, rising off the ponds to breakfast in the sorghum fields up the river. Twenty thousand of them, perhaps more, great white birds with black wing tips rising out of the darkness into the rosy reflected light of dawn. They make a sweeping turn, a cloud of wings rising above the cottonwoods. But cloud is the wrong word. They don't form a disorderly blackbird rabble but a kaleidoscope of goose formations, always shifting, but always orderly. The light catches them—white against the tan velvet of the hills. Then they're overhead, line after line, layer above layer of formations, and the sky is filled with the clamor of an infinity of geese.

—Tony Hillerman, *Hillerman Country*

EXERCISE 3-5 Working individually or with a peer-response group, use RENNS (3f) and techniques for achieving coherence (3g) to develop three of the following topic sentences into paragraphs. When finished, list the RENNS and the coherence techniques you used in each paragraph.

1. Video games reflect current concerns in our culture.
2. The content of trash in the United States says a great deal about US culture.
3. Reality shows on television tend to have several common elements.
4. In many respects, our culture is very wasteful.
5. College students face several true challenges.

3h   How can I arrange a paragraph?

During DRAFTING, you concentrate on getting ideas onto the page or screen. Later, during REVISION, you can experiment to see how your sentences might be arranged for greatest impact. You may find sometimes that only one possible arrangement can work. For example, if you're explaining how to bake a cake, you want to give the directions in a particular order. At other times, you may find that more than one arrangement is possible. For example, if you're writing about solving a problem and therefore using the problem-to-solution arrangement, you might also use the technique of ordering from least to most important—or its reverse. Quick Reference 3.6 lists the most common ways to arrange a paragraph. More about each arrangement follows in this section.

Quick Reference 3.6   ■ ■ ■ ■ ■ ■ ■

Ways to arrange sentences in a paragraph

- By time
- By location
- From general to specific
- From specific to general
- From least to most important
- From problem to solution

ARRANGING BY TIME

In a paragraph arranged according to time, or **chronological order**, events are presented in whatever order they took place. For example, when you tell a story, you write what happened first, then second, then third, and so on. Using a time sequence is a very natural and easy way to organize a paragraph. Paragraph 24 is an example.

24 In 1924, The Dawes Plan renegotiated the sums mandated from Germany as reparations and smoothed debt repayments to the United States. The private American capital that then began to flow to Europe (especially to Germany) created a short burst of prosperity for Europeans. In 1928, however, the booming New York stock market began to siphon money away from European investments, and virtually unregulated financial speculation led to Wall Street's crash in October 1929. The crash produced a banking crisis, for U.S. banks had lent their customers large amounts of money to invest in the stock market. The crash made repayments of these loans impossible and caused banks to fail. Little American capital remained for investment in Europe or elsewhere. Credit of all kinds grew scarce, and renewal of loans already made to Europeans became difficult.

—Donald Kagan, "American Investments"

ARRANGING BY LOCATION

A paragraph arranged according to location, or **spatial order**, leads the reader's attention from one place to another. The movement can be in any direction— from top to bottom, left to right, inside to outside, and so on. Paragraph 25 traces natural disasters across the United States from west to east.

25 In the United States, most natural disasters are confined to specific geographical areas. For example, the West Coast can be hit by damaging earthquakes at any time. Most Southern and Midwestern states can be swept by devastating tornadoes, especially in the spring, summer, and early fall. The Gulf of Mexico and the Atlantic Ocean can experience violent hurricanes in late summer and fall. These different natural disasters, and others as dangerous, teach people one common lesson— advance preparation can mean survival.

—Dawn Seaford, student

ARRANGING FROM GENERAL TO SPECIFIC

The most common pattern for arranging information is from **general to specific**. Typically, the general statement is the TOPIC SENTENCE, and the supporting details (see RENNS, Quick Reference 3.3) explain the specifics. Paragraph 26 is an example.

26 Memory is something we all know intimately. It is a central and unambiguous part of our commonsense world, its presence as indisputable, if unsteady, as the weather. But when we begin to talk about memory, ambiguities and complexities rapidly emerge. How can we grasp memory itself? It is virtually impossible to imagine memory—what it is, how it works, where it lies— without recourse to metaphor. Is memory a storehouse, a computer, a filing system, an encyclopedia, or a landscape, a cathedral, a city? If it is a kind of narrative, is our model to be Proust or Joyce, Virginia Woolf or Christa Wolf?

—Michael Lambek and Paul Antze, "Forecasting Memory"

ARRANGING FROM SPECIFIC TO GENERAL

A less common paragraph arrangement moves from **specific to general**. Paragraph 27 is an example. To achieve the greatest impact, the paragraph starts with details that support the topic sentence, which ends the paragraph.

Replacing the spark plugs is probably the first thing most home auto mechanics do. But too often, the problem lies elsewhere. In the ignition system,
the plug wires, distributor unit, coil, and ignition control unit play just as
27   vital a role as the spark plugs. Moreover, performance problems are by no
means limited to the ignition system. The fuel system and emissions control
system also contain several components that equal the spark plug in importance. The do-it-yourself mechanic who wants to provide basic care for a car
must be able to do more than change the spark plugs.

—Danny Witt, student

ARRANGING FROM LEAST TO MOST IMPORTANT

A paragraph arranged from **least to most important** uses **climactic order**,
which means that the high point—the climax—comes at the end. For a paragraph to be arranged from least to most important, it has to have at least three
items: least, more, most. And remember that the last item always packs the
greatest impact and is the most memorable. Paragraph 28 is an example.

For a year, Hal and I worked diligently on that boat. At times, it was a real
struggle for me to stay on course: as an 11-year-old, my attentions often wan-
dered and the work was not always exciting. But Hal's dedication profoundly
28   influenced me. By his own example, he taught me important lessons about how
to be organized, how to set priorities, and how to be responsible. He also,
through working with me on the design of the boat's electronics, played a pivotal role in developing my passion for science.

—Patrick Regan Buckley, "Lessons in Boat-Building—and Life"

ARRANGING FROM PROBLEM TO SOLUTION

In some cases, an effective arrangement for a paragraph is **problem to solution**.
Usually, the topic sentence presents the problem. The very next sentence presents the main idea of the solution. Then, the rest of the paragraph covers the
specifics of the solution. Paragraph 29 is an example.

When I first met them, Sara and Michael were a two-career couple with a
home of their own, and a large boat bought with a large loan. What interested them in a concept called voluntary simplicity was the birth of their
daughter and a powerful desire to raise her themselves. Neither one of them,
it turned out, was willing to restrict what they considered their "real life" into
29   the brief time before work and the tired hours afterward. "A lot of people
think that as they have children and things get more expensive, the only answer is to work harder in order to earn more money. It's not the only answer,"
insists Michael. The couple's decision was to trade two full-time careers for two
half-time careers, and to curtail consumption. They decided to spend their
money only on things that contributed to their major goal, the construction

of a world where family and friendship, work and play, were all of a piece, a world, moreover, which did not make wasteful use of the earth's resources.

—Linda Weltner, "Stripping Down to Bare Happiness"

EXERCISE 3-6 Working individually or with a peer-response group, re-arrange the sentences in each paragraph below so that it flows logically. To begin, identify the topic sentence, use it as the paragraph's first sentence, and continue from there. For help, consult 3i.

PARAGRAPH A

1. Remember, many people who worry about offending others wind up living according to other people's priorities.
2. Learn to decline, tactfully but firmly, every request that doesn't contribute to your goals.
3. Of all the timesaving techniques ever developed, perhaps the most effective is the frequent use of the word *no*.
4. If you point out that your motivation isn't to get out of work but to save your time to do a better job on the really important things, you'll have a good chance of avoiding unproductive tasks.

—Edwin Bliss, "Getting Things Done:
The ABC's of Time Management"

PARAGRAPH B

1. After a busy day, lens wearers often don't feel like taking time out to clean and disinfect their lenses, and many wearers skip the chore.
2. When buying a pair of glasses, a person deals with just the expense of the glasses themselves.
3. Although contact lenses make the wearer more attractive, glasses are easier and less expensive to care for.
4. However, in addition to the cost of the lenses themselves, contact lens wearers must shoulder the extra expense of cleaning supplies.
5. This inattention creates a danger of infection.
6. In contrast, contact lenses require daily cleaning and weekly enzyming that inconvenience lens wearers.
7. Glasses can be cleaned quickly with water and tissue at the wearer's convenience.

—Heather Martin, student

PARAGRAPH C

1. The researchers found that the participation of women in sport was a significant indicator of the health and living standards of a country.
2. Today, gradually, women have begun to enter sport with more social acceptance and individual pride.

3. In 1952, researchers from the Finnish Institute of Occupational Health who conducted an intensive study of the athletes participating in the Olympics in Helsinki predicted, "Women are able to shake off civil disabilities which millennia of prejudice and ignorance have imposed upon them."

4. Myths die hard, but they do die.

　　　　　　　　　　—Marie Hart, "Sport: Women Sit in the Back of the Bus"

EXERCISE 3-7　Working individually or with a peer-response group, determine the arrangements in these paragraphs. Choose from time, location, general to specific, specific to general, least to most important, and problem to solution. For help, consult 3h.

A.　　A combination of cries from exotic animals and laughter and gasps from children fills the air along with the aroma of popcorn and peanuts. A hungry lion bellows for dinner, his roar breaking through the confusing chatter of other animals. Birds of all kinds chirp endlessly at curious children.
30 Monkeys swing from limb to limb, performing gymnastics for gawking onlookers. A comedy routine by orangutans employing old shoes and garments incites squeals of amusement. Reptiles sleep peacefully behind glass windows, yet they send shivers down the spines of those who remember the quick death many of these reptiles can induce. The sights and sounds and smells of the zoo inform and entertain children of all ages.

　　　　　　　　　　　　　　　　—Deborah Harris, student

B.　　No one even agrees anymore on what "old" is. Not long ago, 30 was middle-aged and 60 was old. Now, more and more people are living into
31 their 70s, 80s and beyond—and many of them are living well, without any incapacitating mental or physical decline. Today, old age is defined not simply by chronological years, but by degree of health and well-being.

　　　　　　　　　　　—Carol Tavris, "Old Age Isn't What It Used to Be"

C.　　Lately, bee researchers have been distracted by a new challenge from abroad. It's, of course, the so-called "killer bee" that was imported into Brazil from Africa in the mid-1950s and has been heading our way ever since. The Africanized bee looks like the Italian bee but is more defensive
32 and more inclined to attack in force. It consumes much of the honey that it produces, leaving relatively little for anyone who attempts to work with it. It travels fast, competes with local bees and, worse, mates with them. It has ruined the honey industry in Venezuela and now the big question is: Will the same thing happen here?

　　　　　　　　　　　　　　—Jim Doherty, "The Hobby That Challenges
　　　　　　　　　　　　　　　　　　　　You to Think Like a Bee"

EXERCISE 3-8　Working individually or collaborating with others, decide what would be the best arrangement for a paragraph on each topic listed here. Choose one or a combination of time, location, general to specific, specific to general, least to most important, and problem to solution. For help, consult 3h.

1. Qualities of annoying people
2. Romantic comedies
3. How to deliver bad news
4. Teaching someone a new job

3i How can rhetorical patterns help me write paragraphs?

Rhetorical patterns (sometimes called *rhetorical strategies*) are techniques for presenting ideas clearly and effectively in academic and other situations. You choose a specific rhetorical strategy according to what you want to accomplish. Quick Reference 3.7 lists the common rhetorical strategies at your disposal.

Quick Reference 3.7   ■ ■ ■ ■ ■ ■ ■

**Common rhetorical patterns
of thought (strategies) for paragraphs**

- Narrative
- Description
- Process
- Examples
- Definition

- Analysis
- Classification
- Comparison and contrast
- Analogy
- Cause-and-effect analysis

Often, your TOPIC SENTENCE will steer you toward a particular pattern. For example, if a topic sentence is "Grilling a great hot dog is easy," the implied pattern—or rhetorical strategy—is to explain the process of how to grill a hot dog. Or if a topic sentence is "To see many different styles of architecture in one US city, visit Chicago," the implied pattern—or rhetorical strategy—is to give examples.

Sometimes, you need to use a combination of rhetorical strategies. For example, in a paragraph on types of color blindness, you might use a combination of definition and classification. A paragraph explaining why one brand of house paint is superior to another might call for comparison and contrast combined with description—and, perhaps, also definition and examples.

NARRATIVE

Narrative writing tells a story. A *narration* relates what is happening or what has happened. Paragraph 33 is an example.

33 Gordon Parks speculates that he might have spent his life as a waiter on the North Coast Limited train if he hadn't strolled into one particular movie house during a stopover in Chicago. It was shortly before World War II began, and on the screen was a hair-raising newsreel of Japanese planes attacking a gunboat. When it was over the camera operator came out on stage and the audience cheered. From that moment on Parks was determined to become a photographer. During his next stopover, in Seattle, he went into a pawnshop and purchased his first camera for $7.50. With that small sum, Parks later proclaimed, "I had bought what was to become my weapon against poverty and racism." Eleven years later, he became the first black photographer at *Life* magazine.

—Susan Howard, "Depth of Field"

DESCRIPTION

Writing a **description** is a rhetorical strategy that appeals to a reader's senses—sight, sound, smell, taste, and touch. *Descriptive writing* paints a picture in words. Paragraph 34 is an example.

34 Walking to the ranch house from the shed, we saw the Northern Lights. They looked like talcum powder fallen from a woman's face. Rouge and blue eye shadow streaked the spires of a white light which exploded, then pulsated, shaking the colors down—like lives—until they faded from sight.

—Gretel Ehrlich, "Other Lives"

PROCESS

Writing about a **process** reports a sequence of actions or pattern by which something is done or made. A process usually proceeds chronologically—first do this, then do that. A process's complexity dictates the level of detail in the writing. For example, paragraph 35 provides an overview of a complicated process. Paragraph 36, on the other hand, gives explicit step-by-step directions.

35 Making chocolate isn't as simple as grinding a bag of beans. The machinery in a chocolate factory towers over you, rumbling and whirring. A huge cleaner first blows the beans away from their accompanying debris—sticks and stones, coins and even bullets can fall among cocoa beans being bagged. Then they go into another machine for roasting. Next comes separation in a winnower, shells sliding out one side, beans falling from the other. Grinding follows, resulting in chocolate liquor. Fermentation, roasting, and "conching" all influence the flavor of chocolate. Chocolate is "conched"—rolled over and over against itself like pebbles in the sea—in enormous circular machines named conches for the shells they once resembled. Climbing a flight of steps to peer into this huge, slow-moving glacier, I was expecting something like molten mud but found myself forced to conclude it resembled nothing so much as chocolate.

—Ruth Mehrtens Galvin, "Sybaritic to Some, Sinful to Others"

Traditionally, oil was extracted by pressing the olives between granite mill-stones. Many nonindustrial mills now use a modern continuous-cycle system.
36 The olives are conveyed up a belt, washed, and cut into pulp. The resulting paste is kneaded and centrifugally "decanted" to separate it into solids, water, and oil.

—Lori de Mori, "Making Olive Oil"

EXAMPLES

A paragraph developed by **examples** presents particular instances of a larger category. For instance, examples of the category "endangered animals" could include the black rhinoceros, South China tiger, Bulmer's fruit bat, and silvery gibbon. Paragraph 37 is an example of this strategy. On the other hand, sometimes one **extended example**, often called an *illustration,* is useful. Paragraph 38 is an example of this technique.

It's hard for us to imagine what it must have been like to live in a culture before the advent of printed books or before you could carry around a ballpoint pen and paper to jot notes. "In a world of few books, and those mostly in communal libraries, one's education had to be remembered, for one could never depend on having continuing access to specific material," writes Mary Carruthers, author of *The Book of Memory*, a study of the role of memory techniques in medieval culture. "Ancient and medieval people reserved their awe for memory. Their greatest geniuses they describe as people of superior
37 memories." Thirteenth-century theologian Thomas Aquinas, for example, was celebrated for composing his Summa Theologica entirely in his head and dictating it from memory with no more than a few notes. Roman philosopher Seneca the Elder could repeat 2,000 names in the order they'd been given to him. Another Roman named Simplicius could recite Virgil by heart—backward. A strong memory was seen as the greatest of virtues since it represented the internalization of a universe of external knowledge. Indeed, a common theme in the lives of the saints was that they had extraordinary memories.

—Joshua Foer, "Remember This"

He was one of the greatest scientists the world has ever known, yet if I had to convey the essence of Albert Einstein in a single word, I would choose *simplicity.* Perhaps an anecdote will help. Once, caught in a downpour, he
38 took off his hat and held it under his coat. Asked why, he explained, with admirable logic, that the rain would damage the hat, but his hair would be none the worse for its wetting. This knack of going instinctively to the heart of the matter was the secret of his major scientific discoveries—this and his extraordinary feeling for beauty.

—Banesh Hoffman, "My Friend, Albert Einstein"

DEFINITION

When you define something, you give its meaning. **Definition** is often used together with other rhetorical strategies. If, for example, you were explaining how to organize a seashell collection, you'd probably want to define the two main types of shells: bivalve and univalve. You can also develop an entire paragraph by using definition, called an **extended definition**. An extended definition discusses the meaning of a word or concept in more detail than a dictionary definition. If the topic is very abstract, the writer tries to put the definition in concrete terms. Sometimes a definition tells what something is not, as well as what it is, as in paragraph 39.

39 Chemistry is that branch of science that has the task of investigating the materials out of which the universe is made. It is not concerned with the forms into which they may be fashioned. Such objects as chairs, tables, vases, bottles, or wires are of no significance in chemistry; but such substances as glass, wool, iron, sulfur, and clay, as the materials out of which they are made, are what it studies. Chemistry is concerned not only with the composition of such substances, but also with their inner structure.

—John Arrend Timm, *General Chemistry*

ANALYSIS

Analysis, sometimes called *division,* divides things up into their parts. It usually starts, often in its topic sentence, by identifying one subject and continues by explaining the subject's distinct parts, as in paragraph 40.

40 Jazz is by its very nature inexact, and thus difficult to define with much precision: humble in its roots, yet an avenue to wealth and fame for its stars; improvised anew with each performance, but following a handful of tried-and-true formulas; done by everybody but mastered by an elite few; made by African Americans, but made the definition of its age by white bands—and predominantly white audiences. Jazz is primarily an instrumental idiom, but nearly all jazz is based on songs with words, and there are great jazz singers. "If you have to ask what jazz is," said Louis Armstrong, "you'll never know."

—D. Kern Holoman, "Jazz"

CLASSIFICATION

Classification groups items according to an underlying, shared characteristic. Paragraph 41 groups—classifies—interior violations of building-safety codes.

41 A public health student, Marian Glaser, did a detailed analysis of 180 cases of building code violation. Each case represented a single building, almost all of which were multiple-unit dwellings. In these 180 buildings, there were an incredible total of 1,244 different recorded violations—about seven per building. What did the violations consist of? First of all, over one-third of the violations were exterior defects: broken doors and stairways, holes in the walls, sagging roofs, broken chimneys, damaged porches, and so on. Another one-third were interior violations that could scarcely be attributed to the most ingeniously destructive rural southern migrant in America. There were, for example, a total of 160 instances of defective wiring or other electrical hazards, a very common cause of the excessive number of fires and needless tragic deaths in the slums. There were 125 instances of inadequate, defective, or inoperable plumbing or heating. There were 34 instances of serious infestation by rats and roaches.

—William Ryan, "Blaming the Victim"

COMPARISON AND CONTRAST

A paragraph developed by *comparison* deals with similarities; a paragraph developed by *contrast* deals with differences. **Comparison and contrast** writing is usually organized one of two ways: You can use *point-by-point organization,* which moves back and forth between the items being compared; or you can use *block organization,* which discusses one item completely before discussing the other. Quick Reference 3.8 lays out the two patterns visually.

Quick Reference 3.8

Comparison and contrast

POINT-BY-POINT STRUCTURE	BLOCK STRUCTURE
Student body: college A, college B	*College A:* student body, curriculum, location
Curriculum: college A, college B	*College B:* student body, curriculum, location
Location: college A, college B	

Paragraph 42 is structured point by point, going back and forth between the two children (whose names are in **boldface**) being compared.

42   My husband and I constantly marvel at the fact that our two sons, born of the same parents and only two years apart in age, are such completely different human beings. The most obvious differences became apparent at their births. Our firstborn, **Mark**, was big and bold—his intense, already wise eyes, broad shoulders, huge and heavy hands, and powerful, chunky legs gave us the impression he could have walked out of the delivery room on his own. Our second son, **Wayne**, was delightfully different. Rather than having the football physique that **Mark** was born with, **Wayne** came into the world with a long, slim, wiry body more suited to running, jumping, and contorting. **Wayne's** eyes, rather than being intense like **Mark's**, were impish and innocent. When **Mark** was delivered, he cried only momentarily, and then seemed to settle into a state of intense concentration, as if trying to absorb everything he could about the strange, new environment he found himself in. Conversely,

Wayne screamed from the moment he first appeared. There was nothing help-less or pathetic about his cry either—he was darn angry!

—Rosanne Labonte, student

Paragraph 43 uses the block pattern for comparison and contrast. The writer first discusses games and then business (each key word is in **boldface**).

43
Games are of limited duration, take place on or in fixed and finite sites, and are governed by openly promulgated rules that are enforced on the spot by neu-tral professionals. Moreover, they're performed by relatively evenly matched teams that are counseled and led through every move by seasoned hands. Scores are kept, and at the end of the game, a winner is declared. **Business** is usually a little different. In fact, if there is anyone out there who can say that the business is of limited duration, takes place on a fixed site, is governed by openly prom-ulgated rules that are enforced on the spot by neutral professionals, competes only on relatively even terms, and performs in a way that can be measured in runs or points, then that person is either extraordinarily lucky or seriously deluded.

—Warren Bennis, "Time to Hang Up the Old Sports Clichés"

ANALOGY

An **analogy** is an extended comparison between objects or ideas from differ-ent classes—things not normally associated. Analogy is particularly effective in explaining unfamiliar or abstract concepts because a comparison can be drawn between what is familiar and what is not. An analogy often begins with a simile or metaphor (12c), as in paragraph 44.

44
Casual dress, like casual speech, tends to be loose, relaxed, and colorful. It often contains what might be called "slang words": blue jeans, sneakers, base-ball caps, aprons, flowered cotton housedresses, and the like. These garments could not be worn on a formal occasion without causing disapproval, but in ordinary circumstances, they pass without remark. "Vulgar words" in dress, on the other hand, give emphasis and get immediate attention in almost any cir-cumstances, just as they do in speech. Only the skillful can employ them with-out some loss of face, and even then, they must be used in the right way. A torn, unbuttoned shirt or wildly uncombed hair can signify strong emotions: pas-sion, grief, rage, despair. They're most effective if people already think of you as being neatly dressed, just as the curses of well-spoken persons count for more than those of the customarily foul-mouthed do.

—Alison Lurie, *The Language of Clothes*

CAUSE-AND-EFFECT ANALYSIS

Cause-and-effect analysis examines outcomes and the reasons for those out-comes. Causes lead to an event or an effect, and effects result from causes. (For a discussion of correct logic for assessing CAUSE AND EFFECT, see 4h.) Paragraph

45 discusses how television (the cause) becomes indispensable (the effect) to parents of young children.

> Once upon a time, flavor research was a matter of asking housewives to munch a few potato chips in the hopes that the company had stumbled on the perfect formula for reconstituting potatoes. But as the science became more sophisticated, and market pressures demanded more novelty and authenticity, flavor scientists had to create new varieties like "Mesquite BBQ" chips to sit alongside regular barbecue flavor. To fill that hungry maw, Dewis and his colleagues work to analyze hundreds of thousands of substances and develop compounds that will please the buying public in four ways—through smell, taste, sensation and emotion. To do so flavor scientists are homing in on molecules, receptors, brain structures and genetic code that will enable them to create flavors tailored to consumers' palates, health condition, demographics, even genotype. The industry doesn't just talk about things tasting good anymore. Now it's about providing an exceptional "flavor experience."

45

> —Tamara Holt, "The Science of Yummy"

EXERCISE 3-9   Working individually or with a peer-response group, decide what rhetorical strategies are used in each of paragraphs 46–50. Choose from any one or a combination of narrative, description, process, example, definition, analysis, classification, comparison and contrast, analogy, and cause and effect. For help, consult 3i.

A.   Another way to think about metamessages is that they frame a conversation, much as a picture frame provides a context for the images in the picture. Metamessages let you know how to interpret what someone is saying by identifying the activity that is going on. Is this an argument or a chat? Is it helping, advising, or scolding? At the same time, they let you know what position the speaker is assuming in the activity, and what position you are being assigned.

46

—Deborah Tannen, *You Just Don't Understand*

B.   I retain only one confused impression from my earliest years: it's all red, and black, and warm. Our apartment was red: the upholstery was of red moquette, the Renaissance dining-room was red, the figured silk hangings over the stained-glass doors were red, and the velvet curtains in Papa's study were red too. The furniture in this awful sanctum was made of black pear wood; I used to creep into the kneehole under the desk and envelop myself in its dusty glooms; it was dark and warm, and the red of the carpet rejoiced my eyes. That is how I seem to have passed the early days of infancy. Safely ensconced, I watched, I touched, I took stock of the world.

47

—Simone de Beauvoir, *Memoirs of a Dutiful Daughter*

C.   In the case of wool, very hot water can actually cause some structural changes within the fiber, but the resulting shrinkage is minor. The fundamental cause of shrinkage in wool is felting, in which the fibers scrunch together

48 in a tighter bunch, and the yarn, fabric, and garment follow suit. Wool fibers are curly and rough-surfaced, and when squished together under the lubricating influence of water, the fibers wind around each other, like two springs interlocking. Because of their rough surfaces, they stick together and can't be pulled apart.

—James Gorman, "Gadgets"

D. **49** After our lunch, we drove to the Liverpool public library, where I was scheduled to read. By then, we were forty-five minutes late, and on arrival we saw five middle-aged white women heading away toward an old car across the street. When they recognized me, the women came over and apologized: They were really sorry, they said, but they had to leave or they'd get in trouble on the job. I looked at them. Every one of them was wearing an inexpensive, faded housedress and, over that, a cheap and shapeless cardigan sweater. I felt honored by their open-mindedness in having wanted to come and listen to my poetry. I thought and I said that it was I who should apologize: I was late. It was I who felt, moreover, unprepared: What in my work, to date, deserves the open-minded attention of blue-collar white women terrified by the prospect of overstaying a union-guaranteed hour for lunch?

—June Jordan, "Waiting for a Taxi"

E. **50** Lacking access to a year-round supermarket, the many species— from ants to wolves—that in the course of evolution have learned the advantages of hoarding must devote a lot of energy and ingenuity to protecting their stashes from marauders. Creatures like beavers and honeybees, for example, hoard food to get them through cold winters. Others, like desert rodents that face food scarcities throughout the year, must take advantage of the short-lived harvests that follow occasional rains. For animals like burying beetles that dine on mice hundreds of times their size, a habit of biting off more than they can chew at the moment forces them to store their leftovers. Still others, like the male MacGregor's bowerbird, stockpile goodies during mating season so they can concentrate on wooing females and defending their arena d'amour.

—Jane Brody, "A Hoarder's Life: Filling the Cache—and Finding It"

EXERCISE 3-10   Working individually or with a peer-response group, reread the paragraphs in Exercise 3-7 and determine the rhetorical strategy (or strategies) being used in each.

3j   What is a transitional paragraph?

Transitional paragraphs form a bridge between one long discussion on a single topic that requires a number of paragraphs and another discussion, usually lengthy, of another topic. Paragraph 51 is an example of a transitional paragraph that allows the writer to move from a long discussion of the extent and sources of anger in our society to a long discussion of possible remedies.

51   So is there any hope for you and your anger? Is there any reason to believe that you will be able to survive the afternoon commute without screaming or tailgating or displaying choice fingers?

—Andrew Santella, "All the Rage"

3k   What are effective concluding paragraphs?

A **concluding paragraph** ends the discussion smoothly by following logically from the essay's introductory paragraph (3c) and the essay's body paragraphs (3d). Always integrate a concluding device into the final paragraph so that the discussion does not end abruptly. A conclusion that is hurriedly tacked on is a missed opportunity to provide a sense of completion and a finishing touch that adds to the whole essay. Quick Reference 3.9 lists strategies for concluding your essay as well as strategies to avoid.

Quick Reference 3.9   ■ ■ ■ ■ ■ ■ ■

Strategies for concluding paragraphs

STRATEGIES TO TRY

- A strategy adapted from those used for introductory paragraphs (3c)—but be careful to choose a different strategy for your introduction and conclusion

- Relating a brief concluding interesting story or anecdote

- Giving one or more pertinent—perhaps surprising—concluding statistics

- Asking one or more provocative questions for further thought

- Using an appropriate quotation to sum up the THESIS STATEMENT

- Redefining a key term for emphasis

- An ANALOGY that summarizes the thesis statement

- A SUMMARY of the main points, but only if the piece of writing is longer than three to four pages

- A statement that urges awareness by the readers

- A statement that looks ahead to the future

- A call to readers

continued >>

> ### Quick Reference 3.9 (continued)
>
> **STRATEGIES TO AVOID**
> * Introducing new ideas or facts that belong in the body of the essay
> * Rewording your introduction
> * Announcing what you've discussed, as in "In this paper, I have explained why oil prices have dropped."
> * Making absolute claims, as in "I have proved that oil prices don't always affect gasoline prices."
> * Apologizing, as in "Even though I'm not an expert, I feel my position is correct."

The same writers who wait to write their introductory paragraph until they've drafted their body paragraphs often also wait to write their concluding paragraph until they've drafted their introduction. They do this to coordinate the beginning and end so that they can make sure they don't repeat the same strategy in both places.

Paragraph 52 is a concluding paragraph that summarizes the main points of the essay.

52 Now the equivalent to molecule fingerprints, DNA profiles have indeed proven to be valuable investigative tools. As the FBI Laboratory continues to develop innovative technologies and share its expertise with criminal justice professionals worldwide, it takes great strides in bringing offenders to swift and sure justice, while clearing innocent individuals and protecting crime victims.

—"DNA Profiling Advancement: The Use of DNA Profiles in Solving Crimes," *The FBI Law Enforcement Bulletin*

Paragraph 53 is a concluding paragraph from an essay on the potential collapse of public schools. It looks ahead to the future and calls for action that involves taking control of them.

53 Our schools provide a key to the future of society. We must take control of them, watch over them, and nurture them if they are to be set right again. To do less is to invite disaster upon ourselves, our children, and our nation.

—John C. Sawhill, "The Collapse of Public Schools"

EXERCISE 3-11 Working individually or in a peer-response group, return to Exercise 3-1, in which you wrote introductory paragraphs for three informally outlined essays. Now, write a concluding paragraph for each.

For more help with your writing, grammar, and research, go to **www.mycomplab.com**

4 ■■■■■ ■ ■

Thinking Critically
About Ideas and Images

4a What is critical thinking?

Thinking isn't something you choose to do, any more than a fish chooses to live in water. To be human is to think. But while thinking may come naturally, being deliberate about how you think doesn't.

Critical thinking means taking control of your conscious thought processes. If you don't, you risk being controlled by the ideas of others. For example, consider the claim "Because climate change is natural, we shouldn't worry about global warming." It's true that the earth's climate has varied over the millenia, but critical readers won't immediately accept that statement without further thought. They might ask, for example, whether the same conditions that caused climate change in the past are the ones causing change today. They might wonder whether the kinds of change happening today are similar to the changes in the past. They might wonder how most scientists would respond to the assertion. It could be true that we shouldn't worry about global warming (though evidence does support the contrary), so a critical reader might ultimately accept the original claim—but not without careful analysis.

The essence of critical thinking is thinking beyond the obvious—beyond the flash of images on a television screen, the alluring promises of glossy advertisements, the evasive statements by some people in the news, the half-truths of propaganda, or even the punchlines of bumper stickers, as in Figure 4.1. Thinking critically means identifying the weaknesses—and the strengths—of an idea, a text, an image, or a presentation. It means analyzing the quality of evidence and how writers or speakers make their cases. It means interpreting, considering implications, imagining alternatives, connecting information and ideas in one situation to information and ideas in another.

The word *critical* here has a neutral meaning. It doesn't mean taking a negative view or finding fault, as when someone criticizes another person for doing something incorrectly. Rather, the term means examining ideas thoroughly and deeply.

As an example of how critical thinking works, consider how the various elements of Figure 4.2 shape our response to the image. When you look at the

"Conservative" is another name for "Selfish"

Liberalism is a mental disorder

Figure 4.1 Two bumper stickers

obvious, surface content of the photograph, you may simply see a number of people standing in line. However, a closer look shows the deeper message that the photographer seeks to convey. The details in the photograph combine to lead viewers to a negative "close reading" of the scene.

Several elements of the photograph convey the idea that these people aren't gathered for a pleasant experience, such as going to a concert. Their body language is slumped and tired. Some people have crossed arms, and others (for example, the

Figure 4.2 Photo of people standing in line

man in the striped shirt) have shifted their weight to one leg. It seems as though they've been in this line a long time, and in fact, it's hard to tell from the picture's angle just how long the line stretches. People stare ahead or blankly into space, not interacting with others around them. They aren't here for fun or socializing.

The setting of the image contributes to the sense of unpleasantness. Although it seems to be a very large room, the ceiling appears quite low. Although the ceiling has numerous lights (indeed, the stretch of lights makes you perceive the room as vast), the image is fairly dark. Both of these qualities contribute to a vague sense that the environment is oppressive or controlled. The physical surroundings echo the collective mood.

There are commonalities and differences among the people. There are men and women of different races. People are dressed in jeans and in shorts, in shirts and in jackets. However, notice what the people have in common. While there's some difference in clothing, nothing is very dressy and nothing is very flashy. Everyone wears fairly casual clothes, with sneakers being the most common footwear. Furthermore, the general age range is comparatively narrow. Are there any children, youths, or elderly? Finally, several people are carrying sheets of paper. Perhaps they're turning in a test, an application, or a form.

In fact, this photograph depicts an unemployment line. Someone who wanted to depict waiting on an unemployment line as an optimistic or pleasant event would have created quite a different image. We're not saying that losing a job is ever pleasant—far from it. However, a different image would have shaped a different response. We imagine that a state unemployment agency that wanted to convey its work as efficient and friendly wouldn't be very happy with this image. We'll return to analyzing images in greater detail, in section 4j, below.

4b What are the elements of critical thinking?

Quick Reference 4.1 describes the general steps of critical thinking, steps that are just as fluid as those in the WRITING PROCESS. Expect sometimes to combine steps, reverse their order, and return to parts of the process you thought you had completed.

Quick Reference 4.1

■ ■ ■ ■ ■ ■ ■

Steps in the critical thinking process

1. **Comprehend** or **summarize.** Understand the **literal** meaning: the "plain" meaning on the surface of the material. Be able to extract and restate its main message or central point or to accurately and objectively describe an image, event, or situation. Add nothing. Read "on the lines."

continued >>

Quick Reference 4.1 (continued)

2. **Analyze.** Examine the material by breaking it into its component parts. Ask about the nature or meaning of each part and how it contributes to the overall meaning or effect.

3. **Infer.** Read "between the lines" to see what's not stated but implied.

4. **Synthesize.** Connect what you've summarized, analyzed, and inferred with your prior knowledge or experiences, with other ideas or perspectives, or with other readings, texts, or situations.

5. **Evaluate.** Read "beyond the lines." Judge the quality of the material or form your own informed opinion about it. Answer such questions as "Is it reasonable? Fair? Accurate? Convincing? Ethical? Useful? Comprehensive? Important?"

4c How do I read to comprehend?

When you read to comprehend, you try to understand the basic, literal meaning of a text. Your goal is to discover the main ideas, the supporting details, or, in a work of fiction, the central details of plot and character.

4c.1 Reading closely and actively

Reading is an active process—a dynamic, meaning-making interaction between the page and your brain. The secret to **reading closely and actively** is to annotate as you read. Annotating means writing notes to yourself in a book or article's margins and using asterisks and other codes to alert you to special material. Some readers start annotating right away, while others wait to annotate after they've previewed the material and read it once. Experiment to determine what works best for you. We recommend your using two different ink colors, one for close reading (blue in the example in Figure 4.3) and one for active reading (black in the example).

Close reading means annotating for content. You might, for example, number and briefly list the steps in a process or summarize major points in the margin. When you review, your marginal notes help you glance over the material and quickly recall what it's about.

Active reading means annotating to make connections between the material and your own knowledge or experiences. This is your chance to converse on paper with the writer. Consider yourself a partner in the making of meaning, a full participant in the exchange of ideas that characterizes a college education. Active reading is a key to ANALYSIS (section 4d), INFERENCE (4e), SYNTHESIS (4f), and EVALUATION (4g).

If you feel uncomfortable writing in a book—even though the practice of annotating texts dates back to the Middle Ages—create a *double-entry notebook*.

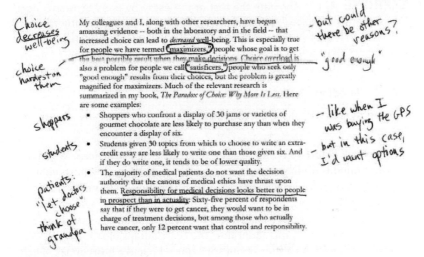

Figure 4.3 A sample of annotated reading

Draw a line down the center of your notebook page. On one side, write content notes (close reading). On the other, write synthesis notes (active reading). Be sure to write down exactly where in the reading you're referring to. Illustrated in Figure 4.4 is a short example from a double-entry notebook.

Content Notes	Synthesis Notes
increased wealth and choice hasn't made people happier	
--14 million people fewer than in 1974 report being "very happy"	I wonder if people define happiness different today than they did 30-40 years ago
--depression and suicide has increased, especially among young people	Scary. There could be lots of causes, and I wonder if wealth and choice are the most important
--demand for counseling has increased at colleges	Could it be that more students seek counseling? Maybe need was there before but people didn't act.

Figure 4.4 Double entry notebook example

EXERCISE 4-1   Annotate the rest of the essay by Barry Schwartz, titled "The Tyranny of Choice," on pages 196–198. Depending on your instructor's directions, either follow the annotation example in Figure 4.3, the double-entry example in Figure 4.4, or try both.

4c.2   Reading systematically

To **read systematically** is to use a structured plan: **Preview**, **Read**, and **Review**.

1. **Preview:** Before you begin reading, start making predictions. When your mind is reading actively, it is guessing what's coming next, either confirming or revising its prediction, and moving on to new predictions. For example, suppose you're glancing through a magazine and come across the title "The Heartbeat." Your mind begins guessing: Is this a love story? Is this about how the heart pumps blood? Maybe, you say to yourself, it's a story about someone who had a heart attack. Then, as you read the first few sentences, your mind confirms which guess was correct. If you see words like *electrical impulse, muscle fibers,* and *contraction,* you know instantly that you're in the realm of physiology.

   - To preview a book, first look at the table of contents. What topics are included? What seems to be the main emphasis? Which sections will be most important? If there's an introduction or preface, skim it.

   - To preview a particular reading (for example, a chapter or an article), read all the headings, large and small. Note the **boldfaced** words (in darker print), and all visuals and their captions, including photographs, drawings, figures, tables, and boxes.

   - Check for introductory notes about the author and head notes, which often precede individual works in collections of essays or short stories. Read pivotal paragraphs, such as the opening and (unless you're reading for suspense) closing.

   - Jot a few questions that you expect—or hope—the reading will answer.

2. **Read:** Read the material closely and actively (see section 4c.1). Identify the main points and start thinking about how the writer supports them.

3. **Review:** Go back to questions you jotted during previewing. Did the reading answer them? (If not, either your predictions could have been wrong, or you didn't read carefully; reread to determine which.) Also, look at the annotations you made through close and active reading. What do these add up to? Where are places you need to go back? Keep in mind that collaborative learning can reinforce what you learn from reading. Ask a friend or classmate to discuss the material with you and quiz you.

Alert: The speed at which you read depends on your purpose for reading. When you're hunting for a particular fact, you can skim the page until you find what you want. When you read about a subject you know well, you might read somewhat rapidly, slowing down when you come to new material. When you're unfamiliar with the subject, you need to work slowly to give your mind time to absorb the new material. ●

Quick Reference 4.2

More ways to help your reading comprehension

- **Make associations.** Link new material to what you already know, especially when you're reading about an unfamiliar subject. You may even find it helpful to read an encyclopedia article or an easier book or article on the subject first in order to build your knowledge base.

- **Simplify tough sentences.** If the author's writing style is complex, "unpack" the sentences: Break them into smaller units or reword them in a simpler style.

- **Make it easy for you to focus.** If your mind wanders, do whatever it takes to concentrate. Arrange for silence or music, for being alone or in the library with others who are studying. Try to read at your best time of day.

- **Allot the time you need.** To comprehend new material, you must allow sufficient time to read, reflect, reread, and study. Discipline yourself to balance classes, working, socializing, and family activities. Alas, reading for comprehension takes time.

- **Master the vocabulary.** If you don't understand key terms in your reading, you can't fully understand the concepts. As you encounter new words, try to figure out their meanings from context clues. Also, many textbooks list key terms and their definitions (called a *glossary*) at the end of each chapter or of the book. Of course, nothing replaces having a good dictionary at hand.

4d How do I analyze a reading?

To analyze something is to break it into parts, just as a chemist does, for example, in order to figure out the compounds in a particular mixture. However, it's easier to define analysis than to understand and apply it to reading. The key is knowing what parts to examine and how.

> ### Quick Reference 4.3 ■ ■ ■ ■ ■ ■ ■
>
> ### Elements of analysis
>
> 1. Separate facts from opinions (4d.1).
> 2. Identify the evidence (4d.2).
> 3. Identify cause and effect (4d.3).
> 4. Describe the tone (4d.4).

4d.1 Separating facts from opinions

A helpful step in analyzing a reading is to distinguish **fact** from **opinion**. *Facts* are statements that can be verified. *Opinions* are statements of personal beliefs. While facts can be verified by observation, research, or experimentation, opinions are open to debate. Problems arise when a writer blurs the distinction between fact and opinion. Critical readers will know the difference.

For example, here are two statements, one a fact, the other an opinion.

1. Women can never make good mathematicians.

2. Although fear of math isn't purely a female phenomenon, girls tend to drop out of math classes sooner than boys, and some adult women have an aversion to math and math-related activity that is akin to anxiety.

Reading inferentially, you can see that statement 1 is clearly an opinion. Is it worthy of consideration? Perhaps it could be open to debate, but the word *never* implies that the writer is unwilling to allow for even one exception. Conversely, statement 2 at least seems to be factual, though research would be necessary to confirm or deny the position.

You may find it practical to label key sentences "facts" or "opinions" as part of your analysis. You could put an "F" or "O" in the margin next to those sentences. Or, you could include a brief note to yourself explaining why certain sentences are opinions.

● **EXERCISE 4-2** Working individually or with a collaborative group, decide
● which of the statements below are facts and which are opinions. When the au-
● thor and source are provided, explain how that information influenced your judgment. For help, consult section 4c.2.

1. The life of people on earth is better now than it has ever been—certainly
   much better than it was 500 years ago.
                                   —Peggy Noonan, "Why Are We So Unhappy When We
                                                              Have It So Good?"

2. The fast food industry pays the minimum wage to a higher proportion of its workers than any other American industry.
   —Eric Schlosser, *Fast Food Nation*

3. Grief, when it comes, is nothing we expect it to be.
   —Joan Didion, *The Year of Living Dangerously*

4. A mind is a terrible thing to waste.
   —United Negro College Fund

5. History is the branch of knowledge that deals systematically with the past.
   —*Webster's New World College Dictionary*, Fourth Edition

6. In 1927, F. E. Tylcote, an English physician, reported in the medical journal *Lancet* that in almost every case of lung cancer he had seen or known about, the patient smoked.
   —William Ecenbarger, "The Strange History of Tobacco"

7. Trucks that must travel on frozen highways in Alaska for most of the year now sometimes get stuck in the mud as the permafrost thaws.
   —Al Gore, *An Inconvenient Truth*

8. You can, Honest Abe notwithstanding, fool most of the people all of the time.
   —Stephen Jay Gould, "The Creation Myths of Cooperstown"

9. You change laws by changing lawmakers.
   —Sissy Farenthold, political activist, *Bakersfield Californian*

10. A critical task for all of the world's religions and spiritual traditions is to enrich the vision—and the reality—of the sense of community among us.
    —Joel D. Beversluis, *A Sourcebook for Earth's Community of Religions*

4d.2 Identifying the evidence

For any opinions or claims, you next need to identify and analyze the evidence that the writer provides. **Evidence** consists of facts, examples, the results of formal studies, and the opinions of experts. A helpful step in analysis is to identify the kind of evidence used (or what evidence is missing).

RECOGNIZING PRIMARY VERSUS SECONDARY SOURCES

Primary sources are firsthand evidence based on your own or someone else's original work or direct observation. Primary sources can take the form of experiments, surveys, interviews, memoirs, observations (such as in ETH-NOGRAPHIES), original creative works (for example, poems, novels, paintings and other visual art, plays, films, or musical compositions).

   Secondary sources report, describe, comment on, or analyze the experiences or work of others. Quick Reference 4.4 illustrates the difference.

Examples of differences between primary and secondary sources

Primary Source	Secondary Source
Professor Fassi interviews thirty single parents and reports his findings in a journal article.	*Time* magazine summarizes Professor Fassi's study in a longer article on single parents.
Medical researcher Molly Doran publishes the results of her experiments with a new cancer drug in the *New England Journal of Medicine.*	*The Washington Post* runs an article that summarizes findings from Doran's study.
The National Assessment of Educational Progress publishes test results on the reading abilities of ninth graders.	National Public Radio refers to the NAEP study in a story on reading in America.
A team of researchers at Bowling Green State University survey 2,259 Ohio citizens about their voting patterns and write an article explaining their findings.	Scholar Maya Dai conducts a study of politics in Colorado; in her review of literature section of her study, she summarizes the Bowling Green study, along with studies in four other states.
Rosa Rodriguez writes a memoir about life as a migrant worker.	Writer Phil Gronowski discusses Rodriguez's memoir in his daily blog.
Gerhard Richter exhibits his paintings at the Art Institute of Chicago.	The *Chicago Tribune* publishes a review of Richter's exhibition.

Primary sources have the advantage of being "closer" to the subject matter or phenomenon. Of course, that doesn't make them perfect. For example, you can't interview only three sophomores and make claims about all college students everywhere. Furthermore, not all eyewitnesses are reliable, so you must judge which ones to believe. Still, readers often find enhanced credibility in primary research. With secondary sources, there's always a risk that the writer isn't reporting the original material accurately, whether intentionally or not.

For example, suppose a primary source author concluded "It would be a mistake to assume that people's poverty level reflects their intelligence," but a secondary source author represents this as "poverty level is connected to intelligence." Problem! The value of a secondhand account hinges on the reliability of the reporter, which depends on the specificity, accuracy, and authority of his or her observations, as well as where he or she published them. Quick Reference 4.5 provides a checklist for evaluating sources.

Quick Reference 4.5 ■ ■ ■ ■ ■ ■ ■

Evaluating sources

- **Is the source authoritative?** Did an expert or a person you can expect to write credibly on the subject write it? If it's a memoir or eyewitness account, does it have the kind of detail and perspective that makes the writer credible?

- **Is the source published in a reliable place?** Does the material appear in a reputable publication—a book published by an established publisher, a respected journal or magazine—or on a reliable Internet site?

- **Is the source well known?** Is the source cited elsewhere as you read about the subject? (If so, the authority of the source is probably widely accepted.)

- **Is the tone balanced?** Is the language relatively objective (and therefore more likely to be reliable), or is it slanted (probably not reliable)?

- **Is the source current?** Is the material up to date and therefore more likely to be reliable, or has later authoritative and reliable research made it outdated? ("Old" isn't necessarily unreliable. In many fields, classic works of research remain authoritative for decades or even centuries.)

- **Are its findings valid (if a primary source)?** Did the experiment, survey, interview, or study seem to be conducted rigorously? Are the conclusions justified by the data?

- **Is it accurate and complete (if a secondary source)?** Does it accurately summarize and interpret the primary resource? Does it leave out anything important?

EXERCISE 4-3   Indicate for each of the passages below whether it contains primary or secondary evidence. Then, decide whether the evidence is reliable or not, and explain why or why not. Refer to section 4d.2 for help.

A.   Midland has the kind of air that hits you like a brick. After a few minutes, your throat burns. After a few days, your skin feels powdery, your eyelids stick, your hair feels dusty and rough. The longer you spend there, the more you become a little bit like the land—you dry out and cake and crack. Not until I spent time in Midland did I fully appreciate the fact that the earth has an actual crust, like bread that has been slowly baked. I became convinced that if I stayed for a while, I would develop one, too.

—Susan Orlean, "A Place Called Midland"

B.   According to a 2005 report of the International Centre for Prison Studies in London, the United States—with 5 percent of the world's population—houses 25 percent of the world's inmates. Our incarceration rate (714 per 100,000 residents) is almost 40 percent greater than those of our nearest competitors (Bermuda, Belarus, and Russia). Other industrial democracies, even those with significant crime problems of their own, are much less punitive: Our incarceration rate is 6.2 times that of Canada, 7.8 times that of France, and 12.3 times that of Japan.

—Glenn C. Loury, "America Incarcerated"

C.   Ordinary human foods can be dangerous to dogs, and the list of potentially hazardous items is growing. Reports from pet owners can prompt an investigation, says Eric Dunayer, senior toxicologist at the ASPCA's Animal Poison Control Center in Urbana, Illinois. In 2006, the center's hotline fielded roughly 116,000 calls. Nearly 200 asked about xylitol, a sugar substitute gaining popularity in baked goods, candy, and gum. "We often see vomiting, followed by weakness, staggering, collapse, and possibly seizures as blood sugar drops," say Dunayer.

—Catherine L. Barker, "Spotting Pet Threats"

EXERCISE 4-4   Individually or with a group, choose one of the following thesis statements and list the kinds of primary and secondary sources you might consult to support the thesis (you can guess intelligently, rather than checking to make sure that the sources exist). Then, decide which sources in your list would be primary and which secondary.

THESIS STATEMENT 1: People who regularly perform volunteer work lead happier lives than those who don't.

THESIS STATEMENT 2: Whether someone regularly performs volunteer work or not ultimately has no effect on their happiness.

EVALUATING EVIDENCE

You can evaluate evidence by asking the following questions to guide your judgment.

- **Is the evidence sufficient?** To be sufficient, evidence can't be skimpy. As a rule, the more evidence, the better. Readers have more confidence in the results of a survey that draws on a hundred respondents rather than on ten. As a writer, you may convince your reader that violence is a serious problem in high schools on the basis of only two examples, but you'll be more convincing with additional examples.

- **Is the evidence representative?** Evidence is representative if it is typical. As a reader, assess the objectivity and fairness of evidence. Don't trust a claim or conclusion about a group based on only a few members rather than on a truly typical sample. For example, a pollster surveying national political views would not get representative evidence by interviewing people only in Austin, Texas, because that group doesn't represent the regional, racial, political, and ethnic makeup of the entire US electorate.

- **Is the evidence relevant?** Relevant evidence is directly related to the conclusion you're drawing. Determining relevance often demands subtle thinking. Suppose you read that one hundred students who had watched television for more than two hours a day throughout high school earned significantly lower scores on a college entrance exam than one hundred students who had not. Can you conclude that students who watch less television perform better on college entrance exams? Not necessarily. Other differences between the two groups could account for the different scores: geographical region, family background, socioeconomic group, or the quality of schools attended.

- **Is the evidence accurate?** Accurate evidence is correct and complete. To be accurate, evidence must come from a reliable source, whether it is primary or secondary. Equally important, evidence must be presented honestly, not misrepresented or distorted.

- **Is the evidence qualified?** Reasonable evidence doesn't make extreme claims. Claims that use words such as *all, always, never,* and *certainly* are disqualified if even one exception is found. Conclusions are more sensible and believable when qualified with words such as *some, many, may, possibly, often,* and *usually.* Remember that today's "facts" may be revised as time passes and knowledge grows. It's a fact today that no life has been found on Mars; a future space mission could change that, however unlikely it might be.

4d.3 Identifying cause and effect

Cause and effect describes the relationship between one event (cause) and another event that happens as a result (effect). The relationship also works in reverse: One event (effect) results from another event (cause). Whether you begin with a cause or with an effect, you're using the same basic pattern.

Cause A → produces → effect B

You may seek to understand the effects of a known cause:

More studying → produces → ?

Or you may seek to determine the cause or causes of a known effect:

? → produces → recurrent headaches

When you're analyzing a reading, look for any claims of cause and effect. (Of course, not all readings will have them.) For any that you find, think carefully through the relationship between cause A and effect B. Just because A happened before B or because A and B are associated with each other doesn't mean A caused B. Consult the guidelines in Quick Reference 4.6.

Quick Reference 4.6   ■ ■ ■ ■ ■ ■ ■

Assessing cause and effect

- **Is there a clear relationship between events?** Related causes and effects happen in sequence: A cause occurs before an effect. First the wind blows; then a door slams; then a pane of glass in the door breaks. But CHRONOLOGICAL ORDER merely implies a cause-and-effect relationship. Perhaps someone slammed the door shut. Perhaps someone threw a base-ball through the glass pane. A cause-and-effect relationship must be linked by more than chronological sequence. The fact that B happens after A doesn't prove that A causes B.

- **Is there a pattern of repetition?** Scientific proof depends on a pattern of repetition. To establish that A causes B, every time A is present, B must occur. Or, put another way, B never occurs unless A is present. The need for repetition explains why the US Food and Drug Admini-stration (FDA) runs thousands of clinical trials before approving a new medicine.

- **Are there multiple causes and/or effects?** Avoid oversimplification. The basic pattern of cause and effect—single cause, single effect (A causes B)—rarely represents the full picture. Multiple causes and/or effects are more typical of real life. For example, it would be oversimplification to assume that a lower crime rate is strictly due to high employment rates. Similarly, one cause can produce multiple effects. For example, advertise-ments for a liquid diet drink might focus on the drink's most appealing effect, rapid weight loss, while ignoring less desirable effects such as lost nutrients and a tendency to regain the weight.

EXERCISE 4-5   For each of the sentences below, explain how the effect might not be a result of the cause given.

EXAMPLE   The number of shoppers downtown increased because the city planted more trees there.

Of course, planting trees might have made the downtown more attractive and drawn more shoppers. However, perhaps there are other reasons: new stores opening, more parking, a suburban mall closed down, and so on.

1. Attendance at baseball games declined because the team raised prices.
2. Test scores improved because the school instituted a dress code.

3. Because of the Internet, Americans are reading fewer books than they did twenty years ago.

4d.4 Describing the tone

Tone refers to the attitude conveyed in writing, mostly by the writer's word choice. A tone can be formal, informal, laid back, pompous, sarcastic, concerned, judgmental, sympathetic, and so on. We discuss tone at greater length in section 8d.

For now, however, as a critical reader, be suspicious of a highly emotional tone in writing. If you find it, chances are the writer is trying to manipulate the audience. As a writer, if you find your tone growing emotional, step back and rethink the situation. No matter what point you want to make, your chance of communicating successfully to an audience depends on your using a moderate, reasonable tone. For instance, the exaggerations below in the NO example (*robbing treasures, politicians are murderers*) might hint at the truth of a few cases, but they're too extreme to be taken seriously. The language of the YES version is far more likely to deliver its intended message.

> NO Urban renewal must be stopped. Urban redevelopment is ruining this country, and money-hungry capitalists are robbing treasures from law-abiding citizens. Corrupt politicians are murderers, caring nothing about people being thrown out of their homes into the streets.

> YES Urban renewal is revitalizing our cities, but it has caused some serious problems. While investors are trying to replace slums with decent housing, they must also remember that they're displacing people who don't want to leave their familiar neighborhoods. Surely, a cooperative effort between government and the private sector can lead to creative solutions.

4e How do I draw inferences?

When you read for **inferences**, you're reading to understand what's suggested or implied but not explicitly stated. Here's an example.

> The band finally appeared an hour after the concert was scheduled to start. The lead singer spent the first two songs staring at the stage and mumbling into his microphone, before finally looking at the audience and saying, "It's great to be here in Portland." The only problem was that they were playing in Denver. At that point the crowd was too stunned even to boo. I started texting some friends to see if they had any more interesting prospects for the evening.

> —Jenny Shi, student

Literally, this paragraph describes what happened at a concert. But there's clearly more going on. Among the inferential meanings are that (1) the band wasn't very enthusiastic about this concert; and (2) this wasn't a very pleasant experience for Jenny or, probably, others at the event. The writer doesn't say this directly, but it's clear from her choice of details.

Drawing inferences takes practice. Quick Reference 4.7 lists questions to help you read "between the lines." A discussion of each point follows the box.

Quick Reference 4.7 ■ ■ ■ ■ ■ ■ ■

Drawing inferences during reading

- What is the point, even if the writer doesn't state it outright?
- How might the writer's position influence his or her perspective?
- Can I detect **bias** in the material?
- What are the implications of the reading?

4e.1 The writer's position

As a reader, when you can "consider the source"—that is, find out exactly who made a statement—you can open up new perspectives. For example, you would probably read an essay for or against capital punishment differently if you knew the writer was an inmate on death row rather than a noninmate who wished to express an opinion. For example, consider the statement, "Freedom isn't the ability to do what you want but rather the ability to do what you should." If you were told this statement was made by a third-world dictator, you would interpret it differently than if you were told it was made by a leader of the American Legion (which it actually was).

Although considering the source can help you draw inferences, take care that you don't fall prey to ARGUMENT TO THE PERSON (4i). Just because someone you don't respect voices an opinion doesn't mean that the position is necessarily wrong.

4e.2 Bias

For inferential reading, you want to detect **bias**, also known as **prejudice**. When writing is distorted by hatred or distrust of individuals, groups of people, or ideas, you as a critical reader want to suspect the accuracy and fairness of the material. Bias can be worded in positive language, but critical readers aren't deceived by such tactics. Similarly, writers can merely imply their bias rather than state it outright. For example, suppose you read, "Poor people like living in crowded conditions because they're used to such surroundings" or "Women are so wonderfully nurturing that they can't succeed in business." As a critical reader, you will immediately detect the bias. Therefore, always question material that rests on a weak foundation of discrimination or narrow-mindedness.

4e.3 What are implications of the reading?

An **implication** takes the form, "If this is true (or if this happens), then that might also be true (or that might be the consequence.)" One way to consider implications, especially for readings that contain a proposal, is to ask, "Who might benefit from an action, and who might lose?" For example, consider the following short argument.

> Because parking downtown is so limited, we should require anyone putting up a new building to construct a parking lot or contribute to parking garages.

It doesn't take much to infer who might benefit: people driving downtown who are looking for places to park. With a little more thought, you can see how store owners could benefit if shoppers have an easier time finding parking. Who might lose? Well, having to provide parking will add to building costs, and these may be passed to customers. More room for parking means less room for building, so the downtown could sprawl into neighborhoods. More parking can encourage more driving, which contributes to congestion and pollution.

Now, benefits may outweigh losses—or the other way around. The point is that if you think about the implications of ideas in a reading, you can generate some inferences.

EXERCISE 4-6   Consider the implications of the following short argument, focusing on who might gain and lose from the following proposal: "In an effort to enhance its prestige, DaVinci College will reduce its enrollment from 10,000 students to 7,000 over the next four years. It will accomplish this reduction by increasing the admissions requirements and more selectively recruiting across the country, not only in the local region."

EXERCISE 4-7   Read the following passages, then (1) list all literal information, (2) list all implied information, and (3) list the opinions stated. Refer to sections 4c.1 and 4c.2 for help.

EXAMPLE   The study found many complaints against the lawyers were not investigated, seemingly out of a "desire to avoid difficult cases."

—Norman F. Dacey

Literal information: Few complaints against lawyers are investigated.

Implied information: The term *difficult cases* implies a cover-up: Lawyers, or others in power, hesitate to criticize lawyers for fear of being sued or for fear of a public outcry if the truth about abuses and errors were revealed.

Opinions: No opinions. It reports on a study.

A.   [T]he sexual balance of power in the world is changing, slowly but surely. New evidence can be found in the 2007 World Development Indicators from the World Bank. It is something to celebrate.

The most obvious changes are in education. In 2004 girls outnumbered boys at secondary schools in almost half the countries of the world (84 of 171). The number of countries in which the gap between the sexes has more or less disappeared has risen by a fifth since 1991. At university level, girls do better still, outnumbering boys in 83 of 141 countries. They do so not only in the rich world, which is perhaps not surprising, but also in countries such as Mongolia and Guyana where university education for anyone is not common.

—*The Economist,* "A Man's World?"

B.   In the misty past, before Bill Gates joined the company of the world's richest men, before the mass-marketed personal computer, before the metaphor of an information superhighway had been worn down to a cliché, I heard Roger Schank interviewed on National Public Radio. Then a computer science professor at Yale, Schank was already well known in artificial intelligence circles. Because those circles did not include me, a new programmer at Sperry Univac, I hadn't heard of him. Though I've forgotten the details of the conversation, I have never forgotten Schank's insistence that most people do not need to own computers.

That view, of course, has not prevailed. Either we own a personal computer and fret about upgrades, or we are scheming to own one and fret about the technical marvel yet to come that will render our purchase obsolete. Well, there are worse ways to spend money, I suppose. For all I know, even Schank owns a personal computer. They're fiendishly clever machines, after all, and they've helped keep the wolf from my door for a long time.

—Paul De Palma, "http://www.when_is_enough_enough?.com"

4f How do I synthesize?

To **synthesize** is to put things together. When analysis and inference generate specific ideas, try to put them together with things you know from your experience or previous learning or from other readings. For example, suppose you read an opinion that reminds you of a similar opinion by an expert you respect. Making that connection is an act of critical thinking. It takes you beyond the reading itself. Or suppose that someone provides evidence for a claim, but that some further reading shows you that their facts are incomplete or even inaccurate. This synthesis allows you to read the first source more critically.

Synthesis also happens between a reading and your own experience. Take the following example.

> Probably no time in life is as liberating or stimulating as the college years. Freed from the drudgery of a career and the obligations of family life, college students have the luxury to explore new ideas and pursue new paths of knowledge. College is a joyful time of endless possibility.

If you're a single parent taking classes at night or someone who is working a couple of jobs and worrying about paying back loans, your perspective probably differs from the author's. Synthesizing the reading and your experience would result in a critical evaluation. We discuss synthesis with additional examples in section 7f.4.

4g How do I evaluate?

When you read to evaluate, you're judging the writer's work. **Evaluative reading** comes after you've summarized, analyzed, and synthesized the material (see Quick Reference 4.1). Reading "between the lines" is usually concerned with recognizing tone, detecting prejudice, differentiating fact from opinion, and determining the writer's position. Reading to evaluate "beyond the lines" requires an overall assessment of the soundness of the writer's reasoning, evidence, or observations, and the fairness and perceptiveness the writer shows, from accuracy of word choice and tone to the writer's respect for the reader.

Evaluating is the step where you make judgments. Ultimately, should we trust the author or not? Should we accept his or her conclusions and recommendations? An important additional strategy for answering questions like these is assessing reasoning processes.

4h How do I assess reasoning processes critically?

To think, read, and write critically, you need to distinguish *sound reasoning* from *faulty reasoning*. **Induction** and **deduction** are two basic reasoning processes, natural thought patterns people use every day to help them think through ideas and make decisions.

4h.1 Inductive reasoning

Inductive reasoning moves from particular facts or instances to general principles. Suppose you go to the Registry of Motor Vehicles to renew your driver's license and have to stand in line for two hours. A few months later you return to get new license plates, and once again you have to stand in line for two hours. You mention your annoyance to a couple of friends who say they had exactly the same experience. You conclude that the registry is inefficient and indifferent to the needs of its patrons. You've arrived at this conclusion by means of induction. Quick Reference 4.8 shows the features of inductive reasoning.

Quick Reference 4.8 ■ ■ ■ ■ ■ ■ ■

Inductive reasoning

- **Inductive reasoning moves from the specific to the general.** It begins with specific evidence—facts, observations, or experiences—and moves to a general conclusion.

- **Inductive conclusions are considered reliable or unreliable, not true or false.** Because inductive thinking is based on a sampling of facts, an inductive conclusion indicates probability—the degree to which the conclusion is likely to be true—not certainty.

- **An inductive conclusion is held to be reliable or unreliable in relation to the quantity and quality of the evidence** (4g) on which it's based.

- **Induction leads to new "truths."** It can support statements about the unknown based on what's known.

4h.2 Deductive reasoning

Deductive reasoning is the process of reasoning from general claims to a specific conclusion. Suppose you know that students who don't study for Professor Sanchez's history tests tend to do poorly. If your friend tells you that she didn't study, you can make a reasonable conclusion about her grade. Your reasoning might go something like this:

PREMISE 1	Students who don't study do poorly on Professor Sanchez's exams.
PREMISE 2	My friend didn't study.
CONCLUSION	Therefore, my friend probably did poorly on the exam.

Deductive arguments have three parts: two **premises** and a conclusion. This three-part structure is known as a **syllogism**. The first and second premises of a deductive argument may be statements of fact or assumptions. They lead to a conclusion, which is the point at which you want to think as precisely as possible because you're into the realm of *validity*.

Whether or not an argument is **valid** has to do with its form or structure. Here, the word *valid* isn't the general term people use in conversation to mean "acceptable" or "well grounded." In the context of reading and writing logical arguments, the word *valid* has a very specific meaning. A deductive argument is *valid* when the conclusion logically follows from the premises; a deductive argument is *invalid* when the conclusion doesn't logically follow from the premises. For example:

VALID DEDUCTIVE ARGUMENT

PREMISE 1	When it snows, the streets get wet. [fact]
PREMISE 2	It is snowing. [fact]
CONCLUSION	Therefore, the streets are getting wet.

INVALID DEDUCTIVE ARGUMENT

PREMISE 1	When it snows, the streets get wet. [fact]
PREMISE 2	The streets are getting wet. [fact]
CONCLUSION	Therefore, it is snowing.

Here's the problem with the invalid deductive argument: It has acceptable premises because they are facts. However, the argument's conclusion is wrong because it ignores other reasons why the streets might be wet. For example, the street could be wet from rain, from street-cleaning trucks that spray water, or from people washing their cars. Therefore, because the conclusion doesn't follow logically from the premises, the argument is invalid.

Another problem in a deductive argument can occur when the premises are implied but not stated—called **unstated assumptions**. An argument can be logically valid even though it is based on wrong assumptions. To show that such an argument is invalid, you need to attack the assumptions, not the conclusion, as wrong. For example, suppose a corporation argues that it can't install pollution-control devices because the cost would cut deeply into its profits. This argument rests on the unstated assumption that a corporation should never do something that would lower its profits. That assumption is wrong, and so is the argument. To show that both are wrong, you need to challenge the assumptions.

Similarly, when a person says that certain information is correct because it's written in the newspaper, that person's deductive reasoning is flawed. The unstated assumption is that everything in a newspaper is correct—which isn't true. Whenever there's an unstated assumption, you need to state it outright and then check that it's true. Quick Reference 4.9 summarizes deductive reasoning.

Quick Reference 4.9

Deductive reasoning

- **Deductive reasoning moves from the general to the specific.** The three-part structure that makes up a deductive argument, or SYLLOGISM, includes two premises and a conclusion drawn from them.

continued >>

> ### Quick Reference 4.9 (continued)
>
> - **A deductive argument is valid if the conclusion logically follows from the premises.**
> - **A deductive conclusion may be judged true or false.** If both premises are true, the conclusion is true. If the argument contains an assumption, the writer must prove the truth of the assumption to establish the truth of the argument.
> - **Deductive reasoning applies what the writer already knows.** Though it doesn't yield new information, it builds stronger arguments than inductive reasoning because it offers the certainty that a conclusion is either true or false.

EXERCISE 4-8   Working individually or with a peer-response group, determine whether each conclusion here is valid or invalid. Be ready to explain your answers. For help, consult section 4h.

1. Faddish clothes are expensive.
   This shirt is expensive.
   This shirt must be part of a fad.
2. When a storm is threatening, small-craft warnings are issued.
   A storm is threatening.
   Small-craft warnings will be issued.
3. The Pulitzer Prize is awarded to outstanding literary works.
   The Great Gatsby never won a Pulitzer Prize.
   The Great Gatsby isn't an outstanding literary work.
4. All states send representatives to the United States Congress.
   Puerto Rico sends a representative to the United States Congress.
   Puerto Rico is a state.
5. Finding a good job requires patience.
   Sherrill is patient.
   Sherrill will find a good job.

4i   How can I recognize and avoid logical fallacies?

Logical fallacies are flaws in reasoning that lead to illogical statements. Though logical fallacies tend to occur when ideas are argued, they can be found in all types of writing. Interestingly, most logical fallacies masquerade as reasonable statements, but in fact, they're attempts to manipulate readers by appealing to their emotions instead of their intellects, their hearts rather than their heads. The name for each logical fallacy indicates the way that thinking has gone wrong.

HASTY GENERALIZATION

A **hasty generalization** draws conclusions from inadequate evidence. Suppose someone says, "My hometown is the best place in the state to live," and gives only two examples to support the opinion. That's not enough. And others might not feel the same way, perhaps for many reasons. Therefore, the person who makes such a statement is indulging in a hasty generalization.

Stereotyping is another kind of hasty generalization. It happens, for example, when someone says, "Everyone from country X is dishonest." Making such a sweeping claim about all members of a particular ethnic, religious, racial, or political group is an example of stereotyping. Other kinds of stereotyping include **sexism**, and **agism**.

FALSE ANALOGY

A **false analogy** draws a comparison in which the differences outweigh the similarities or the similarities are irrelevant. For example, "Old Joe Smith would never make a good president because an old dog can't learn new tricks" is a false analogy. Joe Smith isn't a dog. Also, learning the role of a president bears no comparison to a dog's learning tricks. Homespun analogies like this appear to have an air of wisdom about them, but they tend to fall apart when examined closely.

BEGGING THE QUESTION

Begging the question, also called *circular reasoning,* tries to offer proof by simply using another version of the argument itself. For example, the statement "Wrestling is a dangerous sport because it is unsafe" begs the question. Because *unsafe* is a synonym for *dangerous,* the statement goes around in a circle, getting nowhere. Here's another example of circular reasoning but with a different twist: "Wrestling is a dangerous sport because wrestlers get injured." Here, the support given in the second part of the statement, "wrestlers get injured," is the argument made in the first part of the statement. Obviously, wrestling can be safe when undertaken with proper training and practice.

IRRELEVANT ARGUMENT

An **irrelevant argument** reaches a conclusion that doesn't follow from the premises. Irrelevant argument is also called *non sequitur* (Latin for "it does not follow"). An argument is irrelevant when a conclusion doesn't follow from the premises. Here's an example: "Jane Jones is a forceful speaker, so she'll make a good mayor." You'd be on target if you asked "What does speaking ability have to do with being a good mayor?"

FALSE CAUSE

A **false cause** assumes that because two events are related in time, the first caused the second. False cause is also known as *post hoc, ergo propter hoc* (Latin for "after this, therefore because of this"). For example, if someone claims that a new weather satellite launched last week has caused the rain that's been falling ever since, that person is connecting two events that, while related in time, have no causal relationship to each other. The launching didn't cause the rain.

SELF-CONTRADICTION

Self-contradiction uses two premises that can't both be true at the same time. Here's an example: "Only when nuclear weapons have finally destroyed us will we be convinced of the need to control them." This is self-contradictory because no one would be around to be convinced if everyone has been destroyed.

RED HERRING

A **red herring**, also called *ignoring the question,* tries to distract attention from one issue by introducing a second that's unrelated to the first. Here's an example: "Why worry about pandas becoming extinct when we haven't solved the plight of the homeless?" You'd be on target if you asked, "What do homeless people have to do with pandas?" If the argument were to focus on proposing that the money spent to prevent the extinction of pandas should go instead to the homeless, the argument would be logical; however, the original statement is a fallacy. By using an irrelevant issue, a person hopes to distract the audience, just as putting a herring in the path of a bloodhound would distract it from the scent it's been following.

ARGUMENT TO THE PERSON

An **argument to the person** means attacking the person making the argument rather than the argument itself. It's also known as the *ad hominem* (Latin for "to the man") attack. When someone criticizes a person's appearance, habits, or character instead of the merits of that person's argument, the attack is a fallacy. Here's an example: "We'd take her position on child abuse seriously if she were not so nasty to her husband." You'd be on target if you were to ask, "What does nastiness to an adult, though not at all nice, have to do with child abuse?"

GUILT BY ASSOCIATION

Guilt by association means that a person's arguments, ideas, or opinions lack merit because of that person's activities, interests, or companions. Here's an example: "Jack belongs to the International Hill Climbers Association, which declared bankruptcy last month. This makes him unfit to be mayor of our city." The fact that Jack is a member of a group that declared bankruptcy has nothing to do with Jack's ability to be mayor.

JUMPING ON THE BANDWAGON

Jumping on the bandwagon means something is right or permissible because "everyone does it." It's also called *ad populum* (Latin for "to the people"). This fallacy operates in a statement such as "How could snowboarding be dangerous if thousands of people have done it?" Following the crowd in this example doesn't work because research shows that many people who snowboard eventually suffer serious knee injuries.

FALSE OR IRRELEVANT AUTHORITY

Using **false** or **irrelevant authority** means citing the opinion of someone who has no expertise in the subject at hand. This fallacy attempts to transfer prestige from one area to another. Many advertisements containing celebrity endorsements rely on this tactic—a famous athlete praising a brand of energy drink or a popular movie star lauding a wireless phone service provider.

CARD-STACKING

Card-stacking, also known as *special pleading*, ignores evidence on the other side of a question. From all available facts, people choose only those facts that show the best (or worst) possible case. Many television commercials use this strategy. For example, after three slim, happy consumers praise a diet plan, the announcer adds—in a very low and speedy voice—that results vary. Indeed, even that statement is vague and uninformative.

THE EITHER-OR FALLACY

The **either-or fallacy**, also called *false dilemma,* offers only two alternatives when more exist. Such fallacies tend to touch on emotional issues, so many people accept them until they analyze the statement. Here's an example: "Either go to college or forget about getting a job." This rigid, two-sided statement ignores the truth that many jobs don't require a college education.

TAKING SOMETHING OUT OF CONTEXT

Taking something out of context deliberately distorts an idea or a fact by removing it from its previously surrounding material. For example, suppose that a newspaper movie critic writes, "The plot was predictable and boring, but the music was sparkling." The next day, an advertisement for the movie claims "critics call it 'sparkling.'" Clearly, the ad has taken the critic's words out of context (only the music was called "sparkling"), and it thereby distorts the original meaning.

APPEAL TO IGNORANCE

Appeal to ignorance tries to make an incorrect argument based on something never having been shown to be false—or, the reverse, never having been shown to be true. Here's an example: "Because it hasn't been proven that eating food X doesn't cause cancer, we can assume that it does." The statement is a fallacy because the absence of opposing evidence proves nothing. Such appeals can be very persuasive because they prey on people's superstitions or lack of knowledge. Often, they're stated in the fuzzy language of DOUBLE NEGATIVES.

AMBIGUITY AND EQUIVOCATION

Ambiguity and **equivocation** are statements open to more than one interpretation, thus concealing the truth. Here's an example: Suppose a person is asked, "Is she doing a good job?" and the person answers, "She's performing as expected." The answer is a fallacy because it's open to positive or negative interpretation.

EXERCISE 4-9   Following are letters to the editor of a newspaper. Working alone or with a peer-response group, do a critical analysis of each, paying special attention to logical fallacies.

1. To the Editor:
   I am writing to oppose the plan to convert the abandoned railroad tracks into a bicycle trail. Everyone knows that the only reason the mayor wants to do this is so that she and her wealthy friends can have a new place to play. No one I know likes this plan, and if they did, it would probably be because they're part of the wine and cheese set, too. The next thing you know, the mayor will be proposing that we turn the schools into art museums or the park into a golf course. If you're working hard to support a family, you don't have time for this bike trail nonsense. And if you're not working hard, I don't have time for you.

   Russell Shields

2. To the Editor:
   I encourage everyone to support the bicycle trail project. Good recreation facilities are the key to the success of any community. Since the bike trail will add more recreation opportunities, it will guarantee the success of our town. Remember that several years ago our neighbors over in Springfield decided not to build a new park, and look what happened to their economy, especially that city's high unemployment rate. We can't afford to let the same thing happen to us. People who oppose this plan are narrow-minded, selfish, and almost unpatriotic. As that great patriot John Paul Jones said, "I have not yet begun to fight."

   Susan Thompson

3. To the Editor:
   I'm tired of all this nonsense about pollution and global warming. We had plenty of cold days last winter, and as my dentist said, "If this is global warming, then I'd sure hate to see global cooling." Plus, there were lots of days this summer when I haven't had to turn on my air conditioner. I know there are statistics that some people say show the climate is changing, but you can't trust numbers, especially when they come from liberal

scientists. These people just aren't happy unless they're giving us something to feel guilty about, whether it's smoking, drinking, or driving SUVs. Maybe if they stopped wasting their time worrying about pollution, they could do something useful, like find a cure for cancer.

Marcus Johnson

4j How can I view images with a critical eye?

Our digital age surrounds us with images in publications, on computers, on television, on cell phones. These images shape attitudes and beliefs, often in subtle ways. Consider, for example, how our notions of beauty have been shaped through the years by countless pictures of certain shapes and sizes of people. As a result—and as we suggested in the beginning of this chapter—you need to use critical thinking to analyze images as well as words. Doing so heightens your sensitivity to how others use images and equips you to use them effectively yourself.

You can view images critically in the same way that you can read texts critically by using summary, analysis, synthesis, and evaluation (Quick Reference 4.1) and by using literal, analytic inferential, and evaluative reading (see section 4.c). For example, look at Figure 4.5 with a critical eye.

- *Summarizing* the picture, as well as viewing it literally, you can see—at a minimum—a street full of older houses with modern skyscrapers in the distance.

Figure 4.5 Photo of houses against a city skyline

- *Analyzing* the picture, as well as viewing it inferentially, you can "read be-tween the lines" to see that it's fairly rich with layers of meaning. You can think about the meanings conveyed by the condition of the houses versus those of the modern buildings or about the lives of the people who live and work in each place. You can focus on the message of the comparative sizes of the houses and skyscrapers; on the contrast between this street and those you imagine at the base of the skyscrapers; on why the photographer chose this perspective; on how different captions might give the picture differ-ent meanings. For example, consider the meanings that would be sug-gested by three different captions: "Progress," "Inequality," or "The Neighborhood." Many possible ideas can come to mind as you study the picture critically.

- *Synthesizing* the picture, you can connect what you've analyzed and in-ferred to your previous knowledge and experiences, readings, or even other images.

- *Evaluating* the picture is the last step in viewing it critically. Resist eval-uating prematurely because your evaluation becomes informed by more than a noncritical personal reaction such as "I do/don't like the picture" only after you go through the earlier steps of thinking and reading criti-cally. In evaluating a visual critically, you can speak of how the visual "struck" you at first glance; how it did or didn't gain depth of meaning as you analyzed it, looking at what could be inferred and/or imagined; and how it lent itself to synthesis within the realms of your personal experi-ence and education.

Quick Reference 4.10   ■ ■ ■ ■ ■ ■ ■

Some helpful questions for analyzing visual images

- What does the image show?
- What are its parts? Do the parts belong together (like a lake, trees, and mountains), or do they contrast with one another (such as a woman in a fancy dress sitting on a tractor)? What might be the significance of the re-lationships among the parts?
- If there is a foreground and a background in the image, what is in each and why?
- If the image is a scene, what seems to be going on? What might be its message? If the image seems to be part of a story, what might have hap-pened before or after?

continued >>

Quick Reference 4.10   (continued)

- How do the people, if any, seem to be related? For example, do they appear to be friends, acquaintances, or strangers?

- If the image has a variety of shadings, colorings, and focuses, what's sharply in focus, blurry, bright, in shadows, colorful, or drab? How do such differences, or lack of them, call attention to various parts of the image?

- Can you think of any connections between the image and things you've experienced or learned from school, work, or reading; visits to museums or other cultural sites; watching movies, plays, and television; or other aspects of your life?

- From your observations, what is your evaluation of the image?

EXERCISE 4-10   Working individually or with a peer-response group, use critical thinking to consider one or both of the following photographs: Figure 4.6 and Figure 4.7 on page 134. Write either informal notes or a mini-essay, according to what your instructor requires. Use the questions in Quick Reference 4.10 to generate your summary, analysis, synthesis, and evaluation of the photograph(s).

Figure 4.6 Photo for Exercise 4-10

Figure 4.7 Photo for Exercise 4-10

4k   How can images persuade?

Because they convey lots of information in a small space, and because they can generate powerful emotional responses (*pathos*), images play a strong role in persuasion. (Just think about advertising!) Sometimes persuasion comes through a single well-chosen image: a picture of a bruised child's face demonstrates the cruelty of child abuse; a picture of a grateful civilian hugging a soldier seeks to show that a military action is just and good. In their campaign ads, politicians frequently choose highly unflattering photographs of their opponents, hoping to make them look foolish, incompetent, or unpleasant.

Figure 4.8 is a photograph of a pile of rusted barrels in a beautiful natural setting. The contrast between the barrels and the snow-covered mountains in the background, the lake, and the blue sky is stark and alarming. The barrels stand between viewers and the stunning scenery; they can't be ignored. The photographer has created this juxtaposition to persuade you—but to what purpose? Perhaps this photo makes an argument against pollution. Perhaps it's a statement against industrial development. Perhaps it emphasizes that people can act carelessly. While images can be powerful, they're often more ambiguous than words; images can't state what they mean, although they can move viewers in certain fairly predictable directions. In Figure 4.8, you're aware that the photographer intends to disturb you.

Figure 4.8 Photo of barrels in a natural setting

Frequently, people use a series of images to persuade. Some magazines use photo essays—two or more pictures meant to be viewed in a specific order to achieve a desired effect. An editorial cartoon might include two or more panels to make its point. More often than not, photo essays and editorials include captions or other words along with the images themselves.

4I How can I analyze words combined with images?

Many texts—from Web pages to advertisements, posters, brochures, and so on—are **multimodal** in that they combine words and images. (See section 46a for a further discussion of multimodal texts.) These texts can take advantage of *logos* and *ethos*, in addition to the *pathos* (5g) readily created by pictures alone. Critically analyzing multimodal texts means considering the images (Quick Reference 4.10) and the words separately, and then analyzing how the two elements combine to create a single effect.

Ask yourself, "What is the relationship between the words and the image(s)?" and "Why did the writer choose this particular image for these particular words?"

- Sometimes words and images reinforce one another. A poster with several sentences about poverty, for example, may have a picture of an obviously malnourished person.

- Other times, words and images contrast with one another for effect. Think of a picture of a belching smokestack accompanied by a caption that says, "Everyone deserves fresh air."

- Occasionally, a text might contain images simply to add visual interest. A little decoration is sometimes fine, but always be wary of images that seem simply to be thrown in for the sake of including an image. If there isn't a good reason for a particular combination of words and images, chances are that the document or message is weak.

Document design is the name given to the overall arrangement of words and visuals in a text. Chapter 45 explains several principles of document design.

EXERCISE 4-11   Working individually or with a peer-response group, use critical thinking to analyze either or both of the visual arguments that follow. Write either informal notes or a mini-essay, according to what your instructor requires.

Figure 4.9 Photo for Exercise 4-11

Figure 4.10 Photo for Exercise 4-11

4m What can Images add to my writing?

Occasionally, you might be tempted to add images to your writing because you want to add visual interest. That is a laudable goal, as long as the images support or enhance the message your writing is trying to deliver. However, be wary of throwing in one or more images merely for the sake of including an image. Your readers will rightly assume your images are communicating a message related to the text, and if none emerges, your entire document loses credibility. The best rule for inserting a photograph or other type of illustration into an essay is "When in doubt, leave it out."

There are four basic relationships between an image and a text. The image can simply illustrate or reinforce the text, as when an advertisement for apples contains a picture of an apple. The image can extend the text, as when a text about dangers of pollution, for example, shows a dead animal, even if the text doesn't refer to animals. The image can contrast with the text, creating irony. For example, suppose you see a picture of starving children, and the caption says, "What a great time to be alive!" Finally, the image can simply decorate the text, bearing none of the previous four relationships to the words but simply existing to draw attention.

Of course, some types of writing almost require images. Some posters, advertisements and Web sites, for example, would have far less impact if they contained words alone. For example, Figure 4.11 is a public service advertisement by the World Wildlife Fund, an organization dedicated to conservation and sustainable development. You'll notice that the image not only calls stunning attention to the ad, it reinforces the message in the bottom right corner. The text reads, "A single tin of paint can pollute millions of litres of water." The impact of improperly disposed waste is clearly illustrated by the striking image of a skyscraper-sized paint can as the mouth of an urban river.

Figure 4.11 An advertisement from the World Wildlife Fund

However, sometimes the use of words alone as stylized design elements can emphasize the message the writer is trying to convey. For example, Figure 4.12 is a poster that simply includes some words in various colors and sizes. The result is a powerful visual message about climate change.

As you think about whether to include images in your papers, consult Chapter 45, which discusses DOCUMENT DESIGN, the overall, well-planned arrangement of words and visuals in a text. Also, you may want to consult Chapter 47, which gives advice about MULTIMODAL TEXTS—compositions that extensively combine words, images, and perhaps even more.

Ice
Glacier Permafrost
Ocean Lake River Aquifer
Harvest Spring Fall Winter Plenty
CO_2 H_2SO_4 CO CH_4 N_2O
Industrial Coal "Bigger is Better" Hummer
Conservation Kyoto Future Children
Ross Ice Shelf, Polar Cap, Tibetan Glacier
Drought Hunger War
Despair

Figure 4.12 A poster about global warming

5

Writing Arguments

5a What is a written argument?

When you write an **argument**, you attempt to convince a reader to agree with you on a topic open to debate. You support your position, proposal, or interpretation with EVIDENCE, reasons, and examples. Some people use the terms *argumentative writing* and *persuasive writing* interchangeably. When people distinguish between them, *persuasive writing* is the broader term. It includes advertisements, letters to editors, and emotional speeches, as well as the kind of formal written arguments expected in college courses and other formal situations.

A written argument consists of two main elements:

- The **claim** states the issue and then takes a position on a debatable topic (the position can be written as a THESIS STATEMENT).
- Facts and logical reasoning provide **support** for the claim (the support needs to be in the form of evidence, reasons, and examples).

In daily life, you might think of an argument as a personal conflict or disagreement, begun in anger and involving emotional confrontations. Many radio programs, Web sites, and BLOGS reinforce this impression by featuring people who seem more interested in pushing their own agendas than in trying to persuade reasonably. For academic writing, as well as business and public writing, however, arguments are ways of demonstrating CRITICAL THINKING, calmly and respectfully. On difficult issues, your goal is to persuade an audience to consider your ideas with an open mind, which means that your audience's viewpoints and values need to influence your decisions about content, organization, and style. The passion that underlies a writer's position comes not from angry words but from the force of a balanced, well-developed, clearly written presentation.

In this chapter, you'll learn how to develop an effective claim, or thesis, how to generate support, and how to organize your argument using two strategies: the classical pattern and the Rogerian pattern. In addition, you'll find information about how to analyze and refute opposing arguments.

5b What are common types of arguments?

Many people believe that all writing contains an element of argument. In this view, even seemingly informative pieces like summaries, reports, and analyses attempt to convince readers that the author has done a skillful job and that the result is worth their time and attention. Even if we just concentrate on those writings in which writers are explicitly trying to persuade readers, there are several different types of arguments.

Definition arguments persuade readers to interpret a particular term in a particular way. You might think it strange that definitions are a matter for argument; after all, doesn't the dictionary solve all those questions? But consider how people contest terms like "patriot," "sexual harassment," "success," or even "happiness." What some people might label a work of art, others might term pornography. Is assisted suicide "murder" or "a medical procedure"? What are the characteristics a film must have to be called a romantic comedy?

Evaluation arguments persuade readers that something is good or bad, worthwhile or a waste of time, better or worse than other things like it, and so on. Common examples are movie, music, or television reviews, but every time we judge a politician or new model of car, we're also evaluating. Evaluation arguments have two elements. They argue that a particular set of criteria are important for measuring a particular class of things (for example, "mysteries must keep the audience guessing until the end"), and they argue that the thing being evaluated meets or doesn't meet those criteria ("because you could figure out very early who was the thief, it was a bad film").

Cause-and-effect arguments take one of two different forms. One is to argue that an existing situation results from a particular cause or set of causes. For example, you might take the situation of homelessness and argue that certain causes are most responsible (such as mental illness or minimum wages that are too low). Another is to argue that a cause will result in a certain effect. For example, you might argue that if we built more nuclear power plants, we would reduce global warming. You can see how cause-and-effect arguments are important in making policy decisions.

Proposal arguments convince readers that a particular solution to a problem or a particular way of addressing a need is best. Such arguments need to do two things. First, they must prove the existence of a need or problem that is important enough to require attention. Second, they must offer a solution and demonstrate how it will work and will be more feasible and effective than other possibilities. Suppose you want to convince college administrators to build more student parking. You'd be writing a proposal argument.

5c　How do I choose a topic for an argument?

When you choose a topic for written argument, be sure that it's open to debate. Don't confuse matters of information (facts) with matters of debate. An essay becomes an argument when it makes a claim—that is, *takes a position*—about a debatable topic. An effective way to develop a position is to ask two (or more) opposing questions about a topic.

FACT	Students at Calhoon College must study a foreign language.
DEBATABLE	Should Calhoon College require students to study a foreign language?
ONE SIDE	Calhoon College should not require students to study a foreign language.
OTHER SIDE	Calhoon College should require students to study a foreign language.

Though you need to select one side of a debatable question to defend in your essay, always keep the other side (or sides) in mind. Devoting some space to state and counter opposing viewpoints shows readers that you're well informed and fair-minded. This effect is even stronger if you always maintain a respectful tone by avoiding insults, abstaining from exaggerations, and resisting sarcasm. If you neglect to mention opposing views, your readers could justifiably assume you're not well informed, fair-minded, or disciplined as a thinker.

Instructors sometimes assign students a topic and even the position to take. In such cases, you need to fulfill the assignment skillfully even if you disagree with the point of view. Indeed, experienced debate teams practice arguing all sides of an issue. Being assigned topics or positions is common beyond college, especially in work settings. Perhaps a manager asks you to develop a persuasive marketing campaign or to negotiate a price break from a supplier. Perhaps you'll be told to convince other workers that a new process will save them time and effort.

If you choose your own topic and position, select one that has sufficient substance for college writing. Readers expect you to take an intelligent, defensible position and to support it reasonably and convincingly. For example, "We should prevent censorship in public libraries" is worthy of a college-level essay; "People should wear yellow baseball caps" is not.

Even if you think that all sides of a debatable topic have merit, you need to choose one of them anyway. Don't become paralyzed from indecision. You're not making a lifetime commitment. Concentrate on the merits of one position, and argue that position as effectively as possible, reserving some space to counter objections. Of course, the more thoroughly you think through all sides of the topic, the broader the perspective you'll bring to your writing, and the more likely it is that your writing will be effective. Finally, however, take a position.

5d How do I develop a claim and a thesis statement for my argument?

A CLAIM is a statement that expresses a point of view on a debatable topic. It can be supported by evidence, reasons, and examples (including facts, statistics, names, experiences, and expert testimony). The exact wording of the claim rarely finds its way into the essay, but the claim serves as a focus for your thinking. Later, it serves as the basis for developing your THESIS STATEMENT.

TOPIC	Wild animals as domestic pets
CLAIM	People should not be allowed to own wild animals.
CLAIM	People should be allowed to own wild animals.

To stimulate your thinking about the topic and decide the claim you'll argue, work with the PLANNING techniques discussed in Chapter 2. Another well-favored strategy is to create a two-column list, labeling one column *Pro* or *For,* the other *Con* or *Against.* If there are more than two opposing sides, label the columns accordingly. The columned list displays the quantity and quality of your material so that you can decide whether you're ready to start DRAFTING.

Alex García, the student who wrote the argument essay that appears in section 5n, chose his own topic for a written argument in a first-year college writing class. Alex was a biology major who was fascinated about genetic engineering, especially of food. While exploring this topic, he became interested in the broader issue of organic food and whether it was really better. As a consumer himself, he had a direct stake in this matter. When he began reading articles he found through library research, he thought they would all come out clearly in favor of organic foods. When he found that not all of them did, he knew that the controversy would make a good topic for his argument. Here's how Alex progressed from topic to claim to thesis statement.

TOPIC	Whether organic foods are better than regular ones
MY POSITION	I think people should buy organic foods when they can.
THESIS STATEMENT (FIRST DRAFT)	It is good for people to buy organic foods. [This is a preliminary thesis statement. It clearly states the writer's position, but the word *good* is vague.]

THESIS STATEMENT (SECOND DRAFT)	In order to achieve health benefits and to improve the quality of the environment, organic foods should be purchased by consumers. [This revised thesis statement is better because it states not only the writer's claim but also a reason for the claim. However, it suffers from a lack of conciseness and from the unnecessary passive construction "should be purchased."]
THESIS STATEMENT (FINAL DRAFT)	Research shows that the health and environmental benefits of organic foods outweigh their extra costs. [This final version works well because it states the writer's claim clearly and concisely, with verbs all in the active voice. The writer now has a thesis statement suitable for the time and length given in his assignment. Also, it meets the requirements for a thesis statement given in Quick Reference 2.3.]

EXERCISE 5-1   Working individually or with a peer-response group, develop a claim and a thesis statement for each of the topics listed at the end of the exercise. You may choose any defensible position. For help, consult sections 5a through 5c.

EXAMPLE   TOPIC: Book censorship in high school

CLAIM: Books should not be censored in high school.

THESIS STATEMENT: When books are taken off high school library shelves or are dropped from high school curricula because they are considered inappropriate to read, students are denied an open exchange of ideas.

1. Commercials for weight loss pills on television
2. Taxing new cars according to their mileage
3. Athletes' use of steroids and performance drugs
4. Requiring students to undertake volunteer or community service

5e   What is the structure of a classical argument?

No single method is best for organizing all arguments, but a frequently used structure is the **classical argument**. The ancient Greeks and Romans developed this six-part structure, which is described in Quick Reference 5.1.

The structure of a classical argument

1. **Introductory paragraph:** Sets the stage for the position argued in the essay. It gains the reader's interest and respect (3c).

2. **Thesis statement:** States the topic and position you want to argue (2d).

3. **Background information:** Gives readers the basic information they need for understanding your thesis and its support. As appropriate, you might include definitions of key terms, historical or social context, prior scholarship, and other related material. You can include this as part of your introductory paragraph, or it can appear in its own paragraph placed immediately after the introduction.

4. **Evidence and reasons:** Supports the position you're arguing on the topic. This is the core of the essay. Each reason or piece of evidence usually consists of a general statement backed up with specific details, including examples and other RENNS (that is, reasons, examples, names, numbers, and senses). (See section 3f.) Evidence needs to meet the standards for critical thinking (Chapter 4). Depending on the length of the essay, you might devote one or two paragraphs to each reason or type of evidence. For organization, you might choose to present the most familiar reasons and evidence first, saving the most unfamiliar for last. Alternatively, you might proceed from the least important to the most important point so that your essay builds to a climax, leaving the most powerful impact for the end.

5. **Response to opposing position:** Sometimes referred to as the *rebuttal* or *refutation*. This material mentions and defends against an opposite point of view. Often this refutation, which can be lengthy or brief according to the overall length of the essay, appears in its own paragraph or paragraphs, usually immediately before the concluding paragraph or immediately following the introductory paragraph, as a bridge to the rest of the essay. If you use the latter structure, you can choose to place your thesis statement either at the end of the introductory paragraph or at the end of the rebuttal paragraph. Yet another choice for structure consists of having each paragraph present one type of evidence or reason and then immediately stating and responding to the opposing position. (See 5l for advice on handling opposing arguments.)

6. **Concluding paragraph:** Ends the essay logically and gracefully—never abruptly. It often summarizes the argument, elaborates its significance, or calls readers to action (3k).

5f   How do I support my argument?

Use reasons, examples, and evidence to support an argument's claim. (See
RENNS, Quick Reference 3.3.) One good method for developing reasons for
an argument is to ask yourself *why* you believe your claim. When you respond
"Because . . .," you offer reasons for your claim. Evidence needs to be sufficient,
representative, relevant, accurate, reasonable, and current. Specifically, evidence
consists of facts, statistics, expert testimony, personal experience, and so on.

If you consult SOURCES to find supporting evidence, reasons, or examples,
be sure to use correct DOCUMENTATION within the text of your essay and in your
WORKS CITED or REFERENCES list at the end of your paper (Chapters 36–38).
By doing this, you avoid PLAGIARISM, adopting someone else's ideas and trying
to pass them off as your own. Plagiarism is a serious offense that can result in
your failing a course or even being dismissed from college (Chapter 35).

5g   What types of appeals can provide support?

An effective argument relies on three types of **persuasive appeals**: logical appeals, emotional appeals, and ethical appeals. The ancient Greeks called these
appeals *logos, pathos,* and *ethos.* Quick Reference 5.2 summarizes how to use the
appeals.

Quick Reference 5.2   ■ ■ ■ ■ ■ ■ ■

Guidelines for persuasive appeals

- **Be logical:** Use sound reasoning (*logos*).

- **Enlist the emotions of the reader:** Appeal to the values and beliefs of
  the reader by arousing the reader's "better self" (*pathos*).

- **Establish credibility:** Show that you as the writer can be relied on as a
  knowledgeable person with good sense (*ethos*).

The **logical appeal** (*logos*) is the most widely used and intellectually solid and
sound appeal in arguments. Sound reasoning involves using effective evidence
and reasons. When the student writer Alex Garcia argues that certain foods carry
health risks, he cites research that points to specific diseases (5n). Logical writers
analyze CAUSE AND EFFECT correctly. Also, they use appropriate patterns of
INDUCTIVE REASONING and DEDUCTIVE REASONING, and they distinguish clearly
between fact and opinion. Finally, sound reasoning means avoiding LOGICAL FAL-
LACIES. One strategy for generating logical appeals is the **Toulmin model**, developed by the philosopher Stephen Toulmin, discussed in 5h.

When you use **emotional appeals** (*pathos*), you try to persuade your
readers by appealing to their hearts more than their minds. Such appeals are

generally more effective when you combine them with logical appeals. If an employee asks for a raise and gives reasons like "I have a family to support" or "I need to pay medical bills," that person probably won't get very far. The employee needs in addition to prove how his or her contributions have gone well beyond the job description, dramatically increased sales, or created other advantages.

Emotional appeals can use descriptive language and concrete details or examples to create a mental picture for readers, which is an approach that leads them to feel or understand the importance of your claim. Figure 5.1 provides an example of emotional appeals. You want to appeal to your audience's values and beliefs through honest examples and descriptions that add a sense of humanity and reality to the issue you're arguing. You want, however, to avoid

---

Sleeping Sickness
Untreated, it inevitably Kills

Spread by tsetse flies, this dreaded tropical disease claims more than 66,000 lives a year in 36 African nations. Doctors Without Borders volunteer Rebecca Golden returned from Angola, where a desperate battle against sleeping sickness is being waged after years of war have wrecked that nation's health care system.

"The treatment is a form of arsenic and is extremely painful," says Rebecca. "I was visiting some children receiving their medicine and was amazed at their courage and strength. **When the arsenic entered their bloodstream, they curled their toes, turned their heads, and closed their eyes tightly.** Their choice was to die or take the treatment. They accepted it with such calm. After 20 years of war and lost family members, they seem to accept this as just another part of the survival process."

Your support helps Doctors Without Borders save lives. **In our battle against sleeping sickness and other diseases, your gift can make a vital difference.**

Every Dollar Counts

$35 – Supplies a basic suture kit to repair minor shrapnel wounds.

$75 – Provides 1,500 patients with clean water for a week.

$100 – Provides infection-fighting antibiotics to treat nearly 40 wounded children.

$200 – Supplies 40 malnourished children with special high-protein food for a day.

Visit www.doctorswithoutborders.org

Figure 5.1 An argument that appeals to emotions

manipulating your readers with biased, SLANTED LANGUAGE. Readers see through such tactics and resent them.

When you use **ethical appeals**, or *ethos,* you establish your personal credibility with your audience. Audiences don't trust a writer who states opinions as fact, distorts evidence, or makes claims that can't be supported. They do trust a writer who comes across as honest, knowledgeable, and fair. Ethical appeals can't take the place of logical appeals, but the two work well together. One effective way to make an ethical appeal is to draw on your personal experience. (Some college instructors don't want students to write in the first person, so check with your instructor before you try this technique.) Alex Garcia creates an ethical appeal in his first paragraph when he identifies himself as a shopper with a limited budget who, nonetheless, chooses more expensive options. Another way to make an ethical appeal is to consider a variety of perspectives, reasonably and fairly addressing opposing viewpoints (Quick Reference 5.1). Using reliable SOURCES and a reasonable TONE all communicate that you're being fair-minded.

5h What is the Toulmin model for argument?

One powerful method for generating logical appeals and for analyzing the arguments of others is the Toulmin model. The Toulmin model defines three essential elements in an effective argument: the claim, the support, and the warrants. They describe concepts that you've encountered before (as Quick Reference 5.3 explains). For example, identifying the **warrants** (assumptions that are often unstated) is a good critical thinking strategy.

Quick Reference 5.3   ■ ■ ■ ■ ■ ■ ■

The Toulmin model for argument

- **Claim:** A variation of a thesis statement. If needed, the claim is qualified or limited.

  Alex Garcia makes the following claim in his argument: Health and environmental benefits of organic foods outweigh their extra costs.

- **Support:** REASONS and EVIDENCE, moving from broad reasons to specific data and details, support the claim.

  Alex offers three main reasons: (1) Organic produce is safer for individuals; (2) Organic meats and dairy products are safer for society as a whole; and (3) Organic farming is better for the environment. He then provides evidence for each of those reasons, drawing on source materials.

- **Warrants:** The writer's underlying assumptions, which are often implied rather than stated. Warrants may also need support (also called *backing*).

continued >>

Quick Reference 5.3	(continued)

> Alex's essay has several warrants, among them: (1) We should always make choices that increase our safety; and (2) Preserving the environment enhances our quality of life. (Notice that these warrants are debatable. For example, we routinely make choices that are less safe than their options; going skiing or roller skating is more dangerous than staying at home, for instance. Quality of life is determined by many factors.)

The concept of *warrant* is similar to the concept of *inferences,* a key component of critical thinking (4a). Inferences are not stated outright but are implied "between the lines" of the writing. Similarly, warrants are unspoken underlying assumptions in an argument. Consider the following simple argument: "Johnson should not be elected mayor. She was recently divorced." The *claim* is that Johnson shouldn't be elected. The *support* is that Johnson has been divorced. The unstated *warrant* is "divorced people are not qualified to be mayor." Before they can accept the claim that Johnson shouldn't be elected, readers have to accept this warrant. Of course, a majority of readers would reject the warrant. Thus, this argument is weak. To identify the warrants in an argument, ask "What do I need to assume so that the support is sufficient for establishing each claim?"

The concepts in the Toulmin model can help you write arguments with a critical eye. They can be quite useful on their own as well as applied to the CLASSICAL ARGUMENT structure (Quick Reference 5.1). As you read and revise your own arguments, identify the claim, support, and warrants. If you don't have a clear claim or support, you'll probably have to assume that your argument is weak. Furthermore, make sure that all of your warrants will be convincing to readers. If they aren't, you need to provide backing, or reasons why the warrants are reasonable. For example, consider the following argument: "People should not receive a driver's license until the age of 25 because the accident rate for younger drivers is much higher than for older ones." One of the warrants here is that reducing the number of accidents should have highest priority. Obviously, many 18-to-24-year-old readers will not find that warrant convincing.

EXERCISE 5-2   Individually or with a peer response group, discuss these simple arguments. Identify the claim, support, and warrants for each.

EXAMPLE   The college should establish an honor code. Last semester more than fifty students were caught cheating on exams.

CLAIM: The college should establish an honor code.

SUPPORT: Last semester, more than fifty students were caught cheating on exams.

WARRANTS:

A. Enough students cheat on exams that the college should address the problem.

B. Cheating should be prevented.

C. Students would not have cheated if there had been an honor code.

1. The college should raise student tuition and fees. The football stadium is in such poor repair that the coach is having trouble recruiting players.

2. Vote against raising our taxes. In the past two years, we have already had a 2 percent tax increase.

3. The college should require all students to own laptop computers. Most students will have to use computers in their jobs after graduation.

5i What part does audience play in my argument?

The PURPOSE of written argument is to convince your AUDIENCE either to agree with you or to be open to your position. In writing an argument, you want to consider what your readers already know or believe about your topic. Will the audience be hostile or open-minded to your position? Will it resist or adopt your point of view? What values, viewpoints, and assumptions will your audience hold? (See the questions in Quick Reference 1.5 to help you analyze your audience.)

Unfortunately, some members of some audiences can be persuaded by purely sensational or one-sided claims. Witness the effects on some readers of highly charged advertising or of narrowly one-sided ultraconservative or ultraliberal claims. However, such arguments rarely change the minds of people who don't already agree with them. Critical thinking quickly reveals the weaknesses of such arguments, including a frequent use of LOGICAL FALLACIES (4i). That's why academic audiences expect a higher standard and value, above all, logical appeals and appropriate, adequate support.

In many instances, of course, you can't actually expect to change your reader's mind, which means your goal is to demonstrate that your point of view has its own merit. If you think that your audience is likely to read your point of view with hostility, you might consider using Rogerian argument.

5j How can Rogerian argument help me reach opposing audiences?

Rogerian argument seeks common ground between points of view. The Rogerian approach is based on the principles of communication developed by the psychologist Carl Rogers. According to Rogers, communication is eased when people find common ground in their points of view. For example, the common ground in a debate over capital punishment might be that serious crimes are increasing in numbers and viciousness. Once both sides agree that this is the problem, they might be more willing to consider opposing opinions. Quick Reference 5.4 explains the structure of a Rogerian argument, which can be an effective alternative to CLASSICAL ARGUMENT structure.

Quick Reference 5.4

The structure of a Rogerian argument

1. **Introduction:** Sets the stage for the position that is argued in the essay. It gains the reader's interest and respect (3c).

2. **Thesis statement:** States the topic and position you want to argue (5c and 5d).

3. **Common ground:** Explains the issue, acknowledging that your readers probably don't agree with you. Speculates about and respectfully gives attention to the points of agreement you and your readers might share, especially concerning underlying problems or issues. For example, people on both sides of the gun control issue can share the desire for fewer violent crimes with guns. You might even acknowledge situations in which your reader's position may be desirable. This may take one paragraph or several, depending on the complexity of the issue.

4. **Discussion of your position:** Gives evidence and reasons for your stand on the topic, as in classical argument (see Quick Reference 5.1).

5. **Concluding paragraph:** Summarizes why your position is preferable to your opponent's (3k). You might, for example, explain why a particular situation makes your position desirable.

When it comes to argument, people often "agree to disagree" in the best spirit of intellectual exchange. As you write a Rogerian argument, remember that your audience wants to see how effectively you've reasoned and presented your position. This stance approaches that of a formal oral debate in which all sides are explored with similar intellectual rigor.

5k What is a reasonable tone in an argument?

A reasonable TONE tells your audience that you're being fair-minded. When you anticipate opposing positions and refute them with balanced language and emphasis, you demonstrate that you respect the other side. No matter how strongly you disagree with opposing arguments, never insult the other side. Name-calling reflects poor judgment and a lack of self-control. The saying "It's not what you say but how you say it" needs to be on your mind at all times as you write an argument. Avoid exaggerating, and never show anger. The more emotionally loaded a topic (for example, abortion or capital punishment), the more tempted you might be to use careless, harsh words. For instance, calling the opposing position "stupid" would say more about you as the writer than it would about the issue.

EXERCISE 5-3 Here is the text of a notorious e-mail fraud that has been sent to many people. Hundreds of variations of this e-mail exist, but usually the writer claims to have a large amount of money that he or she wants to transfer to an American bank. The writer wants the recipient's help in making the transfer. This is a complete lie. The writer has no money and is trying to trick people into revealing their bank account numbers to steal their money.

Either alone or in a small group, examine the ways this writer tries to establish emotional and ethical appeals. *Note:* We've reproduced the e-mail with the often incorrect original wording, grammar, and punctuation.

Good day,

It is my humble pleasure to write this letter irrespective of the fact that you do not know me. However, I came to know of you in my private search for a reliable and trustworthy person that can handle a confidential transaction of this nature in respect of this, I got your contact through an uprooted search on the internet. Though I know that a transaction of this magnitude will make any one apprehensive and worried, but I am assuring you that all will be well at the end of the day.

I am Ruth Malcasa, daughter of late Mr. James Malcasa of Somalia, who was killed by the rebel forces on the 24th of December, 2007 in my country Somalia. When he was still alive, he deposited one trunk box containing the sum of USD$10 million dollars in cash (Ten Million dollars). with a private security and safe deposit company here in Lagos Nigeria. This money was made from the sell of Gold and Diamond by my mother and she has already decided to use this money for future investment of the family.

My father instructed me that in the case of his death, that I should look for a trusted foreigner who can assist me to move out this money from Nigeria immediately for investment. Based on this, I solicit for your assistance to transfer this fund into your Account, but I will demand for the following requirement: (1) Could you provide for me a safe Bank Account where this fund will be transferred to in your country after retrieving the box containing the money from the custody of the security company. (2) Could you be able to introduce me to a profitable business venture that would not require much technical expertise in your country where part of this fund will be invested?

I am a Christian and I want you to handle this transaction based on the trust I have established on you. For your assistance in this transaction,

I have decided to compensate you with 10 percent of the total amount at the end of this business. The security of this business is very important to me and as such, I would like you to keep this business very confidential. I shall expect an early response from you. Thank you and God bless. Yours sincerely, Ruth Malcasa.

5l   How do I handle opposing arguments?

Dealing with opposing positions is crucial to writing an effective argument. If you don't acknowledge arguments that your opponents might raise and explain why they are faulty or inferior, you create doubts that you have thoroughly explored the issue. You risk seeming narrow-minded.

The next to last paragraph in Alex Garcia's paper (section 5n), which summarizes opposing arguments, strengthens both his *ethos* (credibility) and his *logos* (logic). He's so confident in his own position that not only can he point out research findings that contradict his position but also concede that this research is reasonably solid. Alex does suggest some promising new research that might eventually support him, but the most important thing he does is explain why, even if organic food is not more nutritious, the other reasons he has argued are strong enough to carry his thesis. He had encountered this counterargument while doing his research. When you do research for your own arguments, look for essays, articles, and opinions that oppose your position, not only ones that agree with yours.

If your research doesn't generate opposing arguments, you need to develop them yourself. Imagine that you're debating someone who disagrees with you; what positions would that person take and why? Note that you can ask a classmate or friend to perform this role. Another strategy is to take the opposite side of the argument and try to develop the best reasons you can for that position. (In some formal debating situations, people are expected to prepare both sides of an issue and only learn immediately before the debate which position they are to argue.)

Once you have generated opposing arguments, you need to refute them, which means you want to show why they're weak or undesirable. Imagine that you're writing about national security and individual rights. You believe that the government shouldn't be allowed to monitor a private citizen's e-mail without a court order, and you have developed a number of reasons for your position. To strengthen your paper, you also generate some opposing arguments, including "People will be safer from terrorism if police can monitor e-mail," "Only people who have something to hide have anything to fear," and "It is unpatriotic to oppose the government's plans." How might you refute these or other opposing claims? Following are some suggestions.

- **Examine the evidence for each opposing argument** (4d–4h). Look especially for missing or contradictory facts. In the given example, you might question the evidence that people would be safer from terrorism if police could monitor e-mail.

- **Use the Toulmin model to analyze the opposing argument** (5h). What are the claims, support, and warrants? Often, it's possible to show that the warrants are questionable or weak. For example, a warrant in the counterarguments above is that the promise of increased safety is worth the price of privacy or individual rights. You might show why this warrant is undesirable.

- **Demonstrate that an opposing argument depends on emotion rather than reasoning.** The assertion that it's unpatriotic to oppose the government is primarily an emotional one.

- **Redefine key terms.** The term *patriotism* can be defined in various ways. You might point out, for example, that at the time of the American Revolution, "patriots" were the people who were opposing the British government then in power.

- **Explain the negative consequences of the opposing position.** Imagine that the opposing position actually won out, and explain how the results would be damaging. For example, if everyone knew that government officials might monitor their computer use, consider how this might affect free speech.

- **Concede an opposing point, but explain that doing so doesn't destroy your own argument.** For example, you might decide to concede that governmental monitoring of e-mails could reduce terrorism. However, you might argue that the increase in safety is not worth the threat to privacy and personal freedom.

- **Explain that the costs of the other position are not worth the benefits.**

EXERCISE 5-4　Individually or with a peer-response group, practice developing objections to specific arguments and responses to those objections. To do this, choose a debatable topic and brainstorm a list of points on that topic, some on one side of the topic, some on another. Following are some arguments to get you started. If you're part of a group, work together to assign the different positions for each topic to different sets of students. Then, conduct a brief debate on which side has more merit, with each side taking turns. At the end, your group can vote for the side that is more convincing.

1. It should be legal/illegal to ride motorcycles without a helmet.
2. Political candidates should/should not use negative advertising.
3. Students should/should not be required to take certain courses in order to graduate.
4. Paid public service (for example, the military or social work) should/should not be required of all 18-to-20-year-olds.

5m   How did one student draft and revise his argument essay?

In his first draft, Alex focused on how organic farming would benefit the environment, and he found lots of studies of how traditional farming practices affect water and soil quality. However, he realized that this argument alone might seem remote to many readers, so he explored how agricultural chemicals affect consumers. Extensive research resulted in a second draft that included not only immediate concerns for individuals but also society at large. While doing that research, he was surprised to encounter evidence that organic foods weren't necessarily more nutritious. Initially, Alex wanted just to ignore it, but then he decided his paper would be stronger if he included and dealt with this opposing viewpoint in his third draft. That draft also was where he developed his introductory paragraph, which until this point he had just sketched generally. Throughout the process, he found the need to check facts and sources in library databases. Before completing the paper, he looked carefully at his use of *pathos* and *ethos* and consulted the revision checklist (see Quick Reference 2.8). Finally, he referred to the special checklist for revising written arguments in Quick Reference 5.5.

Quick Reference 5.5   ■ ■ ■ ■ ■ ■ ■

Revising written arguments

- Is the thesis statement about a debatable topic? (5c and 5d)
- Do the reasons or evidence support the thesis statement? Are the generalizations supported by specific details? (5d)
- Does the argument deal with reader needs and concerns? (5i)
- Does the argument appeal chiefly to reason? Is it supported by an ethical appeal? If it uses an emotional appeal, is the appeal restrained? (5g)
- Is the tone reasonable? (5k)
- Is the opposing position stated and refuted? (5l)

EXERCISE 5-5   Working individually or with a peer-response group, choose a topic from this list. Then, plan an essay that argues a debatable position on the topic. Apply all the principles you've learned in this chapter.

1. Animal experimentation
2. Genetically engineered food
3. Cloning of human beings
4. Taxpayer support for public colleges
5. Home schooling

5n   Final draft of a student's argument essay in MLA style

Alex Garcia

WRIT 1122

Professor Brosnahan

4 May 2008

Why Organic Foods are Worth the Extra Money

A small decision confronts me every time I walk into the grocery store. I see a display of enticing apples for around $1.79 per pound. Next to them is a similar display of the same kind of apples, perhaps just a little smaller and just a little less perfect. These sell for $2.29 per pound. The difference between the two is the tiny sticker that reads "organic." Are those apples worth the extra money, especially when my budget is tight and the other ones appear just fine? Millions of shoppers face this same decision whenever they decide whether to buy organic food, and the right answer seems complicated, especially when the US Department of Agriculture "makes no claims that organically produced food is safer or more nutritious than conventionally produced food" (National). However, current research shows that the health and environmental benefits of organic foods outweigh their extra costs.

Organic foods are produced without using most chemical pesticides, without artificial fertilizers, without genetic engineering, and without radiation (National). In the case of organic meat, poultry, eggs, and dairy products, the animals are raised without antibiotics or growth hormones. As a result, people sometimes use the term "natural" instead of organic,

continued >>

Garcia 2

but "natural" is less precise. Before 2002, people could never be quite sure what they were getting when they bought supposedly organic food, unless they bought it directly from a farmer they knew personally. In 2002, the US Department of Agriculture established standards that food must meet in order to be labeled and sold as organic.

According to environmental scientist Craig Minowa, organic foods tend to cost about 15 percent more than nonorganic, mainly because they are currently more difficult to mass-produce (Minowa). Farmers who apply pesticides often get larger crops from the same amount of land because there is less insect damage. Artificial fertilizers tend to increase the yield, size, and uniformity of fruits and vegetables, and herbicides kill weeds that compete with desirable crops for sun, nutrients, and moisture. Animals who routinely receive antibiotics and growth hormones tend to grow more quickly and produce more milk and eggs. In contrast, organic farmers have lower yields and, therefore, higher costs. These get passed along as higher prices to consumers.

Still, the extra cost is certainly worthwhile in terms of health benefits. Numerous studies have shown the dangers of pesticides for humans. An extensive review of research by the Ontario College of Family physicians concludes that "Exposure to all the commonly used pesticides . . . has shown positive associations with adverse health effects" (Sanborn 173). The risks include cancer, psychiatric effects, difficulties becoming pregnant, miscarriages, and dermatitis. Carefully washing fruits and vegetables can remove some of these dangerous chemicals, but according to the prestigious journal

continued >>

Garcia 3

Fig. 1. A display of organic foods.

Nature, even this does not remove all of them (Giles 797).
Certainly, if there's a way to prevent these poisons entering our
bodies, we should take advantage of it. The few cents saved on
cheaper food can quickly disappear in doctor's bills needed to
treat conditions caused or worsened by chemicals.

Organic meat, poultry, and dairy products can address
another health concern: the diminishing effectiveness of
antibiotics. In the past decades, many kinds of bacteria have
become resistant to drugs, making it extremely difficult to treat
some kinds of tuberculosis, pneumonia, staphylococcus
infections, and less serious diseases (Dangerous 1). True, this
has happened mainly because doctors overly prescribed
antibiotics to patients who expect a pill for every illness.
However, routinely giving antibiotics to all cows and chickens

continued >>

means that these drugs enter our food chain early, giving bacteria lots of chances to develop resistance. A person who switches to organic meats won't suddenly experience better results from antibiotics; the benefit is a more gradual one for society as a whole. However, if we want to be able to fight infections with effective drugs, we need to reserve antibiotics for true cases of need and discourage their routine use in animals raised for food. Buying organic is a way to persuade more farmers to adopt this practice.

Another benefit of organic foods is also a societal one: Organic farming is better for the environment. In his review of several studies, Colin Macilwain concluded that organic farms nurture larger numbers and more diverse kinds of plants and animals than regular farms (797). Organic farms also don't release pesticides and herbicides that can harm wildlife and run into our water supply, with implications for people's health, too. Macilwain notes that those farms also can generate less carbon dioxide, which will help with global warming; also, many scientists believe that organic farming is more sustainable because it results in better soil quality (798). Once again, these benefits are not ones that you will personally experience right away. However, a better natural environment means a better quality of living for everyone and for future generations.

Some critics point out that organic products aren't more nutritious than regular ones. Physician Sanjay Gupta, for example, finds the medical evidence for nutritional advantages is "thin" (60). The *Tufts University Health and Nutrition Letter* also reports that the research on nutritional benefits is mixed, with one important study showing "no

continued >>

Fig. 2. Organic farming betters the environment.

overall differences" ("Is Organic" 8). Nutritional value, which includes qualities such as vitamins and other beneficial substances, is a different measure than food safety. At this point, it seems that nutrition alone is not a sufficient reason to buy organic foods. Perhaps future research will prove otherwise; a 2007 study, for example, showed that organically raised tomatoes have higher levels of flavonoids, nutrients that appear to have many health benefits (Mitchell). In the meantime, however, environmental quality and, most importantly, avoiding chemicals remain convincing reasons to purchase organic food, even if the same cannot yet be claimed for nutrition.

Despite the considerable benefits for purchasing organic products, there remains each consumer's decision in the

continued >>

Garcia 6

grocery store. Are the more expensive apples ultimately worth their extra cost to me? It's true that there are no easily measurable one-to-one benefits, no way to ensure that spending fifty cents more on this produce will directly improve my quality of life by fifty cents. However, countless people are rightly concerned these days about our personal health and the health of the world in which we live, and I am one of them. It's nearly impossible to put a value on a sustainable, diverse natural environment and having the physical health to enjoy it. The long-term benefits of buying organic, for anyone who can reasonably afford to, far outweigh the short-term savings in the checkout line.

continued >>

Garcia 7

Works Cited

"Dangerous Bacterial Infections Are on the Rise." *Consumer Reports on Health* 19 (Nov. 2007): 1–4. Print.

Giles, Jim. "Is Organic Food Better for Us?" *Nature* 428.6985 (22 Apr. 2004): 796–97. Print.

"Is Organic Food Really More Nutritious?" Tufts University Health and Nutrition Letter 25 (Sep. 2007): 8. Web. 25 Apr. 2008.

Gupta, Sanjay, and Shahreen Abedin. "Rethinking Organics." *Time* (20 Aug. 2007): 60. Print.

Macilwain, Colin. "Is Organic Farming Better for the Environment?" *Nature* 428.6985 (22 Apr. 2004): 797–98. Print.

Minowa, Craig. Interview by Louise Druce. "FYI on Organics: Organic Q & A." Organic Consumers Assn. 29 June 2004. Web.

Mitchell, Alyson E., Yun-Jeong Hong, Eunmi Koh, Diane M. Barrett, D. E. Bryant, R. Ford Denison, and Stephen Kaffka. "Ten-Year Comparison of the Influence of Organic and Conventional Crop Management Practices on the Content of Flavonoids in Tomatoes." *Journal of Agricultural Food Chemistry* 55.15 (2007): 6154–59. Web. 30 Apr. 2008.

National Organic Program. "Organic Food Labels and Standards: The Facts." Washington, DC: US Department of Agriculture. Jan. 2007. Web. 26 Apr 2008.

continued >>

Sanborn, Margaret, Donald Cole, Kathleen Kerr, Cathy Vakil,
Luz Helena Sanin, Kate Bassil. *Pesticides Literature
Review: Systematic Review of Pesticide Human Health
Effects*. Toronto: Ontario College of Family Physicians,
2004. Web. 28 Apr. 2008.

6

■ ■ ■ ■ ■ ■

Writing with Others

6a What is writing with others?

Although it may often seem like a lonely act, a surprising amount of writing depends on two or more people working together. Anytime you ask someone else to read your draft and give you feedback for revision, you're working with others. The other person could be a friend, a classmate, a co-worker, a writing tutor (in a campus writing center), or an instructor—after all, your instructor's comments on a draft are designed to guide your revision. In the professional world, a project manager or supervisor will frequently read your reports and proposals and ask you to make changes. Of course, you'll be making suggestions about other people's writings, too. Sections 6c and 6d explain how to give and receive help effectively.

A more direct kind of writing with others happens when two or more people **collaborate** (work together) to complete a single project. This handbook is a prime example. Lynn wrote some sections, then Doug revised them—and vice versa. We planned the book over e-mail, in telephone calls, and in person. Drafts flew back and forth over the Internet. We also worked with editors who suggested—and sometimes required—revisions. Each of us brought different knowledge, experience, and talents.

Collaborative writing projects are extremely common in the business and professional world. Marketing managers, for example, lead teams who conduct consumer research and then—as a group—write up their findings. Often, the size or complexity of a project means that only a team of people can accomplish it in the given amount of time. Different team members bring different skills and expertise. In these professional settings, group members must reach general agreement on how to proceed and contribute equally to a written report.

Collaborative writing assignments are increasingly popular in college courses across the curriculum, especially in business, the sciences, and the social sciences. Even if they aren't required to write full papers, small groups are

Figure 6.1 A collaborative group at work

commonly asked to brainstorm a topic together before individual writing tasks, to discuss various sides of a debatable topic, or to share reactions to an essay or piece of literature the class reads, and so on.

Writing collaboratively enhances confidence when writers support one another. Experience in collaborative writing has benefits beyond your college years because working well with others is a skill that employers value.

Alert: Some instructors and students use the terms *peer-response group* and *collaborative writing* to mean the same thing. In this handbook, we assign the terms to two different situations. We use *collaborative writing* (6b) for students writing an essay, a research paper, or a report together in a group. We use *peer-response group* (6c) for students getting together in small groups to help one another write and revise. ●

6b How can I collaborate with other writers?

Three qualities are essential to collaborative writing. The first is careful planning. Your group needs to decide when and how it will meet (in person, in a telephone call, in an online discussion); what steps it will follow and what the due dates will be; what software you'll use; and who will be responsible for what. Everyone in the group needs to commit to the plan, making changes only after deliberation by everyone.

The second essential quality is a fair division of labor. Almost nothing causes bad feelings more quickly than when some group members feeling like they're doing more than their share. During early planning meetings, the group should figure out the tasks involved in the project and estimate how much time and effort each will take. (You can rebalance things during later meetings, if necessary.)

One basic way a group can divide tasks is according to the different steps in the writing process. One or more people can be in charge of generating ideas or conducting research; one or more can be in charge of writing the first draft; one or more can be in charge of revising; and one or more may be in charge of editing, proofreading, and formatting the final draft. It's hard to separate these tasks cleanly, however, and we warn that writing the first draft often requires more effort than any other element. This approach also means that some group members will be waiting for others to complete their parts.

A second way to divide tasks is to assign part of the project to each person. Many projects can be broken into sections, and using an outline (2f) can help you see what those sections are. Each person can then plan, write, revise, and edit a section, and the other members can serve as a built-in peer-response group to make suggestions for revision. This approach can have the advantage of distributing the work more cleanly at the outset, but it often takes a lot of work at the end to stitch the parts together. It can be difficult when several people try to complete the final editing and compilation.

In reality, you'll probably find your group using a combination of these two approaches. You'll also probably find it useful to assign people basic roles such as leader (or facilitator) and recorder (or secretary). These roles can change during the project, but in our experience, groups find it efficient when someone takes responsibility for calling and leading meetings.

The third essential element of collaborative projects is clear communication. Open and honest communication is vital, and people need to put aside their own egos to build a productive and trusting atmosphere. Keep notes for every meeting so that the group has a clear record of what was decided; one way to do this is to have someone send an e-mail summarizing each meeting. If people disagree over the group's decisions, the group should resolve that disagreement before moving on. You'll also find it effective to ask for regular reports from each group member. These don't have to be long—a few sentences will do it—but they keep everyone informed about others' progress, and they keep you on track, too.

■ ■ ■ ■ ■ ■ ■

Guidelines for collaborative writing

STARTING

1. Learn each other's names and exchange e-mail addresses and phone numbers so that everyone can stay in touch outside of class.

2. Participate actively in the group process. During discussions, help set a tone that encourages everyone to participate by including people who don't like to interrupt, who want time to think before they talk, or who are shy. Conversely, help the group set limits if someone dominates the discussions or makes all the decisions. If you lack experience contributing in a group setting, think about some ways you can try to take an active role.

3. As a group, assign everyone work to be done between meetings. Distribute the responsibilities as fairly as possible. Also, decide whether to choose one discussion leader or to rotate leadership, unless your instructor assigns a particular procedure.

4. Make decisions regarding the technology you'll use. If everyone can use the same word-processing program, for example, that will make sharing drafts or parts of drafts much easier. If not, you can use the "Save As" function in major word processing programs like Microsoft Word to save in a common format. Decide if you'll share materials via e-mail attachments, CDs, flash drives, space on a server, or even through a WIKI (see 46e). If any group members are unfamiliar with these processes, others need to help them learn. (Different areas and levels of expertise are an advantage of working in groups.)

5. Set a timeline and deadlines for the project. Agree on what to do in the event that someone misses a deadline.

PLANNING

6. After discussing the project, brainstorm as a group or use structured techniques for discovering and compiling ideas.

7. Together, agree on the ideas that seem best and allow for a period of INCUBATION, if time permits. Then, discuss your group choices again.

8. As a group, divide the project into parts and distribute assignments fairly. For example, if the project requires research, decide who will do it and how they'll share their findings with others. If one person is going to be responsible for preparing drafts from pieces that others have written, make sure his or her other responsibilities are balanced.

9. As a group, OUTLINE or otherwise sketch an overview of the project to get a preliminary idea of how best to use material contributed by individuals.

continued >>

10. As you work on your part of the project, take notes in preparation for giving your group a progress report.

DRAFTING

11. Draft a THESIS STATEMENT. The thesis statement sets the direction for the rest of the paper. Each member of the group can draft a thesis statement and the group can discuss the advantages of each, but the group needs to agree on one version before getting too far into the rest of the draft. Your group might revise the thesis statement after the whole paper has been drafted, but using a preliminary version gets everyone started in the same direction.

12. Draft the rest of the paper. Decide whether each member of the group should write a complete draft or one part of the whole. For example, each group member might take one main idea and be responsible for drafting that section. Share draft materials among the group members using disks or e-mail attachments (see step 4). If this is impossible, make photocopies. For most group meetings, it will be important to have a paper copy of group materials, so print (or photocopy) copies for everyone.

REVISING

13. Read over the drafts. Are all the important points included?

14. Use the revision checklist (Quick Reference 2.9) and work either as a group or by assigning portions to subgroups. If different people have drafted different sections, COHERENCE and UNITY should receive special attention in revision, as should the introduction and the conclusion.

15. Agree on a final version. Either work as a group, or assign someone to prepare the final draft and make sure every group member has a copy.

EDITING AND PROOFREADING THE WRITING

16. Use the editing checklist (Quick Reference 2.10) to double-check for errors. If you find errors, correct them and print out the page or the whole draft again. No matter how well the group has worked collaboratively, or how well the group has written the paper, a sloppy final version reflects negatively on the entire group.

17. As a group, review printouts or photocopies of the final draft. Don't leave the last stages to a subgroup. Draw on everyone's knowledge of grammar, spelling, and punctuation. Use everyone's eyes for proofreading.

18. If your instructor asks, be prepared to describe your personal contribution to the project and to describe or evaluate the contributions of others.

EXERCISE 6-1   Working in a small group, plan how your group would proceed on one or more of the following collaborative projects, satisfying each of
the three essential criteria for group work. (*Note:* You don't actually have to complete the project; the purpose of this exercise is to develop your planning skills.)

- A report for a public audience in which you evaluate new car models.
- A research project in which you analyze the political views of students on
  your campus.
- A persuasive paper in which you argue whether the United States should
  pass laws to make it harder for American companies to move jobs to
  other countries.

Be prepared to explain your planning to your instructor or to class members in
a way that shows your group has been thoughtful and thorough.

6c   How can I give useful feedback to others?

There are two main ways to give feedback to other writers. One is in a small
group, usually three to five people, who together discuss each group member's
draft out loud. Another way is to work in pairs, providing oral or, more often,
written comments for each other.

6c.1   Working in peer-response groups

In some writing classes, instructors divide students into PEER-RESPONSE GROUPS.
A peer is an "equal": another writer like you. Participating in a peer-response
group makes you part of a respected tradition of colleagues helping colleagues.
Professional writers often seek comments from other writers to improve their
rough drafts. As a member of a peer-response group, you're not expected to be
a writing expert. Rather, you're expected to offer responses as a practiced reader
and as a fellow student writer who understands what writers go through.

 Alert: Some instructors use the term "workshopping" for peer response.
The term comes from creative-writing programs, sometimes called "Writers'
Workshops," where the main learning strategy is to have students discuss each
others' work in progress. ●

The role of peer-response group members is to react and discuss, not to
do the work for someone. Hearing or reading comments from your peers might
be a new experience, one you may find surprising, as well as informative and
helpful. Also, when peers share their writing with your group, you and the
other members get the added advantage of learning other students' approaches
to writing the same assignment.

Peer-response groups are set up in different ways. One arrangement calls for students to pass around and read one another's drafts silently, writing down reactions or questions in the margins or on a response form created by the instructor. Figure 6.2 shows an example of a response form. In another arrangement, students read their drafts aloud, and then each peer responds either orally or in writing on a response form. Yet another arrangement asks for focused responses to

---

Peer Response Questions and Directions

Reviewer's name: _____

Writer's name: _____

*Directions to **Writer***: *Please choose three questions you'd like the reviewer to address. Circle them.*

*Directions to **Reviewer***: *Please read the work and provide clear and detailed answers to each of the THREE questions to which the writer has asked you to respond. Continue on the back, if needed. After you've completed this, talk about your answers with the writer. Then write up a half-page synthesis and suggested plan for further action.*

1. How can this writer make the central argument of this essay stronger, clearer, or more easily accessible to readers?

2. Identify any paragraphs whose purpose is unclear or that seem to be working at cross purposes, and explain how the writer can revise them to make the purpose clear.

3. Does the sequence of the argument build successfully? If not, suggest a way to reorder it and identify transitions that may need clarifying.

4. Writers can offer their readers guidance in a number of ways, such as clearly defining their terms, explaining exactly how the evidence supports their claims, etc. **Identify places in this essay where these forms of guidance could be stronger, and explain specifically how the writer can strengthen them.**

5. Are there places in which you feel the textures or structures of language are serving the writer's purpose effectively? Are there places in which the language could be modified?

Figure 6.2 A peer-response group form

only one or two features of each draft (perhaps each member's thesis statement, or topic sentences and supporting details, or use of transitional words, for example).

Whatever the arrangement of your group, you want to be clear about exactly what you are expected to do, both as a peer-responder and as a writer. If your instructor gives you guidelines for working in a group, follow them carefully. If you've never before participated in a peer-response group, or in the particular kind of group that your instructor forms, consult the guidelines in Quick Reference 6.2; watch what experienced peers do; and ask your instructor questions (your interest shows a positive, cooperative attitude). Otherwise, just dive in knowing that you'll learn as you go.

Quick Reference 6.2 ■ ■ ■ ■ ■ ■ ■

Guidelines for participating in peer-response groups

One major principle needs to guide your participation in a peer-response group: Always take an upbeat, constructive attitude, whether you're responding to someone else's writing or receiving responses from others.

- Think of yourself as a coach, not a judge.
- Consider all writing by your peers as "works in progress."
- After hearing or reading a peer's writing, briefly summarize it to check that you and your peer are clear about what the peer said or meant to say.
- Start with what you think is well done. No one likes to hear only negative comments.
- Be honest in your suggestions for improvement.
- Base your responses on an understanding of the writing process, and remember that you're reading drafts, not finished products. All writing can be revised.
- Give concrete and specific responses. General comments such as "This is good" or "This is weak" don't offer much help. Describe specifically what is good or weak.
- Follow your instructor's system for putting your comments in writing so that your fellow writer can recall what you said. If one member of your group is supposed to take notes, speak clearly so that the person's notes can be accurate. If you're the note taker, be accurate and ask the speaker to repeat what he or she said if the comment went by too quickly.

6c.2 Giving peer response as an individual

Often an instructor will have two people exchange drafts and provide responses and suggestions to each other. All of the general guidelines for peer response in groups apply to situations when you're the only person giving feedback, especially being helpful, specific, and polite.

You might find it useful to play a role if you feel awkward about giving reactions or suggestions to a classmate—especially if you think that some critical comments will help revision. (Instructors sometimes even assign such roles.) For example, instead of responding as yourself, pretend that you're a skeptical member of the writer's target audience. Respond as that person would, even in his or her voice. Separating your own personality from your responses can provide some useful distance. However, you should still aim to be constructive. Of course, you could also take the opposite role, responding as a friendly audience member who agrees with the writer; assuming that role can be particularly helpful if you personally disagree with a draft's position. If you're playing a role as you respond, you should make that clear to the writer by explaining, for example, that you're "playing devil's advocate," a person who is disagreeing on purpose. (The term *devil's advocate* comes from old church debates where one priest was charged with making the "devil's" case, making an argument against the church's position, which would be made stronger as a result of others needing to address challenges.)

As with peer response, your instructor may have you use a response form or follow a set of questions. (See Figure 6.2.) Here are some other questions you might find useful:

- What part of the paper was most interesting or effective?
- If you had to remove one paragraph, which would you sacrifice and why?
- If you had to rearrange two parts of the paper, which would you change and why?
- What is one additional fact, argument, or piece of information that might improve the paper?

Another good strategy is for the writer to generate a couple of questions that he or she would particularly like the reviewer to answer. Avoid questions that require only a *yes* or *no* response. For example:

NOT EFFECTIVE	Is paragraph two on page three effective?
EFFECTIVE	How can I improve paragraph two on page three?
NOT EFFECTIVE	Do you like my tone in the paper?
EFFECTIVE	How would you describe my tone in this paper?

Instead of answering specific questions, the instructor might ask you simply to write to the author about the strengths and weaknesses of the draft. Such responses can take the form of a letter to the author. Peer response can take practice to do well. Our students have found that if they're thoughtful while writing open responses to others, they get useful responses in return. Figure 6.3 shows an example of one student's peer response to another.

Directions. I'll pair you up with another student. Your task is to write a letter in which you play the role of someone who disagrees with the author of the paper; explain as carefully as you can why you disagree. State your own arguments and explain why they lead to a different conclusion. Now, I want you to be polite about this; don't indulge in the extreme language we looked at earlier in the course. However, to be helpful to the author you should be as persuasive as possible—even if you're playing a role that you actually disagree with. Send this letter by v mail, with a copy to me (dhonso@du.edu).

Dear Leslie,

     To begin with I thought your paper was very thorough and well thought out. It was lengthy and covered all the important things you needed to. But as I've been asked to take the role of someone who disagrees, then offer constructive criticism, there are some things that I think would help clarify and convince your readers who are on the fence about your position.

     Your argument is that sex education in schools needs to be complete and that "abstinence only" education is inadequate. You use a lot of statistics and surveys. This is good, it added credibility and "scientific reasoning," but when I see these, I wonder where you found these studies and whether they are themselves factual? You reiterated multiple times that abstinence-only educators use statistics that are untrue or slanted to favor their position. How does the reader know that you haven't made your own facts up or slanted them in your favor? My suggestion would be to label your studies and discuss where they came from and why they're credible. If one of them is from a government agency, you can include the address so if the reader wanted to they could verify the facts. I'm not accusing you of doing this, but it would only make your paper more believable.

     Because I am a strong believer in no sex before marriage, I worry about giving students too much information. I think that sex before marriage causes more problems than it solves. I do believe that giving out specific advice about contraception can encourage people to engage in sex before they are ready. Instead we should encourage students to wait. Can you prove to me that having information doesn't lead to early sexual activity?

     You stated on page two that a study found that consensual sex between two teenagers had no mental health effects on them. I disagree with this finding. Regardless of age and relationship status of the two parties involved, someone often gets hurt by casual sex. If there was a relationship before, it has the potential to be destroyed due to the new baggage. If one of the parties involved uses it as a one night stand and the other person really liked the other, he or she suffers emotional distress that could be extreme. Actually, I'm not sure this point belongs in your paper; because it's controversial, I wonder if your paper would be stronger without it.

Sincerely,
Stephen

Figure 6.3 An example of one student's peer response

EXERCISE 6-2

1. Choose a paper that you're writing (or have written). Create a set of questions that you would ask a peer reviewer to answer.

2. Show your questions to someone else in your class. Ask them to comment on how effective those questions would be for generating constructive comments; let them know that they may also suggest additional questions.

6d How can I benefit from others' help?

Turning to the sometimes sticky issue of how to accept criticism of your writing, we offer you two pieces of personal advice from our own experience.

    First, keep in mind that most students don't like to criticize their peers. They worry about being impolite or inaccurate, or losing someone's friendship. Try, therefore, to cultivate an attitude that encourages your peers to respond as freely and as helpfully as possible. It's particularly important to show that you can listen without getting angry or feeling intruded on.

Second, realize that most people tend to be at least a little defensive about even the best-intentioned and most tactful criticism. Of course, if a comment is purposely mean or sarcastic, you and all the others in your peer-response group have every right to say so, and to not tolerate such comments.

Quick Reference 6.3

■ ■ ■ ■ ■ ■ ■

Making good use of peers' comments

Adopt an attitude that encourages your peers to respond freely. Listen and resist any urge to interrupt during a comment or to jump in to react. A common rule in many writing workshops is that the paper's author must remain silent until the group has finished its discussion. (It's actually useful to hear people misinterpreting what you thought you said or meant.)

Remain open-minded. Your peers' comments can help you see your writing in a fresh way, which, in turn, can help you produce a better-revised draft.

Ask for clarification if a comment isn't clear. If a comment is too general, ask for specifics.

Finally, no matter what anyone says about your writing, it remains yours alone. You retain "ownership" of your writing always, and you don't have to make every suggested change. Use only the comments that you think can move you closer to reaching your intended audience and purpose. Of course, if a comment from your instructor points out a definite problem, and you choose to ignore it, that could have an impact on your grade—though many instructors are open to an explanation of your rationale for deciding to ignore what they said.

⊕ **ESOL Tip:** Students from cultures other than those in the United States or Canada might feel uncomfortable in the role of critic or questioner of other people's writing. Please know, however, that peer-response groups are fairly common in schools and at jobs because people usually think that "two heads are better than one." Sharing and questioning others' ideas—as well as how they are expressed in writing—is an honorable tradition in the United States and Canada. Peer-response groups help writers politely but firmly explore concepts and language, so please feel free to participate fully. In fact, some instructors grade you on your open participation in such activities. ●

6e How can I participate effectively in online discussions?

You might take a course that happens entirely online, where discussion happens through typed remarks via e-mail or a program like Blackboard. However, even courses that meet in traditional classrooms often have an online written component. Contributing to the discussion between class meetings makes you an active learner, allows the instructor to gauge the level of your understanding, and enriches the class by circulating a diversity of opinions.

There are two kinds of online discussions. In **synchronous** discussions, all the participants are online at the same time. The discussions are scheduled in advance and everyone meets online in "real time" for a specific amount of time. Instant messaging is an example of synchronous discussion. In **asynchronous** discussions, participants are online at different times. The discussion is usually open for hours or days, and there may be long periods of time between individual messages.

Whether you're in a completely online course environment or in an enhanced traditional classroom, being prepared for a few key things will help you participate effectively. First, your instructor may post a question and require everyone to respond to it, at least once. Also, your instructor may provide additional directions about the length or content of your posting or about its timing. (For example, he or she might require, "By midnight on Tuesday, post your answer to the discussion question.") Finally, your instructor might give directions about responding to something that others have posted in the discussion. Quick Reference 6.4 contains some additional guidelines about online discussions.

Quick Reference 6.4

Guidelines for online discussions

- Unless specifically instructed to do otherwise, write in complete sentences and paragraphs. Academic discussions are more formal than e-mails or text messages between friends, so don't use the kind of shorthand you might use in those situations.

- Provide a context for your remarks. You might begin your message by summarizing a point from a reading before giving your opinion. Your contribution should be able to stand on its own, or it should clearly connect to the rest of the conversation.

- Respond to other writers. If someone makes a particularly good point, say so—and explain why. If you disagree with someone, politely explain why you disagree and be sure to support your reasoning. Discussions work better when people are actually discussing, and not just speaking while ignoring their audience.

- Be polite and work for the good of the discussion. When people aren't meeting face to face, they can be rude—sometimes even when they don't mean to be. You have to work extra hard to make sure that your TONE is constructive and helpful.

7

Strategies for Writing Typical
Kinds of College Papers

7a   What are typical kinds of papers I'll write in college?

Arguments and research papers are two of the most common types of college
writing. In a written argument you try to persuade readers to take an action,
adopt a position, or see a viewpoint as legitimate even if they ultimately disagree with it. Research papers (sometimes called term papers or seminar papers)
involve gathering information from several sources, which you then summarize, analyze, and synthesize. Because arguments are such a vital part of college
writing, we devote all of Chapter 5 to them. In addition, since there are many
elements in writing a research paper, we devote Chapters 31–36 to this kind
of writing.

College students face many types of writing, and expecting one set of
guidelines to be perfect for every single variety would be unrealistic. Analyzing
the WRITING SITUATION (Chapter 1) and understanding the WRITING PROCESS
(Chapter 2) are important and useful for all writing. But we've found that general advice is even more helpful when combined with strategies for writing particular types of papers. Explaining the most common ones is our purpose in this
chapter. Your instructor may use the term **genre** instead of "type" when describing kinds of papers; the two words basically refer to the same thing.

Consider the following writing assignments you might get in college:

- A lengthy library research paper
- A summary of a reading
- A report on a laboratory experiment
- A proposal
- A personal essay
- An essay exam
- A critical response to a reading

These types of writing obviously differ in terms of length, PURPOSE, CONTEXT,
and SPECIAL CONSIDERATIONS. But notice how each type also uses different

SOURCES (readings vs. experiences vs. observations, for example), how the writer's ROLE changes (for example, from an impartial observer who keeps in the background to a center of attention whose experience and personality are foregrounded), and how format and style can vary. Knowing a few strategies will help you with different kinds of writing.

🔵 **Alert:** Terms that describe different types of writing are often used interchangeably. Most instructors attach specific meanings to each one; we've listed several terms above. Listen closely so you can sort out what terms your instructor uses. If your instructor's use of terms isn't clear, ask for clarification. For example, the words *essay, theme,* and *composition* usually—but not always—refer to written works of about 500 to 1,500 words. *Essay* is probably the most common. Similarly, the word *paper* can mean anything from a few paragraphs to a complex research project; it often refers to longer works. Finally, the general term *piece of writing* can refer to all types of writing ●

7b   What sources will I use in college writing?

A **source** is any form of information that provides ideas, examples, information, or evidence. Commonly, people think of readings (books, articles, Web sites, and so on) when they think of sources, and clearly readings are crucial. In fact, they're so important that we devote most of Chapter 32 to finding and using written sources, and we spend all of Chapters 36 through 38 explaining how to document them. Section 7f provides strategies for writings that make thorough use of readings.

There are other kinds of sources, too. Your own memories and experiences are a source, even though you may not think of them that way. Some academic situations allow or even require personal experiences, while others would definitely exclude them. As with every assignment, check with your instructor. You'll find more about writing from experiences in section 7c.

A second kind of source is direct observation. For example, you might be asked to observe people in a particular setting (let's say standing in line for a concert), take notes on their behaviors, and write a paper that explains what you've seen. You might be asked to attend a lecture and summarize what the speaker had to say or, additionally, to write a reaction to it. You might be asked to gather instances of a particular social or cultural phenomenon and, using analysis, inference, or synthesis, explore the meaning of that phenomenon. For example, an assignment that asks you to analyze how adolescents are portrayed in current television programs would require you carefully to observe several television shows, take notes, and explain your findings. We explain some types of writing about observations in section 7d.

A third kind of source is statistical or quantitative information. Statistical or quantitative information comes to us in the form of numbers ("217 people liked mushroom pizza"), as percentages ("14 percent liked mushroom pizza"), or other statistics. Of course, you might find this information in a published written source: a table of information that reports results from a survey or measurements from a laboratory study. Alternatively, you may be collecting the data yourself. Laboratory courses typically have students perform experiments, make careful measurements, and report their findings. Business, education, or social science courses often have students conduct surveys or interviews. We discuss writing about statistical or quantitative information in section 7e.

Finally, we note that many assignments mix sources. You might be asked to asked to relate one of your experiences to a reading in which someone else reports their own. You might do a study (for example, of public displays of affection or of crowd behaviors at sporting events) that combines direct observations with a survey. We've explained these types separately just to make them clearer.

EXERCISE 7-1　Working alone or in a group, discuss the kinds of sources you might use in each of the following writing questions.

1. Scholar Kyung Kim offers three suggestions for improving American high schools. Would her suggestions have worked at the high school you attended?

2. Are most students at your college liberal or conservative? What about students around the country?

3. What qualities generally seem true of romantic comedy movies that have been released in the past year?

7c　How can I write about experiences?

Some writing assignments may ask you to write about your memories or experiences. Generally, such writings will involve effectively telling a story, often accompanied by some reflection on or analysis of that story.

7c.1　Memoirs and personal essays

In *memoirs,* writers tell what they remember about something that happened to them. While memoirs, like autobiographies, can cover most of a person's life, they often focus on smaller slices, such as a particular incident or a related set of incidents.

Students often think that, unless they're famous or something important or exciting has happened to them, their lives aren't worth writing about. Nothing could be further from the truth. Sure, a juicy story with famous people or dramatic events can be fun to read. But what makes a memoir good is less *what* it's about than *how* the writer writes about it. Consider the following short example.

> I can remember my father driving our car into a filling station at the edge of Birmingham. Two miles after we passed a particular motel, he would turn onto Callahan drive, which was a gravel road.

There's nothing very interesting here, really just some facts and a bare description. But consider this version, in which the author writes about driving from Tennessee to Alabama in the 1950s:

> After lunch, our father would fold up his map and tuck it in the felt visor until we pulled into the filling station on the outskirts of Birmingham. *Are we there yet?* We had arrived when we saw the Moon Winx Motel sign—a heart-stopping piece of American road art, a double-sided neon extravaganza; a big taxicab-yellow crescent with a man-in-the-moon on each side, a sly smile, a blue eye that winked, and that blatant misspelling, that *X* that made us so happy. Two miles beyond the winking moon, the Chrysler's tires would crunch the bed of river pebbles on the Callahan drive. In morning light the pebbles were salmon, ochre, a calcium white—and the water-worn stones, from the one-time bed of the Tombiggee River, closed around our bare feet like cool pockets.

> —Emily Hiestand, *Angela the Upside-Down Girl*

The basic information is no more dramatic than the first version we shared. However, the careful description makes it interesting. The main purpose of a memoir is to create a vivid sense of the experience for its readers. Memoirs have an expressive or literary purpose.

Personal essays are closely related to memoirs (in fact, your instructor may use the terms interchangeably). Once again, you'll want to tell about an experience. Personal essays tend to contain more reflection and to make their points more explicitly. They answer the question "What does this experience mean?" or "How does my experience illustrate a particular idea?"

Important Elements of Memoirs and Personal Essays

- A well-told story. Your readers will want to know what happened. They will also want to know enough background information and context so they can fully understand and appreciate what happened and why it made an impression.

- Lively details. Help your readers see and hear, perhaps even smell, taste, and feel what you were experiencing. Recreate the place and time, the people who were involved. Give readers reason to like (or dislike, as the case may be) the places or people involved by the way you characterize them.

- Reflective or analytic paragraphs or passages. In addition to telling readers what happened, also tell them what you were thinking during the experience (take us inside your head at the time) or what you make of it now, looking backward.

- An effective use of STYLE and TONE (Chapter 8).

Advice on Process

1. Generating
   - In your first draft, concentrate on getting the basic story down. Pretend you're writing to a friend who is interested in what you're saying.

   - Try creating some detailed scenes, describing the physical setting and including some dialogue so readers will get a close sense of being there.

   - Do some FREEWRITING or use other invention strategies about the significance of your story. What did you learn at the time? How about looking back now? How does the experience connect to other experiences, readings, or things you've noticed in the world around you (in movies or on television, for example, or at work, in school, or in family life).

2. Shaping
   - Your basic shape is to tell a story; however, you will also likely have some commentary or reflection (when you "step back" and explain what it all means). You can put that reflection at the beginning, in the middle, or at the end, or you can scatter it in a few places. Choose the strategy that seems most effective.

   - You can begin at the beginning of the story, of course. But you can also begin with some exciting or interesting part from the middle or the end, then go back to the beginning to tell how it all started. You've probably seen movies that have flashbacks, which are examples of this technique.

   - Try to have places in your story where you "slow down," creating a scene in detail, as well as where you "speed up," covering events quickly so you can get to the interesting stuff.

3. Revising
   - Do your story and its details convey your impression of the experience? A common piece of advice is to "show, not tell." Try this experiment. Temporarily leave out any explicit statements about the story and what it means, and show the draft to a friend or peer. Let them tell you what they see as the point or meaning. If they can't—or if their interpretation differs significantly from yours—you need to revise. Put the explicit statements back in for your final draft.

- Are there places where you need more specific detail?
- Are there places where the writing drags too much and needs to be cut?
- Are the reflective or analytic parts thoughtful and interesting, or are they formulaic or obvious?

7c.2 Literacy narratives

A literacy narrative is a specific kind of memoir in which you tell the story of how you developed as a reader and writer. Generally, these stories stretch from your earliest memories to the present day, and we find that students are often surprised at the memories they dig up while writing. First year writing instructors sometimes assign literacy narratives, as do some education or social sciences instructors.

Important Elements of Literacy Narratives

- The elements important to memoirs and personal essays also matter for literacy narratives: a good story, lively details, and reflection.
- Examples of your previous reading, writing, or other language experiences. This may take the form of book titles, papers you remember writing, specific people important in your development as a reader and writer, scenes from school or home, and so on.

Advice on Process

1. Generating and drafting. Several questions can help you generate ideas.
   - What are the earliest books or stories you can remember someone reading to you? The earliest you can remember reading yourself? Can you tell us about more than the titles? Why do you think you remember them?
   - If anyone read to you (a parent, a sibling, a relative, a teacher, etc.), what do you remember about them? Can you create a word picture of that person (or those people)?
   - Where do you remember reading or writing at different points in your life? Was there a particular room in your house or apartment, a particular classroom? Can you describe the setting vividly?
   - What were your favorite books? What topics did you like to read about? What particular writings do you remember?
   - What were your worst experiences reading or writing? What made them bad?

- Who or what were your strongest influences on reading or writing—either for good or ill?
- How did reading and writing "fit in" (or not) with other activities in your life?
- Why do you think you became the type of reader and writer you are today—whatever kind that is?

2. Shaping. The strategies for shaping literacy narratives are the same as those for shaping memoirs and personal essays.

3. Revising and editing. Here are some questions to ask yourself, or to have a peer-response group ask (6c.1), when revising:

- Do all the incidents contribute effectively to the whole narrative? Are there any that need to be cut or shortened?
- Are there places that would be stronger if you created a more vivid scene?
- Are there smooth connections and transitions between the different elements?
- Have you reflected on the meaning of the experiences? Have you included some general observations on what your experiences "add up to" and tell about yourself as a reader and writer?

EXERCISE 7-2

1. Write a memoir about a trip you took, whether it was across town or across the country. The quality of your writing is more important than how unusual the trip was.

2. Write a section of a literacy narrative focusing on one of three periods in your life: birth to age 9; age 10 to 15; age 16 to the present.

7d How can I write about observations?

Writing about observations means writing about things you directly and intentionally see or experience. *Intentionally* is the important word. Sometimes you write about things that you just happened to notice or experience. However, in academic writing situations, observations are almost purposeful and deliberate. You observe as a writer with a specific goal.

7d.1 Reports of observations

Sometimes your assignment is to report about an event. You're asked to attend a presentation or lecture and summarize the talk. You go to a concert, play, or sporting event with the goal of explaining what happened. In these writing situations, your purpose is to inform, and your role is to be an objective reporter, much like a journalist. Other times you may be asked to describe a scene (a landscape, theatre set, classroom), a person, a process, an object (a sculpture, building, machine), or an image. We devote an entire separate section (4j) to viewing and analyzing images.

Important Elements of a Report

- A clear description of what you observed, which is complete and appropriately detailed—but not excessively detailed.
- Objectivity.
- The proper format that your instructor requires.

Advice on Process

1. Generating and drafting
   - Take careful notes. The quality of your report will depend on the clarity and fullness of the details you generate.
   - If you're writing about an event, gather information needed to answer the JOURNALIST'S QUESTIONS (see 2c.4), which are particularly useful for this kind of writing. Write your first draft as soon after the event as possible, while your notes are still fresh.
   - Ask questions, if possible, not only of speakers or performers but also of other people attending the event. Ask what they observed.
   - Be precise with descriptions, noting both major and seemingly minor details.

2. Shaping
   - Orient your readers in the first paragraph. Provide all of the general information (who, what, when, where, how, and why) in your opening.
   - Provide details in body paragraphs. You can organize events or processes either by chronological order (the sequence in which things happened) or by categories or topics.
   - Organize reports about objects by giving a big picture, then moving either spatially (left to right, top to bottom, center to edge) or by features to enhance the description.

3. Revising (questions to ask yourself or to have peers answer)
   - Have you maintained objectivity throughout? Would your report agree with the report of someone else writing about the same thing?

- Did you write an introduction that gives readers a good overall picture?
- Would everything be clear to an audience who hadn't observed what you did?
- Are there any places where you either need more detail or where you need to try to make the report more concise?
- Have you fulfilled all of the assignment's special considerations?

7d.2 Reviews or evaluations

A *review* is a report plus an evaluation: a "reasoned judgment" of whether something is good or bad, fair or unfair, true or false, effective or useless. You're familiar with movie, music, and product reviews, which are designed to help you decide whether to invest your time, attention, or money. Reviews in academic situations show how thoughtfully you can evaluate a presentation, performance, product, event, art work, or some other object.

Elements of Reviews

- Your review needs to contain both a summary or description and one or more evaluations of the source's quality or significance. Your thesis needs to take the form of an evaluation.
- You need to provide reasons for your evaluation, and you need to provide evidence for those reasons.
- Be sure to answer any specific questions your instructor asks and to follow any special considerations of the assignment.

Advice on Process

1. Generating and drafting
   - The advice for reporting applies. In addition, you need to generate an assessment. This involves critical thinking (Chapter 4).
   - Analyze the source, using strategies in section 4d. Pay attention to both content and style.
   - Synthesize, if appropriate. How does the source relate to other ones like it?

2. Shaping
   - Your opening paragraph needs to provide an overview of the event and your thesis.
   - Summarize the source in the early part of the paper (a paragraph or two after your opening) so your audience understands it. Depending

on the type of source you're writing about, this could include a summary of the plot, a description of the setting, a list of songs performed, a physical description of an image or object, or so on.

- Your remaining body paragraphs generally need to begin with a topic sentence that makes an assertion about some feature, followed by an explanation or evidence. You may want to save details from your summary/description, to include when you discuss particular features.

3. Revising and editing

- Is basic information clear?
- Have you included judgments?
- Have you provided enough details and evidence to make your judgments convincing?

7d.3 Interpretations

An interpretation makes an argument about what something means or why it's significant. You might be familiar with interpretations from studying fiction or poetry, and we will talk more about that kind of writing in section 7f and in Chapter 40. However, interpretation is hardly restricted to readings. Consider the following different assignment questions:

- In the painting *Guernica,* what do you think Picasso wants his viewers to feel and understand?
- What is the atmosphere of a particular place (a coffee shop, a shopping mall, a club, and so forth)?
- How are doctors and nurses portrayed on television?

Each of these examples involves both description and interpretation. When you're doing an interpretation, don't feel like you have to "guess the right answer," as if there's one and only one right meaning. Instead, the quality of your work will depend on generating interesting insights that you then support with reasons. Analysis (section 4d) and inference (4e) are especially important for interpretation.

Important Elements of an Interpretation

- A clear explanation of the event, phenomenon, or object that you're interpreting.
- Statements about what the subject of your interpretation means or why it's significant.

- Convincing support, including reasoning, to show why your interpretive statements are convincing.

Advice on Process

1. Generating

   - Summarize and describe very carefully; the act of paying close attention can generate insights.

   - Use strategies of analysis. In particular, see the strategies in Section 4d for looking at elements of the process.

   - Use strategies of inference. In particular, see the strategies in section 4e.

   - Don't be afraid to explore. Brainstorm as many possible interpretations as you can; many of them might be outlandish, but it's better to choose from several possible interpretations than to be stuck with the first thing that comes to mind.

   - Play "the believing game." Believe that you have the authority and expertise to generate an interpretation and boldly put it on paper.

2. Shaping

   - Good interpretations have a thesis that states the meaning or significance that your paper will then go on to explain.

   - Body paragraphs will each offer an explanation for your interpretation, with support and reasoning showing readers why it is plausible.

3. Revising

   - Play "the doubting game." Assume (for the purpose of thinking critically) that your interpretation is flawed. State the flaws. Then revise to address them.

   - Is the balance of summary and interpretation effective? Are there places where you need more reasoning or support?

7d.4 Case Studies

Some **case studies** are careful descriptions and interpretations of individuals, usually focusing on some set of features in relation to a specific situation or issue (for example, "students who work in fast food" or "parents coping with divorce" or "people involved in extreme sports"). The word *case* might suggest a hospital case to be solved, and indeed medical journals publish these kinds of cases; however, *case* also has a more neutral sense of an "instance," and people in case studies usually don't have anything wrong with them, physically or otherwise.

Case studies are important in psychology, social work, education, medicine, and similar fields in which it's useful to form a comprehensive portrait of people in order to understand them and, in some cases, to help them. In some fields, such as education, people do case studies in order to understand or test theories and practices. For example, if you learn that a certain teaching style is effective, you might do a case study of a student in order to understand how it works in a particular instance.

Case studies can also lead to theories or other kinds of research. For example, if you wondered about what factors make people happy at their jobs, you might do a case study (or two or three) of individual workers to generate possible criteria. People about whom you write case studies are called **subjects**. A kind of writing related to a case study is a **profile**, in which you create a portrait in words of a person.

Important Elements of Case Studies of Individuals

- A combination of observation, interview, and discussion of any artifacts you might have from your subject (writings, test results, creative works, and so on).

- A focus on particular traits important to the purpose of the study.

- A combination of report and interpretation or analysis.

- Depending on the type of case study and its purpose, it may include recommendations for a course of action, a discussion of implications, or a commentary on a theory. (For this last, also see section 7f.5.)

Advice on Process

1. Generating

   - Arrange to meet or observe the subject of your case study or profile. Take notes about the meeting, focusing on characteristics, mannerisms, and perhaps interactions with others.

   - Conduct one or more interviews, following our guidelines in Quick Reference 32.1.

   - Look for patterns in your notes. Use clustering to group similar ideas (see section 2c.5). Make each idea a paragraph or two, stating the idea in the form of a topic sentence, then using details from your notes to support your observations.

2. Shaping

   - Learn whether you're to follow a standard report format, for example, one similar to lab reports (section 7e.3).

   - Your opening needs to introduce your subject, explain your purpose for studying him or her, and include a thesis that states your main finding, interpretation, or impression.

- Organize your following paragraphs by qualities you recognized in your subject, for example, by aspects of her or his personality, behavior, attitudes, or interactions. In each case try as best you can to explain "why" your subject has those qualities or aspects.

3. Revising

- Will your readers get a complete and accurate sense of this person?
- Are there any places where your information is "thin," places where you made an interpretation but didn't really back it up?
- Have you included interpretation, trying to explain "why?" If so, have you fully justified your conclusions?
- Is your tone respectful and fair?

7d.5 Ethnographies

The term *case studies* also refers to a kind of research about a particular group of people or situation (consider studies of online video game players, of college basketball players and their study habits, of a store's marketing strategy, of homeless life in Seattle, and so forth). They are closely related to **ethnographies**, another form of FIELD RESEARCH (32c), in that both generally are comprehensive studies of people interacting in a particular situation. Situational case studies and ethnographies commonly occur in courses in business, education, or the social sciences, with anthropology and sociology being prime examples of disciplines that use these studies. Someone might do an ethnography of a classroom in order to understand the interactions and relationships among students. Or they might do a situational case study of an office, a club or social organization, a church, or so on.

Important Elements of Situational Case Studies or Ethnographies

- Thick description. The anthropologist Clifford Geertz coined the term *thick description* to explain the kinds of details needed in ethnographies. Pay attention to everything, from the setting, to observed interactions, to what people say.
- Interpretation. The purpose of an ethnography is to offer an explanation of what the situation means in context.

Advice on Process

1. Generating

- Schedule ample time to observe the situation you're writing about; visit more than once if at all possible.

- Follow the strategies for field research (section 32c).

- Take extensive notes. Double column field research notes (Figure 32.1 on page 520) are particularly effective.

- Interview people who are involved (Quick Reference 32.1), if possible, or have them complete questionnaires that you can analyze.

- Look for patterns in your notes. Group similar information or ideas together and draft sentences that say what each group means; this forms the basis for paragraphs.

2. Shaping

- Some formal case studies and ethnographies take forms similar to lab reports and other empirical studies (7e.3) and have the following sections: Introduction (explaining the issue and perhaps reviewing other literature); Procedures (describing how you chose the setting or people to study, how you gathered information, and so on); Findings (the longest part of the paper, usually, in which you relate what you learned; and Discussion or Conclusions (in which you explain what is significant about what you learned).

- Other case studies put less emphasis on the structure above; instead, they are more narrative, letting the finding unfold like a story, or they are organized according to topics and support materials.

3. Revising

- The questions for revising case studies of individuals (see above) also apply to these writings.

- Would a participant in the scene you're describing share your interpretation? Ethnographers frequently let their subjects read a draft and comment on it.

- What alternative interpretations are available? What conclusions could someone else draw from your notes?

EXERCISE 7-3

1. Write a short report that explains a concert, lecture, or other event to an audience of people who didn't attend it.

2. Write a review of one of the following: a new electronic device, a current movie, a class that you attended, a place where you worked. Your audience is other people who are deciding whether to purchase the device, attend the movie or class, or accept a job at that place.

3. Write a case study of one of your classmates, focusing on their educational experiences, their hobbies or entertainment interests, and their career hopes.

4. Working either alone or with others, write a case study of one of the following situations: people with an activity in common (a team, a musical group, a gathering of video game players); a workplace; a class; a coffee shop.

5. Write an interpretation for a general educated audience of a representation of certain types of people on a particular type of television show. Choose one of the following types of people: adolescents; college students; single parents; white-collar professionals; working-class laborers; gays or lesbians. Then choose one of the following types of shows: sitcoms, crime dramas, medical dramas, reality shows, game shows.

7e　How can I write about quantitative data or information?

Quantitative information or data comes in the form of numbers. Of course, such information can be an important source of detail and evidence in almost any kind of writing. However, some writings especially require writers to translate numbers into words and to explain what they mean.

7e.1　Reports of data

Reporting data is parallel to summarizing. You need to present information clearly and objectively, translating numbers into words. The challenge with these types of assignments is that the numbers seem to "speak for themselves." In other words, if you have a table of information it might seem pointless to write about it. A table is an efficient way to present information, and converting absolutely everything into words would be a waste of time; as a result, reports usually combine words and numbers. To illustrate how this kind of writing works, we've included part of a student paper below. In it, Marcus Kapuranis reports information from the National Survey of Student Engagement, which each year questions first-year college students and college seniors in order to learn about their experiences in a number of areas.

Sample Student Report of Quantitative Data

Kapuranis 1

Marcus Kapuranis

English 1122

Professor Bateman

24 May 2008

Diversity of Student Experiences Reported in the National
Survey of Student Engagement

Part of the 2007 National Survey of Student Engagement
(NSSE) asked college freshmen and seniors to report on their
experiences with people different from themselves. These
differences included racial and ethnic backgrounds as well as
attitudes and beliefs, and the final report provides not only
totals for each group of students but also a breakdown of
responses according to types of college. Responses to three
questions, shown in Figure 1, provide a clear picture of the
national situation.

When asked how often they had serious conversations
with students whose religious beliefs, personal opinions, or
values differed from their own, 12% of first year students
reported "never," 34% said "sometimes," 29% said "often," and
25% said "very often." In response to the same question, seniors
reported similarly. 10% said "never," 35% said "sometimes,"
30% said "often," and 26% said "very often."

First-Year Students Seniors (in percentages)		DRU-VH		DRU-H		DRU		Master's-L		Master's-M		Master's-S		Bac-AS		Bac-DIV		Top 10%		NSSE 2007	
Had serious conversations with students who are very different from you in terms of their religious beliefs, political opinions, or personal values	Never	10	8	12	10	12	10	13	11	16	12	13	10	8	6	15	11	8	6	12	10
	Sometimes	33	33	33	35	34	35	34	35	35	37	34	37	32	34	37	38	29	30	34	35
	Often	31	21	30	30	29	28	29	29	27	27	29	29	30	31	28	28	30	33	29	30
	Very often	27	27	26	26	25	27	24	25	22	23	24	24	30	29	21	23	33	32	25	26
Had serious conversations with students of a different race or ethnicity than your own	Never	14	11	15	12	15	12	18	14	20	16	16	14	14	11	19	15	11	8	16	12
	Sometimes	34	34	34	35	35	33	34	34	35	37	34	36	34	37	37	38	31	32	34	35
	Often	28	29	27	28	27	28	26	27	25	25	27	26	27	26	24	26	20	28	27	28
	Very often	24	27	24	26	23	26	22	25	20	23	23	24	25	26	20	21	31	32	23	25
Institutional emphasis: Encouraging contact among students from different economic, social, and racial or ethnic backgrounds	Very little	12	21	14	20	14	18	14	18	13	17	12	17	11	16	15	19	11	17	13	19
	Some	33	36	34	36	32	34	33	36	33	34	31	34	31	33	33	30	29	35	33	35
	Quite a bit	33	27	32	28	32	29	33	29	33	30	32	30	32	29	32	27	33	28	32	28
	Very much	22	16	21	16	22	19	21	18	22	19	24	20	26	19	23	18	27	20	22	17

Fig. 1. Student experiences with difference.

continued >>

Kapuranis 2

The NSSE study also broke the responses down according to type of institution. There are three categories of "Doctoral Research University" (DRU): those that have "very high" (VH) research levels, those that have "high" (H), and others. There are three categories of "Master's Universities," Large, Medium, and Small (L, M, S), and two categories of "Baccalaureate Colleges," traditional liberal arts and sciences colleges (AS) and those that have a broader range of course and programs (DIV). (This particular study didn't survey two-year colleges, although the *Two-Year College Survey of Student Engagement* does.) The findings across the institutional types were fairly comparable, with the largest differences between traditional liberal arts colleges and medium-size master's universities. The liberal arts colleges had the fewest students (8%) reporting "never" talking to diverse students and most students (30%) reporting "very often" doing so. In contrast the medium-sized master's colleges had the most students (16%) reporting "never" talking to diverse students and the second fewest (22%) reporting "very often."

A second question asked students to report how frequently they had serious conversations with someone of a different race or ethnicity . . .

Kapuranis 5

Work Cited

NSSE: National Survey of Student Engagement. *Experiences That Matter: Enhancing Student Learning and Success Annual Report 2007*. Bloomington: Center for Postsecondary Research, Indiana University, 2007. Web. 14 May 2008.

In his report, Marcus opens with a brief overview of the study and then chooses to include the report itself. When he starts summarizing its findings, he moves from the big picture to the more detailed, and he takes care to explain information (such as the institutional types) that would be unclear to his audience. He selects the most important information, which takes some judgment. After all, you don't want to bore your readers with sentence after sentence telling every single finding, especially because they can read the original itself. Most important for this type of writing, he remains objective, adding nothing to the information that anyone else wouldn't.

Important Elements of Reporting Data

- Clear and accurate translations of numbers into language.
- Judicious selection and summary of data to report.
- Objective reporting, unless your task is to go a step further to analyze or interpret (7e.2).

Advice on Process

1. Generating
   - Ask yourself what is the key information? What do readers most need to see or recognize in this data?
   - If you're stuck, begin by trying to put everything into sentences. You probably won't want to keep all of these sentences in your final draft, because it would get boring; however, you should start writing rather than stare at a blank page.

2. Shaping
   - In the first paragraph, provide a summary or overview of the data you're reporting. Tell its source, how it was gathered, and its purpose. Your thesis will generally forecast the kind of information that follows (as in the case of Marcus Kapuranis's paper above).
   - Group pieces of related information. Each grouping will potentially become a paragraph.
   - Create or reproduce any charts or tables that would be too wordy to translate into language.

3. Revising
   - Do your words accurately report the main information?
   - Will your readers better understand the information through your language, or has your language actually contributed little?

- Have you made the writing as interesting as you can, given the limitations of maintaining objectivity that is faithful to the nature of the task?
- Have you documented the source(s) accurately?

7e.2　Analyses of data

Most papers that emphasize quantitative information go beyond reporting and into analysis or synthesis: drawing conclusions about what the information means or connecting it to other pieces of information or ideas. When you analyze data, you interpret it, going beyond translating numbers into language.

Marcus Kapuranis's paper in section 7e.1 reports how frequently first year students and seniors had serious conversations with people different from them. Here is what a paragraph analyzing that data might say:

> In terms of how often they had serious conversations with students whose religious beliefs, personal opinions, or values differ from their own, first-year students and seniors were disappointingly similar. For example, 34% of first years said "sometimes," almost identical to the 35% of seniors, and 25% of first years said "very often," almost identical to 26% of seniors. The reason this is disappointing is that four years in college seem to have had little effect on students in this dimension. If one of the purposes of college is to have students learn from new knowledge and experiences, one would expect an increase in the frequency of serious encounters with different types of people. Apparently, this isn't happening.

Notice that the analysis reports findings, but it does so in the context of what they might mean. This paragraph emphasizes why the results are disappointing and provides reasons for that interpretation.

Important Elements of Analyses

- A clear report of the data, as explained in section 7e.1.
- Statements that make interpretations, inferences, or evaluations of the data.
- Reasoning and support that convince readers that your statements are justified.

Advice on Process

1. Generating
   - Follow strategies for generating reports of data.
   - Use techniques for analysis (4d) and making inference (4e).

- Brainstorm. For example, try to write ten different statements about what the information means or what its implications might be. Many of them will be silly or invalid, but don't let that stop you. At least one or two will probably be worthwhile.

2. Shaping

- Your basic organization will be a summary of the data (report) followed by analysis. However, you don't want to summarize everything up front—just the most important materials. The reason is that during your analysis, you'll want to quote or cite some of the data. It becomes boring to see the information twice.

3. Revising

- Have you been fair and accurate in the way you've represented the information?
- Have you considered alternative interpretations?
- Have you provided clear and convincing explanations for any analytic, interpretive, or evaluative comments?
- Have you documented your paper appropriately?

7e.3 Lab reports and empirical studies

A **lab report** is a specific and formal way of presenting and discussing the results of experiments or laboratory measurements, in fields such as chemistry, biology, physics, engineering, and other sciences. Lab experiments are one kind of **empirical research**, a name that generally refers to attempts to measure something (from physical substances to behaviors) in order to prove or disprove a theory or hypothesis. Disciplines other than the sciences use experiments, too; among them are psychology and other social sciences, some areas of education (for example, "Does this teaching strategy work better than that teaching strategy?"), economics, and so on. However, those disciplines also use sources like surveys or very specific observations to collect data. Both lab reports and other kinds of empirical research studies tend to have the same standard elements.

Important Sections of Lab Reports and Similar Empirical Studies

- **Introduction.** State your purpose, present background materials (for example, a review of previous studies), and your hypothesis.
- **Methods and materials.** Describe the equipment and procedures.
- **Results.** Accurately and objectively provide information that you acquired through your study.

- **Discussion.** Interpret and evaluate your results, including whether they supported your hypothesis and why or why not.
- **Conclusion.** Discuss the implications of your work, along with any limitations. Suggest further studies.

Take care to keep clear distinctions among each of these sections. Lab reports and empirical studies frequently include two other parts. One is an ABSTRACT, a short overview of the entire report, which appears directly after your title. The other is a list of REFERENCES, which is crucial if you discuss other published research. We provide more information about writing lab reports, as well as an example, in Chapter 41.

EXERCISE 7-4 Following are two tables of data from the General Social Survey. Table A reports responses from the 1970s, and Table B from the 2000s. Write a 100–300 word analysis of the findings.

"Men are better suited for politics than are women"

A. 1970's results, by two age groups, by percent				B. 2000's results, by two age groups, by percent			
	18-40	41-89	TOTAL		18-40	41-89	TOTAL
AGREE	38.3	55.9	47.5	AGREE	20.7	25.5	23.4
DISAGREE	61.7	44.1	52.5	DISAGREE	79.3	74.5	76.6
Total Percent	100.0	100.0	100.0	Total Percent	100.0	100.0	100.0
(Total N)	(2,418)	(2,612)	(5,030)	(Total N)	(1,480)	(1,915)	(3,395)

SDA: Survey Documentation and Analysis. "General Social Survey Quick Tables."
<http://sda.berkeley.edu/archive.htm>

Figure 7.2 Data tables from the General Social Survey

7f How can I write about readings?

Nearly all types of writing about observations have counterparts in writing about reading. You may be asked to write summaries, critical responses, analyses or interpretations, and syntheses. To illustrate some of these types and strategies for doing them, we'll refer to the following part of an essay by Barry Schwartz, titled "The Tyranny of Choice."

> Does increased affluence and increased choice mean we have more happy people? Not at all. Three recently published books—by the psychologist David Myers, the political scientist Robert E. Lane, and the journalist Gregg Easterbrook—point out how the growth of material affluence has not brought with it an increase in subjective well-being. Indeed, they argue that we are actually

experiencing a *decrease* in well-being. In the last 30 years, the number of Americans describing themselves as "very happy" declined by 5 percent, which means that about 14 million fewer people report being very happy today than in 1974. And, as a recent study published in *The Journal of the American Medical Association* indicates, the rate of serious clinical depression has more than tripled over the last two generations, and increased by perhaps a factor of 10 from 1900 to 2000. Suicide rates are also up, not only in the United States, but in almost every developed country. And both serious depression and suicide are occurring among people younger than ever before. Deans at virtually every college and university in the United States can testify to this malaise, as they witness a demand for psychological services that they are unable to meet.

Why are people increasingly unhappy even as they experience greater material abundance and freedom of choice? Recent psychological research suggests that increased choice may itself be part of the problem.

It may seem implausible that there can be too much choice. As a matter of logic, it would appear that adding options will make no one worse off and is bound to make someone better off. If you're content choosing among three different kinds of breakfast cereal, or six television stations, you can simply ignore the dozens or hundreds that get added to your supermarket shelves or cable provider's menu. Meanwhile, one of those new cereals or TV stations may be just what some other person was hoping for. Given the indisputable fact that choice is good for human well-being, it seems only logical that if some choice is good, more choice is better.

Logically true, yes. Psychologically true, no. My colleagues and I, along with other researchers, have begun amassing evidence—both in the laboratory and in the field—that increased choice can lead to *decreased* well-being. This is especially true for people we have termed "maximizers," people whose goal is to get the best possible result when they make decisions. Choice overload is also a problem for people we call "satisficers," people who seek only "good enough" results from their choices, but the problem is greatly magnified for maximizers. Much of the relevant research is summarized in my book, *The Paradox of Choice: Why More Is Less.* Here are some examples:

- Shoppers who confront a display of 30 jams or varieties of gourmet chocolate are less likely to purchase *any* than when they encounter a display of six.

- Students given 30 topics from which to choose to write an extra-credit essay are less likely to write one than those given six. And if they do write one, it tends to be of lower quality.

- The majority of medical patients do not want the decision authority that the canons of medical ethics have thrust upon them. Responsibility for medical decisions looks better to people in prospect than in actuality: Sixty-five percent of respondents say that if they were to get cancer, they would want to be in charge of treatment decisions, but among those who actually have cancer, only 12 percent want that control and responsibility.

- Maximizing college seniors send out more résumés, investigate more different fields, go on more job interviews, and get better, higher-paying jobs than satisficers. But they are less satisfied with the jobs, and are much more stressed, anxious, frustrated, and unhappy with the process.

These examples paint a common picture: Increasing options does not increase well-being, especially for maximizers, even when it enables choosers to do better by some objective standard. We have identified several processes that help explain why increased choice decreases satisfaction. Greater choice:

- Increases the burden of gathering information to make a wise decision.
- Increases the likelihood that people will regret the decisions they make.
- Increases the likelihood that people will *anticipate* regretting the decision they make, with the result that they can't make a decision at all.
- Increases the feeling of missed opportunities, as people encounter the attractive features of one option after another that they are rejecting.

7f.1 Summaries

To *summarize* is to extract the main messages or central points of a reading and restate them in a much briefer fashion. A summary doesn't include supporting evidence or details. It's the gist, the hub, the seed of what the author is saying. Also, it isn't your personal reaction to what the author says. How you summarize depends on your situation and assignment. For example, you can summarize an entire 500-page book in a single sentence, in a single page, or in five or six pages. Most of the time when you get an assignment to write a summary, your instructor will tell you how long it needs to be; if he or she doesn't, it's reasonable for you to ask.

Following are examples of two different levels of summary based on "The Tyranny of Choice" passage above.

SUMMARY IN A SINGLE SENTENCE

Research finds that people with large numbers of choices are actually less happy than people with fewer choices (Schwartz).

SUMMARY IN 50 TO 100 WORDS

Boshoven 1

Kristin Boshoven

English 101

Professor Lequire

5 April 2008

Summary of "The Tyranny of Choice"

Research finds that people with large numbers of choices are actually less happy than people with fewer choices. Although the amount of wealth and choice has increased during the past thirty years, fewer Americans report themselves as being happy, and depression, suicide, and mental health problems have increased. While some choice is good, too many choices hinder decision making, especially among "maximizers," who try to make the best possible choices. Research in shopping, education, and medical settings shows that even when people eventually decide, they experience regret, worrying that the options they didn't choose might have been better (Schwartz).

Boshoven 2

Work Cited

Schwartz, Barry. "The Tyranny of Choice." *Chronicle of Higher Education* (23 Jan. 2004): B6. Print.

Notice that the longer summary begins with the same sentence as the short one, because leading a summary with the reading's main idea is effective. Notice that both summaries put ideas in the author's own words and capture only the main idea.

One decision to make is whether to refer to the author during your summary or to leave him or her out, as in the examples above. Check if your instructor has a preference. The second example above could be rewritten (the four dots are ELLIPSES, showing material left out):

> In "The Tyranny of Research," Barry Schwartz summarizes research that finds. . . . while some choice is good, too many choices. . . .

Important Elements of Summaries

- Inclusion of only the source's main ideas.
- Proportional summary of the source. This means that longer and more important aspects of the original need to get more space and attention in your summary.
- Use of your own words. If there are particular key terms or phrases, include them in quotation marks, but otherwise put everything into your own words.
- Accurate DOCUMENTATION of the original source.

Advice on Process

Note: For more help in writing a summary, see section 35j.

1. Generating
   - Identify TOPIC SENTENCES or main ideas, separating them from examples or illustrations. You want to focus on the main ideas.
   - Take notes in your own words, then put the source away. Write from your notes, going back to check the original only after you've written a first draft.

2. Shaping
   - Begin with a sentence that summarizes the entire reading, unless you're writing a particularly long summary.
   - Follow the order of the original.
   - Include a Works Cited page (Chapter 36) or References (Chapter 37), depending on the required style.

3. Revising
   - Have you maintained objectivity throughout?
   - Have you put things into your own words?
   - Have you been proportional?
   - Have you accurately documented?
   - Is there an even more CONCISE (see Chapter 11) way to state certain things?

7f.2 Critical responses

A **critical response** essay has two missions: to provide a SUMMARY of a source's main idea and to respond to that idea.

A well-written critical response accomplishes these two missions with style and grace. That is, it doesn't say, "My summary is . . ." or "Now, here's what I think. . . ." Instead, you want the two missions to blend together as seamlessly as possible. A critical response essay may be short or somewhat long, depending on whether you're asked to respond to a single passage or to an entire work.

Here's student Kristin Boshoven's short critical response to Barry Schwartz's essay, "The Tyranny of Choice," which we reprinted above. Note that it incorporates the summary she wrote for a previous assignment.

Boshoven 1

Kristin Boshoven

English 101

Professor Lequire

7 April 2008

Too Much Choice: Disturbing but not Destructive

Barry Schwartz argues that people with large numbers
of choices are actually less happy than people with fewer
choices. Although the amount of wealth and choice has
increased during the past thirty years, studies show that fewer
Americans report themselves as being happy. Depression,
suicide, and mental health problems have increased. While
some choice is good, too many choices hinder decision making,
especially among people who Schwartz calls "maximizers,"
people who try to make the best possible choices. Research in
shopping, education, and medical settings shows that even
when people eventually decide, they experience regret,
worrying that the options they didn't choose might have been
better.

---

continued >>

Boshoven 2

Although Schwartz cites convincing evidence for his claims, he ultimately goes too far in his conclusions. Excessive choice does seem to make life harder, not easier, but it alone can't be blamed for whatever unhappiness exists in our society.

My own experience supports Schwartz's finding that that people who have thirty choices of jam as opposed to six (B6) often don't purchase any. About a month ago my husband and I decided to buy an inexpensive global positioning (GPS) device to use in our car. When we went to the store, we were confronted with twenty different models, and even though a helpful salesperson explained the various features to me, we couldn't make up our minds. We decided to do more research, which was a mistake. After weeks of reading reviews in everything from *Consumer Reports* to the *New York Times*, we are close to making a decision. However, I have a sinking feeling that as soon as we buy something, we'll learn that another choice would have been better, or ours will drop $50 in price. In the meantime, we could have been enjoying the use of a GPS for the past month, if we had not worried so much. I could relate similar experiences trying to choose which movie to see, which dentist to visit, and so on. I suspect others could, too, which is why I find Schwartz's argument convincing at this level.

However, when he suggests that the increase of choice is a source of things like depression and suicide, he goes too far. Our society has undergone tremendous changes in the past forty or fifty years, and many of those changes are more likely to cause problems than the existence of too much choice. For example, workers in the 1950s through the 1970s could generally count on holding jobs with one company as long as

continued >>

Boshoven 3

they wanted, even through retirement. A 1950s autoworker, for example, might not have been thrilled in his job (and these were jobs held almost exclusively by men), but at least he could count on it, and it paid enough to buy a house and education for his family. The economic uncertainties of the past twenty years, and especially since 2001, have meant that workers—and now women as well as men—do not have the same job stability as decades ago.

Although I agree that too many choices can lead to anxiety and even unhappiness, there are larger factors. If Americans report more depression and suicide than they once did, a more likely candidate is economic and social uncertainty, not having too many kinds of cereal on the grocery store shelves.

Boshoven 4

Work Cited

Schwartz, Barry. "The Tyranny of Choice." *Chronicle of Higher Education* (23 Jan. 2004): B6. Print.

Important Elements of Critical Responses

- A clear and concise representation of the source.
- Statements of agreement, disagreement, or qualified agreement (you accept some points but not others), accompanied by reasons and evidence for your statements.

Advice on Process

1. Generating
   - Use ACTIVE READING and CRITICAL READING to identify the main points and generate reactions to the article.

- Use techniques for ANALYZING (4d), drawing INFERENCES (4e), and ASSESSING REASONING PROCESSES (4h).

2. Shaping
    - Write a summary of the main idea or central point of the material you're responding to.
    - Write a smooth TRANSITION between the summary and what comes next: your response. This transitional statement, which bridges the two parts, need not be a formal THESIS STATEMENT, but it needs to signal clearly the beginning of your response.
    - Respond to the source based on your prior knowledge and experience.

3. Revising
    - Have you combined summary and response? Have you explained your response in a way that readers will find thoughtful and convincing?
    - Have you fulfilled all documentation requirements? See Chapters 36–38 for coverage of four DOCUMENTATION STYLES (MLA, APA, CM, and CSE). Ask your instructor which style to use.

7f.3   Interpretations and analyses

Interpretations and analyses resemble critical response in that both make claims about a reading. Critical responses ask whether a source is "good," but interpretations and analyses ask what a source "means." You might be most familiar with this kind of writing from previous English or literature courses in which a teacher asked you to interpret a poem, play, or story. In fact, we've devoted much of an entire chapter, along with examples, to writing about literature, Chapter 40.

7f.4   Syntheses

To *synthesize* is to weave together material from several sources. Unsynthesized ideas and information are like separate spools of thread, neatly lined up, possibly coordinated but not integrated. Synthesized ideas and information are threads woven into a tapestry. By synthesizing, you show evidence of your ability to bring ideas together. Synthesis goes beyond summary and comes after it in the critical thinking process (section 4b).

One common synthesizing task is to connect two or more readings or source materials into a single piece of writing. You complete this synthesis after you have summarized, analyzed, and evaluated each of the source materials. Another common type of synthesis is to connect material to what you already know, creating a new final product that is your own.

SYNTHESIZING MULTIPLE SOURCES

Your goal in synthesizing multiple sources is to join two or more texts together into a single writing. The resulting text needs to be more than just a succession of summaries. That is, avoid merely listing who said what about a topic. Such a list isn't a synthesis. It does not create new connections among ideas.

The following example shows how student Tom Mentzer synthesized two sources. Read Source 1 and Source 2 to get familiar with the information he read. Then, read Tom's synthesis that follows.

Source 1

In Shishmaref, calamity has already arrived. The village of 600 Inupiaq lies on the fragile barrier island of Sarichef, where sea ice forms later each year, exposing the land to autumn storms that carve away 50 feet or more of shoreline a season. Two houses have slipped into the sea; 18 others have been moved back from the encroaching ocean; others buckle from the melting permafrost. Ten million dollars has been spent on seawalls, to no avail. Residents have concluded permanent resettlement is their only option.

— Julia Whitty and Robert Knoth, "Sea Change"

Source 2

Global temperatures have risen by about 0.6 degrees Celsius since the nineteenth century. Other measures of climate bolster the theory that the world is getting warmer: satellite measurements suggest that spring arrives about a week earlier now than in the late 1970s, for example, and records show that migratory birds fly to higher latitudes earlier in the season and stay later.

—John Browne, "Beyond Kyoto"

Now read Tom's synthesis. Notice how he used SUMMARY and PARAPHRASE to synthesize the two sources. Also notice how the first sentence in his synthesis weaves the sources together with a new concept.

Example of a Synthesis of Two Sources

Global warming is affecting both the natural and artificial worlds. Rising temperatures have accelerated spring's arrival and changed the migration patterns of birds (Browne 20). They have also changed life for residents of Arctic regions. For example, eighteen families in Shishmaref, Alaska, had to move their houses away from the coast because the permafrost under the beaches had thawed (Whitty and Knoth).

—Tom Mentzer, student

Notice how Tom's synthesis uses in-text citations (MLA style) to signal to the reader which information he has borrowed from the two sources. In the Works

Cited list at the end of his paper, Tom listed full source information for both sources. To learn how to document your sources, see Chapters 36 (MLA), 37 (APA), or 38 (CM, CSE).

SOURCES LISTED IN TOM'S WORKS CITED PAGE

Browne, John. "Beyond Kyoto." *Foreign Affairs* 83.4 (2004): 20–32. Print.

Whitty, Julia, Robert Knoth. "Sea Change." *Mother Jones.* Foundation for National Progress, Sept./Oct. 2007. Web. 2 Jan. 2008.

Process Advice

- Make comparisons with—or contrasts between—concepts, ideas, and information. Do the sources generally agree or generally disagree? What are the bases of their agreement or disagreement? Are there subtle differences or shades of meaning or emphasis?

- Create definitions that combine and extend definitions you encounter in the separate sources.

- Use examples or descriptions from one source to illustrate ideas in another. See the related discussion in section 7f.5.

- Use processes described in one source to explain those in others.

- In revising, ask, "Have I truly synthesized the sources, or have I just written about one and then the other?"

EXERCISE 7-5   Write a one-paragraph synthesis of the passage by Barry Schwartz (printed on pp. 196–198) and the following opening to a short article by Ronni Sandroff, editor of *Consumer Reports on Health:*

> Last time I dropped by my pharmacy in search of a decongestant, I was stopped cold by the wall-sized display of remedies. The brands I had used in the past had multiplied into extended families of products. Yes, I saw *Contac, Excedrin, Tylenol,* and *Vicks,* but each brand came in multiple versions. Products for severe colds, coughs and colds, and headache and flu abounded, and there were further choices: gels, tablets, capsules, extended release, extra strength. I was eager to just grab a product and go, but to find the right one I had to dig out my reading glasses and examine the fine print.
>
> —Ronni Sandroff, "Too Many Choices"

SYNTHESIZING WITH ONE SOURCE

If you're working with only one source, you need to make connections between the source and your prior knowledge, whether from experience, films or television, classes or conversations, or previous readings. Don't be afraid to synthesize. We're always surprised when we find that some students assume that what they think has no value. Nothing could be further from the truth.

In the following example of a synthesis with one source (Source 2 above), student Mikayla Stoller connected her reading to her previous knowledge, in this case a movie she had seen. Her first sentence links the two with a new idea.

Example of a Synthesis with One Source

Even if the existence of global warming is well established, the consequences of it may not be. A 0.6 degrees Celsius rise in temperature over the past century has caused spring to arrive earlier and migrating birds to change their habits (Browne 20). However, some believe that global warming could have the unexpected effect of causing a new ice age. The 2004 movie *The Day after Tomorrow* portrayed New York City as suddenly frozen over with ice because of climate changes. Although most scientists criticized the science in that movie, it seems clear that global warming will alter the world as we know it.

—Mikayla Stoller, student

Mikayla used parenthetical citations in the body of her paragraph and included the full citation in her Works Cited list at the end of her paper.

SOURCE AS LISTED IN MIKAYLA'S WORKS CITED PAGE

Browne, John. "Beyond Kyoto." *Foreign Affairs* 83.4 (2004): 20–32. Print.

Advice on Process

- Use your powers of play. Mentally toss ideas around, even if you make connections that seem outrageous. Try opposites (for example, read about athletes and think about the most nonathletic person you know). Try turning an idea upside down (for example, if you have read about the value of being a good sport, list the benefits of being a bad sport).

- Use the technique of clustering (2c.5) to lay out visually the relationships among elements in your source and other ideas that come to mind.

- Discuss the source with another person. Summarize its content and elicit the other person's opinion or ideas. Deliberately debate that opinion or challenge those ideas.

- Write your personal response to the material. Explain whether you agree or disagree and also the reasons why you respond as you do.

7f.5 Essays that apply theories or concepts (essays of application)

Essays that apply theories or concepts (or **essays of application**) take general information from one source (usually a reading but perhaps from a lecture) and apply it to another, usually for the purpose of interpretation or evaluation. Four example assignments will make this clearer.

1. How does Smith's theory of social deviance explain the behaviors of the criminals who are portrayed in Jones's book?

2. Based on your own experiences, are Beaudoin's categories of high school cliques accurate and sufficient?

3. Which symptoms of depression, as explained by Kho, does the narrator of *The Bell Jar* seem to display? Which does she not?

4. Kevin Sarkis argues that baseball pitchers have progressed further than batters in the past fifty years. Analyze statistics in *The Baseball Abstract* to either confirm or disprove his claim.

Assignments like these require a form of synthesis, in that they combine two or more sources into a single piece of writing. However, the sources have characteristics that distinguish essays of application from other syntheses, which is why we explain them separately. One source explains a theory, concept, or definition; even if it's based on details from formal research or study, its purpose is to offer a generalization about something. The other source is more specific, consisting of stories, experiences, scenarios, observations, quantitative data, or reports of events (perhaps even fictional situations, as in example 3 above), with little or no analysis or interpretation.

Instructors sometime assign essays of application to test how well you grasp concepts; being able to apply an idea to a new situation demonstrates your deeper understanding of it. They may also assign such essays to help you analyze or interpret a situation or body of information in ways you might not have considered. For example, suppose you're asked to read an article that claims that, from a very early age, gender determines the roles assumed by children playing in mixed groups, and then to apply the article to your own observations of children at play. You would pay attention to that situation differently if you were asked to apply a different theory (for example, that physical size determines play roles). Finally, you might apply a theory to a situation in order to test it. Suppose, in the previous example, you observe lots of play situations and find that boys and girls all play the same kinds of roles. A paper resulting from this application will explain why the theory may be invalid.

Important Elements of Essays of Application

- A clear and accurate summary of the theory or concept you're applying.

Advice on Process

1. Generating

   - Use strategies for summary or report (whichever is appropriate) to explain each source.

   - Brainstorm a list of all the possible ways the specific source illustrates the concept or theory. Use analysis and inference.

- Brainstorm a list of all the possible ways the specific source disproves or complicates the concept or theory. Use analysis and inference.
- Use other generating strategies.

2. Shaping

  - Begin your essay in one of two ways. A. Start with a brief summary of the theory or concept, leading to a thesis that states how it applies to the specific source (situation, reading, or information) you're discussing. B. Start with a brief summary of the specific source (situation, reading, or information), leading to a thesis that states how it demonstrates, disproves, or complicates the theory or concept.
  - If you follow opening strategy A, your next paragraph(s) will need to summarize the specific source. If you follow strategy B, your next paragraph(s) will need to summarize the theory or concept.
  - Your next paragraphs will support your thesis, giving reasons (and support) for your assertion.
  - (Optional). Discuss any facts or observations that seem not to fit your thesis. Explain why they, nonetheless, don't mean you're wrong.

3. Revising

  - Have you explained both sources accurately and efficiently, using summary, QUOTATION, or paraphrase?
  - Have you written a strong thesis that applies one source to the other?
  - Have you provided reasons to support your thesis and developed your paragraphs to provide details that show those reasons are solid?
  - Have you used complete and accurate documentation of sources, using the style required by your instructor?

7f.6 Annotated bibliographies

An annotated bibliography is a list of sources that includes, for each one, publishing information, a brief summary, and usually your commentary on the content. Such commentary often addresses how a particular source relates to the other sources in the bibliography (33j).

7f.7 Essay exams

"Essay exam" is a broadly-used term for questions that require you to answer in sentences, usually in a timed situation. Prepare for essay exams by re-reading your class material and by actually doing some writing. Making up a few possible questions is an excellent way of studying, and having yourself answer those practice questions under pressure is good preparation for the real thing. When you receive an essay question, resist the urge to dive right in to writing. Use a margin or scratch paper to jot an informal outline or series of points you want to make. Especially take care to understand the question and respond directly to it. For example, if the question asks you to RESPOND, ANALYZE, SYNTHESIZE, or APPLY, you don't just want to SUMMARIZE. While an essay exam may, rarely, simply invite you to dump information, most of the time it will ask you to perform a very specific task. After you've drafted your answer, save some time to proofread. It's easy to introduce errors when you're writing under pressure.

For more help with your writing, grammar, and research, go to **www.mycomplab.com**

Writing Effectively, Writing with Style

8

Style and Tone in Writing

8a What do style and tone in writing involve?

Style and tone both refer to *how* you say something, in contrast with *what* you're saying. Neither style nor tone are rule bound, the way that grammar is. The sentence structures you shape, from the simple to more complex, contribute to the style of your writing. The words you choose for your sentences create the tone in your sentences. They work in concert. After we discuss how they operate together, we address style and tone separately in this chapter (see 8c and 8d) to differentiate the larger elements of crafting sentences from the smaller elements of skillful word choice.

8b How do style and tone operate in writing?

Style and tone operate together through a combination of the varying levels of formality and personality that you employ. The level of **formality** in writing can be roughly divided into three categories. Formal writing belongs in the structures and language of ceremonies, contracts, policies, or some literary writing. "Formal writing," by the way, doesn't mean dull and drab material. Indeed, lively language always enhances such material. **Informal writing** is casual, colloquial, and sometimes playful, usually found in e-mails, text messages on cell phones, Facebook postings, and certain BLOGS.* Semiformal writing, which sits between these poles, is the style and tone found in academic writing, as well as in much business and public writing. For an audience expecting such communication, its style is clear and efficient, and its tone is reasonable and evenhanded.

Generally, when you write for an audience about whom you know little, a somewhat more formal style and tone is appropriate, though an entirely formal presentation isn't desirable. If informal writings are t-shirts and jeans, and formal writings are tuxedos and evening gowns, then semiformal writings are business-casual attire. Here are examples of writing in the three levels of formality.

> **INFORMAL** It's totally sweet how gas makes stars.
>
> **SEMIFORMAL** Gas clouds slowly transform into stars.

---

*Words printed in SMALL CAPITAL LETTERS are discussed elsewhere in the text and are defined in the Terms Glossary at the back of this book.

FORMAL   The condensations of gas spun their slow gravitational pirouettes, slowly transmogrifying gas cloud into star.
—Carl Sagan, "Starfolk: A Fable"

Personality refers to how much the writer reveals about him- or herself with patterns of sentence structure and choice of words. An intimate style and tone, which treats the reader as a close friend, includes specific personal experiences and opinions. A familiar or polite style and tone includes some experiences or personal thoughts, but only of a kind you might share in a professional relationship with an instructor, supervisor, or colleague. In such writing, the reader can glimpse the writer behind the language, but not as fully as in intimate writing because the emphasis is on the ideas or subject matter. An impersonal style reveals nothing about the writer, so that the content is all that the reader is aware of.

INTIMATE   When our eighth grade teacher assigned Huckleberry Finn by Mark Twain, I got cranky and angry after the first chapter. Why did he lay something so hard on us? I couldn't catch the story or figure out what the dialect was saying.

FAMILIAR/   The next day in class, I was greatly relieved to discover
POLITE   that most other students had run into the same problems as I had reading Huckleberry Finn by Mark Twain.

IMPERSONAL   Our teacher explicated the story line and clarified how to decode the dialect, which enabled the class to appreciate the narrative and its underlying message.

Quick Reference 8.1 lays out the levels of formality and of personality as conveyed by the style and tone you insert into your writing.

Quick Reference 8.1

Major elements that create style and tone in writing

Elements	Levels		
Formality	Informal	Semiformal	Formal
Personality	Intimate	Familiar/Polite	Impersonal

EXERCISE 8.1 Working individually or in a group, describe the style of each of the following paragraphs in terms of formality and personality.

1. I would be willing to bet serious money that right now in your kitchen you have olive oil, garlic, pasta, parmesan cheese, and dried basil (maybe

even fresh basil!). Nothing exotic there, right? They're ingredients we take for granted. But their appearance in our kitchens is a relatively recent phenomenon. Believe me, those big-flavor items did not come over on the Mayflower. It took generations, even centuries, for Americans to expand their culinary horizons to the point where just about everybody cooks Italian and orders Chinese take-out. Heck, the supermarket in my little Connecticut hometown even has a sushi bar.

—Thomas J. Craughwell, "If Only the Pilgrims Had Been Italian"

2. Google has yet to hit upon a strategy that combines the innovation it is known for with an appeal to the self-interest that is the currency of the capital's power brokers. One reason AT&T and Microsoft have succeeded in stoking antitrust interest against Google—quite ironic, given that both companies have been subject to large government antitrust actions—is that they're better versed in the fine points of lobbying. Both companies, for example, hold sway over many lawmakers by frequently reminding them how many employees live in their districts ("jobs" is a metric lawmakers respond to).

—Joshua Green, "Google's Tar Pit"

3. Prices are rising for the black sludge that helps make the world's gears turn. If you think we're talking about oil, think again. Petroleum prices have tumbled from their record highs. No sooner was there relief at the pump, however, than came a squeeze at the pot. That jolt of coffee that a majority of American adults enjoy on a daily basis has gotten more expensive and could go even higher this year. . . .

—New York Times, "Joe Economics"

4. Use Form W-9 only if you are a U.S. person (including a resident alien), to provide your correct TIN to the person requesting it (the requester) and, when applicable, to:
   1. Certify that the TIN you are giving is correct (or you are waiting for a number to be issued),
   2. Certify that you are not subject to backup withholding, or
   3. Claim exemption from backup withholding if you are a U.S. exempt payee.

—Internal Revenue Service, Directions for Form W-9

5. Studies of home-based telework by women yield mixed results regarding the usefulness of telework in facilitating work–life balance. Most research on the social impacts of home-based telework focuses on workers—employees or self-employed—who deliberately choose that alternative work arrangement. Labour force analysts, however, predict an increase in employer-initiated teleworking. As a case study of the workforce of one large, financial-sector firm in Canada, this article considers the conditions of employment of involuntary teleworkers, those required by their employer to work full-time from a home office. In-depth interviews were con-

ducted with a sample of 18 female teleworkers working for the case study firm in a professional occupation.

—Laura C. Johnson, Jean Andrey, and Susan M. Shaw,
"Mr. Dithers Comes to Dinner"

6. I remember vividly the moment that I entered the world of literacy, education, institutional "correctness," and, consequently, identity. I was demonstrating to my older sister how I wrote my name. The memory comes after I had been literally taught how to do it—which strokes of the pencil to use to create the symbols that equate to my name.

—Elise Geraghty, "In the Name of the Father"

8c   How do I write with style?

A well-respected style manual states,

Style, with a capital S, achieves what a rule book never can: it lights the page, draws in readers, earns their delight, makes them gasp or weep, and sometimes captures a place in memory.

—*The New York Times Manual of Style and Usage*

As authors of this handbook, we can report that after seeking to inject the type of style described above into our passages, we always try to distance ourselves from our attempts, so that we can come back another day with a bit less severity or euphoria. Showing our work to each other helps, too.

Writing with style comes more naturally with lots of practice. It rarely shows up on most first drafts. The pleasure of creating a graceful, engaging style in your writing results from experimenting with different structures. And every so often, writers surprise themselves with sentences and passages of enormous power and impact that emerge almost unbidden on the page. Those are magical moments. To write with style, refer to Quick Reference 8.2; as you do, add your own personal hints so that you can make the material your own.

Quick Reference 8.2   ■ ■ ■ ■ ■ ■ ■ ■

How to create good writing style

- Try out different sentence types to maintain readers' interest (see 9a, 9n, 9r).

- Use sentence coordination and subordination to vary the pace (see 9d–9m).

- Vary sentence length to keep your readers' attention (see 9c).

- Experiment with diction or word choice (see 12d, 12e, 12h)

continued >>

> ### Quick Reference 8.2   (continued)
>
> - Use figurative language (see 12c)
> - Employ the gracefulness of parallelism in sentences and larger sections for the pleasure of your readers (see Chapter 10).
> - Be consistent in your level of formality and personality (see 8b)

8d   How do I write with appropriate tone?

Tone in writing involves choosing the right words to deliver your meaning. Tone operates like tone of voice, except that you can't rely on facial expressions and voice intonations to communicate your written message. The language you choose in your writing creates the tone you relay to your readers.

Your choice of words determines the degree to which your readers notice the language itself along with the content that the language is conveying. Well written figurative language (see 12c) can create pleasant surprises for readers. However, if you draw too much attention to your language without communicating a clear message, your writing suffers. Conversely, if you use only simple, one syllable words that create a dull drone, your writing suffers.

Your word choice can result in a wide range of possible tones, some desirable and some not. We list several in Quick Reference 8.3.

> ### Quick Reference 8.3   ∎ ∎ ∎ ∎ ∎ ∎ ∎
>
> #### Some examples of desirable and undesirable tone
>
> | | |
> |---|---|
> | SERIOUS | The advent of space travel supported the predictions of science fiction, especially that of Jules Verne, who wrote in the nineteenth century. |
> | LIGHT OR BREEZY | What a trip to flip through Verne's *From the Earth to the Moon* and find space ships taking off from Tampa, Florida, only 130 miles from today's Cape Canaveral. |
> | SARCASTIC | Some poor slobs probably think Verne is worth worshiping like a god. |
> | MEAN | Verne also made some dumb forecasts. |
> | CONDESCENDING | Although most people struggle to read Jules Verne's sometimes complex books, those who succeed can consider themselves at least reasonably competent readers. |
> | WHINING | Why should Jules Verne be the third most translated writer in the world? He's no big deal. If I put my mind to it, I could write as well as he did. |

Achieving the tone you want in each piece of your writing calls for experimenting with different words with similar meanings. If you consult a thesaurus (which can be a very productive activity), be sure to check the definition of any synonym that's new to you. Lynn once had an excellent student who used the word "profound" instead of "deep," without looking it up in a dictionary. The result was this sentence: "The trenches beneath some parts of that sea were dangerously profound." That misuse ruined an otherwise intelligent passage.

As with style in writing, appropriate tone results from your private trials, rejections, and explorations. Good tone rarely shows up on most first drafts. Quick Reference 8.4 offers you some suggestions for achieving an appropriate tone in your writing. Add your own advice to the list to personalize it.

Quick Reference 8.4   ■ ■ ■ ■ ■ ■ ■

How to use appropriate tone in writing

- Reserve a highly informal tone for conversational writing.
- Use a semiformal level of formality in your academic writing and when you write for supervisors, professionals, and other people you know only from a distance.
- Avoid an overly formal, ceremonious tone.
- Choose a tone that suits your topic and your readers.
- Whatever tone you choose, be consistent in each piece of your writing.

EXERCISE 8-2   Revise each of the sentences to create a very different tone. The sentences in Quick Reference 8.3 provide some examples. For a further challenge, see how many different tones you can create.

1. Many Americans spend much of their leisure time watching professional sports.

2. If you want to waste your money buying organic foods, who am I to stop you?

3. When considering the purchase of clothing in order to possess a serviceable wardrobe, it is imperative to select items in which the color combinations are harmonious and pleasing.

For more help with your writing, grammar, and research,
go to **www.mycomplab.com**

mycomplab

9

Sentence Variety and Style

9a How do sentences affect style?

Sentences affect style through their length (9c), structures like COORDINATION and SUBORDINATION (9k), and types. The main sentence types in English are SIMPLE, COMPOUND, COMPLEX, and COMPOUND-COMPLEX (14q). When any one type dominates a piece of writing, it affects the style, especially if the sentences are also generally the same length. A flurry of short, simple sentences creates a blunt, direct style. Such a style often gains in clarity but loses in interest. A series of long complex or compound-complex sentences creates a lofty, sometimes even stuffy, style. It may achieve sophistication but sacrifice clarity. You can see the difference in the following example, which has two versions of the same piece.

1. Short, simple sentences

   The most worshipped and praised of all ancient sewers was Rome's Cloaca Maxima. It resided within the shrine of the goddess Cloacina. Warriors came here to purge themselves after battle. Young couples purified themselves here before marriage. The lovely Cloacina was an emanation of Venus. Her statue overlooked the imperial city's sewer pipes. The pipes transported 100,000 pounds of ancient *excrementum* [human waste] a day. It was built in the sixth century B.C. by the two Tarquins. It was hailed as one of the three marvels of Rome. The Cloaca became one of the city's great tourist traps. Agrippa rode a boat through it. Nero washed his hands in it.

2. Longer, compound and complex sentences

   The most worshipped and praised of all ancient sewers was Rome's Cloaca Maxima, whose spirit resided within the shrine of the goddess Cloacina, where warriors came to purge themselves after battle and young couples purified themselves before marriage. The lovely Cloacina was an emanation of Venus, and her statue overlooked the imperial city's sewer pipes as they transported 100,000 pounds of ancient *excrementum* [human waste] a day. Built in the sixth century B.C. by the two Tarquins, hailed as one of the three marvels of Rome, the Cloaca became one of the city's great tourist traps. Agrippa rode a boat through it. Nero washed his hands in it.

   —Frederick Kaufman, "Wasteland"

The second version was published in *Harper's Magazine,* which is aimed at a well-educated general AUDIENCE. Notice that even that version ends with two simple sentences. Coming after the longer earlier ones, they offer a refreshing break. In fact, effective and stylistically interesting writing often contains a VARIETY of styles.

9b What are variety and emphasis in writing?

When you write sentences of different lengths and types within a piece of writing, you create **sentence variety**. Working in concert with sentence variety, **emphasis** allows you to add weight to ideas of special importance.

Using techniques of variety and emphasis adds style and clarity to your writing. When readers see variety in your writing, they see you as versatile and in control of language. Usually, the best time to apply the principles of variety and emphasis is while you are REVISING.

9c How do different sentence lengths create variety and emphasis?

To emphasize one idea among many others, you can express it in a sentence noticeably different in length from the sentences surrounding it. In the following example, a four-word sentence between two longer sentences carries the key message of the passage (**boldface** added).

> Today is one of those excellent January partly cloudies in which light chooses an unexpected landscape to trick out in gilt, and then shadow sweeps it away. **You know you're alive.** You take huge steps, trying to feel the planet's roundness arc between your feet.
>
> —Annie Dillard, *Pilgrim at Tinker Creek*

Sometimes a string of short sentences creates impact and emphasis. Yet, at other times, a string of short sentences can be dull to read.

EXERCISE 9-1 The following paragraph is dull because it has only short sentences. Combine some of the sentences to make a paragraph that has a variety of sentence lengths.

> There is a problem. It is widely known as sick-building syndrome. It comes from indoor air pollution. It causes office workers to suffer. They have trouble breathing. They have painful rashes. Their heads ache. Their eyes burn.

Similarly, a string of COMPOUND SENTENCES can be monotonous to read and may fail to communicate relationships among ideas.

EXERCISE 9-2 The following paragraph is dull because it has only compound sentences. Revise it to provide more variety.

> Science fiction writers are often thinkers, **and** they are often dreamers, **and** they let their imaginations wander. Jules Verne was such a writer, **and** he predicted spaceships, **and** he forecast atomic submarines, **but** most people did not believe airplanes were possible.

9d What are coordination and subordination?

Two important sentence structuring methods are **coordination** and **subordination,** which reflect relationships between ideas that you seek to express. Coordination shows the equality of ideas, while subordination shows one idea is more important than others. Using these structures effectively creates variety and emphasis. We explain each of them in sections 9e and 9h, below, but an example will help you see the basic principle:

TWO SENTENCES	The sky turned dark gray. The wind died down.
USING COORDINATION	The sky turned dark gray, **and** the wind died down.
USING SUBORDINATION 1	**As** the sky turned dark gray, the wind died down. [Here, the wind is the focus.]
USING SUBORDINATION 2	**As** the wind died down, the sky turned dark gray. [Here, the sky is the focus.]

9e What is coordination of sentences?

Coordination of sentences is a grammatical strategy to communicate that the ideas in two or more INDEPENDENT CLAUSES are equivalent or balanced. Coordination can produce harmony by bringing related elements together. Whenever you use the technique of coordination of sentences, make sure that it works well with the meaning you want to communicate.

> The sky turned **brighter, and** people emerged happily from buildings.

> The sky turned **brighter;** people emerged happily from buildings.

9f What is the structure of a coordinate sentence?

A **coordinate sentence**, also known as a *compound sentence* (14q), consists of two or more INDEPENDENT CLAUSES joined either by a semicolon or by a comma working in concert with a COORDINATING CONJUNCTION (*and, but, for, or, nor, yet, so*). Here, you can see the pattern for coordination of sentences.

$$\text{Independent clause} \left\{ \begin{array}{l} \text{, and} \\ \text{, but} \\ \text{, for} \\ \text{, or} \\ \text{, nor} \\ \text{, yet} \\ \text{, so} \\ \text{;} \end{array} \right\} \text{independent clause.}$$

9g What meaning does each coordinating conjunction convey?

Each COORDINATING CONJUNCTION has its own meaning. When you choose one, be sure that its meaning accurately expresses the relationship between the equivalent ideas that you want to convey.

- **and** means addition
- **but** and **yet** mean contrast
- **for** means reason or choice
- **or** means choice
- **nor** means negative choice
- **so** means result or effect

🛈 **Alert:** Always use a comma before a coordinating conjunction that joins two INDEPENDENT CLAUSES (24b). ●

9h How can I use coordination effectively?

COORDINATION is effective when each INDEPENDENT CLAUSE is related or equivalent. If they aren't, the result looks like a coordinated sentence, but the ideas are unrelated.

> **NO** Computers came into common use in the 1970s, and they sometimes make costly errors. [The statement in each independent clause is true, but the ideas are not related or equivalent.]

> **YES** Computers came into common use in the 1970s, and now they are indispensable business tools.

Coordination is also most effective when it's not overused. Simply stringing sentences together with COORDINATING CONJUNCTIONS makes relationships among ideas unclear—and the resulting sentence lacks style.

> **NO**   Dinosaurs could have disappeared for many reasons, **and** one theory holds that a sudden shower of meteors and asteroids hit the earth, **so** the impact created a huge dust cloud that caused a false winter. The winter lasted for years, **and** the dinosaurs died.

> **YES**   Dinosaurs could have disappeared for many reasons. One theory holds that a sudden shower of meteors and asteroids hit the earth. The impact created a huge dust cloud that caused a false winter. The winter lasted for years, killing the dinosaurs.

EXERCISE 9-3   Working individually or with a group, revise these sentences to eliminate illogical or overused coordination. If you think a sentence needs no revision, explain why. For help, consult sections 9e through 9h.

EXAMPLE   Fencing, once a form of combat, has become a competitive sport worldwide, and today's fencers disapprove of those who identify fencing with fighting.

Fencing, once a form of combat, has become a competitive sport worldwide, *but* today's fencers disapprove of those who identify fencing with fighting.

1. As depicted in movies, fencing sometimes appears to be reckless swordplay, and fencing requires precision, coordination, and strategy.

2. In the 1800s, fencing became very popular, and it was one of the few sports included in the first modern Olympic Games in 1896, and fencing has been part of the Olympics ever since.

3. Fencing equipment includes a mask, a padded jacket, a glove, and one of three weapons—a foil, épée, or saber—and a fencer's technique and targets differ depending on the weapon used and the fencer's experience.

4. Generally, a fencer specializes in one of the three weapons, but some competitors are equally skilled with all three.

5. The object of fencing is to be the first to touch the opponent five times, and a "president," who is sometimes assisted by a number of judges, officiates at competitions.

9i   What is subordination in sentences?

Subordination is a grammatical strategy to communicate that one idea in a sentence is more important than another idea in the same sentence. To use subordination, you place the more important idea in an INDEPENDENT CLAUSE and the less important—the subordinate—idea in a DEPENDENT CLAUSE. The information you choose to subordinate depends on the meaning you want to deliver.

INDEPENDENT CLAUSE	DEPENDENT

Two cowboys fought a dangerous Colorado snowstorm **while they**

CLAUSE	DEPENDENT CLAUSE

were looking for cattle. **When they came to a canyon,**

INDEPENDENT CLAUSE

they saw outlines of buildings through the blizzard.

To illustrate the difference in writing style when you use subordination, here's a passage with the same message as the example above, but without subordination.

Two cowboys fought a dangerous Colorado snowstorm. They were looking for cattle. They came to a canyon. They saw outlines of buildings through the blizzard.

9j What is the structure of a subordinate sentence?

A subordinate sentence starts the DEPENDENT CLAUSE with either a SUBORDINATING CONJUNCTION or a RELATIVE PRONOUN.

If they are very lucky, the passengers may glimpse dolphins breaking water playfully near the ship.

—Elizabeth Gray, student

Pandas are solitary animals, **which** means they are difficult to protect from extinction.

—Jose Santos, student

For patterns of subordination with dependent clauses, see 9f. Dependent clauses are of two types: ADVERB CLAUSES and ADJECTIVE CLAUSES. An adverb clause starts with a subordinating conjunction. An adjective clause starts with a relative pronoun.

Quick Reference 9.1 ■ ■ ■ ■ ■ ■ ■

Subordination

SENTENCES WITH ADVERB CLAUSES

- **Adverb clause,** independent clause.

    After the sky grew dark, the wind died suddenly.

- Independent clause, **adverb clause.**

    Birds stopped singing, **as they do during an eclipse.**

continued >>

Quick Reference 9.1   (continued)

- Independent clause **adverb clause.**

    The stores closed **before the storm began.**

SENTENCES WITH ADJECTIVE CLAUSES

- Independent clause **restrictive (essential)* adjective clause.**

    Weather forecasts warned of a storm **that might bring a thirty-inch snowfall.**

- Independent clause, **nonrestrictive (nonessential)* adjective clause.**

    Spring is the season for tornadoes, **which may have wind speeds over 220 miles an hour.**

- Beginning of independent clause **restrictive (essential)* adjective clause** end of independent clause.

    Anyone **who lives through a tornado** remembers its power.

- Beginning of independent clause, **nonrestrictive (nonessential)* adjective clause,** end of independent clause.

    The sky, **which had been clear,** turned greenish black.

*For an explanation of RESTRICTIVE and NONRESTRICTIVE ELEMENTS, see section 24f.

9k   What meaning does each subordinating conjunction convey?

Each SUBORDINATING CONJUNCTION has its own meaning. When you choose one, be sure that its meaning accurately expresses the relationship between the ideas that you want to convey. Quick Reference 9.2 lists subordinating conjunctions according to their different meanings.

Quick Reference 9.2   ■ ■ ■ ■ ■ ■ ■

Subordinating conjunctions and their meanings

TIME
after, before, once, since, until, when, whenever, while

After you have handed in your report, you cannot revise it.

REASON OR CAUSE
as, because, since

Because you have handed in your report, you cannot revise it.

continued >>

Quick Reference 9.2 (continued)

PURPOSE OR RESULT
in order that, so that, that

I want to read your report **so that** I can evaluate it.

CONDITION
even if, if, provided that, unless

Unless you have handed in your report, you can revise it.

CONTRAST
although, even though, though, whereas, while

Although you have handed in your report, you can ask to revise it.

CHOICE
than, whether

You took more time to revise **than** I did before the lab report deadline.

PLACE OR LOCATION
where, wherever

Wherever you say, I'll come to hand in my report.

EXERCISE 9-4 Working individually or with a group, combine each pair of sentences, using an adverb clause to subordinate one idea. Then, revise each sentence so that the adverb clause becomes the independent clause. For help, see sections 9f through 9h, especially Quick Reference 9.1.

EXAMPLE The US Mint produces new coins. The US Bureau of Engraving and Printing makes $1, $5, $10, $20, $50, and $100 bills.

    a. While the US Mint produces new coins, the US Bureau of Engraving and Printing makes $1, $5, $10, $20, $50, and $100 bills.

    b. While the US Bureau of Engraving and Printing makes $1, $5, $10, $20, $50, and $100 bills, the US Mint produces new coins.

1. The US Mint can produce more than 50 million coins a day. The US Bureau of Engraving and Printing can produce 20 million notes a day.

2. The Federal Reserve Banks are responsible for both destroying old money and ordering new coins and notes. They must keep the right amount of money in circulation.

3. Coins can stay in circulation for decades. People let them accumulate in jars and drawers in their homes.

4. A $1 bill lasts about fifteen to eighteen months. It reaches its average life span.

5. The US Federal Reserve Banks destroy dirty, worn, and torn bills. The Federal Reserve Banks are destroying more than $40 billion worth of money a year.

EXERCISE 9-5   Working individually or with a group, combine each pair of sentences, using an adjective clause to subordinate one idea to the other. Then, revise each sentence so that the adjective clause becomes the independent clause. Use the relative pronoun given in parentheses. For help, consult sections 9i through 9k, especially Quick Reference 9.1.

EXAMPLE   Aristides was an ancient Greek politician famous for his honesty and judgment. He was known as Aristides the Just. (who)

    a. Aristides, *who* was an ancient Greek politician famous for his honesty and judgment, was known as Aristides the Just.

    b. Aristides, *who* was known as Aristides the Just, was an ancient Greek politician famous for his honesty and judgment.

1. An ancient Greek law allowed voters to banish politicians from their city. It asked citizens to write the name of an unpopular politician on their ballots. (that)

2. A voter was filling out a ballot when Aristides the Just walked by. The voter needed help in spelling *Aristides*. (who)

3. Aristides knew the voter did not recognize him. He asked why the voter wanted to banish that particular politician. (who)

4. The voter said he resented hearing someone called "the Just" all the time. He handed Aristides his ballot. (who)

5. Aristides' reaction demonstrated that the nickname "the Just" was well deserved. His reaction was to write his own name on the voter's ballot even though that person's vote helped banish Aristides. (which)

91   How can I use subordination effectively?

To be effective, a SUBORDINATING CONJUNCTION must communicate a sensible relationship between the INDEPENDENT CLAUSE and the DEPENDENT CLAUSE. See Quick Reference 9.2 for a list of subordinating conjunctions and their different meanings.

    NO   **Because** Beethoven was deaf when he wrote them, his final symphonies were masterpieces. [*Because* is illogical here; it says the masterpieces resulted from the deafness.]

YES   **Although** Beethoven was deaf when he wrote them, his final symphonies were masterpieces. [*Although* is logical here; it says Beethoven wrote masterpieces in spite of his being deaf.]

Subordination is also most effective when you avoid overusing it and crowding too many ideas together in one sentence. This causes readers to lose track of the message. Whenever you write a sentence with two or more dependent clauses, check that your message is clear. If it isn't, you've probably overused subordination.

NO   A new technique for eye surgery, **which is supposed to correct nearsightedness, which previously could be corrected only by glasses,** has been developed, **although many eye doctors do not approve of the new technique because it can create unstable vision, which includes intense glare from headlights on cars and many other light sources.** [The base sentence *A new technique for eye surgery has been developed* is crowded with five dependent clauses attached to it.]

YES   A new technique for eye surgery, **which is supposed to correct nearsightedness,** has been developed. Previously, only glasses could correct nearsightedness. Many doctors do not approve of the new technique **because it can create unstable vision.** The problems include intense glare from car headlights and many other sources of light. [In this revision, one long sentence has been broken into four sentences, which makes the material easier to read and the relationships among ideas clearer. Two dependent clauses remain, which balance well with the other sentence constructions. Some words have been moved to new positions.]

ESOL Tip: If your instructor, manager, or peer reviewers advise that your sentences are too long and complex, limit the number of words in each sentence. Many ESOL instructors recommend that you revise any sentence that contains more than three independent and dependent clauses in any combination. ●

EXERCISE 9-6   Working individually or with a group, correct illogical or excessive subordination in this paragraph. As you revise according to the message you want to deliver, use some dependent clauses as well as some short sentences. (Also, if you wish, apply the principles of coordination discussed in sections 9d through 9g.) For help, consult 9k.

Although many people in the United States consider the hot dog an American invention, it actually originated in Germany in 1852 when butchers in Frankfurt, Germany, stuffed meat into a long casing, which, in honor of the town, they called a "frankfurter." Because one butcher noticed that the frankfurter resembled the shape of his dog, a dachshund, he decided to name the meat roll a "dachshund sausage," a name which caught on in Germany. When Germans brought dachshund sausages to the United States, peddlers sold them on the streets, although the dachshund sausages were so hot that people often burned their fingers because they had trouble holding the meat. When one clever peddler put the sausage in a bun, a *New York Times* cartoonist decided to draw a picture of hot dachshund sausages in buns, although he called them "hot dogs" because he didn't know how to spell *dachshund*.

9m How can I effectively use coordination and subordination together?

Your writing style improves when you use a logical and pleasing variety of SENTENCE TYPES, utilizing COORDINATION and SUBORDINATION to improve the flow of ideas. Here's a paragraph that demonstrates a good balance in the use of coordination and subordination.

> When I was growing up, I lived on a farm just across the field from my grandmother. My parents were busy trying to raise six children and to establish their struggling dairy farm. It was nice to have Grandma so close. While my parents were providing the necessities of life, my patient grandmother gave her time to her shy, young granddaughter. I always enjoyed going with Grandma and collecting the eggs that her chickens had just laid. Usually, she knew which chickens would peck, and she was careful to let me gather the eggs from the less hostile ones.
>
> —Patricia Mapes, student

When you use both coordination and subordination, never use both a COORDINATE CONJUNCTION and a SUBORDINATE CONJUNCTION to express one relationship in one sentence.

NO **Although** the story was well written, **but** it was too illogical.
[The subordinating conjunction *although* expresses the contrast, so also using *but* is incorrect.]

YES **Although** the story was well written, it was too illogical.

YES The story was well written, **but** it was too illogical.

EXERCISE 9-7 Working individually or in a group, use subordination and coordination to combine these sets of short, choppy sentences. For help, consult all sections of this chapter.

EXAMPLE   Owls cannot digest the bones and fur of the mice and birds they
eat. They cough up a furry pellet every day.

Because owls cannot digest the bones and fur of the mice and
birds they eat, they cough up a furry pellet every day.

1. Owl pellets are a rich teaching tool in biology classrooms around the country. The pellets provide an alternative to dissecting frogs and other animals.
2. Inside the pellet are the remains of the owl's nightly meal. They include
   beautifully cleaned hummingbird skulls, rat skeletons, and lots of bird
   feathers.
3. The owl-pellet market has been cornered by companies in New York, California, and Washington. These companies distribute pellets to thousands
   of biology classrooms all over the world.
4. Company workers scour barns and the ground under trees where owls
   nest to pick up the pellets. The pellets sell for $1 each.
5. The owl-pellet business may have a short future. The rural areas of the
   United States are vanishing. Old barns are being bulldozed. All the barns
   are torn down. The owls will be gone, too.

9n   How do occasional questions, commands, or exclamations create variety and emphasis?

The majority of sentences in English are DECLARATIVE—they tell something by
making a statement. Declarative sentences offer an almost infinite variety of
structures and patterns. For variety and emphasis, you might want to use three
alternative types of sentences occasionally.

A sentence that asks a question is called INTERROGATIVE. Occasional questions, placed appropriately, tend to involve readers. A sentence that issues a
mild or strong command is called IMPERATIVE. Occasional mild commands,
appropriately used, gently urge a reader to think along with you. A sentence that
makes an exclamation is called EXCLAMATORY. An occasional exclamatory sentence, appropriate to the context, can enliven writing, but you should use this
sentence type only rarely in ACADEMIC WRITING.

Alert: A declarative statement ends with a period (Chapter 23)—or semicolon (Chapter 25) or colon (Chapter 26). A mild command ends with a period. A strong command and an exclamation end with an exclamation point
(Chapter 23). ●

Here's a paragraph with declarative, interrogative, and imperative sentences.

Imagine what people ate during the winter as little as seventy-five years
ago. They ate food that was local, long-lasting, and dull, like acorn squash,

turnips, and cabbage. Walk into an American supermarket in February and the world lies before you: grapes, melons, artichokes, fennel, lettuce, peppers, pistachios, dates, even strawberries, to say nothing of ice cream. Have you ever considered what a triumph of civilization it is to be able to buy a pound of chicken livers? If you lived on a farm and had to kill a chicken when you wanted to eat one, you wouldn't ever accumulate a pound of chicken livers.

—Phyllis Rose, "Shopping and Other Spiritual
Adventures in America Today"

9o   What are cumulative and periodic sentences?

The **cumulative sentence** is the most common sentence structure in English. Its name reflects the way information accumulates in the sentence until it reaches a period. Its structure starts with a SUBJECT and VERB and continues with modifiers. Another term for a cumulative sentence is *loose sentence* because it lacks a tightly planned structure.

For greater impact, you might occasionally use a **periodic sentence**, also called a *climactic sentence,* which reserves the main idea for the end of the sentence. This structure tends to draw in the reader as it moves toward the period. If overused, however, periodic sentences lose their punch.

> CUMULATIVE   A car hit a shoulder and turned over at midnight last night on the road from Las Vegas to Death Valley Junction.
>
> PERIODIC   At midnight last night, on the road from Las Vegas to Death Valley Junction, a car hit a shoulder and turned over.
> —Joan Didion, "On Morality"

You can build both cumulative and periodic sentences to dramatic—and sometimes excessive—lengths.

EXAMPLE:
How cumulative sentences can grow
1. The downtown bustled with new construction.
2. **The downtown bustled with new construction,** as buildings shot up everywhere, transforming the skyline.
3. **The downtown bustled with new constructio**n, as buildings shot up everywhere, each a mixture of glass and steel, in colors from rust red to ice blue, transforming the skyline from a shy set of bumps to a bold display of mountains

EXAMPLE:
How periodic sentences can grow
1. Marla accepted the job offer.

2. With some reservations about the salary offer and location, **Marla accepted the job offer.**

3. After a day of agonizing and a night without sleep, still having some reservations about the salary offer and location, especially with the company being in an unappealing city more than 400 miles from her fiancé, **Marla accepted the job offer.**

9p How can modifiers create variety and emphasis?

MODIFIERS can expand sentences to add richness to your writing and create a pleasing mixture of variety and emphasis. The longer cumulative and periodic sentence examples in section 9o illustrate the use of modifiers. Your choice of where to place modifiers to expand your sentences depends on the focus you want each sentence to communicate, either on its own or in concert with its surrounding sentences. Be careful where you place modifiers because you don't want to introduce the error known as a MISPLACED MODIFIER.

NO (MISPLACED MODIFIER)	A huge, hairy, grunting thing, I agreed that the bull was scary.
YES	A huge, hairy, grunting thing, the bull was scary, I agreed.

In the No example, it sounds like the writer, I, was huge, hairy, and grunting!

BASIC SENTENCE	The river rose.
ADJECTIVE	The **swollen** river rose.
ADVERB	The river rose **dangerously.**
PREPOSITIONAL PHRASE	The river rose **above its banks.**
PARTICIPIAL PHRASE	**Swelled by melting snow,** the river rose.
ABSOLUTE PHRASE	**Uprooted trees swirling away in the current,** the river rose.
ADVERB CLAUSE	**Because the snows had been heavy that winter,** the river rose.
ADJECTIVE CLAUSE	The river, **which runs through vital farmland,** rose.

EXERCISE 9-8   Working individually or with a group, expand each sentence by adding each kind of modifier illustrated in section 9p.

1. We bought a house.
2. The roof leaked.
3. I remodeled the kitchen.
4. Neighbors brought food.
5. Everyone enjoyed the barbeque.

9q How does repetition affect style?

You can repeat one or more words that express a main idea when your message is suitable. This technique creates a rhythm that focuses attention on the main idea. PARALLELISM (Chapter 10) is another kind of repetition that focuses on grammatical structures as well as words. Here's an example that uses deliberate repetition along with a variety of sentence lengths to deliver its meaning.

> Coal is **black** and it warms your house and cooks your food. The night is **black,** which has a moon, and a million stars, and is beautiful. Sleep is **black,** which gives you rest, so you wake up feeling **good.** I am **black.** I feel very **good** this evening.
>
> —Langston Hughes, "That Word *Black*"

At the same time, don't confuse deliberate repetition with a lack of vocabulary variety.

NO An insurance agent can be an excellent adviser when you want to buy a car. An insurance agent has complete records on most cars. An insurance agent knows which car models are prone to have accidents. An insurance agent can tell you which car models are the most expensive to repair if they are in a collision. An insurance agent can tell you which models are most likely to be stolen. [Although only a few synonyms exist for *insurance agent, car,* and *model,* some do and should be used. Also, the sentence structure here lacks variety.]

YES If you are thinking of buying a new car, an insurance agent, who usually has complete records on most cars, can be an excellent adviser. Any professional insurance broker knows which automobile models are prone to have accidents. Did you know that some cars suffer more damage than others in a collision? If you want to know which vehicles crumple more than others and which are the most expensive to repair, ask an insurance agent. Similarly, some car models are more likely to be stolen, so find out from the person who specializes in dealing with car insurance claims.

9r How else can I create variety and emphasis?

CHANGING WORD ORDER

Standard word order in English places the SUBJECT before the VERB.

> The **mayor** *walked* into the room. [*Mayor,* the subject, comes before the verb *walked.*]

Any variation from standard word order creates emphasis. For example, **inverted word order** places the verb before the subject.

Into the room ***walked*** the **mayor**. [Mayor, the subject, comes after the verb walked.]

CHANGING A SENTENCE'S SUBJECT

The subject of a sentence establishes the focus for that sentence. To create the emphasis you want, you can vary each sentence's subject. All of the sample sentences below express the same information, but the focus changes in each according to the subject (and its corresponding verb).

Our study *showed* that 25 percent of college students' time is spent eating or sleeping. [Focus is on the study.]

College students *eat or sleep* 25 percent of the time, according to our study. [Focus is on the students.]

Eating or sleeping *occupies* 25 percent of college students' time, according to our study. [Focus is on eating and sleeping.]

Twenty-five percent of college students' time *is spent* eating or sleeping, according to our study. [Focus is on the percentage of time.]

EXERCISE 9-9   Working individually or with a group, revise the sentences in each paragraph to change the passage's style. For help, consult the advice in all sections of this chapter.

1.   Thirst is the body's way of surviving. Every cell in the body needs water. People can die by losing as little as 15 to 20 percent of their water requirements. Blood contains 83 percent water. Blood provides indispensable nutrients for the cells. Blood carries water to the cells. Blood carries waste away from the cells. Insufficient water means cells cannot be fueled or cleaned. The body becomes sluggish. The body can survive eleven days without water. Bodily functions are seriously disrupted by a lack of water for more than one day. The body loses water. The blood thickens. The heart must pump harder. Thickened blood is harder to pump through the heart. Some drinks replace the body's need for fluids. Alcohol or caffeine in drinks leads to dehydration. People know they should drink water often. They can become moderately dehydrated before they even begin to develop a thirst.

2.   June is the wet season in Ghana. Here in Accra, the capital, the morning rain has ceased. The sun heats the humid air. Pillars of black smoke begin to rise above the vast Agbobgloshie Market. I follow one plume toward its source. I pass lettuce and plantain vendors. I pass stalls

of used tires. I walk through a clanging scrap market. In the market hunched men bash on old alternators and engine blocks.

—Based on a paragraph by Chris Carroll
in "High Tech Trash"

3.   Because of the development of new economies around the world, with resulting demands for new construction and goods, especially in places like China, there is a high demand for steel, and a new breed of American entrepreneurs is making money in meeting this opportunity. For much of industrial history, steel was made from iron ore and coke, a process that resulted in what might be called "new steel." However, it has now become even more profitable to make recycled steel, melting down junk and recasting it, a process made possible because steel, unlike paper and plastic, can be recycled indefinitely. Because the process saves energy and helps the environment by saving on the amount of ore that has to be mined, manufacturing recycled steel has benefits beyond profitability.

For more help with your
writing, grammar, and research,
go to **www.mycomplab.com**

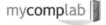

10

Parallelism

10a What is parallelism?

When you write words, PHRASES, or CLAUSES within a sentence to match in their grammatical forms, the result is **parallelism**. Parallelism serves to emphasize information or ideas in writing. The technique relates to the concept of parallel lines in geometry, lines that run alongside each other and never meet.

The deer often come to eat their grain, the wolves to destroy their sheep, the bears to kill their hogs, and the foxes to catch their poultry. [The message of the multiple, accumulating assaults is echoed by the parallel structures.]

—J. Hector St. Jean de Crèvecoeur, *Letters from an American Farmer*

You gain several advantages in using parallel structures:

- You can express ideas of equal weight in your writing.
- You can emphasize important information or ideas.
- You can add rhythm and grace to your writing style.

Many writers attend to parallelism when they are REVISING. If you think while you're DRAFTING that your parallelism is faulty or that you can enhance your writing style by using parallelism, underline or highlight the material and keep moving forward. When you revise, you can return to the places you've marked.

A **balanced sentence** is a type of parallelism in which contrasting content is delivered. The two parallel structures are usually, but not always, INDEPENDENT CLAUSES. A balanced sentence uses COORDINATION. The two coordinate structures are characterized by opposites in meaning, sometimes with one structure cast in the negative.

> By night, the litter and desperation disappeared as the city's glittering lights came on; by day, the filth and despair reappeared as the sun rose.
>
> —Jennifer Kirk, student

Alert: Authorities differ about using a comma, a semicolon, or nothing between the parts of a short balanced sentence. In ACADEMIC WRITING, to avoid appearing to make the error of a COMMA SPLICE, use a semicolon (or revise in some other way), as in the following sentence.

Mosquitoes don't bite; they stab. ●

10b How do words, phrases, and clauses work in parallel form?

When you put words, PHRASES, and CLAUSES into parallel form, you enhance your writing style with balance and grace.

PARALLEL WORDS	Recommended exercise includes running, swimming, and cycling.
PARALLEL PHRASES	Exercise helps people maintain healthy bodies and handle mental pressures.

| PARALLEL CLAUSES | Many people exercise because they want to look healthy, because they need to increase stamina, and because they hope to live longer. |

10c How does parallelism deliver impact?

Parallel structures serve to emphasize the meaning that sentences deliver. Deliberate, rhythmic repetition of parallel forms creates an effect of balance, reinforcing the impact of a message.

> Go back to Mississippi, go back to Alabama, go back to South Carolina, go back to Georgia, go back to Louisiana, go back to the slums and ghettos of our northern cities, knowing that somehow this situation can and will be changed.
>
> —Martin Luther King Jr., "I Have a Dream"

If King had not used PARALLELISM, his message would have made less of an impact on his listeners. His structures reinforce the power of his message. A sentence without parallelism could have carried his message, but with far less effect: *Return to your homes in Mississippi, Alabama, South Carolina, Georgia, Louisiana, or the northern cities, and know that the situation will be changed.*

Here's a longer passage in which parallel structures, concepts, and rhythms operate. Together, they echo the intensity of the writer's message.

> You ask me what is **poverty?** Listen to me. Here I am, dirty, **smelly,** and with no "proper" underwear on and with the stench of my rotting teeth near you. I will tell you. Listen to me. Listen without pity. I cannot use your pity. Listen with understanding. Put yourself in my dirty, worn-out, ill-fitting shoes, and hear me.
>
> **Poverty** is getting up every morning from a dirt- and illness-stained mattress. The sheets have long since been used for diapers. **Poverty** is living in a **smell** that never leaves. This is a **smell** of urine, sour milk, and spoiling food sometimes joined with the strong **smell** of long-cooked onions. Onions are cheap. If you have **smelled** this **smell,** you did not know how it came. It is **the smell** of the outdoor privy. It is **the smell** of young children who cannot walk the long dark way in the night. It is **the smell** of the mattresses where years of "accidents" have happened. It is **the smell** of the milk that has gone sour because the refrigerator long has not worked, and it costs money to get it fixed. It is **the smell** of rotting garbage. I could bury it, but where is the shovel? Shovels cost money.
>
> —Jo Goodwin Parker, "What Is Poverty?"

EXERCISE 10-1 Working individually or with a group, highlight all parallel elements of the Jo Goodwin Parker passage above in addition to those shown in boldface.

10d How can I avoid faulty parallelism?

Faulty parallelism usually results when you join nonmatching grammatical forms.

PARALLELISM WITH COORDINATING CONJUNCTIONS

The coordinating conjunctions are *and, but, for, or, nor, yet,* and *so.* To avoid faulty parallelism, write the words that accompany coordinating conjunctions in matching grammatical forms.

> NO   Love *and* **being married** go together.
>
> YES   **Love *and* marriage** go together.
>
> YES   **Being in love *and* being married** go together.

PARALLELISM WITH CORRELATIVE CONJUNCTIONS

Correlative conjunctions are paired words such as *not only . . . but (also), either . . . or,* and *both . . . and.* To avoid faulty parallelism, write the words joined by correlative conjunctions in matching grammatical forms.

> NO   Differing expectations for marriage *not only* **can lead to disappointment** *but also* **makes the couple angry.**
>
> YES   Differing expectations for marriage *not only* **can lead to disappointment** *but also* **can make the couple angry.**

PARALLELISM WITH *THAN* AND *AS*

To avoid faulty parallelism when you use *than* and *as* for comparisons, write the elements of comparison in matching grammatical forms.

> NO   **Having a solid marriage** can be more satisfying *than* **the acquisition of wealth.**
>
> YES   **Having a solid marriage** can be more satisfying *than* **acquiring wealth.**
>
> YES   **A solid marriage** can be more satisfying *than* **wealth.**

PARALLELISM WITH FUNCTION WORDS

Function words include ARTICLES (*the, a, an*); the *to* of the INFINITIVE (*to* love); PREPOSITIONS (for example, *of, in, about*); and sometimes RELATIVE PRONOUNS.

When you write a series of parallel structures, be consistent in the second and successive structures about either repeating or omitting a function word. Generally, repeat function words only if you think that the repetition clarifies your meaning or highlights the parallelism that you intend.

> NO **To assign** unanswered letters their proper weight, **free** us from the expectations of others, **to give** us back to ourselves—here lies the great, the singular power of self-respect.

> YES **To assign** unanswered letters their proper weight, **to free** us from the expectations of others, **to give** us back to ourselves—here lies the great, the singular power of self-respect.
> —Joan Didion, "On Self-Respect"

I have in my own life a precious friend, a woman of 65 **who has** lived very hard, **who is** wise, **who listens** well, **who has been** where I am and can help me understand it, and **who represents** not only an ultimate ideal mother to me but also the person I'd like to be when I grow up.

> —Judith Viorst, "Friends, Good Friends—and Such Good Friends"

We looked into the bus, which **was** painted blue with orange daisies, **had** picnic benches instead of seats, and **showed** yellow curtains billowing out its windows.

> —Kerrie Falk, student

EXERCISE 10-2   Working individually or with a group, revise these sentences by putting appropriate information in parallel structures. For help, consult sections 10a through 10e.

EXAMPLE   Difficult bosses affect not only their employees' performances but their private lives are affected as well.

Difficult bosses affect not only their employees' performances *but their private lives as well.*

1. According to the psychologist Harry Levinson, the five main types of bad boss are the workaholic, the kind of person you would describe as bullying, a person who communicates badly, the jellyfish type, and someone who insists on perfection.

2. As a way of getting ahead, to keep their self-respect, and for survival purposes, wise employees handle problem bosses with a variety of strategies.

3. To cope with a bad-tempered employer, workers can both stand up for themselves and reasoning with a bullying boss.

4. Often, bad bosses communicate poorly or fail to calculate the impact of their personality on others; being a careful listener and sensitivity to others' responses are qualities that good bosses possess.

5. Employees who take the trouble to understand what makes their bosses tick, engage in some self-analysis, and staying flexible are better prepared to cope with a difficult job environment than suffering in silence like some employees.

EXERCISE 10-3 Working individually or with a group, combine the sentences in each numbered item, using techniques of parallelism. For help, consult sections 10a through 10e.

EXAMPLE College scholarships are awarded not only for academic and athletic ability, but there are also scholarships that recognize unusual talents. Other scholarships even award accidents of birth, like left-handedness.

College scholarships are awarded not only for academic and athletic ability *but also for unusual talents and even for accidents of birth, like left-handedness.*

1. A married couple met at Juniata College in Huntingdon, Pennsylvania. They are both left-handed, and they have set up a scholarship for needy left-handed students attending Juniata.

2. Writers who specialize in humor bankroll a student humor writer at the University of Southern California in Los Angeles. A horse-racing association sponsors a student sportswriter. The student must attend Vanderbilt University in Nashville, Tennessee.

3. The Rochester Institute of Technology in New York State chose 150 students born on June 12, 1979. Each one received a grant of $1,500 per year. These awards were given to select students to honor the school's 150th anniversary, which was celebrated on June 12, 1979.

4. The College of Wooster in Ohio grants generous scholarships to students if they play the bagpipes, a musical instrument native to Scotland. Students playing the traditional Scottish drums and those who excel in Scottish folk dancing also qualify.

5. In return for their scholarships, Wooster's bagpipers must pipe for the school's football team. The terms of the scholarships also require the drummers to drum for the team. The dancers have to cheer the athletes from the sidelines.

EXERCISE 10-4 Working individually or with a group, underline the parallel elements in these three passages. Next, imitate the parallelism in the examples, using a different topic of your choice for each.

A. Our earth is but a small star in a great universe. Yet of it we can make, if we choose, a planet unvexed by war, untroubled by hunger or fear, undivided by senseless distinctions of race, color, or theory.

—Stephen Vincent Benét

B. Some would recover [from polio] almost entirely. Some would die. Some would come through unable to move their legs, or unable to move arms and legs; some could move nothing but an arm, or nothing but a few fingers and their eyes. Some would leave the hospital with a cane, some with crutches, crutches and steel leg braces, or in wheelchairs—white-faced, shrunken, with frightened eyes, light blankets over their legs. Some would remain in an iron lung—a great, eighteen-hundred-pound, casket-like contraption, like the one in which the woman in the magic show (her head and feet sticking out of either end) is sawed in half.

—Charles L. Mee Jr., "The Summer Before Salk"

C. But we always knew that hope is not blind optimism. It's not ignoring the enormity of the task ahead or the roadblocks that stand in our path. It's not sitting on the sidelines or shirking from a fight. Hope is that thing inside us that insists, despite all evidence to the contrary, that something better awaits us if we have the courage to reach for it, and to work for it, and to fight for it. . . .

Hope is what led a band of colonists to rise up against an empire; what led the greatest of generations to free a continent and heal a nation; what led young women and young men to sit at lunch counters and brave fire hoses and march through Selma and Montgomery for freedom's cause.

Hope is what led me here today—with a father from Kenya; a mother from Kansas; and a story that could only happen in the United States of America. Hope is the bedrock of this nation; the belief that our destiny will not be written for us, but by us; by all those men and women who are not content to settle for the world as it is; who have the courage to remake the world as it should be.

—Barack Obama

10e How does parallelism work in outlines and lists?

All items in formal OUTLINES and lists must be parallel in grammar and structure. (For more about outline format and outline development, see section 2f.)

OUTLINES

NO   Reducing Traffic Fatalities

I. Stricter laws
   A. Top speed should be 55 mph on highways.
   B. Higher fines
   C. Requiring jail sentences for repeat offenders
II. The use of safety devices should be mandated by law.

YES   Reducing Traffic Fatalities

    I. Passing stricter speed laws
      A. Making 55 mph the top speed on highways
      B. Raising fines for speeding
      C. Requiring jail sentences for repeat offenders
    II. Mandating by law the use of safety devices

LISTS

NO   Workaholics share these characteristics:
    1. They are intense and driven.
    2. Strong self-doubters
    3. Labor is preferred to leisure by workaholics.

YES   Workaholics share these characteristics:
    1. They are intense and driven.
    2. They have strong self-doubts.
    3. They prefer labor to leisure.

EXERCISE 10-5   Working individually or with a group, revise this outline so that all lines are complete sentences in parallel form. For help, consult sections 2f and 10e.

Improving Health

  I. Exercise
    A. Aerobics
    B. Stretching and strength training
    C. Vary routine
  II. Better Eating Habits
    A. Healthy food
    B. Eat less
    C. Eat more often

11

Conciseness

11a What is conciseness?

Conciseness requires you to craft sentences that are direct and to the point. Its opposite, **wordiness**, means you are filling sentences with empty words and phrases that increase the word count but contribute nothing to meaning. Wordy writing is padded with deadwood, forcing readers to clear away the branches and overgrowth—an annoying waste of time that implies the writer isn't skilled. Usually, the best time to work on making your writing more concise is while you're REVISING.

WORDY ~~As a matter of fact,~~ [T]he [local] television station ~~which is situated in the local area~~ wins ~~a great~~ many awards ~~in the final analysis~~ because of its ~~type of~~ coverage of ~~all kinds of~~ controversial issues.

CONCISE The local television station wins many awards for its coverage of controversial issues.

11b What common expressions are not concise?

Many common expressions we use in informal speech are not concise. Quick Reference 11.1 lists some and shows you how to eliminate them.

Quick Reference 11.1

Cutting unnecessary words and phrases

Empty Word or Phrase	Wordy Example Revised
as a matter of fact	Many marriages~~, as a matter of fact,~~ end in divorce.

continued >>

Quick Reference 11.1   (continued)

Empty Word or Phrase	Wordy Example Revised
at the present time	The revised proposal for outdoor lighting angers many villagers ~~at the present time.~~ *now*
because of the fact that, in light of the fact that, due to the fact that	Because ~~of the fact that~~ the museum has a special exhibit, it stays open late.
by means of	We traveled by ~~means of a~~ car.
factor	The project's final cost was ~~the~~ essential ~~factor~~ to consider.
for the purpose of	Work crews arrived ~~for the purpose of~~ fixing the potholes. *to*
have a tendency to	The team ~~has a tendency~~ to lose home games. *tends*
in a very real sense	~~In a very real sense,~~ all firefighters are heroes. *A*
in the case of	~~In the case of~~ the election, it will be close. *T*
in the event that	~~In the event that~~ you're late, I will buy our tickets. *If*
in the final analysis	~~In the final analysis,~~ no two eyewitnesses agreed on what they saw. *N*
in the process of	We are ~~in the process of~~ reviewing the proposal.
it seems that	~~It seems that~~ the union went on strike over health benefits. *T*
manner	The child spoke ~~in a reluctant manner~~ *reluctantly.*
nature	The movie review was ~~of a~~ sarcastic ~~nature~~.
that exists	The crime rate ~~that exists~~ is unacceptable.
the point I am trying to make	~~The point I am trying to make is~~ television reporters invade our privacy. *T*
type of, kind of	Gordon took a relaxing ~~type of~~ vacation.
What I mean to say is	~~What I mean to say is~~ I love you.

EXERCISE 11-1 Working individually or with a group, revise this paragraph in two steps. First, underline all words that interfere with conciseness. Second, revise each sentence to make it more concise. (You'll need to drop words and replace or rearrange others.)

EXAMPLE It seems that most North Americans think of motor scooters as vehicles that exist only in European countries.

1. <u>It seems that</u> most North Americans think of motor scooters as <u>vehicles that exist</u> only in European countries.
2. Most North Americans think of motor scooters as only European vehicles.

1. As a matter of fact, in the popular imagination, motor scooters are the very essence of European style.
2. Today, over one million scooters are purchased by people in Europe each year, compared with a number that amounts to only 70,000 buyers in the United States.
3. In fact, Europeans have long used fuel-efficient, clean-running scooters for the purpose of getting around in a manner that is relatively easy in congested cities.
4. The use of these brightly colored, maneuverable scooters allows city dwellers to zip through traffic jams and thereby to save time and to save gas.
5. However, sales of scooters, it might interest you to know, are in the process of increasing in North America.
6. What I am trying to say is that motor scooters use much less gasoline than cars, and that as a matter of fact the cost factor is about one-fourth that of an inexpensive new car.
7. In addition, many motor scooters, it is pleasing to note, run on electricity, which in fact makes them noise and emission free.
8. A scooter running by means of electrical power amounts to a cost in the neighborhood of 25 cents to travel 50 miles at 30 miles per hour.
9. Members of many different population groups, from college students to retired persons, have begun to be finding this type of vehicle to be of a useful nature in a very real sense.
10. Traveling by means of an agile, snappy scooter makes getting around a college campus or doing errands in a city neighborhood quick and easy.

11c What sentence structures usually work against conciseness?

Two sentence structures, although appropriate in some contexts, often work against CONCISENESS because they can lead to WORDINESS: writing EXPLETIVE constructions and writing in the PASSIVE VOICE.

AVOIDING EXPLETIVE CONSTRUCTIONS

An expletive construction starts with *it* or *there* followed by a form of the VERB *be*. When you cut the expletive construction and revise, the sentence becomes more direct.

~~It is necessary for~~ stud_^ents ~~to~~ ^{must} fill in both questionnaires.

~~There are~~ eight instructors ~~who~~ teach in the Computer Science Department.

ESOL Tips: (1) *It* in an expletive construction is not a PRONOUN referring to a specific ANTECEDENT. *It* is an "empty" word that fills the SUBJECT position in the sentence but does not function as the subject. The actual subject appears after the expletive construction: *It was the teacher who answered the question.* If concise, the sentence would be *The teacher answered the question.* (2) *There* in an expletive construction does not indicate a place. Rather, *there* is an "empty" word that fills the subject position in the sentence but does not function as the subject. The actual subject appears after the expletive construction: *There are many teachers who can answer the question.* If concise, the sentence would be *Many teachers can answer the question.*

AVOIDING THE PASSIVE VOICE

In general, the passive voice is less concise—as well as less lively—than the ACTIVE VOICE. In the active voice, the subject of a sentence does the action named by the verb.

ACTIVE Professor Higgins teaches public speaking. [*Professor Higgins* is the subject, and he does the action: *He teaches.*]

In the passive voice, the subject of a sentence receives the action named by the verb.

PASSIVE Public speaking is taught by Professor Higgins. [*Public speaking* is the subject, and it receives the action *taught.*]

Unless your meaning justifies using the passive voice, choose the active voice. (For more information, see sections 15n through 15p.)

PASSIVE Volunteer work was done by students for credit in sociology. [The passive phrase *was done by students* is unnecessary for the intended meaning. *Students*, not *volunteer work*, are doing the action and should get the action of the verb.]

ACTIVE **The students did** volunteer work for credit in sociology.

ACTIVE **Volunteer work earned** students credit in sociology. [Since the verb has changed to *earned*, *volunteer work* performs the action of the verb.]

In mistakenly believing the passive voice sounds "mature" or "academic," student writers sometimes deliberately use it. Wordy, overblown sentences suggest that a writer hasn't carefully revised.

> **NO** One very important quality that can be developed during a first job is self-reliance. This strength was gained by me when I was allowed by my supervisor to set up and conduct a survey project on my own.

> **YES** Many individuals develop the important quality of self-reliance during their first job. I gained this strength when my supervisor allowed me to set up and conduct my own survey project.

> **YES** During their first job, many people develop self-reliance, as I did when my supervisor let me set up and conduct my own survey project.

If you are writing on a computer, you may find it helpful to use the word processing application's "Search" or "Find" feature to locate the words "was, is, be, were, and been" in your document as part of your revision. This little trick can help you find possible uses of passive voice and judge whether they are effective or need revision.

11d How else can I revise for conciseness?

Four other techniques can help you achieve CONCISENESS: eliminating unplanned repetition (11d.1); combining sentences (11d.2); shortening CLAUSES (11d.3); and shortening PHRASES and cutting words (11d.4). These techniques involve matters of judgment.

11d.1 Eliminating unplanned repetition

Unplanned repetition lacks conciseness because it delivers the same message more than once, usually in slightly different words. Unplanned repetition, or redundancy, implies that the writer lacks focus and judgment. The opposite— planned repetition—reflects both focus and judgment, as it creates a powerful rhythmic effect (see section 10e). As you revise, check that every word is necessary for delivering your message.

> **NO** Bringing **the project** to **final completion** three weeks early, the supervisor of **the project** earned our **respectful regard.**
> [*Completion* implies *bringing to final; project* is used twice in one sentence; and *regard* implies *respect.*]

YES   Completing the project three weeks early, the supervisor earned our respect. [Eighteen words reduced to eleven by cutting all redundancies.]

NO   **Astonished, the architect circled around the building in amazement.** [*Circled* means "went around," and *astonished* and *in amazement* have the same meaning.]

YES   **Astonished,** the architect **circled** the building. [Nine words reduced to six.]

YES   The architect **circled** the building **in amazement.** [Nine words reduced to seven.]

🌐 **ESOL Tip:** In all languages, words often carry an unspoken message, and native speakers understand the implied meanings of those words. In English, some implied meanings can cause redundancy in writing. For example, *I wrote my blog by computer* is redundant. In American English, *to write a blog* implies *by computer.* As you become more familiar with American English, you'll begin to notice such redundancies. ⬤

11d.2   Combining sentences

Look at sets of sentences in your writing to see if you can fit information contained in one sentence into another sentence. (For more about combining sentences, see Chapter 9, particularly sections 9c, 9e, 9j, and 9m.)

TWO SENTENCES   The *Titanic* hit an iceberg and sank. Seventy-three years later, a team of French and American scientists located the ship's resting site.

SENTENCES COMBINED   Seventy-three years after the *Titanic* hit an iceberg and sank, a team of French and American scientists located the ship's resting site.

TWO SENTENCES   Cameras revealed that the stern of the ship was missing and showed external damage to the ship's hull. Otherwise, the *Titanic* was in excellent condition.

SENTENCES COMBINED   Aside from a missing stern and external damage to the ship's hull, the *Titanic* was in excellent condition.

11d.3   Shortening clauses

Look at clauses in your writing to see if you can more concisely convey the same information. For example, sometimes you can cut a RELATIVE PRONOUN and its verb.

WORDY	The *Titanic,* **which was** a huge ocean liner, sank in 1912.
CONCISE	The Titanic, a huge ocean liner, sank in 1912.

Sometimes you can reduce a clause to a word.

WORDY	The scientists held a memorial service for the passengers and crew **who had drowned.**
CONCISE	The scientists held a memorial service for the **drowned** passengers and crew.

Sometimes an ELLIPTICAL CONSTRUCTION (sections 14p and 22h) can shorten a clause. If you use this technique, be sure that any omitted word is implied clearly.

WORDY	**When they were** confronted with disaster, some passengers behaved heroically, **while** others **behaved** selfishly.
CONCISE	Confronted with disaster, some passengers behaved heroically, others selfishly.

11d.4   Shortening phrases and cutting words

Sometimes you can reduce a phrase or redundant word pair to a single word. Redundant word pairs and phrases include *each and every, one and only, forever and ever, final and conclusive, perfectly clear, few* (or *many*) *in number, consensus of opinion,* and *reason . . . is because.*

NO	**Each and every** person was hungry after the movie.
YES	**Every** person was hungry after the movie.
YES	**Each** person was hungry after the movie.
NO	The **consensus of opinion** was that the movie was disappointing.
YES	The **consensus** was that the movie was disappointing.
YES	**Everyone agreed** that the movie was disappointing.
WORDY	More than fifteen hundred **travelers on that voyage** died in the shipwreck.
CONCISE	More than fifteen hundred **passengers** died in the shipwreck.

Sometimes you can rearrange words so that others can be deleted.

WORDY	Objects **found** inside the ship included **unbroken** bottles of wine and expensive **undamaged** china.

CONCISE   **Undamaged** objects inside the ship included bottles of wine and expensive china.

11e   How do verbs affect conciseness?

ACTION VERBS are strong verbs. *Be* and *have* are weak verbs that often lead to wordy sentences. When you revise weak verbs to strong ones, you can both increase the impact of your writing and reduce the number of words in your sentences. Strong verbs come into play when you revise your writing to reduce PHRASES and to change NOUNS to verbs.

WEAK VERB   The plan before the city council **has to do with** tax rebates.

STRONG VERB   The plan before the city council **proposes** tax rebates.

WEAK VERBS   The board members **were of the opinion** that the changes in the rules were changes they would not accept.

STRONG VERBS   The board members **said** that **they would not accept** the changes in the rules.

REPLACING A PHRASE WITH A VERB

Phrases such as *be aware of, be capable of, be supportive of* can often be replaced with one-word verbs.

I **envy** [not *am envious of*] your mathematical ability.

I **appreciate** [not *am appreciative of*] your modesty.

Your skill **illustrates** [not *is illustrative of*] how hard you studied.

REVISING NOUNS INTO VERBS

Many nouns are derived from verbs. Such nouns usually end with *-ance, -ment,* and *-tion* (*tolerance, enforcement, narration*). When you turn such wordy nouns back into verbs, your writing is more concise.

NO   The **accumulation of** paper lasted thirty years.

YES   The paper **accumulated** for thirty years.

NO   We **arranged for the establishment of** a student advisory committee.

YES   We **established** a student advisory committee.

NO   The building **had the appearance of** having been neglected.

YES   The building **appeared** to have been neglected.

● **EXERCISE 11-2** Working individually or with a group, combine each set
● of sentences to eliminate wordy constructions. For help, consult sections 11c
● through 11e.

EXAMPLE In recent years, ranchers have tried to raise and market many exotic meats. These meats have included emu, ostrich, and bison.
These attempts have failed.

In recent years, ranchers have failed to raise and market many exotic meats, such as emu, ostrich, and bison.

1. Each new attempt of ranchers to raise exotic animals like emu, ostrich,
and bison for the commercial value of their meat follows a pattern. There
is a similar pattern to each new attempt. Each new attempt begins when
a few people make the claim that some exotic animal tastes better than
beef and is more nutritious.

2. Emus were discovered by ranchers. Emus are birds that look like small ostriches. Emus quickly became unprofitable to raise. Only a few consumers
found emu meat tasty.

3. It was found by ostrich ranchers that there was an early, strong demand
for the meat of ostriches. That strong demand soon fizzled out quite a
bit, the ranchers found.

4. There is the American Ostrich Association. The membership of the American Ostrich Association once used to be 3,000. Today, the membership
of the American Ostrich Association now has only 500 people belonging
to it.

5. Bison, also known as buffalo, were a longer-lasting craze. Ranchers had a
strong desire to own the mighty animals; however, the price of bison was
increased greatly by the demand. It became uneconomical for ranchers
to purchase young animals.

6. Also, bison are difficult to raise. They tend to need strong fences to hold
them in. They cannot find enough food to eat. They eat by grazing. The
land of some buffalo ranches consists of poor pasture land or is in mountainous terrain.

7. Recently, the yak has been discovered by ranchers. The yak is an animal
from Central Asia. It is from rugged mountainous areas. For centuries, the
yak has supported the people of the Himalayan region.

8. Yaks have the ability to forage more efficiently compared with bison or
cows. Yaks are easier to care for than bison or cows. Yaks possess a better
resistance to many diseases.

9. Chefs in a few gourmet restaurants are beginning to serve yak meat.
They are devising fancy recipes for it. They are featuring it on their
menus. The meat is mild-tasting and succulent. The meat is also low
in fat.

10. Even though yaks are easy to raise and even are environmentally friendly, there is a problem. The ranchers must overcome that problem before they can raise yaks profitably. That problem is the fact that consumers lack familiarity with yaks. Consumers have a reluctance to try yak meat.

EXERCISE 11-3   Working individually or with a group, revise this paragraph in two steps. First, underline all words that interfere with conciseness. Second, revise the paragraph to make it more concise. (You'll need to drop words and replace or rearrange others.)

EXAMPLE 1. Within a matter of minutes after the completion of a championship game, the winning team's players are enabled to put on caps that have been embroidered with their team's name, the year, as well as the word "champions."

2. Minutes after completing a championship game, the winning team's players receive caps embroidered with their team's name, the year, and the word "champions."

(1) At the present time, caps for sports teams are manufactured in factories located primarily in Asian countries such as China, Korea, and Taiwan. (2) Championship caps are quickly produced and shipped by factories wherever they are needed for both of the two teams playing in a final game or series. (3) The very moment the game ends, a trucking company delivers the caps to the winning team's locker room, and it then immediately and instantly burns the losing team's caps so as to prevent embarrassing anyone. (4) Companies that produce all types of sports apparel know that in most cases there is only a short period of time available for making and earning high profits from merchandise connected to a winning team. (5) Within barely a day or two, they flood the market with all sorts of every kind of t-shirts, jackets, caps, coffee mugs, in addition to banners showing and presenting the winning team's championship information.

For more help with your writing, grammar, and research, go to **www.mycomplab.com**

12

The Impact of Words

12a What is American English?

Evolving over centuries into a rich language, **American English** is the variation of English spoken in the United States. It demonstrates that many cultures have created the US "melting pot" society. Food names are good examples: Africans brought the words *okra, gumbo,* and *goober* (peanut); Spanish and Latin American peoples contributed *tortilla, taco, burrito,* and *enchilada;* Greek speakers gave us *pita,* Cantonese speakers *chow,* Japanese speakers *sushi,* and so on.

In all languages, the meanings of some words change with time. For example, W. Nelson Francis points out in *The English Language* (New York: Norton, 1965) that the word *nice* "has been used at one time or another in its 700-year history to mean: *foolish, wanton, strange, lazy, coy, modest, fastidious, refined, precise, subtle, slender, critical, attentive, minutely accurate, dainty, appetizing, agreeable.*"

12b What is edited American English?

Edited American English, also known as STANDARD ENGLISH, reflects the standards of the written language expected of a textbook. These standards apply in magazines such as *U.S. News & World Report* and *National Geographic;* in newspapers such as the *Washington Post* and the *Wall Street Journal;* and in most nonfiction books. With edited American English, you can achieve the medium or semiformal language level required in ACADEMIC WRITING.

Edited American English isn't a special or fancy dialect for elite groups. Rather, it's a form of the language used by educated people to standardize communication in the larger world. Edited American English conforms to widely established rules of grammar, sentence structure, punctuation, and spelling—as covered in this handbook.

Nonstandard English is legitimately spoken by some groups in our society. With its own grammar and usage customs, it communicates clearly to other speakers of nonstandard English. Yet, one thing is certain: Speakers of nonstandard English often benefit when they can switch, as an academic, business, or public WRITING SITUATION requires, to the medium or semiformal level of language. This means that speakers of nonstandard English never need to re-ject their preferred or home language. Indeed, it's the right of all individuals to decide what works for them in various situations in their lives, and the ability to "code switch" gives them options.

It's true that advertising language and some trendy writings intended for mass audiences frequently ignore the conventions of edited American English. However, such departures from edited American English are not appropriate in academic writing.

12c What is figurative language?

Figurative language uses words for more than their literal meanings. Such words aren't merely decorative or pretentious (12g). Figurative language greatly enhances meaning. It makes comparisons and connections that draw on one idea or image to explain another. Quick Reference 12.1 explains the different types of figurative language and describes one type you should avoid, the **mixed metaphor**.

Quick Reference 12.1   ■ ■ ■ ■ ■ ■ ■ ■

Types of figurative language

- **Analogy:** Comparing similar traits shared by dissimilar things or ideas. Its length can vary from one sentence (which often takes the form of a simile or metaphor) to a paragraph.

  A **cheetah sprinting across the dry plains** after its prey, the **base runner dashed** for home plate, cleats kicking up dust.

- **Irony:** Using words to suggest the opposite of their usual sense.

  Told that a minor repair on her home would cost $2,000 and take two weeks, she said, **"Oh, how nice!"**

- **Metaphor:** Comparing otherwise dissimilar things. A metaphor doesn't use the word *like* or *as* to make a comparison. (See below about not using mixed metaphors.)

  Rush-hour **traffic** in the city **bled out through major arteries** to the suburbs.

- **Personification:** Assigning a human trait to something not human.

  The **book begged** to be read.

- **Overstatement** (also called *hyperbole*): Exaggerating deliberately for emphasis.

  If this paper is late, the professor will **kill** me.

continued >>

| Quick Reference 12.1 | (continued) |

- **Simile:** Comparing dissimilar things. A simile uses the word *like* or *as*.

  Langston Hughes observes that a deferred **dream dries up** "**like a raisin in the sun.**"

- **Understatement:** Emphasizing by using deliberate restraint.

  It feels **warm** when the temperature reaches **105 degrees.**

- **Mixed metaphor:** Combining two or more inconsistent images in one sentence or expression. Never use a mixed metaphor.

  NO The violence of the hurricane reminded me of a train ride. [A train ride is not violent, stormy, or destructive.]

  YES The violence of the hurricane reminded me of a train's crashing into a huge tractor trailer.

EXERCISE 12-1   Working individually or with a group, identify each type of figurative language or figure of speech. Also revise any mixed metaphors. For help, consult section 12c.

1. Good manners are the grease for the wheels of human interaction.
2. Without manners, people would be meaner than junkyard dogs.
3. Being rude is like tracking mud on a freshly mopped floor.
4. If you can't mind your business, at least mind your manners.
5. Good manners are the icing on the cake of human behavior.
6. Being rude should be a criminal offense.
7. Compliments are magicians wielding great power.
8. When you're rude to people, you're playing with fire and getting in over your head.
9. Being polite when you're frustrated is as difficult as driving at night when you're dead tired.
10. He's so tactless that if speech were a weapon, his would be a blunt instrument.

12d   How can using exact diction enhance my writing?

Diction, the term for choice of words, affects the clarity and impact of any writing you do. Your best chance of delivering your intended message to your readers is to choose words that fit exactly with each piece of writing. To choose words correctly—that is, to have good diction—you need to understand the concepts of *denotation* and *connotation* in words.

12d.1   What is denotation in words?

The **denotation** of a word is its exact, literal meaning. It's the meaning you find when you look up the word in a dictionary. A dictionary is your ultimate authority for a word's denotation.

* An **unabridged dictionary** contains the most extensive, complete, and scholarly entries. *Unabridged* means "not shortened." Such dictionaries include all infrequently used words that abridged dictionaries often omit. The most comprehensive, authoritative unabridged dictionary of English is the *Oxford English Dictionary* (OED), which traces each word's history and gives quotations to illustrate changes in meaning and spelling over the life of the word.

* An **abridged dictionary** contains most commonly used words. *Abridged* means "shortened." When an abridged dictionary serves the needs of most college students, the dictionaries are referred to as "college editions." Typical of these is *Merriam-Webster's Collegiate Dictionary* (available online and also in print) and *The New American Webster Handy College Dictionary.*

* A **specialized dictionary** focuses on a single area of language. You can find dictionaries of slang (for example, *Dictionary of Slang and Unconventional English,* ed. Eric Partridge); word origins (for example, *Dictionary of Word and Phrase Origins,* ed. William Morris and Mary Morris); synonyms (for example, *Roget's 21st Century Thesaurus*); usage (for example, *Modern American Usage: A Guide,* ed. Jacques Barzun); idioms (for example, *A Dictionary of American Idioms,* by Adam Makkai); regionalisms (for example, *Dictionary of American Regional English,* ed. Frederic Cassidy); and many others.

ESOL Tip: *The Oxford Dictionary of American English* (Cambridge: Oxford UP, 2005) is particularly useful for students who speak English as a second (or third) language.

12d.2   What is connotation in words?

Connotation refers to ideas implied by a word. Connotations are never completely fixed, for they can vary in differing contexts. Connotations involve associations and emotional overtones that go beyond a word's definition. For example, *home* usually evokes more emotion than its denotation "a dwelling place" or its synonym *house. Home* carries the connotation, for some, of the pleasures of warmth, security, and love of family. For others, however, *home* may carry unpleasant connotations, such as abusive experiences or the impersonal atmosphere of an institution to house the elderly.

USING A THESAURUS

Sometimes a good college dictionary explains the small differences among synonyms, but a thesaurus is devoted entirely to providing synonyms for words. In distinguishing among **synonyms**—the other words close in meaning to a word—a thesaurus demonstrates connotation in operation. As you use a thesaurus, remain very alert to the subtle shades of meaning that create distinctions among words. For instance, using *notorious* to describe a person famous for praiseworthy achievements in public life is wrong. Although *notorious* means "well-known" and "publicly discussed"—which is true of famous people—the connotation of the word is "unfavorably known or talked about." George Washington is famous, not notorious. Jeffrey Dahmer, by contrast, is notorious.

Here's another example, with the word *obdurate,* which means "not easily moved to pity or sympathy." Its synonyms include *inflexible, obstinate, stubborn,* and *hardened.*

> **NO** Footprints showed in the **obdurate** concrete.
>
> **YES** The supervisor remained **obdurate** in refusing to accept excuses.
>
> **YES** My **obdurate** roommates won't let my pet boa constrictor live in the bathtub.

🚫 **Alert:** Most word-processing programs include a thesaurus. But be cautious in using it. Unless you know the exact meaning of an offered synonym, as well as its part of speech, you may choose a wrong word or introduce a grammatical error into your writing. For example, one word-processing program's thesaurus offers these synonyms for *deep* in the sense of "low (down, inside)": *low, below, beneath,* and *subterranean.* None of these words could replace *deep* in a sentence such as *The crater is too deep* [not *too low, too below, too beneath,* or *too subterranean*] *to be filled with sand or rocks.* ●

EXERCISE 12-2 Working individually or with a group, look at each list of words and divide the words among three headings: "Positive" (good connotations); "Negative" (bad connotations); and "Neutral" (no connotations). If you think that a word belongs under more than one heading, you can assign it more than once, but be ready to explain your thinking. For help, consult a good dictionary and 12d.2.

EXAMPLE   grand, big, bulky, significant, oversized

> *Positive:* grand, significant; *Negative:* bulky, oversized; *Neutral:* big

1. harmony, sound, racket, shriek, melody, music, noise, pitch, voice
2. talkative, articulate, chattering, eloquent, vocal, verbose, gossipy, fluent, gabby

3. decorative, beautiful, modern, ornate, overelaborate, dazzling, flashy, elegant, sparkling

4. long, lingering, enduring, continued, drawn-out, stretched, never-ending, unbreakable, incessant

5. calculating, shrewd, crafty, ingenious, keen, sensible, sly, smooth, underhanded

12e How can using specific words enhance my writing?

Specific words identify individual items in a group (*Ford, Honda*). **General words** relate to an overall group (*car*). **Concrete words** identify what can be perceived by the senses, by being seen, heard, tasted, felt, smelled (*padded black leather dashboard*), and convey specific images and details. **Abstract words** denote qualities (*kind*), concepts (*speed*), relationships (*friends*), acts (*cooking*), conditions (*bad weather*), and ideas (*transportation*) and are more general.

Usually, specific and concrete words bring life to general and abstract words. Therefore, whenever you use general and abstract words, try to supply enough specific, concrete details and examples to illustrate them. Here are sentences with general words that come to life when revised with specific words.

GENERAL	His car gets good gas mileage.
SPECIFIC	His Miser gets about 35 mpg on the highway and 30 mpg in the city.
GENERAL	Her car is comfortable and easy to drive.
SPECIFIC	When she drives her new Cushia on a five-hour trip, she arrives refreshed and does not need a long nap to recover, as she did when she drove her ten-year-old Upushme.

What separates most good writing from bad is the writer's ability to move back and forth between the general and abstract and the specific and concrete. Consider these sentences that effectively use a combination of general and specific words to compare cars:

GENERAL   CONCRETE   ┌──── SPECIFIC ────┐   ABSTRACT
My car, a midnight-black Corvette LS1 convertible, has a powerful

┌── SPECIFIC ──┐   GENERAL   SPECIFIC   GENERAL
5.7-liter V8 engine with ride controls, the Tour for regular driving and

SPECIFIC   ┌── CONCRETE ──┐   GENERAL
the Sport for a close-to-the-road feel. In contrast, Harvey's automobile,

<pre>
CONCRETE ┌──────── SPECIFIC ────────┐   ABSTRACT
</pre>
a bright red Dodge Viper SRT-10 convertible, has a mighty

<pre>
┌──────────── SPECIFIC ────────────┐
</pre>
8.3-liter V10 engine with 6-speed manual transmission.

EXERCISE 12-3   Revise this paragraph by providing specific and concrete words and phrases to explain and enliven the ideas presented here in general and abstract language. You may revise the sentences to accommodate your changes in language. For help, consult 12e.

> I hope to get a job as an administrative assistant in the company. At the interview, the person who would be my supervisor was pleasant. We seemed to get along well. The other assistants in the division appeared to be nice. My college courses clearly have prepared me for the position. I think the job would teach me a great deal more. The salary is a bit less than I had hoped for, but the Human Resources representative promised me raises at regular intervals if my work is good. Also, my trip to work would not take too much time for me. If my interviewer calls to offer me the job, I will accept it.

12f   What is gender-neutral language?

Gender-neutral language, also referred to as *gender-free* or *nonsexist language*, relies on terms that don't communicate whether the person is male or female (for example, in replacing *policeman* with *police officer* or *doctors' wives* with *doctors' spouses*).

Sexist language assigns roles or characteristics to people based on their sex and gender. Most people recognize that sexist language discriminates against both men and women. For example, it inaccurately assumes that every nurse and homemaker is female (and therefore referred to as "she"), and that every physician and stockbroker is male (and therefore referred to as "he"). One common instance of sexist language occurs when the pronoun *he* is used to refer to someone whose sex is unknown or irrelevant. Although tradition holds that *he* is correct in such situations, most people believe that using masculine pronouns to represent all humans excludes women and thereby distorts reality.

Nearly all businesses and professional organizations require gender-neutral language in written communications. Their policies exist not only for reasons of accuracy and fairness but also for sound business practice, as they want to be inclusive of potential clients and customers.

Gender-neutral language rejects demeaning STEREOTYPES or outdated assumptions, such as "women are bad drivers" and "men can't cook." In your writing, never describe women's looks, clothes, or age unless you do the same for men or doing so is important to the context. Never use a title for one spouse and the first name for the other spouse: *Phil Miller* (not *Mr. Miller*) and *his wife, Jeannette*, travel on separate planes; or *Jeannette and Phil Miller* live in Idaho. Quick Reference 12.2 gives you guidelines for using gender-neutral language.

EXERCISE 12-4   Working individually or with a group, revise these sentences by changing sexist language to gender-neutral language. For help, consult 12g.

1. Dogs were one of the first animals to be domesticated by mankind.
2. Traditionally, certain breeds of dogs have helped men in their work.
3. On their long shifts, firemen often kept Dalmatians as mascots and companions, whereas policemen preferred highly intelligent and easily trained German shepherds.
4. Another breed, the Newfoundland, accompanied many fishermen on their ocean voyages, and the Newfoundland has been credited with rescuing many a man overboard.
5. Breeds known as hunting dogs have served as the helpers and companions of sportsmen.
6. Maids and cleaning women didn't need dogs, so no breed of dog is associated with women's work.
7. Another group that dogs have not helped is postmen.
8. Everyone who owns a dog should be sure to spend some time exercising his dog and making sure his dog is in good health.
9. No man-made inventions, such as televisions or computers, can take the place of having a dog.
10. Now even though most dogs do not work, they are still man's best friend.

Quick Reference 12.2   ■ ■ ■ ■ ■ ■ ■

How to avoid sexist language

- Avoid using only the masculine pronoun to refer to males and females together. The *he or she* and *his or hers* constructions act as singular PRONOUNS, and they therefore call for singular VERBS. Try to avoid using *he or she* constructions, especially more than once in a sentence or in consecutive sentences. A better solution is revising to the plural. You can also revise to omit the gender-specific pronoun.

NO	A **doctor** has little time to read outside **his** specialty.
YES	A **doctor** has little time to read outside **his or her** specialty.
NO	A successful **stockbroker** knows **he** has to work long hours.
YES	Successful **stockbrokers** know **they** have to work long hours.

continued >>

Quick Reference 12.2 (continued)

> **NO**   **Everyone** hopes that **he or she** will win the scholarship.
> **YES** **Everyone** hopes to win the scholarship.

- Avoid using *man* when referring to both men and women.

> **NO**   **Man** is a social animal.
> **YES** **People** are social animals.
>
> **NO**   The history of **mankind** is predominately violent.
> **YES** **Human** history is predominately violent.
>
> **NO**   Dogs are **men's** best friends.
> **YES** Dogs are **people's** best friends.

- Avoid stereotyping jobs and roles by gender when referring to both men and women.

NO	YES
chairman	chair, chairperson
policeman	police officer
businessman	businessperson, business executive
statesman	statesperson, diplomat
teacher . . . she	teachers . . . they
principal . . . he	principals . . . they

- Avoid expressions that seem to exclude one sex.

NO	YES
the common man	the average person
man-sized sandwich	huge sandwich
old wives' tale	superstition

- Avoid using demeaning and patronizing labels.

NO	YES
male nurse	nurse
gal Friday	assistant
coed	student
My girl can help.	My secretary can help. (*Or, better still:* Ida Morea can help.)

🛈 **Alert:** Increasingly, you see "they" or "their" used as a singular pronoun, as in "If someone puts in the effort, they should be rewarded." The English language continually changes, and perhaps in a few years this growing usage will become perfectly acceptable because it fills a need: English lacks a gender-neutral singular pronoun. Today, however, it is still nonstandard in almost all academic and professional settings. ●

12g What other types of language do I want to avoid?

Language that distorts or tries to manipulate a reader needs to be avoided in ACADEMIC WRITING. These and other types of language to avoid in an academic LEVEL OF FORMALITY are listed, with examples, in Quick Reference 12.3.

Quick Reference 12.3

Language to avoid in academic writing

- Never use **slanted language**, also called *loaded language;* readers feel manipulated by the overly emotional TONE and DICTION.

  NO   Our senator is a deceitful, crooked thug.
  YES Our senator lies to the public and demands bribes.

  NO   Why do labs employ Frankensteins to maim helpless kittens and puppies?
  YES Why do labs employ uncaring technicians who harm kittens and puppies?

- Never use **pretentious language**; readers realize you're showing off.

  NO   As I alighted from my vehicle, my clothing became besmirched with filth.
  YES My coat got muddy as I got out of my car.

  NO   He has a penchant for ostentatiously flaunting recently acquired haberdashery accoutrements.
  YES He tends to show off his new clothes shamelessly.

- Never use **sarcastic language**; readers realize you're being nasty.

  NO   He was a regular Albert Einstein with my questions. [This is sarcastic if you mean the opposite.]
  YES He had trouble understanding my questions.

- Never use **colloquial language**; readers sense you're being overly casual and conversational.

  NO   Christina tanked chemistry.
  YES Christina failed chemistry.

- Never use **euphemisms**, also called *doublespeak;* readers realize you're hiding the truth (more in 12k).

  NO   Our company will **downsize** to meet efficiency standards.
  YES Our company has to cut jobs to maintain our profits.

  NO   We consider our hostages as **foreign guests** being guarded by **hosts**.
  YES We consider our hostages as enemies to be guarded closely.

continued >>

> ### Quick Reference 12.3   (continued)
>
> - Never use NONSTANDARD ENGLISH (see 12b).
> - Never use MIXED METAPHORS (see 12c).
> - Never use SEXIST LANGUAGE or STEREOTYPES (see 12f).
> - Never use REGIONAL LANGUAGE (see 12h).
> - Never use CLICHÉS (see 12i).
> - Never use unnecessary JARGON (see 12j).
> - Never use BUREAUCRATIC LANGUAGE (see 12l).

12h   What is regional language?

Regional language, also called *dialectal language,* is specific to certain geographical areas. For example, a *dragonfly* is a *snake feeder* in parts of Delaware, a *darning needle* in parts of Michigan, and a *snake doctor* or an *ear sewer* in parts of the southern United States. Depending on where you live, soft drinks are known as "soda," "pop," or "coke." Using a dialect in writing for the general reading public tends to shut some people out of the communication. Except when dialect is the topic of the writing, ACADEMIC WRITING rarely accommodates dialect well. Avoid it in academic assignments.

12i   What are clichés?

A **cliché** is a worn-out expression that has lost its capacity to communicate effectively because of overuse. Many clichés are SIMILES or METAPHORS, once clever but now flat. For example, these are clichés: *dead as a doornail, gentle as a lamb,* and *straight as an arrow.*

If you've heard certain expressions repeatedly, so has your reader. Instead of a cliché, use descriptive language that isn't worn out. If you can't think of a way to rephrase a cliché, drop the words entirely.

Interestingly, however, English is full of frequently used word groups that aren't clichés: for example, *up and down* and *from place to place.* These common word groups aren't considered clichés, so you can use them freely. If you're not sure of how to tell the difference between a cliché and a common word group, remember that a cliché often—but not always—contains an image (*busy as a bee* and *strong as an ox*).

EXERCISE 12-5   Working individually or with a group, revise these clichés. Use the idea in each cliché to write a sentence of your own in plain, clear English. For help, consult 12i.

1. The bottom line is that Carl either raises his grade point average or finds himself in hot water.
2. He needs to understand that "When the going gets tough, the tough get going."
3. Carl may not be the most brilliant engineering major who ever came down the pike, but he has plenty of get-up-and-go.
4. When they were handing out persistence, Carl was first in line.
5. The $64,000 question: Will Carl make it safe and sound, or will the college drop him like a hot potato?

12j When is jargon unnecessary?

Jargon is the specialized vocabulary of a particular group. Jargon uses words that people outside that group might not understand. Specialized language exists in every field: professions, academic disciplines, business, various industries, government departments, hobbies, and so on.

Reserve jargon for a specialist AUDIENCE. As you write, keep your audience in mind as you decide whether a word is jargon in the context of your material. For example, a football fan easily understands a sportswriter's use of words such as *punt* and *safety,* but they are jargon words to people unfamiliar with American-style football. Avoid using jargon unnecessarily. When you must use jargon for a nonspecialist audience, be sure to explain any special meanings.

The example below shows specialized language used appropriately; it's taken from a college textbook. The authors can assume that students know the meaning of *eutrophicates, terrestrial,* and *eutrophic.*

> As the lake eutrophicates, it gradually fills until the entire lake will be converted into a terrestrial community. Eutrophic changes (or eutrophication) are the nutritional enrichment of the water, promoting the growth of aquatic plants.
>
> —Davis and Solomon, *The World of Biology*

12k What are euphemisms?

Euphemisms attempt to avoid the harsh reality of truth by using more pleasant, "tactful" words. Good manners dictate that euphemisms sometimes be used in social situations: For example, in US culture, *passed away* is, in some situations, thought to be gentler than *died.* Such uses of euphemisms are acceptable.

In other situations, however, euphemisms drain meaning from truthful writing. Unnecessary euphemisms might describe socially unacceptable behavior (for example, *Johnny has a wonderfully vivid imagination* instead of *Johnny lies*). They also might try to hide unpleasant facts (for example, *She is between assignments* instead of *She's lost her job*). Avoid unnecessary euphemisms.

12l What is bureaucratic language?

Bureaucratic language uses words that are stuffy and overblown. Bureaucratic language (or *bureaucratese*, a word created to describe this style) is marked by unnecessary complexity. This kind of language can take on a formality that complicates the message and makes readers feel left out.

> **NO** In reference to situations delineated above, corporate associates shall determine the existence of extraneous circumstances sufficient to preclude substantive action by management. In the event the evaluation of said circumstances results in an affirmative finding, the associate is directed to enact the policy mandated in section 4.b.7 of the procedures manual, unless said implementation would enact legal pursuits or other actions injurious to the company. Should extraneous circumstances not obtain, the unit supervisor shall be contacted through official communication means in order to pursue a mutually satisfactory conclusion to the occasioning situation.
>
> —from a corporate human resources manual

We would like to give a YES alternative for this example but regret that we can't understand enough of it to do so. If you, gentle reader, can, please contact us at doug.hesse@gmail.com or troykalq@nyc.rr.com.

EXERCISE 12-6   Working individually or with a group, revise these examples of pretentious language, jargon, euphemisms, and bureaucratic language. For help, consult 12g and 12j through 12l.

1. Allow me to express my humble gratitude to you two benefactors for your generous pledge of indispensable support on behalf of the activities of our Bay City's youngsters.
2. No lateral transfer applications will be processed before an employee's six-month probation period terminates.
3. She gave up the ghost shortly after her husband kicked the bucket.
4. Creating nouns in positions meant for verbs is to utter ostentatious verbalizations that will lead inexorably to further obfuscations of meaning.
5. After his operation, he would list to port when he stood up and list to starboard when he sat down.
6. The precious youths were joy riding in a temporarily displaced vehicle.
7. The forwarding of all electronic communiqués must be approved by a staff member in the upper echelon.
8. Coming to a parting of the ways is not as easy as pie.

13

Usage Glossary

A usage glossary presents the customary manner of using particular words and phrases. "Customary manner," however, is not as firm in practice as the term implies. Usage standards change. If you think a word's usage might differ from what you read here, consult a dictionary published more recently than the current edition of this handbook.

The meaning of *informal* or *colloquial* in the definition of a word or phrase is that it's found in everyday or conversational speech, but it needs to be avoided in ACADEMIC WRITING. Another term, *nonstandard,* indicates that the word or phrase, although widely understood in speech and dialect writing, isn't suitable in standard spoken or written English.

Terms of grammar and writing in this Usage Glossary are defined in the Terms Glossary, which begins after the last chapter.

a, an   Use *a* before words that begin with a consonant (*a dog, a grade, a hole*) or a consonant sound (*a one-day sale, a European*). Use *an* before words or acronyms that begin with a vowel sound or a silent *h* (*an owl; an hour; an MRI,* because the *M* is sounded "em"). American English uses *a,* not *an,* before words starting with a pronounced *h: a* (not *an*) *historical event.*

accept, except   The verb *accept* means "agree to; receive." As a preposition, *except* means "leaving out." As a verb, *except* means "exclude; leave out."

The workers wanted to **accept** [verb] management's offer **except** [preposition] for one detail: They wanted the limit on overtime **excepted** [verb] from the contract.

advice, advise   *Advice,* a noun, means "recommendation." *Advise,* a verb, means "recommend; give advice."

I **advise** [verb] you to follow your car mechanic's **advice** [noun].

affect, effect   As a verb, *affect* means "cause a change in; influence." (*Affect* is a noun in psychology.) As a noun, *effect* means "result or conclusion"; as a verb, *effect* means "bring about."

Loud music **affects** people's hearing for life, so some bands have **effected** changes to lower the volume. Many fans, however, don't care about the harmful **effects** of high decibel levels.

aggravate, irritate   *Aggravate* is used colloquially to mean "irritate." In academic writing, use *aggravate* only to mean "intensify; make worse." Use *irritate* to mean "annoy; make impatient."

The coach was **irritated** by reduced time for practice, which **aggravated** the team's difficulties with concentration.

ain't   *Ain't* is a nonstandard contraction. Use *am not, is not,* or *are not* for standard spoken and written English.

all ready, already   *All ready* means "completely prepared." *Already* means "before; by this time."

The team was **all ready** to play, but it had **already** begun to rain.

all right   *All right* is always written as two words, never one (never *alright*).

all together, altogether   *All together* means "in a group; in unison." *Altogether* means "entirely; thoroughly."

The twelve jurors told the judge that it was **altogether** absurd for them to stay **all together** in a single hotel room.

allude, elude   *Allude* means "refer to indirectly." *Elude* means "escape notice."

The detectives **alluded** to budget cuts by saying, "Conditions beyond our control allowed the suspect to **elude** us."

allusion, illusion   An *allusion* is an indirect reference to something. An *illusion* is a false impression or idea.

The couple's casual **allusions** to European tourist sites created the **illusion** that they had visited them.

a lot   *A lot* is informal for *a great deal* or *a great many.* Avoid using it in academic writing. If you must use it, write it as two words (never *alot*).

a.m., p.m.   Use these abbreviations only with numbers, not as substitutes for the words *morning, afternoon,* and *evening.* Some editors consider capital letters wrong for these abbreviations, yet many editors and dictionaries allow both. Whichever you choose, be consistent in each piece of writing.

We will arrive in the **evening** [not p.m.], and we must leave by **8:00 a.m.**

among, amongst, between   Use *among* for three or more items. Use *between* for two items. American English prefers *among* to *amongst.*

My three housemates discussed **among** [not between or amongst] themselves the choice **between** staying in college and getting full-time jobs.

amoral, immoral   *Amoral* means "neither moral (conforming to standards of rightness) nor immoral (the opposite of *moral*)." *Amoral* also means "without any sense of what's moral or immoral." *Immoral* means "morally wrong."

Although many people consider birth control an **amoral** issue, some religions consider using birth control **immoral**.

amount, number   Use *amount* for noncountable things (wealth, work, happiness). Use *number* for countable items.

The **amount** of rice to cook depends on the **number** of guests.

an   See *a, an.*

and/or   This term is appropriate in business and legal writing when either or both of the two items can apply: *We are planning to open additional offices in California **and/or** New York.* In the humanities, writers usually express the alternatives in words: *We are planning to open additional offices in California, New York, or both.*

anymore   Use *anymore* with the meaning "now, any longer" only in negations or questions. In positive statements, instead of *anymore,* use an adverb such as *now.*

No one wants to live without air conditioning **anymore**. Summers are so hot **now** [not anymore] that more people than ever suffer from heatstroke.

anyone, any one   *Anyone* is a singular indefinite pronoun meaning "any person at all." *Any one* (two words), an adjective that modifies a pronoun, means "a member of a group."

Anyone could test-drive **any one** of the display vehicles.

anyplace   *Anyplace* is informal. Use *any place* or *anywhere* instead.

anyways, anywheres   *Anyways* and *anywheres* are nonstandard for *anyway* and *anywhere.*

apt, likely, liable   *Apt* and *likely* are used interchangeably. Strictly, *apt* indicates a tendency or inclination. *Likely* indicates a reasonable expectation or greater certainty than *apt* does. *Liable* usually denotes legal responsibility or implies unpleasant consequences but usage today allows it to mean *likely.*

Evander is **apt** to run stop signs, so he is **likely** to get a ticket. That means he's **liable** for any consequences.

as, as if, as though, like   Use *as, as if,* or *as though,* but not *like,* when the words coming after include a verb.

This hamburger tastes good, **as** [not *like*] a hamburger should. It tastes **as if** [or *as though*, not *like*] it were barbequed over charcoal, not gas.

Both *as* and *like* can function as prepositions in comparisons. However, use *as* to indicate equivalence between two nouns or pronouns, and use *like* to indicate similarity but not equivalence.

My friend Roger served **as** [not *like*] mediator in a dispute about my neighbor's tree that dripped sap on my driveway **like** [not *as*] a leaky water faucet.

assure, ensure, insure   *Assure* means "promise; convince." *Ensure* and *insure* both mean "make certain or secure," but *insure* is reserved for financial or legal matters.

The insurance agent **assured** me that he could **insure** my car, but only I could **ensure** that I would drive safely.

as to   *As to* is nonstandard for *about*.

awful, awfully   *Awful* is an adjective meaning "inspiring awe" and "creating fear." *Awfully* is an adverb meaning "in a way to inspire awe" and "terrifying." Only colloquially are *awful* and *awfully* used to mean "very" or "extremely."

I was **extremely** [not *awfully*] tired yesterday.

a while, awhile   As two words, *a while* (an article and a noun) can function as a subject or object. As one word, *awhile* is an adverb. In a prepositional phrase, the correct form is *for a while, in a while,* or *after a while.*

It took **a while** [article and noun] to drive to the zoo, where we saw the seals bask **awhile** [adverb modifying verb *bask*] in the sun after romping **for a while** [prepositional phrase] in the water.

backup, back up   As a noun, *backup* means "a replacement, fill-in, surrogate; a copy of computer files." As an adjective, *backup* means "alternate; alternative." As a verb, *back up* (two words) means "to serve as a substitute or support"; "to accumulate, as from a stoppage"; and "to make a backup copy of a computer disk or hard drive."

I'll need a **backup** [noun] of your hard drive if I'm going to serve as your **backup** [adjective] computer consultant. I **back up** [verb] all computer disks and drives when I work with them.

bad, badly   *Bad* is an adjective only after linking verbs (*look, feel, smell, taste, sound;* these verbs can function as either linking verbs or action verbs depending on the context). *Badly* is an adverb; it's nonstandard after linking verbs.

Farmers feel **bad** [*feel* is a linking verb, so *bad* is the adjective] because a **bad** [adjective] drought is **badly** [adverb] damaging their crops.

been, being   *Been* and *being* cannot stand alone as main verbs. They work only with auxiliary verbs.

You **are being** [not *being*] honest to admit that you **have been** [not *been*] tempted to eat the whole pie.

being as, being that   *Being as* and *being that* are nonstandard for *because* or *since*.

We had to forfeit the game **because** [not *being as* or *being that*] our goalie was badly injured.

beside, besides   As prepositions, *beside* means "next to, by the side of," and *besides* means "other than, in addition to." As an adverb, *besides* means "also, moreover."

She stood **beside** the new car, insisting that she would drive. No one **besides** her had a driver's license. **Besides,** she owned the car.

better, had better   *Better* is informal for *had better.*

We **had better** [not *better* alone] be careful of the ice.

between   See *among, amongst, between.*

bias, biased   As a noun, *bias* means "a mental leaning for or against something or someone." As an adjective, *biased* means "prejudiced." As a verb, *bias* means "create prejudice." The past tense of this verb is *biased.*

Horace's **bias** [noun] against federal-level politicians grew from his disapproval of their **biased** [adjective] attitudes toward certain foreign countries. Eventually, Horace **biased** [verb] his wife's beliefs about politicians as well.

breath, breathe   *Breath* is a noun; *breathe* is a verb.

Take a deep **breath** [noun] before you start so that you can **breathe** [verb] normally afterward.

bring, take   *Bring* indicates movement from a distant place to a near place. *Take* indicates movement from a near to a distant place.

If you **bring** over sandwiches, we'll have time to **take** [not *bring*] the dog to the vet.

but, however, yet   Use *but, however,* or *yet* alone, not in combination with each other.

The economy is strong, **but** [not *but yet* or *but however*] unemployment is high.

calculate, figure   These are colloquial terms for *estimate, imagine, expect, think,* and the like.

can, may   *Can* signifies ability or capacity. *May* requests or grants permission. In negative expressions, *can* is acceptable for *may.*

> When you **can** [not *may*] get here on time, you **may** [not *can*] be excused early. However, if you are *not* on time, you **cannot** [or *may not*] expect privileges.

can't hardly, can't scarcely   These double negatives are nonstandard for *can hardly* and *can scarcely.*

capitol, capital   *Capitol* means "a building in which legislators meet." *Capital* means a city (Denver, the *capital* of Colorado), wealth, or "most important" (a *capital* offense).

> If the governor can find enough **capital**, the state legislature will agree to build a new **capitol** for our state.

censor, censure   The verb *censor* means "delete objectionable material; judge." The verb *censure* means "condemn or reprimand officially."

> The town council **censured** the mayor for trying to **censor** a report.

chairman, chairperson, chair   Many writers and speakers prefer the gender-neutral terms *chairperson* and *chair* to *chairman.* In general, *chair* is used more than *chairperson.*

choose, chose   *Choose* is the simple form of the verb. *Chose* is the past-tense form of the verb.

> I **chose** a movie last week, so you **choose** one tonight.

cite, site   The verb *cite* means "quote by way of example, authority, or proof." The noun *site* means "a particular place or location."

> The private investigator **cited** evidence from the crime **site** and the defendant's Web **site**.

cloth, clothe   *Cloth* is a noun meaning "fabric." *Clothe* is a verb meaning "dress with garments or fabric."

> "**Clothe** me in red velvet," proclaimed the king, and the royal tailors ran to gather samples of **cloth** to show him.

complement, compliment   As a noun, *complement* means "something that goes well with or completes." As a noun, *compliment* means "praise, flattery." As a verb, *complement* means "brings to perfection; goes well with, completes." As a verb, *compliment* means "praise, flatter."

> The dean's **compliment** was a perfect **complement** to the thrill of my graduating. My parents felt proud when she **complimented** me publicly, an honor that **complemented** their joy.

comprise, include   See *include, comprise.*

conscience, conscious   The noun *conscience* means "a sense of right and wrong." The adjective *conscious* means "being aware or awake."

> Always be **conscious** of what your **conscience** is telling you.

consensus of opinion   This phrase is redundant; use *consensus* only.

> The legislature reached **consensus** on the issue of campaign reform.

continual(ly), continuous(ly)   *Continual* means "occurring repeatedly." *Continuous* means "going on without interruption."

> Larry needed intravenous fluids **continuously** for days, so the nurses **continually** monitored him.

could care less   *Could care less* is nonstandard for *could not care less.*

could of   *Could of* is nonstandard for *could have.*

couple, a couple of   *Couple* means "two," but it can also be nonstandard for *a few* or *several.*

> Rest here for **a few** [not *a couple* or *a couple of*] minutes.

criteria, criterion   A *criterion* is "a standard of judgment." *Criteria* is the plural of *criterion.*

> A sense of history is an important **criterion** for judging political candidates, but voters must consider other **criteria** as well.

data   *Data* is the plural of *datum,* a word rarely used today. Informally, *data* is used as a singular noun that takes a singular verb. In academic or professional writing, *data* is considered plural and takes a plural verb (although this usage is currently viewed as overly formal by some).

> The **data** suggest [not *suggests*] some people are addicted to e-mail.

different from, different than   In academic and professional writing, use *different from* even though *different than* is common in informal speech.

> Please advise us if your research yields data **different from** past results.

disinterested, uninterested The preferred use of *disinterested* means "impartial, unbiased." Colloquially, *disinterested* can mean "not interested, indifferent," but in more formal contexts, *uninterested* is preferred for "not interested, indifferent."

> Jurors need to be **disinterested** in hearing evidence, but never **uninterested**.

don't *Don't* is a contraction for *do not,* never for *does not* (its contraction is *doesn't*).

> She **doesn't** [not don't] like crowds.

effect See *affect, effect.*

elicit, illicit The verb *elicit* means "draw forth or bring out." The adjective *illicit* means "illegal."

> The senator's **illicit** conduct **elicited** a mass outcry from her constituents.

elude See *allude, elude.*

emigrate (from), immigrate (to) *Emigrate* means "leave one country to live in another." *Immigrate* means "enter a country to live there."

> My great-grandmother **emigrated** from Kiev, Russia, to London, England, in 1890. Then, she **immigrated** to Toronto, Canada, in 1892.

enclose, inclose; enclosure, inclosure In American English, *enclose* and *enclosure* are the preferred spellings.

ensure See *assure, ensure, insure.*

enthused *Enthused* is nonstandard for *enthusiastic.*

> Adam was **enthusiastic** [not enthused] about the college he chose.

etc. *Etc.* is the abbreviation for the Latin *et cetera,* meaning "and the rest." For writing in the humanities, avoid using *etc.* Acceptable substitutes are *and the like, and so on,* or *and so forth.*

everyday, every day The adjective *everyday* means "daily." *Every day* (two words) is an adjective with a noun.

> Being late for work has become an **everyday** [adjective] occurrence for me. **Every day** [subject] brings me closer to being fired. I worry about it **every day** [object].

everyone, every one   *Everyone* is a singular, indefinite pronoun. *Every one* (two words) is an adjective and a pronoun, meaning "each member in a group."

Everyone enjoyed **every one** of the comedy skits.

everywheres   *Everywheres* is nonstandard for *everywhere.*

except   See *accept, except.*

explicit, implicit   *Explicit* means "directly stated or expressed." *Implicit* means "implied, suggested."

The warning on cigarette packs is **explicit:** "Smoking is dangerous to health." The **implicit** message is "Don't smoke."

farther, further   Although many writers reserve *farther* for geographical distances and *further* for all other cases, current usage treats them as interchangeable.

fewer, less   Use *fewer* for anything that can be counted (that is, with count nouns): *fewer* dollars, *fewer* fleas, *fewer* haircuts. Use *less* with collective nouns (or other noncount nouns): *less* money, *less* scratching, *less* hair.

firstly, secondly, thirdly   The terms *firstly, secondly,* and *thirdly* are from British English. In American English, use *first, second,* and *third.*

former, latter   When two items are referred to, *former* signifies the first item and *latter* signifies the second item. Never use *former* and *latter* when referring to more than two items.

Brazil and Ecuador are South American countries. Portuguese is the official language in the **former,** Spanish in the **latter.**

go, say   All forms of *go* are nonstandard when used in place of all forms of *say.*

While stepping on my hand, Frank **says** [not goes], "Your hand is in my way."

gone, went   *Gone* is the past participle of *go; went* is the past tense of *go.*

They **went** [not gone] to the concert after Ira **had gone** [not had went] home.

good, well   *Good* is an adjective. As an adverb, *good* is nonstandard. Instead, use *well.*

Good [adjective] maintenance helps cars run **well** [adverb; not good].

good and   *Good and* is a nonstandard intensifier. Instead, use more precise words.

They were **exhausted** [not good and tired].

got, have *Got* is nonstandard for *have*.

What do we **have** [not got] for supper?

hardly Use *hardly* with *can,* never with *can't.*

have, of Use *have,* not *of,* after such verbs as *could, should, would, might,* and *must.*

You *should* **have** [not should of] called first.

have got, have to, have got to Avoid using *have got* when *have* alone delivers your meaning. Also, avoid using *have to* or *have got to* for *must.*

I **have** [not have got] several more sources to read. I **must** [not have got to] finish my reading today.

he/she, s/he, his/her When using gender-neutral language, write out *he or she* or *his or her* instead of using and/or constructions. To be more concise, switch to plural pronouns and antecedents. (For more about gender-neutral language, see 12f.)

Everyone bowed *his or her* head. [**Everyone** bowed *his* head is considered sexist language if women were present when the heads were bowed.]

The **people** bowed **their** heads.

historic, historical The adjective *historic* means "important in history" or "highly memorable." The adjective *historical* means "relating to history." Use *a,* not *an,* before these words because they start with the consonant *h.*

hopefully *Hopefully* is an adverb meaning "with hope, in a hopeful manner," so as an adverb, it can modify a verb, an adjective, or another adverb. However, *hopefully* is nonstandard as a sentence modifier meaning "we hope"; therefore, in academic writing, avoid this usage.

They waited **hopefully** [adverb] for the crippled airplane to land. **We hope** [not Hopefully,] it will land safely.

humanity, humankind, humans, mankind To use gender-neutral language, choose *humanity, humankind,* or *humans* instead of *mankind.*

Some think that the computer has helped **humanity** more than any other twentieth-century invention.

i.e. This abbreviation refers to the Latin term *id est.* In academic writing, use the English translation "that is."

if, whether At the start of a noun clause that expresses speculation or unknown conditions, you can use either *if* or *whether.* However, in such conditional clauses use only *whether* (or *whether or not*) when alternatives are expressed or implied. In a conditional clause that does not express or imply alternatives, use only *if.*

> **If** [not *whether*] you promise not to step on my feet, I might dance with you. Still, I'm not sure **if** [or *whether*] I want to dance with you. Once I decide, I'll dance with you **whether** [not *if*] I like the music or **whether** [not *if*] the next song is fast or slow.

illicit   See *elicit, illicit.*

illusion   See *allusion, illusion.*

immigrate   See *emigrate, immigrate.*

immoral   See *amoral, immoral.*

imply, infer   *Imply* means "hint at or suggest." *Infer* means "draw a conclusion." A writer or speaker *implies;* a reader or listener *infers.*

> When the governor **implied** that she wouldn't seek reelection, reporters **inferred** that she was planning to run for vice president.

include, comprise   The verb *include* means "contain or regard as part of a whole." The verb *comprise* means "consist of or be composed of."

incredible, incredulous   *Incredible* means "extraordinary; not believable." *Incredulous* means "unable or unwilling to believe."

> Listeners were **incredulous** as the freed hostages described the **incredible** hardships they had experienced.

in lieu of   *In lieu of* always means "instead of" or "in the place of." It never means "in light of," "in view of," or "because of."

> **In lieu of** a driver's license for identification, you can present a passport or birth certificate instead.

in regard to, with regard to, as regards, regarding   Use *about, concerning,* and *for* in place of these wordy phrases. Also, avoid the nonstandard *as regards to.*

> **Concerning** [not *in regard to, with regard to, as regards,* or *regarding*] your question, we can now confirm that your payment was received.

inside of, outside of   These phrases are nonstandard when used to mean *inside* or *outside.* When writing about time, never use *inside of* to mean "in less than."

> She waited **outside** [not *outside of*] the apartment house. He changed to clothes that were more informal in **less than** [not *inside of*] ten minutes.

insure   See *assure, ensure, insure.*

irregardless   *Irregardless* is nonstandard for *regardless.*

is when, is where   Never use these constructions when you define something. Instead, use active verbs.

Defensive driving **involves staying** [not *is when you stay*] alert.

its, it's   *Its* is a personal pronoun in the possessive case. *It's* is a contraction of *it is.*

The dog buried **its** bone today. **It's** hot today, which makes the dog restless.

kind, sort   Combine *kind* and *sort* with *this* or *that* when referring to singular nouns. Combine *kinds* and *sorts* with *these* or *those* when referring to plural nouns. Also, never use *a* or *an* after *kind of* or *sort of.*

To stay cool, drink **these kinds** of fluids [not *this kind*] for **this sort of** day [not *this sort of a*].

kind of, sort of   These phrases are colloquial adverbs. In academic writing, use *somewhat.*

The campers were **somewhat** [not *kind of*] dehydrated after the hike.

later, latter   *Later* means "after some time; subsequently." *Latter* refers to the second of two items.

The college library stays open **later** than the town library; also, the **latter** is closed on weekends.

lay, lie   The verb *lay* (**lay,** *laid, laid, laying*) means "place or put something, usually on something else" and needs a direct object. The verb *lie* (**lie,** *lay, lain, lying*), meaning "recline," doesn't need a direct object. Substituting *lay* for *lie,* or the opposite, is nonstandard. *Layed* is not a word.

Lay [not *lie*] down the blanket [direct object], and then place the baby to **lie** [not *lay*] in the shade.

leave, let   *Leave* means "depart." *Leave* is nonstandard for *let. Let* means "allow, permit."

Could you **let** [not *leave*] me use your car tonight?

less   See *fewer, less.*

lie   See *lay, lie.*

like   See *as, as if, as though, like.*

likely See *apt, likely, liable.*

lots, lots of, a lot of These are colloquial constructions. Instead, use *many, much,* or *a great deal.*

mankind See *humanity, humankind, humans, mankind.*

may See *can, may.*

maybe, may be *Maybe* is an adverb; *may be* (two words) is a verb phrase.

> **Maybe** [adverb] we can win, but our team **may be** [verb phrase] too tired.

may of, might of *May of* and *might of* are nonstandard for *may have* and *might have.*

media *Media* is the plural of *medium,* yet colloquial usage now pairs it with a singular verb (for example, *The **media saturates** us with information about every fire*).

morale, moral *Morale* is a noun meaning "a mental state relating to courage, confidence, or enthusiasm." As a noun, *moral* means an "ethical lesson implied or taught by a story or event." As an adjective, *moral* means "ethical."

> One **moral** [noun] of the story is that many people who suffer from low **morale** [noun] still abide by high **moral** [adjective] standards.

most *Most* is nonstandard for *almost.* Also, *most* is the superlative form of an adjective (*some* words, *more* words, *most* words) and of adverbs (*most* suddenly).

> **Almost** [not *Most*] all writers agree that Shakespeare penned the **most** [adjective] brilliant plays ever written.

Ms. *Ms.* is a woman's title free of reference to marital status, equivalent to *Mr.* for men. Generally, use *Ms.* unless a woman requests *Miss* or *Mrs.*

must of *Must of* is nonstandard for *must have.*

nowheres *Nowheres* is nonstandard for *nowhere.*

number See *amount, number.*

of Use *have,* not *of,* after modal auxiliary verbs (*could, may, might, must, should, would*). See also *could of; may of; might of; must of; should of; would of.*

off of *Off of* is nonstandard for *off.*

> Don't fall **off** [not *off of*] the stage.

OK, O.K., okay   These three forms are informal. In academic writing, choose words that express more specific meanings. If you must use the term, choose the full word *okay*.

> The weather was **suitable** [not okay] for a picnic.

on account of, owing to the fact that   Use *because* or *because of* in place of these wordy phrases.

> **Because of the rain** [not *On account of the rain* or *Owing to the fact that it rained*], the picnic was cancelled.

oral, verbal   The adjective *oral* means "spoken or being done by the mouth." The adjective *verbal* means "relating to language" (*verbal* skill) or to words rather than actions, facts, or ideas.

outside of   See *inside of, outside of.*

percent, percentage   Use *percent* with specific numbers: two *percent,* 95 *percent.* Use *percentage* to refer to portions of a whole in general terms.

> Of the eligible US population, **35 percent** votes regularly in national elections. In local elections, **the percentage** [not *the percent*] is much lower.

pixel, pixelation, pixilated   *Pixel,* a relatively new word created from "picture/pix" and "element," is the name for a small dot on a video screen. *Pixelation* (with an *e,* as in *pixel*) is a noun meaning "a film technique that makes people appear to move faster than they are." *Pixilated* (with an *i*), a verb unrelated to *pixels,* derives from *pixie,* meaning "a mischievous elf," and now describes someone who is slightly drunk.

plus   *Plus* is nonstandard for *and, also, in addition,* and *moreover.*

> The band booked three concerts in Hungary, **and** [not *plus*] it will tour Poland for a month. **In addition,** [not *Plus,*] it may perform once in Austria.

precede, proceed   *Precede* is a verb that means "go before." *Proceed* is a verb that means "to advance, go on, undertake, carry on."

> **Preceded** by elephants and music, the ringmaster **proceeded** into the main tent.

pretty   *Pretty* is informal for *rather, quite, somewhat,* or *very.*

> The flu epidemic was **quite** [not *pretty*] severe.

principal, principle   As a noun, *principal* means "chief person; main or original amount." As an adjective, *principal* means "most important." *Principle* is a noun that means "a basic truth or rule."

During the assembly, the **principal** [noun] said, "A **principal** [adjective] value in our democracy is the **principle** [noun] of free speech."

proceed   See *precede, proceed.*

quotation, quote   *Quotation* is a noun, and *quote* is a verb. Don't use *quote* as a noun.

One newspaper reporter **quoted** [verb] the US president, and soon the **quotations** [noun—not *quotes*, which is a verb] were widely broadcast.

raise, rise   *Raise* is a verb (*raise, raised, raised, raising*) that means "lift" or "construct" and needs a direct object. *Rise* (*rise, rose, risen, rising*) means "go upward" and doesn't need a direct object. Substituting *rise* for *raise,* or the opposite, is nonstandard.

When workers **rise** [not *raise*] early, they **raise** [not *rise* or *rise up*] more new walls in a day.

real, really   These words are nonstandard for *very* and *extremely.*

reason is because   This phrase is redundant. To be concise and correct, use *reason is that.*

One **reason** we moved **is that** [not *is because*] our factory was relocated.

reason why   This phrase is redundant. To be concise and correct, use *reason* or *why.*

I don't know **why** [not *the reason why*] they left home.

regarding   See *in regard to, with regard to, as regards, regarding.*

regardless   See *irregardless.*

respectful, respectfully   As an adjective, *respectful* means "marked by respect, showing regard for, or giving honor to." *Respectfully* is the adverb form of *respectful.* Be careful not to confuse these words with *respective* and *respectively* (see next entry).

The child listened **respectfully** [adverb] to the lecture about **respectful** [adjective] behavior.

respective, respectively   *Respective,* a noun, refers to two or more individual persons or things. *Respectively,* an adverb, refers back to two or more individuals or things in the same sequence in which they were originally mentioned.

> After the fire drill, Dr. Daniel Eagle and Dr. Jessica Chess returned to their **respective** offices [that is, he returned to his office, and she returned to her office] on the second and third floors, **respectively** [his office is on the second floor, and her office is on the third floor].

right   *Right* is sometimes used colloquially for *quite, very, extremely,* or similar intensifiers.

> You did **very** [not right] well on the quiz.

rise   See *raise, rise.*

scarcely   Use *scarcely* with *can,* never with *can't.*

secondly   See *firstly, secondly, thirdly.*

seen   *Seen* is the past participle of the verb *see* (*see, saw, **seen**, seeing*). *Seen* is nonstandard for *saw,* a verb in the past tense. Always use *seen* with an auxiliary verb.

> Last night, I **saw** [not seen] the movie that you ***had* seen** [not seen] last week.

set, sit   The verb *set* (*set, set, setting*) means "put in place, position, put down" and needs a direct object. The verb *sit* (*sit, sat, sitting*) means "be seated" and doesn't need a direct object. Substituting *set* for *sit,* or the opposite, is nonstandard.

> Susan **set** [not sat] the sandwiches beside the salad, made Spot **sit** [not set] down, and then **sat** [not set] on the sofa.

shall, will, should   *Shall* was once used with *I* and *we* for future-tense verbs, and *will* was used for all other persons. Today, *shall* is considered highly formal, and *will* is more widely used. Similarly, distinctions were once made between *shall* and *should,* but today *should* is preferred. However, in questions, *should* is used about as often as *shall.*

> We **will** [or shall] depart on Monday, but he **will** [never shall] wait until Thursday to depart. **Should** [or Shall] I telephone ahead to reserve a suite at the hotel?

should of   *Should of* is nonstandard for *should have.*

sit   See *set, sit.*

site   See *cite, site.*

sometime, sometimes, some time   The adverb *sometime* means "at an unspecified time." The adverb *sometimes* means "now and then." *Some time* (two words) is an adjective with a noun that means "an amount or span of time."

Sometime [adverb for "at an unspecified time"] next year, I must take my qualifying exams. I **sometimes** [adverb for "now and then"] worry whether I'll find **some time** [adjective with a noun] to study for them.

sort of See *kind of, sort of.*

stationary, stationery *Stationary* means "not moving; unchanging." *Stationery* refers to paper and related writing products.

Using our firm's **stationery**, I wrote to city officials about a **stationary** light pole that had been knocked over in a car accident.

such *Such* is informal for intensifiers such as *very* and *extremely.* However, *such* is acceptable to mean "of the same or similar kind."

The play got **very** [not such] bad reviews. The playwright was embarrassed by **such** strong criticism.

supposed to, used to The final *-d* is essential in both phrases.

We were **supposed** to [not suppose to] leave early. I **used** to [not use to] wake up before the alarm rang.

sure *Sure* is nonstandard for *surely* or *certainly.*

I was **certainly** [not sure] surprised at the results.

sure and, try and Both phrases are nonstandard for *sure to* and *try to.*

Please **try to** [not try and] reach my doctor.

than, then *Than* indicates comparison; *then* relates to time.

Please put on your gloves, and **then** your hat. It's colder outside **than** you think.

that, which Use *that* with restrictive (essential) clauses only. You can use *which* with both restrictive and nonrestrictive (nonessential) clauses; however, many people reserve *which* to use only with nonrestrictive clauses.

The house **that** [or which] Jack built is on Beanstalk Street, **which** [not that] runs past the reservoir.

that there, them there, this here, these here These phrases are nonstandard for *that, them, this, these,* respectively.

their, there, they're *Their* is a possessive pronoun. *There* means "in that place" or is part of an expletive construction. *They're* is a contraction of *they are.*

They're going to **their** accounting class in the building over **there** near the library. Do you know that **there** are twelve sections of Accounting 101?

theirself, theirselves, themself　These words are nonstandard for *themselves*.

them　Use *them* as an object pronoun only. Do not use *them* in place of the adjectives *these* and *those*.

> Let's buy **those** [not them] delicious looking strawberries.

then　See *than, then*.

thirdly　See *firstly, secondly, thirdly*.

thusly　*Thusly* is nonstandard for *thus*.

till, until　Both are acceptable, although *until* is preferred for academic writing.

to, too, two　*To* is a preposition; it also is part of an infinitive verb. *Too* is an adverb meaning "also; more than enough." *Two* is a number.

> When you go **to** Chicago, visit the Art Institute. Try **to** visit Harry Caray's for dinner, **too**. It won't be **too** expensive because **two** people can share a meal.

toward, towards　Although both are acceptable, writers of American English generally prefer *toward*.

try and, sure and　See *sure and, try and*.

type　*Type* is nonstandard when used to mean *type of*.

> I recommend that you use only that **type of** [not type] glue on plastic.

unique　Never combine *unique* with *more, most,* or other qualifiers.

> Solar heating is **unique** [not somewhat unique] in the Northeast. One **unique** [not very unique] heating system in a Vermont house uses hydrogen for fuel.

uninterested　See *disinterested, uninterested*.

used to　See *supposed to, used to*.

utilize　*Utilize* is considered an overblown word for *use* in academic writing.

> The team **used** [not utilized] all its players to win the game.

verbal, oral　See *oral, verbal*.

wait on　*Wait on* is an informal substitute for *wait for*. *Wait on* is appropriate only when people give service to others.

> I had to **wait for** [not wait on] half an hour for the hotel desk clerk to **wait on** me.

way, ways   When referring to distance, use *way* rather than *ways*.

He is a long **way** [not ways] from home.

Web site, website   Usage at the time of this book's publication calls for two words and a capital *W.* Increasingly, the informal *website* is being used.

well   See *good, well*.

where   *Where* is nonstandard for *that* when *where* is used as a subordinating conjunction.

I read **that** [not where] salt raises blood pressure.

where . . . at   This phrase is redundant; use only *where*.

Where is your house? [not *Where is your house at?*]

whether   See *if, whether*.

which   See *that, which*.

who, whom   Use *who* as a subject or a subject complement; use *whom* as an object (see 16g).

who's, whose   *Who's* is the contraction of *who is*. *Whose* is a possessive pronoun.

Who's willing to drive? **Whose** truck should we take?

will   See *shall, will*.

-wise   The suffix *-wise* means "in a manner, direction, or position." Never attach *-wise* indiscriminately to create new words. Instead, choose words that already exist; when in doubt, consult a dictionary to see if the *-wise* word you have in mind is acceptable.

World Wide Web   Written out, the three words start with a capital *W.* Its abbreviation only in URLs is *www.* When you use only the word *Web,* start it with a capital *W.*

would of   *Would of* is nonstandard for *would have*.

your, you're   *Your* is a possessive pronoun. *You're* is the contraction of *you are*.

You're kind to volunteer **your** time at the senior center.

Understanding Grammar
and Writing Correct Sentences

14

Parts of Speech and Sentence Structures

PARTS OF SPEECH

14a   Why learn the parts of speech?

Knowing the names and definitions of parts of speech gives you a vocabulary for identifying words and understanding how language works to create meaning. No part of speech exists in a vacuum. To identify a word's part of speech correctly, you need to see how the word functions in a sentence. Sometimes the same word functions differently in different sentences, so check the part of speech used in each instance.

> We ate **fish.** [*Fish* is a noun. It names a thing.]
>
> We **fish** on weekends. [*Fish* is a verb. It names an action.]

14b   What is a noun?

A **noun** names a person, place, thing, or idea: *student, college, textbook, education.* Quick Reference 14.1 lists different kinds of nouns.

ESOL Tips: Here are some useful tips for working with nouns.

- Nouns often appear with words that tell how much or how many, whose, which one, and similar information. These words include ARTICLES* (*a, an, the*) and other determiners or limiting adjectives; see section 14f and Chapter 51.
- Nouns sometimes serve as ADJECTIVES. For example, in the term *police officer,* the word *police* serves as an adjective to describe *officer.*
- Nouns in many languages other than English are *inflected.* This means they change form, usually with a special ending, to communicate gender (male, female, neuter); number (singular, plural); and case (see 16a through 16k).
- Words with these suffixes (word endings) are usually nouns: *-ness, -ence, -ance, -ty,* and *-ment.*

---

*Words printed in SMALL CAPITAL LETTERS are discussed elsewhere in the text and are defined in the Terms Glossary at the back of this book.

Quick Reference 14.1

Nouns

PROPER	names specific people, places, or things (first letter is always capitalized)	*Dave Matthews, Paris, Toyota*
COMMON	names general groups, places, people, or things	*singer, city, automobile*
CONCRETE	names things experienced through the senses: sight, hearing, taste, smell, and touch	*landscape, pizza, thunder*
ABSTRACT	names things not knowable through the senses	*freedom, shyness*
COLLECTIVE	names groups	*family, team*
NONCOUNT OR MASS	names "uncountable" things	*water, time*
COUNT	names countable items	*lake, minute*

14c What is a pronoun?

A **pronoun** takes the place of a NOUN. The words or word that a pronoun replaces is called the pronoun's ANTECEDENT. See Quick Reference 14.2 for a list of different kinds of pronouns. For information on how to use pronouns correctly, see Chapters 16 and 17.

David is an accountant. [The noun *David* names a person.]

He is an accountant. [The pronoun *he* refers to its antecedent, *David*.]

The finance committee needs to consult **him**. [The pronoun *him* refers to its antecedent, *David*.]

Quick Reference 14.2

Pronouns

PERSONAL *I, you, its, her, they, ours,* and others	refers to people or things	*I saw **her** take a book to **them**.*
RELATIVE *who, which, that*	introduces certain NOUN CLAUSES and ADJECTIVE CLAUSES	*The book **that** I lost was valuable.*

continued >>

> ### Quick Reference 14.2   (continued)
>
> | | | |
> |---|---|---|
> | **INTERROGATIVE** *which, who, whose, and others* | introduces a question | *Who called?* |
> | **DEMONSTRATIVE** *this, that, these, those* | points out the antecedent | *Whose books are **these**?* |
> | **REFLEXIVE OR INTENSIVE** *myself, themselves, and other -self or -selves words* | reflects back to the antecedent; intensifies the antecedent | *They claim to support **themselves. I myself** doubt it.* |
> | **RECIPROCAL** *each other, one another* | refers to individual parts of a plural antecedent | *We respect **each other**.* |
> | **INDEFINITE** *all, anyone, each, and others* | refers to nonspecific persons or things | ***Everyone** is welcome here.* |

EXERCISE 14-1   Underline and label all nouns (N) and pronouns (P). Refer to 14a through 14c for help.

<pre>
          P   N   P   N   N
EXAMPLE   My mother celebrated her eightieth birthday this summer with

          P   N   N   P   N
          her family and friends; she greatly enjoyed the festivities.
</pre>

1. More and more people live into their eighties and nineties because they get better health benefits and they take better care of themselves.

2. Many elderly people now live busy lives, continuing in businesses or volunteering at various agencies.

3. My mother, Elizabeth, for example, spends four hours each morning as a volunteer for the Red Cross, where she takes histories from blood donors.

4. My neighbors, George and Sandra, who are eighty-six years old, still own and run a card and candy shop.

5. Age has become no obstacle for active seniors as evidenced by the activities they pursue today.

14d   What is a verb?

Main verbs express action, occurrence, or state of being. For information on how to use verbs correctly, see Chapter 15.

I **dance**. [action]

The audience **became** silent. [occurrence]

Your dancing **was** excellent. [state of being]

🛈 **Alert:** If you're not sure whether a word is a verb, try substituting a different TENSE for the word. If the sentence still makes sense, the word is a verb.

> **NO** He is a **changed** man. He is a **will change** man. [*Changed* isn't a verb because the sentence doesn't make sense when *will change* is substituted.]
>
> **YES** The man **changed** his profession. The man **will change** his profession. [*Changed* is a verb because the sentence makes sense when the verb *will change* is substituted.] ●

EXERCISE 14-2   Underline all main verbs. Refer to 14d for help.

EXAMPLE   The study of bats <u>produces</u> some surprising information.

1. Most bats developed many years ago from a shrewlike mammal.

2. One thousand different types of bats exist.

3. Bats comprise almost one quarter of all mammal species.

4. The smallest bat in the world measures only one inch long, while the biggest is sixteen inches long.

5. Bats survive in widely varied surroundings, from deserts to cities.

14e   What is a verbal?

Verbals are verb parts functioning as NOUNS, ADJECTIVES, or ADVERBS. Quick Reference 14.3 lists the three different kinds of verbals.

Quick Reference 14.3   ■ ■ ■ ■ ■ ■ ■

Verbals and their functions

INFINITIVE *to* + verb	1. noun 2. adjective or adverb	*To eat now is inconvenient.* *Still, we have far to go.*
PAST PARTICIPLE *-ed* form of REGULAR VERB or equivalent in IRREGULAR VERB	adjective	*Boiled, filtered water is safe.*
PRESENT PARTICIPLE *-ing* form of verb	1. noun (called a GERUND) 2. adjective	*Eating in diners on the road is an adventure.* *Running water may not be safe.*

ESOL Tip: For information about correctly using the verbals called *infinitives* and *gerunds* as objects, see Chapter 54.

14f What is an adjective?

Adjectives modify—that is, they describe or limit—NOUNS, PRONOUNS, and word groups that function as nouns. For information on how to use adjectives correctly, see Chapter 18.

> I saw a **green** tree. [*Green* modifies the noun *tree*.]
>
> It was **leafy.** [*Leafy* modifies the pronoun *it*.]
>
> The flowering trees were **beautiful.** [*Beautiful* modifies the noun phrase *the flowering trees*.]

ESOL Tip: You can identify some kinds of adjectives by looking at their endings. Usually, words with the SUFFIXES *-ful, -ish, -less,* and *-like* are adjectives.

Determiners, frequently called **limiting adjectives**, tell whether a noun is general (*a* tree) or specific (*the* tree). Determiners also tell which one (*this* tree), how many (*twelve* trees), whose (*our* tree), and similar information.

The determiners *a, an,* and *the* are almost always called **articles.** *The* is a **definite article.** Before a noun, *the* conveys that the noun refers to a specific item (*the* plan). *A* and *an* are **indefinite articles.** They convey that a noun refers to an item in a nonspecific or general way (*a* plan).

Alert: Use *a* when the word following it starts with a consonant: *a carrot, a broken egg, a hip.* Also, use *a* when the word following starts with an *h* that is sounded: *a historical event, a home.* Use *an* when the word following starts with a vowel sound: *an honor, an old bag, an egg.*

ESOL Tip: For information about using articles with COUNT and NONCOUNT NOUNS, and about articles with PROPER NOUNS and GERUNDS, see Chapter 54.

Quick Reference 14.4 lists kinds of determiners. Notice, however, that some words in Quick Reference 14.4 function also as pronouns. To identify a word's part of speech, always check to see how it functions in each particular sentence.

> **That** car belongs to Harold. [*That* is a limiting adjective.]
>
> **That** is Harold's car. [*That* is a demonstrative pronoun.]

Quick Reference 14.4 ■ ■ ■ ■ ■ ■ ■

Determiners (or limiting adjectives)

ARTICLES *a, an, the*	*The news reporter used a cell phone to report an assignment.*
DEMONSTRATIVE *this, these, that, those*	*Those students rent that house.*
INDEFINITE *any, each, few, other, some,* and others	*Few films today have complex plots.*
INTERROGATIVE *what, which, whose*	*What answer did you give?*
NUMERICAL *one, first, two, second,* and others	*The fifth question was tricky.*
POSSESSIVE *my, your, their,* and others	*My violin is older than your cello.*
RELATIVE *what, which, whose, whatever,* and others	*We do not know which road to take.*

14g   What is an adverb?

Adverbs modify—that is, adverbs describe or limit   VERBS, ADJECTIVES, other adverbs, and CLAUSES. For information on how to use adverbs correctly, see Chapter 18.

> Chefs plan meals **carefully.** [*Carefully* modifies the verb *plan.*]
>
> Vegetables provide **very** important vitamins. [*Very* modifies the adjective *important.*]
>
> Those potato chips are **too** heavily salted. [*Too* modifies the adverb *heavily.*]
>
> **Fortunately,** people are learning that overuse of salt is harmful. [*Fortunately* modifies the rest of the sentence, an independent clause.]

Descriptive adverbs show levels of intensity, usually by adding *more* (or *less*) and *most* (or *least*): *more* happily, *least* clearly (18e). Many descriptive adverbs are formed by adding *-ly* to adjectives: *sadly, loudly, normally.* But many adverbs do not end in *-ly*: *very, always, not, yesterday,* and *well* are a few. Some adjectives look like adverbs but are not: *brotherly, lonely, lovely.*

Relative adverbs are words such as *where, why,* and *when.* They are used to introduce ADJECTIVE CLAUSES.

Conjunctive adverbs modify—that is, conjunctive adverbs describe or limit—by creating logical connections to give words meaning. Conjunctive adverbs can appear anywhere in a sentence: at the start, in the middle, or at the end.

However, we consider Isaac Newton an even more important scientist.

We consider Isaac Newton, **however,** an even more important scientist.

We consider Isaac Newton an even more important scientist, **however.**

Quick Reference 14.5 lists the kinds of relationships that conjunctive adverbs can show.

Quick Reference 14.5 ■ ■ ■ ■ ■ ■ ■

Conjunctive adverbs and relationships they express

Relationship	Words
ADDITION	*also, furthermore, moreover, besides*
CONTRAST	*however, still, nevertheless, conversely, nonetheless, instead, otherwise*
COMPARISON	*similarly, likewise*
RESULT OR SUMMARY	*therefore, thus, consequently, accordingly, hence, then*
TIME	*next, then, meanwhile, finally, subsequently*
EMPHASIS	*indeed, certainly*

● **EXERCISE 14-3** Underline and label all adjectives (ADJ) and adverbs
● (ADV). For help, consult 14e through 14g.

ADJ   ADV   ADJ

EXAMPLE Young families carefully looking for a good pet should consider

ADV

domesticated rats.

1. Rats are clean animals that easily bond to their human companions.

2. Two rats are better than one because they are gregarious animals who desperately need social interaction.

3. As intelligent animals, rats can be quickly trained to perform many tricks.

4. Humans consistently have been keeping rats as household pets for over 100 years.

5. Finally, they pose no more health risks than other pets.

14h What is a preposition?

Prepositions are words that convey relationships, usually in time or space. Common prepositions include *in, under, by, after, to, on, over,* and *since*. A

PREPOSITIONAL PHRASE consists of a preposition and the words it modifies. For information about prepositions and commas, see 24k.2.

In the fall, we will hear a concert **by our favorite tenor.**

After the concert, he will fly **to San Francisco.**

🌐 **ESOL Tip:** For a list of prepositions and the IDIOMS they create, see Chapter 53. ●

14i What is a conjunction?

A **conjunction** connects words, PHRASES, or CLAUSES. **Coordinating conjunctions** join two or more grammatically equal words, phrases, or clauses. Quick Reference 14.6 lists the coordinating conjunctions and the relationships they express.

We hike **and** camp every summer. [*And* joins two words.]

We hike along scenic trails **or** in the wilderness. [*Or* joins two phrases.]

I love the outdoors, **but** my family does not. [*But* joins two independent clauses.]

Quick Reference 14.6	■ ■ ■ ■ ■ ■ ■

Coordinating conjunctions and relationships they express	
Relationship	Words
ADDITION	*and*
CONTRAST	*but, yet*
RESULT OR EFFECT	*so*
REASON OR CAUSE	*for*
CHOICE	*or*
NEGATIVE CHOICE	*nor*

Correlative conjunctions are two conjunctions that work as a pair: *both . . . and; either . . . or; neither . . . nor; not only . . . but (also); whether . . . or;* and *not . . . so much as.*

Both English **and** Spanish are spoken in many homes in the United States.

Not only students **but also** businesspeople should study a second language.

Subordinating conjunctions introduce DEPENDENT CLAUSES. Subordinating conjunctions express relationships making the dependent clause in a sentence grammatically less important than the INDEPENDENT CLAUSE in the sentence. Quick Reference 14.7 lists the most common subordinating conjunctions. For information about how to use them correctly, see 9d through 9m.

> **Quick Reference 14.7**   ■ ■ ■ ■ ■ ■ ■
>
> ## Subordinating conjunctions and relationships they express
>
> | Relationship | Words |
> | --- | --- |
> | TIME | *after, before, once, since, until, when, whenever, while* |
> | REASON OR CAUSE | *as, because, since* |
> | RESULT OR EFFECT | *in order that, so, so that, that* |
> | CONDITION | *if, even if, provided that, unless* |
> | CONTRAST | *although, even though, though, whereas* |
> | LOCATION | *where, wherever* |
> | CHOICE | *than, whether* |

Because it snowed, school was canceled.

Many people were happy **after** they heard the news.

14j What is an interjection?

An **interjection** is a word or expression that conveys surprise or a strong emotion. Alone, an interjection is usually punctuated with an exclamation point (!). As part of a sentence, an interjection is usually set off by one or more commas.

Hooray! I won the race.

Oh, my friends missed seeing the finish.

● **EXERCISE 14-4**   Identify the part of speech of each numbered and under-
● lined word. Choose from noun, pronoun, verb, adjective, adverb, preposition,
● coordinating conjunction, correlative conjunction, and subordinating conjunction.
For help, consult 14b through 14i.

$$\overset{1}{}\qquad\overset{2}{}$$

The Mason-Dixon line <u>primarily</u> marks the <u>boundary</u> between Pennsyl-

$$\overset{3}{}$$

vania and Maryland. It was surveyed in the <u>eighteenth</u> century by Charles

$$\overset{4}{}$$

Mason and Jeremiah Dixon, who had <u>previously</u> worked together on a

$$\overset{5}{}$$

<u>scientific</u> expedition to South Africa.

$$\overset{6}{}$$

In 1760, the Calverts of Maryland and the Penns of Pennsylvania <u>hired</u>

$$\overset{7}{}\qquad\qquad\overset{8}{}$$

Mason and Dixon to settle a <u>boundary</u> dispute between their parcels <u>of</u> land.

Mason and Dixon marked their line every five miles using stones shipped from
England, which are called crownstones. These markers were decorated with
two coats-of-arms and can still be found scattered throughout this part of the
country.

Even though Mason and Dixon were British, they had very different backgrounds. Mason was the son of a baker and trained in astronomy. Dixon was a
Quaker, and he specialized in surveying.

The line they drew in America eventually became a symbolic division
between free states and slave states until the end of the Civil War. Because of
the line's importance, it has been the focus of both literature and music, such
as the song "Sailing to Philadelphia" by Mark Knopfler.

SENTENCE STRUCTURES

14k   How is a sentence defined?

A **sentence** is defined in several ways: On a strictly mechanical level, a sentence starts with a capital letter and finishes with a period, question mark, or
exclamation point. Grammatically, a sentence consists of an INDEPENDENT
CLAUSE: *Skydiving is dangerous.* You might hear a sentence described as a
"complete thought," but that definition is too vague to help much. From
the perspective of its purpose, a sentence is defined as listed in Quick Reference 14.8 on page 296.

14l   What are a subject and a predicate in a sentence?

The **subject** and **predicate** of a sentence are its two essential parts. Without
both, a group of words isn't a sentence. Quick Reference 14.9 shows the sentence
pattern with both. Terms used in the Quick Reference are defined after it.

Quick Reference 14.8

Sentences and their purposes

- A **declarative sentence** makes a statement: *Skydiving is dangerous.*
- An **interrogative sentence** asks a question: *Is skydiving dangerous?*
- An **imperative sentence** gives a command: *Be careful when you skydive.*
- An **exclamatory sentence** expresses strong feeling: *How I love skydiving!*

Quick Reference 14.9

Sentence pattern I: Subjects and predicates

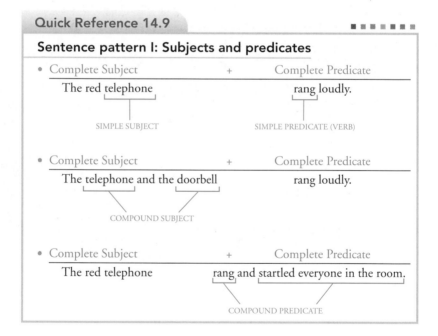

The **simple subject** is the word or group of words that acts, is described, or is acted upon.

The **telephone** rang. [Simple subject, *telephone*, acts.]

The **telephone** is red. [Simple subject, *telephone*, is described.]

The **telephone** was being connected. [Simple subject, *telephone*, is acted upon.]

The **complete subject** is the simple subject and its MODIFIERS.

The red telephone rang.

A **complete compound subject** consists of two or more NOUNS or PRONOUNS and their modifiers.

The telephone and the doorbell rang.

The **predicate** contains the VERB in the sentence. The predicate tells what the subject is doing or experiencing or what is being done to the subject.

The telephone **rang.** [*Rang* tells what the subject, *telephone*, did.]

The telephone **is red.** [*Is* tells what the subject, *telephone*, experiences.]

The telephone **was being connected.** [*Was being connected* tells what was being done to the subject, *telephone*.]

A **simple predicate** contains only the verb.

The lawyer **listened.**

A **complete predicate** contains the verb and its modifiers.

The lawyer **listened carefully.**

A **compound predicate** contains two or more verbs.

The lawyer **listened and waited.**

🌐 **ESOL Tips:** (1) The subject of a declarative sentence usually comes before the predicate, but there are exceptions (9o). In sentences that ask a question, part of the predicate usually comes before the subject. For more information about word order in English sentences, see Chapter 52. (2) In English, don't add a PERSONAL PRONOUN to repeat the stated noun.

> NO   My **grandfather he** lived to be eighty-seven. [The personal pronoun, *he*, mistakenly repeats the stated noun, *grandfather*.]

> YES   My **grandfather** lived to be eighty-seven.

> NO   **Winter storms** that bring ice, sleet, and snow **they** can cause traffic problems. [The personal pronoun, *they*, mistakenly repeats the stated noun, *winter storms*.]

> YES   **Winter storms** that bring ice, sleet, and snow can cause traffic problems. ●

EXERCISE 14-5   Use a slash to separate the complete subject from the complete predicate. For help, consult 14l.

EXAMPLE   A smart shopper / is an intelligent, well-informed consumer.

1. Wise consumers use the Internet to compare prices to discover the best values available.

2. Smart clothing shoppers keep their eyes on the sale racks.

3. They buy summer clothes in the winter and winter clothes in the summer.

4. The financial savings make them content to wait a few months to wear their new clothes.

5. Another good way to earn money for clothing is for people to sell their good used clothing to a resale store.

14m   What are direct and indirect objects?

A **direct object** is a noun, pronoun, or group of words acting as a noun that receives the action of a TRANSITIVE VERB. To check for a direct object, make up a *whom?* or *what?* question about the verb.

An **indirect object** is a noun, pronoun, or group of words acting as a noun that tells *to whom* or *for whom* the action expressed by a transitive verb

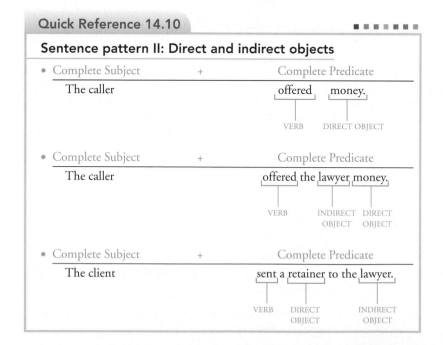

Quick Reference 14.10

Sentence pattern II: Direct and indirect objects

- Complete Subject   +   Complete Predicate

  The caller   offered   money.

                                       VERB   DIRECT OBJECT

- Complete Subject   +   Complete Predicate

  The caller   offered the lawyer money.

                                       VERB   INDIRECT DIRECT
                                               OBJECT   OBJECT

- Complete Subject   +   Complete Predicate

  The client   sent a retainer to the lawyer.

                                       VERB DIRECT   INDIRECT
                                             OBJECT   OBJECT

was done. To check for an indirect object, make up a *to whom? for whom? to what?* or *for what?* question about the verb.

Direct objects and indirect objects always fall in the PREDICATE of a sentence. Quick Reference 14.10 shows how direct and indirect objects function in sentences.

ESOL Tips: (1) In sentences with indirect objects that follow the word *to* or *for,* always put the direct object before the indirect object.

NO	Will you please give **to John** this letter?
YES	Will you please give this letter **to John?**

(2) When a PRONOUN is used as an indirect object, some verbs require *to* or *for* before the pronoun, and others do not. Consult the *Dictionary of American English* (Heinle and Heinle) about each verb when you're unsure.

NO	Please explain **me** the rule. [*Explain* requires *to* before an indirect object.]
YES	Please explain the rule **to me.**
YES	Please give **me** that book. Please give that book **to me.** [*Give* uses both patterns.]

(3) When both the direct object and the indirect object are pronouns, put the direct object first and use *to* with the indirect object.

NO	He gave **me it.**
YES	He gave **it to me.**
YES	Please give **me the letter.** [*Give* does not require *to* before an indirect object.]

(4) Even if a verb does not require *to* before an indirect object, you may use *to* if you prefer. If you do use *to,* be sure to put the direct object before the indirect object.

YES	Our daughter sent **our son** a gift.
YES	Our daughter sent a gift **to our son.**

EXERCISE 14-6   Draw a single line under all direct objects and a double line under all indirect objects. For help, consult 14m.

EXAMPLE   Toni Morrison's award-winning novels give <u>readers</u> the <u>gifts</u> of wisdom, inspiration, and pleasure.

1. Literary critics gave high praise to Toni Morrison for her first novel, *The Bluest Eye,* but the general public showed little interest.

2. *Song of Solomon* won Morrison the National Book Critics Circle Award in 1977, and *Beloved* won her the Pulitzer Prize in 1988.

3. A literary panel awarded Toni Morrison the 1993 Nobel Prize in Literature, the highest honor a writer can receive.

4. Her 1998 novel, *Paradise,* traces for readers the tragic lives of a rejected group of former slaves.

5. Twenty-five years after *The Bluest Eye* was published, Oprah Winfrey selected it for her reader's list, and it immediately became a bestseller.

14n What are complements, modifiers, and appositives?

COMPLEMENTS

A **complement** renames or describes a subject or an object. It appears in the predicate of a sentence.

A **subject complement** is a NOUN, PRONOUN, or ADJECTIVE that follows a LINKING VERB. **Predicate nominative** is another term for a noun used as a subject complement, and **predicate adjective** is another term for an adjective used as a subject complement.

An **object complement** follows a DIRECT OBJECT and either describes or renames the direct object. Quick Reference 14.11 shows how subject and object complements function in a sentence.

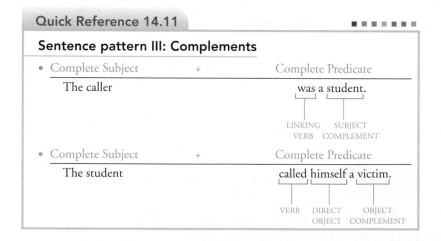

Quick Reference 14.11

Sentence pattern III: Complements

- Complete Subject + Complete Predicate

  The caller   was a student.

                  LINKING   SUBJECT
                  VERB   COMPLEMENT

- Complete Subject + Complete Predicate

  The student   called himself a victim.

                  VERB   DIRECT   OBJECT
                       OBJECT COMPLEMENT

EXERCISE 14-7   Underline all complements and identify each as a subject complement (SUB) or an object complement (OB).

EXAMPLE   Many of the most familiar North American wildflowers are actually

                    SUB
          nonnative <u>plants</u>.

1. The dainty Queen Anne's lace is a native of Europe.
2. The daisies and cornflowers that decorate our roadsides all summer were originally inhabitants of Europe as well.
3. The common purple loosestrife, originally from Asia, came to the North American continent as a garden plant.
4. Many scientists call these plants "alien invasives."
5. Many ecologists consider them threats to the forests, meadows, and wetlands of North America.

MODIFIERS

A **modifier** is a word or group of words that describes or limits other words. Modifiers appear in the subject or the predicate of a sentence.

> The **large red** telephone rang. [The adjectives *large* and *red* modify the noun *telephone*.]
>
> The lawyer answered **quickly.** [The adverb *quickly* modifies the verb *answered*.]
>
> The person **on the telephone** was **extremely** upset. [The prepositional phrase *on the telephone* modifies the noun *person*; the adverb *extremely* modifies the adjective *upset*.]
>
> **Therefore,** the lawyer spoke **gently.** [The adverb *therefore* modifies the independent clause *the lawyer spoke gently*; the adverb *gently* modifies the verb *spoke*.]
>
> **Because the lawyer's voice was calm,** the caller felt reassured. [The adverb clause *because the lawyer's voice was calm* modifies the independent clause *the caller felt reassured*.]

APPOSITIVES

An **appositive** is a word or group of words that renames the noun or pronoun preceding it.

> The student's story, **a tale of broken promises,** was complicated. [The appositive *a tale of broken promises* renames the noun *story*.]
>
> The lawyer consulted an expert, **her law professor.** [The appositive *her law professor* renames the noun *expert*.]

The student, **Joe Jones,** asked to speak to his lawyer. [The appositive *Joe Jones* renames the noun *student.*]

🛈 **Alert:** When an appositive is not essential for identifying what it renames (that is, when it is NONRESTRICTIVE), use a comma or commas to set off the appositive from the rest of the sentence; see 24f. ●

14o   What is a phrase?

A **phrase** is a group of words that does not contain both a SUBJECT and a PREDICATE and therefore cannot stand alone as an independent unit.

NOUN PHRASE

A **noun phrase** functions as a noun in a sentence.

The **modern census** dates back to the seventeenth century.

VERB PHRASE

A **verb phrase** functions as a verb in a sentence.

Two military censuses **are mentioned** in the Bible.

PREPOSITIONAL PHRASE

A **prepositional phrase** always starts with a preposition and functions as a modifier.

William the Conqueror conducted a census **of landowners in newly conquered England in 1086.** [three prepositional phrases in a row, beginning with *of, in, in*]

ABSOLUTE PHRASE

An **absolute phrase** usually contains a noun or pronoun and a present or past participle. An absolute phrase modifies the entire sentence that it's in.

Censuses being the fashion, Quebec and Nova Scotia took sixteen counts between 1665 and 1754.

Eighteenth-century Sweden and Denmark had complete records of their populations, **each adult and child having been counted.**

VERBAL PHRASE

A **verbal phrase** contains a verb part that functions not as a verb, but as a noun or an adjective. Such cases are infinitives, present participles, and past participles.

In 1624, Virginia began **to count its citizens** in a census. [*To count its citizens* is an infinitive phrase.]

Going from door to door, census takers interview millions of people. [*Going from door to door* is a present participial phrase.]

Amazed by some people's answers, census takers always listen carefully. [*Amazed by some people's answers* is a past participial phrase.]

GERUND PHRASE

A **gerund phrase** functions as a noun. Telling the difference between a gerund phrase and a present participial phrase can be tricky because both use the *-ing* verb form. The key is to determine how the phrase functions in the sentence: A gerund phrase functions only as a noun, and a participial phrase functions only as a modifier.

Including each person in the census was important. [This is a gerund phrase because it functions as a noun, which is the subject of the sentence.]

Including each person in the census, Abby spent many hours on the crowded city block. [This is a present participial phrase because it functions as a modifier, namely, an adjective describing Abby.]

EXERCISE 14-8 Combine each set of sentences into a single sentence by converting one sentence into a phrase—a noun phrase, verb phrase, prepositional phrase, absolute phrase, verbal phrase, or gerund phrase. You can omit, add, or change words. Identify which type of phrase you created.

You can combine most sets in several correct ways, but make sure the meaning of your finished sentence is clear. For help, consult 14o.

EXAMPLE   Large chain stores often pose threats to local independent retailers. Smaller store owners must find innovative ways to stay in business.

With large chains posing threats to local independent retailers, smaller store owners must find innovative ways to stay in business. (prepositional phrase)

1. Independent stores develop creative marketing strategies to compete with chain stores. Independent stores figure out ways to offer special features.

2. One independent children's bookstore attracted new customers. It did that by bringing live animals into the store.

3. Animals are popular with children. The store purchased two pet chickens, plus tarantulas, rats, cats, and fish.

4. This children's bookstore did not need to lower prices to draw customers. The store could survive by owning animals that appeal to youngsters.

5. Other sorts of independent stores sometimes take a slightly different approach. They compete by offering better service than the large chain stores can.

6. For example, independent hardware and housewares stores can be service-oriented and customer friendly. They sometimes can thrive financially doing this.

7. Many independent hardware and housewares store owners have begun to offer home-repair and decorating advice as well as to recommend house calls from staff members. They do this to attract and hold customers.

8. These store owners also feature high-end items that chains do not carry. They feature in-store displays and advertise heavily about their high-end items.

9. Independent hardware and housewares stores often stock fine items such as expensive lawn ornaments, costly brand-name paints, and rare Italian tiles. These stores tend to attract wealthier customers.

14p What is a clause?

A **clause** is a group of words with both a SUBJECT and a PREDICATE. Clauses can be either *independent clauses,* also called *main clauses,* or *dependent clauses,* also called *subordinate clauses.*

INDEPENDENT CLAUSES

An **independent clause** contains a subject and a predicate and can stand alone as a sentence. Quick Reference 14.12 shows the basic pattern.

Quick Reference 14.12 ■ ■ ■ ■ ■ ■ ■

Sentence pattern IV: Independent clauses

	Independent Clause	
• Complete Subject	+	Complete Predicate
The telephone		rang.

DEPENDENT CLAUSES

A **dependent clause** contains a subject and a predicate but can't stand alone as a sentence. To be part of a complete sentence, a dependent clause must be joined to an independent clause. Dependent clauses are either adverb clauses or adjective clauses.

ADVERB CLAUSES

An **adverb clause**, also called a subordinate clause, starts with a subordinating conjunction, such as although, because, when, or until. A subordinating conjunction expresses a relationship between a dependent clause and an independent clause; see Quick Reference 14.7 in section 14i. Adverb clauses usually answer some question about the independent clause. How? Why? When? Under what circumstances?

> **If the bond issue passes,** the city will install sewers. [The adverb clause modifies the verb phrase *will install;* it explains under what circumstances.]

> They are drawing up plans **as quickly as they can.** [The adverb clause modifies the verb phrase *drawing up;* it explains how.]

> The homeowners feel happier **because they know the flooding will soon be better controlled.** [The adverb clause modifies the entire independent clause; it explains why.]

Alert: When you write an adverb clause before an independent clause, separate the clauses with a comma; see 24c. ●

ADJECTIVE CLAUSES

An **adjective clause,** also called a *relative clause,* starts with a relative pronoun, such as *who, which,* or *that.* Or an adjective clause can start with a relative adverb, such as *when* or *where.* An adjective clause modifies the noun or pronoun that it follows. Quick Reference 14.13 shows how adverb and adjective clauses function in sentences.

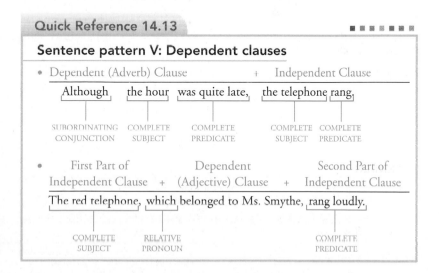

Quick Reference 14.13

Sentence pattern V: Dependent clauses

- Dependent (Adverb) Clause + Independent Clause

Although	the hour	was quite late,	the telephone	rang,
SUBORDINATING CONJUNCTION	COMPLETE SUBJECT	COMPLETE PREDICATE	COMPLETE SUBJECT	COMPLETE PREDICATE

- First Part of Independent Clause + Dependent (Adjective) Clause + Second Part of Independent Clause

The red telephone,	which	belonged to Ms. Smythe,	rang loudly.
COMPLETE SUBJECT	RELATIVE PRONOUN		COMPLETE PREDICATE

> The car **that Jack bought** is practical. [The adjective clause describes the noun *car; that* is a relative pronoun referring to *car.*]

The day **when I can buy my own car** is getting closer. [The adjective clause modifies the noun *day; when* is a relative adverb referring to *day*.]

Use *who, whom, whoever, whomever,* and *whose* when an adjective clause refers to a person or to an animal with a name.

The Smythes, **who collect cars,** are wealthy.

Their dog Bowser, **who is large and loud,** has been spoiled.

Use *which* or *that* when an adjective clause refers to a thing or to an animal that isn't a pet. Sometimes, writers omit *that* from an adjective clause. For grammatical analysis, however, consider the omitted *that* to be implied and, therefore, present.

For help in deciding whether to use *that* or *which,* see Quick Reference 16.4 in section 16s.

🛇 **Alert:** When an adjective clause is NONRESTRICTIVE, use *which* and set it off from the independent clause with commas. Don't use commas with *that* in a RESTRICTIVE CLAUSE.

My car, **which** I bought used, needs major repairs. [The adjective clause is nonrestrictive, so it begins with *which* and is set off with commas.]

The car **that** I want to buy has a CD player. [The adjective clause uses *that* and is restrictive, so it is not set off with commas.] ●

EXERCISE 14-9 Underline the dependent clause in each sentence, and label it an adjectival (ADJ) or an adverbial (ADV) clause. For help, consult 14p.

ADV
EXAMPLE The Stanley Hotel, <u>which is located in Estes Park, Colorado,</u> was built in 1909.

1. The Stanley Hotel is famous because it inspired Stephen King's novel *The Shining*.

2. Although based on King's book, the movie *The Shining* was filmed in England.

3. F. O. Stanley moved to Estes Park when he was diagnosed with tuberculosis.

4. He then built the hotel that now bears his name.

5. Visitors who believe the hotel is haunted claim to see Stanley's ghost in the lobby.

NOUN CLAUSES

Noun clauses function as nouns. Noun clauses can begin with many of the same words that begin adjective clauses: *that, who, which,* and their derivatives, as well as *when, where, whether, why,* and *how.*

Promises are not always dependable. [noun]

What politicians promise is not always dependable. [noun clause]

The electorate often cannot figure out the **truth.** [noun]

The electorate often cannot know **that the truth is being manipulated.** [noun clause]

Because they start with similar words, noun clauses and adjective clauses are sometimes confused with each other. The way to tell them apart is that the word starting an adjective clause has an ANTECEDENT, while the word starting a noun clause doesn't.

Good politicians understand **whom they must please.** [Noun clause; *whom* does not have an antecedent.]

Good politicians **who make promises** know all cannot be kept. [Adjective clause modifies *politicians*, which is the antecedent of *who*.]

ESOL Tip: Noun clauses in INDIRECT QUESTIONS are phrased as statements, not questions: *Kara asked why we needed the purple dye.* Don't phrase a noun clause this way: *Kara asked why **did** [or **do**] we need the purple dye?* If you prefer to change to a DIRECT QUESTION, usually VERB TENSE, PRONOUN, and other changes are necessary; see 22e.

ELLIPTICAL CLAUSES

In an **elliptical clause**, one or more words are deliberately left out for conciseness. For an elliptical clause to be correct, the one or more words you leave out need to be identical to those already appearing in the clause.

Engineering is one of the majors [**that**] **she considered.** [*that*, functioning as a relative pronoun, omitted from adjective clause]

She decided [**that**] **she would rather major in management.** [*that*, functioning as a conjunction, omitted between clauses]

After [**he takes**] **a refresher course,** he will be eligible for a raise. [subject and verb omitted from adverb clause]

Broiled fish tastes better **than boiled fish** [**tastes**]. [second half of the comparison omitted]

EXERCISE 14-10 Use subordinate conjunctions and relative pronouns from the list below to combine each pair of sentences. You may use words more than once, but try to use as many different ones as possible. Some sentence pairs may be combined in several ways. Create at least one elliptical construction.

since	which	if	after	when	as
although	so that	unless	because	even though	that

EXAMPLE   Bluegrass music is associated with American South. It has roots in Irish and Scottish folk music.

Even though it has roots in Irish and Scottish folk music, bluegrass is associated with the American South.

1. Certain aspects of jazz seem to have influenced bluegrass. It involves players of an instrumental ensemble improvising around a standard melody.

2. However, the instruments used in jazz are very different than those played in bluegrass. This style of music usually uses a banjo, fiddle, mandolin, and a dobro.

3. The singing in bluegrass involves tight harmonies and a tenor lead singer. People who listen closely to the vocal arrangements can hear this.

4. Bill Monroe, the founder of bluegrass, added banjo player Earl Scruggs to his band, the Blue Grass Boys. This allowed him to produce a fuller sound.

5. The Blue Grass Boys went into the studio in 1945 to record some songs for Columbia Records. They hit the charts with "Kentucky Waltz" and "Footprints in the Snow."

6. They began touring America with their own large circus tent. They then became one of the most popular acts in country music.

7. Lester Flatt and Earl Scruggs left Bill Monroe's band. They formed their own group called the Foggy Mountain Boys.

8. A famous Flatt & Scruggs song is considered one of the most popular and difficult to play on the banjo. This song is called "Foggy Mountain Breakdown."

9. Most banjo players cannot play "Foggy Mountain Breakdown" at the same speed that Earl Scruggs plays it. Very skilled players can.

10. Bluegrass must continue to attract new and young fans. Otherwise, it will fade into obscurity.

14q   What are the four sentence types?

English uses four **sentence types**: simple, compound, complex, and compound complex. A **simple sentence** is composed of a single INDEPENDENT CLAUSE and no DEPENDENT CLAUSES.

Charlie Chaplin was born in London on April 16, 1889.

A **compound sentence** is composed of two or more independent clauses. These clauses may be connected by a COORDINATING CONJUNCTION (*and, but, for, or, nor, yet, so*), a semicolon alone, or a semicolon and a CONJUNCTIVE ADVERB.

His father died early, **and** his mother spent time in mental hospitals.

Many people enjoy Chaplin films; others do not.

Many people enjoy Chaplin films; **however,** others do not.

A **complex sentence** is composed of one independent clause and one or more dependent clauses.

When times were bad, Chaplin lived in the streets. [dependent clause starting *when*; independent clause starting *Chaplin*]

When Chaplin was performing with a troupe that was touring the United States, he was hired by Mack Sennett, **who owned the Keystone Company.** [dependent clause starting *when*; dependent clause starting *that*; independent clause starting *he*; dependent clause starting *who*]

A **compound-complex sentence** integrates a compound sentence and a complex sentence. It contains two or more independent clauses and one or more dependent clauses.

Chaplin's comedies were immediately successful, and he became rich **because he was enormously popular for playing the Little Tramp, who was loved for his tiny mustache, baggy trousers, big shoes, and trick derby.** [independent clause starting *Chaplin's*; independent clause starting *he*; dependent clause starting *because*; dependent clause starting *who*]

When studios could no longer afford him, Chaplin co-founded United Artists, and then he produced and distributed his own films. [dependent clause starting *when*; independent clause starting *Chaplin*; independent clause starting *then*]

Alerts: (1) Use a comma before a coordinating conjunction connecting two independent clauses; see 24b. (2) When independent clauses are long or contain commas, use a subordinating conjunction—or use a semicolon to connect the sentences; see 25d. ●

EXERCISE 14-11   Decide whether each of the following sentences is simple, compound, complex, or compound-complex. For help, consult 14q.

EXAMPLE   Many people would love to eat a healthy meal at a fast-food restaurant or a food concession at the movies. (*simple*)

1. Fast-food restaurants and healthy meals rarely go together.
2. A fried-chicken sandwich packs an enormous number of calories and fat, and a fried-fish sandwich is no better.

3. A double cheeseburger with bacon at a fast-food restaurant can contain over 1,000 calories and 80 grams of fat, but a plain burger reduces the unhealthy overload considerably.

4. You can purchase other relatively healthy meals at a fast-food restaurant, if you first get to know the chart of nutritional values provided for customers.

5. Even though US government regulations require that nutritional charts be posted on the wall in the public areas of every fast-food restaurant, consumers often ignore the information, and they choose main meals and side dishes with the most flavor, calories, and fat.

6. A healthy meal available at many fast-food restaurants is a salad with low-fat dressing, along with bottled water.

7. The temptations of high fat and calories also entice people at the food concessions in movie theaters.

8. Because calories from sugar have zero nutritional value, health experts use the expression "empty calories" for all sugar products, yet sales of colossal sugar-laden sodas at the movies continue to increase yearly.

9. The silent ingredient in a serving of chips with melted cheese, or nachos, is artery-clogging fat, and the culprits in extra-large candy bars are not only fat but also "empty calories."

10. In truth, many people need to stay away from fast-food restaurants and food concessions at the movies and thereby avoid the tasty temptations of high-calorie foods.

For more help with your writing, grammar, and research,
go to **www.mycomplab.com**

15

Verbs

15a What do verbs do?

A **verb** expresses an action, an occurrence, or a state of being.

> Many people **overeat** on Thanksgiving. [action]
>
> Mother's Day **fell** early this year. [occurrence]
>
> Memorial Day **is** tomorrow. [state of being]

Verbs also reveal when something occurs—in the present, the past, or the future. Verbs convey other information as well; see Quick Reference 15.1. For types of verbs, see Quick Reference 15.2 on page 312.

Quick Reference 15.1

Information that verbs convey

PERSON	First person (the speaker: *I dance*), second person (the one spoken to: *you dance*), or third person (the one spoken about: *the man dances*).
NUMBER	Singular (one) or plural (more than one).
TENSE	Past (*we danced*), present (*we dance*), or future (*we will dance*); see 15g through 15k.
MOOD	Moods are indicative (*we dance*), imperative (commands and polite requests: *Dance*), or conditional (speculation, wishes: *if we were dancing . . .*); see 15l and 15m.
VOICE	Active voice or passive voice; see 15n through 15p.

LINKING VERBS

Linking verbs are main verbs that indicate a state of being or a condition. They link a SUBJECT with one or more words that rename or describe the subject, called a SUBJECT COMPLEMENT. A linking verb is like an equal sign between a subject and its complement. Quick Reference 15.3 on page 312 shows how linking verbs function in sentences.

Quick Reference 15.2 ■ ■ ■ ■ ■ ■ ■

Types of verbs

MAIN VERB	The word in a PREDICATE that says something about the SUBJECT: *She **danced** for the group.*
AUXILIARY VERB	A verb that combines with a main verb to convey information about TENSE, MOOD, or VOICE (15e). The verbs *be, do,* and *have* can be auxiliary verbs or main verbs. The verbs *can, could, may, might, should, would, must,* and others are MODAL AUXILIARY VERBS. They add shades of meaning such as ability or possibility to verbs: *She **might** dance again.*
LINKING VERB	The verb that links a subject to a COMPLEMENT, a word or words that rename or describe the subject: *She **was** happy dancing. Be* is the most common linking verb; sometimes sense verbs (*smell, taste*) or verbs of perception (*seem, feel*) function as linking verbs. See also Quick Reference 15.3.
TRANSITIVE VERB	The verb followed by a DIRECT OBJECT that completes the verb's message: *They **sent** her a fan letter.*
INTRANSITIVE VERB	A verb that does not require a direct object: *Yesterday she **danced.***

Quick Reference 15.3 ■ ■ ■ ■ ■ ■ ■

Linking verbs

- Linking verbs may be forms of the verb *be* (*am, is, was, were;* see 9e for a complete list).

  George Washington   *was*   president.

       SUBJECT   LINKING   COMPLEMENT (PREDICATE
                                VERB   NOMINATIVE: RENAMES SUBJECT)

- Linking verbs may deal with the senses (*look, smell, taste, sound, feel*).

  George Washington   *sounded*   confident.

       SUBJECT   LINKING   COMPLEMENT (PREDICATE
                                VERB   ADJECTIVE DESCRIBES SUBJECT)

- Linking verbs can be verbs that convey a sense of existing or becoming—*appear, seem, become, get, grow, turn, remain, stay,* and *prove,* for example.

  George Washington   *grew*   old.

       SUBJECT   LINKING   COMPLEMENT (PREDICATE
                                VERB   ADJECTIVE DESCRIBES SUBJECT)

continued >>

Quick Reference 15.3 (continued)

- To test whether a verb other than a form of *be* is functioning as a linking verb, substitute *was* (for a singular subject) or *were* (for a plural subject) for the original verb. If the sentence makes sense, the original verb is functioning as a linking verb.

  NO George Washington *grew* a beard → George Washington *was* a beard. [*Grew* is not functioning as a linking verb.]

  YES George Washington *grew* old → George Washington *was* old. [*Grew* is functioning as a linking verb.]

VERB FORMS

15b What are the forms of main verbs?

A **main verb** names an action (*People dance*), an occurrence (*Christmas comes once a year*), or a state of being (*It will be warm tomorrow*). Every main verb has five forms.

- The **simple form** conveys an action, occurrence, or state of being taking place in the present (*I laugh*) or, with an AUXILIARY VERB, in the future (*I will laugh*).

- The **past-tense form** conveys an action, occurrence, or state completed in the past (*I laughed*). REGULAR VERBS add *-ed* or *-d* to the simple form. IRREGULAR VERBS vary (see Quick Reference 15.4 for a list of common irregular verbs).

- The **past participle form** in regular verbs uses the same form as the past tense. Irregular verbs vary; see Quick Reference 15.4. To function as a verb, a past participle must combine with a SUBJECT and one or more auxiliary verbs (*I have laughed*). Otherwise, past participles function as ADJECTIVES (*crumbled cookies*).

- The **present participle form** adds *-ing* to the simple form (*laughing*). To function as a verb, a present participle combines with a subject and one or more auxiliary verbs (*I was laughing*). Otherwise, present participles function as adjectives (*my laughing friends*) or as NOUNS (*Laughing is healthy*).

- The **infinitive** usually consists of *to* and the simple form following *to* (*I started to laugh at his joke*); see 16i. The infinitive functions as a noun or an adjective, not a verb.

🌐 **ESOL Tip:** When verbs function as other parts of speech, they're called VERBALS. Verbals are INFINITIVES, PRESENT PARTICIPLES, and PAST PARTICIPLES. When present participles function as nouns, they're called GERUNDS. For information about using gerunds and infinitives as OBJECTS after certain verbs, see Chapter 54. ●

15c What is the -s, or -es, form of a verb?

The -s **form of a verb** is the third-person singular in the PRESENT TENSE. The ending -s (or -es) is added to the verb's SIMPLE FORM (*smell* becomes *smells,* as in *The bread* **smells** *delicious*).

Be and *have* are irregular verbs. For the third-person singular, present tense, *be* uses *is* and *have* uses *has.*

> The cheesecake **is** popular.
>
> The éclair **has** chocolate icing.

Even if you tend to drop the -s or -es ending when you speak, always use it when you write. Proofread carefully to make sure you haven't omitted any -s forms.

⊘ **Alert:** In informal speech, the LINKING, or *copula,* VERB *to be* sometimes doesn't change forms in the present tense. However, ACADEMIC WRITING requires you to use standard third-person singular forms in the present tense.

> He **is** [not *be*] hungry.
>
> The bakery **has** [not *have*] fresh bread. ●

⊛ **EXERCISE 15-1** Rewrite each sentence, changing the subjects to the word or words given in parentheses. Change the form of the verbs shown in italics to match the new subject. Keep all sentences in the present tense. For help, consult 15c.

EXAMPLE The Oregon giant earthworm *escapes* all attempts at detection. (Oregon giant earthworms)

Oregon giant earthworms escape all attempts at detection.

1. Before declaring the Oregon giant earthworm a protected species, US government agencies *require* concrete proof that it *is* not extinct. (a government agency) (they)

2. A scientist who *finds* one alive will demonstrate that Oregon giant earthworms *do* still exist, in spite of no one's having seen any for over twenty years. (Scientists) (the Oregon giant earthworm)

3. Last seen in the Willamette Valley near Portland, Oregon, the earthworms *are* white, and they *smell* like lilies. (the earthworm) (it)

4. Oregon giant earthworms *grow* up to three feet long. (The Oregon giant earthworm)

5. A clump of soil with a strange shape *indicates* that the giant creatures *continue* to live, but to demonstrate that they *are* not extinct, only a real specimen will do. (clumps of soil) (creature) (it)

15d   What is the difference between regular and irregular verbs?

A **regular verb** forms its PAST TENSE and PAST PARTICIPLE by adding *-ed* or *-d* to the SIMPLE FORM: *type, typed; cook, cooked; work, worked.* Most verbs in English are regular.

In informal speech, some people skip over the *-ed* sound, pronouncing it softly or not at all. In ACADEMIC WRITING, however, you're required to use it. If you're not used to hearing or pronouncing this sound, proofread carefully to see that you have all the needed *-ed* endings in your writing.

> **NO**   The cake was **suppose** to be tasty.
>
> **YES**   The cake was **supposed** to be tasty.

Irregular verbs, in contrast, don't consistently add *-ed* or *-d* to form the past tense and past participle. Some irregular verbs change an internal vowel to make the past tense and past participle: *sing, sang, sung.* Some change an internal vowel and add an ending other than *-ed* or *-d: grow, grew, grown.* Some use the simple form throughout: *cost, cost, cost.* Unfortunately, a verb's simple form doesn't provide a clue about whether the verb is irregular or regular. Quick Reference 15.4 lists frequently used irregular verbs.

Although you can always look up the principal parts of any verb, memorizing any you don't know solidly is much more efficient in the long run. About two hundred verbs in English are irregular.

Alert: For information about changing *y* to *i*, or doubling a final consonant before adding the *-ed* ending, see 31d. ●

Quick Reference 15.4

Common irregular verbs

Simple Form	Past Tense	Past Participle
arise	arose	arisen
awake	awoke *or* awaked	awaked *or* awoken
be (is, am, are)	was, were	been
beat	beat	beaten
become	became	become
begin	began	begun
bend	bent	bent
bite	bit	bitten *or* bit
blow	blew	blown
break	broke	broken
bring	brought	brought
build	built	built
burst	burst	burst
buy	bought	bought
catch	caught	caught
choose	chose	chosen
cling	clung	clung
come	came	come
cost	cost	cost
cut	cut	cut
deal	dealt	dealt
dig	dug	dug
dive	dived *or* dove	dived
do	did	done
draw	drew	drawn
drink	drank	drunk
drive	drove	driven
eat	ate	eaten
fall	fell	fallen
fight	fought	fought
find	found	found
fly	flew	flown
forget	forgot	forgotten *or* forgot
freeze	froze	frozen
get	got	got *or* gotten
give	gave	given
go	went	gone
grow	grew	grown
hang ("to suspend")*	hung	hung
have	had	had

continued >>

Quick Reference 15.4 (continued)

Simple Form	Past Tense	Past Participle
hear	heard	heard
hide	hid	hidden
hurt	hurt	hurt
keep	kept	kept
know	knew	known
lay	laid	laid
lead	led	led
lend	lent	lent
let	let	let
lie	lay	lain
light	lighted *or* lit	lighted *or* lit
lose	lost	lost
make	made	made
mean	meant	meant
prove	proved	proved *or* proven
read	read	read
ride	rode	ridden
ring	rang	rung
rise	rose	risen
run	ran	run
say	said	said
see	saw	seen
seek	sought	sought
send	sent	sent
set	set	set
shake	shook	shaken
shoot	shot	shot
show	showed	shown *or* showed
shrink	shrank	shrunk
sing	sang	sung
sink	sank *or* sunk	sunk
sit	sat	sat
slay	slew	slain
sleep	slept	slept
speak	spoke	spoken
spin	spun	spun
spring	sprang *or* sprung	sprung
stand	stood	stood
steal	stole	stolen
sting	stung	stung
stink	stank *or* stunk	stunk
strike	struck	struck

continued >>

Quick Reference 15.4 (continued)

Simple Form	Past Tense	Past Participle
swear	swore	sworn
swim	swam	swum
swing	swung	swung
take	took	taken
teach	taught	taught
throw	threw	thrown
wake	woke *or* waked	waked *or* woken
wear	wore	worn
wring	wrung	wrung
write	wrote	written

*When it means "to execute by hanging," *hang* is a regular verb: *In wartime, some armies routinely **hanged** deserters.*

EXERCISE 15-2 Write the correct past-tense form of the regular verbs given in parentheses. For help, consult 15d.

EXAMPLE Native North Americans (invent) <u>invented</u> the game of lacrosse.

(1) Ancient lacrosse games (involve) _____ up to 1,000 men and (last) _____ the entire day. (2) Native Americans (play) _____ the game using balls they (create) _____ out of deerskin and wood. (3) Lacrosse (serve) _____ many purposes in tribal life as warriors (train) _____ for battle and (resolve) _____ conflicts. (4) French missionaries eventually (name) _____ the game "la crosse," perhaps referring to the staffs Jesuit bishops (use) _____. (5) Lacrosse (resemble) _____ the Irish sport hurling, so when Irish immigrants (arrive) _____ in America in the 19th century, they (help) _____ to make the game more popular.

EXERCISE 15-3 Write the correct past-tense form of the irregular verbs given in parentheses. For help, consult Quick Reference 15.4 in 15d.

EXAMPLE In August, 1969, the Woodstock music festival (begin) <u>began</u> as thousands of fans (drive) <u>drove</u> to upstate New York for three days of music.

(1) The official name of the festival (is) _____ the Woodstock Music and Art Fair. (2) It (draw) _____ nearly half a million people to Max Yasgur's farm, which (stand) _____ in the small town of Bethel, New

York. (3) The concert (have) _____ to move to Bethel at the last minute after residents of the town of Woodstock (forbid) _____ organizers to hold the festival in their town. (4) Those who (come) _____ to hear music were not disappointed, since several well known artists (sing) _____ to the large crowd. (5) Performers such as Jimi Hendrix, Santana, and Janis Joplin (lend) _____ their talents to the festival. (6) Even though rain clouds occasionally (cast) _____ a shadow on the events, most people (stick) _____ it out the entire three days. (7) According to some reports, two women (give) _____ birth during the festival. (8) Because of the relatively peaceful atmosphere, many people (see) _____ the event as a symbol of countercultural ideals. (9) Filmmaker Michael Wadleigh (strive) _____ to capture that atmosphere in the film *Woodstock*, which he (shoot) _____ and edited with the help of a young Martin Scorsese. (10) The festival also (lead) _____ to a song written by Joni Mitchell called "Woodstock." (11) That song (become) _____ a hit for Crosby, Stills, Nash, and Young, which (make) _____ its debut as a group at Woodstock. (12) Although organizers (try) _____ to turn a profit with the event, they (lose) _____ money because many attendees did not purchase tickets.

15e What are auxiliary verbs?

Auxiliary verbs, also called *helping verbs,* combine with MAIN VERBS to make VERB PHRASES. Quick Reference 15.5 shows how auxiliary verbs work.

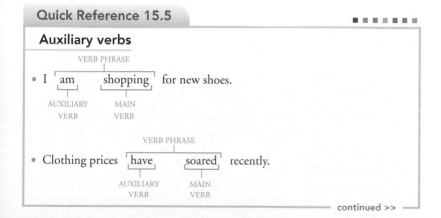

Quick Reference 15.5

Auxiliary verbs

- I | am | shopping | for new shoes.
  - am = AUXILIARY VERB
  - shopping = MAIN VERB
  - VERB PHRASE

- Clothing prices | have | soared | recently.
  - have = AUXILIARY VERB
  - soared = MAIN VERB
  - VERB PHRASE

continued >>

Quick Reference 15.5 (continued)

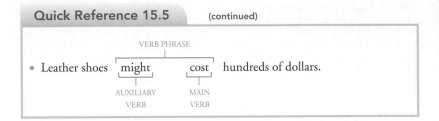

VERB PHRASE

- Leather shoes might cost hundreds of dollars.

AUXILIARY VERB   MAIN VERB

USING *BE, DO, HAVE*

The three most common auxiliary verbs are *be, do,* and *have.* These three verbs can also be main verbs. Their forms vary more than most irregular verbs, as Quick References 15.6 and 15.7 show.

Quick Reference 15.6

Forms of the verb *be*

SIMPLE FORM	be
-*S* FORM	is
PAST TENSE	was, were
PRESENT PARTICIPLE	being
PAST PARTICIPLE	been

Person	Present Tense	Past Tense
I	am	Was
you (singular)	are	Were
he, she, it	is	Was
we	are	Were
you (plural)	are	Were
they	are	Were

Quick Reference 15.7

Forms of the verbs *do* and *have*

SIMPLE FORM	do	have
-*S* FORM	does	has
PAST TENSE	did	had
PRESENT PARTICIPLE	doing	having
PAST PARTICIPLE	done	had

⊕ Alert: In ACADEMIC WRITING, always use the standard forms for *be, do,* and *have,* as shown in Quick References 15.6 and 15.7.

The gym **is** [not be] a busy place.
The gym **is** [not be] filling with spectators. ●

⊕ ESOL Tip: When *be, do,* and *have* function as auxiliary verbs, change their form to agree with a third-person singular subject—and don't add *-s* to the main verb.

> **NO** **Does** the library **closes** at 6:00?
>
> **YES** **Does** the library **close** at 6:00? ●

MODAL AUXILIARY VERBS

Can, could, shall, should, will, would, may, might, and *must* are the nine modal auxiliary verbs. **Modal auxiliary verbs** communicate ability, permission, obligation, advisability, necessity, or possibility. They never change form.

Exercise **can lengthen** lives. [possibility]

She **can jog** for five miles. [ability]

The exercise **must occur** regularly. [necessity, obligation]

People **should protect** their bodies. [advisability]

May I **exercise?** [permission]

⊕ ESOL Tip: For more about modal auxiliary verbs and the meanings they communicate, see Chapter 55. ●

EXERCISE 15-4   Using the auxiliary verbs in the list below, fill in the blanks in the following passage. Use each auxiliary word only once, even if a listed word can fit into more than one blank. For help, consult 15e.

> are   have   may   will   might   can   has

EXAMPLE   Completing a marathon <u>can</u> be the highlight of a runner's life.

(1) The marathon _____ been a challenging and important athletic event since the 19th century. (2) Athletes who _____ training for a marathon _____ use one of the many online training guides.
(3) Running with a partner or friend _____ boost confidence and motivation. (4) Beginning runners _____ find the first few weeks difficult but _____ soon see dramatic improvement in their performance.
(5) Those who _____ successfully finished the race often want to repeat the experience.

15f What are intransitive and transitive verbs?

A verb is **intransitive** when an OBJECT isn't required to complete the verb's meaning: *I sing.* A verb is **transitive** when an object is necessary to complete the verb's meaning: *I need a guitar.* Many verbs have both transitive and intransitive meanings. Some verbs are only transitive: *need, have, like, owe, remember.* Only transitive verbs function in the PASSIVE VOICE. Dictionaries label verbs as transitive (*vt*) or intransitive (*vi*).

Quick Reference 15.8

Using *lie* and *lay*

	lie	lay
SIMPLE FORM	lie	lay
-S FORM	lies	lays
PAST TENSE	lay	laid
PRESENT PARTICIPLE	lying	laying
PAST PARTICIPLE	lain	laid

INTRANSITIVE FORMS

PRESENT TENSE	The hikers **lie** down to rest.
PAST TENSE	The hikers **lay** down to rest.

TRANSITIVE FORMS

PRESENT TENSE	The hikers **lay** their backpacks on a rock.
	[*Backpacks* is a direct object.]
PAST TENSE	The hikers **laid** their backpacks on a rock.
	[*Backpacks* is a direct object.]

The verbs *lie* and *lay* are particularly confusing. *Lie* means "to recline, to place oneself down, or to remain." *Lie* is intransitive (it cannot be followed by an object). *Lay* means "to put something down." *Lay* is transitive (it must be followed by an object). As you can see in Quick Reference 15.8, the word *lay* is both the past tense of *lie* and the present-tense simple form of *lay*. That makes things difficult. Our best advice is memorize them. Yet truthfully, each time we use *lie* and *lay,* we need to pause, think, and recite the list to ourselves.

Two other verb pairs tend to confuse people because of their intransitive and transitive forms: *raise* and *rise* and *set* and *sit.*

Raise and *set* are transitive (they must be followed by an object). *Rise* and *sit* are intransitive (they cannot be followed by an object). Fortunately, although each word has a meaning different from the other words, they don't share forms: *raise, raised, raised; rise, rose, risen;* and *set, set, set; sit, sat, sat.*

EXERCISE 15-5 Underline the correct word of each pair in parentheses. For help, consult 15f.

EXAMPLE During the summer, Caroline enjoys (lying/laying) on the beach.

(1) One day, after (setting/sitting) her chair on the sand, Caroline (lay/laid) her blanket near her umbrella. (2) Worried about getting a sunburn, she (raised/rose) her umbrella and (lay/laid) under it. (3) After a brief nap, Caroline began (rising/raising) to her feet when she realized she had forgotten where she had (lain/laid) her cooler. (4) She soon found it (lying/laying) near her car, just where she had (sat/set) it earlier. (5) She decided to pick it up and (lie/lay) it down near where her blanket (lies/lays).

VERB TENSE

15g What is verb tense?

Verb tense conveys time. Verbs show tense (time) by changing form. English has six verb tenses, divided into simple and perfect groups. The three **simple tenses** divide time into present, past, and future. The simple **present tense** describes what happens regularly, what takes place in the present, and what is consistently or generally true. The simple **past tense** tells of an action completed or a condition ended. The simple **future tense** indicates action yet to be taken or a condition not yet experienced.

> Rick **wants** to speak Spanish fluently. [simple present tense]
>
> Rick **wanted** to improve rapidly. [simple past tense]
>
> Rick **will want** to progress even further next year. [simple future tense]

The three **perfect tenses** also divide time into present, past, and future. They show more complex time relationships than the simple tenses. For information on using the perfect tenses, see section 15i.

The three simple tenses and the three perfect tenses also have **progressive forms**. These forms indicate that the verb describes what is ongoing or continuing. For information on using progressive forms, see section 9j. Quick Reference 15.9 summarizes verb tenses and progressive forms.

Quick Reference 15.9

Simple, perfect, and progressive tenses

SIMPLE TENSES

	Regular Verb	Irregular Verb	Progressive Form
PRESENT	I talk	I eat	I am talking; I am eating
PAST	I talked	I ate	I was talking; I was eating
FUTURE	I will talk	I will eat	I will be talking; I will be eating

PERFECT TENSES

	Regular Verb	Irregular Verb	Progressive Form
PRESENT PERFECT	I have talked	I have eaten	I have been talking; I have been eating
PAST PERFECT	I had talked	I had eaten	I had been talking; I had been eating
FUTURE PERFECT	I will have talked	I will have eaten	I will have been talking; I will have been eating

---

ESOL Tip: Quick Reference 15.9 shows that most verb tenses are formed by combining one or more AUXILIARY VERBS with the SIMPLE FORM, the PRESENT PARTICIPLE, or the PAST PARTICIPLE of a MAIN VERB. Auxiliary verbs are necessary in the formation of most tenses, so never omit them.

> **NO** I **talking** to you.
>
> **YES** I **am talking** to you. ●

15h How do I use the simple present tense?

The **simple present tense** uses the SIMPLE FORM of the verb (15b). It describes what happens regularly, what takes place in the present, and what is generally or consistently true. Also, it can convey a future occurrence with verbs like *start, stop, begin, end, arrive,* and *depart.*

> Calculus class **meets** every morning. [regularly occurring action]
>
> Mastering calculus **takes** time. [general truth]
>
> The course **ends** in eight weeks. [specific future event]

🚫 **Alert:** For a work of literature, always describe or discuss the action in the present tense. This holds true no matter how old the work.

In Shakespeare's *Romeo and Juliet*, Juliet's father **wants** her to marry Paris, but Juliet **loves** Romeo. ●

15i How do I form and use the perfect tenses?

The **perfect tenses** generally describe actions or occurrences that are still having an effect at the present time or are having an effect until a specified time. The perfect tenses are composed of an AUXILIARY VERB and a main verb's PAST PARTICIPLE (15b).

For the **present perfect tense** (see Quick Reference 15.9), use *has* only for the third-person singular subjects and *have* for all other subjects. For the **past perfect**, use *had* with the past participle. For the **future perfect**, use *will have* with the past participle.

PRESENT PERFECT	Our government **has offered** to help. [having effect now]
PRESENT PERFECT	The drought **has created** terrible hardship. [having effect until a specified time—when the rains come]
PAST PERFECT	As soon as the tornado **had passed**, the heavy rain started. [Both events occurred in the past, the tornado occurred before the rain, so the earlier event uses *had*.]
FUTURE PERFECT	Our chickens' egg production **will have reached** five hundred per day by next year. [The event will occur before a specified time.]

15j How do I form and use progressive forms?

Progressive forms describe an ongoing event, action, or condition. They also express habitual or recurring actions or conditions. The **present progressive** uses the present-tense form of *be* that agrees with the subject in PERSON and NUMBER, plus the *-ing* form (PRESENT PARTICIPLE) of the main verb. The **past progressive** uses *was* or *were* to agree with the subject in person and number, and it uses the present participle of the main verb. The **future progressive** uses *will be* and the present participle. The **present perfect progressive** uses *have been* or *has been* to agree with the subject, plus the *-ing* form of the main verb. The **past perfect progressive** uses *had been* and the *-ing* form of the main verb. The **future perfect progressive** uses *will have been* plus the PRESENT PARTICIPLE.

PRESENT PROGRESSIVE	The smog **is stinging** everyone's eyes. [event taking place now]
PAST PROGRESSIVE	Eye drops **were selling** well last week. [event ongoing in the past within stated limits]
FUTURE PROGRESSIVE	We **will be ordering** more eye drops than usual this month. [recurring event that will take place in the future]
PRESENT PERFECT PROGRESSIVE	Scientists **have been warning** us about air pollution for years. [recurring event that took place in the past and may still take place]
PAST PERFECT PROGRESSIVE	We **had been ordering** three cases of eye drops a month until the smog worsened. [recurring past event that has now ended]
FUTURE PERFECT PROGRESSIVE	By May, we **will have been selling** eye drops for eight months. [ongoing condition to be completed at a specific time in the future]

EXERCISE 15-6 Underline the correct verb in each pair of parentheses. If more than one answer is possible, be prepared to explain the differences in meaning between the two choices. For help, consult 15g through 15j.

EXAMPLE According to an article in *National Geographic News,* weird plants (are taking root, would have taken root) in ordinary backyards.

1. Some, smelling like spoiled meat, (will have ruined, are ruining) people's appetites.

2. Stalks similar to male anatomy (typify, are typifying) other examples.

3. *Shockingly large, black, carnivorous,* and *volatile* (describe, is describing) additional unusual plants.

4. Indeed, many unusual plants (live, lived) in places the world over today.

5. Many people now (are planting, planted) these weird items in their backyards.

6. In 1999, in East Lothian, Scotland, Diane Halligan (founded, had founded) The Weird and Wonderful Plant Company because she (was, is) disappointed with the plant selection at her local garden centers.

7. Halligan (chose, is choosing) to open an extraordinary plant store because she (wanted, is wanting) to provide a source of unusual plants for others as well as herself.

8. Marty Harper in Staunton, Virginia, like Halligan in Scotland, (contends, are contending) that his company (fills, would have filled) a niche for himself and others.

9. Harper, after much study on the subject of strange plants, (is indicating, indicates) that Madagascar holds the record for the most weird plants on the planet.

10. Isolated from the rest of the world, Madagascar (has provided, will have provided) a haven for unusual plants to develop undisturbed.

11. *Rafflesia arnoldii* (is, are) the oddest plant Harper (has encountered, will have encountered).

12. Harper, in an interview with *National Geographic*'s John Roach, (reveals, is revealing) that *Rafflesia arnoldii*, a parasitic plant, (has, have) the world's largest bloom, stinks, and (held, holds) in its center six or seven quarts of water.

13. According to Harper, procreation (remains, has remained) the primary reason for the development of the ostensibly outlandish shapes, sizes, odors, and actions of these unusual plants the world over.

14. Douglas Justice, another weird-plant aficionado like Halligan and Harper, (says, is saying) he (wonders, is wondering) what (motivates, motivated) people to choose the odd plants.

15. Harper, however, (exclaims, is exclaiming), "Such plants (make, were making) me smile."

15k How do I use tense sequences accurately?

Verb **tense sequences** communicate time relationships. They help deliver messages about actions, occurrences, or states that take place at different times. Quick Reference 15.10 shows how tenses in the same sentence can vary depending on the timing of actions (or occurrences or states).

Quick Reference 15.10

Tense sequences

If your independent clause contains a simple-present-tense verb, then in your dependent clause you can

* use PRESENT TENSE to show same-time action:

    I **avoid** shellfish because I **am** allergic to it.

* use PAST TENSE to show earlier action:

    I **am** sure that I **deposited** the check.

* use the PRESENT PERFECT TENSE to show (1) a period of time extending from some point in the past to the present or (2) an indefinite past time:

    They **claim** that they **have visited** the planet Venus.

    I **believe** that I **have seen** that movie before.

continued >>

Quick Reference 15.10 (continued)

- use the FUTURE TENSE for action to come:

    The book **is** open because I **will be reading** it later.

If your independent clause contains a past-tense verb, then in your dependent clause you can

- use the past tense to show another completed past action:

    I **closed** the door because you **told** me to.

- use the PAST PERFECT TENSE to show earlier action:

    The sprinter **knew** that she **had broken** the record.

- use the present tense to state a general truth:

    Christopher Columbus **determined** that the world **is** round.

If your independent clause contains a present-perfect-tense or past-perfect-tense verb, then in your dependent clause you can

- use the past tense:

    The bread **has become** moldy since I **purchased** it.

    Sugar prices **had** already **declined** when artificial sweeteners first appeared.

If your independent clause contains a future-tense verb, then in your dependent clause you can

- use the present tense to show action happening at the same time:

    You **will be** rich if you **win** the prize.

- use the past tense to show earlier action:

    You **will** surely **win** the prize if you **remembered** to mail the entry form.

TENSE SEQUENCES

- use the present perfect tense to show future action earlier than the action of the independent-clause verb:

    The river **will flood** again next year unless we **have built** a better dam by then.

If your independent clause contains a future-perfect-tense verb, then in your dependent clause you can

- use either the present tense or the present perfect tense:

    Dr. Chang **will have delivered** five thousand babies by the time she **retires**.

    Dr. Chang **will have delivered** five thousand babies by the time she **has retired**.

🛈 **Alert:** Never use a future-tense verb in a dependent clause when the verb in the independent clause is in the future tense. Instead, use a present-tense verb or present-perfect-tense verb in the dependent clause.

> **NO** The river **will flood** us unless we **will prepare** our defense.
>
> **YES** The river **will flood** us unless we **prepare** our defense. [*Prepare* is a present-tense verb.]
>
> **YES** The river **will flood** us unless we **have prepared** our defense. [*Have prepared* is a present-perfect-tense verb.] ●

Tense sequences may include INFINITIVES and PARTICIPLES. To name or describe an activity or occurrence coming either at the same time as the time expressed in the MAIN VERB or after, use the **present infinitive**.

> I **hope to buy** a used car. [*To buy* comes at a future time. *Hope* is the main verb, and its action is now.]
>
> I **hoped to buy** a used car. [*Hoped* is the main verb, and its action is over.]
>
> I **had hoped to buy** a used car. [*Had hoped* is the main verb, and its action is over.]

The PRESENT PARTICIPLE (a verb's *-ing* form) can describe action happening at the same time.

> **Driving** his new car, the man **smiled.** [The driving and the smiling happened at the same time.]

To describe an action that occurs before the action in the main verb, use the **perfect infinitive** (*to have gone, to have smiled*), the PAST PARTICIPLE, or the **present perfect participle** (*having gone, having smiled*).

> Candida **claimed to have written** fifty short stories in college. [*Claimed* is the main verb, and *to have written* happened first.]
>
> **Pleased** with the short story, Candida **mailed** it to several magazines. [*Mailed* is the main verb, and *pleased* happened first.]
>
> **Having sold** one short story, Candida **invested** in a computer. [*Invested* is the main verb, and *having sold* happened first.]

EXERCISE 15-7   Underline the correct verb in each pair of parentheses that best suits the sequence of tenses. Be ready to explain your choices. For help, consult 15k.

EXAMPLE   When he (is, was) seven years old, Yo-Yo Ma, possibly the world's greatest living cellist, (moves, moved) to the United States with his family.

1. Yo-Yo Ma, who (had been born, was born) in France to Chinese parents, (lived, lives) in Boston, Massachusetts, today and (toured, tours) as one of the world's greatest cellists.

2. Years from now, after Mr. Ma has given his last concert, music lovers still (treasure, will treasure) his many fine recordings.

3. Mr. Ma's older sister, Dr. Yeou-Cheng Ma, was nearly the person with the concert career. She had been training to become a concert violinist when her brother's musical genius (began, had begun) to be noticed.

4. Even though Dr. Ma eventually (becomes, became) a physician, she still (had been playing, plays) the violin.

5. The family interest in music (continues, was continuing), for Mr. Ma's children (take, had taken) piano lessons.

6. Although most people today (knew, know) Mr. Ma as a brilliant cellist, he (was making, has made) films as well.

7. One year, while he (had been traveling, was traveling) in the Kalahari Desert, he (films, filmed) dances of southern Africa's Bush people.

8. Mr. Ma first (becomes, became) interested in the Kalahari people when he (had studied, studied) anthropology as an undergraduate at Harvard University.

9. When he shows visitors around Boston now, Mr. Ma has been known to point out the Harvard University library where, he claims, he (fell asleep, was falling asleep) in the stacks when he (had been, was) a student.

10. Indicating another building, Mr. Ma admits that in one of its classrooms he almost (failed, had failed) German.

MOOD

15I What is "mood" in verbs?

Mood in verbs conveys an attitude toward the action in a sentence. English has three moods: *indicative, imperative,* and *subjunctive.* Use the **indicative mood** to make statements about real things, about highly likely things, and for questions about fact.

INDICATIVE   The door to the tutoring center opened. [real]

She seemed to be looking for someone. [highly likely]

Do you want to see a tutor? [question about a fact]

The **imperative mood** expresses commands and direct requests. Often, the subject is omitted in an imperative sentence, but nevertheless the subject is implied to be either *you* or one of the indefinite pronouns such as *anybody, somebody,* or *everybody.*

Alert: Use an exclamation point after a strong command; use a period after a mild command or a request (23e, 23a). ●

> IMPERATIVE Please shut the door.
>
> Watch out! That screw is loose.

The **subjunctive mood** expresses speculation, other unreal conditions, conjectures, wishes, recommendations, indirect requests, and demands. Often, the words that signal the subjunctive mood are *if, as if, as though,* and *unless.* In speaking, subjunctive verb forms were once used frequently in English, but they're heard far less today. Nevertheless, in ACADEMIC WRITING, you need to use the subjunctive mood.

> SUBJUNCTIVE If I **were** you, I would ask for a tutor.

15m What are subjunctive forms?

For the **present subjunctive**, always use the SIMPLE FORM of the verb for all PERSONS and NUMBERS.

> The prosecutor asks that she **testify** [not testifies] again.
>
> It is important that they **be** [not are] allowed to testify.

For the **past subjunctive**, use the simple past tense: *I wish that I had a car.* The one exception is for the past subjunctive of *be:* Use *were* for all forms.

> I wish that I **were** [not was] leaving on vacation today.
>
> They asked if she **were** [not was] leaving on vacation today.

USING THE SUBJUNCTIVE IN *IF, AS IF, AS THOUGH,* AND *UNLESS* CLAUSES

In dependent clauses introduced by *if, as if, as though,* and sometimes *unless,* the subjunctive describes speculations or conditions contrary to fact.

> If it **were** [not was] to rain, attendance at the race would be disappointing. [speculation]
>
> The runner looked as if he **were** [not was] winded, but he said he wasn't. [a condition contrary to fact]

In an *unless* clause, the subjunctive signals that what the clause says is highly unlikely.

> Unless rain **were** [not was] to create floods, the race will be held this Sunday. [Floods are highly unlikely.]

Not every clause introduced by *if, unless, as if, or as though* requires the subjunctive. Use the subjunctive only when the dependent clause describes speculation or a condition contrary to fact.

INDICATIVE   If she **is** going to leave late, I will drive her to the race. [Her leaving late is highly likely.]

SUBJUNCTIVE   If she **were** going to leave late, I would drive her to the race. [Her leaving late is a speculation.]

USING THE SUBJUNCTIVE IN *THAT* CLAUSES

When *that* clauses describe wishes, requests, demands, or recommendations, the subjunctive can convey the message.

I wish that this race **were** [not *was*] over. [a wish about something happening now]

He wishes that he **had seen** [not *saw*] the race. [a wish about something that is past]

The judges are demanding that the doctor **examine** [not *examines*] the runners. [a demand for something to happen in the future]

Also, MODAL AUXILIARY VERBS *would, could, might,* and *should* can convey speculations and conditions contrary to fact.

If the runner **were** [not *was*] faster, we **would** see a better race. [*Would* is a modal auxiliary verb.]

The issue here is that when an INDEPENDENT CLAUSE expresses a conditional statement using a modal auxiliary verb, you want to be sure that in the DEPENDENT CLAUSE you don't use another modal auxiliary verb.

NO   If I **would have trained** for the race, I **might have won.**

YES   If I **had trained** for the race, I **might have** won.

EXERCISE 15-8   Fill in each blank with the correct form of the verb given in parentheses. For help, consult 15l and 15m.

EXAMPLE   Imagining the possibility of brain transplants requires that we (to be) <u>be</u> open-minded.

(1) If almost any organ other than the brain (to be) _____ the candidate for a swap, we would probably give our consent. (2) If the brain (to be) _____ to hold whatever impulses form our personalities, few people would want to risk a transplant. (3) Many popular movies have asked that we (to suspend) _____ disbelief and imagine the consequences should a

personality actually (to be) _____ transferred to another body. (4) In real life, however, the complexities of a successful brain transplant require that not-yet-developed surgical techniques (to be) _____ used. (5) For example, it would be essential that during the actual transplant each one of the 500 trillion nerve connections within the brain (to continue) _____ to function as though the brain (to be) _____ lying undisturbed in a living human body.

VOICE

15n What is "voice" in verbs?

Voice in a verb tells whether a SUBJECT acts or is acted upon. English has two voices, *active* and *passive*. A subject in the **active voice** performs the action.

> Most clams **live** in salt water. [The subject *clams* does the acting: Clams *live*.]
> They **burrow** into the sandy bottoms of shallow waters. [The subject *they* does the acting: They *burrow*.]

A subject in the **passive voice** is acted upon. The person or thing doing the acting often appears in a PHRASE that starts with *by*. Verbs in the passive voice use forms of *be, have,* and *will* as AUXILIARY VERBS with the PAST PARTICIPLE of the MAIN VERB.

> Clams **are considered** a delicacy by many people. [The subject *clams* is acted upon *by many people.*]
> Some types of clams **are** highly **valued** by seashell collectors. [The subject *types* is acted upon *by seashell collectors.*]

15o How do I write in the active, not passive, voice?

Because the ACTIVE VOICE emphasizes the doer of an action, active constructions are more direct and dramatic. Active constructions usually require fewer words than passive constructions, which makes for greater conciseness (11c). Most sentences in the PASSIVE VOICE can be converted to active voice.

> PASSIVE African tribal masks are often imitated by Western sculptors.
> ACTIVE Western sculptors often imitate African tribal masks.

15p What are proper uses of the passive voice?

Although the active voice is usually best, in special circumstances you need to use the passive voice.

When no one knows who or what did something or when the doer of an action isn't important, writers use the passive voice.

The lock **was broken** sometime after four o'clock. [Who broke the lock is unknown.]

In 1899, the year I was born, a peace conference **was held** at The Hague. [The doers of the action—holders of the conference—aren't important.]

—E. B. White, "Unity"

Sometimes the action in the sentence is more important than the doer of the action. For example, if you want to focus on historical discoveries in a narrative, use the passive voice. Conversely, if you want to emphasize the people making the discoveries, use the active voice.

ACTIVE   Joseph Priestley **discovered** oxygen in 1774. [*Joseph Priestley* is the subject.]

PASSIVE   Oxygen **was discovered** in 1774 by Joseph Priestley. [*Oxygen* is the subject.]

ACTIVE   The postal clerk **sent** the unsigned letter before I **could retrieve** it from the mailroom. [The emphasis is on the doers of the action, *the postal clerk* and *I*, rather than on the events, *sent* and *could retrieve*.]

PASSIVE   The unsigned letter **was sent** before it **could be retrieved** from the postal clerk. [The emphasis is on the events, *was sent* and *could be retrieved*, not on the doers of the action, the unknown sender and *the postal clerk*.]

In former years, the social sciences and natural sciences preferred the passive voice. Recently, style manuals for these disciplines have been advising writers to use the active voice whenever possible. "Verbs are vigorous, direct communicators," point out the editors of the *Publication Manual of the American Psychological Association*. "Use the active rather than the passive voice," they say.*

EXERCISE 15-9   First, determine which sentences are in the active voice and which the passive voice. Second, rewrite each sentence in the other voice, and then decide which voice better suits the meaning. Be ready to explain your choice. For help, consult 15n through 15p.

EXAMPLE   In the West African country of Ghana, a few woodcarvers are creating coffins that reflect their occupants' special interests. (*active; change to passive*)

---

*American Psychological Association, *Publication Manual of the American Psychological Association*, 5th ed. (Washington: APA, 2001) 41.

In the West African country of Ghana, coffins that reflect their occupants' special interests are being created by a few woodcarvers.

1. A coffin in the shape of a green onion was chosen by a farmer.
2. A hunter's family buried him in a wooden coffin shaped like a leopard.
3. A dead chief was carried through his fishing village by friends and relatives bearing his body in a large pink wooden replica of a fish.
4. The family of a wealthy man who greatly admired cars buried him in a coffin shaped like a Mercedes car.
5. Although a few of these fantasy coffins have been displayed in museums, most of them end up buried in the ground.

For more help with your
writing, grammar, and research,
go to **www.mycomplab.com**

16

Pronouns: Case and Reference

PRONOUN CASE

16a What does "case" mean?

Case applies in different ways to PRONOUNS and to NOUNS. For pronouns, case refers to three pronoun forms: the **subjective** (pronoun as a SUBJECT), the **objective** (pronoun as an OBJECT), and the **possessive** (pronouns used in possessive constructions). For nouns, case refers to only one noun form: the possessive. (For help in using apostrophes in the possessive case, see Chapter 27.)

16b What are personal pronouns?

Personal pronouns refer to persons or things. Quick Reference 16.1 shows the case forms of personal pronouns (subjective, objective, and possessive), in both the singular and the plural.

Many of the most difficult questions about pronoun case concern *who/whom* and *whoever/whomever*. For a full discussion of how to choose between them, see 16g.

Quick Reference 16.1   ■ ■ ■ ■ ■ ■ ■

Case forms of personal pronouns

	Subjective	**Objective**	**Possessive**
SINGULAR	I, you, he, she, it	me, you, him, her, it	my, mine, your, yours, his, her, hers, its
PLURAL	we, you, they	us, you, them	our, ours, your, yours, their, theirs

---

16c How do pronouns work in case?

In the subjective case, pronouns function as SUBJECTS.

> **We** were going to get married. [*We* is the subject.]

> John and **I** wanted an inexpensive band for our wedding. [*I* is part of the compound subject *John and I*.]

> **He and I** found an affordable one-person band. [*He and I* is the compound subject.]

In the objective case, pronouns function as OBJECTS.

> We saw **him** perform in a public park. [*Him* is the direct object.]

> We showed **him** our budget. [*Him* is the indirect object.]

> He wrote down what we wanted and shook hands with **us**. [*Us* is the object of the preposition *with*.]

In the possessive case, nouns and pronouns usually indicate ownership or imply a relationship.

> The **musician's contract** was very fair. [The possessive noun *musician's* implies a type of ownership.]

> **His contract** was very fair. [The possessive pronoun *his* implies a type of ownership.]

> The **musicians' problems** stem from playing cheap instruments. [The possessive noun *musicians'* implies a type of relationship.]

> **Their problems** stem from playing with cheap instruments. [The possessive pronoun *their* implies a type of relationship.]

Sometimes, however, the notion of ownership or relationship calls for a major stretch of the imagination in possessive constructions. In such cases, look for the following pattern: noun + the *s* sound + noun. This means that two nouns work together, one of which does the possessing and the other of which is possessed.

> The **musician's arrival** was eagerly anticipated. [The musician neither owns the arrival nor has a relationship with the arrival. Instead, the pattern noun + the *s* sound + noun is operating.]

❗ **Alert:** Never use an apostrophe in personal pronouns: *ours, yours, its, his, hers, theirs* (27c). ●

16d   Which case is correct when *and* connects pronouns?

When *and* connects pronouns, or nouns and pronouns, the result is a **compound construction**. Compounding, which means "putting parts together in a whole," has no effect on case. Always use pronouns in the subjective case when they serve as the subjects of a sentence; also, always use pronouns in the objective case when they serve as objects in a sentence. Never mix cases.

COMPOUND PRONOUN SUBJECT	**He and I** saw the solar eclipse. [*He and I* is a compound subject.]
COMPOUND PRONOUN OBJECT	That eclipse astonished **him and me**. [*Him and me* is a compound object.]

When you're unsure of the case of a pronoun, use the "Troyka test for case" in Quick Reference 16.2. In this four-step test, you drop some of the words from your sentence so that you can tell which case sounds correct.

When pronouns are in a PREPOSITIONAL PHRASE, they are always in the objective case. (That is, a pronoun is always the OBJECT of the preposition.) This rule holds whether the pronouns are singular or plural.

Quick Reference 16.2   ■ ■ ■ ■ ■ ■ ■

Troyka test for case

SUBJECTIVE CASE

STEP 1:   Write the sentence twice, once using the subjective case, and once using the objective case.

continued >>

Quick Reference 16.2	(continued)

STEP 2: Cross out enough words to isolate the element you are questioning.

~~Janet and~~ me

~~Janet and~~ I

> learned about the moon.

STEP 3: Omit the crossed-out words and read each sentence aloud to determine which one sounds right.

NO Me learned about the moon. [This doesn't sound right.]

YES I learned about the moon. [This sounds right, so the subjective case is correct.]

STEP 4: Select the correct version and restore the words you crossed out.

Janet and I learned about the moon.

OBJECTIVE CASE

STEP 1: Write the sentence twice, once using the subjective case, and once using the objective case.

STEP 2: Cross out enough words to isolate the element you are questioning.

The astronomer taught ~~Janet and~~ I

The astronomer taught ~~Janet and~~ me

> about the moon.

STEP 3: Omit the crossed-out words and read each sentence aloud to determine which one sounds right.

NO The astronomer taught I about the moon. [This doesn't sound right.]

YES The astronomer taught me about the moon. [This sounds right, so the objective case is correct.]

STEP 4: Select the correct version and restore the words you crossed out.

The astronomer taught **Janet and me** about the moon.

NO Ms. Lester gave an assignment *to* **Sam and I.** [The prepositional phrase, which starts with the preposition *to*, cannot use the subjective-case pronoun *I*.]

YES Ms. Lester gave an assignment *to* **Sam and me.** [The prepositional phrase, which starts with the preposition *to*, calls for the objective-case pronoun *me*.]

Be especially careful when one or more pronouns follow the preposition *between*.

NO The dispute is *between* **Thomas and I.** [The prepositional phrase, which starts with the preposition *between*, cannot use the subjective-case pronoun *I*.]

YES The dispute is *between* **Thomas and me.** [The prepositional phrase, which starts with the preposition *between*, calls for the objective-case pronoun *me*.]

EXERCISE 16-1 Underline the correct pronoun of each pair in parentheses. For help, consult 16c and 16d.

EXAMPLE Bill and (I, me) noticed two young swimmers being pulled out to sea.

(1) The two teenagers caught in the rip current waved and hollered at Bill and (I, me). (2) The harder (they, them) both swam toward shore, the further away the undercurrent pulled them from the beach. (3) The yellow banners had warned Bill and (I, me) that a dangerous rip current ran beneath the water. (4) I yelled at Bill, "Between you and (I, me), (we, us) have to save them!" (5) (He and I, Him and me) both ran and dove into the crashing waves. (6) As former lifeguards, Bill and (I, me) knew what to do. (7) (We, Us) two remembered that the rule for surviving a rip current is to swim across the current. (8) Only when swimmers are safely away from the current should (they, them) swim toward shore. (9) I reached the teenage girl, who cried, "My boyfriend and (I, me) are drowning." (10) Bill rescued the frightened teenage boy, and when they were safely on shore, the boy looked at (he and I, him and me) and gasped, "Thanks. The two of (we, us) know you saved our lives."

16e How do I match cases with appositives?

You can match cases with APPOSITIVES by putting pronouns and nouns in the same case as the word or words the appositive is renaming. Whenever you're unsure about whether to use the subjective or objective case, use the "Troyka test for case" in Quick Reference 16.2 to get the answer.

We [not *Us*] tennis players practice hard. [Here, the subjective-case pronoun *we* matches the noun phrase *tennis players*, which is the subject of this sentence.]

The winners, **she and I** [not *her and me*], advanced to the finals. [The subjective-case pronoun phrase *she and I* matches the noun *winners*, which is the subject of this sentence.]

The coach tells **us** [not *we*] tennis players to practice hard. [The objective-case pronoun *us* matches the noun phrase *tennis players*, which is the object in this sentence.]

The crowd cheered the winners, **her and me** [not *she and I*]. [The objective-case pronoun phrase *her and me* matches the noun *winners*, which is the object in this sentence.]

16f How does case work after linking verbs?

A pronoun that comes after a LINKING VERB either renames the SUBJECT or shows possession. In both constructions, always use a pronoun in the subjective case. If you're unsure about how to identify a pronoun's case, use the "Troyka test for case" in Quick Reference 16.2.

The contest winner was **I** [not *me*]. [*Was* is a linking verb. *I* renames the subject, which is the noun phrase *contest winner*, so the subjective-case pronoun *I* is correct.]

The prize is **mine.** [*Is* is a linking verb. *Mine* shows possession, so the possessive-case pronoun *mine* is correct.]

EXERCISE 16-2   Underline the correct pronoun of each pair in parentheses. For help, consult 16c through 16f.

EXAMPLE   My college roommate and (<u>I</u>, me) have been interested in the Harlem Renaissance since (<u>we</u>, us) took an American literature survey course as sophomores.

(1) My roommate and (I, me) discovered (we, us) did not know much about the Harlem Renaissance. (2) (We, Us) two began reading the history and literature of the movement and wanted to know more about it. (3) Between (her and me, she and I), (we, us) divided the authors of the Harlem Renaissance into two groups. (4) However, learning about the movement meant more than reading works by the authors, (we, us) found. (5). It also meant (her and me, she and I) needed to study the background that created the movement. (6) (We, Us) learned that many African Americans moved from the South to large industrial cities in the North, a fact that directed (we, us) to other matters. (7) For example, a black middle class arose because (they, them) had industrial jobs, which earned (they, them) more opportunities for

education. (8) (They, them) had a thirst for reading magazines and books by other African Americans. (9) Slowly, a radical group developed a "new consciousness," with the educated writers of the Harlem Renaissance being the most outspoken among (they, them). (10) (We, us), my roommate and (I, me), became even more interested in the Harlem Renaissance then because (she and I, her and me) remembered our parents talking about their participation in the civil rights movement of the 1960s.

16g When should I use *who, whoever, whom,* and *whomever?*

The pronouns *who* and *whoever* are in the SUBJECTIVE CASE. The pronouns *whom* and *whomever* are in the OBJECTIVE CASE.

Informal spoken English tends to blur distinctions between *who* and *whom,* so with these words some people can't rely entirely on what "sounds right." Whenever you're unsure of whether to use *who* or *whoever* or to use *whom* or *whomever,* apply the "Troyka test for case" in Quick Reference 16.2. If you see *who* or *whoever,* test by temporarily substituting *he, she,* or *they.* If you see *whom* or *whomever,* test by temporarily substituting *him, her,* or *them.*

My father tells the same story to **whoever/whomever** he meets.

My father tells the same story to **she/her**. [*Note:* When substituting, stop at *she/her.* The objective case *whomever* is correct because the sentence works when you substitute *her* for *whoever/whomever.* In contrast, the subjective case *whoever* is wrong because the sentence doesn't work when you substitute *she* for *whoever/whomever.*]

My father tells the same story to **whomever** he meets.

The most reliable variation of the test for *who, whom, whoever, whomever* calls for you to add a word before the substituted word set. In this example, the word *if* is added:

I wondered **who/whom** would vote for Ms. Wallace.

I wondered **if he/if him** would vote for Ms. Wallace. [The subjective case *who* is correct because the sentence works when you substitute *if he* for *who/whom.* In contrast, the objective case *whom* is wrong because the sentence doesn't work when you substitute *if him* for *who/whom.*]

I wondered **who** would vote for Ms. Wallace.

Another variation of the test for *who, whom, whoever, whomever* calls for you to invert the word order in the test sentence.

Babies **who/whom** mothers cuddle grow faster and feel happier.

Mothers cuddle ~~they~~/them. [*Note:* When substituting, stop at *they/them*. By inverting the word order in the sentence—that is, by temporarily using *mothers* as the subject of the sentence—and substituting *they/them* for *who/whom*, you see that *them* is correct. Therefore, the objective case *whom* is correct.]

Babies **whom** mothers cuddle grow faster and feel happier.

At the beginning or end of a question, use *who* if the question is about the subject and *whom* if the question is about the object. To determine which case to use, recast the question into a statement, substituting *he* or *him* (or *she* or *her*).

Who watched the space shuttle liftoff? [*He* (not *Him*) *watched the space shuttle liftoff* uses the subjective case, so *who* is correct.]

Ted admires **whom**? [*Ted admires him* (not *he*) uses the objective case, so *whom* is correct.]

Whom does Ted admire? [*Ted admires him* (not *he*) uses the objective case, so *whom* is correct.]

To **whom** does Ted speak about becoming an astronaut? [*Ted speaks to them* (not *they*) uses the objective case, so *whom* is correct.]

EXERCISE 16-3   Underline the correct pronoun of each pair in parentheses. For help, consult 16g.

EXAMPLE   Women (<u>who</u>, whom) both hold jobs outside the home and are mothers serve a "double shift."

(1) Women (who, whom) raise families do as much work at home as at their jobs. (2) In North American society, it is still mainly women (who, whom) cook dinner, clean the house, check the children's homework, read to them, and put them to bed. (3) Nevertheless, self-esteem runs high, some researchers have found, in many women on (who, whom) families depend for both wage earning and child rearing. (4) Compared with women (who, whom) pursue careers but have no children, those (who, whom) handle a double shift experience less anxiety and depression, according to the research. (5) Perhaps the reason for this finding is that those for (who, whom) the extra paycheck helps pay the bills feel pride and accomplishment when they rise to the challenge. (6) However, other studies note that women (who, whom) have both jobs and children experience tremendous stress. (7) Those (who, whom) feel unable both to support and to nurture their children despite their maximum efforts are the women for (who, whom) the dual responsibility is an almost unbearable burden.

16h   What pronoun case comes after *than* or *as*?

When *than* or *as* is part of a sentence of comparison, the sentence sometimes doesn't include words to complete the comparison outright. Rather, by omitting certain words, the sentence implies the comparison. For example, *My two-month-old Saint Bernard is larger than most full-grown dogs [are]* doesn't need the final word *are*.

When a pronoun follows *than* or *as,* the meaning of the sentence depends entirely on whether the pronoun is in the subjective case or the objective case. Here are two sentences that convey two very different messages, depending on whether the subjective case (*I*) or the objective case (*me*) is used.

1. My sister loved that dog more *than* I.

2. My sister loved that dog more *than* me.

In sentence 1, because *I* is in the subjective case, the sentence means *My sister loved that dog more than I [loved it].* In sentence 2, because *me* is in the objective case, the sentence means *My sister loved that dog more than [she loved] me.* In both situations, you can check whether you're using the correct case by supplying the implied words to see if they make sense.

16i   How do pronouns work before infinitives?

Most INFINITIVES consist of the SIMPLE FORMS of verbs that follow *to:* for example, *to laugh, to sing, to jump, to dance.* (A few exceptions occur when the *to* is optional: *My aunt helped the elderly man [to] cross the street;* and when the *to* is awkward: *My aunt watched the elderly man [to] get on the bus.*) For both the SUBJECTS of infinitives and the OBJECTS of infinitives, use the objective case.

> Our tennis coach expects **me** *to serve.* [Because the word *me* is the subject of the infinitive *to serve,* the objective-case pronoun is correct.]

> Our tennis coach expects **him** *to beat* **me.** [Because the word *him* is the subject of the infinitive *to beat,* and *me* is the object of the infinitive, the objective-case pronoun is correct.]

16j   How do pronouns work with *-ing* words?

When a verb's *-ing* form functions as a NOUN, it's called a GERUND: *Brisk **walking** is excellent exercise.* When a noun or PRONOUN comes before a gerund, the POSSESSIVE CASE is required: *His brisk **walking** built up his stamina.* In contrast, when a verb's *-ing* form functions as a MODIFIER, it requires the subjective case for the pronoun, not the possessive case: *He, **walking** briskly, caught up to me.*

Here are two sentences that convey different messages, depending entirely on whether a possessive comes before the *-ing* word.

1. The detective noticed the **man** *staggering*.
2. The detective noticed the **man's** *staggering*.

Sentence 1 means that the detective noticed the *man;* sentence 2 means that the detective noticed the *staggering.* The same distinction applies to pronouns: When *the man* is replaced by *him* or *the man's* by *his,* the meaning is the same as in sentences 1 and 2.

1. The detective noticed **him** *staggering*.
2. The detective noticed **his** *staggering*.

In conversation, such distinctions are often ignored, but use them in ACADEMIC WRITING.

EXERCISE 16-4   Underline the correct pronoun of each pair in parentheses. For help, consult 16h through 16j.

EXAMPLE   Ricky Jay holds the world's record for card throwing; no one can throw a playing card faster than (he/him).

(1) Many magicians agree that no one is better at sleight-of-hand magic than (he/him). (2) Younger magicians often say that Ricky Jay influenced (their/them) to become professional performers. (3) In addition to (him/his) being a respected sleight-of-hand artist, Jay is also a scholar and historian. (4) His interest in strange performers led (him/he) to write *Learned Pigs and Fireproof Women*, which discusses unusual acts and begins with (him/his) explaining their appeal to audiences. (5) Jay's acting career has involved (his/him) performing in several different movies and TV shows. (6) In the James Bond film *Tomorrow Never Dies*, few could have played a villain as well as (he/him). (7) Other roles include (him/his) narrating the introduction to the movie *Magnolia*. (8) Overall, few performers have had such as varied and interesting career as (him/he).

16k   What case should I use for *-self* pronouns?

Two types of pronouns end in *-self:* reflexive pronouns and intensive pronouns.
   A **reflexive pronoun** reflects back on the subject, so it needs a subject in the sentence to be reflected back on. Without a subject, the reflexive pronoun cannot operate correctly.

> The **detective** disguised *himself.* [The reflexive pronoun *himself* reflects back on the subject *detective.*]

Never use a reflexive pronoun to replace a personal pronoun in the subjective case.

NO   My teammates and **myself** will vote for a team captain.

YES   My teammates and **I** will vote for a team captain.

Also, never use a reflexive pronoun to replace a personal pronoun in the objective case. The only exception is when the object restates the subject.

NO   That decision is up to my teammates and **myself**.

YES   That decision is up to my teammates and **me**.

Intensive pronouns, which reflect back in the same way as reflexive pronouns, provide emphasis by making the message of the sentence more intense in meaning.

The detective felt that **his career *itself*** was at risk. [*Itself* intensifies the idea that the detective's career was at risk.]

PRONOUN REFERENCE

16l What is pronoun reference?

The word or group of words that a pronoun replaces is called its **antecedent**. In order for your writing to communicate its message clearly, each pronoun must relate precisely to an antecedent.

> I knew a **woman**, lovely in **her** bones / When small **birds** sighed, **she** would sigh back at **them**.
>
> Theodore Roethke, "I Knew a Woman"

16m What makes pronoun reference clear?

Pronoun reference is clear when your readers know immediately to whom or what each pronoun refers. Quick Reference 16.3 lists guidelines for using pronouns clearly, and the section in parentheses is where each is explained.

Quick Reference 16.3   ■ ■ ■ ■ ■ ■ ■

Guidelines for clear pronoun reference

- Place pronouns close to their ANTECEDENTS (16n).
- Make a pronoun refer to a specific antecedent (16n).
- Do not overuse *it* (16q).
- Reserve *you* only for DIRECT ADDRESS (16r).
- Use *that, which,* and *who* correctly (16s).

16n How can I avoid unclear pronoun reference?

Every pronoun needs to refer to a specific, nearby ANTECEDENT. If the same pronoun in your writing has to refer to more than one antecedent, replace some pronouns with nouns.

> NO   In 1911, **Roald Amundsen** reached the South Pole just thirty-five days before **Robert F. Scott** arrived. **He** [who? Amundsen or Scott?] had told people that **he** [who? Amundsen or Scott?] was going to sail for the Arctic, but **he** [who? Amundsen or Scott?] was concealing **his** [whose? Amundsen's or Scott's?] plan. Soon, **he** [who? Amundsen or Scott?] turned south for the Antarctic. On the journey home, **he** [who? Amundsen or Scott?] and **his** [whose? Amundsen's or Scott's?] party froze to death just a few miles from safety.

> YES   In 1911, **Roald Amundsen** reached the South Pole just thirty-five days before **Robert F. Scott** arrived. **Amundsen** had told people that **he** was going to sail for the Arctic, but **he** was concealing **his** plan. Soon, **Amundsen** turned south for the Antarctic. Meanwhile, on **their** journey home, **Scott** and **his party** froze to death just a few miles from safety.

⬤ Alert: Be careful with the VERBS *said* and *told* in sentences that contain pronoun reference. To maintain clarity, use quotation marks and slightly reword each sentence to make the meaning clear. ⬤

> NO   **Her** mother told **her she** was going to visit **her** grandmother.

> YES   **Her** mother told **her,** "**You** are going to visit your grandmother."

> YES   **Her** mother told **her,** "I am going to visit your grandmother."

Further, if too much material comes between a pronoun and its antecedent, readers can lose track of the meaning.

Alfred Wegener, a German meteorologist and professor of geophysics at the University of Graz in Austria, was the first to suggest that all the continents on earth were originally part of one large landmass. According to this theory, the supercontinent broke up long ago and the fragments drifted apart.

Wegener
~~He~~ named this supercontinent Pangaea.
  ^

[*He* can refer only to Wegener, but material about Wegener's theory intervenes, so using *Wegener* again instead of *he* jogs the reader's memory and makes reading easier.]

When you start a new paragraph, be cautious about beginning it with a pronoun whose antecedent is in a prior paragraph. You're better off repeating the word.

ESOL Tip: Many languages omit a pronoun as a subject because the verb delivers the needed information. English requires the use of the pronoun as a subject. For example, never omit *it* in the following: *Political science is an important academic subject. **It** is studied all over the world.*

EXERCISE 16-5 Revise so that each pronoun refers clearly to its antecedent. Either replace pronouns with nouns or restructure the material to clarify pronoun reference. For help, consult 16n.

EXAMPLE People who return to work after years away from the corporate world often discover that business practices have changed. They may find fiercer competition in the workplace, but they may also discover that they are more flexible than before.

Here is one possible revision: *People who return to work after years away from the corporate world often discover that business practices have changed. Those people may find fiercer competition in the workplace, but they may also discover that business practices are more flexible than before.*

Most companies used to frown on employees who became involved in office romances. They often considered them to be using company time for their own enjoyment. Now, however, managers realize that happy employees are productive employees. With more women than ever before in the workforce and with people working longer hours, they have begun to see that male and female employees want and need to socialize. They are also dropping their opposition to having married couples on the payroll. They no longer automatically believe that they will bring family matters into the workplace or stick up for each other at the company's expense.

One departmental manager had doubts when a systems analyst for research named Laura announced that she had become engaged to Peter, who worked as a technician in the same department. She told her that either one or the other might have to transfer out of the research department. After listening to her plea that they be allowed to work together on a trial basis, the manager reconsidered. She decided to give Laura and Peter a chance to prove that their relationship would not affect their work. The decision paid off. They demonstrated that they could work as an effective research team, right through their engagement and subsequent marriage. Two years later, when Laura was promoted to assistant manager for product development and after he asked to move also, she enthusiastically recommended that Peter follow Laura to her new department.

16o How do pronouns work with *it, that, this,* and *which*?

When you use *it, that, this,* and *which,* be sure that your readers can easily understand what each word refers to.

> **NO** Comets usually fly by the earth at 100,000 mph, whereas asteroids sometimes collide with the earth. **This** interests scientists. [Does *this* refer to the speed of the comets, to comets flying by the earth, or to asteroids colliding with the earth?]

> **YES** Comets usually fly by the earth at 100,000 mph, whereas asteroids sometimes collide with the earth. **This difference** interests scientists. [Adding a noun after *this* or *that* clarifies the meaning.]

> **NO** I told my friends that I was going to major in geology, **which** made my parents happy. [Does *which* refer to telling your friends or to majoring in geology?]

> **YES** My parents were happy **because I discussed my major with my friends.**

> **YES** My parents were happy **because I chose to major in geology.**

Also, the title of any piece of writing stands on its own. Therefore, in your introductory paragraph, never refer to your title with *this* or *that*. For example, if an essay's title is "Geophysics as a Major," the following holds for the first sentence:

> **NO** **This subject** unites the sciences of physics, biology, and paleontology.

> **YES** **Geophysics** unites the sciences of physics, biology, and paleontology.

16p How do I use *they* and *it* precisely?

The expression *they say* can't take the place of stating precisely who is doing the saying. Your credibility as a writer depends on your mentioning a source precisely.

> **NO** **They say** that earthquakes are becoming more frequent. [*They* doesn't identify the authority who made the statement.]

> **YES** **Seismologists** say that earthquakes are becoming more frequent.

The expressions *it said* and *it is said that* reflect imprecise thinking. Also, they're wordy. Revising such expressions improves your writing.

NO   It said in the newspaper that California has minor earthquakes almost daily. [*It said in the newspaper that is wordy.*]

YES   **The newspaper reported** that California has minor earthquakes almost daily.

16q   How do I use *it* to suit the situation?

The word *it* has three different uses in English. Here are examples of correct uses of *it*.

1. PERSONAL PRONOUN: Ryan wants to visit the 18-inch Schmidt telescope, but **it** is on Mount Palomar.

2. EXPLETIVE (sometimes called a *subject filler,* it delays the subject): **It** is interesting to observe the stars.

3. IDIOMATIC EXPRESSION (words that depart from normal use, such as using *it* as the sentence subject when writing about weather, time, distance, and environmental conditions). **It** is sunny. **It** is midnight. **It** is not far to the hotel. **It** is very hilly.

All three uses listed above are correct, but avoid combining them in the same sentence. The result can be an unclear and confusing sentence.

NO   Because our car was overheating, **it** came as no surprise that **it** broke down just as **it** began to rain. [*It is overused here, even though all three uses—2, 1, and 3 on the above list, respectively— are acceptable.*]

YES   **It** came as no surprise that our overheating car broke down just as the rain began. [*The word order is revised so that* it *is used once.*]

🌐 **ESOL Tip:** In some languages, *it* is not used as an expletive. In English, it is. ●

NO   Is a lovely day.

YES   **It** is a lovely day.

16r   When should I use *you* for direct address?

Reserve *you* for **direct address**, writing that addresses the reader directly. For example, we use *you* in this handbook to address you, the student. *You* is not a suitable substitute for specific words that refer to people, situations, or occurrences.

NO	Prison uprisings often happen **when you allow** overcrowding. [The reader, *you*, did not allow the overcrowding.]
YES	Prison uprisings often happen **when prisons are** overcrowded.
NO	In Russia, **you** usually have to stand in long lines to buy groceries. [Are *you*, the reader, planning to do your grocery shopping in Russia?]
YES	**Russian consumers** usually have to stand in long lines to buy groceries.

EXERCISE 16-6   Revise these sentences so that all pronoun references are clear. If a sentence is correct, circle its number. For help, consult 16o through 16r.

EXAMPLE   They say that reaching the summit of Mount Everest is easiest in the month of May.

Experienced climbers say that reaching the summit of Mount Everest is easiest in the month of May. [Revision eliminates imprecise use of *they*, see section 16p.]

1. Climbing Mount Everest is more expensive than you realize.
2. In addition to training, they need to raise as much as $60,000 for the expedition.
3. By contacting the Nepalese embassy in Washington, DC, you can secure the help of Sherpa guides.
4. The government of Nepal requires permits, copies of passports, and letters of recommendation for each climbing team.
5. Climbers will need to pack oxygen bottles, a first aid kit, medications, a satellite phone, walkie-talkies, and a laptop computer. This will ensure a climber's safety.
6. Climbers often use yaks because they are stronger than you and can carry more equipment.
7. They do not offer direct flights, so climbers from America usually need a couple of days to get to Katmandu, Nepal.
8. Once atop the mountain, you should prepare for the descent, which is just as dangerous as the ascent.

16s   When should I use *that, which,* and *who*?

To use the pronouns *that* and *which* correctly, you want to check the context of the sentence you're writing. *Which* and *that* refer to animals and things. Only sometimes do they refer to anonymous or collective groups of people. Quick Reference 16.4 shows how to choose between *that* and *which*. For information about the role of commas with *that* and *which*, see 24f.

Who refers to people and to animals mentioned by name.

John Polanyi, who was awarded the Nobel Prize in Chemistry, speaks passionately in favor of nuclear disarmament. [*John Polanyi* is a person.]

Lassie, who was known for her intelligence and courage, was actually played by a series of male collies. [*Lassie* is the name of an animal.]

Many professional writers reserve *which* for nonrestrictive clauses and *that* for restrictive clauses. Other writers use *that* and *which* interchangeably for restrictive clauses. Current practice allows the use of either as long as you're consistent in each piece of writing. However, for ACADEMIC WRITING, your instructor might expect you to maintain the distinction.

Quick Reference 16.4 ■ ■ ■ ■ ■ ■ ■ ■

Choosing between *that* and *which*

Choice: Some instructors and style guides use either *that* or *which* to introduce a RESTRICTIVE CLAUSE (a DEPENDENT CLAUSE that is essential to the meaning of the sentence or part of the sentence). Others may advise you to use only *that* so that your writing distinguishes clearly between restrictive and NONRESTRICTIVE CLAUSES. Whichever style you use, be consistent in each piece of writing:

* The zoos *that* (or *which*) **most children like** display newborn and baby animals. [The point in this sentence concerns children's preferences. Therefore, the words *most children like* are essential for delivering the meaning and make up a restrictive clause.]

No choice: You are required to use *which* to introduce a nonrestrictive clause (a dependent clause that isn't essential to the meaning of the sentence or part of the sentence).

* Zoos, **which most children like,** attract more visitors if they display newborn and baby animals. [The point in this sentence concerns attracting more visitors to zoos. Therefore, the words *most children like* are not essential to the meaning of the sentence and make up a nonrestrictive clause.]

Alert: Use commas before and after a nonrestrictive clause. Don't use commas before and after a restrictive clause; see 24k.4. ●

EXERCISE 16-7 Fill in the blanks with *that, which,* or *who.* For help, consult 16s.

EXAMPLE Antigua, <u>which</u> is an island in the West Indies, is a popular destination for European and American tourists.

1. Those _____ like to travel to Antigua may enjoy online gambling, _____ is legal on the island.
2. The sport _____ is most popular in Antigua is cricket.
3. Celebrities _____ own homes on the island include Oprah Winfrey, Eric Clapton, and Jamaica Kincaid.
4. The main airport, _____ is named after Prime Minister V. C. Bird, is located in the capital, St. John's.
5. The cruise ships _____ travel to Antigua often stop at St. John's, _____ became the seat of government in 1981.

For more help with your
writing, grammar, and research,
go to **www.mycomplab.com**

17

Agreement

17a What is agreement?

In everyday speech, agreement indicates that people hold the same ideas. Grammatical **agreement** is also based on sameness. Specifically, you need to match SUBJECTS and VERBS; see 17b through 17n. You also need to match PRONOUNS and ANTECEDENTS; see 17o through 17t.

SUBJECT-VERB AGREEMENT

17b What is subject-verb agreement?

Subject-verb agreement means that a SUBJECT and its VERB match in NUMBER (singular or plural) and PERSON (first, second, or third person). Quick Reference 17.1 presents these major concepts in grammatical agreement.

The **firefly glows.** [*Firefly* is a singular subject in the third person; *glows* is a singular verb in the third person.]

Fireflies glow. [*Fireflies* is a plural subject in the third person; *glow* is a plural verb in the third person.]

Grammatical agreement: first, second and third person

- **Number**, as a concept in grammar, refers to *singular* (one) and *plural* (more than one).

- The **first person** is the speaker or writer. *I* (singular) and *we* (plural) are the only subjects that occur in the first person.

  SINGULAR   I see a field of fireflies.

  PLURAL   We see a field of fireflies.

- The **second person** is the person spoken or written to. *You* (for both singular and plural) is the only subject that occurs in the second person.

  SINGULAR   You see a shower of sparks.

  PLURAL   You see a shower of sparks.

- The **third person** is the person or thing being spoken or written about. *He, she, it* (singular) and *they* (plural) are the third-person subject forms. Most rules for subject-verb agreement involve the third person.

  SINGULAR   The **scientist sees** a cloud of cosmic dust.

  PLURAL   The **scientists see** a cloud of cosmic dust.

17c Why is a final -s or -es in a subject or verb so important?

SUBJECT-VERB AGREEMENT often involves one letter: *s* (or *es* for words that end in *-s*). For verbs in the present tense, you form the SIMPLE FORM of third-person singular by adding *-s* or *-es: laugh, laughs; kiss, kisses.* Major exceptions are the verbs *be* (*is*), *have* (*has*), and *do* (*does*), see 9c.

That **student agrees** that **young teenagers watch** too much television.

Those **young teenagers are** taking valuable time away from studying.

That **student has** a part-time job for ten hours a week.

Still, that **student does** well in college.

For a subject to become plural, you add *-s* or *-es* to its end: *lip, lips; princess, princesses.* Major exceptions include most pronouns (*they, it*) and a few nouns that for singular and plural either don't change (*deer, deer*) or change internally (*mouse, mice*). Quick Reference 17.2 shows you how to visualize the basic pattern for agreement using *-s* or *-es*.

Quick Reference 17.2 ■ ■ ■ ■ ■ ■ ■

Basic subject-verb agreement

• The student works long hours. The students work long hours.

SINGULAR SINGULAR   PLURAL PLURAL
SUBJECT VERB   SUBJECT VERB

Here's a device for remembering how agreement works for most subject-verb constructions. Note that the final -*s* or -*es* can take only one path at a time—to the end of the verb or to the end of the subject.

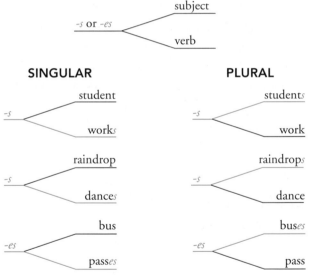

MODEL

-*s* or -*es*
subject
verb

SINGULAR   **PLURAL**

-*s*   student   -*s*   student*s*
        work*s*   work

-*s*   raindrop   -*s*   raindrop*s*
        dance*s*   dance

-*es*   bus   -*es*   bus*es*
        pass*es*   pass

❗**Alert:** When you use an AUXILIARY VERB with a main verb, never add -*s* or -*es* to the main verb: *The coach **can walk*** [not can walks] *to campus. The coach **does like*** [not does likes] *his job.* ●

EXERCISE 17-1   Use the subject and verb in each set to write two complete sentences—one with a singular subject and one with a plural subject. Keep all verbs in the present tense. For help, consult 17c.

EXAMPLE   bird, sing

Singular subject: When a *bird sings*, you will know spring is here.
Plural subject: When *birds sing*, you will know spring is here.

1. chair, rock
2. leaf, fall
3. river, flow
4. clock, tick

5. singer, sing
6. girl, laugh
7. hand, grab
8. loaf, rise

17d Can I Ignore words between a subject and Its verb?

You can ignore all words between a subject and its verb. Focus strictly on the subject and its verb. Quick Reference 17.3 shows you this pattern.

NO **Winners** of the state contest **goes** to the national finals. [*Winners* is the subject; the verb must agree with it. Ignore the words *of the state contest.*]

YES **Winners** of the state contest **go** to the national finals.

The words *one of the* . . . often require a second look. Use a singular verb to agree with the word *one.* Don't be distracted by the plural noun that comes after *of the.* (For information on the phrase *one of the* . . . *who,* see 17l.)

NO **One** of the problems **are** the funds needed for traveling to the national finals.

YES **One** of the problems **is** the funds needed for traveling to the national finals.

Quick Reference 17.3 ■ ■ ■ ■ ■ ■ ■

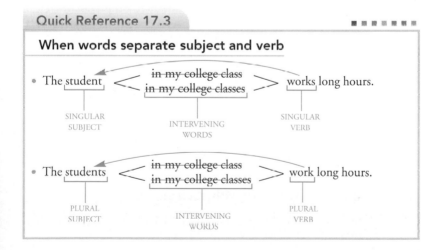

When words separate subject and verb

• The student < in my college class / in my college classes > works long hours.

SINGULAR SUBJECT — INTERVENING WORDS — SINGULAR VERB

• The students < in my college class / in my college classes > work long hours.

PLURAL SUBJECT — INTERVENING WORDS — PLURAL VERB

Similarly, eliminate all word groups between the subject and the verb, starting with *including, together with, along with, accompanied by, in addition to, except,* and *as well as.*

> **NO** The **moon,** *as well as* the planet Venus, **are** visible in the night sky. [*Moon* is the subject. The verb must agree with it. Ignore the words *as well as the planet Venus.*]

> **YES** The **moon,** as well as the planet Venus, **is** visible in the night sky.

17e How do verbs work when subjects are connected by *and*?

When two SUBJECTS are connected by *and,* they create a single COMPOUND SUB-JECT. A compound subject calls for a plural verb. Quick Reference 17.4 shows you this pattern. (For related material on PRONOUNS and ANTECEDENTS, see 17p.)

> The **Cascade Diner** *and* the **Wayside Diner** *have* [not *has*] fried catfish today. [These are two different diners.]

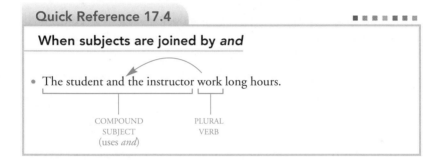

Quick Reference 17.4

When subjects are joined by *and*

- The student and the instructor work long hours.

COMPOUND SUBJECT (uses *and*)

PLURAL VERB

One exception occurs when *and* joins subjects that refer to a single thing or person.

> My **friend** *and* **neighbor** *makes* [not *make*] excellent chili. [In this sentence, the friend is the same person as the neighbor. If they were two different people, *makes* would become *make.*]

> **Macaroni** *and* **cheese** *contains* [not *contain*] carbohydrates, protein, and many calories. [*Macaroni and cheese* is one dish, not two separate dishes, so it requires a singular verb.]

17f How do verbs work with *each* and *every*?

The words *each* and *every* are singular even if they refer to a compound subject. Therefore, they take a singular verb.

> *Each* **human hand and foot** *makes* [not *make*] a distinctive print.

> To identify lawbreakers, *every* **police chief, sheriff, and federal marshal** *depends* [not *depend*] on such prints.

Alert: Use one word, either *each* or *every,* not both at the same time: *Each* [not *Each and every*] *robber has been caught.* (For more information about pronoun agreement for *each* and *every,* see 17i, 17p, and 17r.) ●

17g How do verbs work when subjects are connected by *or*?

As Quick Reference 17.5 shows, when SUBJECTS are joined by *or*—or by the sets *either . . . or, neither . . . nor, not only . . . but (also)*—the verb agrees with the subject closest to it. Ignore everything before the last-mentioned noun or pronoun. Quick Reference 17.5 shows this pattern with *either . . . or*. (For related material on pronouns and antecedents, see 17q.)

Neither spiders *nor* flies upset *me.*

Not only spiders *but also* all other arachnids have four pairs of legs.

A dinner of six clam fritters, four blue crabs, *or* one steamed lobster sounds good.

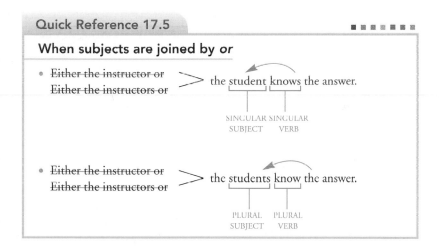

Quick Reference 17.5

When subjects are joined by *or*

- Either the instructor or
  Either the instructors or
  > the student knows the answer.

  SINGULAR SINGULAR
  SUBJECT   VERB

- Either the instructor or
  Either the instructors or
  > the students know the answer.

  PLURAL   PLURAL
  SUBJECT   VERB

17h How do verbs work with inverted word order?

In English sentences, the SUBJECT normally comes before its VERB: *Astronomy is interesting.* **Inverted word order** reverses the typical subject-verb pattern by putting the verb first. Most questions use inverted word order: *Is astronomy interesting?* In inverted word order, find the subject first and then check whether the verb agrees with it.

Into deep space **shoot** probing **satellites.** [The plural verb *shoot* agrees with the inverted plural subject *satellites.*]

On the television screen **appears** an **image** of Saturn. [The singular verb *appears* agrees with the inverted singular subject *image.*]

🚫 **Alert:** When you start a sentence with *there,* check whether the subject is singular or plural, and then choose the right form of *be* to agree with the subject. If your sentence begins with *it,* always use the singular form of *be* (*is, was*) no matter whether the subject is singular or plural.

There *are* nine **planets** in our solar system. [The verb *are* agrees with the subject *planets.*]

There *is* probably no **life** on eight of them. [The verb *is* agrees with the subject *life.*]

It *is* astronomers who explore this theory daily. [The verb *is* agrees with *it,* not with *astronomers.*] ●

EXERCISE 17-2   Supply the correct present-tense form of the verb in parentheses. For help, consult 17c through 17h.

EXAMPLE   Detectives and teachers (to know) <u>know</u> experienced liars can fool almost anybody, but a new computer can tell who is telling the truth.

1. Police officers and teachers often (to wish) _____ they could "read" people's facial expressions.

2. Trained police officers or a smart teacher (to know) _____ facial tics and nervous mannerisms (to show) _____ someone is lying.

3. However, a truly gifted liar, along with well-coached eyewitnesses, (to reveal) _____ very little through expressions or behavior.

4. There (to be) _____ forty-six muscle movements that create all facial expressions in the human face.

5. Neuroscientist Terrence Seinowski, accompanied by a team of researchers, (to be) _____ developing a computer program to recognize even slight facial movements made by the most expert liars.

17i   How do verbs work with indefinite pronouns?

Indefinite pronouns usually refer to nonspecific persons, things, quantities, or ideas. The nonspecific aspect is the reason these pronouns are labeled "indefinite." As part of a sentence, however, the indefinite pronoun is usually clear from the meaning.

Most indefinite pronouns are singular and require a singular verb for agreement. Yet, others are always plural, and a few can be singular *or* plural. Quick

Reference 17.6 clarifies this situation by listing indefinite pronouns according to what verb form they require. (For related material on pronouns and antecedents, see 17o–17r.)

Common indefinite pronouns

ALWAYS PLURAL

both	many

ALWAYS SINGULAR

another	every	no one
anybody	everybody	nothing
anyone	everyone	one
anything	everything	somebody
each	neither	someone
either	nobody	something

SINGULAR OR PLURAL, DEPENDING ON CONTEXT

all	more	none
any	most	some

Here are sample sentences:

SINGULAR INDEFINITE PRONOUNS

Everything about that intersection **is** dangerous.

But whenever **anyone says** anything, **nothing is** done.

Each of us **has** [not *have*] to shovel snow; **each is** [not *are*] expected to help.

Every snowstorm of the past two years **has** [not *have*] been severe.

Every one of them **has** [not *have*] caused massive traffic jams.

SINGULAR OR PLURAL INDEFINITE PRONOUNS
(DEPENDING ON MEANING)

Some of our streams **are** polluted. [*Some* refers to the plural noun *streams*, so the plural verb *are* is correct.]

Some pollution **is** reversible, but **all** pollution **threatens** the balance of nature. [*Some* and *all* refer to the singular noun *pollution*, so the singular verbs *is* and *threatens* are correct.]

All that environmentalists ask **is** to give nature a chance. [*All* has the meaning here of "everything" or "the only thing," so the singular verb *is* is correct.]

Winter has driven the birds south; **all have** left. [*All* refers to the plural noun *birds,* so the plural verb *have* is correct.]

🛑 **Alerts:** (1) Don't mix singular and plural with *this, that, these,* and *those* used with *kind* and *type. This* and *that* are singular, as are *kind* and *type; these* and *those* are plural, as are *kinds* and *types:* **This** [not *These*] **kind** of rainwear is waterproof. **These** [not *This*] **kinds** of sweaters keep me warm. (2) The rules for indefinite pronouns often collide with practices of avoiding SEXIST LANGUAGE. For suggestions, see 17s and 12f. ●

17j How do verbs work with collective nouns?

A **collective noun** names a group of people or things: *family, audience, class, number, committee, team, group,* and the like. When the group of people or things is acting as one unit, use a singular verb. When members of the group are acting individually, use a plural verb. As you're writing, be careful not to shift back and forth between a singular and a plural verb for the same noun.

The senior **class** nervously *awaits* final exams. [The *class* is acting as a single unit, so the verb is singular.]

The senior **class** *were fitted* for their graduation robes today. [The members (of the class) were fitted as individuals, so the verb is plural.]

17k Why does the linking verb agree with the subject, not the subject complement?

Even though a LINKING VERB connects a sentence's SUBJECT to its SUBJECT COMPLEMENT, the linking verb agrees with the subject. It does not agree with the subject complement.

NO The worst **part** of owning a car *are* the bills. [The subject is the singular *part,* so the plural verb *are* is wrong. The subject complement is the plural *bills* and doesn't affect agreement.]

YES The worst **part** of owning a car *is* the bills. [The singular subject *part* agrees with the singular verb *is.* The subject complement doesn't affect agreement.]

17l What verbs agree with *who, which,* and *that?*

If the ANTECEDENT of *who, which,* or *that* is singular, use a singular verb. If the antecedent is plural, use a plural verb.

The scientist will share the prize with the **researchers *who* work** with her. [*Who* refers to *researchers*, so the plural verb *work* is used.]

George Jones is the **student *who* works** in the science lab. [*Who* refers to *student*, so the singular verb *works* is used.]

If you use phrases including *one of the* or *the only one of the* immediately before *who*, *which*, or *that* in a sentence, be careful about the verb you use. *Who*, *which*, or *that* always refers to the plural word immediately following *one of the*, so the verb must be plural. Although *the only one of* is also always followed by a plural word, *who*, *which*, or *that* must be singular to agree with the singular *one*.

Tracy is *one of the* students *who* **talk** in class. [*Who* refers to *students*, so the verb *talk* is plural. *Tracy* is pointed out, but the talking is still done by all of the students.]

Jim is *the only one of the* students *who* **talks** in class. [*Who* refers to *one*, so the verb *talks* is singular. *Jim* is the single person who is talking.]

EXERCISE 17-3 Supply the correct present-tense form of the verb in parentheses. For help, consult 17i through 17l.

EXAMPLE Everybody on a class trip to the coastal waters of the Pacific Ocean (to enjoy) <u>enjoys</u> an opportunity to study dolphins in their natural habitat.

1. A class of college students in marine biology (to take) _____ notes individually while watching dolphins feed off the California coast.

2. Everyone in the class (to listen) _____ as a team of dolphin experts (to explain) _____ some of the mammals' characteristics.

3. A group of dolphins, called a pod, usually (to consist) _____ of 10,000 to 30,000 members.

4. One unique characteristic of dolphins' brains (to be) _____ the sleep patterns that (to keep) _____ one-half of the brain awake at all times.

5. All (to need) _____ to stay awake to breathe, or else they would drown.

17m How do verbs work with amounts, fields of study, and other special nouns?

AMOUNTS

SUBJECTS that refer to time, sums of money, distance, or measurement are singular. They take singular verbs.

Two hours *is* not enough time to finish. [time]

Three hundred dollars *is* what we must pay. [sum of money]

Two miles *is* a short sprint for some serious joggers. [distance]

Three-quarters of an inch *is* needed for a perfect fit. [measurement]

FIELDS OF STUDY

The name for a field of study is singular even if it appears to be plural: *economics, mathematics, physics,* and *statistics.*

Statistics **is** required of science majors. [*Statistics* is a course of study, so the singular verb *is* is correct.]

Statistics **show** that a teacher shortage is coming. [*Statistics* isn't used here as a field of study, so the plural verb *show* is correct.]

SPECIAL NOUNS

Athletics, news, ethics, and *measles* are singular despite their plural appearance. Also, *United States of America* is singular: It is one nation. However, *politics* and *sports* take singular or plural verbs, depending on the meaning of the sentence.

The *news* **gets** better each day. [*News* is a singular noun, so the singular verb *gets* is correct.]

Sports **is** a good way to build physical stamina. [*Sports* is one general activity, so the singular verb *is* is correct.]

Three *sports* **are** offered at the recreation center. [*Sports* are separate activities, so the plural verb *are* is correct.]

Jeans, pants, scissors, clippers, tweezers, eyeglasses, thanks, and *riches* are some of the words that require a plural verb, even though they refer to one thing. However, if you use *pair* with *jeans, pants, scissors, clippers, tweezers,* or *eyeglasses,* use a singular verb for agreement.

Those *slacks* **need** pressing. [plural]

That *pair* of slacks **needs** pressing. [singular]

Series and *means* can be singular or plural, according to the meaning you intend.

Two new TV *series* **are** big hits. [*Series* refers to individual items (two different series), so the plural verb *are* is correct.]

A *series* of disasters **is** plaguing our production. [*Series* refers to a whole group (the whole series of disasters), so the singular verb *is* is correct.]

17n How do verbs work with titles, company names, and words as themselves?

TITLES

A title itself refers to one work or entity (even when plural and compound NOUNS are in the title), so a singular verb is correct.

Breathing Lessons by Anne Tyler **is** a prize-winning novel.

COMPANY NAMES

Many companies have plural words in their names. However, a company should always be treated as a singular unit, requiring a singular verb.

Cohn Brothers **boxes** and **delivers** fine art.

WORDS AS THEMSELVES

Whenever you write about words as themselves to call attention to those words, use a singular verb, even if more than one word is involved.

We **implies** that everyone is included.

During the Vietnam War, *protective reaction strikes* **was** a euphemism for *bombing.*

EXERCISE 17-4   Supply the correct present-tense form of the verb in parentheses. For help, consult 17i through 17n.

EXAMPLE   The movie *Wordplay* is about those who (to enjoy) <u>enjoy</u> solving crossword puzzles.

1. When the movie plays at theaters, the audience often (to consist) _____ of different ages and types of people.

2. For fans of crossword puzzles, the major attraction (to be) _____ the challenges they present.

3. Every creator of puzzles (to know) _____ that in the most successful puzzles all of the clues (to be) _____ interesting.

4. *Setters* (to be) _____ is a term used by crossword puzzle fans to describe someone who creates puzzles.

5. These fans, which (to include) _____ celebrities like Jon Stewart, consider the Sunday puzzle in the *New York Times* one of the most difficult.

EXERCISE 17-5   This exercise covers all of subject-verb agreement (17b through 17n). Supply the correct form of the verb in parentheses.

EXAMPLE   Of the thirty thousand plant species on earth, the rose (to be) <u>is</u> the most universally known.

1. Each plant species (to invite) _____ much discussion about origins and meanings, and when talk turns to flowers, the rose is usually the first mentioned.

2. More fragrant and colorful (to be) _____ other types of flowers, yet roses (to remain) _____ the most popular worldwide.

3. Each of the types of roses (to symbolize) _____ beauty, love, romance, and secrecy.

4. There (to be) _____ more than two hundred pure species of roses and thousands of mixed species, thirty-five of which (to flourish) _____ in the soil of North America.

5. It's impossible to determine exactly where or when the first rose (to be) _____ domesticated, because roses have existed for so many centuries; one of the earliest references dates back to 3000 BC.

6. One myth from Greek mythology (to suggest) _____ that the rose first appeared with the birth of the goddess Aphrodite.

7. Another myth, which focuses on the rose's thorns, (to say) _____ that an angry god shot arrows into the stem to curse the rose forever with arrow-shaped thorns.

8. While theories of this kind (to explain) _____ the significance and evolution of the rose, few people can explain the flower's enduring popularity.

9. Even today, a couple (to demonstrate) _____ love by purchasing red roses.

10. Of all flowers, the best seller (to remain) _____ the rose.

PRONOUN-ANTECEDENT AGREEMENT

17o   What is pronoun-antecedent agreement?

Pronoun-antecedent agreement means that a PRONOUN matches its ANTECEDENT in NUMBER (singular or plural) and PERSON (first, second, or third person). Quick Reference 17.7 shows you how to visualize this pattern of grammatical agreement. You might also want to consult Quick Reference 17.1 in 17b for explanations and examples of the concepts *number* and *person.*

> The **firefly** glows when **it** emerges from **its** nest at night. [The singular pronouns *it* and *its* match their singular antecedent, *firefly.*]

> **Fireflies** glow when **they** emerge from **their** nests at night. [The plural pronouns *they* and *their* match their plural antecedent, *fireflies.*]

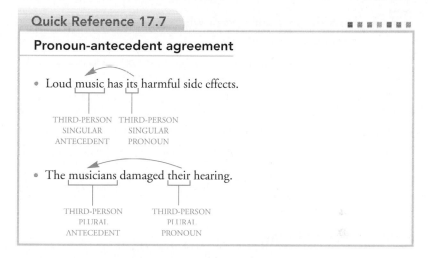

Quick Reference 17.7

Pronoun-antecedent agreement

- Loud music has its harmful side effects.

  THIRD-PERSON THIRD-PERSON
  SINGULAR SINGULAR
  ANTECEDENT PRONOUN

- The musicians damaged their hearing.

  THIRD-PERSON THIRD-PERSON
  PLURAL PLURAL
  ANTECEDENT PRONOUN

17p How do pronouns work when *and* connects antecedents?

When *and* connects two or more ANTECEDENTS, they require a plural pronoun. This rule applies even if each separate antecedent is singular. (For related material on subjects and verbs, see 17e.)

> The Cascade Diner *and* the Wayside Diner closed for New Year's Eve to give **their** [not *its*] employees the night off. [Two separate diners require a plural pronoun.]

When *and* joins singular nouns that nevertheless refer to a single person or thing, use a singular pronoun.

> **My friend *and* neighbor** makes **his** [not *their*] excellent chili every Saturday. [The friend is the same person as the neighbor, so the singular *his* (or *her*) is correct. If two different people were involved, the correct pronoun would be *their*, and *make* would be the correct verb.]

EACH, EVERY

The words *each* and *every* are singular, even when they refer to two or more antecedents joined by *and*. The same rule applies when *each* or *every* is used alone (17i). (For related material on subjects and verbs, see 17f.)

> *Each* **human hand *and* foot** leaves **its** [not *their*] distinctive print.

The rule still applies when the construction *one of the* follows *each* or *every*.

> *Each one of the* **robbers** left **her** [not *their*] fingerprints at the scene.

17q How do pronouns work when *or* connects antecedents?

When ANTECEDENTS are joined by *or*—or by CORRELATIVE CONJUNCTIONS such as *either . . . or, neither . . . nor,* or *not only . . . but (also)*—the antecedents might mix singulars and plurals. For the purposes of agreement, ignore everything before the final antecedent. Quick Reference 17.8 shows you how to visualize this pattern. (For related material on subjects and verbs, see 17g.)

> ~~After the restaurant closes,~~ *~~either~~* ~~the resident mice~~ *~~or~~* **the owner's cat** gets **itself** a meal.

> ~~After the restaurant closes,~~ *~~either~~* ~~the owner's cat~~ *~~or~~* **the resident mice** get **themselves** a meal.

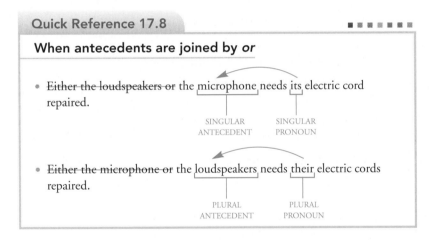

Quick Reference 17.8 ■ ■ ■ ■ ■ ■ ■

When antecedents are joined by *or*

- ~~Either the loudspeakers or~~ the microphone needs its electric cord repaired.

  SINGULAR ANTECEDENT   SINGULAR PRONOUN

- ~~Either the microphone or~~ the loudspeakers needs their electric cords repaired.

  PLURAL ANTECEDENT   PLURAL PRONOUN

17r How do pronouns work when antecedents are indefinite pronouns?

INDEFINITE PRONOUNS usually refer to unknown persons, things, quantities, or ideas. The unknown aspect is the reason these pronouns are labeled "indefinite." But in a sentence, context gives an indefinite pronoun a clear meaning, even if the pronoun doesn't have a specific antecedent. Most indefinite pronouns are singular. Two indefinite pronouns, *both* and *many,* are plural. A few indefinite pronouns can be singular or plural, depending on the meaning of the sentence.

For a list of indefinite pronouns, grouped as singular or plural, see Quick Reference 17.6 in 17i. For more information about avoiding sexist language, especially when using indefinite pronouns, see 17s and 12f. (For related material on subjects and verbs, see 17i.)

SINGULAR INDEFINITE PRONOUNS

Everyone taking this course hopes to get **his or her** [not *their*] college degree within a year.

Anybody wanting to wear a cap and gown at graduation must have **his or her** [not *their*] measurements taken.

Each of the students handed in **his or her** [not *their*] final term paper.

Alert: The use of *their* as a singular indefinite pronoun is becoming more common, even in many respectable publications. Although this usage may become universally accepted in the future, we recommend that you avoid it. ●

SINGULAR *OR* PLURAL INDEFINITE PRONOUNS

When winter break arrives for students, **most** leave **their** dormitories for home. [*Most* refers to *students*, so the plural pronoun *their* is correct.]

As for the luggage, **most** is already on **its** way to the airport. [*Most* refers to *luggage*, so the singular pronoun *its* is correct.]

None thinks that **he or she** will miss graduation. [*None* is singular as used in this sentence, so the singular pronoun phrase *he or she* is correct.]

None of the students has paid **his or her** [not *their*] graduation fee yet. [*None* is singular as used in this sentence, so the singular pronoun phrase *his or her* is correct.]

None are so proud as **they** who graduate. [*None* is plural as used in this sentence, so the plural pronoun *they* is correct.]

17s How do I use nonsexist pronouns?

A word is **nonsexist** when it carries neither male nor female gender. Each PRONOUN in English carries one of three genders: male (*he, him, his*); female (*she, her, hers*); or neutral (*you, your, yours, we, our, ours, them, they, their, theirs, it, its*). Usage today favors nonsexist terms in all word choices. You therefore want to use gender-free pronouns whenever possible. In the past, it was grammatically correct to use only masculine pronouns to refer to INDEFINITE PRONOUNS: "*Everyone open his book.*" Today, however, people feel that the pronouns *he, his, him,* and *himself* exclude women, who make up over half the population. Quick Reference 17.9 shows three ways to avoid using masculine pronouns when referring to males and females together. For more information on gender-neutral language, see 12f.

Questions often arise concerning the use of *he or she* and *his or her*. In general, writers find these gender-free pronoun constructions awkward. To avoid

Quick Reference 17.9

Avoiding the masculine pronoun when referring to males and females together

- **Solution 1:** Use a pair of pronouns—as in the phrase *he or she.* However, avoid using a pair more than once in a sentence or in many sentences in a row. A *he or she* construction acts as a singular pronoun.

  Everyone hopes that **he or she** will win a scholarship.

  A **doctor** usually has time to keep up to date only in **his or her** specialty.

- **Solution 2:** Revise into the plural.

  Many students hope that **they** will win a scholarship.

  Most doctors have time to keep up to date only in **their** specialties.

- **Solution 3:** Recast the sentence.

  Everyone hopes to win a scholarship.

  Few specialists have time for general reading.

them, many writers make the antecedents plural. Doing this becomes problematic when the subject is a SINGULAR INDEFINITE PRONOUN (Quick Reference 17.6 in section 17i). In the popular press (such as newspapers and magazines), the use of the plural pronoun *they* or *them* with a singular antecedent has been gaining favor. Indeed, some experts find that the history of English supports this use. In ACADEMIC WRITING, however, it is better for you not to follow the practice of the popular press. Language practice changes, however, so what we say here is our best advice as we write this book.

17t How do pronouns work when antecedents are collective nouns?

A COLLECTIVE NOUN names a group of people or things, such as *family, group, audience, class, number, committee,* and *team.* When the group acts as one unit, use a singular pronoun to refer to it. When the members of the group act individually, use a plural pronoun. In the latter case, if the sentence is awkward, substitute a plural noun for the collective noun. (For related material on subjects and verbs, see 17j.)

The **audience** was cheering as **it** stood to applaud the performers. [The *audience* was acting as one unit, so the singular pronoun *it* is correct.]

The **audience** put on **their** coats and walked out. [The members of the audience were acting as individuals, so all actions become plural; therefore, the plural pronoun *their* is correct.]

The **family** is spending **its** vacation in Rockport, Maine. [All the family members went to one place together.]

The parallel sentence to the last example above would be *The family are spending their vacations in Maine, Hawaii, and Rome*, which might mean that each family member is going to a different place. But such a sentence is awkward. Therefore, revise the sentence.

The **family members** are spending **their** vacations in Maine, Hawaii, and Rome. [Substituting a plural noun phrase *family members* for the collective noun *family* sounds more natural.]

EXERCISE 17-6   Underline the correct pronoun in parentheses. For help, consult 17o through 17t.

EXAMPLE   Many wonder where inventors like Benjamin Franklin get (his or her, <u>their</u>) creative energy.

1. Many so-called Founding Fathers are famous one or two of (his, his or her, their) accomplishments, but anyone who knows (his, her, his or her, their) history knows that Franklin is known for many things, including (his, her, his or her, their) inventions.

2. The armonica is not one of his well known inventions, but (its, their) design is ingenious.

3. Also called the glass harmonica, the armonica required a person to place (himself, herself, himself or herself) in front of the instrument and to rotate (its, their) glass bowls.

4. The lightning rod and the Franklin stove established his reputation as an inventor, but (it, they) remained in public domain because Franklin refused to secure patents for his inventions.

5. An inventor like Franklin does not limit (his, her, his or her, their) imagination to one field of science.

6. (He, She, He or she, They) can instead pursue many questions and the challenges (they, it) pose.

7. All scientists who study electricity should know that Ben Franklin provided the names (he, she, he or she, they) still use today for positive and negative electrons.

8. Franklin also named the Gulf Stream and mapped (their, its) current

9. Franklin formed the first public lending library in America, which allowed people to borrow (its, their) books and read them at (his, her, his or her, their) leisure.

10. His public service record also includes the reform of the postal system and the establishment of The Academy and College of Philadelphia, which later merged (their, its) students with those of the State of Pennsylvania to become the University of Pennsylvania.

18

Adjectives and Adverbs

18a What are the differences between adjectives and adverbs?

The differences between adjectives and adverbs relate to how they function. **Adjectives** modify NOUNS and PRONOUNS. **Adverbs** modify VERBS, adjectives, and other adverbs. What's the same about adjectives and adverbs is that they're both MODIFIERS—that is, words or groups of words that describe other words.

ADJECTIVE	The **brisk** *wind* blew. [Adjective *brisk* modifies noun *wind*.]
ADVERB	The wind *blew* **briskly**. [Adverb *briskly* modifies verb *blew*.]

Some people think that all adverbs end in *-ly*. But this isn't correct. While many adverbs do end in *-ly* (eat *swiftly,* eat *frequently,* eat *hungrily*), some do not (eat *fast,* eat *often,* eat *seldom*). To complicate matters further, some adjectives end in *-ly* (*lovely* flower, *friendly* dog). Use meaning, not an *-ly* ending, to identify adverbs.

🌐 **ESOL Tips:** (1) In English, the adjective is always singular, even if its noun is plural: *The **hot** [not hots] drinks warmed us up.* (2) Word order in English calls for special attention to the placement of adjectives and adverbs. Here is an example using the adverb *carefully: Thomas closed* [don't place *carefully* here] *the window **carefully*** (see 52b and 52c). ●

EXERCISE 18-1 Underline and label all adjectives (ADJ) and adverbs (ADV). Then, draw an arrow from each adjective and adverb to the word or words it modifies. Ignore *a, an,* and *the* as adjectives. For help, consult 18a.

> EXAMPLE
>
> ADJ   ADV   ADJ
> Leaky faucets are unexpectedly leading to genuine romance
>
> ADJ   ADJ
> in super-sized hardware stores.

1. Today's singles carefully look for possible mates at discount home improvement stores across the country.

2. Understandably, many people find these stores a healthy alternative to dark bars and blind dates.

3. Recently, an employee in the flooring department quietly confided that the best nights for singles are Wednesdays and Thursdays, while weekends generally attract families.

4. A young single mom returns home excitedly because a quick trip to the lumber department for a new door resulted in a date for Saturday night.

5. A lonely widower in his fifties jokingly says he wishes he had developed earlier an interest in wallpapering and gardening.

18b When should I use adverbs—not adjectives— as modifiers?

Adverbs MODIFY verbs, adjectives, and other adverbs. Don't use adjectives as adverbs.

NO The candidate inspired us **great.** [Adjective *great* cannot modify verb *inspired.*]

YES The candidate inspired us **greatly.** [Adverb *greatly* can modify verb *inspired.*]

NO The candidate felt **unusual** energetic. [Adjective *unusual* cannot modify adjective *energetic.*]

YES The candidate felt **unusually** energetic. [Adverb *unusually* can modify adjective *energetic.*]

NO The candidate spoke **exceptional** forcefully. [Adjective *exceptional* cannot modify adverb *forcefully.*]

YES The candidate spoke **exceptionally** forcefully. [Adverb *exceptionally* modifies adverb *forcefully.*]

18c What is wrong with double negatives?

A **double negative** is a nonstandard form. It is a statement with two negative MODIFIERS, the second of which repeats the message of the first. Negative modifiers include *no, never, not, none, nothing, hardly, scarcely,* and *barely.*

NO The factory workers will **never** vote for **no** strike.

YES The factory workers will **never** vote for a strike.

NO The union members did **not** have **no** money in reserve.

YES The union members did **not** have **any** money in reserve.

YES The union members had **no** money in reserve.

Take special care to avoid double negatives with contractions of *not: isn't, don't, didn't, haven't,* and the like (27d). The contraction containing *not* serves as the only negative in a sentence. Don't add a second negative.

NO He **didn't** hear **nothing**.

YES He **didn't** hear **anything**.

NO They **haven't** had **no** meetings.

YES They **haven't** had **any** meetings.

Similarly, be careful to avoid double negatives when you use *nor.* The word *nor* is correct only after *neither* (14i). Use the word *or* after any other negative.

NO Stewart **didn't** eat dinner **nor** watch television last night.

YES Stewart **didn't** eat dinner **or** watch television last night.

YES Stewart **neither** ate dinner **nor** watched television last night.

18d Do adjectives or adverbs come after linking verbs?

LINKING VERBS connect a SUBJECT to a COMPLEMENT. Always use an adjective, not an adverb, as the complement.

The *guests looked* **happy**. [Verb *looked* links subject *guests* to adjective *happy*.]

The words *look, feel, smell, taste, sound,* and *grow* are usually linking verbs, but sometimes they're simply verbs. Check how any of these verbs is functioning in a sentence.

Zora *looks* **happy**. [*Looks* functions as a linking verb, so the adjective *happy* is correct.]

Zora *looks* **happily** at the sunset. [*Looks* doesn't function as a linking verb, so the adverb *happily* is correct.]

BAD, BADLY

The words *bad* (adjective) and *badly* (adverb) are particularly prone to misuse with linking verbs.

NO The students felt **badly**. [This means the students used their sense of touch badly.]

YES The student felt **bad**. [This means the student had a bad feeling about something.]

NO The food smelled **badly**. [This means the food had a bad ability to smell.]

YES The food smelled **bad**. [This means the food had a bad smell to it.]

GOOD, WELL

When the word *well* refers to health, it is an adjective; at all other times, *well* is an adverb. The word *good* is always an adjective.

Evander looks **well**. [This means that Evander seems to be in good health, so the adjective *well* is correct.]

Evander writes **well**. [This means that Evander writes skillfully, so the adverb *well* is correct.]

Use *good* as an adjective, except when you refer to health.

NO She sings **good**. [*Sings* isn't a linking verb, so it calls for an adverb, not the adjective *good*.]

YES She sings **well**. [*Sings* isn't a linking verb, so the adverb *well* is correct.]

EXERCISE 18-2   Underline the correct uses of negatives, adjectives, and adverbs by selecting between the choices in parentheses. For help, consult 18a through 18d.

EXAMPLE   Because she was only five when her father died, Bernice King, Martin Luther King's youngest child, (<u>barely</u>, bare) remembers the details of her father's (solemnly, <u>solemn</u>) funeral, yet her father's image lives (strong, <u>strongly</u>) within her.

1. Although she did feel (badly, bad) about her father's death when she was younger, King's daughter has managed to put his influence on her to good use by speaking (passionately, passionate) about issues her father first introduced.

2. In her (widely, wide) acclaimed book of sermons and speeches, titled *Hard Questions, Hard Answers*, Bernice King strives to deal with the (intensely, intense) topic of race relations.

3. Bernice King believes, as did her father, that all people must connect (genuinely, genuine), or they won't (never, ever) manage to coexist.

4. Bernice King decided to enter the ministry after she heard a (deeply, deep) voice within her directing her to this (extremely, extreme) (spiritually, spiritual) profession.

5. Bernice King entered the public eye in 1993, when she gave a (locally, local) televised Martin Luther King Day sermon at her father's church, and since then she has lived (happily, happy) in her home in Atlanta with memories of her father that are (peacefully, peaceful) recollections.

18e What are comparative and superlative forms?

When you write about comparisons, ADJECTIVES and ADVERBS often carry the message. The adjectives and adverbs also communicate degrees of intensity. When a comparison is made between two things, a **comparative** form is used. When a comparison is made about three or more things, a **superlative** form is used.

REGULAR FORMS OF COMPARISON

Most adjectives and adverbs are regular. They communicate degrees of intensity in one of two ways: either by adding -*er* and -*est* endings or by adding the words *more, most, less,* and *least* (see Quick Reference 18.1).

The number of syllables in the adjective or adverb usually determines whether to use -*er,* -*est* or *more, most* and *less, least.*

- **One-syllable words** usually take -*er* and -*est* endings: *large, larger, largest* (adjectives); *far, farther, farthest* (adverbs).

- **Adjectives of two syllables** vary. If the word ends in -*y,* change the *y* to *i* and add -*er,* -*est* endings: *pretty, prettier, prettiest.* Otherwise, some two-syllable adjectives take -*er,* -*est* endings: *yellow, yellower, yellowest.* Others take *more, most* and *less, least: tangled, more tangled, most tangled; less tangled, least tangled.*

- **Adverbs of two syllables** take *more, most* and *less, least: quickly, more quickly, most quickly; less quickly, least quickly.*

- **Three-syllable words** take *more, most* and *less, least: dignified, more/most dignified, less/least dignified* (adjective); *carefully, more/most carefully, less/least carefully* (adverb).

Quick Reference 18.1 ■ ■ ■ ■ ■ ■ ■

Regular forms of comparison for adjectives and adverbs

POSITIVE	Use when nothing is being compared.
COMPARATIVE	Use when two things are being compared. Add the ending -*er* or the word *more* or *less.*
SUPERLATIVE	Use to compare three or more things. Add the ending -*est* or the word *most* or *least.*

Positive [1]	Comparative [2]	Superlative [3+]
green	greener	greenest
happy	happier	happiest
selfish	less selfish	least selfish
beautiful	more beautiful	most beautiful

! **Alert:** Be careful not to use a double comparative or double superlative. Use either the *-er* and *-est* endings or *more, most* or *less, least*.

He was **younger** [not *more younger*] than his brother.

Her music was the **loudest** [not *most loudest*] on the stereo. ●

IRREGULAR FORMS OF COMPARISON

A few comparative and superlative forms are irregular. Quick Reference 18.2 gives you the list. We suggest that you memorize them so they come to mind easily.

! **Alerts:** (1) Be aware of the difference between *less* and *fewer*. They aren't interchangeable. Use *less* with NONCOUNT NOUNS, either items or values: *The sugar substitute has less* **aftertaste**. Use *fewer* with numbers or COUNT NOUNS: *The sugar substitute has fewer* **calories**. (2) Don't use *more, most* or *less, least* with **absolute adjectives**, that is, adjectives that communicate a noncomparable quality or state, such as *unique* or *perfect*. Something either *is*, or *is not*, one of a kind. No degrees of intensity are involved: *This teapot is* **unique** [not *the most unique*]; *The artisanship is* **perfect** [not *the most perfect*]. ●

Quick Reference 18.2 ■ ■ ■ ■ ■ ■ ■

Irregular forms of comparison for adjectives and adverbs

Positive [1]	Comparative [2]	Superlative [3+]
good (*adjective*)	better	best
well (*adjective* and *adverb*)	better	best
bad (*adjective*)	worse	worst
badly (*adverb*)	worse	worst
many	more	most
much	more	most
some	more	most
little*	less	least

*When you're using *little* for items that can be counted (e.g., pickles), use the regular forms *little, littler, littlest*.

EXERCISE 18-3   Complete the chart that follows. Then, write a sentence for each word in the completed chart. For help, consult 18e.

EXAMPLE   *funny, funnier, funniest:* My brother has a *funny* laugh; he thinks Mom has a *funnier* laugh; the person who has the *funniest* laugh in our family is Uncle Dominic.

POSITIVE	COMPARATIVE	SUPERLATIVE
small	_____	_____
_____	greedier	_____
_____	_____	most complete
gladly	_____	_____
_____	_____	fewest
_____	thicker	_____
some	_____	_____

18f Why avoid a long string of nouns as modifiers?

NOUNS sometimes MODIFY other nouns: *truck driver, train track, security system.* Usually, these terms create no problems. However, avoid using several nouns in a row as modifiers. A string of too many nouns makes it difficult for your reader to figure out which nouns are being modified and which nouns are doing the modifying. You can revise such sentences in several ways.

> **REWRITE THE SENTENCE**
>
> **NO** I asked my adviser to write **two college recommendation letters** for me.
>
> **YES** I asked my adviser to write *letters of recommendation to two colleges* for me.
>
> **CHANGE ONE NOUN TO A POSSESSIVE AND ANOTHER TO AN ADJECTIVE**
>
> **NO** He will take the **United States Navy examination** for **navy engineer training**.
>
> **YES** He will take the *United States Navy's examination* for **naval engineer training**.
>
> **CHANGE ONE NOUN TO A PREPOSITIONAL PHRASE**
>
> **NO** Our **student adviser training program** has won many awards.
>
> **YES** Our *training program for student advisers* has won many awards. [This change requires a change from the singular *adviser* to the plural *advisers*.]

EXERCISE 18-4 Underline the better choice in parentheses. For help, consult this entire chapter.

EXAMPLE Alexis, a huge and powerful six-year-old Siberian tiger, (curious, <u>curiously</u>) explores her new zoo home together with five other tigers.

1. The new tiger home at the world-famous Bronx Zoo is a (special, specially) designed habitat, planted with (dense, denser) undergrowth so that it (close, closely) imitates the tigers' natural wilderness.

2. Like tigers in the wild, the six tigers in this habitat, which (more, many) experts consider the (more authentic, most authentic) of all artificial tiger environments in the world, will face some of the physical challenges and sensory experiences that keep them happy and (healthy, healthier).

3. Research shows that tigers feel (bad, badly) and fail to thrive in zoos without enrichment features placed in (good, well) locations to inspire tigers to stalk (stealthy, stealthily) through underbrush, loll (lazy, lazily) on heated rocks, or tug (vigorous, vigorously) on massive pull toys.

4. Wildlife zoologists think that the new Tiger Mountain exhibit will also serve zoo visitors (good, well) by allowing them to observe and admire the amazing strength, agility, and intelligence of a (rapid, rapidly) dwindling species.

5. Today, (fewer, less) than 5,000 Siberian tigers remain in the wild, which makes it imperative for zoos to raise people's awareness of the (great, greatest) need to prevent the extinction of these big cats that are considered among the (more, most) powerful, beautiful animals in the world.

For more help with your writing, grammar, and research,
go to **www.mycomplab.com**

Sentence Fragments

19a What is a sentence fragment?

A **sentence fragment** looks like a sentence, but it's actually only part of a sentence. That is, even though a sentence fragment begins with a capital letter and ends with a period (or question mark or exclamation point), it doesn't contain an INDEPENDENT CLAUSE. Fragments are merely unattached PHRASES or DEPENDENT CLAUSES.

FRAGMENT	The telephone with redial capacity. [no verb]
CORRECT	The telephone has redial capacity.
FRAGMENT	Rang loudly for ten minutes. [no subject]
CORRECT	The telephone rang loudly for ten minutes.
FRAGMENT	At midnight. [a phrase without a verb or subject]
CORRECT	The telephone rang at midnight.
FRAGMENT	Because the telephone rang loudly. [dependent clause starting with subordinating conjunction *because*]
CORRECT	Because the telephone rang loudly, the family was awakened in the middle of the night.
FRAGMENT	Which really annoyed me. [dependent clause starting with relative pronoun *which*]
CORRECT	The telephone call was a wrong number, which really annoyed me.

Sentence fragments can ruin the clarity of your writing. Moreover, in ACADEMIC WRITING and BUSINESS WRITING, sentence fragments imply that you don't know basic sentence structure or that you're a careless proofreader.

NO	The lawyer was angry. When she returned from court. She found the key witness waiting in her office. [Was the lawyer angry when she returned from court, or when she found the witness in her office?]
YES	The lawyer was angry when she returned from court. She found the key witness waiting in her office.
YES	The lawyer was angry. When she returned from court, she found the key witness waiting in her office.

Let's go beyond the grammatical terms to a more practical approach to recognizing sentence fragments, so that you can avoid them in your writing. To learn to recognize sentence fragments, see 19b; to learn several ways to correct sentence fragments, see 19c and 19d.

Many writers wait until the REVISING and EDITING stages of the WRITING PROCESS to check for sentence fragments. During DRAFTING, the goal is to get ideas down on paper or disk. As you draft, if you suspect that you've written a sentence fragment, simply underline or highlight it in boldface or italics and move on. Later, you can easily find it to check and correct.

19b How can I recognize a sentence fragment?

If you tend to write SENTENCE FRAGMENTS, you want a system for recognizing them. Quick Reference 19.1 shows you a Sentence Test for checking that you haven't written a sentence fragment. Following this Quick Reference, we discuss each question in more detail in 19b.1 through 19b.3.

Quick Reference 19.1   ■ ■ ■ ■ ■ ■ ■

Sentence test to identify sentence fragments

QUESTION 1: IS THE WORD GROUP A DEPENDENT CLAUSE?

A DEPENDENT CLAUSE is a word group that has a subject and a verb but starts with a word that creates dependence—either a SUBORDINATING CON-JUNCTION or a RELATIVE PRONOUN.

FRAGMENT	**When** winter comes early. [starts with *when*, a word that creates dependence]
CORRECT	**When** winter comes early, **ships often rescue the stranded whales.** [adds an independent clause to create a sentence]
FRAGMENT	**Which** can happen quickly. [starts with *which*, a word that creates dependence]
CORRECT	**Whales cannot breathe through the ice and will drown, which** can happen quickly. [adds an independent clause to create a sentence]

QUESTION 2: IS THERE A VERB?

FRAGMENT	Thousands of whales in the Arctic Ocean. [Because a verb is missing, this is a phrase, not a sentence.]
CORRECT	Thousands of whales **live** in the Arctic Ocean. [adds a verb to create a sentence]

QUESTION 3: IS THERE A SUBJECT?

FRAGMENT	Stranded in the Arctic Ocean. [Because a subject is missing, this is a phrase, not a sentence.]
CORRECT	**Many whales** *were* stranded in the Arctic Ocean. [adds a subject (and the verb *were* to *stranded*) to create a sentence]

19b.1 Question 1: Is the word group a dependent clause?

If you answer yes to question 1, you're looking at a sentence fragment. A DEPENDENT CLAUSE is a word group that has a subject and a verb but starts with a word that creates dependence. The only words that create dependence are SUBORDINATING CONJUNCTIONS and RELATIVE PRONOUNS. Such a word before an INDEPENDENT CLAUSE creates a dependent clause, which can't stand alone as a sentence and is therefore a sentence fragment. To become a complete sentence, the fragment needs either to be joined to an independent clause or to be rewritten.

FRAGMENTS WITH SUBORDINATING CONJUNCTIONS

A complete list of subordinating conjunctions appears in Quick Reference 14.7 in 14i. Some frequently used ones are *after, although, because, before, if, unless,* and *when.*

FRAGMENT	**Because** she returned my books. [*Because,* a subordinating conjunction, creates a dependent clause.]
CORRECT	**Because** she returned my books, ***I can study.*** [A comma and the independent clause *I can study* are added, and the sentence becomes complete.]
FRAGMENT	**Unless** I study. [*Unless,* a subordinating conjunction, creates a dependent clause.]
CORRECT	***I won't pass the test*** **unless** I study. [The independent clause *I won't pass the test* is added, and the sentence becomes complete.]

 Alert: When a dependent clause starts with a subordinating conjunction and comes before its independent clause, use a comma to separate the clauses (24c). ●

FRAGMENTS WITH RELATIVE PRONOUNS

Relative pronouns are *that, which, who, whom,* and *whose.*

FRAGMENT	**That** we had studied for all week. [*That,* a relative pronoun, creates a dependent clause here.]
CORRECT	***We passed the exam*** **that** we had studied for all week. [The independent clause *We passed the exam* is added, and the sentence becomes complete.]

When *which, who,* and *whose* begin questions, they function as INTERROGATIVE PRONOUNS, not relative pronouns. Questions are complete sentences, not fragments: *Which* class are you taking? *Who* is your professor? *Whose* book is that?

19b.2 Question 2: Is there a verb?

If you answer no to question 2, you're looking at a sentence fragment. When a VERB is missing from a word group, the result is a PHRASE, not a sentence. You can figure out if a word is a verb by seeing if it can change in TENSE. Verbs have tenses to tell what *is* happening, what *has* happened, or what *will* happen.

> Now the telephone **rings.** [present tense]
>
> Yesterday, the telephone **rang.** [past tense]

When you check for verbs, remember that VERBALS (14e) are not verbs. Verbals might look like verbs, but they don't function as verbs.

FRAGMENT	Yesterday, the students **registering** for classes. [*Registering* is a verbal called a present participle, not a verb.]
CORRECT	Yesterday, the students **were registering** for classes. [Adding the auxiliary verb *were* to the present participle *registering* creates a verb.]
FRAGMENT	Now the students **to register** for classes. [*To register* is a verbal called an infinitive, not a verb.]
CORRECT	Now the students **want to register** for classes. [Adding the verb *want* to the infinitive *to register* creates a verb.]

19b.3 Question 3: Is there a subject?

If you answer no to question 3, you're looking at a sentence fragment. When a SUBJECT is missing from a word group, the result is a PHRASE, not a sentence. To see if a word is a subject, ask, "Who (*or* What) performs the action?"

FRAGMENT	Studied hard for class. [*Who* studied hard for class? unknown]
CORRECT	The students studied hard for class. [*Who* studied hard for class? *The students* is the answer, so a subject makes the sentence complete.]
FRAGMENT	Contained some difficult questions. [*What* contained some difficult questions? unknown]
CORRECT	The test contained some difficult questions. [*What* contained some difficult questions? *The test* is the answer, so a subject makes the sentence complete.]

Be especially careful with COMPOUND PREDICATES—for example, *We **took** the bus to the movie **and walked** home.* If you were to place a period after *movie,* the second part of the compound predicate would be a sentence fragment. Every sentence needs its own subject. To check for this kind of sentence fragment, ask the question "Who?" or "What?" of each verb.

NO	A few students organized a study group to prepare for midterm exams. **Decided to study together for the rest of the course.** [*Who* decided to study together? The answer is *The students* (who formed the group), but this subject is missing.]
YES	A few students organized a study group to prepare for midterm exams. ***The students* decided to study together for the rest of the course.**

IMPERATIVE SENTENCES—commands and some requests—may appear at first glance to be fragments caused by missing subjects. They're not fragments, however. Imperative sentences are complete sentences because their subjects are implied. An implied subject can be *you, anybody, somebody, everybody,* or another INDEFINITE PRONOUN.

Run! [This sentence implies the pronoun *you.* The complete sentence would be *You run!*]

Return all library books to the front desk. [This sentence implies the indefinite pronoun *everyone.* The complete sentence would be *Everyone (should) return all library books to the front desk.*]

EXERCISE 19-1 Identify each word group as either a complete sentence or a fragment. If the word group is a sentence, circle its number. If it's a fragment, tell why it's incomplete. For help, see Quick Reference 19.1 in 19b and sections 19b.1 through 19b.3.

EXAMPLE Although antibacterial soaps have become popular. [Starts with a subordinating conjunction (*although*), which creates dependence, and lacks an independent clause to complete the thought; see Quick Reference 19.1 and section 19c.1]

1. Because antibacterial soaps do not provide protection against viruses.
2. Viruses responsible for a variety of common health problems.
3. Regular soap often successfully eliminates bacteria, viruses, and dirt.
4. Indicate that antibacterial soaps may wash away useful bacteria.
5. Eliminates most of the harmful bacteria as effectively as regular soap.
6. Careful hand washing cannot be stressed enough.
7. To work efficiently, antibacterial soaps, even those purchased in health food stores.

8. Most studies show that antibacterial soaps do not lead to resistant bacteria.

9. Although many people still believe they should not use antibacterial soaps.

10. Bacteria from overuse of antibiotics.

19c What are major ways of correcting fragments?

Once you've identified a SENTENCE FRAGMENT (19b), you're ready to correct it. You can do this in one of two ways: by joining it to an independent clause (19c.1) or by rewriting it (19c.2).

19c.1 Correcting a sentence fragment by joining it to an independent clause

One way you can correct a sentence fragment is by joining it to an INDEPENDENT CLAUSE—that is, to a complete sentence. The first two examples that follow deal with dependent-clause fragments; the examples following the ALERT examine fragments with missing subjects and/or verbs.

FRAGMENT	**Because** the ice was thick. [Although this word group has a subject (*ice*) and verb (*was*), it starts with the subordinating conjunction *because*.]
CORRECT	**Because** the ice was thick, *icebreakers were required to serve as rescue ships.* [Adding a comma and joining the fragment to the independent clause *icebreakers were required to serve as rescue ships* creates a complete sentence.]
CORRECT	*Icebreakers were required to serve as rescue ships* **because** the ice was thick. [Joining the fragment to the independent clause *Icebreakers were required to serve as rescue ships* creates a complete sentence.]
FRAGMENT	**Who** feared the whales would panic. [This fragment starts with the relative pronoun *who*.]
CORRECT	*The noisy motors of the ships worried the crews,* **who** feared the whales would panic. [Joining the fragment to the independent clause *The noisy motors of the ships worried the crews* creates a complete sentence.]

🛈 **Alert:** Be careful with all words that indicate time, such as *after, before, since,* and *until.* They aren't always subordinating conjunctions. Sometimes they function as ADVERBS—especially if they begin a complete sentence. At other times, they function as PREPOSITIONS. When you see one of these words that indicate time, realize that you aren't necessarily looking at a dependent-clause fragment.

> **Before,** the whales had responded to classical music. [This is a complete sentence in which *Before* is an adverb that modifies the independent clause *the whales had responded to classical music.*]

> **Before the whales had responded to classical music,** some crew members tried rock and roll music. [If the word group before the comma stood on its own, it would be a sentence fragment because it starts with *Before* functioning as a subordinating conjunction.] ●

FRAGMENT	**To announce new programs for crime prevention.** [*To announce* starts an infinitive phrase, not a sentence.]
CORRECT	*The mayor called a news conference last week* **to announce** new programs for crime prevention. [The infinitive phrase starting with *to announce* is joined with an independent clause.]
FRAGMENT	**Hoping for strong public support.** [*Hoping* starts a present-participle phrase, not a sentence.]
CORRECT	**Hoping** for strong public support, *she gave examples of problems throughout the city.* [The present-participle phrase starting with *Hoping* is joined with an independent clause.]
FRAGMENT	**Introduced by her assistant.** [*Introduced* starts a past-participle phrase, not a sentence.]
CORRECT	**Introduced** by her assistant, *the mayor began with an opening statement.* [The past-participle phrase starting with *Introduced* is joined with an independent clause.]
FRAGMENT	**During the long news conference.** [*During* functions as a preposition—starting a prepositional phrase, not a sentence.]
CORRECT	*Cigarette smoke made the conference room seem airless* **during** the long news conference. [The prepositional phrase starting with *during* is joined with an independent clause.]
FRAGMENT	**A politician with fresh ideas.** [*A politician* starts an appositive phrase, not a sentence.]

CORRECT   *Most people respected the mayor,* **a politician** with fresh ideas. [The appositive phrase starting with *a politician* is joined with an independent clause.]

EXERCISE 19-2   Find and correct any sentence fragments. If a sentence is correct, circle its number. For help, consult 19a through 19c.

EXAMPLE   Even though lice are a common problem for young children.

Correct: Lice are a common problem for young children.

1. Even though lice are not dangerous and do not spread disease, parents tend to worry about their children. Who have been infected with this parasite.
2. Although good hygiene is important, it does not prevent lice infestation. Which can occur on clean, healthy scalps.
3. Spread only through direct contact. Lice are unable to fly or jump.
4. Evidence of lice has been found on ancient Egyptian mummies, which suggests that lice have been annoying humans for a long time.
5. While lice can spread among humans who share combs or pillows or hats. Lice cannot be spread from pets to humans.
6. Doctors may prescribe special shampoos and soaps. To help get rid of the lice on a child's head.
7. Because lice do not like heat, experts recommend putting infected sheets and stuffed animals and pillows in a dryer for thirty minutes.
8. Just one is called a *louse*, and a louse egg is called a *nit.* Which is where we get the words *lousy* and *nit-pick.*
9. Using a hair dryer after applying a scalp treatment can be dangerous. Because some treatments contain flammable ingredients.
10. Although lice cannot live for more than twenty-four hours without human contact.

19c.2 Correcting a sentence fragment by rewriting it

A second way you can correct a sentence fragment is by rewriting it as an INDEPENDENT CLAUSE—that is, as a complete sentence. The first two examples below deal with dependent-clause fragments; the others examine fragments with missing subjects and/or verbs.

FRAGMENT   **Because the ice was thick.** [Although this word group has a subject (*ice*) and verb (*was*), it starts with the subordinating conjunction *because*.]

CORRECT   The ice was thick. [The fragment starting with *Because* is rewritten to become a complete sentence.]

FRAGMENT	**Who** feared the whales would panic. [This fragment starts with the relative pronoun *who*.]
CORRECT	*The crew* feared the whales would panic. [The fragment starting with *Who* is rewritten to become a complete sentence.]
FRAGMENT	**To announce** new programs for crime prevention. [*To announce* starts an infinitive phrase, not a sentence.]
CORRECT	*The mayor called a news conference last week because she wanted* **to announce** new programs for crime prevention. [The infinitive phrase starting with *To announce* is rewritten to become a complete sentence.]
FRAGMENT	**Hoping** for strong public support. [*Hoping* starts a present-participle phrase, not a sentence.]
CORRECT	*She was* **hoping** for strong public support. [The present-participle phrase starting with *Hoping* is rewritten to become a complete sentence.]
FRAGMENT	**Introduced** by her assistant. [*Introduced* starts a past-participle phrase, not a sentence.]
CORRECT	**Introduced** by her assistant, *the mayor began with an opening statement.* [The past-participle phrase starting with *Introduced* is rewritten to become a complete sentence.]
FRAGMENT	**During** the long news conference. [*During* functions as a preposition that starts a prepositional phrase, not a sentence.]
CORRECT	*It was hard to breathe* **during** the long news conference. [The prepositional phrase starting with *During* is rewritten to become a complete sentence.]
FRAGMENT	**A politician** with fresh ideas. [*A politician* starts an appositive phrase, not a sentence.]
CORRECT	*She seemed to be* **a politician** with fresh ideas. [The appositive phrase is rewritten to become a complete sentence.]

19d How can I fix a fragment that is part of a compound predicate?

A COMPOUND PREDICATE contains two or more VERBS. When the second part of a compound predicate is punctuated as a separate sentence, it becomes a sentence fragment.

FRAGMENT	The reporters asked the mayor many questions about the new program. **And then discussed her answers among themselves.** [*And then discussed* starts a compound predicate fragment, not a sentence.]
CORRECT	The reporters asked the mayor many questions about the new program and then discussed her answers among themselves. [The compound predicate fragment starting with *And then discussed* is joined to the independent clause.]
CORRECT	The reporters asked the mayor many questions about the new program. *Then the reporters* **discussed** her answers among themselves. [The compound predicate fragment starting with *And then discussed* is rewritten as a complete sentence.]

EXERCISE 19-3 Go back to Exercise 19-1 and revise the sentence fragments into complete sentences. In some cases, you may be able to combine two fragments into one complete sentence.

19e What are the two special fragment problems?

Two special fragment problems sometimes involve lists and examples. Lists and examples must be part of a complete sentence, unless they are formatted as a column.

You can connect a list fragment by attaching it to the preceding independent clause using a colon or a dash. You can correct an example fragment by attaching it to an independent clause (with or without punctuation, depending on the meaning) or by rewriting it as a complete sentence.

FRAGMENT	You have a choice of desserts. **Carrot cake, chocolate silk pie, apple pie, or peppermint ice cream.** [The list cannot stand on its own as a sentence.]
CORRECT	You have a choice of desserts: carrot cake, chocolate silk pie, apple pie, or peppermint ice cream. [A colon joins the sentence and the list.]
CORRECT	You have a choice of desserts—carrot cake, chocolate silk pie, apple pie, or peppermint ice cream. [A dash joins the sentence and the list.]
FRAGMENT	Several good places offer brunch. **For example, the restaurants Sign of the Dove and Blue Yonder.** [Examples can't stand on their own as a sentence.]

CORRECT	Several good places offer brunch—**for example,** the restaurants Sign of the Dove and Blue Yonder.
CORRECT	Several good places offer brunch. **For example,** *there are* the restaurants Sign of the Dove and Blue Yonder.

19f How can I recognize intentional fragments?

Professional writers sometimes intentionally use fragments for emphasis and effect.

> But in the main, I feel like a brown bag of miscellany propped against a wall. Pour out the contents, and there is discovered a jumble of small things priceless and worthless. **A first-water diamond, an empty spool, bits of broken glass, lengths of string, a key to a door long since crumbled away, a rusty knife-blade, old shoes saved for a road that never was and never will be, a nail bent under the weight of things too heavy for any nail, a dried flower or two still a little fragrant.**
>
> —Zora Neale Hurston, *How It Feels to Be Colored Me*

Being able to judge the difference between an acceptable and unacceptable sentence fragment comes from years of reading the work of skilled writers. For ACADEMIC WRITING, most instructors don't accept sentence fragments in student writing until a student demonstrates a consistent ability to write well-constructed, complete sentences. As a rule, avoid sentence fragments in academic writing.

EXERCISE 19-4 Revise this paragraph to eliminate all sentence fragments. In some cases, you can combine word groups to create complete sentences; in other cases, you must supply missing elements to rewrite. Some sentences may not require revision. In your final version, check not only the individual sentences but also the clarity of the whole paragraph. For help, consult 19a through 19d.

EXAMPLE   Although the subject of many amusing anecdotes. Diogenes remains an influential figure in Greek philosophy.

Correct: Although the subject of many amusing anecdotes, Diogenes remains an influential figure in Greek philosophy.

(1) Throughout his career as a philosopher and Cynic, Diogenes cultivated a following. That included the likes of Aristotle and Alexander the Great. (2) Diogenes was an important member of the Cynics, a group of people who rejected conventional life. The word *Cynic* comes from the Greek word for dog. (3) Diogenes lived like a beggar and slept in a tub. Which he carried around with him wherever he went. (4) He rejected the pursuit of wealth and once destroyed his wooden bowl. Because he saw a peasant boy

drinking water with his hands. (5) Although none of his writings have survived, Diogenes produced dialogues and a play. That allegedly describes a social utopia in which people live unconventional lives. (6) Since he often walked around Athens in broad daylight with a lamp looking for an honest man. (7) When Plato defined *man* as a featherless biped, Diogenes plucked a chicken and said, "Here is Plato's man." (8) According to legend, Diogenes was once sunbathing when he was approached by Alexander the Great. Who was a fan of the eccentric Cynic. (9) Alexander asked if he could do anything for Diogenes. Which the philosopher answered by saying, "Don't block my sunlight." (10) Because Diogenes is a strange and interesting character. He has inspired works by such writers and artists as William Blake, Anton Chekhov, and Rabelais.

EXERCISE 19-5   Revise this paragraph to eliminate all sentence fragments. In some cases, you can combine word groups to create complete sentences; in other cases, you must supply missing elements to revise word groups. Some sentences may not require revision. In your final version, check not only the individual sentences but also the clarity of the whole paragraph. Refer to 19a through 19e for help.

(1) The English games cricket and rounders. (2) Are the forerunners of the American game baseball. (3) Which became popular in America in the nineteenth century. (4) According to the *New York Morning News,* in an article from 1845. (5) Members of the New York Knickerbockers Club played the first reported baseball game. (6) Taking place at Elysian Fields in Hoboken, New Jersey. (7) Creating one of baseball's first teams, and writing "20 Original Rules of Baseball." (8) Alexander Cartwright is often called The Father of Baseball. (9) By scholars and historians of the game. (10) His new rules, which became known as Knickerbocker Rules. (11) Changed baseball in a number of ways. (12) Such as giving each batter three strikes and each inning three outs. (13) The first game, therefore. (14) That used the Knickerbocker Rules was played on June 19, 1846, in New Jersey. (15) Acting as umpire for this game. (16) Cartwright charged six-cent fines for swearing. (17) The Knickerbockers lost this game by 22 points to a team. (18) That was known as "The New York Nine."

20

Comma Splices and Run-On Sentences

20a What are comma splices and run-on sentences?

Comma splices and run-on sentences are somewhat similar errors: One has a comma by itself between two complete sentences, and one has no punctuation at all between two complete sentences.

A **comma splice**, also called a *comma fault,* occurs when a comma, rather than a period, is used incorrectly between complete sentences. The word *splice* means "to fasten ends together," which is a handy procedure, except when splicing has anything to do with sentences.

A **run-on sentence**, also called a *fused sentence* and a *run-together sentence,* occurs when two complete sentences run into each other without any punctuation. Comma splices and run-on sentences create confusion because readers can't tell where one thought ends and another begins.

COMMA SPLICE	The icebergs broke off from the **glacier, they** drifted into the sea.
RUN-ON SENTENCE	The icebergs broke off from the **glacier they** drifted into the sea.
CORRECT	The icebergs broke off from the **glacier. They** drifted into the sea.

There is one exception. You can use a comma between two independent clauses, but only if the comma is followed by one of the seven coordinating conjunctions: *and, but, for, or, nor, yet, so.* A comma in such a construction is correct; see Chapter 24.

CORRECT	The icebergs broke off from the glacier, and they drifted into the sea.

⚠ **Alert:** Occasionally, when your meaning allows it, you can use a colon or a dash to join two independent clauses. ●

Many writers wait until the REVISING and EDITING stages of the WRITING PROCESS to check for comma splices and run-on sentences. During DRAFTING, the goal is to put ideas down on paper or disk. As you draft, if you suspect that you've written a comma splice or a run-on sentence, simply underline or highlight it in boldface or italics, and move on. Later, you can easily find it to check and correct.

20b How can I recognize comma splices and run-on sentences?

When you know how to recognize an INDEPENDENT CLAUSE, you'll know how to recognize COMMA SPLICES and RUN-ON SENTENCES. An independent clause can stand alone as a complete sentence. An independent clause contains a SUBJECT and a PREDICATE. Also, an independent clause doesn't begin with a word that creates dependence—that is, it doesn't begin with a SUBORDINATING CONJUNCTION or a RELATIVE PRONOUN.

Interestingly, almost all comma splices and run-on sentences are caused by only four patterns. If you become familiar with these four patterns, listed in Quick Reference 20.1, you'll more easily locate them in your writing.

Alert: To proofread for comma splices, cover all words on one side of the comma and see if the words remaining form an independent clause. If they do, next cover all words you left uncovered, on the other side of the comma. If the second side of the comma is also an independent clause, you're looking at a comma splice. (This technique doesn't work for run-on sentences because a comma isn't present.) ●

Quick Reference 20.1   ■ ■ ■ ■ ■ ■ ■ ■

Detecting comma splices and run-on sentences

- Watch out for a PRONOUN starting the second independent clause.

  NO   The physicist Marie Curie discovered **radium, she** won two Nobel Prizes.

  YES   The physicist Marie Curie discovered **radium. She** won two Nobel Prizes.

- Watch out for a CONJUNCTIVE ADVERB (such as *furthermore, however, similarly, therefore,* and *then;* see Quick Reference 14.5, section 14g, for a complete list) starting the second independent clause.

  NO   Marie Curie and her husband, Pierre, worked together at **first, however**, he died tragically at age forty-seven.

  YES   Marie Curie and her husband, Pierre, worked together at **first. However**, he died tragically at age forty-seven.

continued >>

> **Quick Reference 20.1**   (continued)
>
> - Watch out for a TRANSITIONAL EXPRESSION (such as *in addition, for example, in contrast, of course,* and *meanwhile;* see Quick Reference 3.5, section 3g.1, for a reference list) starting the second independent clause.
>
>   **NO**   Marie Curie and her husband won a Nobel Prize for the discovery of **radium, in addition, Marie** herself won another Nobel Prize for her work on the atomic weight of radium.
>
>   **YES**   Marie Curie and her husband won a Nobel Prize for the discovery of **radium; in addition, Marie** herself won another Nobel Prize for her work on the atomic weight of radium.
>
> - Watch out for a second independent clause that explains, says more about, contrasts with, or gives an example of what's said in the first independent clause.
>
>   **NO**   Marie Curie died of leukemia in **1934, exposure** to radioactivity killed her.
>
>   **YES**   Marie Curie died of leukemia in **1934. Exposure** to radioactivity killed her.

Experienced writers sometimes use a comma to join very short independent clauses, especially if one independent clause is negative and the other is positive: *Mosquitoes don't **bite, they** stab.* In ACADEMIC WRITING, however, many instructors consider this an error, so you'll be safe if you use a period. (Another option is a semicolon, if the two independent clauses are closely related in meaning: *Mosquitoes don't **bite; they** stab.*)

20c   How can I correct comma splices and run-on sentences?

Once you have identified a COMMA SPLICE or a RUN-ON SENTENCE, you're ready to correct it. You can do this in one of four ways, as shown in Quick Reference 20.2 and discussed further in sections 20c.1 through 20c.4.

20c.1   Using a period to correct comma splices and run-on sentences

You can use a period to correct comma splices and run-on sentences by placing the period between the two sentences. For the sake of sentence variety and emphasis (Chapter 9), however, you want to choose other options as well, such as those shown in 20c.3 and 20c.4. Strings of short sentences rarely establish relationships and levels of importance among ideas.

Quick Reference 20.2

Ways to correct comma splices and run-on sentences

* Use a period between the INDEPENDENT CLAUSES (20c.1).
* Use a semicolon between the INDEPENDENT CLAUSES (20c.2).
* Use a comma together with a COORDINATING CONJUNCTION (20c.3).
* Revise one independent clause into a DEPENDENT CLAUSE (20c.4).

COMMA SPLICE	A shark is all **cartilage, it** doesn't have a bone in its body.
RUN-ON SENTENCE	A shark is all **cartilage it** doesn't have a bone in its body.
CORRECT	A shark is all **cartilage. It** doesn't have a bone in its body. [A period separates the independent clauses.]

COMMA SPLICE	Sharks can smell blood from a quarter mile **away, they** then swim toward the source like a guided missile.
RUN-ON SENTENCE	Sharks can smell blood from a quarter mile **away they** then swim toward the source like a guided missile.
CORRECT	Sharks can smell blood from a quarter mile **away. They** then swim toward the source like a guided missile. [A period separates the independent clauses.]

20c.2 Using a semicolon to correct comma splices and run-on sentences

You can use a semicolon to correct comma splices and run-on sentences by placing the semicolon between the two sentences. Use a semicolon only when the separate sentences are closely related in meaning. For the sake of sentence variety and emphasis, however, you'll want to choose other options, such as those shown in 20c.1, 20c.3, and 20c.4; for correct semicolon use, see Chapter 25.

COMMA SPLICE	The great white shark supposedly eats **humans, research** shows that most white sharks spit them out after the first bite.
RUN-ON SENTENCE	The great white shark supposedly eats **humans research** shows that most white sharks spit them out after the first bite.

CORRECT	The great white shark supposedly eats **humans; research** shows that most white sharks spit them out after the first bite. [A semicolon separates two independent clauses that are close in meaning.]

20c.3   Using a comma together with a coordinating conjunction to correct comma splices and run-on sentences

You can connect independent clauses with a comma together with a coordinating conjunction (*and, but, for, or, nor, yet, so*) to correct a comma splice. You can also correct a run-on sentence by inserting a comma followed by a coordinating conjunction.

Alert: Use a comma before a coordinating conjunction that links independent clauses (24b). ●

When you use a coordinating conjunction, be sure that your choice fits the meaning of the material. *And* signals addition; *but* and *yet* signal contrast; *for* and *so* signal cause; and *or* and *nor* signal alternatives.

COMMA SPLICE	All living creatures give off weak electrical charges in the **water, special** pores on a shark's skin can detect these signals.
RUN-ON SENTENCE	All living creatures give off weak electrical charges in the **water special** pores on a shark's skin can detect these signals.
CORRECT	All living creatures give off weak electrical charges in the **water,** and **special** pores on a shark's skin can detect these signals.

EXERCISE 20-1   Revise the comma splices and run-on sentences by using a period, a semicolon, or a comma and coordinating conjunction. For help, consult sections 20c.1 through 20c.3.

EXAMPLE   Every two years, a very popular "Celebration of Books" takes place at Oklahoma State University at Tulsa writers from across the United States gather along with readers to discuss the art of writing.

Revised: Every two years, a very popular "Celebration of Books" takes place at Oklahoma State University at *Tulsa. Writers* from across the United States gather along with readers to discuss the art of writing.

1. During the "Celebration of Books," aspiring writers can ask published authors questions about writing, for example, many people wish to know how to find an agent.

2. Besides asking about agents, would-be writers also query published authors about writing techniques many questions deal with whether to write using a computer or by longhand.

3. The "Celebration of Books" offers panel discussions on a variety of topics, including memoir writing, poetry development, and techniques of plotting short stories other panels cover writing the western novel and true crime stories.

4. The "Celebration of Books" appeals to readers, many of whom can see their favorite authors in person speaking on panels and in more informal settings such as receptions and book signings fans of authors greatly enjoy such opportunities.

5. In addition to writers, many well-known artists and musicians are honored at the "Celebration of Books," its Advisory Board recommended this expansion years ago to widen the conference's appeal.

20c.4 Revising one independent clause into a dependent clause to correct comma splices and run-on sentences

You can correct a comma splice or run-on sentence by revising one of the two independent clauses into a dependent clause. This method is suitable only when one idea can logically be subordinated to the other. Also, be careful never to end the dependent clause with a period or semicolon. If you do, you've created the error of a SENTENCE FRAGMENT.

CREATE DEPENDENT CLAUSES
WITH SUBORDINATING CONJUNCTIONS

One way to create a dependent clause is to insert a SUBORDINATING CONJUNCTION (such as *because, although, when,* and *if*—see Quick Reference 14.7, section 14i, for a complete list). Always choose a subordinating conjunction that fits the meaning of each particular sentence: *because* and *since* signal cause; *although* signals contrast; *when* signals time; and *if* signals condition. Dependent clauses that begin with a subordinating conjunction are called ADVERB CLAUSES.

COMMA SPLICE	Homer and Langley Collyer had packed their house from top to bottom with **junk, police** could not open the front door to investigate a reported smell.
RUN-ON SENTENCE	Homer and Langley Collyer had packed their house from top to bottom with **junk police** could not open the front door to investigate a reported smell.
CORRECT	**Because** Homer and Langley Collyer had packed their house from top to bottom with **junk, police** could not open the front door to investigate a reported smell. [*Because* starts a dependent clause that is joined by a comma with the independent clause starting with *police*.]

COMMA SPLICE	Old newspapers and car parts filled every room to the **ceiling, enough** space remained for fourteen pianos.
RUN-ON SENTENCE	Old newspapers and car parts filled every room to the **ceiling enough** space remained for fourteen pianos.
CORRECT	**Although** old newspapers and car parts filled every room to the **ceiling, enough** space remained for fourteen pianos. [The subordinating conjunction *although* starts a dependent clause that is joined by a comma with the independent clause starting with *enough*.]

Alert: Place a comma between an introductory dependent clause and the independent clause that follows (24c). ●

CREATE DEPENDENT CLAUSES WITH RELATIVE PRONOUNS

You can create a dependent clause with a RELATIVE PRONOUN (*who, whom, whose, which, that*). Dependent clauses with a relative pronoun are called ADJECTIVE CLAUSES.

COMMA SPLICE	The Collyers had been crushed under a pile of **newspapers, the newspapers** had toppled onto the brothers.
RUN-ON SENTENCE	The Collyers had been crushed under a pile of **newspapers the newspapers** had toppled onto the brothers.
CORRECT	The Collyers had been crushed under a pile of **newspapers *that* had toppled** onto the brothers. [The relative pronoun *that* starts a dependent clause and is joined with the independent clause starting with *The Collyers*, after deletion of *the newspapers*.]

Alert: Sometimes you need commas to set off an adjective clause from the rest of the sentence. This happens only when the adjective is NONRESTRICTIVE (nonessential), so check carefully (24f). ●

EXERCISE 20-2 Working individually or with your peer-response group, identify and then revise the comma splices and run-on sentences. Circle the numbers of correct sentences. For help, consult 20b through 20c.4.

EXAMPLE

COMMA SPLICE	Artists occasionally need a catalyst to set them on the road to their careers, for B. B. King, a tractor acted as that catalyst.

RUN-ON SENTENCE	Artists occasionally need a catalyst to set them on the road to their careers for B. B. King, a tractor acted as that catalyst.
CORRECT	Artists occasionally need a catalyst to set them on the road to their **careers; for** B. B. King, a tractor acted as that catalyst.

(1) B. B. King, the great blues guitarist and singer, born Riley B. King in Itta Bena, Mississippi, began his working life as a sharecropper and tractor driver, he earned one dollar a day at a plantation owned by Johnson Barrett in Indianola, Mississippi. (2) As a side venture to his farm work, King sang with the excellent St. John's Gospel Singers he wanted the group to leave Mississippi to find riches and recognition in the music world. (3) In 1946, King left the group, he had tried very hard to urge them to go with him. (4) King was working hard all day in Mr. Barrett's fields, driving a tractor, he always returned to the barn at the end of the day, jumping off the tractor to the ground. (5) One day, the sudden movement made the tractor charge ahead and break off its exhaust stack King had already turned off the engine. (6) A terrified young King, fearing his boss's anger over the damaged tractor, ran away to Memphis with his guitar and $2.50, his fear kept him there for many months. (7) After a year of unsuccessfully pursuing a music career, King became discouraged and returned to Indianola he went back to work for Johnson Barrett. (8) By 1948, King had saved enough money as a tractor driver, sharecropper, and street musician to try his luck again making a living as a musician and singer, he returned to Memphis and finally found recognition and fortune, not only in that city but internationally. (9) By 1999, B. B. King had been nominated for twenty Grammy Awards, he won his ninth in that year for *Blues on the Bayou*, in the category of the Best Traditional Blues Recording. (10) In 1998, B. B. King was installed in the Grammy Hall of Fame, after having received the Grammy Lifetime Achievement Award in 1987, among his most dramatic honors were honorary PhDs granted by Yale University and the University of Mississippi.

20d How can I correctly use a conjunctive adverb or other transitional expression between independent clauses?

CONJUNCTIVE ADVERBS and other TRANSITIONAL EXPRESSIONS link ideas between sentences. When these words fall between sentences, a period or semicolon must immediately precede them—and a comma usually immediately follows them.

Conjunctive adverbs include such words as *however, therefore, also, next, then, thus, furthermore,* and *nevertheless* (see Quick Reference 14.5, section 14g, for a complete list). Be careful to remember that conjunctive adverbs are not COORDINATING CONJUNCTIONS (*and, but,* and so on; see 20c.3).

COMMA SPLICE	Buying or leasing a car is a matter of individual preference**, however,** it's wise to consider several points before making a decision.
RUN-ON SENTENCE	Buying or leasing a car is a matter of individual preference **however** it's wise to consider several points before making a decision.
CORRECT	Buying or leasing a car is a matter of individual preference**. However,** it's wise to consider several points before making a decision.
CORRECT	Buying or leasing a car is a matter of individual preference**; however,** it's wise to consider several points before making a decision.

Transitional expressions include *for example, for instance, in addition, in fact, of course,* and *on the one hand/on the other hand* (see Quick Reference 3.5 section 3g.1, for a complete list).

COMMA SPLICE	Car leasing requires a smaller down payment**, for example,** in many cases, you need only $1,000 or $2,000 and the first monthly payment.
RUN-ON SENTENCE	Car leasing requires a smaller down payment **for example** in many cases, you need only $1,000 or $2,000 and the first monthly payment.
CORRECT	Car leasing requires a smaller down payment**. For example,** in many cases, you need only $1,000 or $2,000 and the first monthly payment.
CORRECT	Car leasing requires a smaller down payment**; for example,** in many cases, you need only $1,000 or $2,000 and the first monthly payment.

❗ **Alert:** A conjunctive adverb or a transitional expression is usually followed by a comma when it starts a sentence (24c). ●

EXERCISE 20-3 Revise comma splices or run-on sentences caused by incorrectly punctuated conjunctive adverbs or other transitional expressions. If a sentence is correct, circle its number. For help, consult 20d.

EXAMPLE Yearly, the US National Aeronautics and Space Administration (NASA) requests federal funding for space exploration, however, many US citizens wonder what practical value the space program offers.

Corrected: Yearly, the U.S. National Aeronautics and Space Administration (NASA) requests federal funding for space *exploration.*
However, many US citizens wonder what practical value the space
program offers. [comma splice; corrected by inserting a period before a conjunctive adverb]

1. US citizens may not realize products developed by NASA directly affect
   their lives. For example, NASA has developed or improved a number of
   goods and services now available to the general public.

2. People may be surprised to learn that bar coding on products grew out
   of NASA's need to keep track of thousands of spacecraft components, indeed, bar codes allow merchants to track what they sell and to record
   items for reordering.

3. Methods of medical imaging today are based on NASA's developing
   ways to process signals for sending images from space, in addition, the
   ear thermometer, popular for use with adults and children, developed out
   of NASA technology to identify the birth of stars.

4. Firefighters now wear fire-resistant suits because of space technology furthermore, NASA research created protective lenses that now save
   welders' eyes from harmful radiation.

5. Not all items coming from NASA's experiments result in medical advances or safety for workers, for instance, thermal gloves, ski boots, and
   failsafe flashlights are now available to the general public as a direct result of NASA's work.

EXERCISE 20-4   Revise all comma splices and run-on sentences, using as
many different methods of correction as you can.

(1) Energy psychology represents fairly new methods joining Eastern lines
of thought to the mind and body and Western psychology and psychotherapy,
according to an article by Leonard Holmes, PhD, proponents of energy
psychology contend that striking acupuncture points and at the same time
recalling an anxiety-producing incident can alleviate anxiety and phobias.
(2) Holmes inquires whether this idea is true in fact, he goes on to question
the connection the acupuncture points have to anxiety. (3) In the early 1980s,
Roger Callahan, PhD, popularized procedures utilizing energy psychology, he
called the procedures "The Callahan Technique" or "Thought Field Therapy."
(4) In the beginning, Callahan's training programs were costly, generally
hundreds of dollars, now, on the other hand, they are moderately priced.
(5) Other therapists such as clinical psychologist David Feinstein, PhD, have
joined the ranks promoting energy psychology, interestingly, Feinstein sells
an interactive CD-ROM that presents guidance in energy psychology/
psychotherapy. (6) A qualified therapist can use the CD-ROM laypersons
should not experiment with the contents of the CD-ROM. (7) Today,
proponents of energy psychology contend it results in the successful handling

of problems such as trauma, abuse, depression, and addictive cravings, other uses for energy psychology, or "Emotional Freedom Techniques" (EFT), as Gary Craig calls them on his Web site, include treatment for medical conditions such as headaches and breathing difficulties. (8) Craig, not a licensed health professional, contends the "missing piece to the healing puzzle" is EFT he quotes from supposedly scientific clinical trials indicating that patients have seen dramatic results in their conditions because of EFT. (9) Holmes thinks energy psychotherapy is still too early in its development to be widely applied he cautions the general public to avoid trying it on their own. (10) Holmes advises extreme caution for psychologists about continuing to use EFT more needs to be known from research.

For more help with your writing, grammar, and research, go to **www.mycomplab.com**

Misplaced and Dangling Modifiers

MISPLACED MODIFIERS

21a What is a misplaced modifier?

A **modifier** is a word or group of words that describes or limits another word or group of words. A **misplaced modifier** is positioned incorrectly in a sentence, which means, therefore, that it describes the wrong word and changes the writer's meaning. Always place a modifier as close as possible to what it describes.

AVOIDING SQUINTING MODIFIERS

A **squinting modifier** is misplaced because it modifies both the word that comes before it and the word that follows it. Check that your modifiers are placed so that they communicate the meaning you intend.

NO   The football player being recruited **eagerly** believed each successive offer would be better. [What was eager? The recruitment or the player's belief?]

YES   The football player being recruited believed **eagerly** that each successive offer would be better.

YES   The football player being **eagerly** recruited believed that each successive offer would be better.

PLACING LIMITING WORDS CAREFULLY

Words such as *only, not only, just, not just, almost, hardly, nearly, even, exactly, merely, scarcely,* and *simply* serve to limit the meaning of a word according to where they are placed. When you use such words, position them precisely. Consider how moving the placement of the word *only* changes the meaning of this sentence: *Professional coaches say that high salaries motivate players.*

Only professional coaches say that high salaries motivate players. [No one else says this.]

Professional coaches **only** say that high salaries motivate players. [The coaches probably do not mean what they say.]

Professional coaches say **only** that high salaries motivate players. [The coaches say nothing else.]

Professional coaches say that **only** high salaries motivate players. [Nothing except high salaries motivates players.]

Professional coaches say that high salaries **only** motivate players. [High salaries do nothing other than motivate players.]

Professional coaches say that high salaries motivate **only** players. [High salaries do motivate the players but not the coaches and managers.]

21b   How can I avoid split infinitives?

An INFINITIVE is a VERB form that starts with *to: to motivate, to convince, to create* are examples (14e). A **split infinitive** occurs when words are placed between the word *to* and its verb. The effect is awkward.

NO   Orson Welles's radio drama "War of the Worlds" managed ***to, in October 1938, convince*** listeners that they were hearing an invasion by Martians. [*In October 1938* is misplaced because the words come between *to* and *convince.*]

YES   **In October 1938,** Orson Welles's radio drama "War of the Worlds" managed ***to convince*** listeners that they were hearing an invasion by Martians.

Often, the word that splits an infinitive is an ADVERB ending in *-ly*. In general, place adverbs either before or after the infinitive.

NO People feared that they would no longer be able **to *happily* live** in peace.

YES People feared that they would no longer be able **to live *happily*** in peace.

The rule about split infinitives has changed recently. Current usage says that when the best placement for a single adverb is actually between *to* and the verb, use that structure freely.

Welles wanted **to *realistically* portray** a Martian invasion for the radio audience.

If you want to avoid splitting infinitives in your ACADEMIC WRITING, revise to avoid the split:

Welles wanted his "Martian invasion" **to sound *realistic*** for the radio audience. [The adverb *realistically* was changed to the adjective *realistic*.]

21c How can I avoid other splits in my sentences?

When too many words split—that is, come between—a SUBJECT and its VERB or between a verb and its OBJECT, the result is a sentence that lurches rather than flows from beginning to end.

NO The **announcer,** because the script, which Welles himself wrote, called for perfect imitations of emergency announcements, **opened** with a warning that included a description of the "invasion." [The subject *announcer* is placed too far away from the verb *opened*, so this split is too large.]

YES Because the script, which Welles himself wrote, called for perfect imitations of emergency announcements, the **announcer opened** with a warning that included a description of the "invasion." [The subject and verb, *announcer opened*, aren't split.]

NO Many churches **held** for their frightened communities **"end of the world" prayer services.** [The verb *held* is placed too far away from the object *"end of the world" prayer services*, so this split is too large.]

YES Many churches **held "end of the world" prayer services** for their frightened communities. [The verb and object, *held "end of the world" prayer services*, aren't split.]

EXERCISE 21-1 Revise these ten sentences to correct misplaced modifiers, split infinitives, and other splits. If a sentence is correct, circle its number. For help, consult 21a through 21c.

EXAMPLE   The city of Deadwood is known for its many notorious residents made popular by a TV show including Wild Bill Hickok and Calamity Jane.

Made popular by a TV show, the city of Deadwood is known for its many notorious residents, including Wild Bill Hickok and Calamity Jane.

1. Deadwood, because of its location near the Deadwood Gulch and the Black Hills of South Dakota, was named for the dead trees found in that canyon.

2. The city's founding, during a gold rush that attracted a quarter of a million miners to the area, was in 1876.

3. The main source of revenue for the city was gambling, which was outlawed in 1905 but reinstated in 1989.

4. Today, tourists who visit Deadwood often gamble and enjoy the historical reenactments of the town's famous events.

5. Deadwood nearly was the home to a dozen of famous characters from the Old West.

6. Serving as the sheriff of Hays City and Abilene, Wild Bill Hickok worked to with an iron fist tame the lawless towns of the frontier.

7. Hickok moved to Deadwood after he without much success performed in a Wild West show.

8. During a poker game at Nuttall & Mann's saloon, Jack McCall shot for unknown reasons Will Bill.

9. The cards Hickok was holding included a pair of black aces, a pair of black eights, and an unknown fifth card now known as the dead man's hand.

10. The legends of Deadwood and Wild Bill in the stories of fiction writers and TV shows continue to grow.

EXERCISE 21-2 Using each list of words and phrases, create all the possible logical sentences. Insert commas as needed. Explain differences in meaning among the alternatives you create. For help, consult 21a through 21c.

EXAMPLE   exchange students
learned to speak French
while in Paris
last summer

A. Last summer,/exchange students/learned to speak French/while in Paris.

B. While in Paris,/exchange students/learned to speak French/last summer.

C. Exchange students/learned to speak French/while in Paris/last summer.

D. Exchange students/learned to speak French/last summer/while in Paris.

1. chicken soup
according to folklore
helps
cure colds

2. tadpoles
instinctively
swim
toward
their genetic relatives

3. the young driver
while driving
in the snow
skidded carelessly

4. climbed
the limber teenager
a tall palm tree
to pick a ripe coconut
quickly

5. and cause mini-avalanches
ski patrollers
set explosives
often
to prevent
big avalanches

DANGLING MODIFIERS

21d   How can I avoid dangling modifiers?

A **dangling modifier** describes or limits a word or words that never actually appear in the sentence. Aware of the intended meaning, the writer unconsciously supplies the missing words, but the reader gets confused. To correct a dangling modifier, state clearly your intended SUBJECT in the sentence.

> **NO** **Having read Faulkner's short story "A Rose for Emily," *the ending* surprised us.** [This sentence says *the ending* was reading the story, which is impossible.]

> **YES** Having read Faulkner's short story "A Rose for Emily," **we were surprised by the ending.** [Second half of sentence is rewritten to include the subject *we*.]

> **YES** **We** read Faulkner's short story "A Rose for Emily" **and were surprised by the ending.** [Sentence is rewritten to include the subject *We*.]

> **NO** **When courting Emily, *the townspeople* gossiped about her.** [This sentence says *the townspeople* were courting Emily, which isn't true.]

> **YES** **When Emily was being courted *by Homer Barron,*** the townspeople gossiped about her. [First half of sentence is rewritten to include the name of the person doing the courting: *Homer Barron*.]

A major cause of dangling modifiers is the unnecessary use of the PASSIVE VOICE. Whenever possible, use the ACTIVE VOICE.

NO **To earn money, china painting lessons** were offered by Emily to wealthy young women. [*China painting lessons* cannot *earn money. Were offered by Emily* is in the passive voice.]

YES **To earn money, Emily** offered china painting lessons to wealthy young women. [Change to the active voice; *Emily offered* corrects the problem.]

EXERCISE 21-3 Identify and correct any dangling modifiers in these sentences. If a sentence is correct, circle its number. For help, consult 21d.

EXAMPLE To understand what happened to Krakatoa, the volcano and its history must be studied

Corrected: To understand what happened to Krakatoa, one must study the volcano and its history.

1. In 1883, massive destruction was caused by the eruption of the volcano Krakatoa, an event recently examined in the book *Krakatoa: The Day the World Exploded.*

2. Exploding with a force 13,000 times stronger than the bomb dropped on Hiroshima, people thousands of miles away heard the eruption.

3. The loudest sound historically reported was generated by the explosion, with devastating tsunamis soon following.

4. Ejecting tons of debris into the air, the volcano destroyed or damaged hundreds of nearby villages.

5. Beginning to erupt around late July, larger eruptions didn't start until the middle of August.

6. Reaching over 100 feet in height and traveling at devastating speeds, major destruction was caused on the coastlines of Sumatra.

7. Lasting much longer than expected, people in nearby areas felt aftershocks until February of 1884.

8. To understand the magnitude of this volcanic eruption, changes in weather patterns were studied by scientists.

9. Darkening the sky for days afterwards and producing unusual sunsets, the ash and gases from the volcano temporarily lowered the average temperature of the earth.

10. Affecting the art of its time, the background of Edvard Munch's famous painting *The Scream* was inspired by Krakatoan sunsets.

21e How can I proofread successfully for misplaced and dangling modifiers?

Sentence errors like MISPLACED MODIFIERS and DANGLING MODIFIERS are hard to spot because of the way the human brain works. Writers know what they mean to say when they write. When they PROOFREAD, however, they often misread what they've written for what they intended to write. The mind unconsciously adjusts for the error. In contrast, readers see only what's on the paper or screen. We suggest that you read your writing aloud, or have someone else read it to you, to proofread it for these kinds of problems.

For more help with your
writing, grammar, and research,
go to **www.mycomplab.com**

22

Shifting and Mixed Sentences

SHIFTING SENTENCES

22a What is a shifting sentence?

A **shift** within a sentence is an unnecessary, abrupt change in PERSON, NUMBER, SUBJECT, VOICE, TENSE, MOOD, or DIRECT or INDIRECT DISCOURSE. These shifts blur meaning. Sometimes a shift occurs between two or more sentences in a paragraph. If you set out on one track (writing in FIRST PERSON, for example), your readers expect you to stay on that same track (and not unnecessarily shift to THIRD PERSON, for example). When you go off track, you have written a shifting sentence or paragraph.

22b How can I avoid shifts in person and number?

Who or what performs or receives an action is defined by the term *person*. FIRST PERSON (*I, we*) is the speaker or writer; SECOND PERSON (*you*) is the one being spoken or written *to;* and THIRD PERSON (*he, she, it, they*) is the person or thing being spoken or written *about.*

The essential point is that shifts are incorrect unless the meaning in a particular context makes them necessary.

> **NO** I enjoy reading financial forecasts of the future, but **you** wonder which will turn out to be correct. [The first person *I* shifts to the second person *you*.]

> **YES** I enjoy reading financial forecasts of the future, but **I** wonder which will turn out to be correct.

NUMBER refers to whether words are *singular* (one) or *plural* (more than one) in meaning. Do not start to write in one number and then shift for no reason to the other number.

> **NO** Because **people** are living longer, **an employee** now retires later. [The plural *people* shifts to the singular *employee*.]

> **YES** Because **people** are living longer, **employees** now retire later.

In ACADEMIC WRITING, reserve *you* for addressing the reader directly. Use the third person for general statements.

> **NO** I like my job in customer service because **you** get to solve people's problems. [*I* is in the first person, so a shift to the second person *you* is incorrect.]

> **YES** I like my job in customer service because **I** get to solve people's problems.

> **NO** **People** enjoy feeling productive, so when a job is unsatisfying, **you** usually become depressed. [*People* is in the third person, so a shift to the second person *you* is incorrect.]

> **YES** **People** enjoy feeling productive, so when a job is unsatisfying, **they** usually become depressed.

Be careful with words in the singular (usually NOUNS) used in a general sense, such as *employee, student, consumer, neighbor,* and *someone.* These words are always third-person singular. The only pronouns for these ANTECEDENTS in the third-person singular are *he, she,* and *it.* Remember that *they* is plural, so the word *they* can't be used with singular nouns.

> **NO** When **an employee** is treated with respect, **they** are more motivated to do a good job. [*Employee* is third-person singular, so the shift to the third-person plural *they* is incorrect.]

YES   When **an employee** is treated with respect, **he or she** is more motivated to do a good job.

YES   When **employees** are treated with respect, **they** are more motivated to do a good job.

YES   **An employee** who is treated with respect is more motivated to do
a good job.

YES   **Employees** who are treated with respect are more motivated to
do a good job.

🛈 Alert: When you use INDEFINITE PRONOUNS (such as *someone, everyone,*
or *anyone*), you want to use GENDER-NEUTRAL LANGUAGE. For advice, see 17s
and 12f. ●

EXERCISE 22-1   Eliminate shifts in person and number between, as well as
within, sentences. Some sentences may not need revision. For help, consult 22b.

(1) First-time visitors to the Mall of America may be overwhelmed by its
size, but you will also see its helpful design. (2) A shopper will notice that the
mall is divided into architecturally distinct areas so they won't get lost. (3) The
four sides of the mall have different themes and matching décor, so it is easy
to navigate. (4) The architects named the four sides the North Garden, South
Avenue, East Broadway, and West Market. (5) He or she also called the fourth
floor's collection of nightclubs the Upper East Side to reflect an urban
environment. (6) In spite of skeptics who thought the mall would never make
money, it has been consistently successful in renting its retail space and
attracting shoppers. (7) The amusement park in the middle of the mall remains
an important draw for families and children, and they have roller coasters and
water rides. (8) Couples can enjoy fine dining and high-end shopping, and
you can even get married in the mall's wedding chapel.

22c How can I avoid shifts in subject and voice?

A SHIFT in SUBJECT is rarely justified when it is accompanied by a shift in VOICE.
The voice of a sentence is either *active* (*People expect changes*) or *passive* (*Changes
are expected*). Some subject shifts, however, are justified by the meaning of a passage: for example, *People look forward to the future, but the future holds many secrets.*

NO   Most **people expect** major improvements in the future, but some
hardships are also **anticipated.** [The subject shifts from *people* to
hardships, and the voice shifts from active to passive.]

YES   Most **people expect** major improvements in the future, but **they**
also **anticipate** some hardships.

YES   Most **people expect** major improvements in the future but also **anticipate** some hardships.

22d   How can I avoid shifts in tense and mood?

TENSE refers to the time in which the action of a VERB takes place—past, present, or future: *We **will go** to the movies after we **finish** dinner.* An unnecessary tense SHIFT within or between sentences can make the statement confusing or illogical.

NO   A campaign to clean up movies in the United States **began** in the 1920s as civic and religious groups **try** to ban sex and violence from the screen. [The tense incorrectly shifts from the past *began* to the present *try.*]

YES   A campaign to clean up movies in the United States **began** in the 1920s as civic and religious groups **tried** to ban sex and violence from the screen.

NO   Film producers and distributors **created** the Production Code in the 1930s. At first, violating its guidelines **carried** no penalty. Eventually, however, films that **fail** to get the board's seal of approval **do not receive** wide distribution. [This shift occurs between sentences—the past tense *created* and *carried* shift to the present tense *fail* and *do not receive.*]

YES   Film producers and distributors **created** the Production Code in the 1930s. At first, violating its guidelines **carried** no penalty. Eventually, however, films that **failed** to get the board's seal of approval **did not receive** wide distribution.

MOOD indicates whether a sentence is a statement or a question (INDICATIVE MOOD), a command or request (IMPERATIVE MOOD), or a conditional or other-than-real statement (SUBJUNCTIVE MOOD). A shift in mood creates an awkward construction and can cause confusion.

NO   The Production Code included two guidelines on violence: **Do not show** the details of brutal killings, and movies **should not be** explicit about how to commit crimes. [The verbs shift from the imperative mood *do not show* to the indicative mood *movies should not be.*]

YES   The Production Code included two guidelines on violence: **Do not show** the details of brutal killings, and **do not show** explicitly how to commit crimes. [This revision uses the imperative mood for both guidelines.]

YES   The Production Code included two guidelines on violence: Movies **were not to show** the details of brutal killings or explicit ways to commit crimes.

NO   The code's writers worried that **if a crime were to be** accurately **depicted** in a movie, **copycat crimes will follow.** [The sentence shifts from the subjunctive mood *if a crime were to be depicted* to the indicative mood *copycat crimes will follow.*]

YES   The code's writers worried that **if a crime were to be** accurately **depicted** in a movie, **copycat crimes would follow.**

22e   How can I avoid shifts between indirect and direct discourse?

Indirect discourse is not enclosed in quotation marks because it reports, rather than quotes, something that someone said. In contrast, **direct discourse** is enclosed in quotation marks because it quotes exactly the words that someone said. It's incorrect to write direct discourse and omit the quotation marks. Also, it's incorrect to write sentences that mix indirect and direct discourse. Such SHIFT errors confuse readers, who can't tell what was said and what is being merely reported.

NO   A critic said that board members were acting as censors and **what you are doing is unconstitutional.** [*Said that* sets up indirect discourse, but *what you are doing is unconstitutional* is direct discourse; it also lacks quotation marks and the changes in language that distinguish spoken words from reported words.]

YES   A critic said that board members were acting as censors and **that what they were doing was unconstitutional.** [This revision uses indirect discourse consistently.]

YES   A critic, in stating that board members were acting as censors, added, **"What you are doing is unconstitutional."** [This revision uses discourse correctly, with quotation marks and other changes in language to distinguish spoken words from reported words.]

Whenever you change your writing from direct discourse to indirect discourse (when you decide to paraphrase rather than quote someone directly, for example), you need to make changes in VERB TENSE and other grammatical features for your writing to make sense. Simply removing the quotation marks is not enough.

NO He asked **did we enjoy the movie?** [This version has the verb form needed for direct discourse, but the pronoun *we* is wrong and quotation punctuation is missing.]

YES He asked **whether we enjoyed the movie.** [This version is entirely indirect discourse, and the verb has changed from *enjoy* to *enjoyed*.]

YES He asked, **"Did you enjoy the movie?"** [This version is direct discourse. It repeats the original speech exactly, with correct quotation punctuation.]

EXERCISE 22-2 Revise these sentences to eliminate incorrect shifts within sentences. Some sentences can be revised in several ways. For help, consult 22b through 22e.

EXAMPLE In 1942, the US government is faced with arresting five million people for not paying their federal income taxes.

In 1942, the US government *was faced* with arresting five million people for not paying their federal income taxes.

1. Congress needed money to pay for US participation in World War II, so a new tax system was proposed.
2. Tax payments were due on March 15, not April 15 as it is today.
3. For the first time, Congress taxed millions of lower-income citizens. Most people do not save enough to pay the amount of taxes due.
4. When a scientific poll showed lawmakers that only one in seven Americans had saved enough money, he became worried.

EXERCISE 22-3 Revise this paragraph to eliminate incorrect shifts between sentences and within sentences. For help, consult 22b through 22e.

(1) According to sociologists, people experience role conflict when we find ourselves trying to juggle too many different social roles. (2) When people reach overload, he or she decided, "to cut back somewhere." (3) For example, a well-known politician might decide not to run for reelection because family life would be interfered with by the demands of the campaign. (4) In other cases, you may delay having children so they can achieve early career success. (5) A person might say to themselves that I can't do this right now and focus instead on career goals. (6) In yet another example, a plant manager might enjoy social interaction with employees but consequently find themselves unable to evaluate him or her objectively. (7) In short, sociologists find that although not all role conflicts cause problems, great hardships are suffered by some individuals faced with handling difficult balancing acts.

(8) People can minimize role conflicts, however, if we learn to compartmentalize our lives. (9) A good example of this is people saying that I'm going to stop thinking about my job before I head home to my family.

MIXED SENTENCES

22f What is a mixed sentence?

A mixed sentence has two or more parts, with the first part starting in one direction and the rest of the parts going off in another. This mixing of sentence parts leads to unclear meaning. To avoid this error, as you write each sentence, remember how you started it and make sure that whatever comes next in the sentence relates grammatically and logically to that beginning.

NO Because our side lost the contest eventually motivated us to do better. [*Because our side lost the contest* starts the sentence in one direction, but *eventually motivated us to do better* goes off in another direction.]

YES Because our side lost the contest, **we** eventually became motivated to do better.

YES Our side lost the contest, **which** eventually motivated us to do better.

NO Because television's first transmissions in the 1920s included news programs became popular with the public. [The opening dependent clause starts off on one track (and is not correctly punctuated), but the independent clause goes off in another direction. What does the writer want to emphasize, the first transmissions or the popularity of news programs?]

NO Because television's first transmissions in the 1920s included news, programs became popular with the public. [The revision helps but is partial: the dependent clause talks about the news, but the independent clause goes off in another direction by talking about the popularity of the programs in general.]

YES Television's first transmissions in the 1920s included news programs, **which were** popular with the public. [Dropping *because* and adding *which were* solves the problem by keeping the focus on news programs throughout.]

NO By increasing the time for network news to thirty minutes increased the prestige of network news programs. [A prepositional phrase, such as *by increasing,* can't be the subject of a sentence.]

YES Increasing the time for network news to thirty minutes increased the prestige of network news programs. [Dropping the preposition *by* clears up the problem.]

YES By increasing the time for network news to thirty minutes, **the network executives** increased the prestige of network news programs. [Inserting a logical subject, *the network executives*, clears up the problem.]

The phrase *the fact that* lacks CONCISENESS, and it also tends to cause a mixed sentence.

NO The fact that quiz show scandals in the 1950s prompted the networks to produce even more news shows.

YES The fact **is** that quiz show scandals in the 1950s prompted the networks to produce even more news shows. [Adding *is* clarifies the meaning.]

YES Quiz show scandals in the 1950s prompted the networks to produce even more news shows. [Dropping *the fact that* clarifies the meaning.]

22g How can I correct a mixed sentence due to faulty predication?

Faulty predication, sometimes called *illogical predication*, occurs when a SUBJECT and its PREDICATE don't make sense together.

NO The purpose of television was invented to entertain people. [A *purpose* cannot be *invented*.]

YES The purpose of television was to entertain people.

YES Television was invented to entertain people.

Faulty predication often results from a lost connection between a subject and its SUBJECT COMPLEMENT.

NO Walter Cronkite's outstanding **characteristic** as a newscaster **was credible.** [The subject complement *credible* could logically describe *Walter Cronkite*, but *Walter Cronkite* is not the sentence's subject. Rather, the sentence's subject is his *characteristic*. Therefore, the sentence lacks a subject complement that would name a characteristic of *Walter Cronkite as a newscaster*.]

YES Walter Cronkite's outstanding **characteristic** as a newscaster **was credibility.** [When *credibility* is substituted for *credible*, the sentence is correct.]

> **YES** Walter Cronkite was credible as a newscaster. [When *Walter Cronkite* becomes the sentence's subject, *credible* is correct.]

In ACADEMIC WRITING, avoid nonstandard constructions such as *is when* and *is where*. They should be avoided not only because they are nonstandard, but also because they usually lead to faulty predication.

> **NO** A disaster **is when** TV news shows get some of their highest ratings.
>
> **YES** TV news shows get some of their highest ratings during a disaster.

In academic writing, avoid constructions such as *the reason . . . is because.* Using both *reason* and *because* makes the construction redundant (it says the same thing twice). Instead, use either *the reason . . . is that* or *because* alone.

> **NO** One **reason** that TV news captured national attention in the 1960s **is because** it covered the Vietnam War thoroughly.
>
> **YES** One **reason** TV news captured national attention in the 1960s **is that** it covered the Vietnam War thoroughly.
>
> **YES** TV news captured national attention in the 1960s **because** it covered the Vietnam War thoroughly.

EXERCISE 22-4 Revise the mixed sentences so that the beginning of each sentence fits logically with its end. If a sentence is correct, circle its number. For help, consult 22f and 22g.

EXAMPLE The reason a newborn baby may stare at her hands or feet is because she can only focus on nearby objects.

> *A newborn baby may stare at her hands or feet* because she can only focus on nearby objects.

1. By showing babies plain, black-and-white images will help them learn to recognize shapes and focus their vision.

2. Even though babies can see their parents' faces will not respond with a smile until they are a few weeks old.

3. Babies may gaze intently into a small, unbreakable mirror attached to the inside of their cribs.

4. While following an object with her eyes is when eye coordination develops.

5. Because of a newborn's limited ability to see color forces him to focus only on bright colors.

6. The reason babies occasionally cross their eyes is because they are perfecting their tracking skills.

7. Whether a light sleeper or a heavy sleeper, a typical baby does not need complete silence in order to rest well.

8. The fact that newborns can vary dramatically in their sensitivity to sounds and ability to sleep in noisy environments.

9. The reason that a two-month-old baby turns her head toward her parents' voice is because she is beginning to recognize familiar sounds.

10. Through changing his facial expression indicates he may find a particular sound soothing or comforting.

22h What are correct elliptical constructions?

An **elliptical construction** deliberately leaves out one or more words in a sentence for CONCISENESS.

> Victor has his book and Joan's. [This means *Victor has his book and Joan's book.* The second *book* is left out deliberately.]

For an elliptical construction to be correct, the one or more words you leave out need to be identical to those already appearing in the sentence. For instance, the sample sentence above about Victor and Joan would have an incorrect elliptical construction if the writer's intended meaning were *Victor has his book, and Joan has her own book.*

> NO   During the 1920s in Chicago, the cornetist Manuel Perez **was leading** one outstanding jazz group, and Tommy and Jimmy Dorsey another. [The words *was leading* cannot take the place of *were leading,* which is required after *Tommy and Jimmy Dorsey.*]

> YES   During the 1920s in Chicago, the cornetist Manuel Perez **was leading** one outstanding jazz group, and Tommy and Jimmy Dorsey **were leading** another.

> YES   During the 1920s in Chicago, the cornetist Manuel Perez **led** one outstanding jazz group, and Tommy and Jimmy Dorsey another. [*Led* is correct with both *Manuel Perez* and *Tommy and Jimmy Dorsey,* so *led* can be omitted after *Dorsey.*]

22i What are correct comparisons?

When you write a sentence in which you want to compare two or more things, make sure that no important words are omitted.

> NO   Individuals driven to achieve make **better** business executives. [*Better* is a word of comparison (18e), but no comparison is stated.]

> YES   Individuals driven to achieve make **better** business executives **than do people not interested in personal accomplishments.**

> NO   Most personnel officers value high achievers **more than risk takers.** [*More* is a word of comparison, but it's unclear whether the

sentence says *personnel officers value high achievers over risk takers* or *personnel officers value high achievers more than risk takers value them.*]

YES Most personnel officers value high achievers **more than they value** risk takers.

YES Most personnel officers value high achievers **more than** risk takers **do.**

22j How can I proofread successfully for little words I forget to use?

If you're rushing or distracted as you write, you might unintentionally omit little words, such as ARTICLES, PRONOUNS, CONJUNCTIONS, and PREPOSITIONS. Lynn does, unfortunately. She solves this by reading her writing aloud, word by word; or, better still, she asks someone else to read it aloud because she tends to fill in mentally any missing words in her own work.

NO On May 2, 1808, citizens Madrid rioted against French soldiers and were shot.

YES On May 2, 1808, citizens **of** Madrid rioted against French soldiers and were shot.

NO The Spanish painter Francisco Goya recorded both the riot the execution in a pair of pictures painted 1814.

YES The Spanish painter Francisco Goya recorded both the riot **and** the execution in a pair of pictures painted **in** 1814.

EXERCISE 22-5 Revise this paragraph to create correct elliptical constructions, to complete comparisons, and to insert any missing words. For help, see 22h through 22j.

(1) A giant tsunami is as destructive and even larger than a tidal wave. (2) The word *tsunami* is Japanese for "harbor wave," for this kind wave appears suddenly in harbor or bay. (3) A tsunami begins with rapid shift in ocean floor caused by an undersea earthquake or volcano. (4) The wave this produces in the open sea is less than three feet high, but it can grow to a height of a hundred feet as it rushes and strikes against the shore. (5) For this reason, tsunamis are much more dangerous to seaside towns than ships on the open sea. (6) In 1960, a huge tsunami that struck coasts of Chile, Hawaii, and Japan killed total of 590 people. (7) In 2004, a huge tsunami that struck coasts of Indonesia, Thailand, Malaysia, and other countries killed total 275,000 people.

Using Punctuation and Mechanics

23

Periods, Question Marks, and Exclamation Points

Periods, question marks, and **exclamation points** are collectively called *end punctuation* because they occur at the ends of sentences.

I love you. Do you love me? I love you!

PERIODS

23a When does a period end a sentence?

A **period** ends a statement, a mild command, or an INDIRECT QUESTION.* Never use a period to end a DIRECT QUESTION, a strong command, or an emphatic declaration.

END OF A STATEMENT

A journey of a thousand miles must begin with a single step.

—Lao-tsu, *The Way of Lao-tsu*

MILD COMMAND

Put a gram of boldness into everything you do.

—Baltasar Gracian

INDIRECT QUESTION

I asked if they wanted to climb Mt. Everest. [As an indirect question, this sentence reports that a question was asked. If it were a direct question, it would end with a question mark: *I asked, "Do you want to climb Mt. Everest?"*]

23b How do I use periods with abbreviations?

Most **abbreviations**, though not all, call for periods. Typical abbreviations with periods include *Mt., St., Dr., Mr., Ms., Mrs., Jr., Fri., Feb., a.m.,* and *p.m.* (For more about *a.m.* and *p.m.,* see Chapter 22, "Usage Glossary," and section 30j; for more about abbreviations in general, see 30i through 30l.)

---

*Words printed in SMALL CAPITAL LETTERS are discussed elsewhere in the text and are defined in the Terms Glossary at the back of this book.

⚠️ **Alert:** Spell out the word *professor* in ACADEMIC WRITING; never abbreviate it. ●

Abbreviations without periods include the postal codes for states (for example, IL, CO) and the names of some organizations and government agencies (for example, CBS and NASA).

> **Ms.** Yuan, who works at **NASA,** lectured to **Dr.** Garcia's physics class at 9:30 **a.m.**

⚠️ **Alert:** When the period of an abbreviation falls at the end of a sentence that calls for a period, the period of the abbreviation serves also to end the sentence. If, however, your sentence ends in a question mark or an exclamation point, put it after the period of the abbreviation.

> The phone rang at 4:00 **a.m.**
>
> It's upsetting to answer a wrong-number call at 4:00 **a.m.!**
>
> Who would call at 4:00 **a.m.?** ●

QUESTION MARKS

23c When do I use a question mark?

A **question mark** ends a **direct question**, one that quotes the exact words the speaker used. (In contrast, an **indirect question** reports a question and ends with a period.)

> How many attempts have been made to climb Mt. Everest? [An indirect question would end with a period: *She wants to know how many attempts have been made to climb Mt. Everest.*]

⚠️ **Alert:** Never use a question mark with a period, comma, semicolon, or colon.

> **NO** She asked, "How are you?."
>
> **YES** She asked, "How are you?" ●

Questions in a series are each followed by a question mark, whether or not each question is a complete sentence.

> After the fierce storm, the mountain climbers debated what to do next. Turn back? Move on? Rest for a while?

⚠️ **Alert:** When questions in a series are not complete sentences (as in the preceding example), you can choose whether to capitalize the first letter, but be consistent within each piece of writing. ●

Sometimes a statement or mild command is phrased as a question to be polite. In such cases, a question mark is optional, but be consistent in each piece of writing.

Would you please send me a copy.

or

Would you please send me a copy?

23d When can I use a question mark in parentheses?

The only time to use a question mark in parentheses (?) is if a date or other number is unknown or doubtful. Never use (?) to communicate that you're unsure of information.

Mary Astell, a British writer of pamphlets on women's rights, was born in 1666 **(?)** and died in 1731.

The word *about* is often a more graceful substitute for (?): *Mary Astell was born* **about** *1666.*

Also, never use (?) to communicate IRONY or sarcasm. Choose words to deliver your message.

NO Having altitude sickness is a pleasant **(?)** experience.

YES Having altitude sickness is **as** pleasant **as having a bad case of the flu.**

EXCLAMATION POINTS

23e When do I use an exclamation point?

An **exclamation point** ends a strong command or an emphatic declaration. A strong command is a firm and direct order: *Look out behind you!* An emphatic declaration is a shocking or surprising statement: *There's been an accident!*

! Alert: Never combine an exclamation point with a period, comma, semicolon, or colon.

NO "There's been an accident**!,**" she shouted.

YES "There's been an accident**!**" she shouted.

YES "There's been an accident," she shouted. [Use this form if you prefer not to use an exclamation point.] ●

23f What is considered overuse of exclamation points?

In ACADEMIC WRITING, words, not exclamation points, need to communicate the intensity of your message. Reserve exclamation points for an emphatic declaration within a longer passage.

> When we were in Nepal, we tried each day to see Mt. Everest. But each day we failed. **Clouds defeated us!** The summit never emerged from a heavy overcast.

Also, using exclamation points too frequently suggests an exaggerated sense of urgency.

NO Mountain climbing can be dangerous. You must know correct procedures! You must have the proper equipment! Otherwise, you could die!

YES Mountain climbing can be dangerous. You must know correct procedures. You must have the proper equipment. Otherwise, you could die!

Never use (!) to communicate amazement or sarcasm. Choose words to deliver your message.

NO At 29,035 feet (!), Mt. Everest is the world's highest mountain. Yet, Chris (!) wants to climb it.

YES At **a majestic** 29,035 feet, Mt. Everest is the world's highest mountain. Yet, Chris, **amazingly,** wants to climb it.

EXERCISE 23-1 Insert any needed periods, question marks, and exclamation points and delete any unneeded ones. For help, consult all sections of this chapter.

EXAMPLE Dr Madan Kataria, who calls himself the Giggling Guru (!), established the world's first laughter club in 1995.

Dr. Madan Kataria, who calls himself the Giggling Guru, established the world's first laughter club in 1995.

1. More than 1,000 (?) laughter clubs exist throughout the world, each seeking to promote health by reducing stress and strengthening the immune system!

2. Dr Madan Kataria, a physician in Bombay, India, developed a yoga-like (!) strategy based on group (!) laughter and then set up laughter clubs.

3. Laughter clubs say, "Yes!" when asked, "Is laughter the best medicine."

4. The clubs' activities include breathing and stretching exercises and playful (?) behaviors, such as performing the opera laugh (!), the chicken laugh (!), and the "Ho-Ho, Ha-Ha" (?) exercise.

5. According to the German psychologist Dr Michael Titze, "In the 1950s people used to laugh eighteen minutes a day (!), but today we laugh not more than six (?) minutes per day, despite huge rises in the standard of living."

EXERCISE 23-2 Insert needed periods, question marks, and exclamation points. For help, consult all sections of this chapter.

Weather experts refer to a rise in surface temperature of the Pacific Ocean as El Niño, but La Niña refers to a drop in ocean temperature What effects can these changes cause In the spring of 1998, the cold water of La Niña surfaced quickly and produced chaotic and destructive weather In the American Northeast, rainfall amounts for June were three times above normal But no one expected the strangest consequence: snow in June Can you imagine waking up on an early summer morning in New England to snow Throughout the summer, most New England states failed to experience a single heat wave, which requires more than three days of 90 degree weather During that winter, the Great Lakes experienced record warmth, but California suffered from disastrously cold air A citrus freeze caused $600 million of damage That's more than half a billion dollars

For more help with your writing, grammar, and research, go to **www.mycomplab.com**

Commas

24a What is the role of the comma?

Commas are the most frequently used marks of punctuation, occurring twice as often as all other punctuation marks combined. A comma must be used in certain places, it must not be used in other places, and it's optional in still other places. This chapter helps you sort through the various rules.

For quick access to most answers when you have a comma question, consult Quick Reference 24.1. The sections in parentheses indicate where you can find fuller explanations.

Quick Reference 24.1

Key uses of commas

**COMMAS WITH COORDINATING CONJUNCTIONS
LINKING INDEPENDENT CLAUSES (24b)**

Postcards are ideal for brief greetings, **and** they can also be miniature works of art. [*and* is a coordinating conjunction]

COMMAS AFTER INTRODUCTORY ELEMENTS (24c)

Although most postcards cost only a quarter, one recently sold for thousands of dollars. [clause]

On postcard racks, several designs are usually available. [phrase]

For example, animals are timeless favorites. [transitional expression]

However, most cards show local landmarks. [word]

COMMAS WITH ITEMS IN A SERIES (24d)

Places, paintings, and people appear on postcards. [*and* between last two items]

Places, paintings, people, animals occupy dozens of display racks. [no *and* between last two items]

COMMAS WITH COORDINATE ADJECTIVES (24e)

Some postcards feature **appealing, dramatic** scenes.

NO COMMAS WITH CUMULATIVE ADJECTIVES (24e)

Other postcards feature **famous historical** scenes.

COMMAS WITH NONRESTRICTIVE ELEMENTS (24f)

Four years after the first postcard appeared, the US government began to issue prestamped postcards. [nonrestrictive element introduces independent clause]

The Golden Age of postcards, **which lasted from about 1900 to 1929,** yielded many especially valuable cards. [nonrestrictive element interrupts independent clause]

Collectors attend postcard shows, **which are similar to baseball-card shows.** [nonrestrictive element ends independent clause]

NO COMMAS WITH RESTRICTIVE ELEMENTS (24f)

Collectors **who attend these shows** may specialize in a particular kind of postcard. [restrictive clause]

continued >>

Quick Reference 24.1   (continued)

COMMAS WITH QUOTED WORDS (24h)

One collector told me, "Attending a show is like digging for buried treasure." [quoted words at end of sentence]

"I always expect to find a priceless postcard," he said. [quoted words at start of sentence]

"Everyone there," he joked, "believes a million-dollar card is hidden in the next stack." [quoted words interrupted mid-sentence]

24b How do commas work with coordinating conjunctions?

Never use a comma when a coordinating conjunction links only two words, two PHRASES, or two DEPENDENT CLAUSES.

NO   Habitat for Humanity depends on volunteers for **labor, and donations** to help with its construction projects. [*Labor* and *donations* are two words; the conjunction explains their relationship. No comma is needed.]

YES   Habitat for Humanity depends on volunteers for **labor and donations** to help with its construction projects.

NO   Each language has **a beauty of its own, and forms of expression** that are duplicated nowhere else. [*A beauty of its own* and *forms of expression* are only two phrases.]

YES   Each language has **a beauty of its own and forms of expression** that are duplicated nowhere else.

—Margaret Mead, "Unispeak"

Do use a comma when a coordinating conjunction links two or more INDEPENDENT CLAUSES. Place the comma before the coordinating conjunction.

The sky turned dark gray, **and** the wind died suddenly.

The November morning had just begun, **but** it looked like dusk.

Shopkeepers closed their stores early, **for** they wanted to get home.

Soon high winds would start, **or** thick snow would begin silently.

Farmers could not continue harvesting, **nor** could they round up their animals in distant fields.

People on the road tried to reach safety, **yet** a few unlucky ones were stranded.

The firehouse whistle blew four times, **so** everyone knew a blizzard was closing in.

Exceptions

- When two independent clauses are very short and they contrast with each other, you can link them with a comma without using a coordinating conjunction: *Mosquitoes don't bite, they stab.* Some instructors consider this an error, so in ACADEMIC WRITING, you'll never be wrong if you use a period or semicolon (Chapter 25) instead of a comma.

- When one or both independent clauses linked by a coordinating conjunction happen to contain other commas, dropping the coordinating conjunction and using a semicolon instead of the comma can help clarify meaning.

  > With temperatures below freezing, the snow did not melt; and people wondered, gazing at the white landscape, when they would see grass again.

Alerts: (1) Never put a comma *after* a coordinating conjunction that joins independent clauses.

 NO   A house is renovated in two weeks **but,** an apartment takes a week.

 YES   A house is renovated in two weeks, **but** an apartment takes a week.

(2) Never use a comma alone between independent clauses, or you'll create the error known as a COMMA SPLICE (see Chapter 20).

 NO   Five inches of snow fell in two hours, driving was hazardous.

 YES   Five inches of snow fell in two hours, **and** driving was hazardous. ●

EXERCISE 24-1
Working individually or in a group, combine each pair of sentences using the coordinating conjunction shown in parentheses. Rearrange words when necessary. For help, consult 24b.

EXAMPLE   Children spend less time playing outdoors than ever before. That has been found to be a significant problem. (and)

   Children spend less time playing outdoors than ever before, **and** that has been found to be a significant problem.

1. If your parents ever said to you, "Go outside and burn off some energy," you should thank them. They did you a big favor. (for)

2. Spending time outside as children is good for people. Now there is scientific proof. (and)

3. As children play outside, their senses are stimulated. That helps them learn in numerous ways. (and)

4. For example, children's vision is fully stimulated by being outside. They should spend more time playing outdoors than reading or watching TV, which stimulates only a narrow part of their vision. (so)

5. When children spend time playing outside, they may engage in intense physical activity. They may be less active but still discover the magic of the natural world. (or)

6. The outdoors can be a child's greatest source of stimulation. Many parents don't realize this. (yet)

7. Sadly enough, recess at many schools has been reduced. Children miss out on an opportunity for what scientists now know is another form of education. (so)

8. But as people learn more about the many benefits of outdoor play for children, parents will not allow children to spend so much time on indoor activities. Schools will not continue to reduce recess time. (nor)

9. Instead, school leaders may heed renowned educators such as Maria Montessori, Rudolf Steiner, and Howard Gardner, who understood the close connection between movement and learning. Children will once again enjoy the benefits of a longer recess. (and)

10. Enjoying the natural world may be part of our genetic makeup. It only makes sense that children should be encouraged to get their vitamin D from sunlight and to use up some energy. (so)

24c   How do commas work with introductory clauses, phrases, and words?

A comma follows any introductory element that comes before an INDEPENDENT CLAUSE. An introductory element can be a CLAUSE, PHRASE, or words. Because these elements are not sentences by themselves, you need to join them to independent clauses.

When the topic is dieting, many people say sugar craving is their worst problem. [introductory dependent clause]

Between 1544 and 1689, sugar refineries appeared in London and New York. [introductory prepositional phrase]

Beginning in infancy, we develop lifelong tastes for sweet foods. [introductory participial phrase]

Sweets being a temptation for many adults, most parents avoid commercial baby foods that contain sugar. [introductory absolute phrase]

For example, fructose comes from fruit, but it's still sugar. [introductory transitional expression]

Nevertheless, many people think fructose isn't harmful. [introductory conjunctive adverb]

To satisfy a craving for ice cream, even timid people sometimes brave midnight streets. [introductory infinitive phrase]

EXCEPTION

When an introductory element is short, and the sentence can be understood easily, some writers omit the comma. However, in ACADEMIC WRITING, you'll never be wrong if you use the comma.

    YES   In 1992, the Americans with Disabilities Act was passed. [preferred]

    YES   In 1992 the Americans with Disabilities Act was passed.

An **interjection** is an introductory word that conveys surprise or other emotions. Use a comma after an interjection at the beginning of a sentence: *Oh, we didn't realize that you're allergic to cats. Yes, your sneezing worries me.*

Alert: Use a comma before and after a transitional expression that falls in the middle of a sentence. When the transitional expression starts a sentence, follow it with a comma. When the transitional expression ends a sentence, put a comma before it.

By the way, the parade begins at noon. [introductory transitional expression with comma after it]

The parade**, by the way,** begins at noon. [transitional expression with comma before and after it, in middle of sentence]

The parade begins at noon**, by the way.** [transitional expression with comma before it, at end of sentence]

However, our float isn't finished. [introductory conjunctive adverb with comma after it]

Our float**, however,** isn't finished. [conjunctive adverb with comma before and after it, in middle of sentence]

Our float isn't finished**, however.** [conjunctive adverb with comma before it, at end of sentence]

EXERCISE 24-2

Working individually or with a group, combine each set of sentences into one sentence according to the direction in parentheses. Use a comma after the introductory element. You can add, delete, and rearrange words as needed. For help, consult 24c.

EXAMPLE People have known that humor is good for them. They have known this for a long time. (Begin with *for a long time*.)

For a long time, people have known that humor is good for them.

1. People laugh. Scientists study them to find out what actually happens. (Begin with *when*.)
2. Scientists track our physiological reactions. They discover the chemicals we produce while we are laughing. (Begin with *in fact*.)
3. Our brains use dopamine when we laugh. Dopamine is a chemical we produce that makes us feel good. (Begin with *produced*.)
4. We sometimes activate our tear ducts by laughing. That reduces stress. (Begin with *interestingly*.)
5. Scientists tested people's saliva immediately after they laughed. Scientists concluded that immune systems may benefit from laughter. (Begin with *immediately*.)
6. Blood pressure and heart rates tend to go below baseline after we laugh. People should be happy about this effect because that's what happens after we exercise well. (Begin with *although*.)
7. Laughter causes the inner lining of our blood vessels to expand. This expansion produces good chemicals in our bodies. (Begin with *in addition*.)
8. One of these good chemicals is nitric oxide. It reduces inflammation and clotting. (Begin with *in the human body*.)
9. Laughter may even help with pain management. Laughter seems to have an analgesic effect. (Begin with *seeming*.)
10. Humor has so many physical benefits, and it makes us feel better. Try to enjoy a few laughs every day. (Begin with *because*.)

24d How do commas work with items in a series?

A **series** is a group of three or more elements—words, PHRASES, or CLAUSES— that match in grammatical form and are of equal importance in a sentence.

Marriage requires **sexual, financial, and emotional** discipline.

—Anne Roiphe, "Why Marriages Fail"

Culture is a way of **thinking, feeling, believing**.

—Clyde Kluckhohn, *Mirror for Man*

My love of flying goes back to those early days **of roller skates, of swings, and of bicycles.**

—Tresa Wiggins, student

We have been taught **that children develop by ages and stages, that the steps are pretty much the same for everybody, and that to grow out of the limited behavior of childhood, we must climb them all.**

—Gail Sheehy, *Passages*

Many general publications omit the comma between the next to last item of a series and the coordinating conjunction. Recently, practice is changing even in ACADEMIC WRITING, which means that some instructors require the use of a comma here and others consider it an error. Check with your instructor.

NO The sweater comes in **blue, green, pink and black.** [Do the sweaters come in three or four colors?]

YES The sweater comes in **blue, green, pink, and black.** [The comma before *and* clarifies that the sweaters come in four colors.]

At all times, however, follow the "toast, juice, and ham and eggs" rule. That is, when one of the items in a series contains *and,* don't use a comma in that item.

When items in a series contain commas or other punctuation, separate them with SEMICOLONS instead of commas (25e).

If it's a bakery, they have to sell cake; if it's a photography shop, they have to develop film; and if it's a dry-goods store, they have to sell warm underwear.

—Art Buchwald, "Birth Control for Banks"

Numbered or lettered lists within a sentence are considered items in a series. With three or more items, use commas (or semicolons if the items themselves contain commas) to separate them.

To file your insurance claim, please enclose (1) a letter requesting payment, (2) a police report about the robbery, **and** (3) proof of purchase of the items you say are missing.

🛑 **Alert:** In a series, never use a comma before the first item or after the last item, unless a different rule makes it necessary.

NO Many **artists, writers, and composers, have indulged** in daydreaming.

YES Many artists, writers, and composers have indulged in daydreaming.

NO Such dreamers include, Miró, Debussy, Dostoevsky, and Dickinson.

YES Such dreamers include Miró, Debussy, Dostoevsky, and Dickinson.

YES Such dreamers include**, of course,** Miró, Debussy, Dostoevsky, and Dickinson. [As a transitional expression, *of course* is set off from the rest of the sentence by commas before and after it (24c).] ●

EXERCISE 24-3 Insert commas to separate the items in a series. If a sentence needs no commas, explain why. For help, consult 24d.

EXAMPLE Families from New York New Jersey and Pennsylvania raise the puppies that become Seeing Eye dogs.

Families from *New York*, *New Jersey*, *and Pennsylvania* raise the puppies that become Seeing Eye dogs.

1. To socialize future Seeing Eye dogs, families with children ages 9 to 14 care for specially bred German shepherds retrievers and mixed-breed puppies for up to 16 months.

2. One youngster in each family becomes the pup's primary caretaker and is responsible for feeding training and grooming the future Seeing Eye dog.

3. While living with their families, the pups learn basic obedience commands, such as sit stay come and down.

4. Groups of families get together frequently to take their Seeing Eye dogs-in-training on outings, so that the puppies become familiar with things that frighten some dogs, such as riding in cars being in crowds walking on slippery floors and hearing loud noises.

5. When the puppies grow up, the families have the pain of giving them up but the satisfaction of knowing that their dogs will lead happy and productive lives while improving the quality of life for their future owners.

24e How do commas work with coordinate adjectives?

Coordinate adjectives are two or more ADJECTIVES of equal weight that describe—that is, modify—a NOUN. In contrast, **cumulative adjectives** build meaning from word to word, as they move toward the noun. The key to applying this rule is recognizing when adjectives are coordinate and when they aren't. Quick Reference 24.2 tells you how.

The audience cheered when the **pulsating, rhythmic** music filled the stadium. [*Pulsating* and *rhythmic* are coordinate adjectives.]

Each band had a **distinctive musical** style. [*Distinctive* and *musical* aren't coordinate adjectives.]

Quick Reference 24.2

Tests for coordinate and cumulative adjectives

If either one of these tests works, the adjectives are coordinate and require a comma between them.

- Can the order of the adjectives be reversed without changing the meaning or creating nonsense? If yes, use a comma.

  NO The concert featured **new several** bands. [*New several* makes no sense.]

  YES The **huge, restless** crowd waited for the concert to begin. [*Restless, huge* still carries the same meaning, so these are coordinate adjectives.]

- Can *and* be sensibly inserted between the adjectives? If yes, use a comma.

  NO The concert featured **several and new** bands. [*Several and new* makes no sense.]

  YES The **huge and restless** crowd waited. [Modifier *huge and restless* makes sense, so these are coordinate adjectives.]

! **Alert:** Don't put a comma between a final coordinate adjective and the noun it modifies.

　　NO Hundreds of **roaring, cheering, yelling, fans** filled the stadium.

　　YES Hundreds of **roaring, cheering, yelling fans** filled the stadium. ●

EXERCISE 24-4   Insert commas to separate coordinate adjectives. If a sentence needs no commas, explain why. For help, consult 24e.

EXAMPLE　Only corn grown for popcorn pops consistently because all other kinds of corn lack tough enamel-like shells.

　　　　　　Only corn grown for popcorn pops consistently because all other kinds of corn lack *tough, enamel-like* shells.

1. The outside of an unpopped popcorn kernel is a hard plastic-like coating.

2. Inside an unpopped kernel is a soft starchy substance combined with water.

3. Applying heat causes the water molecules to expand until the pressure pops the dark yellow kernel.

4. The popped kernel turns itself inside out and absorbs air into its white pulpy matter.

5. The thinner softer shells of nonpopcorn corn don't allow water to heat to the high popping temperature.

24f How do commas work with nonrestrictive elements?

A **restrictive element** contains information (a descriptive word, clause, or phrase) that's essential for a sentence to deliver its message; thus, it is often called an *essential element*. A **nonrestrictive element** contains information that's not essential for a sentence to deliver its meaning, and therefore, it is often called a *nonessential element*. The key is in recognizing what's essential (restrictive) and what's nonessential (nonrestrictive) in a sentence. Quick Reference 24.3 defines and explains the differences in the meanings of these terms.

Quick Reference 24.3

■ ■ ■ ■ ■ ■ ■

Restrictive and nonrestrictive defined

RESTRICTIVE

A restrictive element contains information essential for the sentence to deliver its message. By being essential, the words in the element limit—that is, "restrict"—the meaning in some way. Don't use commas with restrictive elements.

> Many US states retest drivers **who are over sixty-five** to check their driving competency.

The information *who are over sixty-five* is essential to understanding the sentence because it limits or restricts the meaning of *drivers* to only those over the age of sixty-five. Drivers *under* sixty-five are not included. To check whether an element is essential, drop it and read the sentence. If the meaning of the sentence changes, then the information element is essential in delivering the message intended in the sentence. This means the element is restrictive (essential), and commas are not used.

NONRESTRICTIVE

A nonrestrictive element contains information that's *not* essential for the sentence to deliver its message. By being nonessential, the words in the element don't limit—or "restrict"—the meaning. Use commas with nonrestrictive (nonessential) elements.

> My parents**, who are both over sixty-five,** took a defensive-driving course.

The information *who are both over sixty-five* is not essential because the words *my parents* carry the sentence's message so that we know who took a defensive driving course. (Information about their age is "extra" to this message, so commas are required.)

Quick Reference 24.4 shows the pattern for comma use with nonrestrictive elements. The pattern for restrictive elements calls for no commas.

Commas with nonrestrictive elements

Nonrestrictive element, independent clause.

Beginning of independent clause, nonrestrictive element, end of independent clause.

Independent clause, nonrestrictive element.

Restrictive and nonrestrictive elements can fall at the beginning, in the middle, or at the end of a sentence. To test whether an element is nonrestrictive, read the sentence without the element. If the meaning of the sentence does not change, the element is nonrestrictive.

MORE EXAMPLES OF RESTRICTIVE ELEMENTS

Some people **in my neighborhood** enjoy jogging. [The reader needs the information *in my neighborhood* to know which people enjoy jogging. The information is essential, so no commas are used.]

Some people **who are in excellent physical condition** enjoy jogging. [The reader needs the information *who are in excellent physical condition* to know which people enjoy jogging. The information is essential, so no commas are used.]

The agricultural scientist **Wendy Singh** has developed a new fertilization technique. [*Wendy Singh* is essential to identify exactly which agricultural scientist developed the new technique, so no commas are used.]

MORE EXAMPLES OF NONRESTRICTIVE ELEMENTS

An energetic person, Anna Hom enjoys jogging. [Without knowing that Anna Hom is *an energetic person,* the reader can understand that she enjoys jogging. The information is nonessential, so a comma is used.]

Anna Hom**, who is in excellent physical condition,** enjoys jogging. [Without knowing Anna Hom's *physical condition,* the reader can understand that Anna Hom enjoys jogging. The information is nonessential, so commas are used.]

Anna Hom enjoys jogging**, which is also Adam's favorite pastime.** [Without knowing about *Adam's favorite pastime,* the reader can understand that Anna Hom enjoys jogging. The information is nonessential, so commas are used.]

The agricultural scientist**, a new breed of farmer,** explains how to control a farming environment. [Without knowing that the scientist is *a new breed of farmer,* the reader can understand that the agricultural scientist explains how to control a farming environment. The information is nonessential, so commas are used.]

EXERCISE 24-5   Using your knowledge of restrictive and nonrestrictive elements, insert commas as needed. If a sentence is correct, explain why. For help, consult 24f.

EXAMPLE   During the summer when butterflies are most active gardeners can attract them by planting the right flowers.

During the summer, when butterflies are most active, gardeners can attract them by planting the right flowers.

1. In spring as birds and bees look for water and food certain plants and trees provide those needs and thus attract the greatest number of airborne visitors.

2. Gardeners who learn to attract birds may find they have fewer problems with insects and other unwelcome pests.

3. During suburban sprawl when cities eat up more and more land birds have to adapt by putting their nests in buildings.

4. Birds are attracted to pines and evergreens where they can find food and shelter.

5. Hungry birds who are not picky will enjoy a feeder stocked with black oil sunflower seeds.

6. Birds also need to eat insects which provide a higher protein content than seeds.

7. Some common plants such as butterfly weed and lantana are ideal for attracting butterflies.

8. Because they have the nectar that butterflies want these plants enhance any butterfly garden.

9. As butterflies pass by a garden looking for bright colors and strong fragrances they will notice flowers planted in large clumps.

10. Gardens that are favorable to birds and butterflies will also invite honeybees and other pollinators.

24g How do commas set off parenthetical expressions, contrasts, words of direct address, and tag sentences?

Parenthetical expressions are "asides." They add information but aren't necessary for understanding the message of a sentence. Set them off with parentheses or commas.

American farmers **(according to US government figures)** export more wheat than they sell at home.

A major drought, **sad to say,** wiped out this year's wheat crop.

Expressions of **contrast** state what is *not* the case. Set them off with commas.

Feeding the world's population is a serious**, though not impossible,** problem.

We must work against world hunger continuously**, not only when famines strike.**

Words of **direct address** name the person or group being spoken to (addressed). Set them off with commas.

Join me**, brothers and sisters,** to end hunger.

Your contribution to the Relief Fund**, Steve,** will help us greatly.

A **tag sentence** is a normal sentence that ends with a "tag," an attached phrase or question. Set off a tag with a comma. When the tag is a question, the sentence ends with a question mark. This holds whether or not the **tag question** is formed with a CONTRACTION.

People will give blood regularly**, I hope.**

The response to the blood drive was impressive**, wasn't it?**

EXERCISE 24-6   Add commas to set off any parenthetical or contrasting elements, words of direct address, and tag sentences. Adjust end punctuation as necessary. For help, consult 24g.

EXAMPLE   Writer's block it seems to me is a misunderstood phenomenon.

　　　　　Writer's block*, it seems to me,* is a misunderstood phenomenon.

1. An inability to write some say stems from lack of discipline and a tendency to procrastinate.

2. In other words the only way to overcome writer's block is to exert more willpower.

3. But writer's block is a complex psychological event that happens to conscientious people not just procrastinators.

4. Such people strangely enough are often unconsciously rebelling against their own self-tyranny and rigid standards of perfection.

5. If I told you my fellow writer that all it takes to start writing again is to quit punishing yourself, you would think I was crazy wouldn't you?

24h　How do commas work with quoted words?

Explanatory words are *said, stated, declared,* and other words that introduce DIRECT DISCOURSE. When they fall in the same sentence, quoted words are set off from explanatory words.

Speaking of ideal love, the poet William Blake wrote, "Love seeketh not itself to please."

"My love is a fever," said William Shakespeare about love's passion.

"I love no love," proclaimed the poet Mary Coleridge, "but thee."

EXCEPTION

When the quoted words are blended into the grammatical structure of your sentence, don't use commas to set them off. These are instances of INDIRECT DIS-COURSE, usually occurring with *as* and *that*.

The duke describes the duchess **as** "too soon made glad."

The duchess insists **that** "appearing glad often is but a deception."

Alert: When the quoted words end with an exclamation point or a question mark, retain that original punctuation, even if explanatory words follow.

QUOTED WORDS	*"O Romeo! Romeo!"*
NO	"O Romeo! Romeo**!,**" whispered Juliet from her window.
NO	"O Romeo! Romeo**,**" whispered Juliet from her window.
YES	"O Romeo! Romeo**!**" whispered Juliet from her window.

QUOTED WORDS	*"Wherefore art thou Romeo?"*
NO	"Wherefore art thou Romeo**?,**" Juliet urgently asked.
NO	"Wherefore art thou Romeo**,**" Juliet urgently asked.
YES	"Wherefore art thou Romeo**?**" Juliet urgently asked.

EXERCISE 24-7   Punctuate the following dialogue correctly. If a sentence is correct, explain why. For help, consult 24h.

EXAMPLE   "Can you tell me just one thing?," asked the tourist.

"Can you tell me just one thing**?"** asked the tourist.

1. "I'm happy to answer any questions you have" said the rancher to the tourist.

2. "Well, then" said the tourist "I'd like to know how you make ends meet on such a tiny ranch."

3. "Do you see that man leaning against the shed over there?" asked the rancher.

4. The rancher continued "He works for me, but I don't pay him any money. Instead, I have promised him that after two years of work, he will own the ranch."

5. "Then, I'll work for him, and in two more years, the ranch will be mine again!," said the rancher with a smile.

24i How do commas work in dates, names, addresses, correspondence, and numbers?

When you write dates, names, addresses, correspondence, and numbers, use commas according to accepted practice. Quick References 24.5 through 24.8 provide some guidelines.

Quick Reference 24.5 ■ ■ ■ ■ ■ ■ ■

Commas with dates

- Use a comma between the date and the year: *July 20, 1969.*
- Use a comma between the day and the date: *Sunday, July 20.*
- Within a sentence, use a comma on both sides of the year in a full date: *Everyone planned to be near a TV set on July 20, 1969, to watch the lunar landing.*
- Never use a comma when only the month and year, or the month and day, are given. Also, never use a comma between the season and year.

  YES   People knew that one day in **July 1969** would change the world.

  YES   News coverage was especially heavy on **July 21.**

  YES   In **summer 1969** a man walked on the moon.

- Never use a comma in an inverted date, a form used in the US military and throughout the world except in the United States.

  YES   People stayed near their televisions on **20 July 1969** to watch the lunar landing.

Quick Reference 24.6 ■ ■ ■ ■ ■ ■ ■

Commas with names, places, and addresses

- When an abbreviated academic degree (*MD, PhD*) comes after a person's name, use a comma between the name and the title (*Angie Eng, MD*), and also after the title if other words follow in the sentence: *The jury listened closely to the expert testimony of **Angie Eng, MD, last week.***

continued >>

Quick Reference 24.6   (continued)

- When an indicator of birth order or succession (*Jr., Sr., III, IV*) follows a name, never use a comma: *Martin Luther **King Jr.*** or *Henry **Ford II***
- When you invert a person's name, use a comma to separate the last name from the first: ***Troyka, David***
- When city and state names are written together, use a comma to separate them: ***Philadelphia, Pennsylvania.*** If the city and state fall within a sentence, use a comma after the state as well: *My family settled in **Philadelphia, Pennsylvania,** before I was born.*
- When a complete address is part of a sentence, use a comma to separate all the items, except the state and ZIP code: *I wrote to **Shelly Kupperman, 1001 Rule Road, Upper Saddle River, NJ 07458,** for more information about the comma.*

Quick Reference 24.7

Commas in correspondence

- For the opening of an informal letter, use a comma: **Dear Betty,**
- For the opening of a business or formal letter, use a colon:
  Dear Ms. Kiviat:
- For the close of a letter, use a comma:
  Sincerely yours,   **Best regards,**   **Love,**

Quick Reference 24.8

Commas with numbers

- Counting from right to left, put a comma after every three digits in numbers with more than four digits.
  72,867   156,567,066
- A comma is optional in most four-digit numbers. Be consistent within each piece of writing.
  $1776 $1,776
  1776 miles   1,776 miles
  1776 potatoes   1,776 potatoes

continued >>

Quick Reference 24.8 (continued)

- Never use a comma in a four-digit year: **1990** (*Note:* If the year has five digits or more, do use a comma: **25,000 BC.**)
- Never use a comma in an address of four digits or more: *12161 Dean Drive*
- Never use a comma in a page number of four digits or more: *see page 1338*
- Use a comma to separate related measurements written as words: *five feet, four inches*
- Use a comma to separate a scene from an act in a play: *act II, scene iv* (or *act 2, scene 4*)
- Use a comma to separate references to a page and a line: *page 10, line 6*

EXERCISE 24-8 Insert commas where they are needed. For help, consult 24i.

EXAMPLE On June 1 1984 the small German-French production company released a feature film called *Paris Texas*.

On June 1, 1984, the small German-French production company released a feature film called *Paris, Texas*.

1. Made by the noted German director Wim Wenders, *Paris Texas* was set in an actual town in Lamar County Texas with a population of 24699.

2. The movie's title was clearly intended to play off the slightly more famous Paris in France.

3. The custom of naming little towns in the United States after cosmopolitan urban centers in the Old World has resulted in such places as Athens Georgia and St. Petersburg Florida.

4. As of December 1 2005 the American St. Petersburg was estimated to have nearly 250000 citizens and the American Athens nearly 109000.

5. By comparison, St. Petersburg Russia and Athens Greece were estimated to have populations of 4 million and 1 million, respectively.

24j How do commas clarify meaning?

A comma is sometimes needed to clarify the meaning of a sentence, even though no rule calls for one. The best solution is to revise the sentence.

NO   Of the gymnastic team's twenty five were injured.

YES   Of the gymnastic team's **twenty, five** were injured.

YES   Of **twenty on** the gymnastic team, five were injured. [preferred]

NO	Those who can practice many hours a day.
YES	**Those who can,** practice many hours a day.
YES	**They** practice many hours a day **when they can.** [preferred]
NO	George dressed and performed for the sellout crowd.
YES	**George dressed,** and performed for the sellout crowd.
YES	**After** George dressed, **he** performed for the sellout crowd. [preferred]

EXERCISE 24-9   Working individually or with a group, insert commas to prevent misreading. For help, consult 24j.

EXAMPLE   For scientists tracking and measuring hurricanes is still an inexact science.

For scientists, tracking and measuring hurricanes is still an inexact science.

1. Lasting for thirteen days in August 1992 Hurricane Andrew after 2005's Katrina was the second most expensive hurricane.

2. Andrew was rated a category four smaller than 2005's Katrina when it made landfall in south Florida.

3. The highest gust officially recorded 164 miles per hour at 130 feet above the ground occurred before Andrew shut down the National Hurricane Center's measuring devices.

4. The thousands of vortexes within Andrew as with many high-intensity storms are what caused the worst damage.

5. Andrew difficult to measure accurately was upgraded from a category four to a category five hurricane ten years after it occurred.

24k   How can I avoid misusing commas?

Throughout this chapter, Alert notes remind you about comma misuses as they relate to each comma rule. Most of these misuses are overuses—inserting a comma where one is unnecessary. This section summarizes the Alert notes and lists other frequent misuses of the comma.

When advice against overusing a comma clashes with a rule requiring one, follow the rule that requires the comma.

The town of Kitty Hawk, North Carolina, attracts thousands of tourists each year. [Even though the comma after *North Carolina* separates the subject and its verb (which it normally shouldn't), the comma is required here because of the rule that calls for a comma when the name of a state follows the name of a city within a sentence (24i).]

24k.1 Commas with coordinating conjunctions

Never use a comma after a COORDINATING CONJUNCTION that joins two INDEPENDENT CLAUSES, unless another rule makes it necessary (24b). Also, don't use a comma to separate two items joined with a coordinating conjunction—there must be at least three (24d).

NO   The sky was dark gray **and,** it looked like dusk.

YES   The sky was dark gray**,** and it looked like dusk.

NO   **The moon, and the stars** were shining last night.

YES   **The moon and the stars** were shining last night.

24k.2 Commas with subordinating conjunctions and prepositions

Never put a comma after a SUBORDINATING CONJUNCTION or a PREPOSITION, unless another rule makes it necessary.

NO   **Although,** the storm brought high winds, it did no damage.

YES   **Although the storm brought high winds,** it did no damage. [comma follows full subordinated dependent clause, not the subordinate conjunction that begins it]

NO   The storm did no damage **although,** it brought high winds.

YES   The storm did no damage **although it brought high winds.** [no comma after a subordinating conjunction]

NO   People expected worse **between,** the high winds and the heavy downpour.

YES   People expected worse **between the high winds and the heavy downpour.** [preposition begins sentence element that needs no comma before or after]

24k.3 Commas in a series

Never use a comma before the first, or after the last, item in a series, unless another rule makes it necessary (24d).

NO   The gymnasium was decorated **with, red, white, and blue** ribbons for the Fourth of July.

NO   The gymnasium was decorated with **red, white, and blue, ribbons** for the Fourth of July.

YES   The gymnasium was decorated with **red, white, and blue** ribbons for the Fourth of July.

Never put a comma between a final COORDINATE ADJECTIVE and the NOUN that the adjectives modify. Also, don't use a comma between adjectives that are not coordinate (24e).

NO He wore an **old, baggy, sweater.**

YES He wore an **old, baggy sweater.** [coordinate adjectives]

NO He has **several, new sweaters.**

YES He has **several new sweaters.** [noncoordinate, or cumulative, adjectives]

24k.4 Commas with restrictive elements

Never use a comma to set off a RESTRICTIVE (essential) element from the rest of a sentence (24f).

NO **Vegetables, stir-fried in a wok,** are crisp and flavorful. [The words *stir-fried in a wok* are essential, so they are not set off with commas.]

YES **Vegetables stir-fried in a wok** are crisp and flavorful.

24k.5 Commas with quotations

Never use a comma to set off INDIRECT DISCOURSE; use a comma only with DIRECT DISCOURSE (24h).

NO Jon said **that, he likes** stir-fried vegetables.

YES Jon said **that he likes** stir-fried vegetables.

YES **Jon said,** "I like stir-fried vegetables."

24k.6 Commas that separate a subject from its verb, a verb from its object, or a preposition from its object

A comma does not make sense between these elements, though in some cases another comma rule might supersede this guideline (as in the first example in section 24k).

NO **The brothers Wright, made** their first successful airplane flights on December 17, 1903. [As a rule, a comma doesn't separate a subject from its verb.]

YES **The brothers Wright made** their first successful airplane flights on December 17, 1903.

NO These inventors enthusiastically **tackled, the problems** of powered flight and aerodynamics. [As a rule, a comma doesn't separate a verb from its object.]

YES These inventors enthusiastically **tackled the problems** of powered flight and aerodynamics.

NO Airplane hobbyists **from, all over the world** visit Kitty Hawk's flight museum. [As a rule, a comma doesn't separate a preposition from its object.]

YES Airplane hobbyists **from all over the world** visit Kitty Hawk's flight museum.

EXERCISE 24-10 Some commas have been deliberately misused in these sentences. Delete misused commas. If a sentence is correct, explain why. For help, consult all parts of this chapter, especially 24j and 24k.

EXAMPLE The Harlem Renaissance was a cultural and artistic movement, that began around 1919 and lasted until the early 1930s.

The Harlem Renaissance was a cultural and artistic movement that began around 1919 and lasted until the early 1930s.

1. Although, this movement is named for Harlem, its impact spread to urban areas throughout the country, and the world.
2. During the Harlem Renaissance, artists in many fields found new ways to express the different facets, of black life in America.
3. The migration of millions of African Americans from the rural South to the urban North in the early twentieth century, helped make the Harlem Renaissance possible.
4. W. E. B. Du Bois played an important role in the Harlem Renaissance, for he edited the magazine, that became the official publication of the NAACP.
5. Furthermore, Du Bois rose to prominence by becoming, the first African American to receive a PhD. from Harvard University.
6. The music, of the Harlem Renaissance, became a vital tool for expressing and celebrating, the culture of those who lived there.
7. In particular, many people listened to jazz after, musicians from the South moved north and began playing it in clubs, theaters, and private homes.
8. The Harlem Renaissance produced diverse, original, writers, and they created everything from plays to poems.
9. For example, Claude McKay wrote novels that those in, literary studies, still study today.
10. The political and cultural gains achieved by African Americans during this time paved, the way for future generations.

24l How can I avoid comma errors?

You can avoid most comma errors with these two bits of advice:

- As you write or reread what you've written, never insert a comma simply because you happen to pause to think or take a breath before moving on.

Pausing isn't a reliable guide for writers, although that myth continues to thrive. Throughout the United States, and indeed the world, people's breathing rhythms, accents, and thinking patterns vary greatly.

- As you're writing, if you're unsure about a comma, insert it and circle the spot. Later, when you're EDITING, check this handbook for the rule that applies.

For more help with your
writing, grammar, and research,
go to **www.mycomplab.com**

25

Semicolons

25a What are the uses of a semicolon?

While a period signals the complete separation of INDEPENDENT CLAUSES, a **semicolon** indicates only a partial ("semi") separation. Use a semicolon in only two situations. A semicolon can replace a period between sentences that are closely related in meaning (25b and 25c). Also, a semicolon belongs between sentence structures that already contain one or more commas (25d) and with certain lists (25e). Quick Reference 25.1 shows different patterns for using semicolons.

25b When can I use a semicolon, instead of a period, between independent clauses?

The choice between a period and a semicolon for separating independent clauses depends on whether your meaning is better communicated by a complete separation (period) or a partial separation (semicolon).

The desert known as Death Valley became a US National Park in 1994; it used to be a US National Monument.

This is my husband's second marriage; it's the first for me.

—Ruth Sidel, "Marion Deluca"

Quick Reference 25.1

Semicolon patterns

- Independent clause; independent clause. [25b]
- Independent clause; conjunctive adverb, independent clause. [25c]
- Independent clause; transitional expression, independent clause. [25c]
- Independent clause, one that contains a comma; coordinating conjunction followed by independent clause. [25d]
- Independent clause; coordinating conjunction followed by independent clause, one that contains a comma. [25d]
- Independent clause, one that contains a comma; coordinating conjunction followed by independent clause, one that contains a comma. [25d]
- Independent clause containing a series of items, any of which contains a comma; another item in the series; and another item in the series. [25e]

🛑 **Alert:** Never use a comma alone between independent clauses—this rule will prevent you from creating the error known as a COMMA SPLICE (Chapter 20). ●

25c When else can I use a semicolon between independent clauses?

When the second of a set of independent clauses closely related in meaning starts with a CONJUNCTIVE ADVERB or with a TRANSITIONAL EXPRESSION, you can choose to separate the clauses with a semicolon instead of a period. Also, insert a comma following a conjunctive adverb or transitional expression that starts an independent clause. Although some professional writers today omit the comma after short words (*then, next, soon*), the rule remains for most ACADEMIC WRITING. Quick Reference 25.1 shows this pattern for using semicolons.

> The average annual rainfall in Death Valley is about two inches; **nevertheless,** hundreds of plant and animal species survive and even thrive there. [conjunctive adverb]

> Photographers have spent years recording desert life cycles; **as a result,** we can watch bare sand flower after a spring storm. [transitional expression]

! **Alert:** Never use only a comma between independent clauses that are connected by a conjunctive adverb or word of transition—this rule will prevent you from creating the error known as a COMMA SPLICE. ●

25d How do semicolons work with coordinating conjunctions?

As a general rule, when INDEPENDENT CLAUSES are linked by a COORDINATING CONJUNCTION, good practice calls for a comma, not a period or semicolon, before the coordinating conjunction (24b). However, when one or more of the independent clauses already contain a comma, link the independent clauses by substituting a semicolon for the period. This can help your reader see the relationship between the ideas more clearly. Quick Reference 25.1 shows the various combinations of this pattern.

> When the peacock has presented his back, the spectator will usually begin to walk around him to get a front view**; but** the peacock will continue to turn so that no front view is possible.
>
> —Flannery O'Connor, "The King of the Birds"

> Our Constitution is in actual operation; everything appears to promise that it will last**; but** in this world, nothing is certain but death and taxes.
>
> —Benjamin Franklin, in a 1789 letter

> For anything worth having, one must pay the price**; and** the price is always work, patience, love, self-sacrifice.
>
> —John Burroughs

25e When should I use semicolons between items in a series?

When a sentence contains a series of items that are long or that already contain one or more commas, separate the items with semicolons. Punctuating this way groups the elements so that your reader can see where one item ends and the next begins. Quick Reference 25.1 shows this pattern.

> The assistant chefs chopped onions, green peppers, and parsley**;** sliced chicken and duck breasts into strips**;** started a broth simmering**; and** filled a large, shallow copper pan with oil.

25f How do I avoid misusing the semicolon?

NOT USING A SEMICOLON AFTER AN INTRODUCTORY PHRASE

If you use a semicolon after an introductory phrase, you create the error known as a sentence fragment (Chapter 19).

NO	**Open until midnight;** the computer lab is well used. [Using a semicolon turns an introductory phrase into a sentence fragment.]
YES	**Open until midnight,** the computer lab is well used.

NOT USING A SEMICOLON WITH A DEPENDENT CLAUSE

If you use a semicolon with a DEPENDENT CLAUSE, you create the error known as a sentence fragment.

NO	**Although the new dorms have computer facilities;** many students still prefer to go to the computer lab. [Using a semicolon turns a dependent clause into a sentence fragment.]
YES	**Although the new dorms have computer facilities,** many students still prefer to go to the computer lab.

NOT USING A SEMICOLON TO INTRODUCE A LIST

When the words that introduce a list form an independent clause, use a colon, never a semicolon (26b).

NO	**The newscast featured three major stories;** the latest pictures of Uranus, a speech by the president, and dangerous brush fires in Nevada. [*The newscast featured three major stories* is an independent clause, so the punctuation before the list should be a colon, not a semicolon.]
YES	**The newscast featured three major stories:** the latest pictures of Uranus, a speech by the president, and dangerous brush fires in Nevada.

EXERCISE 25-1 Insert semicolons as needed in these items. Also, fix any incorrectly used semicolons. If a sentence is correct, explain why. For help, consult all sections of this chapter.

EXAMPLE Bicycle racing is as popular in Europe as baseball or basketball is in the United States, it is even more heavily commercialized.

Bicycle racing is as popular in Europe as baseball or basketball is in the United States; it is even more heavily commercialized.

1. The Tour de France is the world's best-known bicycle race, the 94-year-old Giro d'Italia runs a close second.

2. Both are grueling, three-week-long events that require cyclists to cover over 2,000 miles of difficult, mountainous terrain, and both are eagerly anticipated, draw enormous crowds along their routes, and receive extensive media coverage.

3. That media attention leads to marketing opportunities for the events' sponsors; which place ads along the race's route, in the nearby towns, and on the cyclists themselves.

4. Martin Hvastija, a participant in the 2003 Giro d'Italia, had no chance of winning the race, nevertheless, he drew extensive media attention for his sponsors.

5. His method was simple; he managed to ride out in front of the field for a few brief miles.

6. Although he had no chance of winning the race; newscasters beamed his image around the world during the short time he was a front-runner, during the same period; showing the world the brightly colored advertising logos on his jersey.

7. In addition to sponsoring individual athletes, corporations plaster ads all over the towns that the race goes through, they toss samples, coupons, and gadgets to spectators from promotional vehicles that ride the route an hour ahead of the cyclists, and they run ads during TV and radio coverage of the race.

8. In 2003, the organizers of the Giro took in over $8 million in fees from advertisers and $12 million in broadcast rights from the Italian state-owned TV network, RAI, however, these figures were down a bit from the previous year.

9. An additional source of revenues for race organizers is fees from the towns where the race starts and ends each day, as a result, organizers determine the actual course according to which cities are willing to pay the $120,000 charge.

10. Media watchers think the Giro d'Italia could become even more profitable and popular, especially among young adults, but only if it took a cue from the Tour de France by encouraging; more international press coverage, more star riders, and even heavier corporate sponsorship.

EXERCISE 25-2 Combine each set of sentences into one sentence so that it contains two independent clauses. Use a semicolon correctly between the two clauses. You may add, omit, revise, and rearrange words. Try to use all the patterns in this chapter, and explain the reasoning behind your decisions. More than one revision may be correct. For help, consult all sections of this chapter.

EXAMPLE   Although not as well known as Thomas Edison, the inventor Nikola Tesla was a revolutionary and important scientist. One biographer calls him "the man who invented the twentieth century."

Although not as well known as Thomas Edison, the inventor Nikola Tesla was a revolutionary scientist; one biographer calls him "the man who invented the twentieth century."

1. Tesla was born in what is now Croatia and studied at the Technical University at Graz, Austria. He excelled in physics, mechanical engineering, and electrical engineering.

2. Tesla's accomplishments include inventing alternating current. He also contributed to the fields of robotics, computer science, and wireless

technology. And he helped increase knowledge of nuclear physics, ballistics, and electromagnetism.

3. The Italian inventor Guglielmo Marconi and Tesla both claimed to have invented the radio. However, the US Supreme Court, in 1943, upheld Tesla's radio patent and officially credited him as the device's inventor.

4. In 1901, Tesla began construction of a tower that he claimed would create a global network of wireless communication and be able to control the weather. Unfortunately, Tesla soon lost funding and never finished the project.

5. At his lab in Colorado Springs, he was able to produce artificial lightning. This scene was vividly portrayed in the 2006 film *The Prestige*.

For more help with your
writing, grammar, and research,
go to **www.mycomplab.com**

26

Colons

26a What are the uses of a colon?

A **colon** is a full stop that draws attention to the words that follow. It can be placed only at the end of an INDEPENDENT CLAUSE. A colon introduces a list, an APPOSITIVE, or a QUOTATION. Quick Reference 26.1 shows different patterns for using a colon.

Quick Reference 26.1

Colon patterns

- Independent clause: list. [26b]
- Independent clause: appositive. [26b]
- Independent clause: "Quoted words." [26b]
- Independent clause: Independent clause that explains or summarizes the prior independent clause. [26c]

26b When can a colon introduce a list, an appositive, or a quotation?

When a complete sentence—that is, an INDEPENDENT CLAUSE—introduces a list, an APPOSITIVE, or a QUOTATION, place a colon before the words being introduced. These words don't have to form an independent clause themselves, but a complete sentence before the colon is essential.

INTRODUCING LISTED ITEMS

When a complete sentence introduces a list, a colon is required, as demonstrated in the following example.

> **If you really want to lose weight, you must do three things:** eat smaller portions, exercise, and drink lots of water. [The required independent clause comes before the listed items, so a colon is correct.]

When the lead-in words at the end of an independent clause are *such as, including, like,* or *consists of,* never use a colon. In contrast, if the lead-in words at the end of an independent clause are *the following* or *as follows,* do use a colon.

> **The students demanded improvements *such as*** an expanded menu in the cafeteria, improved janitorial services, and more up-to-date textbooks.

> **The students demanded *the following:*** an expanded menu in the cafeteria, improved janitorial services, and more up-to-date textbooks.

INTRODUCING APPOSITIVES

An APPOSITIVE is a word or words that rename a NOUN or PRONOUN. When an appositive is introduced by an independent clause, use a colon.

> **Only cats are likely to approve of one old-fashioned remedy for cuts:** a lotion of catnip, butter, and sugar. [The required independent clause comes before the appositive: *a lotion of catnip, butter, and sugar* renames *old-fashioned remedy.*]

INTRODUCING QUOTATIONS

When an independent clause introduces a quotation, use a colon after it. (If the words introducing a quotation don't form an independent clause, use a comma.)

> **The little boy in *E.T.* did say something neat:** "How do you explain school to a higher intelligence?" [The required independent clause comes before the quotation.]

> —George F. Will, "Well, I Don't Love You, E.T."

26c When can I use a colon between two independent clauses?

When a second INDEPENDENT CLAUSE explains or summarizes a first independent clause, you can use a colon to separate them. Quick Reference 26.1 shows this pattern for using a colon.

🛑 **Alert:** You can choose to use a capital letter or a lowercase letter for the first word of an independent clause that follows a colon. Whichever you choose, be consistent within a piece of writing. We use a capital letter in this handbook.

> We will never forget the first time we made dinner together: He got stomach poisoning and was too sick to go to work for four days.
>
> —Lisa Baladendrum, student ●

26d What standard formats require a colon?

A variety of standard formats in American English require a colon. Also, colons are used in many DOCUMENTATION STYLES, as shown in Chapters 36, 37, and 38.

TITLE AND SUBTITLE

A Brief History of Time: From the Big Bang to Black Holes

HOURS, MINUTES, AND SECONDS

The plane took off at 7:15 p.m.

The runner passed the halfway point at 1:23:02.

🛑 **Alert:** In the military, hours and minutes are written without colons and with four digits on a 24-hour clock: *The staff meeting originally scheduled for Tuesday at **0930** will be held Tuesday at **1430** instead.* ●

REFERENCES TO BIBLE CHAPTERS AND VERSES

Psalms 23:1–3

Luke 3:13

MEMOS

Date: January 9, 2009
To: Dean Kristen Olivero
From: Professor Daniel Black
Re: Student Work-Study Program

SALUTATION IN A BUSINESS LETTER

Dear Dr. Jewell:

26e When is a colon wrong?

INDEPENDENT CLAUSES

A colon can introduce a list, an APPOSITIVE, or a QUOTATION, but only when an INDEPENDENT CLAUSE does the introducing. Similarly, a colon can be used between two independent clauses when the second summarizes or explains the first. In following these rules, be sure that you're dealing with independent clauses, not other word groups.

> **NO** The cook bought: eggs, milk, cheese, and bread. [*The cook bought* isn't an independent clause.]
>
> **YES** The cook bought eggs, milk, cheese, and bread.

Never use a colon to separate a PHRASE or DEPENDENT CLAUSE from an independent clause. Otherwise, you'll create the error known as a SENTENCE FRAGMENT.

> **NO** Day after day: the drought dragged on. [*Day after day* is a phrase, not an independent clause.]
>
> **YES** Day after day, the drought dragged on.
>
> **NO** After the drought ended: the farmers celebrated. [*After the drought ended* is a dependent clause, not an independent clause.]
>
> **YES** After the drought ended, the farmers celebrated.

LEAD-IN WORDS

Never use a colon after the lead-in words *such as, including, like,* and *consists of.*

> **NO** The health board discussed many problems **such as:** poor water quality, aging sewage treatment systems, and the lack of alternative water supplies. [A colon is incorrect after *such as.*]
>
> **YES** The health board discussed poor water quality, aging sewage treatment systems, and the lack of alternative water supplies. [*Such as* is dropped and the sentence slightly revised so that the colon is not needed.]
>
> **YES** The health board discussed many problems, **such as** poor water quality, an aging sewage treatment system, and the lack of alternative water supplies. [Comma before *such as* tells the reader that the list coming up is nonrestrictive (nonessential)—it illustrates *problems.*]
>
> **YES** The health board discussed many problems: poor water quality, aging sewage treatment systems, and the lack of alternative water supplies. [If *such as* is dropped, a colon after the independent clause is correct.]

EXERCISE 26-1   Insert colons where needed and delete any not needed. If a sentence is correct, explain why. For help, consult all sections of this chapter.

EXAMPLE   The twentieth century saw a flowering of Irish literature, W. B. Yeats, G. B. Shaw, Samuel Beckett, and Seamus Heaney all won the Nobel Prize for Literature.

The twentieth century saw a flowering of Irish literature: W. B. Yeats, G. B. Shaw, Samuel Beckett, and Seamus Heaney all won the Nobel Prize for Literature.

1. People who work the night shift are typically deprived of essential sleep, an average of nine hours a week.

2. The Iroquois of the Great Lakes region lived in fortified villages and cultivated: corn, beans, and squash.

3. Five nations originally formed the Iroquois Confederacy: the Mohawk, the Oneida, the Onondaga, the Cayuga, and the Seneca.

4. Later, these five Iroquois nations were joined by: the Tuscarora.

5. Shouting: "Come back!" Adam watched the vehicle speed down the highway.

6. When a runner breaks through that unavoidable wall of exhaustion, a very different feeling sets in; an intense sense of well-being known as the "runner's high."

7. However: the "runner's high" soon disappears.

8. Two new nations were born on the same day in 1947, India and Pakistan achieved their independence from Britain at midnight on August 15.

9. Date   December 8, 2008
   To   English 101 Instructors
   From   Dean of Instruction
   Re   Classroom Assignments

10. Only a hurricane could have kept Lisa from meeting Nathaniel at 8:00 p.m.; unfortunately, that night a hurricane hit.

11. George's interests were typical of a sixteen-year-old's, cars, music, and dating.

12. Like many people who have never learned to read or write, the woman who told her life story in *Aman; The Story of a Somali Girl* was able to remember an astonishing number of events in precise detail.

27

■ ■ ■ ■ ■ ■

Apostrophes

27a What is the role of the apostrophe?

The **apostrophe** plays four roles in writing: It creates the POSSESSIVE CASE of NOUNS, forms the possessive case of INDEFINITE PRONOUNS, stands for one or more omitted letters in a word (a CONTRACTION), and can help form plurals of letters and numerals.

In contrast, here are two roles the apostrophe doesn't play: It doesn't belong with plurals of nouns, and it doesn't form the plural of PERSONAL PRONOUNS in the possessive case.

27b How do I use an apostrophe to show a possessive noun?

An apostrophe works with a NOUN to form the POSSESSIVE CASE, which shows ownership or a close relationship.

OWNERSHIP	The **writer's** pen ran out of ink.
CLOSE RELATIONSHIP	The **novel's** plot is complicated.

Possession in nouns can be communicated in two ways: by a PHRASE starting with *of* (*comments **of** the instructor; comments **of** Professor Furman*) or by an apostrophe and the letter *s* (*the instructor's comments; Professor Furman's comments*). Here's a list of specific rules governing the usage of *'s*.

- **Add *'s* to nouns not ending in -s:**

    She felt a **parent's** joy. [*Parent* is a singular noun not ending in -s.]

    They care about their **children's** education. [*Children* is a plural noun not ending in -s.]

- **Add *'s* to singular nouns ending in -s:** You can add *'s* or the apostrophe alone to show possession when a singular noun ends in -s. In this handbook, we use *'s* to clearly mark singular-noun possessives, no matter what letter ends the noun. Whichever rule variation you choose, be consistent within each piece of writing.

The **bus's** (or **bus'**) air conditioning is out of order.

Chris's (or **Chris'**) ordeal ended.

If you encounter a tongue-twisting pronunciation (*Charles **Dickens's** novel*), you may decide not to add the additional -*s* (*Charles **Dickens'** novel*). You must, however, be consistent in each piece of writing.

- **Add only an apostrophe to a plural noun ending in -*s*:**

  The **boys'** statements were taken seriously.

  Three **months'** maternity leave is in the **workers'** contract.

- **Add *'s* to the last word in compound words and phrases:**

  His **mother-in-law's** corporation has bought out a competitor.

  The **tennis player's** strategy was brilliant.

  We want to hear the **caseworker's** recommendation.

- **Add *'s* to each noun in individual possession:**

  Shirley's and **Kayla's** houses are next to each other. [Shirley and Kayla each own a house; they don't own the houses jointly.]

- **Add *'s* to only the last noun in joint or group possession:**

  Kareem and Brina's house has a screened porch. [Kareem and Brina own one house.]

  Avram and Justin's houses always have nice lawns. [Avram and Justin jointly own more than one house.]

27c   How do I use an apostrophe with possessive pronouns?

When a POSSESSIVE PRONOUN ends with *s* (*hers, his, its, ours, yours,* and *theirs*), never add an apostrophe. Below is a list of PERSONAL PRONOUNS and their possessive forms.

Personal Pronouns	Possessive Forms
I	my, mine
you	your, yours
he	his
she	her, hers
it	its
we	our, ours
they	their, theirs
who	whose

27d How do I use an apostrophe with contractions?

In a **contraction**, an apostrophe takes the place of one or more omitted letters. Be careful not to confuse a contraction with a POSSESSIVE PRONOUN. Doing so is a common spelling error, one that many people—including employers—consider evidence of a poor education. Whether or not that's fair, it's usually true.

it's (contraction for *it is*)	**its** (possessive pronoun)
they're (contraction for *they are*)	**their** (possessive pronoun)
who's (contraction for *who is*)	**whose** (possessive form of *who*)
you're (contraction for *you are*)	**your** (possessive pronoun)

> **NO** The government has to balance **it's** budget.
>
> **YES** The government has to balance **its** budget.
>
> **NO** The professor **who's** class was canceled is ill.
>
> **YES** The professor **whose** class was canceled is ill.

In choosing whether or not to use a contraction, consider that many instructors think contractions aren't appropriate in ACADEMIC WRITING. Nevertheless, the *MLA Handbook* accepts contractions, including '90s for *the 1990s*. In this handbook, we use contractions because we're addressing you, the student. We suggest, however, that before you use contractions in your academic writing, you check with your instructor. Here's a list of common contractions.

Common Contractions

aren't = *are not*	she's = *she is*
can't = *cannot*	there's = *there is*
didn't = *did not*	they're = *they are*
don't = *do not*	wasn't = *was not*
he's = *he is*	we're = *we are*
I'd = *I would, I had*	weren't = *were not*
I'm = *I am*	we've = *we have*
isn't = *is not*	who's = *who is*
it's = *it is*	won't = *will not*
let's = *let us*	you're = *you are*

❗ Alert: One contraction required in all writing is *o'clock* (which stands for *of the clock,* an expression used long ago). ●

27e How do I use an apostrophe with possessive indefinite pronouns?

An apostrophe works with an INDEFINITE PRONOUN (see list in Quick Reference 17.6 in 17i) to form the POSSESSIVE CASE, which shows ownership or a close relationship.

OWNERSHIP	Everyone's dinner is ready.
CLOSE RELATIONSHIP	Something's aroma is appealing.

Possession in indefinite pronouns can be communicated in two ways: by a PHRASE starting with *of* (*comments of everyone*) or by an apostrophe and the letter *s* (*everyone's comments*).

27f How do I form the plural of miscellaneous elements?

Until recently, the plural of elements such as letters meant as letters, words meant as words, numerals, and symbols could be formed by adding either *'s* or *s*. The most current MLA guidelines endorse the use of *s* only, with the exception of adding *'s* to letters meant as letters. MLA recommends using italics for letters meant as letters and words meant as words. The examples below reflect MLA practices.

PLURAL OF LETTERS MEANT AS LETTERS	Printing *M's* and *N's* confuses young children.
	Printing *m's* and *n's* confuses young children.
PLURAL OF LETTERS MEANT AS WORDS	He was surprised to get all **B**s in his courses.
PLURAL OF WORDS MEANT AS WORDS	Too many *ifs* in a contract make me suspicious.
PLURAL OF NUMBERS	Her e-mail address contains many 7**s**.
PLURAL OF YEARS	I remember the 1990s well.
PLURAL OF SYMBOLS	What do those &s mean?

27g When is an apostrophe wrong?

If you're a writer who makes the same apostrophe errors repeatedly, memorize the rules you need (some you're likely to know almost without thought). Then you won't be annoyed by "that crooked little mark," a nickname popular with students who wish the apostrophe would go away. Quick Reference 27.1 lists the major apostrophe errors.

Quick Reference 27.1 ■ ■ ■ ■ ■ ■ ■

Leading apostrophe errors

- Never use an apostrophe with the PRESENT-TENSE VERB.

    Cholesterol **plays** [not **play's**] an important role in how long we live.

- Always use an apostrophe after the -*s* in a POSSESSIVE plural of a noun.

    Patients' [not **Patients**] questions seek detailed answers.

- Never add an apostrophe at the end of a nonpossessive noun ending in -*s*.

    Medical **studies** [not **studies'** or **study's**] show this to be true.

- Never use an apostrophe to form a nonpossessive plural.

    Teams [not **Team's**] of doctors have studied the effects of cholesterol.

EXERCISE 27-1 Rewrite these sentences to insert *'s* or an apostrophe alone to make the words in parentheses show possession. (Delete the parentheses.) For help, consult 27b and 27e.

EXAMPLE All boxes, cans, and bottles on a (supermarket) shelves are designed to appeal to (people) emotions.

All boxes, cans, and bottles on a *supermarket's* shelves are designed to appeal to *people's* emotions.

1. A (product) manufacturer designs packaging to appeal to (consumers) emotions through color and design.

2. Marketing specialists know that (people) beliefs about a (product) quality are influenced by their emotional response to the design of its package.

3. Circles and ovals appearing on a (box) design supposedly increase a (product user) feelings of comfort, while bold patterns and colors attract a (shopper) attention.

4. Using both circles and bold designs in (Arm & Hammer) and (Tide) packaging produces both effects in consumers.

5. (Heinz) ketchup bottle and (Coca-Cola) famous logo achieve the same effects by combining a bright color with an old-fashioned, "comfortable" design.

6. Often, a (company) marketing consultants will custom-design products to appeal to the supposedly "typical" (adult female) emotions or to (adult males), (children), or (teenagers) feelings.

7. One of the (marketing business) leading consultants, Stan Gross, tests (consumers) emotional reactions to (companies) products and their packages by asking consumers to associate products with well-known personalities.

8. Thus, (test takers) responses to (Gross) questions might reveal that a particular brand of laundry detergent has (Russell Crowe) toughness, (Oprah Winfrey) determination, or (someone else) sparkling personality.

9. Manufacturing (companies) products are not the only ones relying on (Gross) and other corporate (image makers) advice.

10. (Sports teams) owners also use marketing specialists to design their (teams) images, as anyone who has seen the angry bull logo of the Chicago Bulls basketball team will agree.

EXERCISE 27-2   Rewrite these sentences so that each contains a possessive noun. For help, consult 27b and 27e.

EXAMPLE   The light of a firefly gives off no heat.

A *firefly's* light gives off no heat.

1. The scientific name of a firefly is *lampyridae,* but the nicknames of the bug include *glowworm* and *lightning bug.*

2. More than two thousand species of fireflies can be found throughout the temperate climates of the world.

3. The light of a firefly is caused by a chemical reaction in the organs of the abdomen.

4. Fireflies played a role in the mythology of ancient Mayans and were often compared to the light of a star.

5. Although it may be in the interest of nobody to know, fireflies are not flies at all; they are, according to the classifications of scientists, beetles.

28

Quotation Marks

28a   What is the role of quotation marks?

Quotation marks are used most often to enclose **direct quotations**—the exact spoken or written words of a speaker or writer. Quotation marks also set off some titles, and quotation marks can call attention to words used in a special sense.

Double quotation marks (" ") are standard. In most computer fonts, the opening marks differ slightly in appearance from the closing marks. The opening marks look like tiny 6s, the closing marks like tiny 9s. In some computer fonts, the opening and closing marks look the same (" " or " "). Single quotation marks (' or ' ') are used for quotations within quotations: *Gregory said, "I heard the man shout 'Help me' but could not reach him in time."* Quotation marks operate only in pairs: to open and to close. When you proofread your writing, check carefully that you've inserted the closing mark.

Please note, before you continue reading this chapter, that we use MLA STYLE to format the examples here and in other chapters. This affects the documentation features and the lengths of "short" and "long" quotations. These factors vary with different documentation styles. For MLA style, used in most English courses, see Chapter 36. For APA STYLE, see Chapter 37.

28b   How do I use quotation marks with short direct quotations?

DIRECT QUOTATIONS are exact words from print or nonprint sources. In MLA STYLE, a quotation is considered *short* if it occupies no more than four typed lines. Use double quotation marks at the start and finish of a short quotation. Give DOCUMENTATION information after a short quotation, before the sentence's ending period.

SHORT QUOTATIONS

Gardner has suggested the possibility of a ninth intelligence: existential, "the proclivity to pose (and ponder) questions about life, death, and ultimate realities" (72).

Susana Urbina, who surveyed many studies about intelligence, found that intelligence "is such a multifaceted concept that no single quality can define it . . ." (1130).

28c Are quotation marks used with long quotations?

No. With a long DIRECT QUOTATION, don't use quotation marks. In MLA STYLE, a quotation is *long* if it occupies more than four typed lines. Instead of using quotation marks with a long quotation, indent all its lines as a block (that is, the quotation is "set off" or "displayed"). This format makes quotation marks unnecessary. Give DOCUMENTATION information after the period that ends the quotation.

LONG QUOTATIONS

Gardner uses criteria by which to judge whether an ability deserves to be categorized as an "intelligence." Each must confer

> a set of skills of problem solving--enabling the individual to resolve genuine problems or difficulties [author's emphasis] that he or she encounters and laying the groundwork for the acquisition of new knowledge. (*Frames* 60-61)

In the Gardner example above, note that a capital letter is *not* used to start the quotation. The lead-in words (*Each must confer*) are an incomplete sentence, so they need the quotation to complete the sentence.

Goleman also emphasizes a close interaction of the emotional and rational states with the other intelligences that Gardner has identified:

> These two minds, the emotional and the rational, operate in tight harmony for the most part, intertwining their very different ways of knowing to guide us through the world. Ordinarily there is a balance between emotional and rational minds, with emotion feeding into and informing the operations of the rational mind, and the rational mind refining and sometimes vetoing the inputs of the emotions. (9)

In the Goleman example above, note that a capital letter starts the quotation because the lead-in words are a complete sentence. (A colon can—but isn't required to—end the lead-in sentence because it's an independent clause; see 26b.)

Alert: Whether a quotation is one word or occupies many lines, always document its SOURCE. Also, when you quote material, be very careful to record the words exactly as they appear in the original. ●

28d How do I use quotation marks for quotations within quotations?

In MLA STYLE, practice varies between short and long quotations when a quotation contains internal quotation marks. In short quotations of prose, use single quotation marks for any internal quotation marks, and use double quotation marks for the entire quotation. Give DOCUMENTATION information after the entire quotation, before the sentence's ending period. For other documentation styles, check each style's manual.

In long quotations of prose—those that are displayed (set off in a block) and not enclosed in quotation marks—keep the double quotation marks as they appear in the original. Give DOCUMENTATION information after the long quotation following any closing punctuation, and before the period that ends a short quotation.

SHORT QUOTATIONS: USE SINGLE WITHIN DOUBLE QUOTATION MARKS (MLA STYLE)

With short quotations, the double quotation marks show the beginning and end of words taken from the source; the single quotation marks replace double marks used in the source.

ORIGINAL SOURCE

Most scientists concede that they don't really know what "intelligence" is. Whatever it might be, paper and pencil tests aren't the tenth of it.

—Brent Staples, "The IQ Cult," p. 293

STUDENT'S USE OF THE SOURCE

Brent Staples argues in his essay about IQ as an object of reverence: "Most scientists concede that they don't really know what 'intelligence' is. Whatever it might be, paper and pencil tests aren't the tenth of it" (293).

LONG QUOTATIONS: USE QUOTATION MARKS AS IN SOURCE

All long quotations must be set off (displayed) without being enclosed in quotation marks. Therefore, show any double and single quotation marks exactly as the source does.

28e How do I use quotation marks for quotations of poetry and dialogue?

POETRY (MLA STYLE)

A quotation of poetry is *short* if it includes three lines or fewer of the poem. As with prose quotations (28d), use double quotation marks to enclose the material. If the poetry lines have internal double quotation marks, change them to single quotation marks. To show when a line of poetry breaks to the next line, use a slash (/) with one space on each side. Give DOCUMENTATION information after a short poetry quotation, before the period that ends the sentence (see also 29e).

> As Auden wittily defined personal space, "some thirty inches from my nose / The frontier of my person goes" (*Complete* 205).

A quotation of poetry is *long* if it includes more than three lines of the poem. As with prose quotations (28d), indent all lines as a block, without quotation marks to enclose the material. Start new lines exactly as they appear in your source. Give documentation information after the long quotation and after the period that ends the quotation.

Alert: When you quote lines of poetry, follow the capitalization of your source.

DIALOGUE (MLA AND APA STYLES)

Dialogue, also called DIRECT DISCOURSE, presents a speaker's exact words. Enclose direct discourse in quotation marks. In contrast, INDIRECT DISCOURSE reports what a speaker said. Don't enclose indirect discourse in quotation marks. In addition to these differences in punctuation, PRONOUN use and VERB TENSES also differ for these two types of discourse.

DIRECT DISCOURSE	The mayor said, **"I** intend to veto that bill.**"**
INDIRECT DISCOURSE	The mayor said **that he intended** to veto that bill.

Whether you're reporting the words of a real speaker or making up dialogue in a short story, use double quotation marks at the beginning and end of a speaker's words. This tells your reader which words are the speaker's. Also, start a new paragraph each time the speaker changes.

> "I don't know how you can see to drive," she said.
> "Maybe you should put on your glasses."
> "Putting on my glasses would help you to see?"
> "Not me; you," Macon said. "You're focused on the windshield instead of the road."
>
> —Anne Tyler, *The Accidental Tourist*

In American English, if two or more paragraphs present a single speaker's words, use double opening quotation marks at the start of each paragraph, but save the closing double quotation marks until the end of the last quoted paragraph.

EXERCISE 28-1 Working individually or with a group, decide whether each sentence below is direct or indirect discourse and then rewrite each sentence in the other form. Make any changes needed for grammatical correctness. With direct discourse, put the speaker's words wherever you think they belong in the sentence. For help, consult 28b through 28e.

EXAMPLE A school counselor told Betty, a senior at Whatsamatta U, that she needed to take one more three-unit elective to graduate in May.

A school counselor told Betty, a senior at Whatsamatta U, "You need to take one more three-unit elective to graduate in May."

1. "Betty, would you be interested in taking an introductory electronics course?" asked the counselor.

2. Betty asked why she would take such a course when she was a nursing major.

3. The counselor looked Betty straight in the eye and said, "Some knowledge of electronics may not be part of your major, but it's a very important modern subject, nevertheless."

4. Betty wondered whether it might give her a greater understanding of all the electronics used in medical diagnosis and treatment today. But she also asked if there wasn't another elective that might do more to enhance her nursing career.

5. The counselor was quiet for a moment and then declared, "And don't forget, electronics is something you can always fall back on, Betty. And the more you have to fall back on, the softer the landing."

28f How do I use quotation marks with titles of short works?

When you refer to certain short works by their titles, enclose the titles in quotation marks (other works, usually longer, need to be in italics; see 30g). Short works include short stories, essays, poems, articles from periodicals, pamphlets, brochures, songs, and individual episodes of a series on television or radio.

What is the rhyme scheme of Andrew Marvell's "Delight in Disorder"? [poem]

Have you read "The Lottery"? [short story]

The best source I found is "The Myth of Political Consultants." [magazine article]

"Shooting an Elephant" describes George Orwell's experiences in Burma. [essay]

Titles of some other works are neither enclosed in quotation marks nor written in italics. For guidelines, see Quick Reference 30.1 in 30e and Quick Reference 30.2 in 30g.

Alert: When placing the title of your own piece of writing on a title page or at the top of a page, never use quotation marks. ●

EXERCISE 28-2 Working individually or with a group, correct any misuses of quotation marks. For help, consult 28f.

1. The song America the Beautiful by Katharine Lee Bates celebrates the natural beauty and the ideals that many people associate with the United States.

2. Ralph Waldo Emerson's essay The American Scholar praises the ideals of independence and self-reliance in American education and was first heard as an oration delivered to the "Phi Beta Kappa Society."

3. However, not only the ideals, but also the harsh realities of life in America for Filipino immigrants form the basis of Carlos Bulosan's autobiography, America Is in the Heart.

4. A film that honestly and poignantly reveals the realities facing a family of Irish immigrants in New York City and their hopes for a better life is In America.

5. The poet Langston Hughes in his poem Let America Be America Again is fierce in his criticism of the way poor people and minorities are often treated in the United States.

28g How do I use quotation marks for words used as words?

When you refer to a word as a word, you can choose to either enclose it in quotation marks or put it in italics. Whichever you choose, be consistent throughout each piece of writing.

NO	Many people confuse affect and effect.
YES	Many people confuse "affect" and "effect."
YES	Many people confuse *affect* and *effect*.

Always put quotation marks around the English translation of a word or PHRASE. Also, use italics for the word or phrase in the other language.

My grandfather usually ended arguments with *de gustibus non disputandum est* ("there is no disputing about tastes").

Many writers use quotation marks around words or phrases meant ironically or in other nonliteral ways.

The proposed tax "reform" is actually a tax increase.

Some writers put technical terms in quotation marks and define them—but only the first time they appear. Never reuse quotation marks after a term has been introduced and defined.

"Plagiarism"—the undocumented use of another person's words or ideas—can result in expulsion. Plagiarism is a serious offense.

Some student writers put quotation marks around words that they sense might be inappropriate for ACADEMIC WRITING, such as a SLANG term or a CLICHÉ used intentionally to make a point. However, when possible, use different language—not quotation marks. Take time to think of accurate, appropriate, and fresh words instead. If you prefer to stick with the slang or cliché, use quotation marks.

They "eat like birds" in public, but they "stuff their faces" in private.

They **eat almost nothing** in public, but they **eat hefty heaps of food** in private.

A nickname doesn't call for quotation marks, unless you use the nickname along with the full name. When a person's nickname is widely known, you don't have to give both the nickname and the full name. For example, use *Senator Ted Kennedy* or *Senator Edward Kennedy,* whichever is appropriate in context. Because he's well known, don't use *Senator Edward "Ted" Kennedy.*

EXERCISE 28-3   Working individually or with a group, correct any misuses of quotation marks. If you think a sentence is correct, explain why. For help, consult 28g.

EXAMPLE   The word asyndeton simply means that a conjunction has been omitted, as when Shakespeare writes, A woman mov'd is like a fountain troubled, / Muddy, ill seeming, thick, bereft of beauty.

The word **"**asyndeton**"** simply means that a conjunction has been omitted, as when Shakespeare writes, **"**A woman mov'd is like a fountain troubled, / Muddy, ill seeming, thick, bereft of beauty.**"**

1. Shakespeare's phrases such as the sound and the fury from *Macbeth* and pale fire from *The Tempest* have been used by authors such as William Faulkner and Vladimir Nabokov as titles for their books.

2. Shakespeare's understanding of human nature was "profound" and helped him become a "prolific" writer.

3. Many words used commonly today, such as "addiction" and "alligator," were first used in print by Shakespeare.

4. To understand the difference between the words sanguinary and *sanguine* is important for a reader of Shakespeare because the former means bloody and the latter means optimistic.

5. In the play *Romeo and Juliet,* one of Shakespeare's most famous quotations is What's in a name? That which we call a rose / By any other name would smell as sweet.

28h How do I use quotation marks with other punctuation?

COMMAS AND PERIODS WITH QUOTATION MARKS

A comma or period that is grammatically necessary is always placed inside the closing quotation mark.

> Jessica enjoyed F. Scott Fitzgerald's story "The Freshest Boy," so she was eager to read his novels. [comma before closing quotation mark]
>
> Max said, "Don't stand so far away from me." [comma before opening quotation mark (24k.5); period before closing quotation mark]
>
> Edward T. Hall coined the word "proxemia." [period before closing quotation mark]

SEMICOLONS AND COLONS WITH QUOTATION MARKS

A semicolon or colon is placed outside the closing quotation mark, unless it is part of the quotation.

> Computers offer businesses "opportunities that never existed before"; some workers disagree. [semicolon after closing quotation mark]
>
> We have to know each culture's standard for "how close is close": No one wants to offend. [colon after closing quotation mark]

QUESTION MARKS, EXCLAMATION POINTS, AND DASHES WITH QUOTATION MARKS

If the punctuation marks belong to the words enclosed in quotation marks, put them inside the quotation marks.

> "Did I Hear You Call My Name?" was the winning song.
>
> "I've won the lottery!" Arielle shouted.
>
> "Who's there? Why don't you ans—"

If a question mark, an exclamation point, or a dash doesn't belong to the material being quoted, put the punctuation outside the quotation marks.

> Have you read Nikki Giovanni's poem "Knoxville, Tennessee"?
>
> If only I could write a story like David Wallace's "Girl with Curious Hair"!

Weak excuses—a classic is "I have to visit my grandparents"—change little.

When you use quotation marks and want to know how they work with capital letters, see 30d; with brackets, 29c; with ellipsis points, 29d; and with the slash, 29e.

28i When are quotation marks wrong?

Never enclose a word in quotation marks to call attention to it, to intensify it, or to be sarcastic.

NO I'm "very" happy about the news.

YES I'm very happy about the news.

Never enclose the title of your paper in quotation marks (or underline it). However, if the title of your paper contains another title that requires quotation marks, use those marks only for the included title.

NO "The Elderly in Nursing Homes: A Case Study"

YES The Elderly in Nursing Homes: A Case Study

NO Character Development in Shirley Jackson's Story The Lottery

YES Character Development in Shirley Jackson's Story "The Lottery"

EXERCISE 28-4 Correct any errors in the use of quotation marks and other punctuation with quotation marks. If you think a sentence is correct, explain why. For help, consult 28e through 28i.

1. Dying in a shabby hotel room, the witty writer Oscar Wilde supposedly said, "Either that wallpaper goes, or I do".

2. Was it the Russian novelist Tolstoy who wrote, "All happy families resemble one another, but each unhappy family is unhappy in its own way?"

3. In his poem A Supermarket in California, Allen Ginsberg addresses the dead poet Walt Whitman, asking, Where are we going, Walt Whitman? The doors close / in an hour. Which way does your beard point tonight?

4. Toni Morrison made this reply to the claim that "art that has a political message cannot be good art:" She said that "the best art is political" and that her aim was to create art that was "unquestionably political" and beautiful at the same time.

5. Benjamin Franklin's strange question—"What is the use of a newborn child?—" was his response to someone who doubted the usefulness of new inventions.

29

Other Punctuation Marks

This chapter explains the uses of **dashes, parentheses, brackets, ellipsis points, slashes,** and **hyphens.** These punctuation marks aren't used often, but each serves a purpose and gives you options with your writing style.

DASH

29a When can I use a dash in my writing?

The **dash,** or a pair of dashes, lets you interrupt a sentence to add information. Such interruptions can fall in the middle or at the end of a sentence. To make a dash, hit the hyphen key twice (--). Do not put a space before, between, or after the hyphens. Some word processing programs automatically convert two hyphens into a dash; either form is correct. In print, the dash appears as an unbroken line approximately the length of two hyphens joined together (—). If you handwrite, make the dash at least twice as long as a hyphen.

USING DASHES FOR SPECIAL EMPHASIS

If you want to emphasize an example, a definition, an appositive, or a contrast, you can use a dash or dashes. Some call a dash "a pregnant pause"—that is, take note, something special is coming. Use dashes sparingly so that you don't dilute their impact.

EXAMPLE
The caretakers—those who are helpers, nurturers, teachers, mothers—are still systematically devalued.

—Ellen Goodman, "Just Woman's Work?"

DEFINITION
Although the emphasis at the school was mainly language—speaking, reading, writing—the lessons always began with an exercise in politeness.

—Elizabeth Wong, *Fifth Chinese Daughter*

APPOSITIVE

Two of the strongest animals in the jungle are vegetarians—the elephant and the gorilla.

—Dick Gregory, *The Shadow That Scares Me*

CONTRAST

Fire cooks food—and burns down forests.

—Smokey the Bear

Place what you emphasize with dashes next to or nearby the material it refers to so that what you want to accomplish with your emphasis is not lost.

> **NO** The current **argument is**—one that faculty, students, and coaches debate fiercely—whether to hold athletes to the same academic standards as others face.
>
> **YES** The current **argument**—one that faculty, students, and coaches debate fiercely—**is** whether to hold athletes to the same academic standards as others face.

USING DASHES TO EMPHASIZE AN ASIDE

An **aside** is a writer's comment, often the writer's personal views, on what's been written. Generally, this technique isn't appropriate for academic writing, so before you insert an aside, carefully consider your writing purpose and your audience.

> Television showed us the war. It showed us the war in a way that was—if you chose to watch television, at least—unavoidable.

—Nora Ephron, *Scribble Scribble*

Alerts: (1) If the words within a pair of dashes require a question mark or an exclamation point, place it before the second dash.

> A first date—do you remember?—stays in the memory forever.

(2) Never use commas, semicolons, or periods next to dashes. If such a need arises, revise your writing.

(3) Never enclose quotation marks in dashes except when the meaning requires them. These two examples show that, when required, the dash stops before or after the quotation marks; the two punctuation marks do not overlap.

> Many of George Orwell's essays—"A Hanging," for example—draw on his experiences as a civil servant.
>
> "Shooting an Elephant"—another Orwell essay—appears in many anthologies. ●

EXERCISE 29-1   Write a sentence about each topic, shown in italics. Use dashes to set off what is asked for, shown in roman, in each sentence. For help, consult 29a.

EXAMPLE   *punctuation mark,* an aside

> Sometimes I get confused—but what's new?—about the difference between a colon and a semicolon.

1. *ice cream flavor,* an aside
2. *a shape,* a definition
3. *sport,* an appositive
4. *public transportation,* an example
5. *occupation,* a contrast

6. *musical instrument,* a definition
7. *TV show,* an aside
8. *American president,* an example
9. *country,* an appositive
10. *animal,* a contrast

PARENTHESES

29b   When can I use parentheses in my writing?

Parentheses let you interrupt a sentence to add various kinds of information. Parentheses are like dashes (29a) in that they set off extra or interrupting words—but unlike dashes, which emphasize material, parentheses de-emphasize what they enclose. Use parentheses sparingly because overusing them can make your writing lurch, not flow.

USING PARENTHESES TO ENCLOSE INTERRUPTING WORDS

EXPLANATION

After they've finished with the pantry, the medicine cabinet, and the attic, they will throw out the red geranium (too many leaves), sell the dog (too many fleas), and send the children off to boarding school (too many scuffmarks on the hardwood floors).

> —Suzanne Britt, "Neat People vs. Sloppy People"

EXAMPLE

Though other cities (Dresden, for instance) had been utterly destroyed in World War II, never before had a single weapon been responsible for such destruction.

> —Laurence Behrens and Leonard J. Rosen,
> *Writing and Reading Across the Curriculum*

ASIDE

The older girls (non-graduates, of course) were assigned the task of making refreshments for the night's festivities.

> —Maya Angelou, *I Know Why the Caged Bird Sings*

The sheer decibel level of the noise around us is not enough to make us cranky, irritable, or aggressive. (It can, however, affect our mental and physical health, which is another matter.)

—Carol Tavris, *Anger: The Misunderstood Emotion*

USING PARENTHESES FOR LISTED ITEMS
AND ALTERNATIVE NUMBERS

When you number listed items within a sentence, enclose the numbers (or letters) in parentheses. Never use closing parentheses to set off numbers in a displayed list; use periods.

Four items are on the agenda for tonight's meeting: (1) current treasury figures, (2) current membership figures, (3) the budget for renovations, and (4) the campaign for soliciting additional public contributions.

❶ Alerts: For listed items that fall within a sentence, (1) use a colon before a list only if an INDEPENDENT CLAUSE comes before the list, and (2) use commas or semicolons to separate three or more items, but be consistent within a piece of writing. If, however, any item contains punctuation itself, use a semicolon to separate the items. ●

In legal writing and in some BUSINESS WRITING, you can use parentheses to enclose a numeral that repeats a spelled-out number.

The monthly rent is three hundred fifty dollars (\$350).

Your order of fifteen (15) gross was shipped today.

In ACADEMIC WRITING, especially in subjects in which the use of figures or measurements is frequent, enclose alternative or comparative forms of the same number in parentheses: *2 mi (3.2 km)*.

USING OTHER PUNCTUATION WITH PARENTHESES

When a complete sentence enclosed in parentheses stands alone, start it with a capital letter and end it with a period. When a sentence in parentheses falls within another sentence, never start with a capital or end with a period.

NO Looking for his car keys (He had left them at my sister's house.) wasted an entire hour.

YES Looking for his car keys (he had left them at my sister's house) wasted an entire hour.

YES Looking for his car keys wasted an entire hour. (He had left them at my sister's house.)

If the material before the parenthetical material requires a comma, place that comma after the closing parenthesis unless you're using commas to set off numbers in a list.

NO   Although clearly different from my favorite film,2 (*The Wizard of Oz*) *Gone With the Wind* is also outstanding.

YES   Although clearly different from my favorite film (*The Wizard of Oz*), *Gone With the Wind* is also outstanding.

YES   Dorothy wore (1) a white blouse, (2) a blue pinafore, and (3) ruby slippers.

You can use a question mark or an exclamation point within parentheses that occur in a sentence.

Looking for clues (what did we expect to find?) wasted four days.

Place parentheses around quotation marks that come before or after any quoted words.

NO   Alberta Hunter "(Down Hearted Blues)" is known for singing jazz.

YES   Alberta Hunter ("Down Hearted Blues") is known for singing jazz.

BRACKETS

29c When do I need to use brackets in my writing?

Brackets allow you to enclose words that you want to insert into quotations, but only in the specific cases discussed below.

ADJUSTING A QUOTATION WITH BRACKETS

When you use a quotation, you might need to change the form of a word (a verb's tense, for example), add a brief definition, or fit the quotation into the grammatical structure of your sentence. In such cases, enclose the material you have inserted into the quotation in brackets. (These examples use MLA style for parenthetical references; see 36b.)

ORIGINAL SOURCE

Current research shows that successful learning takes place in an active environment.

—Deborah Moore, "Facilities and Learning Styles," p. 22

QUOTATION WITH BRACKETS

Deborah Moore supports a student-centered curriculum and agrees with "current research [which] shows that successful learning takes place in an active environment" (22).

ORIGINAL SOURCE

The logic of the mind is *associative;* it takes elements that symbolize a reality, or trigger a memory of it, to be the same as that reality.

—Daniel Goleman, *Emotional Intelligence,* p. 294

QUOTATION WITH BRACKETS

The kinds of intelligence are based in the way the mind functions: "The logic of the mind is *associative* [one idea connects with another]; it takes elements that symbolize a reality, or trigger a memory of it, to be the same as that reality" (Goleman 294).

USING BRACKETS TO POINT OUT AN ERROR IN A SOURCE OR TO ADD INFORMATION WITHIN PARENTHESES

In words you want to quote, sometimes page-makeup technicians or authors make a mistake without realizing it—a wrong date, a misspelled word, or an error of fact. You fix that mistake by putting your correction in brackets, without changing the words you want to quote. This tells your readers that the error was in the original work and not made by you.

USING [SIC] TO SHOW A SOURCE'S ERROR

Insert *sic* (without italics), enclosed in brackets, in your MLA-style essays and research papers to show your readers that you've quoted an error accurately. *Sic* is a Latin word that means "so," or "thus," which says "It is so (or thus) in the original."

USE FOR ERROR

A journalist wrote, "The judge accepted an [sic] plea of not guilty.

USE FOR MISSPELLING

The building inspector wrote about the consequence of doubling the apartment's floor space: "With that much extra room per person, the tennants [sic] would sublet."

USING BRACKETS WITHIN PARENTHESES

Use brackets to insert information within parentheses.

That expression **(first used in *A Fable for Critics* [1848] by James R. Lowell)** was popularized in the early twentieth century by Ella Wheeler Wilcox.

ELLIPSIS POINTS

29d How do I use ellipsis points in my writing?

The word *ellipsis* means "omission." **Ellipsis points** in writing are a series of three spaced dots (use the period key on the keyboard). You're required to use ellipsis points to indicate you've intentionally omitted words—perhaps even a sentence or more—from the source you're quoting. These rules apply to both prose and poetry.

The *MLA Handbook* no longer recommends that ellipsis points you have inserted be enclosed in brackets to make it clear to your reader that the omission is yours. See Chapter 36 for more information.

29d.1 Using ellipsis points with prose

ORIGINAL SOURCE

These two minds, the emotional and the rational, operate in tight harmony for the most part, intertwining their very different ways of knowing to guide us through the world. Ordinarily, there is a balance between emotional and rational minds, with emotion feeding into and informing the operations of the rational mind, and the rational mind refining and sometimes vetoing the inputs of the emotions. Still, the emotional and rational minds are semi-independent faculties, each, as we shall see, reflecting the operation of distinct, but interconnected, circuitry in the brain.

—Daniel Goleman, *Emotional Intelligence*, p. 9

QUOTATION OF SELECTED WORDS, NO ELLIPSIS NEEDED

Goleman explains that the "two minds, the emotional and the rational" usually provide "a balance" in our daily observations and decision making (9).

QUOTATION WITH ELLIPSIS MID-SENTENCE

Goleman emphasizes the connections between parts of the mind: "Still, the emotional and rational minds are semi-independent faculties, each . . . reflecting the operation of distinct, but interconnected, circuitry in the brain (9).

QUOTATION WITH ELLIPSIS AND PARENTHETICAL REFERENCE

Goleman emphasizes that the "two minds, the emotional and the rational, operate in tight harmony for the most part . . ." **(9).** [Note: In MLA style, place a sentence-ending period after the parenthetical reference.]

QUOTATION WITH ELLIPSIS ENDING THE SENTENCE

On page 9, Goleman states: "These two minds, the emotional and the rational, operate in tight harmony for the most part. . . ."   [*Note:* In MLA style, when all needed documentation information is written into a sentence—that is, not placed in parentheses at the end of the sentence—there's no space between the sentence-ending period and an ellipsis.]

QUOTATION WITH SENTENCE OMITTED

Goleman explains: "These two minds, the emotional and the rational, operate in tight harmony for the most part, intertwining their very different ways of knowing to guide us through the world. . . . Still, the emotional and rational minds are semi-independent faculties" (9).

QUOTATION WITH WORDS OMITTED FROM THE MIDDLE OF ONE SENTENCE TO THE MIDDLE OF ANOTHER

Goleman states: "Ordinarily, there is a balance between emotional and rational minds . . . reflecting the operation of distinct, but interconnected, circuitry in the brain" (9).

QUOTATION WITH WORDS OMITTED FROM THE BEGINNING OF A SENTENCE AND FROM THE MIDDLE OF ONE SENTENCE TO A COMPLETE OTHER SENTENCE

Goleman explains: ". . . there is a balance between emotional and rational minds. . . . Still, the emotional and rational minds are semi-independent faculties, each, as we shall see, reflecting the operation of distinct, but interconnected, circuitry in the brain" (9).

When you omit words from a quotation, you also omit punctuation related to those words, unless it's needed for the sentence to be correct.

Goleman explains: "These two minds . . . operate in tight harmony" (9). [comma in original source omitted after *minds*]

Goleman explains that the emotional and rational minds work together while, "still, . . . each, as we shall see, [reflects] the operation of distinct, but interconnected, circuitry in the brain" (9).   [comma kept after *still* because it's an introductory word; *still* changed to begin with lowercase letter because it's now in the middle of the sentence; form of *reflecting* changed to improve the sense of sentence]

29d.2 Using ellipsis points with poetry

When you omit one or more words from a line of poetry, follow the rules stated above for prose. However, when you omit a full line or more from poetry, use a full line of spaced dots.

ORIGINAL SOURCE

Little Boy Blue

Little boy blue, come blow your horn,
The sheep's in the meadow, the cow's in the corn
Where is the little boy who looks after the sheep?
He's under the haystack, fast asleep.

QUOTATION WITH LINES OMITTED

Little Boy Blue

Little boy blue, come blow your horn,

. . . .

Where is the little boy who looks after the sheep!
He's under the haystack, fast asleep.

SLASH

29e When can I use a slash in my writing?

The **slash** (/), also called a *virgule* or *solidus,* is a diagonal line that separates or joins words in special circumstances.

USING A SLASH TO SEPARATE QUOTED LINES OF POETRY

When you quote more than three lines of a poem, no slash is involved; you merely follow the rules in 28e. When you quote three lines or fewer, enclose them in quotation marks and run them into your sentence—and use a slash to divide one line from the next. Leave a space on each side of the slash.

One of my mottoes comes from the beginning of Anne Sexton's poem "Words": "Be careful of words, / even the miraculous ones."

Capitalize and punctuate each line of poetry as in the original—but even if the quoted line of poetry doesn't have a period, use one to end your sentence. If your quotation ends before the line of poetry ends, use ellipsis points (29d).

USING A SLASH FOR NUMERICAL FRACTIONS IN MANUSCRIPTS

To type numerical fractions, use a slash (with no space before or after the slash) to separate the numerator and denominator. In mixed numbers—that is, whole numbers with fractions—leave a space between the whole number and its fraction: 1 2/3, 3 7/8. Do not use a hyphen. (For information about using spelled-out and numerical forms of numbers, see 30m through 30o.)

USING A SLASH FOR *AND/OR*

When writing in the humanities, try not to use word combinations connected with a slash, such as *and/or*. In academic disciplines in which such combinations are acceptable, separate the words with a slash. Leave no space before or after the slash. In the humanities, listing both alternatives in normal sentence structure is usually better than separating choices with a slash.

> **NO**   The best quality of reproduction comes from 35 mm slides/direct-positive films.

> **YES**   The best quality of reproduction comes from 35 mm slides **or** direct-positive films.

EXERCISE 29-2   Supply needed dashes, parentheses, brackets, ellipsis points, and slashes. If a sentence is correct as written, circle its number. In some sentences, when you can use either dashes or parentheses, explain your choice. For help, consult all sections of this chapter.

EXAMPLE   Two tiny islands in the English Channel Jersey and Guernsey have breeds of cows named after them.

Two tiny islands in the English Channel—Jersey and Guernsey—have breeds of cows named after them.

1. In *The Color Purple* a successful movie as well as a novel, Alice Walker explores the relationships between women and men in traditional African American culture.

2. W. C. Fields offered two pieces of advice on job hunting: 1 never show up for an interview in bare feet, and 2 don't read your prospective employer's mail while he is questioning you about your qualifications.

3. A series of resolutions was passed 11–0 with one council member abstaining calling on the mayor and the district attorney to improve safety conditions and step up law enforcement on city buses.

4. All the interesting desserts ice cream, chocolate fudge cake, pumpkin pie with whipped cream are fattening, unfortunately.

5. Thunder is caused when the flash of lightning heats the air around it to temperatures up to 30,000°F 16,666°C.

6. Christina Rossetti wonders if the end of a life also means the end of love in a poem that opens with these two lines: "When I am dead, my dearest, Sing no sad songs for me."

7. After the internationally famous racehorse Dan Patch died suddenly from a weak heart, his devoted owner, Will Savage, died of the same condition a mere 32 1/2 hours later.

8. In his famous letter from the Birmingham jail on April 16, 1963, Martin Luther King Jr. wrote: "You the eight clergymen who had urged him not to hold a protest deplore the demonstrations taking place in Birmingham."

9. The world's most expensive doll house sold for $256,000 at a London auction contains sixteen rooms, a working chamber organ, and a silver clothes press but no toilet.

10. The person renting this apartment agrees to pay seven hundred fifty dollars $750 per month in rent.

11. Railroad entrepreneur George Francis Train his real name! dreamed of creating a chain of great cities across the United States, all connected by his Union Pacific Railroad.

12. Patients who pretend to have ailments are known to doctors as "Munchausens" after Baron Karl Friedrich Hieronymus von Münchhausen he was a German army officer who had a reputation for wild and unbelievable tales.

EXERCISE 29-3   Follow the directions for each item. For help, consult all sections of this chapter.

EXAMPLE   Write a sentence about getting something right using a dash.

I tried and failed, I tried and failed again—and then I did it.

1. Write a sentence that quotes only three lines of the following sonnet by William Shakespeare:

Let me not to the marriage of true minds
Admit impediments. Love is not love
Which alters when it alteration finds,
Or bends with the remover to remove.
O, no! it is an ever-fixèd mark
That looks on tempests and is never shaken;
It is the star to every wand'ring bark,
Whose worth's unknown, although his height be taken.
Love's not Time's fool, though rosy lips and cheeks
Within his bending sickle's compass come;
Love alters not with his brief hours and weeks,
But bears it out even to the edge of doom.
 If this be error, and upon me proved,
 I never writ, nor no man ever loved.

2. Write a sentence using parentheses to enclose a brief example.

3. Write a sentence using dashes to set off a definition.

4. Write a sentence that includes four numbered items in a list.

5. Quote a few sentences from any source you choose. Omit words without losing meaning or use brackets to insert words to maintain meaning or grammatical structure. Use ellipsis points to indicate the omission, and place the parenthetical reference where it belongs.

HYPHEN

29f When do I need a hyphen in my writing?

A **hyphen** serves to divide words at the end of a line, to combine words into compounds, and to communicate numbers.

29g When do I use a hyphen at the end of a line?

Generally, try not to divide a word with a hyphen at the end of a line. (In printed books, hyphens are acceptable because of the limits on line length.) Word processing programs can be set either to space the words in a line (in order to avoid dividing words at the end of a line) or to hyphenate words automatically. If you must divide a word, or if the computer divides one automatically, try hard not to divide the last word on the first line of a paper, the last word in a paragraph, or the last word on a page.

When you can't avoid using a hyphen at the end of a line, break the word only between syllables. If you aren't sure about the syllables in a word, consult a dictionary. Never divide words that are short, contain only one syllable, or are pronounced as one syllable.

   wealth   envy   screamed

Divide words between two consonants according to pronunciation.

   full-ness   omit-ting   punc-ture

Never divide a word when only one or two letters would be left or carried over to another line.

   alive   touchy   helicop-ter

29h How do I use a hyphen with prefixes and suffixes?

Prefixes are syllables in front of a **root**—a word's core, which carries the origin or meaning. Prefixes modify meanings. **Suffixes** also have modifying power, but they follow roots. Some prefixes and suffixes are attached to root words with hyphens, but others are not. Quick Reference 29.1 shows you how to decide.

Quick Reference 29.1   ■ ■ ■ ■ ■ ■ ■

Hyphens with prefixes and suffixes

- Use hyphens after the prefixes *all-, ex-, quasi-,* and *self-.*

  YES all-inclusive   self-reliant

- Never use a hyphen when *self* is a root word, not a prefix.

  NO self-ishness   self-less

  YES selfishness   selfless

- Use a hyphen to avoid a distracting string of letters.

  NO antiintellectual   belllike   prooutsourcing

  YES anti-intellectual   bell-like   pro-outsourcing

- Use a hyphen to add a prefix or suffix to a numeral or a word that starts with a capital letter.

  NO post1950   proAmerican   Rembrandtlike

  YES post-1950   pro-American   Rembrandt-like

- Use a hyphen before the suffix *-elect.*

  NO presidentelect

  YES president-elect

- Use a hyphen to prevent confusion in meaning or pronunciation.

  YES re-dress (means *dress again*)   redress (means *set right*)

  YES un-ionize (means *remove the ions*)   unionize (means *form a union*)

- Use a hyphen when two or more prefixes apply to one root word.

  YES pre- and post-Renaissance

29i How do I use hyphens with compound words?

A compound word puts two or more words together to express one concept. Compound words come in three forms: an open-compound word, as in *night shift;* hyphenated words, as in *tractor-trailer;* and a closed-compound word, as in *handbook.* Quick Reference 29.2 lists basic guidelines for positioning hyphens in compound words.

Quick Reference 29.2

Hyphens with compound words

- Divide a compound word already containing a hyphen only after that hyphen, if possible. Also, divide a closed-compound word only between the two complete words, if possible.

NO	self-con-scious	sis-ter-in-law	mas-terpiece
YES	self-conscious	sister-in-law	master-piece

- Use a hyphen between a prefix and an open-compound word.

  NO　antigun control [*gun control* is an open-compound word]

  YES　anti-gun control

- Use a hyphen for most compound words that precede a noun but not for most compound words that follow a noun.

  YES　well-researched report　report is well researched

- Use hyphens when a compound modifier includes a series.

  YES　two-, three-, or four-year program

- Never use a hyphen when a compound modifier starts with an *-ly* adverb.

NO	happily-married couple	loosely-tied package
YES	happily married couple	loosely tied package

- Use a hyphen with most COMPARATIVE (*-er*) and SUPERLATIVE (*-est*) compound forms, but not when the compound modifier includes *more/most* or *less/least.*

  NO　better fitting shoe

  YES　better-fitting shoe

  NO　least-significant factors

  YES　least significant factors

- Never use a hyphen when a compound modifier is a foreign phrase.

  YES　*post hoc* fallacies

- Never use a hyphen with a possessive compound.

NO	a full-week's work	eight-hours' pay
YES	a full week's work	eight hours' pay

EXERCISE 29-4   Provide the correct form of the words in parentheses, according to the rules in 29f through 29i. Explain your reasoning for each.

1. The tiger is (all powerful) _____ in the cat family.

2. (Comparison and contrast) _____ studies of tigers and lions show that the tiger is the (more agile) _____ and powerful.

3. Male tigers and lions look similar except for their hair length: Tigers have (ultra short) _____ hair and male lions have (extra long) _____ hair in their manes.

4. The tiger's body is a (boldly striped) _____ yellow, with a white (under body) _____.

5. The Bengal tiger, the largest of the family, is aggressive and (self confident) _____.

6. In India, where the Bengal tiger is called a (village destroyer) _____, it goes (in to) _____ villages to hunt for food.

7. Entire villages have been temporarily abandoned by (terror stricken) _____ people who have seen a Bengal tiger nearby.

8. Villagers seek to protect their homes by destroying tigers with traps, (spring loaded) _____ guns, and (poisoned arrows) _____.

9. Bengal tigers are also called (cattle killers) _____, although they attack domestic animals only when they cannot find wild ones.

10. Many people who do not live near a zoo get to see tigers only in (animal shows) _____, although (pro animal) _____ activists try to prevent tigers from being used this way.

For more help with your writing, grammar, and research,
go to **www.mycomplab.com**

mycomplab

30

Capitals, Italics, Abbreviations, and Numbers

CAPITALS

30a When do I capitalize a "first" word?

FIRST WORD IN A SENTENCE

Always capitalize the first letter of the first word in a sentence.

> Four inches of snow fell last winter.

A SERIES OF QUESTIONS

If questions in a series are complete sentences, start each with a capital letter. If, however, the questions aren't complete sentences, you can choose to capitalize or not. Whatever your choice, be consistent in each piece of writing. In this handbook, we use capitals for a series of questions.

> What facial feature would most people like to change? Eyes? Ears? Nose?

> What facial feature would most people like to change? eyes? ears? nose?

SMALL WORDS IN TITLES OR HEADINGS

Capitalize small words (*the, a, an,* and short PREPOSITIONS such as *of, to*) in a title or heading only when they begin the title or when the source capitalizes these small words.

Always capitalize *I,* no matter where it falls in a sentence or group of words: *I love you now, although I didn't use to.* The same holds for *O,* the INTERJECTION: *You are, O my fair love, a burning fever; O my gentle love, embrace me.* In contrast, never capitalize the interjection *oh,* unless it starts a sentence or is capitalized in words you're quoting.

AFTER A COLON

When a complete sentence follows a colon, you can choose to start that sentence with either a capital or a lowercase letter, but be consistent in each piece of writing. When the words after a colon are not a complete sentence, do not capitalize.

> She reacted instantly: She picked up the ice cream and pushed it back into her cone.

> She reacted instantly: she picked up the ice cream and pushed it back into her cone.

> She bought four pints of ice cream: vanilla, chocolate, strawberry, and butter pecan.

Alert: A colon can follow only a complete sentence (an INDEPENDENT CLAUSE; see 26a). ●

FORMAL OUTLINE

In a formal outline, start each item with a capital letter. Use a period only when the item is a complete sentence.

30b When do I use capitals with listed items?

A LIST RUN INTO A SENTENCE

If run-in listed items are complete sentences, start each with a capital and end each with a period (or question mark or exclamation point). If the run-in listed items are incomplete sentences, start each with a lowercase letter and end each with a comma—unless the items already contain commas, in which case use semicolons. If you list three or more items that are incomplete sentences, use *and* before the last item.

> **YES** We found three reasons for the delay: (1) Bad weather held up delivery of materials. (2) Poor scheduling created confusion. (3) Improper machine maintenance caused an equipment failure.

> **YES** The reasons for the delay were (1) bad weather, (2) poor scheduling, **and** (3) equipment failure.

> **YES** The reasons for the delay were (1) bad weather, which had been predicted; (2) poor scheduling, which is the airline's responsibility; **and** (3) equipment failure, which no one can predict.

A DISPLAYED LIST

In a displayed list, each item starts on a new line. If the items are sentences, capitalize the first letter and end with a period (or question mark or exclamation point). If the items are not sentences, you can use a capital letter or not. Whichever you choose, be consistent in each piece of writing. Punctuate a displayed list as you would a run-in list.

YES We found three reasons for the delay:
1. Bad weather held up delivery of materials.
2. Poor scheduling created confusion.
3. Improper machine maintenance caused an equipment failure.

YES The reasons for the delay were
1. bad weather,
2. poor scheduling, and
3. equipment failure.

Alerts: (1) If a complete sentence leads into a displayed list, you can end the sentence with a colon. However, if an incomplete sentence leads into a displayed list, use no punctuation. (2) Use PARALLELISM for items in a list. For example, if one item is a sentence, use sentences for all the items (10e); or if one item starts with a VERB, start all items with a verb in the same TENSE; and so on. ●

30c When do I use capitals with sentences in parentheses?

When you write a complete sentence within parentheses that falls within another sentence, don't start with a capital or end with a period—but do use a question mark or exclamation point, if needed. When you write a sentence within parentheses that doesn't fall within another sentence, capitalize the first word and end with a period (or question mark or exclamation point).

> I did not know till years later that they called it the Cuban Missile Crisis. But I remember Castro. (We called him Castor Oil and were awed by his beard.) We might not have worried so much (what would the communists want with our small New Hampshire town?) except we lived 10 miles from a U.S. air base.
>
> —Joyce Maynard, "An 18-Year-Old Looks Back on Life"

30d When do I use capitals with quotations?

If a quotation within your sentence is itself less than a complete sentence, never capitalize the first quoted word. If the quotation you have used in your sentence is itself a complete sentence, capitalize the first word.

Mrs. Enriquez says that students who are learning a new language should visit that country and "absorb a good accent with the food."

Talking about students who live in a new country Mrs. Enriquez says, "They'll absorb a good accent with the food."

When you write DIRECT DISCOURSE—which you introduce with verbs such as *said, stated, reported,* and others (see 35k) followed by a comma, capitalize the first letter of the quoted words. However, never capitalize a partial quotation, and never capitalize the continuation of a one-sentence quotation within your sentence.

Mrs. Enriquez said, "Students who are learning a new language should visit that country. They'll absorb a good accent with the food." [complete sentence]

Mrs. Enriquez told me that the best way to "absorb a good accent" in a language is to visit the country and eat its food. [part of a quotation integrated in a sentence]

"Of course," she continued with a smile, "the accent lasts longer than the food." [continuation of a one-sentence quotation]

30e When do I capitalize nouns and adjectives?

Capitalize PROPER NOUNS (nouns that name specific people, places, and things): *Abraham Lincoln, Mexico, World Wide Web.* Also, capitalize **proper adjectives** (adjectives formed from proper nouns): *a Mexican entrepreneur, a Web address.* Don't capitalize ARTICLES (*the, a, an*) that accompany proper nouns and proper adjectives, unless they start a sentence.

When a proper noun or adjective loses its very specific "proper" association, it also loses its capital letter: *french fries, pasteurized.* When you turn a common noun (*lake*) into a proper noun (*Lake Mead*), capitalize all words.

Expect sometimes that you'll see capitalized words that this handbook says not to capitalize. For example, a corporation's written communications usually capitalize its own entities (*our Board of Directors or this Company*), even though the rule calls for lowercase (*the board of directors, the company*). Similarly, the administrators of your school might write *the Faculty* and *the College* (or *the University*), even though the rule calls for a lowercase *f, c,* and *u.* How writers capitalize can depend on AUDIENCE and PURPOSE in each specific context.

Quick Reference 30.1 is a capitalization guide. If you don't find what you need, locate an item in it (or in Quick Reference 30.2 on page 492) that's close to what you want, and use it as a model.

Quick Reference 30.1

Capitalization

	Capitals	Lowercase Letters
NAMES	Mother Teresa (*also, used as names:* Mother, Dad, Mom, Pa)	my mother [relationship]
	Doc Holliday	the doctor [role]
TITLES	President Truman	the president
	Democrat [party member]	a democrat [believer in democracy]
	Representative Harold Ford	the congressional representative
	Senator Edward M. Kennedy	a senator
	Queen Elizabeth II	the queen
GROUPS OF PEOPLE	Caucasian [race]	white, black [*also* White, Black]
	African American, Hispanic [ethnic group]	
	Irish, Korean, Canadian [nationality]	
	Jewish, Catholic, Protestant, Buddhist [religious affiliation]	
ORGANIZATIONS	Congress	the legislative branch of the US government
	the Ohio State Supreme Court	the state supreme court
	the Republican Party	the party
	National Gypsum Company	the company
	Chicago Cubs	a baseball team
	American Medical Association	a professional group
	Sigma Chi	a fraternity
	Alcoholics Anonymous	a self-help group
PLACES	Los Angeles	the city
	the South [region]	turn south [direction]
	the West Coast	the US states along the western seaboard
	Main Street	the street
	Atlantic Ocean	the ocean
	the Black Hills	the hills

continued >>

Quick Reference 30.1 (continued)

	Capitals	Lowercase Letters
BUILDINGS	the Capitol [in Washington, DC]	the state capitol
	Ace High School	a high school
	Front Road Café	a restaurant
	Highland Hospital	a hospital
SCIENTIFIC TERMS	Earth [as one of nine planets]	the earth [otherwise]
	the Milky Way, the Galaxy [as name]	our galaxy, the moon, the sun
	Streptococcus aureus	a streptococcal infection
	Gresham's law	the theory of relativity
LANGUAGES, SCHOOL COURSES	Spanish, Chinese	
	Chemistry 342	a chemistry course
	History 111	my history class
	Introduction to Photography	a photography course
NAMES OF SPECIFIC THINGS	Black Parrot tulip	a climbing rose
	Purdue University	the university
	Heinz ketchup	ketchup, sauce
	a Toyota Camry	a car
	Twelfth Dynasty	the dynasty
	the *Boston Globe*	a newspaper
TIMES, SEASONS, HOLIDAYS	Monday, Fri.	today
	September, February	a month
	the Roaring Twenties	the decade
	the Christmas season	spring, summer, autumn, winter, the fall semester
	Kwanzaa, New Year's Day	a feast day, the holiday
	Passover, Ramadan	a religious holiday or observance
HISTORICAL EVENTS AND DOCUMENTS	World War II	the war
	Battle of the Bulge	the battle
	the Great Depression (of the 1930s)	the depression [any serious economic downturn]
	the Reformation	the eighteenth century
	Paleozoic	an era or age, prehistory
	the Bill of Rights	fifth-century manuscripts

continued >>

Quick Reference 30.1 (continued)

	Capitals		Lowercase Letters
RELIGIOUS	Athena, God		a goddess, a god
TERMS		Islam	a religion
	the Torah, the Koran (or Qur'an)		a holy book
	the Bible		biblical
LETTER PARTS	Dear Ms. Schultz: Sincerely, Yours truly,		
PUBLISHED	"The Lottery"		[Capitalize first letter
AND RELEASED	*A History of the United*		of first word and all
MATERIAL	*States to 1877*		other major words]
	Jazz on Ice		the show, a performance
	Nixon Papers		the archives
	Mass in B Minor		the B minor mass
ACRONYMS AND	NASA, NATO, UCLA,		
INITIALISMS	AFL-CIO, DNA		
COMPUTER	Gateway, Dell		a computer company
TERMS	Microsoft Word, WordPerfect		computer software
	Netscape Navigator		a browser
	the Internet		a computer network
	World Wide Web, the Web		www
	Web site, Web page		a home page, a link
PROPER	Victorian		southern
ADJECTIVES	Midwestern		transatlantic
	Indo-European		alpine

EXERCISE 30-1   Individually or with a group, add capital letters as needed. See 30a through 30e for help.

1. The state of california is best known as the golden state, but other nicknames include the land of milk and honey, the el dorado state, and the grape state.

2. Most people think of san Francisco as northern california, but the city of Eureka, from the greek word meaning "I have found it," is 280 miles north of san Francisco, and the state line is another 90 miles north of eureka.

3. South of san Francisco on the california coast is santa Barbara, which hosts the annual Dickens Universe, a weeklong series of studies and celebrations of the famous writer charles dickens.

4. The highest point in the contiguous United States is mt. Whitney at 14,495 feet high, and the lowest place in the contiguous United States is bad Water in death valley at 282 feet below sea level, both located in california.

5. Having approximately 500,000 detectable seismic tremors per year, california rocks, literally.

6. Because the tehema county fairgrounds are located in red bluff, california hosts the largest three-day rodeo in the united States.

7. Numerous songs have been written about california, including "california girls" by the beach boys and the theme of the tv show *the beverly hillbillies.*

8. san Bernardino county with almost three million acres is the largest county in the united states.

9. Hollywood and movie stars are what many people associate california with, and well they might because two of California's governors, ronald reagan and arnold schwarzenegger, were actors before they became governors.

10. When told all these fantastic facts about california, a stereotypical valley girl would respond, "whatever."

ITALICS

30f What are italics?

Italic typeface slants to the right (*like this*); **roman typeface** does not (like this). MLA STYLE requires italics, not underlining, in all documents.

ROMAN   your writing
ITALICS   *your writing*

30g How do I choose between using italics and quotation marks?

As a rule, use italics for titles of long works (*Juno,* a movie) or for works that contain subsections (*Masterpiece Theater,* a television show). Generally, use quotation marks for titles of shorter works ("Smells like Teen Spirit," a song) and for titles of subsections within longer works such as books (Chapter 1, "Loomings").

Quick Reference 30.2 is a guide for using italics, quotation marks, or nothing. If you don't find what you need, locate an item that is as much like what you want as possible and use it as a model.

Quick Reference 30.2

Italics, quotation marks, or nothing

Italics	Quotation Marks or Nothing
TITLES AND NAMES	
Sense and Sensibility [a novel]	title of student essay
Death of a Salesman [a play]	act 2 [part of a play]
A Beautiful Mind [a film]	the Epilogue [a part of a film or book]
Collected Works of O. Henry [a book]	"The Last Leaf" [a story in a book]
Simon & Schuster Handbook for Writers [a textbook]	"Agreement" [a chapter in a book]
The Prose Reader [a collection of essays]	"Putting in a Good Word for Guilt" [an essay]
Iliad [a book-length poem]	"Nothing Gold Can Stay" [a short poem]
Scientific American [a magazine]	"The Molecules of Life" [an article in a magazine]
Symphonie Fantastique [a long musical work]	Violin Concerto No. 2 in B-flat Minor [a musical work identified by form, number, and key—neither quotation marks nor italics]
U2 18 Singles [an album]	"With or Without You" [a song]
Lost [a television series]	"Something Nice Back Home" [an episode of a television series]
Kids Count [a Web site title]	Excel [a software program]
the *Los Angeles Times* [a newspaper]*	
OTHER WORDS	
semper fidelis [words in a language other than English]	burrito, chutzpah [widely understood non-English words]
What does *our* imply? [a word meant as a word]	
the *abc*'s; the letter *x* [letters meant as letters]	6s and 7s; & [numerals and symbols]

*When *The* is part of a newspaper's title, don't capitalize or italicize it in MLA-style or CM-style documentation. In APA-style and CSE-style documentation, capitalize and italicize *The*.

30h Can I use italics for special emphasis?

Some professional writers, especially writers of nonfiction and self-help material, occasionally use italics to clarify a meaning or stress a point. In ACADEMIC WRITING, however, you're expected to convey special emphasis through your choice of words and sentence structure, not with italics (or underlining). If your message absolutely calls for it, use italics sparingly—and only after you're sure nothing else will do.

> Many people we *think* are powerful turn out on closer examination to be merely frightened and anxious.
>
> —Michael Korda, *Power!*

EXERCISE 30-2   Edit these sentences for correct use of italics (or underlining), quotation marks, and capitals. For help, consult 30a through 30h.

1. The article "the Banjo" in the Encyclopaedia Britannica calls the Banjo "America's only national instrument" because it combines the traditional mbanza (an instrument native to certain southern areas of africa) and some European stringed instruments.

2. The writer of a humor column at a newspaper called The "Globe and Mail" has described an imaginary newspaper called The mop and pail, where things are more ridiculous than in Real Life.

3. "Porgy and Bess," a Folk Opera by George and ira Gershwin and Du Bose Heyward, introduced the beautiful, haunting song *Summertime.*

4. Marlon Brando persuaded the Director of *The Godfather* to cast him as the Elderly don Corleone by auditioning with cotton-stuffed cheeks and mumbling hoarsely.

5. When the name of a Small Business begins with the letter a repeated many times, as in AAAAAbc "Auto Body," we know its marketing plan includes being listed First in the telephone directory.

ABBREVIATIONS

30i What are standard practices for using abbreviations?

Some abbreviations are standard in all writing circumstances (*Mr.*, not *Mister,* in a name; *St.* Louis, the city, not *Saint* Louis). In some situations, you may have a choice whether to abbreviate or spell out a word. Choose what seems suited to your PURPOSE for writing and your AUDIENCE, and be consistent within each piece of writing.

NO   The great painter Vincent Van Gogh was **b.** in Holland in 1853, but he lived most of his life and died in **Fr.**

YES   The great painter Vincent Van Gogh was **born** in Holland in 1853, but he lived most of his life and died in **France.**

NO   Our field hockey team left after Casey's **psych** class on **Tues., Oct.** 10, but the flight had to make an unexpected stop (in **Chi.**) before reaching **L.A.**

YES   Our field hockey team left after Casey's **psychology** class on **Tuesday, October** 10, but the flight had to make an unexpected stop (in **Chicago**) before reaching **Los Angeles.**

NO   Please confirm in writing your order for one **doz.** helmets in **lg** and **x-lg.**

YES   Please confirm in writing your order for one **dozen** helmets in **large** and **extra large.**

⓵ **Alerts:** (1) Many abbreviations call for periods (*Mrs., Ms., Dr.*), but the practice is changing. The trend today is to drop the periods (*PS,* not *P.S.; MD,* not *M.D.; US,* not *U.S.*), yet firm rules are still evolving.

(2) **Acronyms** (pronounceable words formed from the initials of a name) generally have no periods: *NASA* (National Aeronautics and Space Administration) and *AIDS* (*a*cquired *i*mmune *d*eficiency *s*yndrome).

(3) **Initialisms** (names spoken as separate letters) usually have no periods (*IBM, ASPCA, UN*).

(4) US Postal abbreviations for states have no periods (30k).

(5) When the final period of an abbreviation falls at the end of a sentence, that period serves also to end the sentence. ●

30j How do I use abbreviations with months, time, eras, and symbols?

MONTHS

According to MLA STYLE, abbreviations for months belong only in "Works Cited" lists, tables, charts, and the like. Write out the full spelling, never the abbreviation, in your ACADEMIC WRITING.

TIMES

Use the abbreviations *a.m.* and *p.m.* only with exact times: *7:15 a.m.; 3:47 p.m.* Although some publication styles use the capitalized versions, *A.M.* and *P.M.*, MLA style calls for the use of lowercase letters.

🛑 Aler t: Never use *a.m.* and *p.m.* in place of the words *morning, evening,* and *night.*

NO   My hardest final exam is in the **a.m.** tomorrow, but by early **p.m.**, I'll be ready to study for the rest of my finals.

YES   My hardest final exam is in the **morning** tomorrow, but by early **evening**, I'll be ready to study for the rest of my finals. ●

ERAS

In MLA style, use capital letters, without periods, in abbreviations for eras. Some writers prefer using *CE* ("common era") in place of *AD* (Latin for *anno Domini,* "in the year of our Lord") as the more inclusive term. In addition, many writers prefer using *BCE* ("before the common era") in place of *BC* ("before Christ").

When writing the abbreviations for eras, place *AD* before the year (*AD 476*) and all the others after the year (*29 BC; 165 BCE; 1100 CE*).

SYMBOLS

In MLA style, decide whether to use symbols or spelled-out words according to your topic and the focus of your document (see also 30m). However, never use a freestanding symbol, such as *$, %,* or *¢* in your sentences; always use it with a numeral. With many exceptions, spell out both the symbol and the numeral accompanying it (*twenty centimeters*), unless the number is more than one or two words (*345 centimeters,* not *three hundred forty-five centimeters*).

The exceptions include *$18; 7 lbs.; 24 KB; 6:34 a.m., 5″; 32°*; and numbers in addresses, dates, page references, and decimal fractions (*8.3*). In writing about money, the form *$25 million* is an acceptable combination of symbol, numeral, and spelled-out word.

In confined spaces, such as charts and tables, use symbols with numerals (*20¢*). In documents that focus on technical matters, use numerals but spell out the unit of measurement (*2,500 pounds*)—in MLA style. In other documentation styles, such as APA, CM, and CSE, the guidelines differ somewhat, so you need to check each style's manual.

30k   How do I use abbreviations for other elements?

TITLES

Use either a title of address before a name (*Dr. Daniel Klausner*) or an academic degree after a name (*Daniel Klausner, PhD*), not both. However, because *Jr., Sr., II, III,* and so forth are part of a given name, you can use both titles of address and academic degree abbreviations: *Dr. Martin Luther King Jr.; Gavin Alexander II, MD.*

Alerts: (1) Insert a comma both before and after an academic degree that follows a person's name, unless it falls at the end of a sentence: *Joshua Coleman, LLD, is our guest speaker,* or *Our guest speaker is Joshua Coleman, LLD.* (2) Never put a comma before an abbreviation that is part of a given name: *Steven Elliott Sr., Douglas Young III.* ●

NAMES AND TERMS

If you use a term frequently in a piece of writing, follow these guidelines: The first time you use the term, spell it out completely and then put its abbreviation in parentheses immediately after. In later references, use the abbreviation alone.

Spain voted to continue as a member of the **North Atlantic Treaty Organization (NATO)**, to the surprise of other **NATO** members.

When referring to the United States, use the abbreviation *US* as a modifier before a noun (*the US ski team*), but spell out *United States* when you use it as a noun (*the ski team from the United States*).

ADDRESSES

If you include a full address in a piece of writing, use the two-letter postal abbreviation for the state name. For any other combination of a city and a state, or a state by itself, spell out the state name; never abbreviate it.

Alert: When you write the names of a US city and state within a sentence, use a comma before and after the state.

NO   Portland**,** Oregon is much larger than Portland, Maine.

YES   Portland**,** Oregon**,** is much larger than Portland, Maine.

If you include a ZIP code, however, don't use a comma after the state. Do place the comma after the ZIP code. ●

SCHOLARLY WRITING (MLA STYLE)

MLA style permits abbreviations for a selection of scholarly terms. These are listed in Quick Reference 30.3. Never use them in the body of your ACADEMIC WRITING. Reserve them for your "Works Cited" lists and for any notes you might write in a separate list at the end of your research paper.

Quick Reference 30.3

Major scholarly abbreviations—MLA style

anon.	anonymous	**i.e.**	that is
b.	born	**ms., mss.**	manuscript,
c. *or* ©	copyright		manuscripts
c. *or* **ca.**	circa *or* about	**NB**	note well (*nota bene*)
	[with dates]	**n.d.**	no date (of
cf.	compare		publication)
col., cols.	column, columns	**p., pp.**	page, pages
d.	died	**par.**	paragraph
ed., eds.	edition, edited by,	**pref.**	preface, preface by
	editor(s)	**rept.**	report, reported by
e.g.	for example	**rev.**	review, reviewed by;
esp.	especially		revised, revised by
et al.	and others	**sec., secs.**	section, sections
ff.	following pages,	**v.** *or* **vs.**	versus [*v.* in legal
	following lines,		cases]
	folios	**vol., vols.**	volume, volumes

30l When can I use *etc.*?

The abbreviation *etc.* comes from the Latin *et cetera,* meaning "and the rest." In ACADEMIC WRITING, don't use *etc.* Accepted substitutes include *and the like, and so on, and so forth,* among others. Even better is a more concrete description. An acceptable use of *etc.* is in tables and charts.

> **NO** We took paper plates, plastic forks, **etc.,** to the picnic.
>
> **YES** We took paper plates, plastic forks, **and other disposable items** to the picnic.

! Alert: If you do write *etc.,* always put a comma after the period if the abbreviation falls in the middle of a sentence. ●

EXERCISE 30-3   Working individually or with a group, revise these sentences for correct use of abbreviations. For help, consult 30i through 30l.

1. Originally named the Geo. S. Parker Company, located in Salem, Mass., the toy co. changed its name to Parker Bros. when Chas. joined the business in 1888.

2. Sev. of their games have become quite famous, esp. Monopoly and Clue, both of which were released in the 20th cent.

3. The obj. of the game Monopoly (meaning "dominating the mkt.") is to get the most $ by purchasing, renting, & selling real est.

4. Clue, another pop. brd. game, is a murder mys. in which players move from 1 rm. to another, making accusations to reveal the i.d. of the murderer, the weapon used, and the room where the crime took place.

5. On a cold day in Jan., when the snow is 3 ft. deep and it's dark by early eve., passing the hrs. with your fam. and friends playing a board game is great fun.

NUMBERS

30m When do I use spelled-out numbers?

Your decision to write a number as a word or as a figure depends on what you're referring to and how often numbers occur in your piece of writing. The guidelines we give in this handbook are for MLA STYLE, which focuses on writing in the humanities. For other disciplines, follow the guidelines in their style manuals.

When you write numbers for more than one category in a piece of writing, reserve figures for some categories of numbers and spelled-out words for other categories. Never mix spelled-out numbers and figures for a particular category.

> NO   In **four** days, our volunteers increased from **five** to **eight** to 17 to **233.**

> YES   In **four** days, our volunteers increased from **5** to **8** to 17 to **233.**
> [Numbers referring to volunteers are in numerals, while *four* is spelled out because it refers to a different category: days.]

🛇 Alert: When you write a two-word number, use a hyphen between the spelled-out words, starting with *twenty-one* and continuing through *ninety-nine.* ●

If you use numbers infrequently in a document, spell out all numbers that call for no more than two words: *fifty-two cards, twelve hundred students.* If you use specific numbers often in a document (temperatures when writing about climate, percentages in an economics essay, or other specific measurements of time, distance, and other quantities), use figures: *36 inches, 11 nanoseconds.* If you give only an approximation, spell out the numbers: *About twelve inches of snow fell.*

In the humanities, the names of centuries are always spelled out: *the eighteenth century.*

When you write for courses in the humanities, never start a sentence with a figure. Spell out the number—or better still, revise the sentence so that the number doesn't need to fall at the beginning. For practices in other disciplines, consult their manuals.

NO $375 **dollars** for each credit is the tuition rate for nonresidents.

YES   ~~Three hundred seventy five dollars for each credit is the tuition~~ ~~rate for nonresidents.~~

YES   The tuition rate for nonresidents is $375 for each credit.

30n What are standard practices for writing numbers?

Quick Reference 30.4 shows standard practices for writing numbers. Consider it a basic guide, and rely on the manual of each documentation style for answers to other questions you may have.

Quick Reference 30.4	■ ■ ■ ■ ■ ■ ■

Specific numbers in writing

DATES	August 6, 1941
	1732–1845
	from 34 BC to AD 230 (*or* 34 BCE to 230 CE)
ADDRESSES	10 Downing Street
	237 North 8th Street
	Export Falls, MN 92025
TIMES	8:09 a.m., 6:00 p.m.
	six o'clock (*not* 6 o'clock)
	four in the afternoon *or* 4 p.m. (*not* four p.m.)
DECIMALS	0.01
AND FRACTIONS	98.6
	3.1416
	7/8
	12 1/4
	a sixth
	three-quarters (*not* 3-quarters)
	one-half
CHAPTERS	Chapter 27, page 2
AND PAGES	p. 1029 *or* pp. 660–62 (MLA style)
SCORES	a 6–0 score
AND STATISTICS	29% (or twenty-nine percent)
	a 5 to 1 ratio (*and* a ratio of 5:1)
	a one percent change (*and* at the 1 percent level)

continued >>

Quick Reference 30.4	(continued)

IDENTIFICATION NUMBERS	94.4 on the FM dial please call (012) 345–6789
MEASUREMENTS	67.8 miles per hour 2 level teaspoons a 700-word essay 8-by-10-inch photograph 2 feet 1.5 gallons 14 liters
ACT, SCENE, AND LINE	act 2, scene 2 (*or* act II, scene ii) lines 75–79
TEMPERATURES	40°F *or* −5°F 20° Celsius
MONEY	$1.2 billion $3.41 25¢ (*or* twenty-five cents) $10,000

EXERCISE 30-4 Revise these sentences so that the numbers are in correct form, either spelled out or as figures. For help, consult 30m and 30n.

1. At five fifteen p.m., the nearly empty city streets filled with 1000's of commuters.

2. A tarantula spider can survive without food for about two years and 3 months.

3. By the end of act one, scene five, Romeo and Juliet are in love and at the mercy of their unhappy fate.

4. Sound travels through air at a speed of 1,089 feet per second, but in water it travels four hundred and fifty percent faster, at four thousand, eight hundred fifty-nine feet per second.

5. 21 years old and unhappily married, Cleopatra met middle-aged Julius Caesar in forty-eight BCE.

6. An adult blue whale, which can weigh one hundred tons—the combined weight of 30 elephants—has gained over seven-point-five pounds an hour since infancy.

7. On the morning of August thirteen, nineteen hundred thirty, 3 huge meteorites smashed into the Amazon jungle.

8. 2 out of every 5 people who have ever lived on earth are alive today, according to 1 estimate.

9. The house at six hundred and fifty-three Oak Street—the 1 that children think is haunted—has been empty for 8 years, waiting for a buyer willing to pay its price of $ six million, forty-nine thousand dollars.

10. The 1912 sinking of the *Titanic*, in which one thousand five hundred and three people drowned, is widely known, but few people remember that more than three thousand people lost their lives aboard the ferryboat *Doña Paz* when it hit an oil tanker in the Philippines in nineteen eighty-seven.

30o How do I use hyphens with spelled-out numbers?

A **spelled-out number** uses words, not figures. Quick Reference 30.5 gives you guidelines.

Alert: Use figures rather than words for a fraction written in more than two words. If your context calls for figures, use hyphens only between the words of the numerator and only between the words of the denominator—but never between the numerator and the denominator: two one-hundredths (*2/100*), thirty-three ten-thousandths (*33/10,000*). ●

Quick Reference 30.5 ■ ■ ■ ■ ■ ■ ■ ■

Hyphens with spelled out numbers

- Use a hyphen between two-word numbers from *twenty-one* through *ninety-nine,* whether they stand alone or are part of a larger number.

  YES thirty-five two hundred thirty-five

- Use a hyphen in a COMPOUND-WORD modifier formed from a number and a word, whether the number is in words or figures.

  YES fifty-minute class [*also* 50-minute class]

  YES three-to-one odds [*also* 3-to-1 odds]

- Use a hyphen between the numerator and the denominator of two-word fractions.

  YES one-half two-fifths seven-tenths

- Use a hyphen between compound nouns joining two units of measure.

  YES light-years kilowatt-hours

31

Spelling

31a   What makes a good speller?

You might be surprised to hear that good spellers don't know how to spell and hyphenate every word they write. What they do know, however, is to check if they're not sure of a word's spelling. If your inner voice questions a spelling, do what good spellers do—consult a dictionary.

What do you do if even the first few letters of a word seem mysterious? Our best advice is that you think of an easy-to-spell SYNONYM for the word you need; look up that synonym in a thesaurus; and among the synonyms, find the word you need to spell.

Many people incorrectly believe that only naturally skilled spellers can write well. The truth is that correct spelling matters a great deal in final drafts, but not in earlier drafts. The best time to check spellings you doubt is when you're EDITING.

The various origins and ways that English-speaking people around the world pronounce words make it almost impossible to rely solely on pronunciation to spell a word. What you can rely on, however, are the proofreading hints and spelling rules explained in this chapter.

Alert: Word-processing software usually includes a spell-check program, which claims to spot spelling errors because the words typed in don't match the spellings in the software's dictionary. Such programs have one major drawback. The programs can't detect that you've spelled a word incorrectly if what you've typed is a legitimate spelling of a legitimate word. For example, if you mean *top* but type *too,* or if you mean *from* and type *form,* no spell-check program will "see" that mistake. In these and similar cases, only the human eye (that is, a reader) can discover the errors. ●

31b   How can I proofread for errors in spelling and hyphen use?

Many spelling errors are the result of illegible handwriting, slips of the pen, or typographical mistakes. Catching these "typos" requires especially careful proofreading, using the techniques in Quick Reference 31.1.

■ ■ ■ ■ ■ ■ ■ ■

Proofreading for errors in spelling

- Slow down your reading speed to allow yourself to concentrate on the individual letters of words rather than on the meaning of the words.

- Stay within your "visual span," the number of letters you can identify with a single glance (for most people, about six letters).

- Put a ruler or large index card under each line as you proofread, to focus your vision and concentration.

- Read each paragraph in reverse, from the last sentence to the first. This method can keep you from being distracted by the meaning of the material.

31c How are plurals spelled?

In American English, plurals take many forms. The most common form adds -s or -es at the end of the word. The following list covers all variations of creating plurals.

- **Adding -s or -es:** Plurals of most words are formed by adding -s, including words that end in "hard" -ch (sounding like k): *leg, legs; shoe, shoes; stomach, stomachs.* Words ending in -s, -sh, -x, -z, or "soft" -ch (as in *beach*) are formed by adding -es to the singular: *lens, lenses; tax, taxes; beach, beaches.*

- **Words ending in -o:** Add -s if the -o is preceded by a vowel: *radio, radios; cameo, cameos.* Add -es if the -o is preceded by a consonant: *potato, potatoes.* With a few words, you can choose the -s or -es plural form, but current practice generally supports adding -es: *cargo, cargoes; tornado, tornadoes; zero, zeros* or *zeroes.*

- **Words ending in -f or -fe:** Some words ending in -f and -fe are made plural by adding -s: *belief, beliefs.* Others require changing -f or -fe to -ves: *life, lives; leaf, leaves.* Words ending in -ff or -ffe simply add -s: *staff, staffs; giraffe, giraffes.*

- **Compound words:** For most compound words, add -s or -es at the end of the last word: *checkbooks, player-coaches.* In a few cases, the first word is made plural: *sister-in-law, sisters-in-law; miles per hour.* (For information about hyphens in compound words, see 31g.)

- **Internal changes and endings other than -s:** A few words change internally or add endings other than -s to become plural: *foot, feet; man, men; crisis, crises; child, children.*

- **Foreign words:** The best advice is to check your dictionary. In general, many Latin words ending in *-um* form the plural by changing *-um* to *-a*: *curriculum, curricula; datum, data; medium, media.* Also, Latin words that end in *-us* usually form the plural by changing *-us* to *-i*: *alumnus, alumni; syllabus, syllabi.* Additionally, Greek words that end in *-on* usually form the plural by changing *-on* to *-a*: *criterion, criteria; phenomenon, phenomena.*

- **One-form words:** Some words have the same form in both the singular and the plural: *deer, elk, fish.* You need to use modifiers, as necessary, to indicate which form you mean: ***one** deer, **nine** deer.*

EXERCISE 31-1 Write the correct plural form of these words. For help, consult 31c.

1. yourself
2. sheep
3. photo
4. woman
5. appendix
6. millennium
7. lamp
8. runner-up
9. criterion
10. lunch
11. echo
12. syllabus
13. wife
14. get-together
15. crisis

31d How are suffixes spelled?

A **suffix** is an ending added to a word that changes the word's meaning or its grammatical function. For example, adding the suffix *-able* to the VERB *depend* creates the ADJECTIVE *dependable*.

- **-y words:** If the letter before a final *-y* is a consonant, change the *-y* to *-i* and add the suffix: *try, tries, tried.* In the case of *trying* and similar words, the following rule applies: Keep the *-y* when the suffix begins with *-i* (*apply, applying*). If the letter before the final *-y* is a vowel, keep the final *-y: employ, employed, employing.* These rules don't apply to IRREGULAR VERBS (see Quick Reference 15.4 in section 15d).

- **-e words:** Drop a final *-e* when the suffix begins with a vowel, unless doing this would cause confusion: for example, *be + ing* can't be written *bing,* but *require* does become *requiring; like* does become *liking.* Keep the final *-e* when the suffix begins with a consonant: *require, requirement; like, likely.* Exceptions include *argue, argument; judge, judgment; true, truly.*

- **Words that double a final letter:** If the final letter is a consonant, double it *only* if it passes three tests: (1) Its last two letters are a vowel followed by a consonant; (2) it has one syllable or is accented on the last syllable;

(3) the suffix begins with a vowel: *drop, drop**ped**; begin, begin**ning**; forget, forget**table**.*

- **-cede, -ceed, -sede words:** Only one word in the English language ends in -*sede: super**sede**.* Only three words end in -*ceed: ex**ceed**, pro**ceed**, suc**ceed**.* All other words with endings that sound like "seed" end in -*cede: con**cede**, inter**cede**, pre**cede**.*

- **-ally and -ly words:** The suffixes -*ally* and -*ly* turn words into adverbs. For words ending in -*ic,* add -*ally: logic**ally**, statistic**ally**.* Otherwise, add -*ly: quick**ly**, sharp**ly**.*

- **-ance, -ence, and -ible, -able:** No consistent rules govern words with these suffixes. When in doubt, look up the word.

31e What is the *ie, ei* rule?

The famous rhymed rule for using *ie* and *ei* is usually true:

I before *e* [bel**ie**ve, f**ie**ld, gr**ie**f],
Except after *c* [c**ei**ling, conc**ei**t],
Or when sounded like "ay"—
As in n**ei**ghbor and w**ei**gh [**ei**ght, v**ei**n].

There are major exceptions (sorry!) to the *ie, ei* rule, listed here. Our best advice is that you memorize them.

- *ie:* consc**ie**nce, financ**ie**r, sc**ie**nce, spec**ie**s

- *ei:* **ei**ther, n**ei**ther, l**ei**sure, s**ei**ze, counterf**ei**t, for**ei**gn, forf**ei**t, sl**ei**ght (as in *sl**ei**ght of hand*), w**ei**rd

EXERCISE 31-2   Follow the directions for each group of words. For help, consult 31d and 31e.

1. Add -*able* or -*ible:* (a) profit; (b) reproduce; (c) control; (d) coerce; (e) recognize.

2. Add -*ance* or -*ence:* (a) luxuri____; (b) prud____; (c) devi____; (d) resist____; (e) independ____.

3. Drop the final -*e* as needed: (a) true + ly; (b) joke + ing; (c) fortunate + ly; (d) appease + ing; (e) appease + ment.

4. Change the final -*y* to -*i* as needed: (a) happy + ness; (b) pry + ed; (c) pry + ing; (d) dry + ly; (e) beautify + ing.

5. Double the final consonant as needed: (a) commit + ed; (b) commit + ment; (c) drop + ed; (d) occur + ed; (e) regret + ful.

6. Insert *ie* or *ei* correctly: (a) rel____f; (b) ach____ve; (c) w____rd; (d) n____ce; (e) dec____ve.

31f How are homonyms and other frequently confused words spelled?

Homonyms are words that sound exactly like other words: *to, too, two; no, know.* The different spellings of homonyms tend to confuse many writers. The same holds for words that sound almost alike (*accept, except; conscience, conscious*).

Another reason for spelling problems is so-called swallowed pronunciation, which means one or more letters at the end of a word aren't pronounced clearly. For example, the *-d* ending in *used to* or *prejudiced* or the *-ten* ending in *written* are often swallowed rather than pronounced. When writers spell as they mispronounce, spelling errors result.

For more information about word usage that affects spelling, see Chapter 13, "Usage Glossary." Quick Reference 31.2 lists homonyms and other words that can be confused and lead to misspellings.

Quick Reference 31.2

Homonyms and other frequently confused words

• ACCEPT	to receive
EXCEPT	with the exclusion of
• ADVICE	recommendation
ADVISE	to recommend
• AFFECT	to influence [verb]; emotion [noun]
EFFECT	result [noun]; to bring about or cause [verb]
• AISLE	space between rows
ISLE	island
• ALLUDE	to make indirect reference to
ELUDE	to avoid
• ALLUSION	indirect reference
ILLUSION	false idea, misleading appearance
• ALREADY	by this time
ALL READY	fully prepared
• ALTAR	sacred platform or place
ALTER	to change
• ALTOGETHER	thoroughly
ALL TOGETHER	everyone or everything in one place
• ARE	PLURAL form of *to be*
HOUR	sixty minutes
OUR	plural form of *my*

continued >>

Quick Reference 31.2   (continued)

• ASCENT	the act of rising or climbing
ASSENT	consent [noun]; to consent [verb]
• ASSISTANCE	help
ASSISTANTS	helpers
• BARE	nude, unadorned
BEAR	to carry; an animal
• BOARD	piece of wood
BORED	uninterested
• BRAKE	device for stopping
BREAK	to destroy, make into pieces
• BREATH	air taken in
BREATHE	to take in air
• BUY	to purchase
BY	next to, through the agency of
• CAPITAL	major city; money
CAPITOL	government building
• CHOOSE	to pick
CHOSE	PAST TENSE of *choose*
• CITE	to point out
SIGHT	vision
SITE	a place
• CLOTHES	garments
CLOTHS	pieces of fabric
• COARSE	rough
COURSE	path; series of lectures
• COMPLEMENT	something that completes
COMPLIMENT	praise, flattery
• CONSCIENCE	sense of morality
CONSCIOUS	awake, aware
• COUNCIL	governing body
COUNSEL	advice [noun]; to advise [verb]
• DAIRY	place associated with milk production
DIARY	personal journal
• DESCENT	downward movement
DISSENT	disagreement

continued >>

Quick Reference 31.2 (continued)

• DESERT	to abandon [verb]; dry, usually sandy area [noun]
DESSERT	final, sweet course in a meal
• DEVICE	a plan; an implement
DEVISE	to create
• DIE	to lose life (dying) [verb]; one of a pair of dice [noun]
DYE	to change the color of something (dyeing)
• DOMINANT	commanding, controlling
DOMINATE	to control
• ELICIT	to draw out
ILLICIT	illegal
• EMINENT	prominent
IMMANENT	living within; inherent
IMMINENT	about to happen
• ENVELOP	to surround
ENVELOPE	container for a letter or other papers
• FAIR	light-skinned; just, honest
FARE	money for transportation; food
• FORMALLY	conventionally, with ceremony
FORMERLY	previously
• FORTH	forward
FOURTH	number four in a series
• GORILLA	animal in ape family
GUERRILLA	fighter conducting surprise attacks
• HEAR	to sense sound by ear
HERE	in this place
• HOLE	opening
WHOLE	complete; an entire thing
• HUMAN	relating to the species *Homo sapiens*
HUMANE	compassionate
• INSURE	to buy or give insurance
ENSURE	to guarantee, protect
• ITS	POSSESSIVE form of *it*
IT'S	CONTRACTION for *it is*
• KNOW	to comprehend
NO	negative

continued >>

Quick Reference 31.2   (continued)

• LATER	after a time
LATTER	second one of two things
• LEAD	a heavy metal [noun]; to guide [verb]
LED	past tense of *lead*
• LIGHTNING	storm-related electricity
LIGHTENING	making lighter
• LOOSE	unbound, not tightly fastened
LOSE	to misplace
• MAYBE	perhaps [adverb]
MAY BE	might be [verb]
• MEAT	animal flesh
MEET	to encounter
• MINER	a person who works in a mine
MINOR	underage; less important
• MORAL	distinguishing right from wrong; the lesson of a fable, story, or event
MORALE	attitude or outlook, usually of a group
• OF	PREPOSITION indicating origin
OFF	away from; not on
• PASSED	past tense of *pass*
PAST	at a previous time
• PATIENCE	forbearance
PATIENTS	people under medical care
• PEACE	absence of fighting
PIECE	part of a whole; musical arrangement
• PERSONAL	intimate
PERSONNEL	employees
• PLAIN	simple, unadorned
PLANE	to shave wood; aircraft
• PRECEDE	to come before
PROCEED	to continue
• PRESENCE	being at hand; attendance at a place or in something
PRESENTS	gifts
• PRINCIPAL	foremost [adjective]; school head [noun]
PRINCIPLE	moral conviction, basic truth

continued >>

Quick Reference 31.2   (continued)

•	QUIET	silent, calm
	QUITE	very
•	RAIN	water that falls to earth [noun]; to fall like rain [verb]
	REIGN	to rule
	REIN	strap to guide or control an animal [noun]; to guide or control [verb]
•	RAISE	to lift up
	RAZE	to tear down
•	RESPECTFULLY	with respect
	RESPECTIVELY	in that order
•	RIGHT	correct; opposite of *left*
	RITE	ritual
	WRITE	to put words on paper
•	ROAD	path
	RODE	past tense of *ride*
•	SCENE	place of an action; segment of a play
	SEEN	viewed
•	SENSE	perception, understanding
	SINCE	measurement of past time; because
•	STATIONARY	standing still
	STATIONERY	writing paper
•	THAN	in comparison with; besides
	THEN	at that time; next; therefore
•	THEIR	possessive form of *they*
	THERE	in that place
	THEY'RE	contraction of *they are*
•	THROUGH	finished; into and out of
	THREW	past tense of *throw*
	THOROUGH	complete
•	TO	toward
	TOO	also; indicates degree (*too much*)
	TWO	number following *one*
•	WAIST	midsection of the body
	WASTE	discarded material [noun]; to squander, to fail to use up [verb]

continued >>

Quick Reference 31.2 (continued)

- WEAK — not strong
  WEEK — seven days
- WEATHER — climatic condition
  WHETHER — if, when alternatives are expressed or implied
- WHERE — in which place
  WERE — past tense of *be*
- WHICH — one of a group
  WITCH — female sorcerer
- WHOSE — possessive form of *who*
  WHO'S — contraction for *who is*
- YOUR — possessive form of *you*
  YOU'RE — contraction for *you are*
  YORE — long past

EXERCISE 31-3 Circle the correct homonym or commonly confused word of each group in parentheses.

   Imagine that you (are, our) standing in the middle of a busy sidewalk, with a worried look on (your, you're, yore) face. In your hand (your, you're, yore) holding a map, (which, witch) you are puzzling over. If that happened in (real, reel) life, (its, it's) almost certain that within (to, too, two) or three minutes a passerby would ask if you (where, were) lost and would offer you (assistance, assistants). That helpful passerby, (buy, by) taking a (personal, personnel) interest in your problem, is displaying a quality known as empathy—the ability (to, too, two) put oneself in another person's place. Some researchers claim that empathy is an instinct that (human, humane) beings share with many other animals. Other scientists wonder (weather, whether) empathy is instead a (conscience, conscious) (moral, morale) choice that people make. Whatever explanation for the origin (of, off) empathy is (right, rite, write), such empathy generally has a positive (affect, effect)—especially if (your, you're, yore) a person who (maybe, may be) (to, too, two) lost to (know, no) (where, were) (to, too, two) turn.

31g What are compound words?

A **compound word** puts together two or more words to express one concept.

   Open compound words remain as separate words, such as *decision making*, *problem solving*, and *editor in chief*.

Hyphenated compound words use a hyphen between the words, such as *trade-in, fuel-efficient,* and *tax-sheltered.* For punctuation advice about hyphens, see 29i.

Closed compound words appear as one word, such as *proofread, citywide,* and *workweek.*

Single-word compounds usually start as open (two-word) compounds and then become hyphenated compounds before ending up as closed compounds. To check whether a compound term consists of closed, hyphenated, or open words, consult an up-to-date dictionary.

For more help with your writing, grammar, and research, go to **www.mycomplab.com**

Research and Writing

32

Types and Uses of Research in Writing

32a What is the role of research in writing?

Research is a systematic process of gathering information to answer a question. You're doing research when you're trying to decide which college to attend, which MP3 player to buy, or which summer job to accept. Perhaps you find facts or information, in print or online. You analyze and evaluate what you learn and then make a decision.

Other kinds of research are more formal. People wanting to start small businesses usually have to research the local business climate and present their findings to lenders to get a loan. Citizens wanting to oppose a new construction project have to research its impact and present their findings in a careful way to elected officials.

The amount of research in a piece of writing can vary, depending on your audience, purpose, and type of writing (see 1b; 7a). You might be familiar with RESEARCH PAPERS* or TERM PAPERS, which are dense with sources, synthesizing information to support a thesis. Chapter 33 will help you with extended formal research projects.

However, any essay might potentially benefit from even a little research. Finding a crucial fact might improve an argument. Consider the original and revised paragraphs below:

ORIGINAL	The homeless situation is even more serious when we understand the variety of people who lack a place to sleep every night. It's not just a problem that afflicts single men or individuals with physical or mental problems. Many families are homeless.
RESEARCHED	The homeless situation is even more serious when we understand the variety of people who lack a place to sleep every night. It's not just a problem that afflicts single men or individuals with physical or mental problems. According to the U.S. Department of

---

*Words printed in SMALL CAPITAL LETTERS are discussed elsewhere in the text and are defined in the Terms Glossary at the back of this book.

Housing and Urban Development, of the 750,000 homeless people in America, nearly 40% are families (Eaton-Robb).

WORK CITED

Eaton-Robb, Pat. "Number of Homeless Families Rises." *USA Today* 10 Oct. 2007. Web. 15 Oct. 2007.

In the second version, the writer specifically answers the research question, "How many families are homeless?" Whenever writing has a vague term like "a lot" or "many" or "some," research can improve it with more precise information. Of course, you might also find facts that complicate your argument. For example, trying to persuade people to oppose "the death tax" (taxes paid by a deceased person's estate) may become more difficult when you learn that it affects only the wealthiest two percent of Americans who leave heirs over $2 million.

EXERCISE 32-1   The following paragraph has a number of general statements. Generate a list of all the possible research questions you might pursue to strengthen the paragraph.

> **EXAMPLE**   "If we fail to act on global warming, our coastal cities will be damaged by rising ocean levels."
>
> **POSSIBLE QUESTIONS**   How will global warming affect oceans? How much will oceans rise? Which cities will be affected?

> In a troubling reversal of roles, boys are now considerably more at risk in school than are girls. Girls used to be denied many opportunities in schools and colleges, as boys enjoyed several unfair advantages. Now, however, girls are graduating from high schools at much higher rates. They are performing better on standardized tests and entering colleges and universities at much higher levels, to the extent that several colleges now have programs specifically targeted to attract and admit more male students. Women substantially outnumber men in admission to medical and law schools. A number of factors is responsible, but unless we take actions to ensure academic quality and success for both boys and girls, we will need to create affirmative action programs for men.

32b   What are reasons for doing research?

Writers do research for several reasons and at different points in the writing process, from generating and planning to revising.

1. **To find a fact or piece of information.** Sometimes you simply need to answer a direct question of "how much?" or "when?" or "where?" or "who?" In each case, you need to find a credible source and extract only

the specific information necessary to answer the question. Example: How does the cost of college today compare to the cost twenty years ago?

2. **To understand an issue or situation more fully.** Sometimes you need to learn basic information about a topic, even before writing. You're trying to learn not only information new to you but also the range of viewpoints or opinions on a particular topic. Rather than identifying a single fact from a source, you're reading many sources, sometimes with a goal of synthesizing them, sometimes with the goal of generating more specific research questions. Example: What are the effects of globalization?

3. **To synthesize current information.** Even if you know a good deal about a topic, you may need to bring together the most current information. A **review of the literature** is a synthesis of the latest knowledge on a particular topic. It may be part of a longer project, as in the case of SCIENCE REPORTS (41i.1), or it may be the project itself as in the case of SCIENCE REVIEWS (41i.2). Example: What treatments are now possible for Alzheimer's disease?

4. **To identify a specific opinion or point of view.** A good strategy in argumentative writing is to state and refute counter arguments. You might research in order to find out what people who disagree with you believe and, more important, why. You can then explain the shortcomings of their views or explain why your position is better. You might also look for expert viewpoints that support your own. Example: What are the main arguments in favor of censoring cable television programs? For more information on writing arguments, see Chapter 5.

5. **To create new knowledge.** Writers often do kinds of research that make new knowledge rather than find knowledge others have already created. This is the kind of research that chemists and biologists do, but so do psychologists, sociologists, journalists and so on. This kind of research includes experiments, surveys, interviews, ethnographies, and observations. For example, if you were writing a guide to coffee houses in a certain area, you'd need to visit all of them, take notes, and present your findings to readers. Field research (32e) is a general name for this kind of research.

32c What is the process of doing research?

Although the research process varies according to the specific reason you're doing research (32b) and to your writing situation (1a), a few general steps are common to most projects involving research.

1. **Develop a research question.** What is the question that you need to answer by conducting research? Some questions might be very specific, such as when you're looking for a piece of data; consider, for example, "What was the population of Canada in 1880?" or "How much methane is produced by dairy cattle in the United States?" With substantial projects, however, your research question involves more than looking for a single fact. Consider, for example, "What is the most practical way to reduce global warming caused by automobile emissions?" or "How might the depiction of college students on television influence general attitudes about higher education?" Section 33e has more advice about developing effective research questions.

2. **Decide what kinds of sources will best answer your question.** Some research questions are best answered by finding appropriate PUBLISHED SOURCES, generally through the library (Chapter 34). Others might require **field research**, gathering data firsthand through surveying, interviewing, or observing (32e). We talk about kinds of sources in 32d.

3. **Develop a search strategy.** Once you determine the sources you need, develop a plan for finding them. How will you search the library, for example (34b)? Whom will you contact to interview? When will you visit a location for direct observations, and how will you take notes once you're there? Be purposeful in designing your strategy so you'll be effective and efficient.

4. **Gather your sources.** This is the stage where you not only find appropriate books and articles, for example, but also take notes (33k). Your goal is to accumulate more than enough materials so that you feel confident you can answer your research question.

5. **Interpret your source materials.** Having a bunch of reading notes, a lot of survey answers, a transcript of an interview, or a list of direct observations is only part of the process. Organizing and interpreting them to understand how they answer your research question is just as vital. This stage can also tell you whether your search strategy has been successful or whether you need to gather even more sources. Look for themes or patterns. Look not only for information and ideas that seem to fit together but also for conflicts or tensions.

6. **Draft, revise, edit, and proofread your paper.** The general writing processes that we explained in Chapter 2 also apply to researched writing. In sections 33l–33n, we explain how to apply specifically those processes to writing research papers.

32d What kinds of sources do writers use?

A **source** is any form of information that provides ideas, examples, information, or evidence, and different kinds of college writing require different kinds of sources (7b). You're probably most familiar with PUBLISHED SOURCES: books, magazine or journal articles, sources from organizational Web sites, and so on. Being able to use published sources effectively is so fundamental, especially to academic writing, that we've devoted two chapters entirely to them. Chapter 34 talks about finding and evaluating published sources and Chapter 35 talks about using them and avoiding plagiarism.

However, writers use other sources, too. As we discussed in Chapter 7, these include interviews; surveys; direct observations of situations, places, or people; performances or lectures; museums; and so on.

🌐 **ESOL Tip:** In the United States, PLAGIARISM is a major offense in academic writing. In some cultures, it's customary to take material from scholarly authorities on your topic. However, this practice is forbidden in the United States unless you use quotation marks around the exact words and then state the place where you found those words. For detailed information about how to avoid plagiarism, see Chapter 35. ●

A source is either primary or secondary. **Primary sources** are firsthand evidence based on your own or someone else's original work or direct observation. Primary sources can take the form of experiments, surveys, interviews, memoirs, FIELD RESEARCH (32e), or original creative works (for example, poems, novels, paintings and other art, plays, films, or musical compositions). **Secondary sources** report, describe, comment on, or analyze the experiences or work of others. Quick Reference 4.4 on page 114 illustrates the difference.

Suppose you're researching student attitudes toward marriage. Surveying several students would be primary research. Consulting scholars' books and articles about students and marriage would be secondary research. Your decision to use primary or secondary sources depends on your RESEARCH QUESTION or the nature of your assignment.

32e What is field research?

Field research involves going into real-life situations to observe, survey, interview, or join some activity firsthand. A field researcher might, for example, go to a factory, a lecture, a day-care center, or a mall— anywhere that people engage in everyday activities. A field researcher might also interview experts and other identified individuals. Because field research yields original data, it's a PRIMARY SOURCE.

Conducting field research takes careful planning. Be sure to allow time to gather the data you want, ANALYZE it, and then SYNTHESIZE it with other sources and with your own knowledge and experience. Field research often involves events that can't be revisited. Therefore, record as much information as possible during your research and decide later what information you can use. Afterwards, while your memory is fresh, go over your notes and highlight major types of information. Also, fill in any details you might not have written down.

32e.1 Surveying

Surveys use several questions to gather information from a number of people, asking about experiences, situations, opinions, or attitudes. Responses to multiple choice or true/false questions are easy for people to complete and for researchers to summarize and report, as totals or averages. Open-ended questions, in which people are asked to respond in writing to a question, require more effort on the part of researchers and people completing the survey. However, they sometimes have the advantage of providing more complete or accurate information.

If you want to survey a group of people, allow time to write, reflect on, and revise a questionnaire. Test the questionnaire on a few people. Revise any questions that don't work well. For advice, see Quick Reference 32.1.

Quick Reference 32.1

Guidelines for developing a questionnaire

1. Define what you want to learn.
2. Identify the appropriate type and numbers of people to answer your survey so that you get the information you need.
3. Write questions to elicit the information.
4. Use appropriate language when phrasing questions so that they are easy to understand.
5. Make sure that your wording does not imply what you want to hear.
6. Decide whether to include open-ended questions that allow people to write their own answers.
7. Test a draft of the questionnaire on a small group of people. If any question is misinterpreted or difficult to understand, revise and retest it.

When you report findings from a survey, keep within your limitations. For example, if the only people who answer your survey are students at a particular college or people at a particular shopping mall, you can't claim your results represent "all college students" or "all Americans and Canadians." For further advice on writing about quantitative information, see section 3e.

32e.2 Observing people and situations

CASE STUDIES (7d.4) and ETHNOGRAPHIES (7d.5) are examples of researching people in specific situations. For observations of behavior (for example, the audience at a sporting event or elementary school children at play during recess), you can take notes during the activity. Permission to videotape instead of taking notes is hard to get because of privacy concerns. Try to remain objective so that you can see things clearly. One strategy is to take notes in a two-column format. On the left, record only objective observations; on the right, record comments or possible interpretations. Figure 32.1 is an example of a double-column note strategy.

32e.3 Interviewing

An expert can offer valuable information, a new point of view, and firsthand facts, statistics, and examples. Probably the best place to start is with the faculty at your college. Your instructors are also scholars and researchers with expertise in many areas. They may suggest good additional sources, as well as other experts to contact. Indeed, your family and friends might qualify as

Notes	Comment/Analyses
Small conference room; round table covered with papers	
JP suggests fundraising plan	JP seems nervous. Her normal behavior, or is it this situation?
AR and CT lean forward; SM leans back	
SM interrupts JP's plan, asks for more; CT silent	The fact that JP and AR are women might explain SM's response. Or is it that he's more senior?
JP continues proposal	
SM looks out window, taps pencil	Seems to have made up his mind. A power move?

Figure 32.1 A double-column field research note

experts, if they've been involved with an issue you're researching. Corporations, institutions, and professional organizations often have public relations offices that can answer questions or put you in contact with experts.

Make every attempt to conduct interviews in person so that you can observe body language and facial expressions as you talk. However, if distance is a problem, you can conduct interviews over the phone or online. Quick Reference 32.2 provides specific suggestions for conducting interviews.

Quick Reference 32.2

■ ■ ■ ■ ■ ■ ■

Conducting research interviews

- Arrange the interview well in advance, conduct background research, prepare specific questions, and show up on time.

- Rehearse how to ask your questions without reading them (perhaps highlight the key word in colored ink). Looking your interviewee in the eye as you ask questions establishes ease and trust. If you're interviewing on the telephone, be organized and precise.

- Create a shortcut symbol or letter for key terms you expect to hear during the interview. This cuts down on your time needed to look away from your interviewee.

- Take careful notes, listening especially for key names, books, and other print materials, or online sources.

- Use standard 8 1/2-by-11-inch paper so that you have room to write.

- Bring extra pens or pencils.

- Never depend on recording an interview. People have become very reluctant to permit anyone to record them, and many will cancel appointments on the spot if recording is even mentioned.

32e.4 Gathering data about things or practices

Some kinds of primary research involve looking at objects, artifacts, or practices, describing or counting what you observe, and reporting what you find. Consider three research questions:

1. How are women portrayed on the covers of national magazines?

2. What are the most popular colors to paint houses in middle-class neighborhoods and in wealthy neighborhoods?

3. Are characters with foreign-sounding names or accents in current movies more likely to be heroes or villains?

You might be able to answer these questions by finding published sources, interviewing experts, or using existing means. However, it is more likely that you'd need to collect this information yourself, by directly and systematically looking at examples. In the examples above, you'd need to examine dozens of magazine covers, look at many houses, or view several movies. Quick Reference 32.3 summarizes steps for this kind of research.

Quick Reference 32.3 ■ ■ ■ ■ ■ ■ ■

Research using direct observations

1. Identify your research question.

2. Identify the sample (the group of individual examples) that you're going to examine, count, describe, or analyze.

3. Develop a system for recording your observations.

4. After recording all observations, look for patterns, make conclusions, or draw inferences.

5. If appropriate to your purpose, explore questions such as "Why are things as I found them?" or "What might be the implications of my findings?"

EXERCISE 32-2 For each of the research questions, what kinds of research would be appropriate? If more than one type would work, explain all that apply.

1. What types of television programs most appeal to college students?

2. Do men and women behave differently in fast food restaurants?

3. What factors led to the genocide in Rwanda in the 1990s?

4. What are the working conditions in a job that interests me?

5. How do clothing displays in upscale stores differ from clothing displays in discount stores?

33

Writing Research Papers

33a What is a research paper?

A **research paper** (sometimes called a *term paper*) is a specific kind of re-searched writing common in many college courses. In Chapter 32, we explained roles that researching plays in many writing situations, and we also character-ized different kinds of sources. Research paper assignments usually require the use of several published sources (Chapter 34) throughout. Your mission is to synthesize those sources into a project of fairly significant length.

Every research activity, formal or informal, involves two processes:

1. Gathering information
2. Analyzing, synthesizing, and evaluating what you've gathered

Academic research writing (and many business and public reports), involves a third process:

3. Writing an accurately documented paper based on your ANALYSIS, SYNTHESIS, and EVALUATION of what you've gathered

Some research papers use information from PRIMARY SOURCES and FIELD RESEARCH. However, most use information from SECONDARY and PUBLISHED SOURCES.

Research is an absorbing, creative activity. It lets you come to know a sub-ject deeply and leads to fresh insights. The entire process, especially when re-peated in a number of courses and settings, helps to shape you into a self-reliant learner. Nevertheless, many researchers—inexperienced and experienced—feel intimidated at the beginning of a research project. We find that research writ-ing goes most easily when you deliberately break it down into organized steps using a manageable research plan.

33b How do I plan a research project?

Research takes time, so budget your efforts intelligently. As soon as you get an assignment for a research paper, plan your schedule, using Quick Reference 33.1 as a model. Because no two research paper projects are alike, adapt these steps to your own needs. You might, for example, need only one day for some steps but two weeks for others. So, while you need to stay flexible, you also want to be realistic and keep your eye on the calendar.

■ ■ ■ ■ ■ ■ ■

Sample schedule for a research project

Assignment received _____

Assignment due date _____

PLANNING	FINISH BY (DATE)

1. Start my research log (33c). _____
2. Choose a topic suitable for research (33d). _____
3. Draft my research question (33e). _____
4. Understand my writing situation (33f). _____
5. Take practical steps (33g):
   a. Gather materials and supplies. _____
   b. Learn how to use my college library. _____
6. Determine what documentation style I need to use (33h). _____

RESEARCHING

7. Plan my "search strategy," but modify as necessary (34b). _____
8. Decide the kinds of research I need to do:
   a. Field research (32d). If yes, schedule tasks. _____
   b. Published sources (34). _____
9. Locate and evaluate sources (34d, 34j). _____
10. Compile a working bibliography (33i) or annotated bibliography (33j). _____
11. Take content notes from sources I find useful (33k). _____

WRITING

12. Draft my thesis statement (33l). _____
13. Outline, as required or useful (33m). _____
14. Draft my paper (33n). _____
15. Use correct parenthetical citations (34b–34c; 35b–35c; 36a, 36c). _____
16. Revise my paper (33o). _____
17. Compile my final bibliography (Works Cited or References), using the documentation style required (Chapters 36–38). _____

33c What is a research log?

A **research log** is your diary of your research process. Use a separate notebook for the log, or create a new folder or file on the computer. Whichever format you rely on, make your research schedule one of the first entries.

Although much of your research log will never find its way into your research paper itself, what you write in it greatly increases your efficiency. A well-kept log traces your line of reasoning as your project evolves, tells where you've ended each work session, and suggests what your next steps might be. It can also provide information about your process in a way that helps your instructor note your effort and determine how best to help you. In your log, always record the date as well as the following elements:

- Your **current step** in your search for information.
- The **search strategy** you used to find that information.
- The **name, location,** and other details of exactly where you found the information.
- The **main point** of the information you found.
- The exact **file or folder name** in which you've stored your detailed content notes.
- Your suggested **next step** for when you return to your research.
- Your evolving **overall thoughts** and insights as you move through the research and writing processes; particularly pay attention to the movements away from gathering material to organizing it, from organizing to drafting, and from drafting to revising.

Figure 33.1 (page 526) shows a selection from the research log of Andrei Gurov, who wrote the MLA-style research paper shown in section 36e.

33d How do I choose and narrow a research topic?

Sometimes, of course, you don't get to choose a research topic. Research in the workplace and many public arenas often emerges from specific situations. A doctor needs to decide the best way to treat a patient. An office manager needs to make a decision about purchasing new computers. An actor needs to research a time period to better portray an historical character.

Some instructors assign a specific topic for research (for example, "What are the most compelling scientific theories to explain false memory?"). Others leave more choice to you, assigning a general subject area appropriate to a specific course (for example, "memory" in a psychology course) and expecting you to narrow it to a manageable topic. Still other instructors expect you to choose

October 20: Because I'm not sure where online to start searching for sources about déjà vu, I've decided to use the "Research Navigator" our professor told us is available at <prenhall.com/troyka>. [Pause] Done—sure enough, when I clicked on the cover of this book, then on "research," and finally on the EBSCO database, I could navigate my way to a number of sources. I filed them in the folder offered and printed out what looked like the best ones. One problem I noted immediately: because the topic of déjà vu seems largely to be studied by psychologists and neuroscientists, the researchers use only the first initial of their first names. That's okay for APA style, but MLA requires the full first name. That's a problem I'll have to tackle.

Figure 33.1 A selection from the research log of Andrei Gurov, who wrote the MLA-style research paper shown in section 36e

a topic on your own (for example, "Write a research paper on a topic of current interest or importance"). This last example happens most often in composition courses, where instructors often emphasize learning research skills more than mastering a particular content area.

33d.1 Choosing a topic on your own

The freedom to choose any topic you want can sometimes be overwhelming. Don't panic. Instead, use some of the strategies for generating ideas in Quick Reference 33.2.

33d.2 Narrowing a general topic into a workable one

Whether you're working with a topic of your choice or an assigned one, you want to check that it's sufficiently narrow for the time frame and other requirements of your research paper. Also, you want to be sure that the narrowed topic is worthy of a college research project.

- **Expect to consider various topics before making your final choice.** Give yourself time to think. Keep your mind open to flashes of insight and to alternative ideas. At the same time, be careful not to let indecision paralyze you.

Quick Reference 33.2

■ ■ ■ ■ ■ ■ ■ ■

Finding general ideas for research

- **Talk with others.** Ask instructors or other experts in your area of interest what issues currently seem "hot" to them. Ask them to recommend readings or the names of authorities on those issues.

- **Browse some textbooks.** Read the table of contents and major headings of textbooks for subjects that interest you. As you narrow your focus, note the names of important books and experts, often mentioned in reference lists at the end of chapters or in the final pages of the book.

- **Browse the library or a well-stocked bookstore.** Stroll through the **stacks** (the rows of bookshelves) to find subjects that interest you. Look at books as well as periodicals. Thumb through popular magazines, and browse academic journals in fields that interest you.

- **Browse the Internet.** Many search engines provide topic directories. Click on some general categories and review subcategories until you locate specific topics that interest you. Then try further subject searches or KEYWORD searches (34d) to see where they lead.

- **Read encyclopedia articles about your interests.** General encyclopedias survey a wide range of topics, while specialized encyclopedias concentrate on a specific area. Never, however, stop with encyclopedias—they are too basic for college-level research.

- **Get ready.** Carry a small notebook and a pen, a laptop, or a PDA. Ideas have a way of popping into your mind when you least expect them. Jot down your thoughts on the spot so that they don't slip away.

- **Select a topic that interests you.** Your topic will be a companion for a while, sometimes for most of a semester. Select a topic that arouses your interest and allows you the pleasure of satisfying your intellectual curiosity.

- **Choose a sufficiently narrow topic.** You want to be successful within the time and length given by the assignment. Avoid topics that are too broad, such as "emotions." A better choice would be "how people perceive and respond to anger in others."

- **Choose a topic worth researching.** Avoid trivial topics that prevent you from doing what instructors and others expect of a student researcher.

  NO   The colors of MP3 players.

  YES   The legal issues of sharing downloaded music.

- **Choose a topic that has a sufficient number of appropriate sources available.** If you can't find useful sources—ones that relate directly to your topic and ones that are credible, not simply plentiful—drop the topic.

- **Talk with a professor in your field of interest, if possible.** Before the meeting, read a little about your topic so that you can ask informed questions. Ask whether you've narrowed your topic sufficiently and productively. Also, ask for the titles of major books and the names of major authorities on your topic.

A good academic topic allows you to demonstrate your critical thinking abilities. There are two broad ways of doing this. First, you might choose a topic on which intelligent people have formed different opinions. Then, you might analyze your sources and draw on your own experiences to decide which position appears best. The purpose of such a paper would be to attempt to PERSUADE readers that you've considered the various positions and reached a reasonable conclusion.

Alternatively, you might choose to INFORM readers in a paper that synthesizes several sources related to a complex subject. Writing a SYNTHESIS means pulling together extensive information from varied sources to examine essential points that relate to a topic. For example, imagine you've been assigned to write the sample research paper about déjà vu in section 36e. After you've read a dozen articles on the topic of déjà vu, you might try to identify three or four key points and then organize information from your reading around those points. Your goal is to clarify complicated or scattered information for your readers.

For a more detailed narrative of Andrei Gurov's research process and the final draft of his research paper, see 36e.1 and 36e.2.

33e What is a research question?

A **research question** about your topic is the controlling question that drives your research. Few research paper assignments are phrased as questions. Therefore, most research writing calls on you to ask a thought-provoking, underlying question and then to search for answers to it. Regarding research as a quest for an answer gives your work a specific focus: You can't know whether you've found useful source material unless you know what you're looking for.

Research questions, whether stated or implied, and the strategies needed to answer them vary widely. Your purpose might be to present and explain information: "How does penicillin destroy bacteria?" Or your purpose might be to argue one side of an issue: "Is Congress more important than the Supreme Court in setting social policy?" You can then consult various sources in an attempt to work toward an answer.

Attempt is an important word in relation to research. Some research questions lead to a final, definitive answer, but some do not. The previous question about penicillin leads to a reasonably definitive answer (you describe how the antibiotic penicillin destroys the cell walls of some bacteria); this means your writing has an informative purpose. The other question about social policy has no definitive answer, so you're asked to offer an informed opinion based on facts and authoritative viewpoints gathered from your research; this means your writing has a persuasive purpose.

To formulate a research question, begin by BRAINSTORMING a list of questions that come to mind about your topic. Write your list of ideas in your research log (33c).

Suppose, for example, the topic you want to write about is "homelessness." Here are some typical questions you might ask.

- Why can't a rich country like the United States eliminate homelessness?
- Who is homeless?
- How do people become homeless?
- Is it true that many families—not just adults—are homeless?
- Is the homelessness problem getting better or worse?
- What are we doing to solve the problem of homelessness?
- What is it like to be homeless?

Some questions will interest you more than others, so begin with one of those. If a question leads to a dead end, pursue another. Only when you find yourself accumulating answers—or in the case of questions without definitive answers, accumulating viewpoints—is it likely you're dealing with a usable research question. Once you have an explicitly stated research question, you can streamline your research by taking notes from those sources that help you answer your research question. If your research paper requires you to state an informed opinion, keep in mind that dealing with opposing positions is crucial to writing an effective argument (see section 5l).

Stay flexible as you work. The results of your research may lead you to modify the research question slightly. Actually, such modifying is part of the "moving ahead and circling back" that characterizes research writing. When you've finished researching and notetaking in response to your final research question, you have a starting place for formulating your preliminary THESIS STATEMENT (see 2d).

33f How does the writing situation shape my research paper?

Your TOPIC, PURPOSE, AUDIENCE, ROLE, and SPECIAL CONSIDERATIONS (1b) all influence your research paper. If you receive an assignment to argue for a position but instead you inform readers about possible positions, your paper will fall short. The same would happen if you were assigned to write a ten-page paper, in MLA style, for an audience of people knowledgeable on a certain topic and instead you wrote fifteen pages in APA style, for a very general audience. When you receive a research paper assignment, make sure to understand if you're being asked to write for a specific situation. Maybe the assignment will specify only a few elements of the situation but not all; follow, then, the ones required.

Even if you receive a very open assignment, you'll find it useful to create a writing situation for that paper, especially a purpose and audience. Doing so will give you a guidepost to see if you're on the right track. To decide whether your paper will have an informative purpose or a persuasive purpose, see what your research question asks. If the answer to it involves giving facts, information, and explanation, your purpose is to inform. For example, "How have computers changed over time?" calls for INFORMATIVE WRITING. Conversely, if the answer involves offering an educated opinion based on contrasting views and supporting evidence, your purpose is to persuade. For example, "Why should people be aware of current developments in computers?" calls for PERSUASIVE WRITING. You may find that during your research or writing process, a different purpose would make more sense. Usually, it makes sense to change to the new purpose, adjusting your thesis in the process. However, if your instructor has asked for a proposal or otherwise approved your research project, you'll want to check to make sure the new direction is OK.

AUDIENCES for research papers can vary. Your instructor, of course, is always an audience. However, in some cases he or she will read as a representative of other, larger audiences, and you'll want to meet their expectations. For example, if you're writing about the topic of déjà vu for a specialized audience (1d.2) that knows psychology and expects your paper to have the characteristics of writing in that field, your research paper will differ slightly from one on the very same topic but for a general educated audience (1d.1). Your sense of audience can guide your decisions about content, prior knowledge, assumptions, level of detail and explanations needed, STYLE, TONE, and so on. Section 1d provides advice for analyzing audience.

33g What practical steps can help me work efficiently?

To conduct your research with greatest efficiency, you need to do some footwork before you start researching. First, gather the materials listed in Quick Reference 33.3 so that they're organized and ready for use at a moment's notice. Second, become familiar with your college library, especially its catalogs and databases (34d). Third, be sure to become skilled with finding and evaluating appropriate resources on the Internet (34k–34m).

Quick Reference 33.3

■ ■ ■ ■ ■ ■ ■

Materials you might need for research

1. A copy of your assignment.

2. This handbook, especially Part Five, or access to the Internet so that you can read the book online and use its guidelines.

3. Your research log (33c).

4. Index cards for taking notes (unless you use a laptop). If you use different colors of index cards, you might color-code the different categories of information you find. Also, you might use one size for bibliography cards and the other for content note cards. Another coding strategy is to use pens of different ink colors or self-sticking dots of various colors.

5. Money or a debit card for copy machines or printers.

6. A flash drive or other means for storing downloaded source materials, if you're not exclusively using your own computer.

7. If you use index cards and other paper, a small stapler, paper clips, and rubber bands.

8. A separate bag or backpack with wheels to carry research-project materials and books you check out from the library. (Librarians joke about researchers with wheelbarrows.)

33g.1 Learning how to use library resources

When you learn how your college library functions, your research efficiency increases. Though almost all libraries in the United States and Canada are organized around the same principles for organizing information, physical layouts and procedures differ considerably. If you visit your college library for the sole purpose of figuring out what's located where, you'll feel comfortable and confident when you work there.

Some college libraries provide orientations through English courses; some offer individual training sessions; and most offer informative Web sites or handouts about their resources. Quick Reference 33.4 provides a checklist for familiarizing yourself with your library.

33g.2 Deciding how you'll use the computer

How you use the computer in the research process is largely a matter of personal preference. Some students use a computer only for finding sources and for DRAFTING and REVISING the paper itself. These students do the rest of their research steps by hand on index cards and sheets of paper: keeping their

Quick Reference 33.4

■ ■ ■ ■ ■ ■ ■

Learning your library's resources

- How do you get access to the library's catalog and databases, both from inside the library and through the Internet? What are the log-in procedures?

- How does the library's catalog work?

- What periodical indexes or databases does your library have, online or in print? (*Indexes* and *databases* are lists of articles in journals and magazines, grouped by subject areas.)

- Where is the general reference collection? (You can't check out reference books, so when you need to use them, build extra time into your schedule to spend at the library.)

- Where is the special reference collection? (Same rules apply as for general reference books.)

- Are the book and journal stacks open (fully accessible shelves) or closed (request each item by filling out a form to hand to library personnel)? If the latter, become familiar with the required procedures not only for asking for a book or journal but also for picking it up when it's ready.

- Where are the library's physical collections of periodicals (journals, magazines, and newspapers) stored? Libraries are increasingly moving from paper to digital storage, but some publications might still exist only in print. Most libraries place periodicals published recently in open areas, and they place older ones in bound volumes, on microfilm or microfiche, or online. Learn to use whatever system is in place at your library.

- How do you identify when periodical articles exist digitally, in versions that you can read completely online rather than only from a paper copy? When you find that an article has a digital version, how do you access it?

- What, if anything, is stored on microfilm or microfiche? If you think you'll use that material, take the time to learn how to use the machines. (We find that each library's machines work differently—and many of them have stumped us on occasion.)

- Does the library have special collections, such as local historical works or the writings of persons worthy of such an exclusive honor?

research log (33c), compiling their WORKING BIBLIOGRAPHY (33i), taking content notes (33k), and so forth.

Other students carry out their entire research process on computer. They set up folders for every phase of their project. To accumulate print sources for their working bibliography, these students download them onto a computer hard drive or a flash drive—always carefully recording the origin of the source in the documentation style they've selected (33h). They type their research log, working bibliography, and content notes directly into computer files.

33h What documentation style should I use?

A **documentation style** is a system for providing information about each source you've used in your research paper. Documentation styles vary from one academic discipline to another. The humanities often use MLA (Modern Language Association) style (Chapter 36). The social sciences frequently use APA (American Psychological Association) style (Chapter 37). Biology and other natural sciences often use CSE (Council of Science Editors) style (Chapter 38). CM (*Chicago Manual*) style is used in various disciplines, generally in the humanities (Chapter 38). Instructors almost always have precise expectations about which style they want you to use. Find it out, and follow it to the letter! Using the wrong documentation style—or using the right one badly—is like showing up to a formal wedding wearing flip-flops and a ripped shirt. You don't want an instructor to minimize your research and writing effort because he or she is so distracted by careless documentation.

Determining the required documentation style at the start of the process helps to guarantee that you'll write down the exact details you need to document your sources. You'll need to document all secondary sources. If you're doing primary research, decide what you must document before you begin. Your instructor may have special requirements, such as asking you to submit your research notes or results from observations, questionnaires, surveys, interviews, or anything else that produces primary data.

33i What is a working bibliography?

A **working bibliography** is a preliminary list of the PRIMARY and SECONDARY SOURCES you gather in your research. It contains information about the source and where others might find it. The following is a list of basic elements to include (see more detailed information about documenting specific types of sources in Chapters 36–38).

Books	Periodical Articles	Online Sources
Author(s)	Author(s)	Author (if available); editor or sponsor of site
Title	Title	Title of document and title of site

Books	Periodical Articles	Online Sources
Publisher and place of publication	Name of periodical, volume number, issue number	Name of database or sponsor of online source
Year of publication	Date of issue	Date of electronic publication
Call number	Page numbers of article	Electronic address (URL) Date you accessed the source

Begin your working bibliography as soon as you start identifying sources. Compiling a working bibliography will help you find out what is available on a particular subject before you do extensive reading and notetaking. If your search turns up very few sources, you may want to change your topic. If it reveals a vast number of sources, you definitely want to narrow your topic or even choose a different one. At the outset, don't leave anything out; even an unpromising source may later prove useful. Expect to add and drop sources throughout the research writing process. As a rough estimate, your working bibliography needs to be about twice as long as the list of sources you end up using. You can record your working bibliography on note cards or on a computer.

On the one hand, note cards have the advantage of being easy to sift through and rearrange. You can also carry them with you when you do library research. At the end of your writing process, you can easily sort and alphabetize them to prepare your final bibliography. Write only one source on each card. Figure 33.2 displays a handwritten bibliography note card by Andrei Gurov for his MLA-style research paper in section 36e.

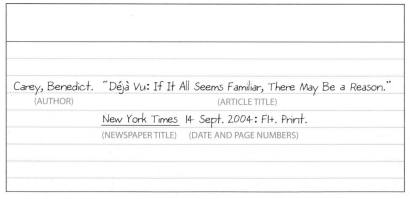

Figure 33.2 Sample bibliography note card in MLA style

On the other hand, putting your working bibliography on a computer saves you from having to type your list of sources later. If you use a computer for this purpose, clearly separate one entry from another. You can organize the list alphabetically, by author, or according to your subtopics.

Your library may even have a program like RefWorks or EndNote that allows you to download bibliographic information directly onto your computer, and then easily reformat it to the appropriate documentation style.

Whichever method you use, when you come across a potential source, immediately record the information exactly as you need it to fulfill the requirements of the DOCUMENTATION STYLE you need to use for your assignment (33h). Spending a few extra moments at this stage can save you hours of work and frustration later on.

33j What is an annotated bibliography?

An **annotated bibliography** includes not only publishing information about your sources but also your brief summary of each one, and perhaps a commentary. Figure 33.3 shows part of an annotated bibliography for sources used in the APA-style student paper in Chapter 37.

McKenna, K. Y., Green, A. S., & Gleason, M. E. (2003). Relationship formation on the Internet: What's the big attraction? *Journal of Social Issues, 58,* 9–31.

> Two studies show that people who share "true selves" over the Internet often form closer relationships than when they meet face to face. One study surveyed Internet users. A second study found that students who meet first on the Internet tend to like each other better than students who meet first in person.

Miyake, K., & Zuckerman, M. (1993). Beyond personality impressions. *Journal of Personality, 61*(3), 411–436.

> This research study examines how both physical and vocal attractiveness affect judges' responses to individuals. The researchers found that, for five different personality measures, judges rate more attractive people more highly.

Figure 33.3 Section from an annotated bibliography in APA style

33k How do I take content notes?

When you write **content notes,** you record information from your sources. As with your working bibliography, you can make content notes either in a computer file or on index cards.

- If you're using index cards, put a heading on each card that gives a precise link to one of your bibliography items. Include the source's title and the numbers of the pages from which you're taking notes.

- On the computer, keep careful track of the source of each idea. One strategy is to open a new file for each. Later, after you've taken notes on many of your sources, you can determine what subtopics are important for your paper. You can then open a new file for each topic and use the "Cut" and "Paste" functions to gather notes from all of your sources under each topic.

- On every note card or every file in your computer, do one of three things: (1) Copy exact words from a source in a quotation, enclosing it in quotation marks; (2) write a paraphrase of the source; or (3) write a summary of the source. Keeping track of the kind of note you're taking will help you avoid PLAGIARISM. You might use the codes *Q* for QUOTATION, *P* for PARAPHRASE, and *S* for SUMMARY. Or you might use a different typeface or ink color.

- As you're taking notes, separately record your own reactions and ideas, but take care to differentiate your ideas from those found in your sources. You might write your own thoughts in a different colored ink (note card) or font (computer); you might use the back of your note cards or a computer's "Comment" feature. You can also record your thinking in your RESEARCH LOG.

Figure 33.4 shows one of Andrei Gurov's note cards for his paper in section 36e.2.

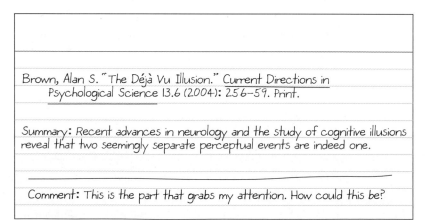

Brown, Alan S. "The Déjà Vu Illusion." *Current Directions in Psychological Science* 13.6 (2004): 256–59. Print.

Summary: Recent advances in neurology and the study of cognitive illusions reveal that two seemingly separate perceptual events are indeed one.

Comment: This is the part that grabs my attention. How could this be?

Figure 33.4 A handwritten content note card in MLA style

331 How do I draft a thesis statement for a research paper?

Drafting a THESIS STATEMENT for a research paper marks the transition from the research process to the writing process. A thesis statement in a research paper sets out the central theme, which you need to sustain throughout the paper (see section 2d, especially Box 2.3). As with any piece of writing, your research paper must fulfill the promise of its thesis statement.

You might begin thinking of a preliminary thesis statement at some middle point in the research process, although it's perfectly acceptable to wait until you've completely finished researching. To start your thesis statement, you might try to convert your RESEARCH QUESTION into a preliminary thesis statement. Remember that a good thesis statement makes an assertion that conveys your point of view about your topic and foreshadows the content of your paper (see Quick Reference 2.3 in 2d). And not least, remember that your research needs to support your thesis statement. Ask yourself whether the material you've gathered from sources can effectively give support. If not, revise your thesis statement, conduct further research, or do both.

Here are examples of subjects narrowed to topics, focused into research questions, and then cast as thesis statements.

SUBJECT	*nonverbal communication*
TOPIC	Personal space
RESEARCH QUESTION	How do standards for personal space differ among cultures?
INFORMATIVE THESIS STATEMENT	Everyone has expectations concerning the use of personal space, but accepted distances for that space are determined by each person's culture.
PERSUASIVE THESIS STATEMENT	To prevent intercultural misunderstandings, people must be aware of cultural differences in standards for personal space.
SUBJECT	*computers*
TOPIC	artificial intelligence
RESEARCH QUESTION	How close are researchers to developing artificial intelligence in computers?
INFORMATIVE THESIS STATEMENT	Scientists disagree about whether computers need emotions to have artificial intelligence.
PERSUASIVE THESIS STATEMENT	Because emotions play a strong role in human intelligence, computers must have emotions before they can truly have artificial intelligence.

Andrei Gurov (whose research paper appears in section 36e) revised his preliminary thesis statement twice before he felt that it expressed the point he wanted to make. Andrei also took the key step of checking that he would be able to support it sufficiently with sources throughout the paper.

FIRST PRELIMINARY THESIS STATEMENT

Déjà vu can be explained by a variety of scientific theories. [Andrei realized that this draft thesis would lead to a paper that would merely list, paragraph by paragraph, each theory, and that the paper would lack synthesis.]

SECOND PRELIMINARY THESIS STATEMENT

Many people believe feelings of déjà vu have mysterious origins, but science has shown this is not true. [Andrei liked this statement better because it began to get at the complexity of the topic, but he wanted to work on it more because he felt the second part was too general.]

FINAL THESIS STATEMENT

Although a few people today still prefer to believe that feelings of déjà vu have mysterious or supernatural origins, recent research in cognitive psychology and the neurosciences has shed much rational light on the phenomenon.

33m How do I outline a research paper?

Some instructors require an OUTLINE of your research paper, either before you hand in the paper or along with the paper. In such cases, your instructor is probably expecting you to be working from an outline as you write your drafts. Your research log often comes in handy when you group ideas, especially for a first draft of your paper—and as you make an *informal outline* for it. An outline can serve as a guide as you plan and write your paper. For directions on composing a *formal outline,* see section 2f. To see a topic outline of Andrei Gurov's research paper, turn to section 36e.

33n How do I draft a research paper?

DRAFTING and REVISING a research paper is like drafting and revising any other piece of writing (Chapter 2). Yet to write a research paper, you need extra time for planning, drafting, thinking, redrafting, rethinking, and creating a final draft because you need to demonstrate all of the following:

- You've followed the steps of the research processes presented in Chapters 32–35.

- You understand the information that you've located during your research.
- You've evaluated the SOURCES you've used in your research.
- You haven't PLAGIARIZED your material from someone else (35b).
- You've used sources well in your writing, correctly employing QUOTATIONS, PARAPHRASES, and SUMMARIES (35f–35k).
- You've moved beyond SUMMARY to SYNTHESIS so that your sources are interwoven with each other and with your own thinking, not merely listed one by one (4f).
- You've used DOCUMENTATION accurately. (For MLA STYLE, see Chapter 36; for APA STYLE, see Chapter 37; for other documentation styles, see Chapter 38)

Expect to write a number of drafts of your research paper. The first draft is your chance to discover new insights and connections. Successive drafts help you master the information you've learned and add it authoritatively to the knowledge you already had about the topic. In the first draft, organize the broad categories of your paper. Quick Reference 33.5 suggests some ways to write your first draft.

33o How do I revise a research paper?

Before you write each new draft, read your previous draft with a sharp eye. For best results, take a break of a few days (or at least a few hours) before beginning this process. This gives you distance from your material, and a clearer vision of what you need to revise. For a more objective point of view, consider asking a few people you respect to read and react to your first, or perhaps your second, draft.

One key to REVISING any research paper is to examine carefully the evidence you have included. **Evidence** consists of facts, statistics, expert studies and opinions, examples, and stories. As a reader, you expect writers to provide solid evidence to back up their claims and conclusions. Similarly, when you write, readers expect you to provide evidence that clearly supports your claims and conclusions. Use RENNS (3f) to see if you can develop paragraphs more fully. Identify each of the points you have made in your paper, including your thesis and all your subpoints. Then ask the questions in Quick Reference 33.6.

Experienced writers know that writing is really *rewriting*. Research papers are among the most demanding composing assignments, and most writers revise several times. Once you've produced a *final draft,* you're ready to edit (2j), proofread (2k), and format (2c.5) your work. Check for correct grammar,

Quick Reference 33.5 ■ ■ ■ ■ ■ ■ ■

Suggestions for drafting a research paper

- Some writers categorize their notes and write a section at a time. They organize the notes into broad categories by making a separate group for each topic. As patterns begin to emerge, these writers might move material from one category to another. Each category becomes a section of the first draft. This method not only assures writers that their first draft will include all of the material from their research, but reveals any gaps in information that call for additional research. Of course, you may discover that some of your research doesn't fit your topic and thesis. Put it aside; it might be useful in a later draft.

- Some writers generate a list of questions that their paper needs to address, then answer each question, one at a time, looking for the content notes that will help them. For example, writing on the topic of organic foods, some possible questions might be, "What are organic foods? What benefits do people see for eating them? Why do they cost more than regular foods? Does everyone agree that they are beneficial?" Generating and answering questions can be a way of turning a mass of information into manageable groupings.

- Some writers finish their research and then slowly review half of the information they've gathered. Next, setting aside that information, they write a partial first draft by drawing on the information they remember from their reading. Then, they use the same process with the second half of the information that they've gathered. Finally, with their two partial drafts and all of their research notes in front of them, they write a complete first draft. Writers who use this method say it gives them a broad overview of their material quickly and identifies any gaps in information that they need to fill in with further research.

- Some writers stop at various points during their research and use FREEWRITING to get their ideas into words. Writers who use this method say that it helps them recognize when they need to adjust their RESEARCH QUESTION or change the emphasis of their search. After a number of rounds of researching and freewriting, these writers find that they can complete their first draft relatively easily.

- Some writers review their sources and create an OUTLINE before drafting (2f). Some find a formal outline helpful, while others use a less formal approach.

Quick Reference 33.6

Questions for evaluating your evidence

- **Is the evidence sufficient?** To be sufficient, evidence can't be thin or trivial. As a rule, the more evidence you present, the more convincing your thesis will be to readers.

- **Is the evidence representative?** Representative evidence is customary and normal, not based on exceptions. When evidence is representative, it provides a view of the issue that reflects the usual circumstances rather than rare ones.

- **Is the evidence relevant?** Relevant evidence relates directly to your thesis or topic sentences. It illustrates your reasons straightforwardly and never introduces unrelated material.

- **Is the evidence accurate?** Accurate evidence is correct, complete, and up to date. It comes from a reliable SOURCE. Equally important, you present it honestly, without distorting or misrepresenting it.

- **Is the evidence reasonable?** Reasonable evidence is not phrased in extreme language, such as *all, never,* or *certainly.* Reasonable evidence is well thought out and free of logical fallacies (4i).

punctuation, capitalization, and spelling. (No amount of careful research and good writing can make up for an incorrectly presented, sloppy, error-laden document.)

Consult Quick References 2.8 and 2.9 to remind yourself of the general principles of revising, and consult the research paper revision checklist in Quick Reference 33.7. One of the best things you might do is apply the strategies of critical thinking (Chapter 4) to your own writing. Read your own paper as if you were an outside critical reader. Additionally, have a classmate or trusted friend provide peer response (6c).

To see one example of the research writing process in action, turn to section 36e. There you'll see the final draft of an MLA-style research paper; a narrative of decisions that the student made during his research process; and commentary (on the text page facing each page of the student's paper) that gives you insight into specific aspects of his paper.

For an APA style research paper, turn to section 37h. There you'll see the final draft of a student's paper and a narrative of the decisions that the student made during his research process.

Quick Reference 33.7 ■ ■ ■ ■ ■ ■ ■ ■

Revising a research paper

If the answer to any of the following questions is no, you need to revise. The section numbers in parentheses tell you where to find useful information.

WRITING

- Does your introductory paragraph lead effectively into the material? (3b)
- Have you met the basic requirements for a written thesis statement? (2d)
- Do your thesis statement and the content of your paper address your research question(s)? (33e)
- Have you developed effective body paragraphs? (3d; 3f, Quick Reference 3.3)
- Does the concluding paragraph end your paper effectively? (3k)
- Does your paper satisfy a critical thinker? (Chapter 4)

RESEARCH

- Have you included appropriate and effective evidence? (3d and Quick Reference 33.6)
- Have you deleted irrelevant or insignificant information? (3g)
- Have you used quotations, paraphrases, and summaries well? (35f–35k)
- Have you integrated your source material well without plagiarizing? (35c)

FORMAT AND DOCUMENTATION

- Have you used the correct format for your parenthetical citations or other documentation style? (Chapters 36–38)
- Does each citation tie into an item in your WORKS CITED (MLA style) or REFERENCES (APA style) list of sources at the end of your paper? (36d and 37f)
- Does the paper exactly match the format you've been assigned to follow? Check margins, spacing, title, headings, page number, font, and so on (Chapter 45).

34

Finding and Evaluating Published Sources

34a What is a published source?

A **published source** is a book, article, Web page, or other type of writing that appears in print or in electronic format. While the kinds of field research we discuss in section 32e require you to gather information and turn it into words, in published sources other writers have already done that work. However, it's up to you to decide whether they have done it accurately, fairly, and well. Your goal is to find sources needed to answer your research question, evaluate their quality, and SYNTHESIZE them into your own writing, using QUOTATION, SUMMARY, or PARAPHRASE. Published sources are PRIMARY if they are firsthand reports of experiments, observations, and so on, or if they are creative works like poems, letters, or stories. A SECONDARY published source is one that reports, describes, or comments on someone else's work. Section 4d explains the differences.

34b What is a search strategy?

A **search strategy** is an organized procedure for locating and gathering information to answer your specific RESEARCH QUESTION. Some research, such as finding one particular fact or piece of information, doesn't require an extensive strategy (34b). Others, such as fully understanding an issue or synthesizing current knowledge, require care and planning. Using a search strategy means working systematically rather than haphazardly.

Following are three frequently used search strategies. If no single one meets your requirements, create your own.

The **expert method** is useful when you know your topic well enough to begin "at the top," with the best current thinking by experts on that subject. You'll begin by reading their books and articles to identify the main subtopics, positions, or issues. You'll ask yourself: What is in agreement? What is in dispute? What are the main questions under investigation?

Of course, the expert method means that you have to know who the experts are, and sometimes that's difficult. Talk with people who are generally knowledgeable about your topic, learn what you can from them, and ask them to refer you to work by experts on the topic. Your professors are an obvious place to start.

For example, if you're researching Internet dating, a psychology instructor may be able to tell you who are the leading experts on that topic. In some cases, you might be able to interview an expert in person, on the phone, or through e-mail. Turn to section 32e.3 for detailed advice about conducting effective interviews.

The **chaining method** is useful when you know only general things about your topic or can't tell who the experts are. Start by reading or skimming reference books or some current articles in scholarly journals, popular magazines, or newspapers. As you do, pay close attention to people who are cited in those readings or in any bibliographies at the end. Then search for works by those people or look for the specific books or articles mentioned.

For example, suppose you read an article on Internet dating in *Time* magazine, and that article quotes a scholar named Monica Whitty, who seems to be an expert. You use your library's catalog or databases to see if Whitty has published anything, and you discover she has co-authored a book *Cyberspace Romances: The Psychology of Online Relationships*. You then find and browse that book both to see how it contributes to your research question and also to find the names of other scholars, publications, and key terms. You keep following the links in this chain until you're confident you've identified expert sources and you have gathered the breadth and depth of information you'll need.

The **questioning method** means breaking your overall research question into several smaller questions, then finding sources to answer each of them. This method has the advantage of allowing you to see if your sources cover all the areas important to your research question. Suppose your research question is, "How successful are relationships that begin on the Internet?" The list of questions you brainstorm might include, "Who participates in Internet dating? Are there typical ways Internet relationships develop? How may Internet contacts result in actual meetings?" Generating a list of questions like this can give your search a direction and purpose.

You may find yourself switching or combining methods. That's fine. "Flexibility with focus" is the guiding principle for experienced researchers. Discovering early in the process what sources are available allows you time to find those that are harder to locate; to use interlibrary loan if an item isn't available in your library or online; to wait for someone to return checked-out books you need; or to schedule interviews, arrange visits, or conduct surveys.

As you locate, assemble, and evaluate sources, expect to accumulate much more information than you'll actually use. Indeed, the quality of a research paper depends partly on your ability to eliminate inadequate or repetitive sources and to recognize what is valuable material. Turn to section 34j for detailed guidelines for evaluating sources.

One more piece of advice: Avoid getting too far along in your search until you're reasonably certain you're going in a useful direction. Rather than spend endless hours simply gathering sources, read and analyze some of your materials to make sure your topic is a good one. Your RESEARCH LOG can be useful for this purpose.

34c What are library-based sources?

In an age when the Internet contains billions of pages of information, it might seem almost prehistoric to talk about libraries. After all, the **library** is where generations of college students have traditionally gone to find sources: books and periodicals organized by catalogs and indexes. However, notice that we've referred to "library-based" sources and not necessarily to the library itself. In many respects, the function that a library performs is even more important than its physical building. Librarians and scholars have systematically gathered and organized sources so that students and researchers can find the best ones efficiently and reliably. Many libraries give you online access to their holdings, so you might use library-based sources without ever setting foot in the building itself.

Still, the building itself continues to be a vital place for all research. One key advantage of going to the library is your chance to consult face-to-face with librarians. They train for their profession by learning how to advise students and other researchers about using library resources to the greatest advantage. Never hesitate to ask questions about how to proceed or where to find a resource.

Catalogs list sources—usually books, but also films, recordings, and documents—that the library owns (34d). **Databases** contain extensive lists of articles, reports, and books, organized and searchable in many ways (34d). Your library will own or provide access to many sources included in a database, but it almost certainly won't have all of them. Catalogs and databases exist in electronic formats that you can access and search from computers in the library or, often, by connecting to the library online. Both college and public libraries subscribe to database services, although they may be limited depending on the library's size. Many businesses and corporations also subscribe to databases, making them available to people associated with the company. A law firm, for example, likely subscribes to LexisNexis, which provides searchable access to legal cases and decisions.

If you're accessing a database by connecting to the library online, you need to use a **browser** (such as Firefox or Internet Explorer), a software program that gives you access to the Web.

34d How do I use catalogs and databases?

Sources that you identify through catalogs and scholarly databases are almost always more reliable and appropriate than sources you find by simply browsing the Web. The reliability of scholarly databases stems from their origins: Only experts and professionals who judge works to have merit compile them.

The best way to access a database at your library is to go to your college library's Web site, whether you're online in the library, at home, or in a dormitory. Each home page of a library shows the resources available through that Web site, although more might be available in the library itself. Most college libraries subscribe to one or more database services, such as EBSCO, ProQuest, or First-Search. Because your tuition pays for these services, you can take advantage of them without further expense, but you'll need an ID or password to gain access.

Each entry in a database contains bibliographic information, including a title, author, date of publication, and publisher (in the case of books or reports) or periodical (in the case of articles). The entry might also provide an abstract, or summary, of the material. Once you locate an entry that seems promising, you need to find the actual book or complete article itself, and we explain how to do that below in sections 34e (for books) and 34f (for periodicals).

EXERCISE 34-1 Working either individually or as part of a group, access your library's Web site. List all of the types of information available. In particular, list the indexes and databases you can search and the subject areas each one covers. Note whether any of the databases have full-text versions of articles.

USING KEYWORDS

When you search library databases, **keywords**, also called *descriptors* or *identifiers*, are your lifeline to success. Keywords are the main words in a source's title or the words that the author or editor has identified as central. Without keywords, you'd have great difficulty accessing sources listed in electronic databases.

When you search using keywords, chances are you'll come up with a large or even overwhelming number of sources. Much of what turns up won't be relevant to your topic. Two main ways to make keyword searches more efficient are using guided searches (answers to prompts) and using Boolean expressions (keyword combinations).

USING GUIDED SEARCHES

Guided searches, also called *advanced searches,* allow you to look through a database or search engine by answering prompts provided in an onscreen form. A typical search involves selecting a range of dates of publication (for example, after 2006 or between 1990 and 1995) and specifying only a certain language (such as English) or a certain format (such as books). Figure 34.1 is an example of a search for sources that have the words *déjà vu* in their titles and sources that use *false memory* as another keyword but are not about *crime.*

USING BOOLEAN EXPRESSIONS

Using **Boolean expressions** means that you search a database or search engine by typing keyword combinations that narrow and refine your search. To combine keywords, use the words *AND, OR,* and *NOT,* or the symbols that represent those words. Boolean expressions, generally placed between keywords,

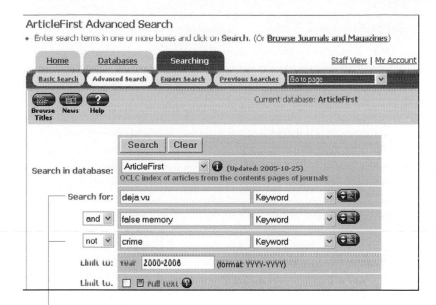

Users can list the keywords
they want to search for or
not to search for

Figure 34.1 A guided or advanced search

instruct the search engine to list only those Web sites in which your keywords
appear in certain combinations and to ignore others. Quick Reference 34.1
explains a few ways to search with keywords more effectively, using the subject
"relationships" as an example.

> **Quick Reference 34.1**   (continued)
>
> **OR:**   Expands a search's boundaries by including more than one keyword. If you want to expand your search to include sources about relationships begun through either instant messaging or chat rooms, try the expression *relationships AND attractiveness AND Internet AND instant messaging OR chat rooms*. You'll get pages mentioning relationships and attractiveness only if they also mention instant messaging or chat rooms.
>
> **" ":**   Quotation marks direct a search engine to match your exact word order on a Web page. For example, a search for "online relationships" will find pages that contain the exact phrase *online relationships*. However, it won't return pages with the phrase *relationships online*. If you search for *James Joyce* without using quotation marks, most engines will return all pages containing the words *James* and *Joyce* anywhere in the document; however, a search using "James Joyce" brings you closer to finding Web sites about the Irish writer.

34e   How do I find books?

A library's **book catalog**, which lists its entire collection, exists as a computer database in almost every modern library. You can find a book by searching by **author**, by **title**, by **subject**, and by KEYWORD. Figure 34.3 shows the home page for a typical type of catalog, this one at the Library of Congress. Note

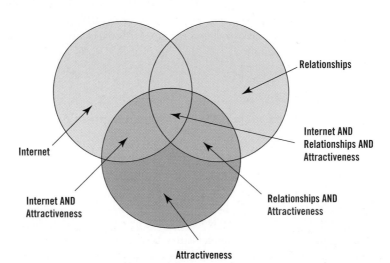

Figure 34.2 A Venn diagram showing overlaps among *relationships, attractiveness,* and *Internet* (see Quick Reference 34.1)

URL for Library of Congress Catalog

Begin here for new search

Advanced search

General help areas

Links

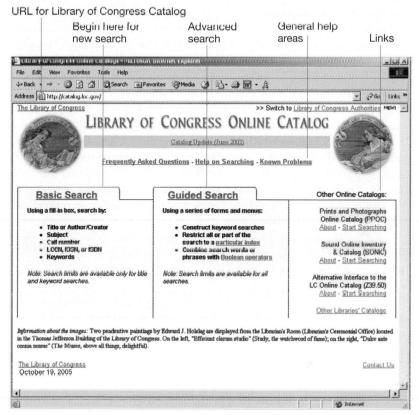

Figure 34.3 Library of Congress Online Catalog

that it allows you to search by title, author, subject, call number, or keyword; to search particular indexes; or to search using BOOLEAN EXPRESSIONS.

Suppose you're using the EXPERT SEARCH STRATEGY and a source recommends that you find a book by the **author** Thomas L. Friedman, but you don't know its title. You can search the catalog for books by this author. A screen on your library's computer will have a place for you to type "Friedman, Thomas" in a space for "author." (Usually, you enter last name, then first name, but check which system your library uses.) If your library owns any books by Thomas Friedman, the computer will display their titles and other bibliographic information, such as the library call number. Then you can use the call number to request the book or to find it yourself.

Among the books you might find when searching for "Friedman, Thomas" is *The World Is Flat: A Brief History of the Twenty-first Century* (New York: Farrar, Straus and Giroux, 2005). Suppose you know that book's **title**, but not its author, and want to see if your library owns a copy. Your library's online catalog will have a place for you to type in the title; some systems omit words like *the* or *a,* so that in this case, you would type in only "World Flat Brief History Twenty-first Century."

Suppose, however, you don't know an author's name or a book title. You have only a research topic, and you need to find sources. In this case, you need to search by **subject**, using the terms listed in the *Library of Congress Subject Headings (LCSH).* The *LCSH* is a multivolume catalog available, primarily in book form, in the reference section of every library. A version of the information in the *LCSH* is online at http://authorities.loc.gov. The *LCSH* lists only **subject headings**, which are organized from most general to most narrow. Suppose you're researching the topic of "globalization." If you enter that term into a space for subject searches in your own library's "Search" screen, *The World Is Flat: A Brief History of the Twenty-first Century* by Thomas Friedman will be listed if the book is available.

Finally, you may wish to search by **keyword** in your library's holdings. If you were researching a paper on the future of jobs in the changing world economy, you could find Friedman's book using the keywords *economy, globalization, outsourcing, employment,* and so on.

An entry in the library's book catalog contains a great deal of useful information: a book's title, author, publisher, date and place of publication, and length, along with its location in the library. A full-record catalog entry (a complete set of information about the source rather than a brief listing that may have only author, title, and call number) lists additional subjects covered in that book. The list of additional subjects can provide valuable clues for further searching.

Many libraries allow you to print out this information, send it to your e-mail account, or download and save it. Whether you choose one of these options or copy the information yourself directly into your WORKING BIBLIOGRAPHY, it's crucial to record the **call number** exactly as it appears, with all numbers, letters, and decimal points. The call number tells where the book is located in the library's stacks (storage shelves). If you're researching in a library with *open stacks* (that is, you're permitted to go where books are shelved), the call number leads you to the area in the library where you can find all books on the same subject. Simply looking at what's on the shelves may yield useful sources. Keep in mind that in physically browsing the stacks, however, you're missing sources that other students have checked out or that are "on hold" at the library's reserve desk. The book catalog generally will contain information about whether a book is checked out or on reserve.

A call number is especially crucial in a library or special collection with *closed stacks* (that is, a library where you fill in a call slip, hand it in at the call desk, and wait for the book to arrive). Such libraries don't permit you to browse the stacks, so you have to rely entirely on the book catalog. If you fill in the wrong number or an incomplete number, your wait will be in vain.

34f   How do I find periodicals?

Periodicals are newspapers, magazines, and journals published at set intervals. Different kinds of periodicals will meet different research purposes. Quick Reference 34.2 describes several important types.

Quick Reference 34.2   ■ ■ ■ ■ ■ ■ ■

Types of periodicals

Type	Characteristics	Useful for
JOURNALS	Scholarly articles written by experts for other experts; usually focus on one academic discipline or field; published relatively infrequently (often 3–6 times per year, generally not more than once per month); examples are *College Composition and Communication* and *American Journal of Public Health.*	The most reliable expert research on a particular subject; detailed articles and extensive bibliographies that can point to other sources or experts; may also have book reviews
NEWS MAGAZINES	Short to modest length articles on current events or topics that are of interest to a broad readership; have lots of photographs and graphics; may have opinions or editorials, as well as reviews; generally are published weekly; examples are *Time* and *U.S. News and World Report.*	Easily understandable and timely introductions to current topics; often can point to more expert sources, topics, and keywords
SPECIAL INTEREST OR "LIFESTYLE" MAGAZINES	Written for audiences (including fans and hobbyists) interested in a particular topic; include news and features on that topic; generally published monthly, with entertainment as an important goal; examples include *Outside, Rolling Stone, Wired.*	Providing "how to" information on their topics of focus, as well as technical information or in-depth profiles of individuals, products, or events; many include reviews related to emphasis; the more serious examples are well-written and reliable

continued >>

Quick Reference 34.2 (continued)

Type	Characteristics	Useful for
"INTELLECT- UAL" OR LITERARY MAGAZINES	Publish relatively longer articles that provide in-depth analysis of issues, events, or people; may include creative work as well as nonfiction; aimed at a general well-educated audience; usually published monthly (though sometimes more or less often); examples include *The Atlantic, Harper's, The New Yorker.*	Learning about a topic in depth but in way more accessible than scholarly journals; becoming aware of major controversies and positions; learning who experts are and what books or other sources have been published; reading arguments on topics
TRADE MAGAZINES	Focus on particular businesses, industries and trade groups; discuss new products, legislation, or events that will influence individuals or businesses in that area; examples include *National Hog Farmer, Sound and Video Contractor.*	Specialized information focusing on applying information or research in particular settings; seeing how specific audiences or interest groups may respond to a particular position
NEWS- PAPERS	Publish articles about news, sports, and cultural events soon after they happen; contain several sections, including opinions and editorials, lifestyle (home, food, movies, etc.), sports and so on; most appear daily, though some smaller ones are weekly or twice-weekly; examples are *The Washington Post; The Rocky Mountain News; The DeWitt, Iowa, Observer.*	Very current information on things as they happen; national newspapers (such as the *New York Times*) cover world events and frequently have analysis and commentary; local newspapers cover small happenings you likely won't find elsewhere; opinion sections and reviews are stimulating sources of ideas and positions

To use periodicals efficiently, consult databases or **indexes** to periodicals, which allow you to search by subject, title, keyword, or author. Most exist as online databases that are updated frequently. Your library very likely subscribes to several of the ones that you'll need, and you can access them through the library's Web site.

Alert: The terms DATABASE and INDEX are often used interchangeably, but there are differences between the two. Before electronic means of storing information in databases became common, periodical information was organized in lists of references called indexes, which existed only in print. A very few still do, but most are now electronic. An index only had bibliographic information. A database, however, often includes not only that information but also connections to the articles themselves. A database is more comprehensive than an index. Generally, if you're referring to online lists of sources, you can't go wrong simply using the broader term database. ●

34f.1   Using databases to find periodicals

Your library's home page generally provides different ways to access various databases. Figure 34.4 shows an example. Users who know the name of a database can go directly to it. However, users who know only a general field can "Search by Category" and see an alphabetical list of subject areas. When you choose a category, you'll see a list of all the databases for that area. For example, Figure 34.4 shows the subject databases for anthropology. It's important to choose the right database for your search because the wrong one may miss some of the best sources for your paper.

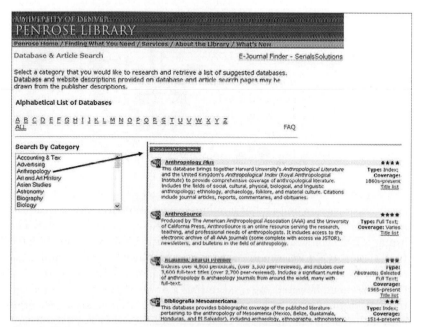

Figure 34.4 Listing of indexes that include relevant articles

General databases index articles in journals, magazines, and newspapers. Large libraries have many general databases. Among common ones are the following:

- *Academic Search Premier* covers thousands of general and scholarly publications in the social sciences, humanities, education, computer sciences, engineering, language and linguistics, arts and literature, medical sciences, and ethnic studies. Most of the sources in this database are available in full text. This database is suitable for academic research projects, as long as you take care to focus on journal articles and well-regarded general publications.

- *General Reference Center Gold* covers current events, popular culture, business and industry, the arts and sciences, and sports published in newspapers, reference books, and periodicals; it focuses on general interest periodicals.

- *LexisNexis Academic* provides abstracts of news, business, and legal information. Sources include foreign news publications; regional US news services; radio and television transcripts; federal and state case law; medical, legislative and industry news; and so on.

Specialized databases are more appropriate than general ones for much college-level research. They list articles in journals published by and for expert, academic, or professional readers. Many specialized databases include the abstract, or summary, that is printed at the beginning of each scholarly article. Examples of specialized databases include *General Science Abstracts, Business Abstracts, Humanities Index, Social Sciences Abstracts, MLA International Bibliography,* and *PsycINFO.*

You search periodical indexes by using KEYWORDS. Shown in Figure 34.5 are three screens from a keyword search of *PsycINFO* for Andrei Gurov's research paper that appears in section 36e.2.

34f.2   Locating the articles themselves

Periodical indexes help you locate the titles of specific articles on your topic. Once you have the listing, though, how do you get your hands on the article itself? Often you can find a full-text online version of the article to read, download, or print. A full-text version may be either in HTML format or PDF. The listing will tell you which one; if you have a choice, we recommend using the PDF version, which is easier to cite because it has the layout of a common article. Figure 34.6 shows location information in a typical database entry.

Sometimes, however, you need to find a printed copy of the periodical. Often the listing in the database will tell you whether your library owns a print copy and what its call number is. Otherwise, you'll need to check if the periodical is listed in the library's catalog. Search for the periodical name you want

Keyword search

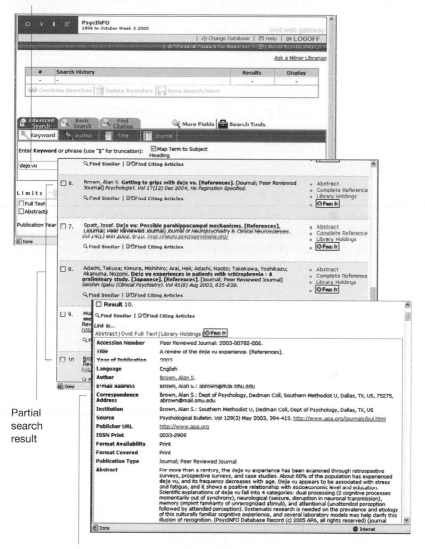

Partial
search
result

One article selected from database

Figure 34.5 Keyword search of *PsycINFO*

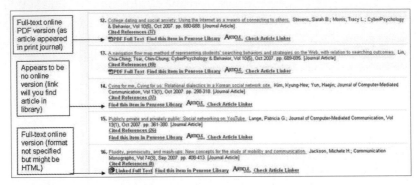

Figure 34.6 Location information in a database

(for example, *American Literature* or *The Economist*), not for the article's author or title. If your library subscribes to that periodical, you can use its call number to find its location. You then need to find the specific article you want by looking for the issue in which the article you're looking for is printed.

Few libraries subscribe to all of the periodicals listed in specialized databases. For advice on locating sources that your college doesn't own, see 34i.

EXERCISE 34-2   Use two databases that are available through your library to conduct two searches for one or more of the terms below. (Alternatively, your instructor may suggest a different term or have you pursue a topic of your own choosing.)

If possible, choose one general and one specialized database. Compile a brief report that compares the sources you generate. You might address questions like these: How many sources did each search turn up? Is there any overlap? What kinds of periodicals are represented in each database? What access does your library provide to the several sources you find most interesting in each search? Note: If you're generating lots of hits, restrict your search to the past year or two.

Suggested terms for searching (with type of specialized database to consult in parentheses): *memory* (psychology); *globalization* (business, economics, sociology); *cloning* (biology); *global warming* (geology, geography, political science); *obesity* (medicine, psychology).

34g   How do I use reference works?

Reference works include encyclopedias, almanacs, yearbooks, fact books, atlases, dictionaries, biographical reference works, and bibliographies. Some references are *general,* providing information on a vast number of subjects, but without any depth. Others are *specialized,* providing information on selected topics, often for more expert or professional audiences.

34g.1 General reference works

Reference works are the starting point for many college and other advanced researchers—but they're no more than a starting point. **General reference works** by themselves are insufficient for academic research. Still, they help researchers identify useful KEYWORDS, find examples, and verify facts. Most widely used reference works are available in electronic versions, usually online. Check your library's Web site to see if the reference work you want is available online through a subscription or license the library has purchased. For example, your library may have a subscription to the *Gale Virtual Reference Library,* which allows libraries to choose up to 1000 reference books available to users online. You can also check your library's catalog. Finally, you can search the World Wide Web by entering the work's name to see if it's available there. (For example, *Encyclopaedia Britannica* is at http://www.britannica.com.) Be aware that often you have to pay a fee for works you don't access through the library.

GENERAL ENCYCLOPEDIAS

Articles in multivolume general encyclopedias, such as the *Encyclopaedia Britannica,* summarize information on a wide variety of subjects. The articles can give you helpful background information and the names of major figures and experts in the field. Best of all, many articles end with a brief bibliography of major works on the subject. General encyclopedias aren't the place to look for information on recent events or current research, although sometimes they cover a field's ongoing controversies up until the date that the reference was published.

ALMANACS, YEARBOOKS, FACT BOOKS

Almanacs, yearbooks, and fact books are huge compilations of facts in many subject areas. They're often available both in print and online. They're excellent for verifying information from other sources and, in some cases, for finding supporting facts and figures. Almanacs, such as *The World Almanac,* present capsule accounts of a year's events and data about government, politics, economics, science and technology, sports, and many other categories. *Facts on File,* which is indexed online by LexisNexis, covers world events in a weekly digest and in an annual one-volume yearbook. The annual *Statistical Abstract of the United States* (accessed online through http://www.census.gov) contains a wealth of data on the United States. *Demographic Yearbook* and the *United Nations Statistical Yearbook* carry worldwide data.

ATLASES AND GAZETTEERS

Atlases (such as *The Times Atlas of the World*) contain maps of our planet's continents, seas, and skies. Gazetteers (such as *The Columbia Gazetteer of the World,* available online for a fee at http://www.columbiagazetteer.org) provide comprehensive geographical information on topography, climates, populations, migrations, natural resources, crops, and so on.

DICTIONARIES

Dictionaries define words and terms. In addition to general dictionaries, specialized dictionaries exist in many academic disciplines to define words and phrases specific to a field.

BIOGRAPHICAL REFERENCE WORKS

Biographical reference books give brief factual information about famous people—their accomplishments along with pertinent events and dates in their lives. Biographical references include the *Who's Who* series, *The Dictionary of American Biography*, and many others. Specialized biographical references in various fields are also available.

BIBLIOGRAPHIES

Bibliographies list books, articles, documents, films, and other resources and provide publication information so that you can find those sources. Some bibliographies are comprehensive and list sources on a wide range of topics. Others list only sources on a particular subject. Specialized bibliographies can be very helpful in your research process. Annotated or critical bibliographies describe and evaluate the works that they list. These resources are increasingly available online but require you either to access them through a library's paid subscription service or to pay a fee each time you use them.

34g.2 Specialized reference works

Specialized reference works provide more authoritative and specific information than do general reference works. Specialized reference works are usually appropriate for college-level research because the information is more advanced and detailed. They can be invaluable for introducing you to the controversies and KEYWORDS in a subject area. In particular, finding authors' names in such books can help you begin to accumulate a list of credible authors.

There are hundreds of specialized references. Some examples include the *Encyclopedia of Banking and Finance*, the *Oxford Companion to American Literature*, the *Encyclopedia of Chemistry*, the *Dictionary of American Biography*, and the *International Encyclopedia of Film*.

Because hundreds of one-volume works are highly specific, we haven't listed them here. Check what specialized reference books your college library has available that might help you in your search. They may be listed in the library's catalog or in a references database, such as the *Gale Virtual Reference Library*.

34h How do I find government publications?

Government publications are available in astounding variety. You can find information on laws and legal decisions, regulations, population, weather patterns, agriculture, national parks, education, and health, to name just a few topics. Since the middle 1990s, most government documents have been available through the World Wide Web. The Government Printing Office maintains the *Catalog of U.S. Government Publications* at http://www.gpoaccess.gov.

The GPO site has a searchable database. Information about legislation is also available at the Web site THOMAS, a service of the Library of Congress, which you can access at http://thomas.loc.gov. A directory of all federal government sites that provide statistical information is at http://www.fedstats.gov.

The LexisNexis database service provides access to a huge number of other governmental reports and documents. For example, it includes the *Congressional Information Service (CIS),* which indexes all papers produced by US congressional panels and committees. These documents include the texts of hearings (for example, testimony about homelessness) and reports (for example, a comparative study of temporary shelters for homeless people).

34i What if my library doesn't have a source I need?

Almost no library owns every book or subscribes to every periodical. However, many libraries are connected electronically to other libraries' book catalogs and can give you access to additional holdings. Often you or a librarian can request materials from other libraries through interlibrary loan (generally free of charge). Alternatively, your college may have a different document delivery system (perhaps at a cost to you).

34j How do I evaluate sources?

Finding a source is only part of your effort. Your next step is to evaluate the quality of each source. Your critical thinking skills (Chapter 4) will be important in this effort. First, decide whether the information in the source relates to your topic in more than a vague, general sense. Then, ask how a source might help you answer your research question (33e). Finally, using the criteria in Quick Reference 34.3, evaluate each source with a cold, critical eye.

ESOL Tip: The definition of *authority* can differ across cultures. However, in the United States, a source must meet specific criteria to be considered authoritative. A source is not reliable simply because the author or speaker is an important member of the community, claims to have knowledge about a topic, or publishes material in print or online. When considering whether to use a source for your research, ask yourself the questions in Quick Reference 34.3. ●

Quick Reference 34.3　　　■ ■ ■ ■ ■ ■ ■

Evaluating sources

1. **Is the source authoritative?** Generally, encyclopedias, textbooks, and academic journals (*The American Scholar, Journal of Counseling and Development*) are authoritative. Books published by university presses (Indiana University Press) and by publishers that specialize in scholarly books are also trustworthy. Material published in newspapers, in general-readership magazines (*Newsweek, U.S. News & World Report*), and by established commercial publishers (Prentice Hall) are usually reliable, but you want to apply the other criteria in this list with special care, cross-checking names and facts whenever possible. Web sites maintained by professional organizations, such as the National Council of Teachers of English at http://www.ncte.org, are authoritative.

2. **Is the author an expert?** Biographical material in the article or book may tell you if the author is an expert on the topic. Look up the author in a reputable, up-to-date biographical dictionary. Alternatively, enter the author's name in an Internet search engine. Look to see if the author has a degree in this field and whether he or she is affiliated with a reliable institution. Also, if an author is often cited by professionals in the field and published in journals, he or she is probably considered an expert.

3. **Is the source current?** Check the publication date. Research is ongoing in most fields, and information is often modified or replaced by new findings. Check databases and online subject directories to see if newer sources are available.

4. **Does the source support its information sufficiently?** Are its assertions or claims supported with sufficient evidence? Separate facts from opinions (4d.1) and see if the writer relies too much on opinion. If the author expresses a point of view, check what kind of evidence he or she offers to back up that position (4d.2). If there are claims of cause and effect, ask yourself if they're justified (4d.3). If the writer resorts to logical fallacies, reject the source (4i). Use wise judgment and don't take chances.

5. **Is the author's tone balanced?** If the TONE is unbiased and the reasoning is logical, the source is probably useful (4d.4, 4e.2). Some warning signs of biased tone are name calling, sarcasm, stereotyping, or absolute assertions about matters that are open to interpretation (using *always, everyone,* and similar words).

34k   What should I know about searching the Web?

Sources from the library or from library databases have the advantage of being selected by experts. While you still have to evaluate them, they have passed a screening process. On the other hand, anyone can put anything on the Web. This makes the Web a rich source of information, but it also makes finding what you need difficult, and it opens the possibility of encountering inaccurate or biased materials. Therefore, searching library databases remains a crucial method of finding many scholarly sources.

34l   How do I search the Web?

Finding information on the Web has become so common that "google" has become a verb. The principles for searching the Web are much like those for searching databases (34d). Once you use a browser to get on the Web, you can search for sites by using a SEARCH ENGINE or by typing an address (called a URL, for "universal resource locator" or "uniform resource locator") into the search box. **Search engines** are programs designed to hunt the Internet for sources on specific topics that you identify by using keywords (34l.1) or through subject directories (34l.2). Some commonly used search engines include Google (http://www.google.com) or Yahoo (http://www.yahoo.com).

As the Internet matures, search engines are constantly acquiring new features. A special page on the Google search engine, Google Scholar (http://scholar.google.com) and its Advanced Scholar Search function permit scholarly searches that have features in common with the searches of library databases.

Alert: When you cite a URL as a source, such as the Web site for MyCompLab, the Modern Language Association (MLA) tells you to surround it with angle brackets, such as <www.MyCompLab.com>. However, don't use angle brackets when you type a URL in the locator box at the top of a Web page'. ●

As you know, the Internet contains many types of sources. We've listed a few of the main ones in Quick Reference 34.4.

34l.1   Using keywords

In the same way you use KEYWORDS to find materials in library databases (34d), you can use them to find information on the Internet. Type a word or group of words in the search box on the opening page of the search engine, and click on the "Search" or "Enter" button. The engine scans for your word(s) in Web pages, and then lists sites that contain them.

Quick Reference 34.4

■ ■ ■ ■ ■ ■ ■

Types of sources on the Internet

Periodicals and news sites. Many newspapers and magazines put content online, although some of them give access to all of their material only to subscribers. Some periodicals put only print content online, while others have extra content that appears only on the Web. Finally, there are periodicals that exist only online. Examples include *Salon.com* and *Kairos* (http://english.ttu.edu/Kairos/).

Mainstream news organizations (for example, CNN or MSNBC) frequently have sites, too, in which they publish video and sound clips as well as articles.

Organizational Web sites. Interest groups, clubs, businesses, museums, universities, and similar organizations frequently have Web sites. They often provide basic facts and information about the organization, but they may include articles, reports, research findings, position papers, policy statements, and so on. Some of them can be very authoritative and useful; others require more evaluation and care, especially when the organization is promoting itself, as is reasonable.

Government Web sites. Federal, state, and local governments maintain Web sites to provide all sorts of information to their citizens. This frequently includes not only news about laws or events, but often research or articles. (In his argument paper about organic food in Chapter 5, Alex Garcia found the US Department of Agriculture's Web site very helpful.) A number of GOVERNMENT DOCUMENTS can also help researchers (34h). The Library of Congress is a powerful source for many kinds of digital information and its Web site includes many useful and usable public access materials, like images and recordings, that are not available on commercial sites.

Blogs. Much of what appears now on the Web is in the form of blogs, regular short articles published by people ranging from experts to amateurs. Blogs tend to be highly opinionated, so evaluate them carefully, but several well-regarded scholars and other experts do keep blogs.

Images, sounds, and videos. Both as parts of other sites and in sites of their own, images, sounds, and videos appear on the Web. A podcast or a documentary may offer expert information on a particular topic. There may be a video of a press conference or a recording of a speech. The Online Speech Bank at http://www.americanrhetoric.com, for example, has over 5,000 recordings and videos.

341.2   Using subject directories

Subject directories provide an alternative to keyword searches. These directories list topics (education, computing, entertainment, and so on) or resources and services (shopping, travel, and so on), with links to Web sites on those topics and resources. Most search engines' home pages have one or more subject directories. In addition, there are some independent subject directories. Some examples are *Educator's Reference Desk* (http://www.edurcf.org), *Internet Public Library* (http://www.ipl.org), and *Refdesk.com* (http://www.refdesk.com).

Clicking on a general category within a subject directory will take you to lists of increasingly specific categories. Eventually, you'll get a list of Web pages on the most specific subtopic you select. These search engines also allow you to click on a category and enter keywords for a search. For example, suppose that you are using Google to search for information on organic food. As Figure 34.7 shows, you'll first go to Google's general category of "Health." Under "Health" you'll find the category of "Nutrition," and within "Nutrition," you'll find a link to "Organic Food," a page that lists dozens of additional categories and sources.

Quick Reference 34.5 summarizes the information in this section by providing some general guidelines for using search engines and directories with keywords.

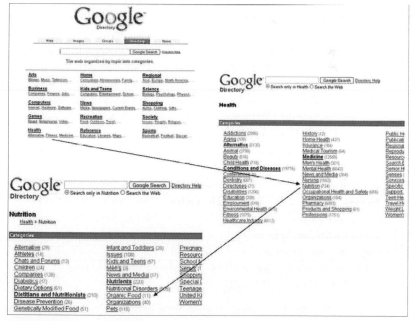

Figure 34.7 A Google subject directory for "Organic Food"

Quick Reference 34.5

■ ■ ■ ■ ■ ■ ■

Tips on using search engines and directories

- Use keyword combinations or BOOLEAN EXPRESSIONS (Quick Reference 34.1) unless you have a very specific, narrow topic with unique keywords. A search for even a moderately common topic may produce thousands of hits, many of which won't be relevant to your topic. You might also switch to a subject directory.

- Most search engines attempt to search as much of the World Wide Web as possible. But because the Web is vast and unorganized, different search engines will give different results for the same search. Try using more than one search engine, or use a **metasearch engine** that searches several search engines at once, such as Dogpile (http://dogpile.com).

- Use the "Advanced Search" page, if one is available. It allows you to search or sort by date, language, file format, and domain type, as well as by various combinations of keywords.

- When you find a useful site, go to the toolbar at the top of the screen and click on "Bookmark" or "Favorites" and then click on "Add." This will make it easy for you to return to a good source.

- Use the "History" or "Go" function to track the sites you visit, in case you want to revisit one you previously thought was not helpful.

- Sources on the Web may come in various formats. Most common are Web pages in html (Hypertext Markup Language) format. However, you may also encounter Word or Excel documents, PowerPoint slides, or PDF (portable document format) files, each of which requires specific software. PDF files, which require the free Adobe Acrobat Reader that you can download from http://www.adobe.com, allow people to preserve documents in their original formats.

EXERCISE 34-3   Use a search engine of your choice to search for sources on "déjà vu." (To make the search easier, you may omit the accents.) For each option below, record how many hits occur.

1. Enter the phrase *"deja vu"*
2. Enter the word *"memory"*
3. Enter the phrase *"memory" AND "deja vu"*
4. Enter the phrase *"deja vu" AND "consciousness"*
5. To any of the searches above, add the word *"research"*
6. Repeat this exercise by searching another topic that interests you.

34m How do I evaluate Web sources?

The same strategies for evaluating library sources, discussed in 34c, apply to evaluating Web sources. Ask yourself if the Web source is well supported with evidence and free from fallacies or bias. Use strategies for critical thinking and analysis in Chapter 4.

However, you need to evaluate Web sources with additional care for two reasons. First, because anyone can post anything on the Web, some sources may very well be plagiarized. Second, many sources on the Web have been written by individuals posing as experts and, as a result, may offer false or misleading information.

You're always accountable for the sources you choose. Most sites also contain material that will help you assess their credibility, such as a bibliography, links to the author or editor, or a description of the sponsoring organization. You want to discard sites that do not contain such verifying information, however useful they may seem. Err on the side of caution.

An important question to ask about any Web site is why the information exists and why it was put on the Internet. What motives might the site's authors have? Are you asked to take action of any kind? If yes, take special care to judge the source's bias. For example, the World Wildlife Fund can ask for contributions and still maintain a Web site that contains reliable information. Conversely, a hate group or extreme political organization can't be trusted to be objective. Quick Reference 34.6 summarizes the questions to ask about Web sites.

Quick Reference 34.6

Judging the reliability of Web sources

Reliable sources are . . .	Questionable sources are . . .
From educational, not-for-profit, or government organizations. One sign is an Internet address ending in *.edu*, *.org*, *.gov*, or a country abbreviation such as *.us* or *.uk*. However, if any of these organizations fail to list their sources, don't use them. After all, many colleges and universities now host student Web sites, which also end in *.edu*.	**From commercial organizations advertising to sell a product** (*.com*)**; Web sites that are advertisements or personal pages; junk mail.** These sites may or may not list sources. If they fail to, don't use them. If they do, check that the sources are legitimate, not a front for some commercial enterprise.

continued >>

Quick Reference 34.6 (continued)

From expert authors. Experts have degrees or credentials in their fields that you can check. See if their names appear in other reliable sources, in bibliographies on your topic, or in reference books in your college's library. Check whether the site's author gives an e-mail address for questions or comments.

From anonymous authors or authors without identifiable credentials. Chat rooms, discussion groups, bulletin boards, and similar networks are questionable when they don't give credentials or other qualifying information.

From reliable print sources. Online versions of the *New York Times, Time* magazine, and other publications that are produced by the publisher are just as reliable as the print versions.

Secondhand excerpts and quotations. Materials that appear on a site that is not the official site of the publisher (such as a quotation taken from the *New York Times*) may be edited in a biased or inaccurate manner. Such sources may be incomplete and inaccurate.

Well supported with evidence. The information is presented in a balanced, unbiased fashion.

Unsupported or biased. These sites carry declarations and assertions that have little or no supporting evidence.

Current. The site's information is regularly updated.

Outdated. The site's information hasn't been updated in a year or more.

For more help with your writing, grammar, and research, go to **www.mycomplab.com**

mycomplab

35

Using Sources and Avoiding Plagiarism

35a   How do I use sources well?

Using sources well means using QUOTATIONS (35h), PARAPHRASES (35i), and SUMMARIES (35j) to create a synthesis of those materials and your own thoughts. It also means documenting your sources and avoiding PLAGIARISM. Generally, you'll begin this process after you've located most of your sources and evaluated them (Chapter 34), written a WORKING BIBLIOGRAPHY (33i), and taken content notes (33k). Of course, during the process of DRAFTING, you might discover the need to do some additional research, and that's fine. Be careful, though, to avoid a trap into which we see some writers fall—endlessly researching to put off the challenging work of drafting.

Pulling together a SYNTHESIS of your sources and your own thinking about the topic means:

* Mastering the information from each source
* Finding relationships among the pieces of information from various sources
* Adding your own thinking to the mix

To write effectively, organize your paper around a logical sequence based on the main points in your synthesis. Further, support each main point and important subpoint with specific evidence, explanations, ideas, or facts drawn from your sources. You'll also want to support your points with ideas generated through your own CRITICAL THINKING (Chapter 4), especially through ANALYSIS (4d), INFERENCE (4e), SYNTHESIS (4f), EVALUATION (4g), and assessment of authors' reasoning processes (4h). If your PURPOSE is persuasive rather than informative, remember to present opposing viewpoints evenhandedly and then refute them reasonably (5e, 5l).

All SOURCE-BASED WRITING needs to be:

* Accurate
* Effective
* Honest (the only way to avoid plagiarism)

A crucial part of honesty is using correct documentation (Chapters 36–38). **Documentation** means making two types of entries in your research paper each time you use a source:

1. Writing a parenthetical citation for each quotation, paraphrase, and summary you take from sources (for examples in MLA STYLE, see 36c; for APA, see 37c).

2. Composing a BIBLIOGRAPHY for the end of your paper. MLA calls this list of sources WORKS CITED, while APA calls it REFERENCES. This list needs to include full bibliographic information on each source from which you have quoted, paraphrased, and summarized in your paper (for examples, see 36d for MLA style, 37f for APA, or 38 for CMS or CSE).

Today's bibliographies differ from those of the past. The root word *biblio-* means "book," so traditionally, the bibliographic information referred to a book's title, author, publisher, and place and year of publication. In the age of digital technology, researchers include in their bibliographies not only print sources but also electronic sources.

Documentation is vital for three reasons. It tells readers where to find your sources in case they want to consult those sources in greater depth or verify that you've used them properly. It lends credibility and weight to your writing, strengthening your ethos as someone who has done the careful work needed to develop well-supported papers. It also gives credit to others for their work. A **documentation style** refers to a specific system for providing information on sources used in a research paper. Documentation styles vary among the disciplines. This handbook presents four documentation styles in Chapters 36–38. Refer to the directory on the first page of each documentation chapter for a detailed index of where to find MLA, APA, CM, and CSE style information.

35b What is plagiarism?

Plagiarism is presenting another person's words, ideas, or visual images as if they were your own. Plagiarizing is like stealing: It is a form of academic dishonesty or cheating. Plagiarism is a serious offense that can be grounds for a failing grade or expulsion from a college. Beyond that, you're hurting yourself. If you're plagiarizing, you're not learning.

Plagiarism isn't something that just college instructors get fussy about. In the workplace, it can get you fired and hinder your being hired elsewhere. Plagiarism at work also has legal implications; words, ideas, and images, especially those that describe or influence business practices and decisions, are *intellectual property*. Using someone else's intellectual property without permission or credit is a form of theft that may land you in court. Furthermore, plagiarism in any setting—academic, business, or civic—hurts your credibility and reputation. Quick Reference 35.1 lists the major types of plagiarism.

Quick Reference 35.1

■ ■ ■ ■ ■ ■ ■ ■

Types of plagiarism

You're plagiarizing if you . . .

- Buy a paper from an Internet site, another student or writer, or any other source and pass it off as your own.

- Turn in any paper that someone else has written, whether the person has given it to you, you've downloaded it from the Internet, or you've copied it from any other source.

- Change selected parts of an existing paper and claim the paper as your own.

- Neglect to put quotation marks around words that you quote directly from a source, even if you document the source.

- Copy or paste into your paper any *key terms, phrases, sentences,* or *longer passages* from another source without using documentation to tell precisely where the material came from. This is equally true for both library-based sources and sources you find on the Internet.

- Use *ideas* from another source without correctly citing and documenting that source, even if you put the ideas into your own words.

- Combine ideas from many sources and pass them off as your own without correctly citing and documenting the sources.

- Take language, ideas, or visual images from anyone (colleagues, companies, organizations, and so on) without obtaining permission or crediting them.

ESOL Tip: Perhaps you come from a country or culture that considers it acceptable for students to copy the writing of experts and authorities. Some cultures, in fact, believe that using another's words, even without citing them, is a sign of respect or learning. However, this practice is considered unacceptable in American and most Western settings. It is plagiarism, and you need to avoid it by using the strategies we discuss in this chapter. ●

35c How do I avoid plagiarism?

You can avoid plagiarism two ways. First, be very systematic and careful when you take content notes and when you quote, paraphrase, or summarize materials. Second, become comfortable with the concept of DOCUMENTATION, which you need each time you use a source. Quick Reference 35.2 describes the main strategies you can use to avoid plagiarism.

Another important way to avoid plagiarism is to dive willingly into any interim tasks your instructors build into research assignments. For example, many instructors set interim deadlines such as a date for handing in a WORKING BIBLIOGRAPHY (33i) or an ANNOTATED BIBLIOGRAPHY (33j). Further, some instructors want to read and coach you about how to improve one or more of your research paper drafts. In some cases, they might want to look over a research log (33c), content notes (33k), and/or photocopies of your sources.

Quick Reference 35.2

■ ■ ■ ■ ■ ■ ■

Strategies for avoiding plagiarism

- Use DOCUMENTATION to acknowledge your use of the ideas or phrasings of others, taken from the sources you've compiled on your topic.

- Become thoroughly familiar with the documentation style that your instructor tells you to use for your research paper (Chapters 36–38). To work efficiently, make a master list of the information required to document all sources that you quote, paraphrase, or summarize according to your required documentation style.

- Write down absolutely all the documentation facts that you'll need for your paper, keeping careful records as you search for sources. Otherwise, you'll waste much time trying to retrace your steps to get a documentation detail you missed.

- Use a consistent system for taking CONTENT NOTES, making sure to maintain the distinction between your own thinking and the ideas that come directly from a source. Perhaps use different colors of ink or another coding system to keep these three uses of sources separate:

  1. Quotations from a source (documentation required)

  2. Material paraphrased or summarized from a source (documentation required)

  3. Thoughts of your own triggered by what you've read or experienced in life (no documentation required)

- Write clear, perhaps oversized, quotation marks when you're directly quoting a passage. Make them so distinct that you can't miss seeing them later.

- Consult with your instructor if you're unsure about any phase of the documentation process.

Never assume that your instructor can't detect plagiarism. Instructors have keen eyes for writing styles that are different from the ones students generally produce and from your own style in particular. They recognize professionally drawn visuals and charts. Instructors can access Web sites that electronically check your submitted work against all material available online. Further, services such as http://www.turnitin.com allow instructors to check your writing against hundreds of thousands of papers for free or for sale on the World Wide Web and the Internet. (Also, that site adds your paper to its huge database of student papers so that no one can plagiarize your work.) Moreover, when instructors receive papers that they suspect contain plagiarized passages, they can check with other professors to see whether a student paper looks familiar.

35d How do I work with Internet sources to avoid plagiarism?

Online sources can both greatly help researchers and create new possible problems. Because it's so easy to download source materials, it's potentially easy to misrepresent someone else's work as your own, even if you don't intend to be dishonest.

You might be tempted to download a completed research paper from the Internet. *Don't*. That's intellectual dishonesty, which can get you into real trouble. Or you might be tempted to borrow wording from what you wrongly consider an "obscure" Internet source. *Don't*. Not only is this intellectual dishonesty, but instructors will easily detect it. Even if you have absolutely no intention of plagiarizing, being careless, especially with cutting and pasting, can easily lead to trouble. Quick Reference 35.3 suggests ways to avoid plagiarism when you're working with digital or online sources.

35e What don't I have to document?

You don't have to document common knowledge or your own thinking. **Common knowledge** is information that most educated people know, although they may need to remind themselves of certain facts by looking up information in a reference book. For example, here are a few facts of common knowledge that you don't need to document.

- Bill Clinton was the US president before George W. Bush.
- Mercury is the planet closest to the sun.
- Normal human body temperature is 98.6 degrees Fahrenheit.
- All the oceans on our planet contain salt water.

Sometimes, of course, a research paper doesn't contain common knowledge. For example, Andrei Gurov, whose research paper appears in 36e.2, had only very general common knowledge about the topic of déjà vu. Most of his

Quick Reference 35.3 ▪ ▪ ▪ ▪ ▪ ▪ ▪

Guidelines for avoiding plagiarizing online sources

- Never cut material from an online source and paste it directly in your paper. You can too easily lose track of which language is your own and which comes from a source.

- Keep material that you downloaded or printed from the Internet separate from your own writing, whether you intend to QUOTE, SUMMARIZE, or PARAPHRASE the material. Be careful how you manage copied files. Use another color or a much larger font as a visual reminder that this isn't your work. Just as important, make sure that you type in all of the information you need to identify each source, according to the documentation style you need to use.

- Copy or paste downloaded or printed material into your paper only when you intend to use it as a direct quotation or visual. Immediately place quotation marks around the material, or set off a long passage as a block quotation. Be sure to document the source at the same time as you copy or paste the quotation into your paper. Don't put off documenting the passage until later because you may forget to do it or do it incorrectly.

- Summarize or paraphrase materials *before* you include them in your paper. If you have printed or downloaded Internet sources to separate files, don't copy directly from those files into your paper. Summarize or paraphrase the sources in a different file, and then paste the summaries or paraphrases into your paper. Document the source of each passage at the same time as you insert it in your paper. If you put off this task until later, you may forget to do it or get it wrong.

- Use an Internet service to check a passage you're not sure about. If you're concerned that you may have plagiarized material by mistake, try submitting one or two sentences that concern you to http://www.google.com. To make this work, always place quotation marks around the sentences you want to check when you type them into the search window.

paper consists of ideas and information that he quotes, paraphrases, and summarizes from sources.

A very important component of a research paper that doesn't need documentation is **your own thinking,** which is based on what you've learned as you built on what you already knew about your topic. Sara Cardini, whose paper appears in section 2l, knew an extensive amount about anime from years of personal experience and reading, so her own thinking is evident throughout her paper. Still, even that paper might have been stronger had she included some research to add more specific support for her observations.

Your own thinking consists of your ANALYSIS, SYNTHESIS, and interpretation of new material as you read or observe it. You don't have to document your own thinking. Your own thinking helps you formulate a THESIS STATEMENT and organize your research paper by composing TOPIC SENTENCES that carry along your presentation of information. For example, suppose that you're drawing on an article about the connections between emotions and logic in people. While reading the article, you come to a personal conclusion that computers can't have emotions. This idea is not stated anywhere in the article you are reading or in any other source you use. Certainly, you need to cite the ideas from the article that led to your conclusion, but you don't need to cite your own thinking. On the other hand, if you find a source that states this very idea, you should cite it. Among other things, doing so will add force to your paper and strengthen your credibility.

35f What must I document?

You must document everything that you learn from a source. This includes ideas as well as specific language. Expressing the ideas of others in your own words doesn't release you from the obligation to tell exactly where you got those ideas—you need to use complete, correct documentation. Here's an example in action.

SOURCE

Park, Robert L. "Welcome to Planet Earth." *The Best American Science Writing 2001*. Ed. Jesse Cohen. New York: Ecco-Harper, 2001. 302–08. Print. [This source information is arranged in MLA documentation style.]

ORIGINAL (PARK'S EXACT WORDS)

The widespread belief in alien abductions is just one example of the growing influence of pseudoscience. Two hundred years ago, educated people imagined that the greatest contribution of science would be to free the world from superstition and humbug. It has not happened. (304)

PLAGIARISM EXAMPLE

Belief in alien kidnappings illustrates the influence of pseudoscience. In the nineteenth century, educated people imagined that science would free the world from superstition, but they were wrong.

Even though the student changed some wording in the example above, the ideas aren't original to her. To avoid plagiarism she's required to document the source. The underlined phrases are especially problematic examples of plagiarism because they're Park's exact wording.

CORRECT EXAMPLE (USING QUOTATION, PARAPHRASE, AND DOCUMENTATION)

Robert Park calls people's beliefs in alien kidnapping proof of "the growing influence of pseudoscience" (304). Centuries of expectation that science would conquer "superstition and humbug" are still unfulfilled (304).
[This citation is arranged in MLA documentation style.]

The writer of the correct example above has used Park's ideas properly through a combination of quotation and paraphrase and documentation. For example, she correctly quotes the phrase "the growing influence of pseudoscience," and she paraphrases the statement "Two hundred years ago, educated people imagined that the greatest contribution of science would be to free the world," rephrasing it as "Centuries of expectation that science would conquer." She also gives the author's name in the sentence and twice includes parenthetical citations, which would lead the reader to find the source on the WORKS CITED page. Sections 35g through 35j explain exactly how to use sources effectively and document correctly.

35g How can I effectively integrate sources into my writing?

Integrating sources means blending information and ideas from others with your own writing. Before trying to integrate sources into your writing, you need to ANALYZE and SYNTHESIZE your material. Analysis requires you to break ideas down into their component parts so that you can think them through separately. Do this while reading your sources and reviewing your notes. Synthesis requires you to make connections among different ideas, seeking relationships and links that tie them together.

35h How can I use quotations effectively?

A **quotation** is the exact words of a source enclosed in quotation marks. Well-chosen quotations can lend a note of authority and enliven a document with someone else's voice. Think, for example, of a good marketing campaign. A company can incorporate real-life quotes to help support its claim that a product or service works effectively. In academic writing, you achieve some of the same benefits by supporting your work with quotations.

You face conflicting demands when you use quotations in your writing. Although quotations provide support, you can lose coherence in your paper if you use too many of them. If more than a quarter of your paper consists of quotations, you've probably written what some people call a "cut and paste special"—

merely stringing together a bunch of someone else's words. Doing so gives your readers—including instructors—the impression that you've not bothered to develop your own thinking and you're letting other people do your talking.

In addition to avoiding too many quotations, you also want to avoid using quotations that are too long. Readers tend to skip over long quotations and lose the drift of the paper. Also, your instructor might assume that you just didn't take the time required to PARAPHRASE or SUMMARIZE the material. Generally, paraphrases and summaries are more effective for reconstructing someone else's argument. If you do need to quote a long passage, make absolutely sure every word in the quotation counts. Edit out irrelevant parts, using ellipsis points to indicate deleted material (29d and 35h.1). Quick Reference 35.4 provides guidelines for using quotations. Sections 35h.1 and 35h.2 give examples of acceptable and unacceptable quotations.

Quick Reference 35.4

■ ■ ■ ■ ■ ■ ■ ■

Guidelines for using quotations

1. Use quotations from authorities on your subject to support or refute what you write in your paper.

2. Never use a quotation to present your THESIS STATEMENT or a TOPIC SENTENCE.

3. Select quotations that fit your message. Choose a quotation for these reasons:

   * Its language is particularly appropriate or distinctive.
   * Its idea is particularly hard to paraphrase accurately.
   * The source's authority is especially important to support your thesis or main point.
   * The source's words are open to interpretation.

4. Never allow quotations to make up more than a quarter of your paper. Instead, rely on paraphrases (35i) and summaries (35j).

5. Quote accurately. Always check each quotation against the original source—and then recheck it.

6. Integrate quotations smoothly into your writing.

7. Avoid PLAGIARISM (35b–35d).

8. Document quotations carefully.

35h.1 Making quotations fit smoothly with your sentences

When you use quotations, the greatest risk you take is that you'll end up with incoherent, choppy sentences. You can avoid this problem by making the words you quote fit smoothly with three aspects of your writing: grammar, style, and logic. Here are some examples of sentences that don't mesh well with quotations, followed by revised versions.

SOURCE

Goleman, Daniel. *Emotional Intelligence.* New York: Bantam, 1995. 9. Print. [This source information is arranged in MLA documentation style.]

ORIGINAL (GOLEMAN'S EXACT WORDS)

These two minds, the emotional and the rational, operate in tight harmony for the most part, intertwining their very different ways of knowing to guide us through the world.

INCOHERENT GRAMMAR PROBLEM

Goleman explains how the emotional and rational minds "intertwining their very different ways of knowing to guide us through the world" (9). [Corrected: Goleman explains how emotional and rational minds mix "their very different ways of knowing to guide us through the world" (9).]

INCOHERENT STYLE PROBLEM

Goleman explains how the emotional minds based on reason work together by "intertwining their very different ways of knowing to guide us through the world" (9). [Corrected: Goleman explains how the emotional and rational minds work together by "intertwining their very different ways of knowing to guide us through the world" (9).]

INCOHERENT LOGIC PROBLEM

Goleman explains how the emotional and rational minds work together by "their very different ways of knowing to guide us through the world" (9). [Corrected: Coleman explains how the emotional and rational minds work together by combining "their very different ways of knowing to guide us through the world" (9).]

CORRECT USE OF THE QUOTATION

Goleman explains how the emotional and rational minds work together by "intertwining their very different ways of knowing to guide us through the world" (9). [This citation is arranged in MLA documentation style.]

After writing sentences that contain quotations, read the material aloud and listen to whether the language flows smoothly and gracefully. Perhaps you need to add a word or two placed in brackets (29c) within the quotation so that the wording works grammatically and effortlessly with the rest of your sentence. Of course, make sure your bracketed additions don't distort the meaning of the quotation. For example, the following quotation comes from the same page of the source quoted above. The bracketed material explains what the phrase *these minds* refers to in the original quotation—this helps the reader understand what was clear in the context of the original source but isn't clear when quoted in isolation.

ORIGINAL (GOLEMAN'S EXACT WORDS)

In many or most moments, these minds are exquisitely coordinated; feelings are essential to thought, thought to feeling.

QUOTATION WITH EXPLANATORY BRACKETS

"In many or most moments, these minds [emotional and rational] are exquisitely coordinated; feelings are essential to thought, thought to feeling" (Goleman 9). [This citation is arranged in MLA documentation style.]

Another way to create a smooth integration of a quotation into your sentence is to delete some words, always using an ellipsis where the deletion occurs (29d). You also might delete any part of the quotation that interferes with conciseness and the focus you intend in your sentence. When you use an ellipsis, make sure that the remaining words accurately reflect the source's meaning and that your sentence structure still flows smoothly.

ORIGINAL (GOLEMAN'S EXACT WORDS)

These two minds, the emotional and the rational, operate in tight harmony for the most part, intertwining their very different ways of knowing to guide us through the world (9).

QUOTATION WITH ELLIPSIS

Goleman contends that, generally, "these two minds, the emotional and the rational, operate in tight harmony . . . to guide us through the world" (9). [This citation is arranged in MLA documentation style.]

In the preceding example, the words "for the most part, intertwining their very different ways of knowing" have been deleted from the original material so that the quotation is more concise and focused.

35h.2 Using quotations to enhance meaning

Perhaps the biggest complaint instructors have about student research papers is that sometimes quotations are simply stuck in, for no apparent reason. Whenever you place words between quotation marks, they take on special significance for your message as well as your language. Without context-setting information in the paper, the reader can't know exactly what logic leads the writer to use a particular quotation.

Furthermore, always make sure your readers know who said each group of quoted words. Otherwise, you've used a *disembodied quotation* (some instructors call them "ghost quotations"), which reflects poorly on your writing.

SOURCE

Wright, Karen. "Times of Our Lives." *Scientific American* Sept. 2002: 58-66. Print. [This source information is arranged in MLA documentation style.]

ORIGINAL (WRIGHT'S EXACT WORDS)

In human bodies, biological clocks keep track of seconds, minutes, days, months and years. (66)

INCORRECT (DISEMBODIED QUOTATION)

The human body has many subconscious processes. People don't have to make their hearts beat or remind themselves to breathe. "In human bodies, biological clocks keep track of seconds, minutes, days, months and years" (Wright 66).

CORRECT

The human body has many subconscious processes. People don't have to make their hearts beat or remind themselves to breathe. However, other processes are less obvious and perhaps more surprising. Karen Wright observes, for example, "In human bodies, biological clocks keep track of seconds, minutes, days, months and years" (66).

Rarely can a quotation begin a paragraph effectively. Start your paragraph by relying on your TOPIC SENTENCE, based on your own thinking. Then, you can fit in a relevant quotation somewhere in the paragraph, if it supports or extends what you have said.

Another strategy for working quotations smoothly into your paper is to integrate the name(s) of the author(s), the source title, or other information into your paper. You can prepare your reader for a quotation using one of these methods:

- Mention in your sentence directly before or after the quotation the name(s) of the author(s) you're quoting.
- Mention in your sentence the title of the work you're quoting from.
- Give additional authority to your material. If the author of a source is a noteworthy figure, you gain credibility when you refer to his or her credentials.
- Mention the name(s) of the author(s), with or without the name of the source and any author credentials, along with your personal introductory lead-in to the material.

Here are some examples, using the original source material from Karen Wright on page 578, of effective integration of an author's name, source title, and credentials, along with an introductory analysis.

AUTHOR'S NAME

Karen Wright explains that "in human bodies, biological clocks keep track of seconds, minutes, days, months and years" (66).

AUTHOR'S NAME AND SOURCE TITLE

Karen Wright explains in "Times of Our Lives" that "in human bodies, biological clocks keep track of seconds, minutes, days, months and years" (66).

AUTHOR'S NAME AND CREDENTIALS

Karen Wright, an award-winning science journalist, explains that "in human bodies, biological clocks keep track of seconds, minutes, days, months and years" (66).

AUTHOR'S NAME WITH STUDENT'S INTRODUCTORY ANALYSIS

Karen Wright reviews evidence of surprising subconscious natural processes, explaining that "in human bodies, biological clocks keep track of seconds, minutes, days, months and years" (66).

🛈 **Alert:** After using an author's full name in the first reference, you can decide to use only the author's last name in subsequent references. This holds unless another source has that same last name. ●

EXERCISE 35-1   Working individually or with a group, read the following original material, from page 60 of "What Makes You Who You Are" by Matt Ridley in *Time* (2 June 2003). Then, read items 1 through 5 and explain why each is an incorrect use of a quotation. Next, revise each numbered sentence so that it correctly uses a quotation. End each quotation with this MLA-style parenthetical reference: (Ridley 60).

ORIGINAL (RIDLEY'S EXACT WORDS)

Human beings differ from chimpanzees in having complex, grammatical language. But language does not spring fully formed from the brain; it must be learned from other language-speaking human beings. This capacity to learn is written into the human brain by genes that open and close a critical window during which learning takes place. One of those genes, FoxP2, has recently been discovered on human chromosome 7 by Anthony Monaco and his colleagues at the Wellcome Trust Centre for Human Genetics in Oxford. Just having the FoxP2 gene, though, is not enough. If a child is not exposed to a lot of spoken language during the critical learning period, he or she will always struggle with speech.

UNACCEPTABLE USES OF QUOTATIONS

1. Scientists are learning more about how people learn languages. "Human beings differ from chimpanzees in having complex, grammatical language" (Ridley 60).

2. People might assume that individuals can acquire speaking abilities through hard individual work, "but language must be learned from other language-speaking human beings" (Ridley 60).

3. Helping the language learning process "by genes that open and close a critical window during which learning takes place" (Ridley 60).

4. In 2002, one gene important for language development "has recently been discovered on human chromosome 7 by Anthony Monaco and his colleagues" (Ridley 60).

5. Parents should continually read to and speak with young children, because "if children are not exposed to a lot of spoken language during the critical learning period of childhood, they will always struggle with speech" (Ridley 60).

EXERCISE 35-2   Working individually or with your peer-response group, do the following:

1. For a paper that argues how a person should choose a spouse, write a two- to three-sentence passage that includes your own words and a quotation from the following paragraph, from page 70 of "What's Love Got to Do with It?" by Anjula Razdan in *Utne* (May-June 2003). After the quoted words, use this parenthetical reference: (Razdan 70).

   ORIGINAL (RAZDAN'S EXACT WORDS)
   Fast forward a couple hundred years to a 21st-century America, and you see a modern, progressive society where people are free to choose their mates, for the most part, based on love instead of social or economic gain. But for many people, a quiet voice from within wonders: Are we really better off? Who hasn't at some point in their life—at the end of an ill-fated relationship or midway through dinner with the third "date-from-hell" this month—longed for a matchmaker to find the right partner? No hassles. No effort. No personal ads or blind dates.

2. For a paper arguing that biologists need more funding to speed up our understanding of the earth's living creatures before many more of them become extinct, quote from the Wilson material in Exercise 35-6 (section 35j). Be sure to include at least one numerical statistic in your quotation. (For documentation purposes, keep in mind that Wilson's article appears on pages 29–30 in the original source.)

3. Write a two- to three-sentence passage that includes your own words and a quotation from a source you're currently using for a paper assigned in one of your courses. If you have no such assignment, choose any material suitable for a college-level research paper. Your instructor might request a

photocopy of the material from which you're quoting, so make a copy to have on hand.

35i How can I write good paraphrases?

A **paraphrase** precisely restates in your own words and your own writing style the written or spoken words of someone else. Select for paraphrase only the passages that carry ideas you need to reproduce in detail. Because paraphrasing calls for a very close approximation of a source, avoid trying to paraphrase more than a paragraph or two; for longer passages, use SUMMARY instead. Expect to write a number of drafts of your paraphrases, each time getting closer to effectively rewording and revising the writing style so that you avoid PLAGIARISM. Quick Reference 35.5 provides guidelines for writing paraphrases.

Quick Reference 35.5

Guidelines for writing paraphrases

1. Decide to paraphrase authorities on your subject to support or counter what you write in your paper.

2. Never use a paraphrase to present your THESIS STATEMENT or a TOPIC SENTENCE.

3. Say what the source says, but no more.

4. Reproduce the source's sequence of ideas and emphases.

5. Use your own words and writing style to restate the material. If some technical words in the original have no or awkward synonyms, you may quote the original's words—but do so very sparingly. For example, you can use the term *human chromosome 7* if you're paraphrasing the original source by Matt Ridley in Exercise 35-1.

6. Never distort the source's meaning as you reword and change the writing style.

7. Expect your material to be as long as, and often longer than, the original.

8. Integrate your paraphrases smoothly into your writing.

9. Avoid plagiarism (35b–35d).

10. Enter all DOCUMENTATION precisely and carefully.

Here's an example of an unacceptable paraphrase and an acceptable one.

SOURCE

Hulburt, Ann. "Post-Teenage Wasteland?" *New York Times Magazine* 9 Oct. 2005: 11-12. Print. [This source information is arranged in MLA documentation style.]

ORIGINAL (HULBURT'S EXACT WORDS)

[T]he available data suggest that the road to maturity hasn't become as drastically different as people think—or as drawn out, either. It's true that the median age of marriage rose to 25 for women and almost 27 for men in 2000, from 20 and 23, respectively, in 1960. Yet those mid-century figures were record lows (earnestly analyzed in their time). Moreover, Americans of all ages have ceased to view starting a family as the major benchmark of grown-up status. When asked to rank the importance of traditional milestones in defining the arrival of adulthood, poll respondents place completing school, finding full-time employment, achieving financial independence and being able to support a family far above actually wedding a spouse or having kids. The new perspective isn't merely an immature swerve into selfishness; postponing those last two steps is good for the future of the whole family (11).

UNACCEPTABLE PARAPHRASE (UNDERLINED WORDS ARE PLAGIARIZED)

Data suggest that the road to maturity hasn't changed as much as people think. True, the median age of marriage was 25 for women and 27 for men in 2000, up from 20 and 23 in 1960. Yet those 1960 figures were record lows. Furthermore, Americans have stopped regarding beginning a family as the signpost of grown-up status. When they were asked to rank the importance of traditional benchmarks for deciding the arrival of adulthood, people rated graduating from school, finding a full-time job, gaining financial status, and being a breadwinner far above marrying or having kids. This new belief isn't merely immature selfishness; delaying those last two steps is good for the future of the whole family (Hulburt 11).

ACCEPTABLE PARAPHRASE

According to Ann Hulburt, statistics show that people are wrong when they believe our society is delaying maturity. She acknowledges that between 1960 and 2000, the median age at which women married rose from 20 to 25 (for men it went from 23 to 27), but points out that the early figures were extreme lows. Hulburt finds that Americans no longer equate adulthood with starting a family. Polls show that people rank several other "milestones" above marriage and children as signaling adulthood. These include finishing school, securing a full-time job, and earning enough to be independent and to support a family. Hulburt concludes that we should regard postponing marriage and children not as being selfish or immature but as investing in the family's future (11).

[This citation is arranged in MLA documentation style.]

The first attempt to paraphrase is not acceptable. The writer simply changed a few words. What remains is plagiarized because the passage keeps most of the original's language, has the same sentence structure as the original, and uses no quotation marks. The documentation is correct, but its accuracy doesn't make up for the unacceptable paraphrasing. The second paraphrase is acceptable. It captures the meaning of the original in the student's own words.

EXERCISE 35-3   Working individually or with your peer-response group, read the original material, a paragraph from page 49 of *Uniforms: Why We Are What We Wear* by Paul Fussell (Boston: Houghton, 2002). Then, read the unacceptable paraphrase, and point out each example of plagiarism. Finally, write your own paraphrase, starting it with a phrase naming Fussell and ending it with this parenthetical reference: (49).

ORIGINAL (FUSSELL'S EXACT WORDS)

Until around 1963, part of the routine for Levi's wearers was shrinking the trousers to fit, and the best way to do that was to put them on wet and let them dry on your body. This gave the wearer the impression that he or she was actually creating the garment, or at least emphasizing one's precious individuality, and that conviction did nothing to oppose the illusion of uniqueness precious to all American young people (49).

UNACCEPTABLE PARAPHRASE

Paul Fussell says that until around 1963 Levi's wearers used to shrink new trousers to fit. The best way to do that was to put them on wet and let them dry while wearing them. Doing this created the impression that wearers were actually creating the garment or emphasizing their precious individuality. It reinforced the illusion of uniqueness precious to all American teens (49).

EXERCISE 35-4   Working individually or with your peer-response group, do the following:

1. For a paper on the place of censorship in the coverage of military conflicts, paraphrase the following paragraph from page 65 of *Regarding the Pain of Others* by Susan Sontag (New York: Farrar, 2003). Start with words mentioning Sontag, and end with this parenthetical reference: (65).

   ### ORIGINAL (SONTAG'S EXACT WORDS)

   There had always been censorship, but for a long time it remained desultory, at the pleasure of generals and heads of state. The first organized ban on press photography at the front came during the First World War; both the German and French high commands allowed only a few selected military photographers near the fighting. (Censorship of the press by the British General Staff was less inflexible.) And it took another fifty years, and the relaxation of censorship with the first televised war coverage, to understand what impact shocking photographs could have on the domestic public. During the Vietnam era, war photography became, normatively, a criticism of war. This was bound to have consequences: Mainstream media are not in the business of making people feel queasy about the struggles for which they are being mobilized, much less of disseminating propaganda against waging war.

2. In one of your sources for a current research assignment, locate a paragraph that is at least 150 words in length and write a paraphrase of it. If you have no such assignment, choose any material suitable for a college-level paper. Your instructor may request that you submit a photocopy of the original material, so make a copy to have on hand.

35j   How can I write good summaries?

A **summary** differs from a PARAPHRASE (35i) in one important way: A paraphrase restates the original material completely, but a summary provides only the main point of the original source. A summary is much shorter than a paraphrase. Summarizing is the technique you'll probably use most frequently in writing your research paper, both for taking notes and for integrating what you have learned from sources into your own writing.

As you summarize, you trace a line of thought. This involves deleting less central ideas and sometimes transposing certain points into an order more suited to summary. In summarizing a longer original—say, ten pages or more—you may find it helpful first to divide the original into subsections and summarize each. Then, group your subsection summaries and use them as the basis for further condensing the material into a final summary. You'll probably have to revise a summary more than once. Always make sure that a summary accurately reflects the source and its emphases.

When you're summarizing a source in your CONTENT NOTES, resist the temptation to include your personal interpretation along with something the author says. Similarly, never include in your summary your own judgment about the point made in the source. Your own opinions and ideas, although they have value, don't belong in a summary. Instead, jot them down immediately when they come to mind, but separate them clearly from your summary. Write your notes so that when you go back to them you can be sure to distinguish your opinions or ideas from your summary. On a computer, highlight your personal writing with a screen of yellow or some other color, or use an entirely different font for it. Quick Reference 35.6 provides guidelines for writing good summaries.

Guidelines for writing summaries

1. Use summaries from authorities on your subject to support or refute what you write in your paper.

2. Identify the main points you want to summarize and condense them using your own words without losing the meaning of the original source.

3. Never use a summary to present your THESIS STATEMENT or a TOPIC SENTENCE.

4. Keep your summary short.

5. Integrate your summaries smoothly into your writing.

6. Avoid PLAGIARISM (35b–35d).

7. Enter all DOCUMENTATION precisely and carefully.

Here's an example of an unacceptable summary and an acceptable one.

SOURCE

Tanenbaum, Leora. *Catfight: Women and Competition.* New York: Seven Stories, 2002. 117-18. Print. [This source information is arranged in MLA documentation style.]

ORIGINAL (TANENBAUM'S EXACT WORDS)

Until recently, most Americans disapproved of cosmetic surgery, but today the stigma is disappearing. Average Americans are lining up for procedures—two-thirds of patients report family incomes of less than $50,000 a year—and many of them return for more. Younger women undergo "maintenance" surgeries in a futile attempt to halt time. The latest fad is Botox, a purified and diluted form of botulinum toxin that is injected between the eyebrows to eliminate frown lines. Although the procedure costs between $300 and $1000 and must be repeated every few months, roughly 850,000 patients have had it performed on them. That number will undoubtedly shoot up now that the FDA has approved Botox for cosmetic use. Even teenagers are making appointments with plastic surgeons. More than 14,000 adolescents had plastic surgery in 1996, and many of them are choosing controversial procedures such as breast implants, liposuction, and tummy tucks, rather than the rhinoplasties of previous generations.

UNACCEPTABLE SUMMARY (UNDERLINED WORDS ARE PLAGIARIZED)

<u>Average Americans are lining up</u> for surgical <u>procedures. The latest fad is Botox,</u> a toxin injected <u>to eliminate frown lines.</u> This is an insanely

foolish waste of money. <u>Even teenagers are making appointments with plastic surgeons</u>, many of them for <u>controversial procedures such as breast implants, liposuction, and tummy tucks</u> (Tanenbaum 117-18).

ACCEPTABLE SUMMARY

Tanenbaum explains that plastic surgery is becoming widely acceptable, even for Americans with modest incomes and for younger women. Most popular is injecting the toxin Botox to smooth wrinkles. She notes that thousands of adolescents are even requesting controversial surgeries (117-18). [This citation is arranged in MLA documentation style.]

The unacceptable summary above has several major problems: It doesn't isolate the main point. It plagiarizes by taking much of its language directly from the source. Examples of plagiarized language include all the underlined phrases. Finally, the unacceptable summary includes the writer's interpretation ("This is an insanely foolish waste of money") rather than objectively representing the original. The acceptable summary concisely isolates the main point, puts the source into the writer's own words, calls attention to the author by including her name in the summary, and remains objective throughout.

EXERCISE 35-5   Working individually or with your peer-response group, read the original material from pages 23–24 of *Diversity: The Invention of a Concept* by Peter Wood (San Francisco: Encounter, 2003). Then, read the unacceptable summary. Point out each example of plagiarism. Finally, write your own summary, starting it with a phrase mentioning Wood and ending it with this parenthetical reference: (23-24).

ORIGINAL (WOOD'S EXACT WORDS)
    Among the many meanings of diversity, let's for the moment distinguish two: the actual racial and ethnic condition of America, which I will call *diversity I,* and the diversiphile ideal of how American society should recognize and respond to its racial and ethnic composition, which I will call *diversity II.* In principle, it ought to be easy to distinguish between these two meanings. One refers to the facts, the other to hopes or wishes. *Diversity I* is the sort of thing that we might expect could be counted, or at least approximated, with wide agreement. We know with reasonable certainty, for example, that about 13 percent of the U.S. population considers itself of African descent. We can and do argue with one another over the significance of this fact, but the fact itself is not seriously in dispute.
    Diversity II, by contrast, is an ideal. It expresses a vision of society in which people divide themselves into separate groups, each with profound traditions of its own, but held together by mutual esteem, respect and tolerance. It would be futile, however, to look for general agreement about the exact details of this ideal.

UNACCEPTABLE, PLAGIARIZED SUMMARY

Peter Wood distinguishes between *diversity I*, the actual racial and ethnic condition of America, and *diversity II*, the diversiphile ideal of how American society should recognize and respond to its racial and ethnic composition. *Diversity I* could be counted or approximated with wide agreement. *Diversity II* is an ideal vision of society, but there can be no general agreement about the exact nature of this ideal (23-24).

EXERCISE 35-6 Working individually or with your peer-response group, do the following:

1. Summarize the following paragraph from pages 29–30 of "Vanishing Before Our Eyes" by Edward O. Wilson in *Time* (24 Apr. 2000). Start your summary with a phrase mentioning the author, and end with this parenthetical reference: (29-30).

   ORIGINAL (WILSON'S EXACT WORDS)
   By repeated sampling, biologists estimate that as few as 10% of the different kinds of insects, nematode worms, and fungi have been discovered. For bacteria and other microorganisms, the number could be well below 1%. Even the largest and most intensively studied organisms are incompletely cataloged. Four species of mammals, for example, have recently been discovered in the remote Annamite Mountains along the Vietnam-Laos border. One of them, the saola or spindlehorn, is a large cowlike animal distinct enough to be classified in a genus of its own. Earth, as far as life is concerned, is still a little-known planet.

2. Write a summary of your paraphrase of the Sontag material in Exercise 35-4. Use the parenthetical reference given there.

3. Write a summary of a passage from a source you're currently using for a paper assigned in one of your courses. If you have no such assignment, choose any material suitable for a college-level research paper. Your instructor might request a photocopy of the material you're summarizing, so make a copy to have on hand.

35k Which verbs can help me weave source material into my sentences?

The verbs listed in Quick Reference 35.7 can help you work quotations, paraphrases, and summaries smoothly into your writing. Some of these verbs imply your position toward the source material (for example, *argue, complain, concede, deny, grant, insist,* and *reveal*). Other verbs imply a more neutral stance (for example, *comment, describe, explain, note, say,* and *write*). For many examples of effective use of such verbs, see the student research papers presented in sections 36e.2 and 37h.2.

Quick Reference 35.7

Verbs useful for integrating quotations, paraphrases, and summaries

acknowledges	discusses	organizes
agrees	distinguishes	points out
analyzes	between/among	prepares
argues	emphasizes	promises
asks	endeavors to	proves
asserts	establishes	questions
balances	estimates	recognizes
begins	explains	recommends
believes	expresses	refutes
claims	finds	rejects
comments	focuses on	remarks
compares	grants	reports
complains	illuminates	reveals
concedes	illustrates	says
concludes	implies	sees
confirms	indicates	shows
connects	informs	signals
considers	insists	specifies
contends	introduces	speculates
contradicts	maintains	states
contrasts	means	suggests
declares	negates	supports
demonstrates	notes	supposes
denies	notices	thinks
describes	observes	wishes
develops	offers	writes

36

MLA Documentation with Case Study

Following are two directories that point you to guidance you'll find in this chapter. The first lists examples of MLA in-text parenthetical citations. The second lists examples of MLA Works Cited entries.

MLA-STYLE DIRECTORY

MLA

MLA

36a　What is MLA style?

A DOCUMENTATION STYLE is a standard format that writers follow to tell readers what SOURCES they used in conducting their research and how to find those sources. Different disciplines follow different documentation styles. The one most frequently used in the humanities (Chapter 40) is from the Modern Language Association (MLA).

MLA style requires you to document your sources in two connected, equally important ways.

1. Within the text of the paper, use parenthetical documentation, as described in section 36b. Section 36c shows twenty models of in-text parenthetical documentation, each for a different type of source.

2. At the end of the paper, provide a WORKS CITED list of the sources you used in your paper. Title this list "Works Cited." It should include only the sources you've actually used in your research paper, not any

---

Important MLA Style Changes

As part of our continuing efforts to ensure that this book provides the most current information on documentation styles, the guidelines and examples in this chapter have been adapted from the Third Edition of *The MLA Style Manual and Guide to Scholarly Publishing* (2008). According to the MLA's Web site, this edition of the *MLA Style Manual* provides documentation style guidelines that will be used in MLA publications beginning in 2009. Thus, the guidelines in the sixth edition of the *MLA Handbook for Writers of Research Papers* should only be followed until the seventh edition is released in spring 2009. If you need more information regarding MLA style updates, check http://www.mla.org.

Although MLA citations should include the minimum amount of information necessary to allow readers to locate the original source, there are several new requirements for entries in works cited lists:

- Include the **medium of publication** for each entry, such as "Print" or "Web."
- Include the URL *only* when the reader probably could not locate the source without it.
- Include both an issue and volume number for scholarly journals.
- Use italics for titles instead of underlining for all works cited entries.

See Quick Reference 36.1 on page 600 for more guidance on these requirements.

you've consulted but haven't used. Section 36d gives instructions for composing a Works Cited list, followed by ninety-six models, each based on different kinds of sources (book, article, Web site, and so on) that you might use.

For an example of a research paper that uses MLA-style parenthetical documentation and a Works Cited list, see section 36e.2. As you read the research paper, notice how the two requirements for crediting sources work together so that readers can learn the precise origin of QUOTATIONS, PARAPHRASES, and SUMMARIES.

36b   What is MLA in-text parenthetical documentation?

MLA-style **parenthetical documentation** places SOURCE information in parentheses within the sentences of your research papers. Also called an *in-text citation,* this information is given each time that you quote, summarize, or paraphrase source materials. It signals materials used from outside sources and enables readers to find the originals.

If you include an author's name (or, if none, a shortened title of the work) in the sentence to introduce the source material, you include in parentheses only the page number where you found the material:

According to Brent Staples, IQ tests give scientists little insight into intelligence (293). [Author name cited in text; page number cited in parentheses.]

For readability and good writing technique, try to introduce names of authors (or titles of sources) in your own sentences. If you don't include this information in your sentence, you need to insert it before the page number, in parentheses. There is no punctuation between the author's name and the page number:

IQ tests give scientists little insight into intelligence (Staples 293).

[Author name and page number cited in parentheses.]

When possible, position a parenthetical reference at the end of the quote, summary, or paraphrase it refers to—preferably at the end of a sentence, unless that would place it too far from the source's material. When you place the parenthetical reference at the end of a sentence, insert it before the sentence-ending period.

If you're citing a quotation enclosed in quotation marks, place the parenthetical information after the closing quotation mark but before sentence-ending punctuation.

Coleman summarizes research that shows that "the number, rate, and direction of time-zone changes are the critical factors in determining the

MLA

extent and degree of jet lag symptoms" (67). [Author name cited in text; page number cited in parentheses.]

The one exception to this rule concerns quotations that you set off in BLOCK STYLE, meaning one inch from the left margin. (MLA style requires that quotations longer than four typed lines be handled this way.) For block quotations, put the parenthetical reference after the period.

> Bruce Sterling worries that people are pursuing less conventional medical treatments, and not always for good reasons:
>> Medical tourism is already in full swing. Thailand is the golden shore for wealthy, sickly Asians and Australians. Fashionable Europeans head to South Africa for embarrassing plastic surgery. Crowds of scrip-waving Americans buy prescription drugs in Canada and Mexico. (92)

36c What are MLA guidelines for parenthetical documentation?

This section shows examples of how to handle parenthetical documentation in the text of your papers. The directory at the beginning of this chapter corresponds to the numbered examples in the following pages. Most of these examples show the author's name or the title included in the parenthetical citation, but remember that it's usually more effective to include that information in your sentences in the paper itself.

1. Paraphrased or Summarized Source—MLA

According to Brent Staples, IQ tests give scientists little insight into intelligence (293). [Author name cited in text; page number cited in parentheses.]

In "The IQ Cult," the journalist Brent Staples states that IQ tests give scientists little insight into intelligence (293). [Title of source, author name, and author credentials cited in text; page number cited in parentheses.]

IQ tests give scientists little insight into intelligence (Staples 293). [Author name and page number cited in parentheses.]

2. Source of a Short Quotation—MLA

Given that "thoughts, emotions, imagination and predispositions occur concurrently . . . [and] interact with other brain processes" (Caine and Caine 66), it is easy to understand why "whatever [intelligence] might be, paper and pencil tests aren't the tenth of it" (Staples 293).

Coles asks, "What binds together a Mormon banker in Utah with his brother, or other coreligionists in Illinois or Massachusetts?" (2).

3. Source of a Long Quotation—MLA

A long quotation in MLA style consists of more than four typed lines. It's set off block style, indented one inch or ten spaces from the left margin. Never put quotation marks around a set-off quotation because the indentation and block style communicate that the material is quoted. At the end of an indented quotation, place the parenthetical reference after the end punctuation mark.

> Gray and Viens explain how, by tapping into a student's highly developed spatial-mechanical intelligence, one teacher can bolster a student's poor writing skills:
>
> > The teacher asked that during "journal time" Jacob create a tool dictionary to be used as a resource in the mechanical learning center. After several entries in which he drew and described tools and other materials, Jacob confidently moved on to writing about other things of import to him, such as his brothers and a recent birthday party. Rather than shy away from all things linguistic--he previously had refused any task requiring a pencil--Jacob became invested in journal writing. (23-24)

4. One Author—MLA

Give an author's name as it appears on the source: for a book, on the title page; for an article, directly below the title or at the end of the article.

> One test asks four-year-olds to choose between one marshmallow now or two marshmallows later (Gibbs 60).

Many nonprint sources also name an author; for CDs or DVDs, for example, check the printed sleeve or cover. For an online source, look at the beginning or end of the file for a link to the author, or at the site's home page. (For more information about citing electronic sources, see items 18 through 20.)

5. Two or Three Authors—MLA

Give the names in the same order as in the source. Spell out *and.* For three authors, use commas to separate the authors' names.

> As children get older, they begin to express several different kinds of intelligence (Todd and Taylor 23).

> Another measure of emotional intelligence is the success of inter- and intrapersonal relationships (Voigt, Dees, and Prigoff 14).

MLA

6. More Than Three Authors—MLA

If your source has more than three authors, you can name them all or use the first author's name only, followed by *et al.,* either in a parenthetical reference or in your sentence. In MLA citations, do not underline or italicize *et al.*

> Emotional security varies, depending on the circumstances of the social interaction (Carter et al. 158).

⚠ Alerts: (1) The abbreviation *et al.* stands for "and others." The Latin term *et* means "and" and requires no period. The term *al* is an abbreviation of *alii,* so it requires a period. (2) When an author's name followed by *et al.* is a subject, use a plural verb.

> Carter et al. have found that emotional security varies, depending on the circumstances of the social interaction (158). ●

7. More Than One Source by an Author—MLA

When you use two or more sources by an author, include the relevant title in each citation. In parenthetical citations, use a shortened version of the title. For example, in a paper using two of Howard Gardner's works, *Frames of Mind: The Theory of Multiple Intelligences* and "Reflections on Multiple Intelligences: Myths and Messages," use *Frames* and "Reflections." Shorten the titles as much as possible, keeping them unambiguous to readers and starting them with the word by which you alphabetize each work in your Works Cited list. Separate the author's name and the title with a comma, but do not use punctuation between the title and the page number. When you incorporate the title into your own sentences, you can omit a subtitle, but never shorten the main title.

> Although it seems straightforward to think of multiple intelligences as multiple approaches to learning (Gardner, *Frames* 60-61), an intelligence is not a learning style (Gardner, "Reflections" 202-03).

8. Two or More Authors with the Same Last Name—MLA

Use each author's first initial and full last name in each parenthetical citation. This is the only instance in MLA style where you use an initial in a parenthetical reference. If both authors have the same first initial, use the full name in all instances.

> According to Anne Cates, psychologists can predict how empathetic an adult will be from his or her behavior at age two (41), but other researchers disagree (T. Cates 171).

9. Work with a Group or Corporate Author—MLA

When a corporation or other group is named as the author of a source you want to cite, use the corporate name just as you would an individual's name.

In a five-year study, the Boston Women's Health Collective reported that
these tests are usually unreliable (11).

A five-year study shows that these tests are usually unreliable (Boston
Women's Health Collective 11).

10. Work Listed by Title—MLA

If no author is named, use the title in citations. In your own sentences, use the
full main title and omit a subtitle, if any. For parenthetical citations, shorten
the title as much as possible (making sure that the shortened version refers unambiguously to the correct source), and always make the first word the one by
which you alphabetize it. "Are You a Day or Night Person?" is the full title of
the article in the following citation.

The "morning lark" and "night owl" connotations are typically used to
categorize the human extremes ("Are You" 11).

11. Multivolume Work—MLA

When you cite more than one volume of a multivolume work, include the relevant volume number in each citation. Give the volume number first, followed
by a colon and one space, and then the page number(s).

By 1900, the Amazon forest dwellers had been exposed to these viruses
(Rand 3: 202).

Rand believes that forest dwellers in Borneo escaped illness from
retroviruses until the 1960s (4: 518-19).

12. Material from a Novel, Play, Poem, or Short Story—MLA

Literary works frequently appear in different editions. When you cite material
from literary works, providing the part, chapter, act, scene, canto, stanza, or line
numbers usually helps readers locate what you are referring to more than page
numbers alone. Unless your instructor tells you not to, use Arabic numerals for
these references, even if the literary work uses Roman numerals. For novels
that use them, give part and/or chapter numbers after page numbers. Use a
semicolon after the page number but a comma to separate a part from a chapter.

Flannery O'Connor describes one character in *The Violent Bear It Away*
as "divided in two—a violent and a rational self" (139; pt. 2, ch. 6).

For plays that use them, give act, scene, and line numbers. Use periods between these numbers. For short stories, use page numbers.

Among the most quoted of Shakespeare's lines is Hamlet's soliloquy
beginning "To be, or not to be: that is the question" (3.1.56).

MLA

> The old man in John Collier's short story "The Chaser" says about his
> potions, "I don't deal in laxatives and teething mixtures . . ." (79).

For poems and plays that use them, give canto, stanza, and line numbers. Use
periods between these numbers.

> In "To Autumn," Keats's most melancholy image occurs in the lines "Then in
> a wailful choir the small gnats mourn / Among the river swallows" (3.27-28).

13. Bible or Sacred Text—MLA

Give the title of the edition you're using, the book (in the case of the Bible),
and the chapter and verse. Spell out the names of books in sentences, but use
abbreviations in parenthetical references.

> He would certainly benefit from the advice in Ephesians to "get rid of all
> bitterness, rage, and anger" (*New International Version Bible*, 4.31).

> He would certainly benefit from the advice to "get rid of all bitterness,
> rage, and anger" (*New International Version Bible*, Eph. 4.31).

14. Work in an Anthology or Other Collection—MLA

You may want to cite a work you have read in a book that contains many works
by various authors and that was compiled or edited by someone other than the
person you're citing. Your in-text citation should include the author of the selection you're citing and the page number. For example, suppose you want to
cite the poem "Several Things" by Martha Collins, in a literature text edited by
Pamela Annas and Robert Rosen. Use Collins's name and the title of her work
in the sentence and the line numbers (see item 12) in a parenthetical citation.

> In "Several Things," Martha Collins enumerates what could take place in
> the lines of her poem: "Plums could appear, on a pewter plate / A dead
> red hare, hung by one foot. / A vase of flowers. Three shallots" (2-4).

15. Indirect Source—MLA

When you want to quote words that you found quoted in someone else's work,
put the name of the person whose words you're quoting into your own sentence.
Give the work where you found the quotation either in your sentence or in a
parenthetical citation beginning with *qtd. in.*

> Martin Scorsese acknowledges the link between himself and his films: "I
> realize that all my life, I've been an outsider. I splatter bits of myself all
> over the screen" (qtd. in Giannetti and Eyman 397).

> Giannetti and Eyman quote Martin Scorsese as acknowledging the link
> between himself and his films: "I realize that all my life, I've been an
> outsider. I splatter bits of myself all over the screen" (397).

16. Two or More Sources in One Reference—MLA

If more than one source has contributed to an idea, opinion, or fact in your paper, cite them all. Suppose, as in the following example, that three sources all make the same point. An efficient way to credit all is to include them in a single parenthetical citation, with a semicolon separating each block of information.

> Once researchers agreed that multiple intelligences existed, their next step was to try to measure or define them (West 17; Arturi 477; Gibbs 68).

17. Entire Work—MLA

References to an entire work usually fit best into your own sentences.

> In *Convergence Culture*, Henry Jenkins explores how new digital media create a culture of active participation rather than of passive reception.

18. Electronic Source with Page Numbers—MLA

The principles that govern in-text parenthetical citations of electronic sources are exactly the same as the ones that apply to books, articles, or other sources. When an electronically accessed source identifies its author, use the author's name for parenthetical references. If no author is named, use the title of the source. When an electronic source has page numbers, use them exactly as you would the page numbers of a print source.

> Learning happens best when teachers truly care about their students' complete well-being (Anderson 7).

19. Electronic Source with Paragraph Numbers—MLA

When an electronic source has numbered paragraphs (instead of page numbers), use them for parenthetical references, with two differences: (1) Use a comma followed by one space after the name (or title); and (2) use the abbreviation *par.* for a reference to one paragraph or *pars.* for a reference to more than one paragraph, followed by the number(s) of the paragraph(s) you are citing. Note that the practice of numbering paragraphs is rare.

> Artists seem to be haunted by the fear that psychoanalysis might destroy creativity while it reconstructs personality (Francis, pars. 22-25).

20. Electronic Source Without Page or Paragraph Numbers—MLA

Many online or digital sources don't number pages or paragraphs. Simply refer to those works in their entirety. Here are two examples referring to "What Is Artificial Intelligence?" by John McCarthy; this Web site does not use page numbers or paragraph numbers. Include the name of the author in your sentence; it is also helpful to include the title.

MLA

According to McCarthy, the science of artificial intelligence includes efforts beyond trying to simulate human intelligence.

In "What Is Artificial Intelligence?" John McCarthy notes that the science of artificial intelligence includes efforts beyond trying to simulate human intelligence.

36d What are MLA guidelines for a Works Cited list?

In MLA-STYLE DOCUMENTATION, the Works Cited list gives complete bibliographic information for each SOURCE used in your paper. Include only the sources from which you quote, paraphrase, or summarize. Never include sources that you consulted but don't refer to in the paper. Quick Reference 36.1 gives general information about the Works Cited list. The rest of this chapter gives models of many specific kinds of Works Cited entries.

Quick Reference 36.1

■ ■ ■ ■ ■ ■ ■ ■

Guidelines for an MLA-style Works Cited list

TITLE
Use "Works Cited" (without quotation marks) as the title.

PLACEMENT OF LIST
Start a new page numbered sequentially with the rest of the paper, following the Notes pages, if any.

CONTENT AND FORMAT
Include all sources quoted from, paraphrased, or summarized in your paper. Start each entry on a new line and at the regular left margin. If the entry uses more than one line, indent the second and all following lines one-half inch (or five spaces) from the left margin. Double-space all lines.

SPACING AFTER PUNCTUATION
When typewriters were common, it improved readability to leave two spaces after punctuation at the end of a sentence. Computers have made this practice no longer necessary. The *MLA Handbook* uses one space, as does this book. Either style is acceptable. However, you should use two spaces if that's the style your instructor prefers. Always put only one space after a comma or a colon.

ARRANGEMENT OF ENTRIES
Alphabetize by author's last name. If no author is named, alphabetize by the title's first significant word (ignore *A, An,* or *The*).

continued >>

Quick Reference 36.1 (continued)

AUTHORS' NAMES

Use first names and middle names or middle initials, if any, as given in the source. Don't reduce to initials any name that is given in full. For one author or the first-named author in multiauthor works, give the last name first. Use the word *and* with two or more authors. List multiple authors in the order given in the source. Use a comma between the first author's last and first names and after each complete author name except the last. After the last author's name, use a period: **Fein, Ethel Andrea, Bert Griggs, and Delaware Rogash.**

Include *Jr., Sr., II,* or *III* but no other titles and degrees before or after a name. For example, an entry for a work by Edward Meep III, MD, and Sir Richard Bolton would start like this: **Meep, Edward, III, and Richard Bolton.**

CAPITALIZATION OF TITLES

Capitalize all major words and the first and last words of all titles and subtitles. Don't capitalize ARTICLES (*a, an, the*), PREPOSITIONS, COORDINATING CONJUNCTIONS (*and, but, for, nor, or, so, yet*), or *to* in infinitives in the middle of a title.

SPECIAL TREATMENT OF TITLES

Use quotation marks around titles of shorter works (poems, short stories, essays, articles). Italicize titles of longer works (books, periodicals, plays).

When a book title includes the title of another work that is usually italicized (as with a novel, play, or long poem), the preferred MLA style is not to italicize the incorporated title: *Decoding* Jane Eyre. For an alternative that MLA accepts, see item 20 in 36d.1.

If the incorporated title is usually enclosed in quotation marks (such as a short story or short poem), keep the quotation marks and italicize the complete title of the book: *Theme and Form in "I Shall Laugh Purely": A Brief Study.*

Drop *A, An,* or *The* as the first word of a periodical title.

PLACE OF PUBLICATION

If several cities are listed for the place of publication, give only the first. MLA doesn't require US state names no matter how obscure or confusing the city names might be. For an unfamiliar city outside the United States, include an abbreviated name of the country or Canadian province.

PUBLISHER

Use shortened names as long as they are clear: *Random* for *Random House.* For companies named for more than one person, name only the first: *Prentice* for *Prentice Hall.* For university presses, use the capital letters *U* and *P* (without periods): **Oxford UP; U of Chicago P**

continued >>

MLA

PUBLICATION MONTH ABBREVIATIONS

Abbreviate all publication months except *May, June,* and *July.* Use the first three letters followed by a period (*Dec., Feb.*) except for September (*Sept.*).

PAGE RANGES

Give the page range—the starting page number and the ending page number, connected by a hyphen—of any paginated electronic source and any paginated print source that is part of a longer work (for example, a chapter in a book, an article in a journal). A range indicates that the cited work is on those pages and all pages in between. If that isn't the case, use the style shown next for discontinuous pages. In either case, use numerals only, without the word *page* or *pages* or the abbreviation *p.* or *pp.*

Use the full second number through *99.* Above that, use only the last two digits for the second number unless to do so would be unclear: 113-14 is clear, but 567-602 requires full numbers.

DISCONTINUOUS PAGES

A source has discontinuous pages when the source is interrupted by material that's not part of the source (for example, an article beginning on page 32 but continued on page 54). Use the starting page number followed by a plus sign (+): 32+.

MEDIUM OF PUBLICATION

Include the MEDIUM OF PUBLICATION for each Works Cited entry. For example, every entry for a print source must include "Print" at the end, followed by a period (if required, certain supplementary bibliographic information like translation information, name of a book series, or the total number of volumes in a set should follow the medium of publication). Every source from the World Wide Web must include "Web" at the end, followed by a period and the date of access. The medium of publication also needs to be included for broadcast sources ("Television", "Radio"), sound recordings ("CD", "LP", "Audiocassette"), as well as films, DVDs, videocassettes, live performances, musical scores and works of visual arts, and so on. (See examples 34–96.)

ISSUE AND VOLUME NUMBERS FOR SCHOLARLY JOURNALS

Include both an issue and volume number for each Works Cited entry for scholarly journals. This applies both to journals that are continuously paginated and those that are not.

WORKS CITED INFORMATION REQUIRED FOR ONLINE SOURCES

The following publication information should be listed for all online sources:

1. Name of the author, director, narrator, performer, editor, compiler, or producer of the work. If no author is given, begin the entry with the title of the work.

continued >>

MLA

2. Title of the work. Italicize the title, unless it is part of a larger work. Titles that are part of a larger work should be enclosed in quotation marks.

3. Title of the overall Web site (in italics) if this is distinct from the title of the work.

4. Version or edition of the site.

5. Publisher or sponsor of the site. If this information is not available, use n.p. (for no publisher).

6. Date of publication (day, month, and year, if available). If no date is given, use n.d.

7. Medium of publication. For all online sources, the medium of publication is "Web."

8. Date of access (day, month, and year).

URLs IN ELECTRONIC SOURCES

Entries for online citations should include the URL only when the reader probably could not locate the source without it.

If the entry requires a URL, enclose it in angle brackets <like this>. Put the URL before the access date and end it with a period. If your computer automatically creates a hyperlink when you type a URL (the text changes color, the URL is underlined, or both) format the URL to look the same as the rest of the entry by changing the font color to black, removing the underline, and making any other changes. In some applications, like Microsoft Word, you can use the command "remove hyperlink," which you can find on the "Insert" menu or by right-clicking on the hyperlink.

If a URL must be divided between two lines, only break the URL after a slash and do not use a hyphen.

36d.1   Following MLA guidelines for specific sources in a Works Cited list

The Works Cited directory above corresponds to the numbered entries in this section. Not every possible documentation model is shown in this chapter. You may find that you have to combine features of models to document a particular source. You'll also find more information in the *MLA Handbook for Writers of Research Papers*. Figure 36.1 provides another tool to help you find the Works Cited model you need: a decision-making flowchart.

BOOKS

Citations for books have three main parts: author, title, and publication information (place of publication, publisher, and date of publication). Figure 36.2 (p. 605) illustrates where to find this information and the proper citation format.

MLA

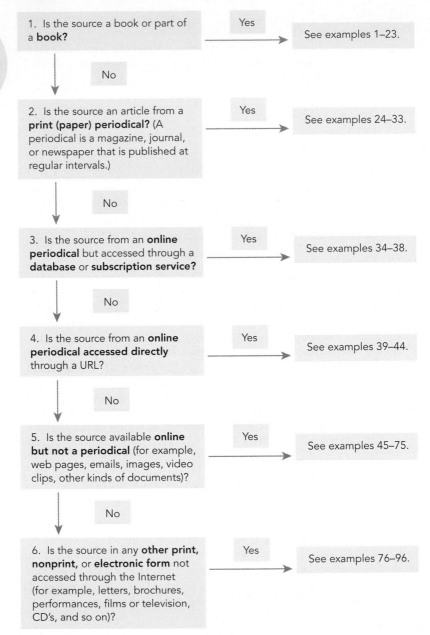

1. Is the source a book or part of a **book?**
Yes → See examples 1–23.

No ↓

2. Is the source an article from a **print (paper) periodical?** (A periodical is a magazine, journal, or newspaper that is published at regular intervals.)
Yes → See examples 24–33.

No ↓

3. Is the source from an **online periodical** but accessed through a **database** or **subscription service?**
Yes → See examples 34–38.

No ↓

4. Is the source from an **online periodical accessed directly** through a URL?
Yes → See examples 39–44.

No ↓

5. Is the source available **online but not a periodical** (for example, web pages, emails, images, video clips, other kinds of documents)?
Yes → See examples 45–75.

No ↓

6. Is the source in any **other print, nonprint,** or **electronic form** not accessed through the Internet (for example, letters, brochures, performances, films or television, CD's, and so on)?
Yes → See examples 76–96.

Figure 36.1 MLA Works Cited visual directory

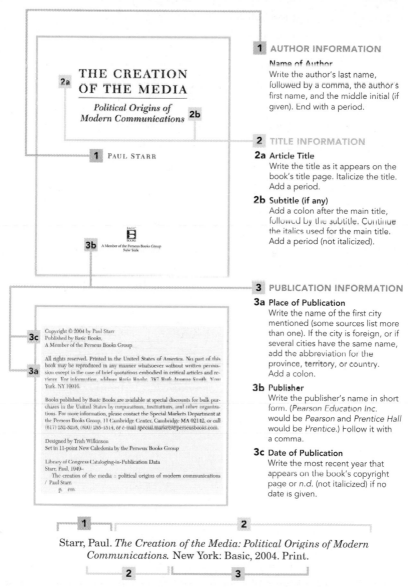

1 AUTHOR INFORMATION

Name of Author
Write the author's last name, followed by a comma, the author's first name, and the middle initial (if given). End with a period.

2 TITLE INFORMATION

2a Article Title
Write the title as it appears on the book's title page. Italicize the title. Add a period.

2b Subtitle (if any)
Add a colon after the main title, followed by the subtitle. Continue the italics used for the main title. Add a period (not italicized).

3 PUBLICATION INFORMATION

3a Place of Publication
Write the name of the first city mentioned (some sources list more than one). If the city is foreign, or if several cities have the same name, add the abbreviation for the province, territory, or country. Add a colon.

3b Publisher
Write the publisher's name in short form. (*Pearson Education Inc.* would be *Pearson* and *Prentice Hall* would be *Prentice.*) Follow it with a comma.

3c Date of Publication
Write the most recent year that appears on the book's copyright page or *n.d.* (not italicized) if no date is given.

Starr, Paul. *The Creation of the Media: Political Origins of Modern Communications.* New York: Basic, 2004. Print.

Figure 36.2 Locating and citing source information in a book

1. Book by One Author—MLA

Bradway, Becky. *Pink Houses and Family Taverns*. Bloomington: Indiana UP,
2002. Print.

2. Book by Two or Three Authors—MLA

Edin, Kathryn, and Maria Kefalas. *Promises I Can Keep: Why Poor Women Put
Motherhood before Marriage*. Berkeley: U of California P, 2005. Print.

Lynam, John K., Cyrus G. Ndiritu, and Adiel N. Mbabu. *Transformation of
Agricultural Research Systems in Africa: Lessons from Andreiya*. East
Lansing: Michigan State UP, 2004. Print.

3. Book by More Than Three Authors—MLA

Give only the first author's name, followed by a comma and the phrase *et al.*
(abbreviated from the Latin *et alii*, meaning "and others"), or list all names in
full and in the order in which they appear on the title page.

Saul, Wendy, et al. *Beyond the Science Fair: Creating a Kids' Inquiry
Conference*. Portsmouth: Heinemann, 2005. Print.

4. Two or More Works by the Same Author(s)—MLA

Give author name(s) in the first entry only. In the second and subsequent entries, use three hyphens and a period to stand for exactly the same name(s). If
the person served as editor or translator, put a comma and the appropriate abbreviation (*ed.* or *trans.*) following the three hyphens. Arrange the works in alphabetical (not chronological) order according to book title, ignoring labels
such as *ed.* or *trans.*

Jenkins, Henry. *Convergence Culture: Where Old and New Media Collide*. New
York: New York UP, 2006. Print.

---. *Fans, Bloggers, and Gamers: Exploring Participatory Culture*. New York:
New York UP, 2006. Print.

5. Book by Group or Corporate Author—MLA

Cite the full name of the corporate author first, omitting the first articles *A, An,*
or *The*. When a corporate author is also the publisher, use a shortened form of
the corporate name in the publication information.

American Psychological Association. *Publication Manual of the American
Psychological Association*. 5th ed. Washington: APA, 2001. Print.

Boston Women's Health Collective. *Our Bodies, Ourselves for the New Century*.
New York: Simon, 1998. Print.

6. Book with No Author Named—MLA

If there is no author's name on the title page, begin the citation with the title. Alphabetize the entry according to the first significant word of the title ignoring *A, An* or *The*.

The Chicago Manual of Style. 15th ed. Chicago: U of Chicago P, 2003. Print.

7. Book with an Author and an Editor—MLA

If your paper refers to the work of the book's author, put the author's name first; if your paper refers to the work of the editor, put the editor's name first.

Brontë, Emily. *Wuthering Heights*. Ed. Richard J. Dunn. New York: Norton, 2002.
Print.

Dunn, Richard J., ed. *Wuthering Heights*. By Emily Brontë. New York: Norton,
2002. Print.

8. Translation—MLA

Kundera, Milan. *The Unbearable Lightness of Being*. Trans. Michael Henry
Heim. New York: Harper, 1999. Print.

9. Work in Several Volumes or Parts—MLA

If you're citing only one volume, put the volume number before the publication information. If you wish, you can give the total number of volumes at the end of the entry. MLA recommends using Arabic numerals, even if the source uses Roman numerals (*Vol. 6* rather than *Vol. VI*).

Chrisley, Ronald, ed. *Artificial Intelligence: Critical Concepts*. Vol. 1. London:
Routledge, 2000. Print. 4 vols.

10. Anthology or Edited Book—MLA

In the following example, *ed.* stands for "editor," so use *eds.* when more than one editor is named; also see items 9, 11, and 12.

Purdy, John L., and James Ruppert, eds. *Nothing but the Truth: An Anthology of
Native American Literature*. Upper Saddle River: Prentice, 2001. Print.

11. One Selection from an Anthology or an Edited Book—MLA

Give the author and title of the selection first and then the full title of the anthology. Information about the editor starts with *Ed.* (for "Edited by"), so don't use *Eds.* when there is more than one editor. Give the name(s) of the editor(s) in normal order rather than reversing first and last names. Give the page range at the end.

Trujillo, Laura. "Balancing Act." *Border-Line Personalities: A New Generation
of Latinas Dish on Sex, Sass, and Cultural Shifting*. Ed. Robyn Moreno and
Michelle Herrera Mulligan. New York: Harper, 2004. 61-72. Print.

12. More Than One Selection from the Same Anthology or Edited Book—MLA

If you cite more than one selection from the same anthology, you can list the anthology as a separate entry with all the publication information. Also, list each selection from the anthology by author and title of the selection, but give only the name(s) of the editor(s) of the anthology and the page number(s) for each selection. List selections separately in alphabetical order by author's last name.

Bond, Ruskin. "The Night Train at Deoli." Chaudhuri 415-18.

Chaudhuri, Amit, ed. *The Vintage Book of Modern Indian Literature*. New York: Vintage, 2004. Print.

Vijayan, O.V. "The Rocks." Chaudhuri 291-96.

13. Signed Article in a Reference Book—MLA

A "signed article" means that the author of the article is identified. If the articles in the book are alphabetically arranged, you don't need to give volume and page numbers.

Burnbam, John C. "Freud, Sigmund." *The Encyclopedia of Psychiatry, Psychology, and Psychoanalysis*. Ed. Benjamin B. Wolman. New York: Holt, 1996. Print.

14. Unsigned Article in a Reference Book—MLA

Begin with the title of the article. If you're citing a widely used reference work, don't give full publication information. Instead, give only the edition and year of publication.

"Ireland." *The New Encyclopaedia Britannica: Macropaedia*. 15th ed. 2002. Print.

15. Second or Later Edition—MLA

If a book isn't a first edition, the edition number appears on the title page. Place the abbreviated information (*2nd ed., 3rd ed.*, etc.) between the title and the publication information. Give only the latest copyright date for the edition you're using.

Gibaldi, Joseph. *MLA Handbook for Writers of Research Papers*. 6th ed. New York: MLA, 2003. Print.

16. Introduction, Preface, Foreword, or Afterword—MLA

Give first the name of the writer of the part you're citing and then the name of the cited part, capitalized but not underlined or in quotation marks. After the book title, write *By* or *Ed.* and the full name(s) of the book's author(s) or editor(s), if different from the writer of the cited material. If the writer of the cited material is the same as the book author, include only the last name after

By. Following the publication information, give inclusive page numbers for the cited part, using Roman or Arabic numerals as the source does.

Hesse, Doug. Foreword. *The End of Composition Studies.* By David W. Smit.
    Carbondale: Southern Illinois UP, 2004. ix-xiii. Print.

When the introduction, preface, foreword, or afterword has a title (as in the next example), include it in the citation before the section name.

Fox-Genovese, Elizabeth. "Mothers and Daughters: The Ties That Bind."
    Foreword. *Southern Mothers.* Ed. Nagueyalti Warren and Sally Wolff.
    Baton Rouge: Louisiana State UP, 1999. iv-xviii. Print.

17. Unpublished Dissertation or Essay—MLA

State the author's name first, then the title in quotation marks (not italicized), then a descriptive label (such as *Diss.* or *Unpublished essay*), followed by the degree-granting institution (for dissertations), and, finally, the date. Treat published dissertations as books.

Stuart, Gina Anne. "Exploring the Harry Potter Book Series: A Study of
    Adolescent Reading Motivation." Diss. Utah State U, 2006. Print.

18. Reprint of an Older Book—MLA

Republishing information can be found on the copyright page. Give the date of the original version before the publication information for the version you're citing.

O'Brien, Flann. *At Swim-Two-Birds.* 1939. Normal: Dalkey Archive, 1998. Print.

19. Book in a Series—MLA

Goldman, Dorothy J. *Women Writers and World War I.* New York: Macmillan,
    1995. Print. Lit. and Soc. Ser.

Mukherjee, Meenakshi. *Jane Austen.* New York: St. Martin's, 1991. Print. Women
    Writers Ser.

20. Book with a Title Within a Title—MLA

The MLA recognizes two distinct styles for handling normally independent titles when they appear within an italicized title. (Use whichever style your instructor prefers.) When using the MLA's preferred style, do not italicize the embedded title or set it within quotation marks.

Lumiansky, Robert M., and Herschel Baker, eds. *Critical Approaches to Six
    Major English Works:* Beowulf *Through* Paradise Lost. Philadelphia: U of
    Pennsylvania P, 1968. Print.

However, because MLA also accepts a second style for handling such embedded titles, you can set the normally independent titles within quotation marks and italicize them.

Lumiansky, Robert M., and Herschel Baker, eds. *Critical Approaches to Six
    Major English Works: "Beowulf" Through "Paradise Lost."* Philadelphia:
    U of Pennsylvania P, 1968. Print.

21. Bible or Sacred Text—MLA

Bhagavad-Gita. Trans. Juan Mascaro. Rev. ed. New York: Penguin, 2003. Print.

The Holy Bible: New International Version. New York: Harper, 1983. Print.

The Qur'an. Trans. Abdullah Yusuf Ali. 13th ed. Elmhurst: Tahrike Tarsile
    Qur'an, 1999. Print.

22. Government Publication—MLA

For government publications that name no author, start with the name of the government or government body. Then name the government agency. *GPO* is a standard abbreviation for *Government Printing Office*, the publisher of most US government publications.

United States. Cong. House. Committee on Resources. *Coastal Heritage Trail
    Route in New Jersey.* 106th Cong., 1st sess. H. Rept. 16. Washington: GPO,
    1999. Print.

---. ---. Senate. Select Committee on Intelligence. *Report on the U.S.
    Intelligence Community's Prewar Intelligence Assessment of Iraq.*
    108th Cong., 1st sess. Washington: GPO, 2004. Print.

23. Published Proceedings of a Conference—MLA

Rocha, Luis Mateus, et al., eds. *Artificial Life X: Proceedings of the Tenth
    International Conference on the Simulation and Synthesis of Living
    Systems.* Bloomington, IN. 3-7 June 2006. Cambridge: MIT P, 2006.
    Print.

PERIODICAL PUBLICATIONS—PRINT VERSIONS

Citations for periodical articles contain three major parts: author information, title information, and publication information. Figure 36.3 shows a citation for an article in a scholarly journal (see item 27).

24. Signed Article in a Weekly or Biweekly Periodical—MLA

Brink, Susan. "Eat This Now!" *US News and World Report* 28 Mar. 2005: 56-58. Print.

1 AUTHOR INFORMATION

Name of Author
Write the author's last name, followed by a comma, the author's first name, and the middle initial (if given). End with a period.

2 TITLE INFORMATION

2a Article Title
Begin with a quotation mark, write the title (with subtitle, if there is one), include a period, and end with a closing quotation mark. Capitalize all major words.

2b Journal Title and Volume
Italicize the title. Capitalize all major words. Include the volume number and issue number, separated by a period.

3 PUBLICATION INFORMATION

3a Date of Publication
Include the year of publication in parentheses, followed by a colon.

3b Page Numbers
Provide the page numbers on which the article begins and ends, separated by a hyphen. For numbers up to 99, include both digits. For higher numbers, include only the last two digits (145-57) unless doing so would be unclear (295-307). End with a period.

Malinowitz, Harriet. "Business, Pleasure, and the Personal Essay." *College English* 65.3 (2003): 305-22. Print.

Figure 36.3 Locating and citing sources from a journal article

25. Signed Article in a Monthly or Bimonthly Periodical—MLA

Fallows, James. "The $1.4 Trillion Question." *The Atlantic* Jan.-Feb. 2008: 36-48. Print.

26. Unsigned Article in a Weekly or Monthly Periodical—MLA

"The Price Is Wrong." *Economist* 2 Aug. 2003: 58-59. Print.

27. Article in a Scholarly Journal

Adler-Kassner, Linda, and Heidi Estrem. "Rethinking Research Writing: Public
Literacy in the Composition Classroom." *WPA: Writing Program
Administration* 26.3 (2003): 119-31. Print.

28. Article in a Collection of Reprinted Articles—MLA

First include the original publication information, then *Rpt.* and information
about the place the article was republished.

Brumberg, Abraham. "Russia after Perestroika." *New York Review of Books* 27
June 1991: 53-62. Rpt. in *Russian and Soviet History*. Ed. Alexander Dallin.
Vol. 14 of *The Gorbachev Era*. New York: Garland, 1992. 300-20. Print.

Textbooks used in college writing courses often collect previously printed articles.

Rothstein, Richard. "When Mothers on Welfare Go to Work." *New York Times*
5 June 2002: A20. Rpt. in *Writing Arguments: A Rhetoric with Readings*. Ed.
John D. Ramage, John C. Bean, and June Johnson. New York: Longman,
2004. 263. Print.

29. Signed Article in a Daily Newspaper—MLA

Omit *A, An,* or *The* as the first word in a newspaper title. Give the day, month,
and year of the issue (and the edition, if applicable). If sections are designated,
give the section letter as well as the page number. If an article runs on noncon-
secutive pages, give the starting page number followed by a plus sign (for example, *23+* for an article that starts on page 23 and continues on a later page).

Green, Penelope. "The Slow Life Picks Up Speed." *New York Times* 31 Jan. 2008,
natl. ed.: D1+. Print.

30. Unsigned Article in a Daily Newspaper—MLA

"Oscars Ready Plans to Deal with Strike." *Denver Post* 31 Jan. 2008: B3. Print.

If the city of publication is not part of the title, put it in square brackets after
the title, not italicized.

"Hackers Hit Northwestern Computer Net." *Pantagraph* [Bloomington] 26 Mar.
2005: A5. Print.

31. Editorial, Letter to the Editor, or Review—MLA

After the author's name or title, provide information about the type of publication.

"Primary Considerations." Editorial. *Washington Post* 27 Jan. 2008: B6. Print.

Finanger, Emily. Letter. *Outside* Feb. 2008: 14. Print.

Shenk, David. "Toolmaker, Brain Builder." Rev. of *Beyond Big Blue: Building
the Computer That Defeated the World Chess Champion,* by Feng-Hsiung
Hsu. *American Scholar* 72 (Spring 2003): 150-52. Print.

MLA

32. Article in a Looseleaf Collection of Reprinted Articles—MLA

Give the citation for the original publication first, followed by the citation for the collection.

Hayden, Thomas. "The Age of Robots." *US News and World Report* 23 Apr. 2001:
44+. Print. *Applied Science* 2002. Ed. Eleanor Goldstein. Boca Raton: SIRS,
2002. Art. 66.

33. Abstract in a Collection of Abstracts—MLA

To cite an abstract, first give information for the full work: the author's name, the title of the article, and publication information about the full article. If a reader could not know that the cited material is an abstract, write the word *Abstract*, not italicized, followed by a period. Give publication information about the collection of abstracts. For abstracts identified by item numbers rather than page numbers, use the word *item* before the item number.

Marcus, Hazel R., and Shinobu Kitayamo. "Culture and the Self: Implications
for Cognition, Emotion, and Motivation." *Psychological Review* 88 (1991):
224 53. *Psychological Abstracts* 78 (1991): item 23878. Print.

PERIODICALS—ONLINE VERSIONS FROM SUBSCRIPTION SERVICES

A large (and increasing) number of periodicals are available in digital versions online, as well as in print; some periodicals are available only online. Online periodicals fall into two categories: (1) periodicals you access through a DATABASE or **subscription service** paid for by your library or company, such as EBSCO or FirstSearch, or through an online service to which you personally subscribe (examples 34–38); and (2) periodicals you directly access by entering a specific URL (examples 39–44). Articles you access through a subscription service are the most important for academic research. Of course, many other online sources are not from periodicals; we explain them in examples 45–75.

ALERT: Online periodical articles are frequently available in both "HTML" (hypertext mark-up language) and "PDF" (portable document format) versions. The PDF versions are almost always preferable for research because they present an image of articles exactly as they appear in print. This means the PDF version of an article has page numbers, images and graphics, side-bar stories, headings, and so on. As a result, PDFs are easier to cite. The HTML version of an article does include all of the text; however, because it has been formatted to work efficiently in databases, it contains no page numbers or graphics. HTML versions load more quickly on your computer, but citing them is less precise. If you have a choice, always use the PDF version.

34. Subscription Service: Article with a Print Version—MLA

Jackson, Gabriel. "Multiple Historic Meanings of the Spanish Civil War."
   Science and Society 68.3 (2004): 272-76. *Academic Search Elite*. Web.
   7 Mar. 2005.

VandeHei, Jim. "Two Years after White House Exit, Clinton Shaping Democratic
   Party." *Washington Post* 21 June 2003, final ed.: A1. *Academic Universe*.
   Web. 5 May 2005.

Figure 36.4 illustrates citing an article that has a print version but has been accessed through a subscription service.

35. Subscription Service: Material with No Print Version—MLA

Siemens, Raymond G. "A New Computer-Assisted Literary Criticism?"
   Computers and the Humanities 36.3 (2002). *America Online*. Web.
   12 Nov. 2002.

36. Subscription Service: Abstract—MLA

The example below is for the same abstract shown in item 33, but here it is accessed from an online database (*PsycINFO*) by means of a library subscription service. The name of the library shows where the source was accessed, and *10 Apr. 2004* is the date it was accessed.

Marcus, Hazel R., and Shinobu Kitayamo. "Culture and the Self: Implications
   for Cognition, Emotion, and Motivation." *Psychological Abstracts* 78 (1991).
   PsycINFO. Web. 10 Apr. 2004.

37. Subscription Service Access with a Keyword: Article in a Periodical with a Print Version—MLA

Electronic versions of sources that also appear in print start with information about the print version. Here's an entry for a journal article accessed through a computer service; it also has a print version.

Wynne, Clive D. L. "'Willy' Didn't Yearn to Be Free." Editorial. *New York Times*
   27 Dec. 2003: *New York Times Online*. America Online. Web. 29 Dec. 2003.
   Keyword: nytimes.

Information applying to the print version of this article in the *New York Times* ends with the publication date and information about the online version starts with the title of the database, *New York Times Online. America Online* is the service through which the database was accessed, and *29 Dec. 2003* is the access date. The keyword *nytimes* was used to access *New York Times Online*.

1 AUTHOR INFORMATION

Name of Author
Write the author's last name, followed by a comma, the author's first name, and the middle initial (if given). End with a period.

2 TITLE INFORMATION

Article Title
State the full title of the article, enclosed in quotation marks. Use a period before the closing quotation mark.

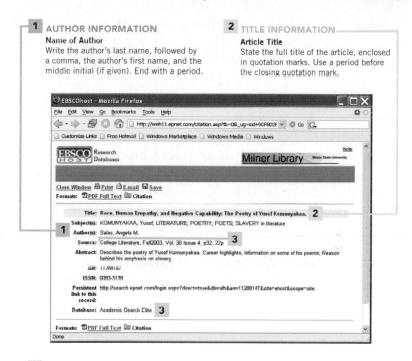

3 PUBLICATION INFORMATION

3a **Name of Periodical**
Provide the journal title (italicized).

3b **Volume and Issue Numbers**
Leave one space after the journal title and provide the volume and issue numbers, separated by a period.

3c **Date of Publication**
Provide the year of publication, in parentheses, followed by a colon.

3d **Page Numbers**
Provide the inclusive page numbers for the complete article, not just the portion you used. End with a period.

3e **Title of Database**
Italicize the name of the database. End with a period.

3f **Medium of Publication**
Provide the medium of publication consulted (*Web*), followed by a period.

3g **Date of Access**
Provide the day, month, and year that you accessed the article online. End with a period.

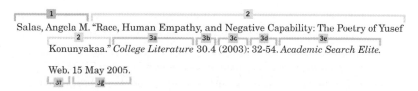

Salas, Angela M. "Race, Human Empathy, and Negative Capability: The Poetry of Yusef Konunyakaa." *College Literature* 30.4 (2003): 32-54. *Academic Search Elite.* Web. 15 May 2005.

Figure 36.4 Locating and citing source information for a journal found in an online database

38. Subscription Service Access Showing a Path—MLA

When you access a source by choosing a series of keywords, menus, or topics, end the entry with the "path" of words you used. Use semicolons between items in the path, and put a period at the end.

Futrelle, David. "A Smashing Success." *Money.com* 23 Dec. 1999. America Online. Web. 26 Dec. 1999. Path: Personal Finance; Business News; Business
Publications; Money.com.

PERIODICALS—ONLINE VERSIONS ACCESSED DIRECTLY

You can access some online versions of periodicals directly, without going through a paid subscription service. Newspapers and magazines often publish some of their articles from each issue online this way. Often, however, you can't access every single article—or any older articles—without being a subscriber.

39. Online Version of a Print Magazine Article—MLA

The example below is for the online version of the same article cited in 25, above. In addition to the print information, include the date you accessed the online version. (If the page numbers from the print version are available, include them, too, before the access date.)

Fallows, James. "The $1.4 Trillion Question." *The Atlantic.com*. Atlantic
Monthly Group, Jan.-Feb. 2008. Web. 2 May 2008.

If the article is unsigned, begin with the title.

"Too Smart to Marry." *The Atlantic.com*. Atlantic Monthly Group, 14 Apr. 2005.
Web. 7 Mar. 2005.

40. Online Version of a Print Journal Article—MLA

Hoge, Charles W., et al. "Mild Traumatic Brain Injury in U.S. Soldiers
Returning from Iraq." *New England Journal of Medicine* 358.5 (2008):
453-63. Web. 10 Sept. 2008.

41. Periodical Article Published Only Online—MLA

Many periodicals are published only online; others have "extra" online content that doesn't appear in print. Figure 36.5 illustrates how to cite an article that appears only online.

Ramirez, Eddy. "Comparing American Students with Those in China and
India." *U.S. News and World Report*. U.S. News and World Report, 30 Jan.
2008. Web. 4 Mar. 2008.

Shipka, Jody. "This Was (Not!!) an Easy Assignment." *Computers and
Composition Online*. Computers and Composition Online, Fall 2007.
Web. 2 May 2008.

MLA

1 **AUTHOR INFORMATION**
Name of Author
Write the author's last name, followed by a comma, the author's first name, and the middle initial (if given). End with a period.

2 **TITLE INFORMATION**
Article Title
State the full title of the article, enclosed in quotation marks. Unless the title contains its own closing punctuation (question mark), use a period before the closing quotation mark.

3 **PUBLICATION INFORMATION**
3a **Title of the Overall Web Site**
Provide the title of the Web site (italicized), followed by a period.
3b **Publisher or Sponsor of the Web Site**
Leave one space after the title of the overall Web site and provide the publisher or sponsor of the Web site. If this information is not available, use "n.p." End with a comma.
3c **Date of Publication**
Provide the day, month, and year of publication, followed by a period. If no date is available, use "n.d."
3d **Medium of Publication**
Provide the medium of publication consulted (Web), followed by a period.
3e **Date of Access**
Provide the day, month, and year that you accessed the article online. End with a period.

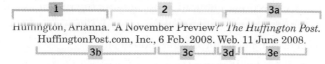

Huffington, Arianna. "A November Preview?" *The Huffington Post.*
HuffingtonPost.com, Inc., 6 Feb. 2008. Web. 11 June 2008.

Figure 36.5 Locating and citing source information for an article published only online

42. Online Version of a Print Newspaper Article—MLA

If the article is signed, begin with the author's name, last name first.

Wilson, Janet. "EPA Fights Waste Site near River." *Los Angeles Times*. Los
Angeles Times, 5 Mar. 2005. Web. 7 Mar. 2005.

If the article is unsigned, begin with the article title.

"Remnant of Revolutionary War Washes Ashore." *CNN.com*. Cable News
Network, 28 Mar. 2005. Web. 29 Mar. 2005.

43. Online Editorial or Letter to the Editor—MLA

"Garbage In, Garbage Out." Editorial. *Los Angeles Times*. Los Angeles
Times, 2 Feb. 2008. Web. 22 Mar. 2008.

Ennis, Heather B. Letter to the Editor. *U.S. News and World Report*. U.S. News
and World Report, 20 Dec. 2007. Web. 22 Dec. 2007.

44. Online Material from a Newspaper or News Site Published Only Online—MLA

Harris, Edward. "Rain Forests Fall at 'Alarming' Rate." *denverpost.com*.
Denver Post, 3 Feb. 2008. Web. 3 Feb. 2008.

OTHER INTERNET SOURCES

This section shows models for online sources. For such sources, provide as
much of the following information as you can.

- The author's name, if given.
- In quotation marks, the title of a short work (Web page, brief document, essay, article, message, and so on); or italicized, the title of a book.
- Publication information for any print version, if it exists.
- The name of an editor, translator, or compiler, if any, with an abbreviation such as *Ed., Trans.,* or *Comp.* before the name.
- The italicized title of the Internet site (scholarly project, database, online periodical, professional or personal Web site). If the site has no title, describe it: for example, *Home page.*
- The date of electronic publication (including a version number, if any) or posting or the most recent update.
- The name of a sponsoring organization, if any.
- The medium of publication.
- The date you accessed the material.

- The URL in angle brackets (< >), only when the reader probably could not locate the source without it. If you must break a URL at the end of a line, break only after a slash and do not use a hyphen.

45. Online Book—MLA

Chopin, Kate. *The Awakening.* 1899. *PBS Electronic Library.* 10 Dec. 1998. PBS. Web. 13 Nov. 2008.

46. Online Book in a Scholarly Project—MLA

Herodotus. *The History of Herodotus.* Trans. George Rawlinson. 1947. *Internet Classics Archive.* Ed. Daniel C. Stevenson. 11 Jan. 1998. MIT. Web. 15 May 2006.

47. Online Government-Published Book—MLA

Start with the name of the government or government body, and then name the government agency, the title, the work's author (if known), the publication date, the access date, and the URL, if the reader needs it.

United States. Cong. Research Service. *Space Stations.* By Marcia S. Smith. 12 Dec. 1996. Web. 4 Dec. 2007.

MLA also permits an alternative format, with the author's name first, then title, then government body.

Huff, C. Ronald. *Comparing the Criminal Behavior of Youth Gangs and At-Risk Youths.* United States. Dept. of Justice. Natl. Inst. of Justice. Oct. 1998. Web. 5 Aug. 2008.

48. Professional Home Page—MLA

Provide as much of the following information as you can find.

- If available, include the name of the person who created or put up the home page. If first and last names are given, reverse the order of the first author's name.
- For a professional home page, include the name of the sponsoring organization.
- Include the date you accessed the material.

Association for the Advancement of Artificial Intelligence. Web. 17 Mar. 2008.

49. Personal Home Page—MLA

Follow guidelines for professional home pages, with the following changes. Give the name of the person who created the page, last name first. Include the page's title, if there is one, italicized; if there is no title, add the description *Home page,* not italicized, followed by a period.

Hesse, Doug. Home page. Web. 1 Nov. 2007. <http://portfolio.du.edu/dhesse>.

MLA

1 TITLE

Title of the Work
State the full title of the work cited, enclosed in quotation marks. Use a period before the closing quotation mark.

2 PUBLICATION INFORMATION

2a Title of the Overall Web Site
Provide the title of the Web site (italicized), followed by a period.

2b Publisher or Sponsor of the Web Site
Leave one space after the title of the overall Web site and provide the publisher or sponsor of the Web site. If this information is not available, use "n.p." End with a comma.

2c Date of Publication
Provide the available date (day, month, and year) of publication, followed by a period. If no date is available, use "n.d."

2d Medium of Publication
Provide the medium of publication consulted (Web), followed by a period.

2e Date of Access
Provide the day, month, and year that you accessed the article online. End with a period.

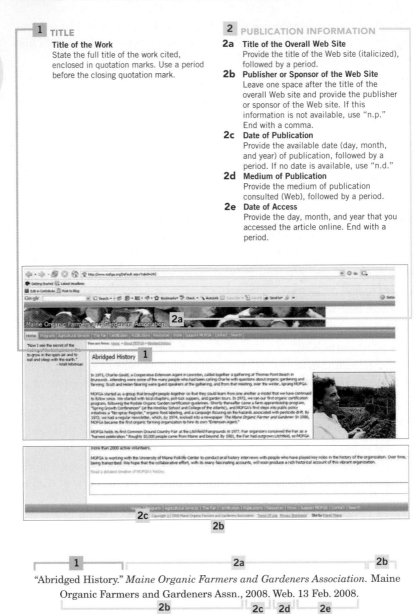

"Abridged History." *Maine Organic Farmers and Gardeners Association.* Maine Organic Farmers and Gardeners Assn., 2008. Web. 13 Feb. 2008.

Figure 36.6 Locating and citing source information for a Web page with no author

MLA

50. Page from a Web Site—MLA

Provide as much information as you can (see Figure 36.6).

"Protecting Whales from Dangerous Sonar." *National Resources Defense
     Council*. NRDC, 9 Nov. 2005. Web. 12 Dec. 2005.

"Abridged History." *Maine Organic Farmers and Gardeners Association*.
     Maine Organic Farmers and Gardeners Assn., 2007. Web. 13 Dec. 2007.

51. Entire Internet Site—MLA

WebdelSol.Com. Ed. Michael Neff. 2008. Web. 11 Nov. 2008.

52. Academic Department Home Page—MLA

Write the name of the academic department, followed by the words *Dept. home
page.* (Do not put any words in quotations or in italics.) Also include the name
of the institution and the date you accessed the page.

Writing. Dept. home page. Grand Valley State U. Web. 26 Feb. 2008.

53. Course Home Page—MLA

St. Germain, Sheryl. Myths and Fairytales: From *Inanna* to *Edward Scissorhands*.
     Course home page. Summer 2003. Dept. of English, Iowa State U. Web. 20
     Feb. 2005. <http://www.public.iastate.edu/~sgermain/531.homepage.html>.

54. Government or Institutional Web Site—MLA

Home Education and Private Tutoring. Pennsylvania Department of Education,
     2005. Web. 15 Dec. 2005.

55. Online Poem—MLA

Browning, Elizabeth Barrett. "Past and Future." *Women's Studies Database
     Reading Room*. U of Maryland. Web. 9 June 2003.

56. Online Work of Art—MLA

Provide artist, title of work, creation date (optional), the museum or individual who owns it, the place and the access date.

van Gogh, Vincent. *The Starry Night*. 1889. Museum of Mod. Art, New York.
     Web. 5 Dec. 2003. Keyword: Starry Night.

In this example, the keyword "Starry Night" is what a researcher types into a
search box on the museum's Web site.

1 TITLE

Title of the Work
State the full title of the work cited, enclosed in quotation marks. Use a period before the closing quotation mark.

2 PUBLICATION INFORMATION

2a Title of the Overall Web Site
Provide the title of the Web site (italicized), followed by a period.

2b Publisher or Sponsor of the Web Site
Leave one space after the title of the overall Web site and provide the publisher or sponsor of the Web site. If this information is not available, use "N.p." End with a comma.

2c Date of Publication
Provide the day, month, and year of publication, followed by a period. If no date is available, use "n.d."

2d Medium of Publication
Provide the medium of publication consulted (*Web*), followed by a period.

2e Date of Access
Provide the day, month, and year that you accessed the article online. End with a period.

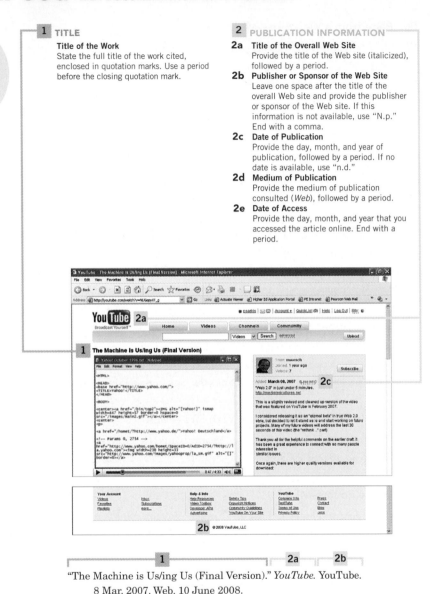

"The Machine is Us/ing Us (Final Version)." *YouTube.* YouTube. 8 Mar. 2007. Web. 10 June 2008.

Figure 36.7 Locating and citing source information for an online video

57. Online Image or Photograph—MLA

As with images from print publications (see item 88), include information about the photographer and title, if known. Otherwise, describe the photograph briefly and give information about the Web site and the access date.

Bourke-White, Margaret. "Fort Peck Dam, Montana." 1936. Gelatin silver print. Metropolitan Museum of Art, New York. Web. 5 Aug. 2008.

58. Online Interview—MLA

Pope, Carl. Interview by Amy Standen. *Salon.com*. Salon Media Group, 29 Apr. 2002. Web. 27 Jan. 2005.

59. Online Video or Film Clip—MLA

See Figure 36.7.

Reeves, Matt, dir. *Cloverfield*. Trailer. Bad Robot, 2008. Web. 18 Jan. 2008.

60. Online Cartoon—MLA

Harris, Sidney. "We have lots of information technology." Cartoon. *New Yorker* 27 May 2002. Web. 9 Feb. 2007.

61. Online Television or Radio Program—MLA

Chayes, Sarah. "Concorde." *All Things Considered*. Natl. Public Radio. 26 July 2000. Web. 7 Dec. 2001.

"The Beginning of the End." *Lost*. ABC. 30 Jan. 2008. Web. 1 Feb. 2008.

62. Online Discussion Posting—MLA

To cite an online message, give the author's name (if any), the title of the message in quotation marks, and then *Online posting*. Give the date of the posting and the name of the bulletin board, if any. Then give the access date and, in angle brackets, the URL if needed.

Firrantello, Larry. "Van Gogh on Prozac." Online posting. 23 May 2005. *Salon Table Talk*. Web. 7 June 2005. <http://tabletalk.salon.com/ webx?50@931.xC34anLmwOq.1@.773b2ad1>.

Be cautious about using online postings as sources. Some postings contain cutting-edge information from experts, but some contain trash. Unfortunately, it is nearly impossible to find out whether people online are who they claim to be.

63. Real-Time Communication—MLA

Give the name of the speaker or writer, a title for the event (if any), the forum, date, and access date.

Berzsenyi, Christyne. Online discussion of "Writing to Meet Your Match: Rhetoric, Perceptions, and Self-Presentation for Four Online Daters." *Computers and Writing Online*. 13 May 2007. AcadianaMoo. Web. 13 May 2007.

64. E-Mail Message—MLA

Start with the name of the person who wrote the e-mail message. Give the title or subject line in quotation marks. Then describe the source (*e-mail*) and identify the recipient. End with the date.

Pessin, Eliana. "Scottish Writers." Message to Georgia Dobyns. 11 Nov. 2007.
     Email.

65. Part of an Online Book—MLA

Teasdale, Sara. "Driftwood." *Flame and Shadow*. Ed. A. Light. N.p., 1920.
     Project Gutenberg. 1 July 1996. Web. 18 Aug. 2008.

66. Online Review—MLA

Travers, Peter. Rev. of *No Country for Old Men*, dir. Joel Coen and Ethan Coen.
     Rollingstone.com. Rolling Stone, 1 Nov. 2007. Web. 25 Nov. 2007.

67. Online Abstract—MLA

Avery, Christopher, et al. "A Revealed Preference Ranking of U.S. Colleges and
     Universities." NBER Working Paper No. W10803. Abstract. Web. 11 Oct. 2004.

68. Posting on a Blog—MLA

McLemee, Scott. "To Whom It May Concern." *Quick Study*. 1 Jan. 2008. Web.
     14 May 2008.

69. Online Sound Recording or Clip—MLA

Komunyakaa, Yusef. "My Father's Love Letters." Poets.org Listening Booth.
     Academy of American Poets, 5 May 1993. Web. 27 Apr. 2005.

70. Online Advertisement—MLA

Samsung. Advertisement. *RollingStone*. 8 Nov. 2005. Web.

71. Online Manuscript or Working Paper—MLA

deGrandpre, Andrew. "Baseball Destined to Die in Hockey Town." 2002.
     Unpublished article. Web. 7 Mar. 2005.

72. Podcast—MLA

A podcast is an audio recording that is posted online. Include as much of the following information as you can identify: author, title, sponsoring organization or Web site, date posted, and date accessed.

"Business Marketing with Podcast: What Marketing Professionals Should
     Know." *Podblaze.com*. The Info Gurus, 13 Oct. 2005. Web. 19 Oct. 2005.

73. Online Slide Show—MLA

Erickson, Britta, narr. *Visionaries from the New China.* July 2007. Web. 11 Sept. 2008.

74. Online Photo Essay—MLA

Nachtwey, James. "Crime in Middle America." *Time* 2 Dec. 2006. Web. 5 May 2007.

75. Online Map, Chart, or Other Graphic—MLA

"Hurricane Rita." Graphic. *New York Times Online.* New York Times. 24 Sept. 2005. Web. 24 Sept. 2005.

OTHER PRINT, NONPRINT, AND ELECTRONIC SOURCES

76. Published or Unpublished Letter—MLA

Begin the entry with the author of the letter. Note the recipient, too.

Irvin, William. Letter to Lesley Osburn. 7 Dec. 2007. Print.

Williams, William Carlos. Letter to his son. 13 Mar. 1935. *Letters of the Century: America 1900-1999.* Ed. Lisa Grunwald and Stephen J. Adler. New York. Dial, 1999. 225-26. Print.

77. Microfiche Collection of Articles—MLA

A microfiche is a transparent sheet of film (a *fiche*) with microscopic printing that needs to be read through a special magnifier. Each fiche holds several pages, with each page designated by a grid position. A long document may appear on more than one fiche.

Wenzell, Ron. "Businesses Prepare for a More Diverse Work Force." *St. Louis Post Dispatch* 3 Feb. 1990: 17. Microform. *NewsBank: Employment* 27 (1990): fiche 2, grid D12.

78. Map or Chart—MLA

Colorado Front Range Mountain Bike Topo Map. Map. Nederland: Latitude 40, 2001. Print.

79. Report or Pamphlet—MLA

Use the format for books, to the extent possible.

National Commission on Writing in America's Schools and Colleges. *The Neglected "R": The Need for a Writing Revolution.* New York: College Board, 2003. Print.

80. Legal Source—MLA

Include the name of the case, the number of the case (preceded by *No.*), the name of the court deciding the case, and the date of the decision.

Brown v. Board of Ed. No. 8. Supreme Ct. of the US. 8 Oct. 1952. Print.

81. Interview—MLA

Note the type of interview—for example, "Telephone," "Personal" (face-to-face), or "E-mail."

Friedman, Randi. Telephone interview. 30 Aug. 2008.

For a published interview, give the name of the interviewed person first, identify the source as an interview, and then give details as for any published source: title; author, preceded by the word *By;* and publication details.

Winfrey, Oprah. "Ten Questions for Oprah Winfrey." By Richard Zoglin. *Time*
15 Dec. 2003: 8. Print.

82. Lecture, Speech, or Address—MLA

Kennedy, John Fitzgerald. Greater Houston Ministerial Assn. Rice Hotel,
Houston. 12 Sept. 1960. Address.

83. Film, Videotape, or DVD—MLA

Give the title first, and include the director, the distributor, and the year. For older films that were subsequently released on tape or DVD, provide the original release date of the movie *before* the type of medium. For video downloads, include the download date and the source. Other information (writer, producer, major actors) is optional but helpful. Put first names first.

Shakespeare in Love. Screenplay by Marc Norman and Tom Stoppard. Dir.
John Maddon. Prod. David Parfitt, Donna Gigliotti, Harvey Weinstein,
Edward Zwick, and Mark Norman. Perf. Gwyneth Paltrow, Joseph
Fiennes, and Judi Dench. Miramax, 1998. Film.

It Happened One Night. Screenplay by Robert Riskin. Dir. and Prod. Frank Capra.
Perf. Clark Gable and Claudette Colbert. 1934. Sony Pictures, 1999. DVD.

It Happened One Night. Screenplay by Robert Riskin. Dir. and Prod. Frank
Capra. Perf. Clark Gable and Claudette Colbert. Columbia 1934. 2007.
4 Mar. 2008. MPEG file.

84. Musical Recording—MLA

Put first the name most relevant to what you discuss in your paper (performer, conductor, the work performed). Include the recording's title, the medium for any recording other than a CD (*LP, audiocassette*), the name of the issuer (*Vanguard*), and the year the work was issued.

Smetana, Bedrich. *My Country.* Czech Philharmonic Orch. Cond. Karel Anserl.
LP. Vanguard, 1975. CD.

Springsteen, Bruce. "Lonesome Day." *The Rising.* Sony, 2002. CD.

Radiohead. "Jigsaw Falling into Place." *In Rainbows.* Radiohead, 2007. MP3 file.

85. Live Performance (Play, Concert, etc.)—MLA

All My Sons. By Arthur Miller. Dir. Calvin McLean. Center for the Performing
Arts, Normal, IL. 27 Sept. 2005. Performance.

86. Work of Art, Photograph, or Musical Composition—MLA

Cassatt, Mary. *La Toilette.* 1890. Oil on canvas. Art Institute of Chicago.

Mydans, Carl. *General Douglas MacArthur Landing at Luzon,* 1945. Gelatin silver print. Soho Triad Fine Art Gallery, New York. 21 Oct.-28 Nov. 1999.

Don't underline or put in quotation marks music identified only by form, number, and key.

Schubert, Franz. Symphony no. 8 in B minor. Print.

Italicize any work that has a title, such as an opera or ballet or a named symphony.

Schubert, Franz. *Unfinished Symphony.* Print.

To cite a published score, use the following format.

Schubert, Franz. *Symphony in B Minor (Unfinished).* Ed. Martin Cusid. New
York: Norton, 1971. Print.

87. Television or Radio Program—MLA

Include at least the title of the program or series (underlined), the network,
the local station and its city, and the date of the broadcast.

*Not for Ourselves Alone: The Story of Elizabeth Cady Stanton and Susan B.
Anthony.* Writ. Andrei Burns. Perf. Julie Harris, Ronnie Gilbert, and Sally
Kellerman. Prod. Paul Barnes and Andrei Burns. PBS. WNET, New York.
8 Nov. 1999. Television.

Supply the title of a specific episode (if any) in quotation marks before the title
of the program (italicized) and the title of the series (if any) neither italicized
nor in quotation marks.

"The Middle of Nowhere." *This American Life.* Prod. Ira Glass. Chicago Public
Radio. KCFR-AM, Denver. 7 Dec. 2007. Radio.

Note that many radio programs also exist as podcasts (see item 72).

88. Image or Photograph in a Print Publication—MLA

To cite an image or a photograph that appears as part of a print publication (perhaps as an illustration for an article), give the photographer (if known), the
title or caption of the image, and complete publication information, as for an
article. If the image has no title, provide a brief description.

Greene, Herb. "Grace Slick." *Rolling Stone* 30 Sept. 2004: 102. Print.

MLA

89. Advertisement—MLA

American Airlines. Advertisement. ABC. 24 Aug. 2003. Television.

Canon Digital Cameras. Advertisement. *Time* 2 June 2003: 77. Print.

90. Video Game or Software—MLA

Guitar Hero III: Legends of Rock. Santa Monica: Activision, 2007.

91. Nonperiodical Publications on CD, DVD, or Magnetic Tape—MLA

Citations for publications on DVD, CD-ROM, or other recording formats follow guidelines for print publications, with two additions: list the publication medium (for example, *CD*), and give the vendor's name.

Perl, Sondra. *Felt Sense: Guidelines for Composing.* Portsmouth: Boynton, 2004.
     CD.

92. Materials on CD or DVD with a Print Version—MLA

Before the maturity of the Internet, many print materials were previously stored on CD-ROMs.

"The Price Is Right." *Time* 20 Jan. 1992: 38. *Time Man of the Year.* CD-ROM. New
     York: Compact, 1993.

Information for the print version ends with the article's page number, 38. The title of the CD-ROM is *Time Man of the Year,* its producer is the publisher Compact, and its copyright year is 1993. Both the title of the print publication and the title of the CD-ROM are italicized.

93. Materials on CD or DVD with No Print Version—MLA

"Artificial Intelligence." *Encarta 2003.* CD-ROM. Redmond: Microsoft, 2003.

Encarta 2003 is a CD-ROM encyclopedia with no print version. "Artificial Intelligence" is the title of an article in *Encarta 2003.*

94. Book in Digital Format—MLA

Many books are now available for downloading from the Internet in digital format, to be read on special players.

Gilbert, Elizabeth. *Eat, Pray, Love.* New York: Viking, 2007. Kindle Edition.

95. PowerPoint or Similar Presentation—MLA

Delyser, Ariel. "Political Movements in the Philippines." University of Denver.
     7 Apr. 2006. PowerPoint.

MLA

96. Work in More Than One Publication Medium—MLA

Shamoon, Linda, et al., eds. *Coming of Age: The Advanced Writing Curriculum. Coming of Age Course Descriptions.* Portsmouth: Boynton, 2000. CD-ROM, print.

This book and CD-ROM come together. Each has its own title, but the publication information—*Portsmouth: Boynton, 2000*—applies to both.

36d.2 Using content or bibliographic notes in MLA style

In MLA style, footnotes or endnotes serve two specific purposes: (1) You can use them for content (ideas and information) that does not fit into your paper but is still worth relating; and (2) you can use them for bibliographic information that would intrude if you were to include it in your text. Place a note number at the end of a sentence, if possible. Put it after any punctuation mark except the dash. Do not put any space before a note number, and put one space after it. Raise the note number a little above the line of words, as shown in the following examples.

TEXT OF PAPER

Eudora Welty's literary biography, *One Writer's Beginnings*, shows us how both the inner world of self and the outer world of family and place form a writer's imagination.[1]

CONTENT NOTE—MLA

[1]Welty, who valued her privacy, always resisted investigation of her life. However, at the age of seventy-four, she chose to present her own autobiographical reflections in a series of lectures at Harvard University.

TEXT OF PAPER

Barbara Randolph believes that enthusiasm is contagious (65).[1] Many psychologists have found that panic, fear, and rage spread more quickly in crowds than positive emotions do, however.

BIBLIOGRAPHIC NOTE—MLA

[1]Others who agree with Randolph include Thurman 21, 84, 155; Kelley 421-25; and Brookes 65-76.

36e A student's MLA-style research paper

36e.1 Researching and writing the paper

The following is student writer Andrei Gurov's assignment for an MLA-style research paper.

MLA

Write an MLA-style research paper on the general subject of "memory." You are required to write 1,800 to 2,000 words, using a variety of sources. Your final paper is due in six weeks. Interim deadlines for parts of the work will be announced. To complete this assignment, you need to engage in three interrelated processes: conducting research, understanding the results of that research, and writing a paper based on the first two processes. Consult the *Simon & Schuster Handbook for Writers,* especially Chapters 33–35 for guidance on how to complete this assignment, and Chapter 36 for guidance on MLA-style parenthetical citations and Works Cited entries. You may also consult the MLA Web site at http://www.mla.org.

Andrei's instructor also assigned a bonus exercise asking students to chronicle their research processes in a brief informal narrative. This exercise could help students see what worked well for them and what didn't, and then they could apply that knowledge when researching future papers. The following is from Andrei's narrative about how he researched his topic and sources for his MLA-style paper about déjà vu.

I started by immediately filling in the research schedule suggested in section 33b of our handbook. I also looked for ideas in Box 33.2: Finding General Ideas for Research. In the past, brainstorming has worked well for me, so I just started listing anything that came to mind about the assigned topic of "memory" (e.g., how much memory is on my iPod, past vacations, my sister's wedding, relatives, when I broke my collarbone, forgetfulness, flashbacks). I had a lot of personal memories to write about, but those wouldn't have worked because I couldn't have done formal research on them.

So, I turned to the Web and searched Google using the keyword "memory." The computer screen practically exploded

continued >>

with 326 million hits, and they generally pointed to four large categories: brain memory, computer memory, entertainment venues, and music. I didn't expect so many directions. In an attempt to narrow this down, I tried some Boolean NOT instructions, but even eliminating "computer + music + entertainment + girls" made little difference. Then I realized I hadn't used Google Scholar, which has been recommended for academic research. So, I tried again, and although I reduced the number of hits, I still would've spent a lifetime trying to sort through all of these resources.

I knew I needed something else to spark ideas. As advised by Box 33.2 in my handbook, I decided to flip through other textbooks. My anthropology book came with a study skills guide that offered some tips about memory retention. That could've been a topic, but it really didn't interest me enough to want to learn more about it. My intro sociology textbook had some information about eyewitness testimony and false memory--both pretty interesting, so I kept those topics in reserve. Then, a chapter in my intro psychology textbook (Saul Kassin's *Psychology*, 4th ed.) turned up a topic that I'd always been curious about: déjà vu. I'd experienced that weird feeling of being somewhere before--even though I'd never been there in my life--and was really curious to know what caused it. So, I decided to narrow my formal research question to "What is known today about the experience of déjà vu?"

Back in front of the computer, I did online searches using "déjà vu." Google Scholar brought up 14 million hits. AltaVista brought up only music DVDs. I went to good old Yahoo and got

continued >>

MLA

mostly music DVDs along with a few popular press articles. Searching with Mozilla Firefox, I typed in "memory + deja vu" and got 726,000 hits, which, under the circumstances, seemed relatively small. But very few of the resources seemed as relevant as the ones on the first few pages of Google Scholar. To help me determine how scholarly many of the online resources were, I went to the library and skimmed Alan S. Brown's 2004 scholarly book *The Déjà Vu Experience* and Weiten's *Psychology: Themes and Variations*. I found I'd been fooled three times out of eleven. When I read the printouts, I knew almost immediately that two of the three unreliable sources were bad, but figuring out the third one took me a while longer.

In my research, I took notes and carefully recorded my sources. (I created a lot of new documents on my computer and gave each a descriptive name that I'd understand.) Then, I organized the notes into folders. At that point, I felt ready to do some planning. I knew my audience was mainly my instructor, but because my first draft was going to be peer-edited, I wanted to make sure my paper also appealed to other students in my class. I wasn't too sure about which purpose I wanted to tackle. Originally, I had wanted to write with a persuasive purpose and argue against the concept of déjà vu having anything to do with witchcraft, reincarnation, and that stuff. But the more I read, the more I became convinced that I wanted to educate people about the scientific aspects of déjà vu experiences. Therefore, I switched to an informative purpose.

I used the note documents that I had created, making sure that I kept track of when I was quoting, summarizing,

continued >>

and paraphrasing (I hardly paraphrased at all). As much as possible, I kept revising so that I could work into my sentences the author and document title because I preferred to include only page numbers in my parenthetical citations. Having had a bad experience in high school with losing track of my sources, I kept a separate document as my working bibliography, which would make it easier to list each of my sources in my Works Cited list at the end of my paper.

At this stage, I felt ready to write my first draft. I sat on the floor and surrounded myself with all my printed notes sorted into categories. I then wrote a very rough draft with numbers where I thought notes would fit. Next, I went to the computer and strung my paper together. Unfortunately, but not too surprisingly, my first draft ran on for too many pages. It was time to cut. My major cuts had to do with (a) at least two pages about other terms related to déjà vu but not the same as déjà vu, and (b) a table reporting an unscientific survey I had taken of the déjà vu memories of each member in a family of fifteen.

I then worked through the paper and worked on conciseness of language (I found lots of repetition) and tried to draft my concluding paragraph. It was a struggle. I had to synthesize complicated material in a fairly limited space. I kept wanting to introduce new information, but I knew that would only set me off track and confuse readers. If you look at the next page of this narrative, you'll see my first try at a concluding paragraph, which I show in block format. (You can compare it with the one in my final draft at the end of my paper.) [Page 652.] I rejected it because it's closer to a conclusion

continued >>

that might work, if it were better organized, at the end of a paper about the paranormal and déjà vu. It definitely didn't work for the paper I wrote.

> We know more today than we did hundreds of years ago about the phenomenon of déjà vu. But there is more to be learned. In the last two decades, the real investigations have begun. Alan S. Brown seems to be the researcher who has led the field into an age of enlightenment, and many more mentioned in this paper are his fellow researchers. No longer can people settle for explanations that involve reincarnation and visits from the dead. No longer can we accept that spirits from the "other side" are coming back to visit us in the form of visions.

Overall, my research and writing process went well. In giving an account of it, I've simplified the details to keep the assignment brief. However, I will say that learning how to brainstorm ideas and how to do keyword searches effectively definitely saved me some anxiety, time, and effort in getting the topic and the information I needed.

36e.2 Formatting the MLA-style research paper

TITLE PAGE

MLA style doesn't call for a title page for research papers or any other types of writing. Many instructors, however, do require one. If you're asked to use a title page, follow the format of the example on page 635. Never assign a page number to a title page.

Whether or not you use a title page, use the headings shown on the first page of the sample research paper on page 638. If you're required to hand in a formal outline with your paper, place the outline after the title page, unless told to do otherwise by your instructor.

Title page of Andrei Gurov's MLA-style research paper

MLA style doesn't call for a title page; however, many instructor's who do require one follow this format.

One-third down from top of page

Déjà Vu: At Last a Subject for Serious Study

Double-space title if more than one line

by

Andrei Gurov

Lowercase "by" and double-space

Professor Ryan

University of Middle Byrd

English 101, Section A4

12 December 2007

Instructor

Institution

Course and section

Date order: day month year

MLA

MLA

PAGE 1 OF PAPER WITH OR WITHOUT A TITLE PAGE

On the first page of your paper, in the upper right corner, type your last name, followed by a space, and then followed by the numeral 1 placed one-half inch below the top edge of the page and one inch in from the right margin. Next, at the left margin, one inch in from the left side, type the four lines with the information shown on the first page of the sample paper on page 638. Finally, type your paper's title centered one double space below the last of the four lines that you just finished typing flush left.

Double-space after the title, and start your paper, indenting the first line of the first—and all—paragraphs five character spaces. The indent in Microsoft Word is a hanging indent of 0.5″ for "first line."

OUTLINES

Even though MLA doesn't officially endorse using outlines, some instructors, including Andrei Gurov's, require that students submit formal outlines with their research papers. In this handbook, you'll find examples of two formal outlines in section 2f. The traditional formal outline follows long-established conventions for using numbers and letters to show relationships among ideas. A less traditional formal outline includes these elements but also includes the planned content for a research paper's introductory and concluding paragraphs. Both the traditional and the less traditional outlines can be sentence outlines (composed entirely of complete sentences) or topic outlines (composed only of words and phrases). In your outlines, however, never mix the two styles.

The outline on page 637 is for Andrei Gurov's research paper about déjà vu. To format the outline, he used the less traditional outline, which was what his instructor preferred and asked her class to use. In the name-page number line in the upper right corner of his outline, Andrei typed his last name, left one space, and then typed the lowercase Roman numeral *i* for the page number, the conventional way of indicating any page that comes before the first page of the essay itself. He placed that information one-half inch from the top of the page and made sure it ended one inch in from the right edge of the paper. He then left a half-inch space below the name-number heading and centered the word *Outline*. The thesis statement in the outline matches the last sentence of the first paragraph of his paper (see p. 638).

Even if your instructor doesn't require an outline, you'll probably find that developing one to go with a later draft of your paper will help you clarify the overall organization and logic of your research paper (or, indeed, any essay you write). Examining the paper's "skeleton" enables you to focus on the overall shape of the paper and may reveal gaps in your paper's development that you can fill in.

PAGE NUMBERING AFTER THE FIRST PAGE OF THE PAPER

In the upper right corner, type your last name, followed by a space, and then followed by the Arabic numeral of the page in sequence (2, 3, and so on). Place

MLA

1"

Outline

Double-space

I. Introduction

  A. The meaning of the term déjà vu

  B. Thesis statement: Although a few people today still
prefer to believe that feelings of déjà vu have
mysterious and supernatural origins, recent research
in cognitive psychology and the neurosciences has
shed much rational light on the phenomenon.

II. Percentage of people who report experiencing déjà vu

III. Misunderstandings of the phenomenon of déjà vu

  A. Precognition

  B. False memory

IV. New psychological and medical theories of déjà vu

  A. Human sight's two pathways

  B. Implanted memories

    1. Natural: from old memories long forgotten

    2. Manipulated: from subliminal stimulation

    3. Inattentional blindness

V. Conclusion

  A. Many years of paranormal explanations of déjà vu

  B. Scientific research after 1980

  C. Much promise for further research

this name-number heading one-half inch below the top edge of the page and one inch in from the right margin. Number the pages consecutively, including the last page of your Works Cited. Many writers use the "header and footer" word-processing function that inserts last names and sequential page numbers, updating automatically. This feature is especially convenient during revision, when your writing causes your pages to fall differently than they originally did.

MLA

↕ 1"

Andrei Gurov

Professor Ryan

English 101, Section A4

12 December 2007

Put identifying
information in
upper left corner.

Use 1/2-inch
top margin,
1-inch bottom
and side
margins;
double-space
throughout.

↕ ½"
Gurov 1   1

Center title.   Déjà Vu: At Last a Subject for Serious Study

"Brain hiccup" might be another name for *déjà vu*, French   2

for "already seen." During a moment of déjà vu, a person

relives an event that in reality is happening for the first time.

The hiccup metaphor seems apt because each modern

scientific explanation of the déjà vu phenomenon involves

a doubled event, as this paper will demonstrate. However,

such modern scientific work was long in coming. In his article

Quotation
marks around
phrases show
they appeared
separately in
the source.

"The Déjà Vu Illusion," today's leading researcher in the field,

Alan S. Brown at Southern Methodist University, states that

"for over 170 years, this most puzzling of memory illusions

has intrigued scholars" but was hampered when "during

The ellipsis in-
dicates words
omitted from
a quotation.

the behaviorist era . . . the plethora of parapsychological and

psychodynamic interpretations" multiplied rapidly (256). Thus,   3

notions of the supernatural and magic halted the scientific

study of déjà vu for almost two centuries. By the first quarter

of the twentieth century, it began again slowly. Although a   4

few people today still prefer to believe that feelings of déjà vu

have mysterious or supernatural origins, recent research in

cognitive psychology and the neurosciences has shed much

rational light on the phenomenon.

continued >>

(Proportions shown in this paper are adjusted to fit space limitations of this book. Follow
actual dimensions discussed in this book and your instructor's directions.)

COMMENTARY

1 **Computer tip.** Following MLA style, Andrei uses his last name and the page number as a header (meaning "at the top" of his pages) throughout the paper. He doesn't use a footer (meaning "at the bottom" of his pages). To do this, he accesses the "header and footer" option in the "View" choice on the toolbar in his Microsoft Word word processing program and inserts the proper information so that it will appear automatically on each page.

2 **Introductory strategy.** Andrei hopes to attract his readers' interest by making up the unusual phrase "brain hiccups," which ties into the dual visual processing that he describes later in his paper. He also refers briefly to the paranormal and immediately discredits it by quoting the leading modern researcher into déjà vu, Alan S. Brown.

3 **PROCESS NOTE:** I use a quotation from Brown's journal article "The Déjà Vu Illusion," so I include the page number in parentheses.

4 **Thesis statement.** The last sentence of Andrei's introductory paragraph is his THESIS STATEMENT. He drafted two preliminary thesis statements, shown in section 33l. The thesis statement is a bridge from his introduction to the rest of his paper and helps his readers anticipate the main message of his paper. All of his topic sentences have to tie into his thesis statement.

MLA

Header has student's last name and page number.

Some people report never having experienced déjà vu, and the percentages vary for the number of people who report having lived through at least one episode of it. In 2004, Brown reports that of the subjects he has interviewed, an average of 66 percent say that they have had one or more déjà vu experiences during their lives (*Experience* 33). However, in early 2005 in "Strangely Familiar," Uwe Wolfradt reports that "various studies indicate that from 50 to 90 percent of the people [studied] can recall having had at least one such déjà vu incident in their lives."

World Wide Web source has no page numbers or paragraph numbers.

Perhaps part of the reason for this variation in the range of percentages stems from a general misunderstanding of the phrase *déjà vu*, even by some of the earlier scientific researchers twenty or more years ago. Indeed, in today's society, people throw around the term *déjà vu* without much thought. For example, it is fairly common for someone to see or hear about an event and then say, "Wow. This is déjà vu. I had a dream that this exact same thing happened." However, dreaming about an event ahead of time is a different phenomenon known as *precognition*, which relates to the paranormal experience of extrasensory perception. To date, precognition has never been scientifically demonstrated. As Johnson explains about dreams, however,

Use block indent of 1-inch (or ten spaces) for a quotation longer than four typed lines.

> . . . there is usually very little "data," evidence, or documentation to confirm that a Precognition has taken place. If a person learns about some disaster and THEN [author's emphasis] tells people that he/she has foreseen it the day before, that may or may not

continued >>

COMMENTARY

5 **Summarizing and citing a source by an author of two different sources used in this paper.** Andrei summarizes the percentage information that Brown gives in his book *The Déjà Vu Experience.* Then Andrei cites his source with a shortened title and page number. He includes a title because he has been drawing on two of Brown's writings for this paper—one book and one journal article that he accesses online—and he knows that he needs to make a clear distinction between them whenever he cites them.

6 **The writer inserting words to fit a quotation into the writer's sentence.** Nothing is wrong with Uwe Wolfradt's sentence, but Andrei needs to add the word *studied* to make the meaning clear within his research paper. To do this in proper MLA form, Andrei put his added word in brackets to indicate that he is adding the word—that is, the word is not in the original text by Uwe Wolfradt.

7 **Figuring out a page number from an online source.** Andrei found the article "Strangely Familiar" by Uwe Wolfradt online through his search using http://www.googlescholar.com. Even though the citation for the article on the opening screen page says that the page spread is pages 32–37, and Andrei might feel quite safe in assuming that his information is on the first page—namely, page 32—he can't be sure, so he can't include a page number.

8 **PROCESS NOTE:** I kept being distracted about using the word *déjà vu* as a term or as the name of an experience. As I was drafting, I purposely overlooked the problem, but I circled each use so that I could tackle the issue on my final draft.

9 **PROCESS NOTE:** I'm fairly certain that my instructor will know that this quotation is not from a source, but it's rather one I made up from everyday speech.

10 **No capital letter to start block-indented quotation.** Andrei took this quotation from the middle of a sentence in the source, so he can't start it with a capital letter. The ellipsis indicates he omitted words to make the quotation fit stylistically.

11 **How "[author's emphasis]" is used.** Whenever a source uses a typographical technique of emphasis—such as italics or all capital letters—the writer who quotes that source is required to indicate that the emphasis belongs to the source, not to the writer. In MLA style, "[author's emphasis]" is required so that the reader won't think the emphasis has been made by the writer of the paper.

MLA

Gurov 3

be true, because there is usually not corroborative   12

confirmation of what the person claims.

Thus, precognition, a phenomenon talked about

frequently but one that has never held up under scientific

scrutiny, is definitely not the same as déjà vu.

False memory is another phenomenon mislabeled *déjà*

vu. It happens when people are convinced that certain events

took place in their lives, even though the events never

happened. This occurs when people have strong memories of

many unrelated occurrences that suddenly come together into

a whole that's very close to the current experience. It seems

Introductory like a déjà vu experience. This occurs from the "converging

phrase

smoothly elements of many different but related experiences. When this

leads into

direct abstract representation, which has emerged strictly from the

quotation. melding together of strongly associated elements, happens to

correspond to the present experience, a déjà vu may be the

outcome" (Brown, *Experience* 160). To illustrate lab-induced   13

false memory, Brown in *Experience* cites investigations in   14

which subjects are shown lists of words related to sleep;

however, the word *sleep* itself is not on the list. In recalling

the list of words, most subjects insist that the word *sleep* was

indeed on the list, which means that the memory of a word that

was never there is false memory. This is exactly what happens

when well-intentioned eyewitnesses believe they recall certain

criminal acts even though, in fact, they never saw or

Put only page experienced the events at all (159).

number in

parentheses In the last twenty years especially, new theories

when author

is named have come to the fore as a result of rigorous work from

in text. psychological and medical points of view. In *Experience*,   15

Brown surveys the literature and concludes that this relatively

continued >>

MLA

COMMENTARY

12 **MLA style for a block-indent quotation.** MLA style requires that when a quotation takes up four or more lines in a research paper that it be set off in a block. A block indent calls for all lines to be indented ten spaces from the left margin. The quoted material in the block has to end with a period. Then the source information has to come after the period in parentheses. Because Andrei's online source did not provide page, paragraphs, or screen numbers, he could not include a parenthetical citation after the quotation.

13 **PROCESS NOTE:** I want to use Brown in two different ways in this paragraph because I've drawn on Brown as a major reference throughout my paper. I don't want to only use quotations or only summaries. Here I use a quotation but don't call attention to the source. I place all source information in parentheses after the end of the quotation. I include a shortened version of the title of the source because I've used two different sources by the same author to write this paper.

14 **PROCESS NOTE:** To follow up on Process Note 13, this time I summarize Brown's words and fit in his name and the shortened title of the source.

15 **PROCESS NOTE:** I now need to write a paragraph of transition from what was *not* déjà vu to what was. My plan is to write about two types of phenomena that aren't déjà vu, and then write about three types of phenomena that are. I checked my outline to make sure I was adhering to my plan.

MLA

Gurov 4

young field of investigation is dividing itself into four categories: (1) dual processing, (2) memory, (3) neurological, and (4) attentional. This paper briefly discusses the first and second as each relates to the third. Next, I discuss the fourth as it relates to the second.

16

Brain-based studies of the human sense of sight are one heavily researched theory of déjà vu that has been partially explained in the last two decades. Such studies focus on the dual pathways by which the sight of an event reaches the brain (Glenn; Carey F1). For example, the left hemisphere processes information from the right eye and the right hemisphere processes information from the left eye. The brain is incapable of storing data with respect to time and is only able to "see" events in relation to others. Each eye interprets data separately, at the same precise time. According to research, the human brain can perceive two visual stimuli at one instant as long as they are "seen" less than 25 milliseconds apart. Since the human brain is capable of interpreting both signals within this time, when events are perceived normally, they are seen and recognized by the brain as one single event (Weiten 69, 97-99, 211).

17

18

Put author and page number in parentheses when author is not named in the sentence.

Paragraph summarizes several pages of source material, as parenthetical citation shows.

Occasionally, however, the neurological impulses that carry data from each eye to the brain are delayed. As Johnson explains, the person might be fatigued or have had his or her attention seriously distracted (as when crossing the street at a dangerous intersection). As a result, one signal may reach the brain in under 25 milliseconds, while the other signal is slowed and reaches the brain slightly more than 25 milliseconds later. Even a few milliseconds' delay makes the second incoming signal arrive late--and, without fail, the brain interprets the

19

continued >>

COMMENTARY

16 PROCESS NOTE: Every time I type the word *attentional* (using Microsoft Word) into my paper, a red wavy line pops up under it, which means a misspelling. However, because the word is spelled that way consistently in all my sources, I've just ignored the red wavy line and added the word, with confidence, to my personal dictionary provided by the Microsoft Word program.

17 Two sources for one piece of information. When two sources contain the same information, MLA style permits the citing of both sources. Each source is given with its page number; don't provide a page number if you're using a one-page source or an online source with no page numbers. A semicolon divides the sources.

18 Words used in a nonliteral way. The words *see* and *seen* here do not carry their literal meaning related to conscious sight. Rather, they refer to subconscious sight. Therefore, they belong in quotation marks.

19 PROCESS NOTE: Earlier in the paper, I devoted two paragraphs to each of two non-déjà vu topics. Now, I'm giving more attention to each of the three types of legitimate déjà vu phenomena that I've chosen to discuss (dual pathways of sight, implanted memories, and inattentional blindness). This paragraph is the second I'm writing about dual pathways of sight.

MLA

Gurov 5

stimuli as two separate events rather than one event. The person thus has the sensation of having seen the event before because the brain has recognized the milliseconds-later event as a memory.

Implanted memories is another well-researched 20
explanation for the déjà vu phenomenon. Examples of this originate in both the natural and the lab-induced experiences of people. For instance, perhaps a person walks into the kitchen of a new friend for the first time and, although the person has never been there before, the person feels certain that he or she has. With hypnosis and other techniques, researchers could uncover that the cupboards are almost exactly like those that the person had forgotten were in the kitchen of the person's grandparents' house and that the scent of baking apple pie is identical to the smell the person loved when walking into the grandparents' home during holidays (Carey F1).

Thomas McHugh, a researcher at MIT, believes he has even discovered the specific "memory circuit" in the brain that is the source of this kind of déjà vu (Lemonick). This circuit allows people to complete memories with just a single cue. For example, you can remember much about a football game you saw even if someone just mentions the two teams involved. Sometimes, however, the circuit "misfires," and it signals that a new memory is actually part of the pattern of an old one.

Wolfradt describes a lab-induced experiment in which 21
psychologist Larry L. Jacoby in 1989 manipulated a group of subjects so that he could implant a memory that would lead to a déjà vu experience for each of them. He arranged for his subjects to assemble in a room equipped with a screen in front. He flashed on the screen one word so quickly that no one was

continued >>

MLA

COMMENTARY

20 **PROCESS NOTE:** I'm now starting to write about the second of the three types of déjà vu that I'm covering in this paper. I'm intentionally using the word *another* in my topic sentence to bridge from dual pathways of sight to implanted memories. Because there are so many concepts and examples of them in this paper, I'm trying to be very clear in my transitions.

21 **PROCESS NOTE:** Specific examples are very important to me as I write this paper. It's far too easy for me to write on and on about theory and concepts. As I'm writing this paper, I find myself often cutting generalizations to make room for details. When I've read my sophomore and junior friends' papers from when they were freshmen, I'm surprised to see how few specifics and concrete details they put in their freshman composition papers—and their grades and the comments they got reflect this fact.

Gurov 6

consciously aware they had seen the word. Jacoby was certain, however, that the visual centers of the brain of each subject had indeed "seen" the word. Later, when he flashed the word leaving it on the screen long enough for the subjects to consciously see it, everyone indicated they had seen the word somewhere before. All the subjects were firmly convinced that the first time they had seen the word, it absolutely was not on the screen at the front of the room they were in. Some became annoyed at being asked over and over. Since Jacoby's work, lab-induced memory research has become very popular in psychology. In fact, it has been given its own name: *priming*.

Inattention, or what some researchers call "inattentional blindness," is also an extensively researched explanation for the déjà vu experience. Sometimes people can see objects without any impediment right before them but still not process the objects because they're paying attention to something else (Brown, *Experience* 181). The distraction might be daydreaming, a sudden lowering of energy, or simply being drawn to another object in the environment. As David Glenn explains in "The Tease of Memory":

> Imagine that you drive through an unfamiliar town but pay little attention because you're talking on a cellphone [sic]. If you then drive back down the same streets a few moments later, this time focusing on the landscape, you might be prone to experience déjà vu. During your second pass, the visual information is consciously processed in the hippocampus [of the brain] but feels falsely "old"

22

23

continued >>

COMMENTARY

22 **PROCESS NOTE:** When I wrote my first draft, I felt that my discussion of implanted memories was pretty weak. I did some further research and was happy to find enough information to write this additional paragraph in my second draft. It is, to me, a dramatic demonstration of laboratory-manipulated implanted memory.

23 **Using [sic].** This quotation spells "cell phone" as one word. Therefore, Andrei uses [sic] to tell his readers that he knows this is a misspelling.

because the images from your earlier drive still
linger in your short term memory.   24
The busy lifestyle today would seem to lead to many
distractions of perception and thus to frequent experiences of
déjà vu; however, these are no more frequently reported than
any other causes reported concerning déjà vu.

One compelling laboratory experiment studying   25
inattention is described by Carey in "Déjà Vu: If It All Seems
Familiar, There May Be a Reason." He recounts a test with
many college students from Duke University in Durham, North
Carolina. The students were asked to look at a group of
photographs of the campus of Southern Methodist University in
Dallas, Texas, that were flashed before them at a very quick
speed. A small black or white cross was superimposed on each
photograph, and the students were instructed to find the cross
and focus on it (F6). Brown in *Experience* explains that the
researchers assumed that the quick speed at which the
photographs had been shown would result in no one's having
noticed the background scenes. A week's time passed, and
the same students were shown the pictures again, this time
without the crosses. Almost all insisted that they had been to
the college campus shown in the photos, which was physically
impossible for that many students since they lived in Durham,
North Carolina, and the college in the photographs was in
Dallas, Texas (182-83). This means that the scenes in the
photographs did indeed register in the visual memories of the
students in spite of the quick speed and the distraction of
looking only for the crosses.

continued >>

COMMENTARY

24 **PROCESS NOTE:** Here's how I wasted a day of researching for this paper. I know it's not unusual for freshmen to go off the topic and waste their time, so I am trying to stay very conscious of what I am doing so that I can learn what NOT to do in the future. What happened was that I was becoming aware that psychologists have named many phenomena that are closely related to déjà vu, each somewhat different from it and from each other. For example, Brown in *Experience* names over twenty relatives of déjà vu, while other sources name as few as eight. This captured my interest, but once I got into writing up the information, I began to realize that I was going off my topic. I'll list here some that had potential but that, in the end, I never used in my paper:

- **Déjà eprouvé:** A sense that this act has already been attempted and didn't work out.

- **Déjà senti:** A mental feeling that one is *feeling* something again. It is limited to feeling, and does not include a sense of being in a place.

- **Déjà visité:** The knowledge of a large place, such as an entire village, but knowing still that one has never been there.

- **Jamais vu:** This is the opposite of déjà vu. Even though one knows something has happened before, the experience feels completely unfamiliar.

- **Presque vu:** This is the sense of almost, but not quite, remembering something—as in "it's on the tip of my tongue."

25 **PROCESS NOTE:** To stay on the topic, I needed a third type of déjà vu—for which I used inattentional blindness—to drive home my thesis statement.

MLA

Gurov 8

26

The worlds of psychology and neurology have learned much since the age of paranormal interpretations of déjà vu experiences, starting around 1935. That is when rational science energetically began its disciplined investigations of brain-based origins of the déjà vu phenomenon. Concepts such as dual processing of sight, implanted memories, and inattentional blindness, among other theories, have gone far in opening the door to the possibilities of many more inventive theories to explain incidents of déjà vu. The leading researcher in the field today, Alan S. Brown, is among the strongest voices urging a vast expansion of investigations into this still relatively unexplored phenomenon. He is optimistic this will happen, given his whimsical remark to Carlin Flora of *Psychology Today:* "We are always fascinated when the brain goes haywire."

Concluding paragraph summarizes paper.

continued >>

COMMENTARY

26 **PROCESS NOTE:** In my second draft, I decided to check whether all my topic sentences tied together with each other. I remembered that neither the introductory nor the concluding paragraphs have topic sentences. Here's a list of my thesis and topic sentences.

THESIS STATEMENT: Although a few people today still prefer to believe that feelings of déjà vu have mysterious or supernatural origins, recent research in cognitive psychology and the neurosciences has shed much rational light on the phenomenon.

- Some people report never having experienced déjà vu, and the percentages vary for the number of people who report having lived through at least one episode of it.

- Perhaps part of the reason for this variation in the range of percentages stems from a general misunderstanding of the phrase *déjà vu,* even by some of the earlier scientific researchers twenty or more years ago.

- False memory is another phenomenon mislabeled *déjà vu.*

- In the last twenty years especially, new theories have come to the fore as a result of rigorous work from psychological and medical points of view.

- Brain-based studies of the human sense of sight are one heavily researched theory of déjà vu that has been partially explained in the last two decades.

- Occasionally, however, the neurological impulses that carry data from each eye to the brain are delayed.

- Implanted memories is another well-researched explanation for the déjà vu phenomenon.

- Wolfradt describes a lab-induced experiment in which psychologist Larry L. Jacoby in 1989 manipulated a group of subjects so that he could implant a memory that would lead to a déjà vu experience for each of them.

- Inattention, or what some researchers call "inattentional blindness," is also an extensively researched explanation for the déjà vu experience.

- One compelling laboratory experiment studying inattention is described by Carey in "Déjà Vu: If It All Seems Familiar, There May Be a Reason."

MLA

Gurov 9

Works Cited

Brown, Alan S. *The Déjà Vu Experience: Essays in Cognitive Psychology.* New York: Psychology, 2004. Print.

--- . "The Déjà Vu Illusion." *Current Directions in Psychological Science* 13.6 (2004): 256-59. Print.

Carey, Benedict. "Déjà Vu: If It All Seems Familiar, There May Be a Reason." *New York Times* 14 Sept. 2004: F1+. *LexisNexis.* Web. 11 Nov. 2007.

Flora, Carlin. "Giving Déjà Vu Its Due." *Psychology Today* Mar.-Apr. 2005: 27. *Academic Search Premier.* Web. 7 Nov. 2007.

Glenn, David. "The Tease of Memory." *Chronicle of Higher Education* 23 July 2004: A12. Print.

Johnson, C. "A Theory on the Déjà Vu Phenomenon." 8 Dec. 2001. Web. 20 Nov. 2007.

Lemonick, Michael D. "Explaining Déjà Vu." *Time* 20 Aug. 2007. *Academic Search Premier.* Web. 5 Dec. 2007.

Thompson, Rebecca G., et al. "Persistent Déjà Vu: A Disorder of Memory." *International Journal of Geriatric Psychiatry* 19.9 (2004): 906-07. Print.

Weiten, Wayne. *Psychology: Themes and Variations.* Belmont: Wadsworth, 2005. Print.

Wolfradt, Uwe. "Strangely Familiar." *Scientific American Mind* 16.1 (2005): 32-37. *Academic Search Elite.* Web. 7 Nov. 2007.

Works Cited begins on a new page.

Double-space throughout.

List sources in alphabetical order.

27

28

29

30

MLA

COMMENTARY

27 **Working versus final bibliography.** In keeping with MLA style, Andrei developed a working bibliography using those sources referred to in his research paper. His bibliography contained over twice the number of sources in his Works Cited. He dropped sources he considered less authoritative and ones that were not specifically targeted to the subjects that he chose to discuss related to déjà vu.

28 **Balance of source types.** Andrei's final list of Works Cited contains ten works, five from online databases and five from print sources—a proportion that is typical of today's college-level research papers.

29 **What is LexisNexis?** LexisNexis is an online database, available to students through their college library, that contains a large number of research and other scholarly collections, including the LexisNexis Academic and Library Solutions. Originally a document service for law students and lawyers, it now includes areas of study such as government, business, and environmental issues.

30 **What is Academic Search Premier?** Academic Search Premier is a widely used online database in English studies and the humanities. It's available to students through their college library and gives access to over one hundred reference databases, thousands of online journals, lists of book titles at some libraries, linking services, and much more.

For more help with your writing, grammar, and research, go to **www.mycomplab.com**

mycomplab

37

APA Documentation with Case Study

Following are two directories that point you to guidance you'll find in this chapter. The first lists examples of APA in-text citations. The second lists examples of APA References entries.

APA STYLE DIRECTORY

APA

37a What is APA documentation style?

The American Psychological Association (APA) sponsors a DOCUMENTATION system widely used in the social sciences. APA style involves two equally important features that need to appear in research papers.

1. Within the body of your paper, use **in-text citations,** in parentheses, to acknowledge your SOURCES. This chapter explains the proper way to provide APA in-text citations. Section 37b explains how they work, and section 37c shows sixteen models, each of which gives one or more examples of different types of sources.

2. At the end of your paper, provide a list of the sources you used—and only those sources. Title this list, which contains complete bibliographic information about each source, **References.** It needs to appear on a separate page at the end of your research paper. It includes only the sources you've actually used in your paper, not any you've consulted but haven't used. Section 37f gives instructions for

composing your References pages, followed by seventy-five models, each based on a different kind of source (book, article, Web site, and so on) that you might use.

For an example of a research paper that uses APA style in-text citations in parentheses and a References list, see section 37h. As you read the paper, notice how the two requirements for crediting sources work together so that readers can learn the precise origin of the material that is quoted, paraphrased, and summarized.

37b   What are APA parenthetical in-text citations?

The APA-STYLE DOCUMENTATION guidelines here follow the recommendations of the *Publication Manual of the American Psychological Association,* Fifth Edition (Washington, DC: American Psychological Association, 2001) and *APA Style Guide to Electronic References* (Washington, DC: American Psychological Association, 2007). For possible updates to information, you may wish to check the APA's Web site at http://www.apastyle.org.

APA style requires parenthetical IN-TEXT CITATIONS that identify a SOURCE by the author's name (or a shortened version of the title if there is no author) and the copyright year. For readability and a good writing style, you can often incorporate the name, and sometimes the year, into your sentence. Otherwise, place this information in parentheses, located as close as possible to the material you quote, paraphrase, or summarize. Your goal is to tell readers precisely where they can find the original material.

APA style requires page numbers for DIRECT QUOTATIONS and recommends them for PARAPHRASES and SUMMARIES. Some instructors expect you to give page references for paraphrases and summaries, and others don't; so find out your instructor's preference to avoid any problems in properly crediting your sources.

Put page numbers in parentheses, using the abbreviation *p.* before a single page number and *pp.* when the material you're citing falls on more than one page. For a direct quotation from an electronic source that numbers paragraphs, give the paragraph number (or numbers). Handle paragraph numbers as you do page numbers, but use *para.* or ¶ (the symbol for paragraph) rather than *p.* or *pp.*

The APA *Publication Manual* recommends that if you refer to a work more than once in a paragraph, you give the author's name and the date at the first mention and then give only the name after that. An exception occurs if you're citing two or more works by the same author, or if two or more authors have the same last name. In such cases, each separate citation must include the date to identify which work you're citing.

37c What are APA guidelines for in-text citations?

The following numbered examples show how to cite various kinds of sources in the body of your research paper. Remember, though, that you often can introduce source names, including titles when necessary, and sometimes even years, in your own sentences rather than in the parenthetical IN-TEXT CITATIONS.

1. Paraphrased or Summarized Source—APA

People from the Mediterranean prefer an elbow-to-shoulder distance from each other (Morris, 1977). [Author name and date cited in parentheses; note comma.]

Desmond Morris (1977) notes that people from the Mediterranean prefer an elbow-to-shoulder distance from each other. [Author name cited in text; date cited in parentheses.]

2. Source of a Short Quotation—APA

A recent report of reductions in SAD-related "depression in 87 percent of patients" (Binkley, 1990, p. 203) reverses the findings of earlier studies. [Author name, date, and page reference in parentheses immediately following the quotation.]

Binkley (1990) reports reductions in SAD-related "depression in 87 percent of patients" (p. 203). [Author name followed by the date in parentheses incorporated into the words introducing the quotation; page number in parentheses immediately following the quotation.]

3. Source of a Long Quotation (and Format of Quotation)—APA

Incorporate a direct quotation of fewer than forty words into your own sentence and enclose it in quotation marks. Place the parenthetical in-text citation after the closing quotation mark and, if the quotation falls at the end of the sentence, before the sentence-ending punctuation. When you use a quotation longer than forty words, set it off in block style indented one-half inch or five spaces from the left margin. Never enclose a set-off quotation in quotation marks because the placement in block style carries the message that the material is quoted. Place the parenthetical reference citation one space after the end punctuation of the last sentence.

DISPLAYED QUOTATION (FORTY OR MORE WORDS)

Jet lag, with its characteristic fatigue and irregular sleep patterns, is a common problem among those who travel great distances by jet airplane to different time zones:

> Jet lag syndrome is the inability of the internal body rhythm to rapidly resynchronize after sudden shifts in the timing. For a variety of reasons, the system attempts to maintain stability and resist temporal change. Consequently, complete adjustment can often be delayed for several days—sometimes for a week—after arrival at one's destination. (Bonner, 1991, p. 72)

4. One Author—APA

In a parenthetical reference in APA style, a comma and a space separate a name from a year, and a year from a page reference. (Note: Examples 1 through 3 are also citations of works by one author.)

> One of his questions is "What binds together a Mormon banker in Utah with his brother, or other coreligionists in Illinois or Massachusetts?" (Coles, 1993, p. 2).

5. Two Authors—APA

If a work has two authors, give both names in each citation.

> One report describes 2,123 occurrences (Krait & Cooper, 2003).

> The results that Krait and Cooper (2003) report would not support the conclusions Davis and Sherman (1999) draw in their review of the literature.

When you write a parenthetical in-text citation naming two (or more) authors, use an ampersand (&) between the final two names, but write out the word *and* for any reference in your own sentence.

6. Three, Four, or Five Authors—APA

For three, four, or five authors, use the last names of all the authors in the first reference. In all subsequent references, use only the first author's last name followed by *et al.* (a Latin term meaning "and others"). Note that *et al.* is followed by a period and is not italicized.

FIRST REFERENCE

In one study, only 30% of the survey population could name the most commonly spoken languages in five Middle Eastern countries (Ludwig, Rodriquez, Novak, & Ehlers, 2008).

SUBSEQUENT REFERENCE

Ludwig et al. (2008) found that most Americans could identify the language spoken in Saudi Arabia.

7. Six or More Authors—APA

For six or more authors, name the first author followed by *et al.* in all in-text references, including the first.

These injuries can lead to an inability to perform athletically, in addition to initiating degenerative changes at the joint level (Mandelbaum et al., 2005).

8. Author(s) with Two or More Works in the Same Year—APA

If you use more than one source written in the same year by the same author(s), alphabetize the works by their titles for the References list and assign letters in alphabetical order to the years—(2007a), (2007b), (2007c). Use the year-letter combination in parenthetical references. Note that a citation of two or more such works lists the years in alphabetical order.

Most recently, Torrevillas (2007c) draws new conclusions from the results of eight experiments conducted with experienced readers (Torrevillas, 2007a, 2007b).

9. Two or More Authors with the Same Last Name—APA

Include first initials for every in-text citation of authors who share a last name. Use the initials appearing in the References list. (In the second example, a parenthetical citation, the name order is alphabetical, as explained in item 12.)

R. A. Smith (2008) and C. Smith (1999) both confirm these results.

These results have been confirmed independently (C. Smith, 1999; R. A. Smith, 2008).

10. Work with a Group or Corporate Author—APA

If you use a source in which the "author" is a corporation, agency, or group, an in-text reference gives that name as author. Use the full name in each citation, unless an abbreviated version of the name is likely to be familiar to your audience. In that case, use the full name and give its abbreviation at the first citation; then, use the abbreviation for subsequent citations.

This exploration will continue into the 21st century (National Aeronautics and Space Administration [NASA], 2004). [In subsequent citations, use the abbreviated form, NASA, alone.]

11. Work Listed by Title—APA

If no author is named, use a shortened form of the title for in-text citations. Ignoring *A*, *An*, or *The*, make the first word the one by which you alphabetize the title in your References. The following example refers to an article fully titled "Are You a Day or Night Person?"

> Scientists group people as "larks" or "owls" on the basis of whether individuals are more efficient in the morning or at night ("Are You," 1989).

12. Reference to More Than One Source—APA

If more than one source has contributed to an idea or opinion in your paper, cite the sources alphabetically by author in one set of parentheses; separate each block of information with a semicolon, as in the following example.

> Conceptions of personal space vary among cultures (Morris, 1977; Worchel & Cooper, 1983).

13. Personal Communication, Including E-Mail and Other Nonretrievable Sources—APA

Telephone calls, personal letters, interviews, and e-mail messages are "personal communications" that your readers can't access or retrieve. Acknowledge personal communications in parenthetical references, but never include them in your References list at the end of your paper.

> Recalling his first summer at camp, one person said, "The proximity of 12 other kids made me—an only child with older, quiet parents— frantic for eight weeks" (A. Weiss, personal communication, January 12, 2005).

14. References to Retrievable Online Sources—APA

When you quote, paraphrase, or summarize an online source that is available to others, cite the author (if any) or title and the date as you would for a print source, and include the work in your References list.

> It's possible that similarity in personality is important in having a happy marriage (Luo & Clonen, 2005, p. 324).

15. Reference to an Online Source with No Pages—APA

If an online source doesn't provide page numbers, use the paragraph number, if available, preceded by the abbreviation *para*. It is rare, however, to number paragraphs. If you can't decipher a page or paragraph number, cite a heading if possible.

(Anderson, 2003, para. 14)

(Migueis, 2002, Introduction)

16. Source Lines for Graphics and Table Data—APA

If you use a graphic from another source or create a table using data from another source, provide a note at the bottom of the table or graphic, crediting the original author and the copyright holder. Here are examples of two source lines—one for a graphic from an article, the other for a graphic from a book.

GRAPHIC USING DATA FROM AN ARTICLE—APA

Note. The data in columns 1 and 2 are from "Advance Organizers in Advisory Reports: Selective Reading, Recall, and Perception" by L. Lagerwerf et al., 2008, *Written Communication, 25*(1), p. 68. Copyright 2008 by Sage Publications. Adapted with permission of the author.

GRAPHIC FROM A BOOK—APA

Note. From *The Road to Reality: A Complete Guide to the Laws of the Universe* (p. 270), by R. Penrose, 2005, New York: Alfred Knopf. Copyright 2004 by R. Penrose. Reprinted with permission of the publisher.

37d What are APA guidelines for writing an abstract?

As the APA *Publication Manual* explains, "an abstract is a brief, comprehensive summary" (p. 12) of a longer piece of writing. The APA estimates that an abstract should be no longer than about 120 words. Your instructor may require that you include an abstract at the start of a paper; if you're not sure, ask. Make the abstract accurate, objective, and exact. Actually, as you study the social sciences, you may become familiar with effective abstracts because many disciplines have online abstracts of longer sources. See 37g for guidelines on formatting an abstract page. The student paper in 37h.2 has an abstract you can study as an example.

37e What are APA guidelines for content notes?

Content notes in APA-style papers add relevant information that can't be worked effectively into a text discussion. Use consecutive Arabic numerals for note numbers, both within your paper and on any separate page following the last text page of your paper. Try to arrange your sentence so that the note number falls at the end. Use a numeral raised slightly above the line of words and immediately after the final punctuation mark. See 37g for instructions on formatting the Footnotes page.

37f What are APA guidelines for a References list?

The REFERENCES list at the end of your research paper provides complete bibliographic information for readers who may want to access the sources you draw on for your paper.

Include in a References list all the sources you QUOTE, PARAPHRASE, or SUMMARIZE in your paper so that readers can find the same sources with reasonable effort. Never include in your References list any source that's not generally available to others (see item 13 in 37c). Quick Reference 37.1 presents general format guidelines.

Quick Reference 37.1

Guidelines for an APA-style References list

TITLE
The title is "References" (centered without quotation marks, italics, or underlining).

PLACEMENT OF LIST
Start a new page. Number it sequentially with the rest of the paper and place it immediately after the body of the paper.

CONTENTS AND FORMAT
Include all quoted, paraphrased, or summarized sources in your paper that are not personal communications, unless your instructor tells you to include all the references you have consulted, not just those you have to credit. Start each entry on a new line, and double-space all lines. APA recommends that student papers follow journal formatting by using a *hanging indent* style: The first line of each entry begins flush left at the margin, and all other lines are indented. The hanging indent makes source names and dates more prominent. Type the first line of each entry full width, and indent subsequent lines one-half inch. The easiest way to do this is using the word processor's ruler bar.

Shuter, R. (1977). A field study of nonverbal communication in Germany, Italy, and the United States. *Communication Monographs, 44,* 298–305.

SPACING AFTER PUNCTUATION
APA calls for one space after end-punctuation marks.

continued >>

APA

ARRANGEMENT OF ENTRIES

Alphabetize by the author's last name. If no author is named, alphabetize by the first significant word (ignore *A, An,* or *The*) in the title of the work.

AUTHORS' NAMES

Use last names, first initials, and middle initials, if any. Reverse the order for all authors' names, and use an ampersand (&) before the last author's name: Mills, J. F., & Holahan, R. H.

Give names in the order in which they appear on the work (on the title page of a book or under the title of an article or other printed work). Use a comma between each author's last name and first initial and after each complete name except the last. Use a period after the last author's name.

DATES

Date information follows the name information and is enclosed in parentheses. Place a period followed by one space after the closing parenthesis.

For books, articles in journals that have volume numbers, and many other print and nonprint sources, the year of publication or production is the date to use. For articles from most general-circulation magazines and newspapers, use the year followed by a comma and then the exact date that appears on the issue (month and day for daily and weekly publications, month alone for monthly and bimonthly publications, and season for quarterly publications). Capitalize any words and use no abbreviations. Individual entries that follow show how much information to give for various sources.

CAPITALIZATION OF TITLES

For book, article, and chapter titles, capitalize the first word, the first word after a colon between a title and subtitle, and any proper nouns. For names of journals and proceedings of meetings, capitalize the first word, all nouns, verbs, adverbs, and adjectives, and any other words four or more letters long.

SPECIAL TREATMENT OF TITLES

Use no special treatment for titles of shorter works (poems, short stories, essays, articles). Italicize titles of longer works (books, names of newspapers or journals). If an italic typeface is unavailable, draw an unbroken line beneath the title *and* beneath the punctuation.

Don't drop any words, such as *A, An,* or *The,* from the titles of periodicals (such as newspapers, magazines, and journals).

PUBLISHERS

Use a shortened version of the publisher's name except for an association, corporation, or university press. Drop *Co., Inc., Publishers,* and the like, but retain *Books* or *Press.*

continued >>

| Quick Reference 37.1 | (continued) |

PLACE OF PUBLICATION

For US publishers, give the city and add the state (use the two-letter postal abbreviations listed in most dictionaries) for all US cities except Baltimore, Boston, Chicago, Los Angeles, New York, Philadelphia, and San Francisco. For publishers in other countries, give city and country spelled out; no country name is needed with Amsterdam, Jerusalem, London, Milan, Moscow, Paris, Rome, Stockholm, Tokyo, and Vienna. However, if the state or country is part of the publisher's name, omit it after the name of the city.

ABBREVIATIONS OF MONTHS

Don't abbreviate the names of months in any context.

PAGE NUMBERS

Use all digits, omitting none. For references to books or newspapers only, use *p.* and *pp.* before page numbers. List all discontinuous pages, with numbers separated by commas: pp. 32, 44–45, 47–49, 53.

REFERENCES ENTRIES: BOOKS

Citations for books have four main parts: author, date, title, and publication information (place of publication and publisher). Each part ends with a period.

AUTHOR   DATE   TITLE

Wood, P. (2003). *Diversity: The invention of a concept.*

PUBLICATION INFORMATION

San Francisco: Encounter Books.

REFERENCES ENTRIES: ARTICLES

Citations for periodical articles contain four major parts: author, date, title of article, and publication information (usually, the periodical title, volume number, and page numbers). Each part ends with a period.

AUTHOR   DATE   ARTICLE TITLE

Wood, W., Witt, M. G., & Tam, L. (2005). Changing circumstances, disrupting

                                          VOLUME   PAGE
PERIODICAL TITLE   NUMBER   RANGE

habits. *Journal of Personality and Social Psychology, 88,* 918–933.

REFERENCES ENTRIES: ELECTRONIC AND ONLINE SOURCES

Styles for documenting electronic and online sources continue to evolve. The *APA Style Guide to Electronic References* (Washington, D.C.: American Psychological Association, 2007) is available on the APA Web page http://www.apastyle.org/elecref.html and is the best source for current guidelines on these formats. This guide updates the *Publication Guide of the American Psychological Association* (5th ed.).

continued >>

APA

APA

When citing electronic or online sources, include the name(s) of author(s) the same way as for books and journals. Always include the publication date in parentheses after the author(s) name(s), followed by a period. Titles of books, periodicals, and whole Web sites should be italicized; titles of articles or pages in a Web site should not use italics. Articles retrieved online should always list the volume and issue number; this is a change from previous APA guidelines.

You then include retrieval information for the electronic source. For articles with DOI (Digital Object Identifier) numbers, this is simply the letters "doi" followed by a colon, then the number. Figure 37.1 (page 670) shows how to find publication information in a journal article with a DOI. Figure 37.1a shows how the source is listed in a database. Figure 37.1b shows the actual page of the article itself. We illustrate this below and in example 39.

For nearly all other references, retrieval information begins with the words "Retrieved from," sometimes followed by the date you actually retrieved it, then the URL and, occasionally, additional information, such as database names. We provide more detailed information about documenting electronic resources beginning on page 676.

In the meantime, however, here are three examples of electronic source entries. The first is for an article that does not have a DOI number. Because it is for a permanent version of the article, you don't include a date in your "retrieved from" statement.

AUTHOR DATE ARTICLE TITLE

Overbye, D. (2005, June 28). Remembrance of things future: The mystery

ONLINE
NEWSPAPER TITLE RETRIEVAL INFORMATION

of time. *The New York Times.* Retrieved from http://www.nytimes.com

Notice that the only punctuation in the URL is part of the address. Don't add a period after a URL.

The second example is for an electronic article that has a DOI number. Note that this is for the article in Figure 37.1.

AUTHOR DATE ARTICLE TITLE

Agliata, A.K., Tantelff-Dunn, S., & Renk, K. (2007). Interpretation of teasing

PUBLICATION INFORMATION

during early adolescence. *Journal of Clinical Psychology, 63*(1), 23–30,

DOI

doi: 10.1002/jclp.20302

continued >>

| Quick Reference 37.1 | (continued) |

A third example is for an article from a Web site. Because Web sites may change, the retrieval statement includes the date retrieved as well as the URL. This example has no author.

ARTICLE TITLE   DATE

Think again: Men and women share cognitive skills. (2006).

PUBLICATION INFORMATION   RETRIEVAL INFORMATION

American Psychological Association. Retrieved January 18, 2006,

URL

from http://www.psychologymatters.org/thinkagain.html

The following samples of entries may appear in an APA References list. You can find others in the *Publication Manual of the American Psychological Association* or at http://www.apastyle.org. For quick help deciding which example you should follow, see the decision flowchart in Figure 37.2 (page 671).

PRINT REFERENCES—BOOKS

1. Book by One Author—APA

Note that all entries use the hanging indent style: The first line of an entry is flush to the left margin, and all other lines in the entry are indented one-half inch.

Bradway, B. (2002). *Pink houses and family taverns*. Bloomington: Indiana University Press.

2. Book by Two Authors—APA

Edin, K., & Kefalas, M. (2005). *Promises I can keep: Why poor women put motherhood before marriage*. Berkeley: University of California Press.

3. Book by Three or More Authors—APA

For a book by three to six authors, include all the authors' names. For a book by more than six authors, use only the first six names followed by *et al.*

Lynam, J. K., Ndiritu, C. G., & Mbabu, A. N. (2004). *Transformation of agricultural research systems in Africa: Lessons from Kenya*. East Lansing: Michigan State University Press.

APA

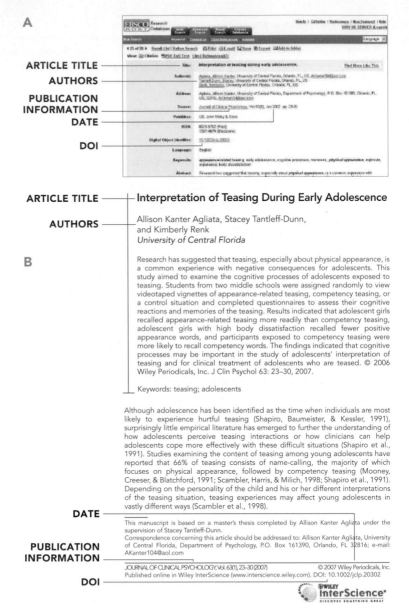

Figure 37.1 Publication information in a journal article with a DOI

APA

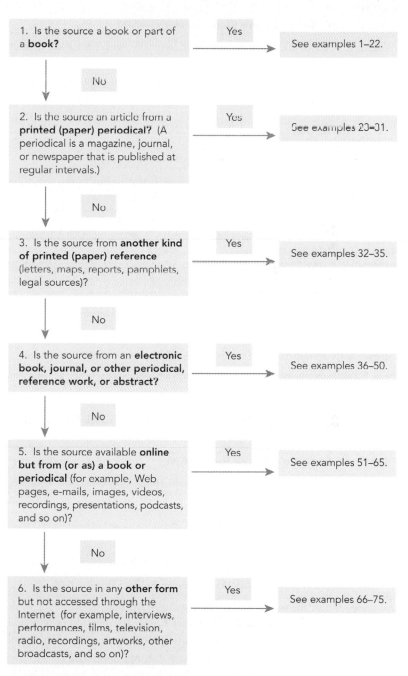

Figure 37.2 APA References visual directory

4. Two or More Books by the Same Author(s)—APA

Arrange references by the same author chronologically, with the earlier date of publication listed first.

Jenkins, H. (1992). *Textual poachers: Television fans and participatory culture.* New York: Routledge.

Jenkins, H. (2006). *Convergence culture: Where old and new media collide.* New York: New York University Press.

5. Book by a Group or Corporate Author—APA

Cite the full name of the corporate author first. If the author is also the publisher, use the word *Author* as the name of the publisher.

American Psychological Association. (2001). *Publication manual of the American Psychological Association* (5th ed.). Washington, DC: Author.

Boston Women's Health Collective. (1998). *Our bodies, ourselves for the new century.* New York: Simon & Schuster.

6. Book with No Author Named—APA

The Chicago manual of style (15th ed.). (2003). Chicago: University of Chicago Press.

7. Book with an Author and an Editor—APA

Brontë, E. (2002). *Wuthering heights* (R. J. Dunn, Ed.). New York: Norton.

8. Translation—APA

Kundera, M. (1999). *The unbearable lightness of being* (M. H. Heim, Trans.). New York: HarperPerennial. (Original work published 1984)

9. Work in Several Volumes or Parts—APA

Chrisley, R. (Ed.). (2000). *Artificial intelligence: Critical concepts* (Vols. 1–4). London: Routledge.

10. Anthology or Edited Book—APA

Purdy, J. L., & Ruppert, J. (Eds.). (2001). *Nothing but the truth: An anthology of Native American literature.* Upper Saddle River, NJ: Prentice Hall.

11. One Selection from an Anthology or an Edited Book—APA

Give the author of the selection first. The word *In* introduces the larger work from which the selection is taken. Note that names are inverted only in the author position; in all other circumstances, they are written in standard form.

Trujillo, L. (2004). Balancing act. In R. Moreno & M. H. Mulligan (Eds.), *Borderline personalities: A new generation of Latinas dish on sex, sass, and cultural shifting* (pp. 61–72). New York: HarperCollins.

12. Selection from a Work Already Listed in References—APA

Provide full information for the already-cited anthology (second example below), along with information about the individual selection. Put entries in alphabetical order.

Bond, R. (2004). "The night train at Deoli." In A. Chaudhuri (Ed.), *The Vintage book of modern Indian literature* (pp. 415–418). New York: Vintage Books.

Chaudhuri, A. (Ed.). (2004). *The Vintage book of modern Indian literature.* New York: Vintage Books.

13. Signed Article in a Reference Book—APA

Use *In* to introduce the larger work from which the selection is taken.

Burnbam, J. C. (1996). Freud, Sigmund. In B. B. Wolman (Ed.), *The encyclopedia of psychiatry, psychology, and psychoanalysis* (p. 220). New York: Holt.

14. Unsigned Article in a Reference Book—APA

Ireland. (2002). In *The new encyclopaedia Britannica: Macropaedia* (15th ed., Vol. 21, pp. 997–1018). Chicago: Encyclopaedia Britannica.

15. Second or Subsequent Edition—APA

A book usually doesn't announce that it's a first edition. However, after the first edition, the edition number appears on the title page. In your entry, place the abbreviated information (*2nd ed., 3rd ed.,* and so on) after the title and in parentheses.

Gibaldi, J. (2003). *MLA handbook for writers of research papers* (6th ed.). New York: Modern Language Association.

16. Introduction, Preface, Foreword, or Afterword—APA

If you're citing an introduction, preface, foreword, or afterword, give its author's name first. After the year, give the name of the part cited. If the writer of the material you're citing is not the author of the book, use the word *In* and the author's name before the title of the book.

Hesse, D. (2004). Foreword. In D. Smit, *The end of composition studies* (pp. ix–xiii). Carbondale: Southern Illinois University Press.

17. Unpublished Dissertation or Essay—APA

Stuart, G.A. (2006). *Exploring the Harry Potter book series: A study of adolescent reading motivation.* Unpublished doctoral dissertation, Utah State University.

18. Reprint of an Older Book—APA

O'Brien, F. (1998). *At Swim-Two-Birds*. Normal, IL: Dalkey Archive Press.
(Original work published 1939)

You can find republishing information on the copyright page.

19. Book in a Series—APA

Give the title of the book but not of the whole series.

Goldman, D. J. (1995). *Women writers and World War I*. New York: Macmillan.

20. Book with a Title Within a Title—APA

Never italicize a title within a title, even though it would appear in italic type-face if it were by itself.

Lumiansky, R. M., & Baker, H. (Eds.). (1968). *Critical approaches to six major English works:* Beowulf *through* Paradise Lost. Philadelphia: University of Pennsylvania Press.

21. Government Publication—APA

Use the complete name of a government agency as author when no specific person is named.

U.S. Congress. House Subcommittee on Health and Environment of the Committee on Commerce. (1999). *The nursing home resident protection amendments of 1999* (99-0266-P). Washington, DC: U.S. Government Printing Office.

U.S. Senate Special Committee on Aging. (1998). *The risk of malnutrition in nursing homes* (98-0150-P). Washington, DC: U.S. Government Printing Office.

22. Published Proceedings of a Conference—APA

Rocha, L., Yaeger, L., Bedau, M., Floreano, D., Goldstone, R. & Vespignani, A. (Eds.). (2006, June). *Artificial life X: Proceedings of the tenth international conference on the simulation and synthesis of living systems*. Bloomington, IN. Cambridge: MIT Press.

PRINT REFERENCES—PERIODICALS

23. Article in a Journal with Continuous Pagination—APA

Give the volume number, italicized after the journal title. In the 2001 edition of the APA style manual, only the volume number appears. The new (2007) APA style for electronic references directs writers also to include the issue number in parentheses, immediately after the volume number. We have followed that new practice in the example below.

Tyson, P. (1998). The psychology of women. *Journal of the American Psychoanalytic Association, 46*(3), 361–364.

24. Article in a Journal That Pages Each Issue Separately—APA

Give the volume number, italicized with the journal title. Give the issue number in parentheses; don't italicize it and leave no space before it. Note that the new APA practice now uses this style for journals with continuous pagination, too (see item 23).

Adler-Kassner, L., & Estrem, H. (2003). Rethinking research writing: Public
literacy in the composition classroom. *WPA: Writing Program
Administration, 26*(3), 119–131.

25. Signed Article in a Weekly or Biweekly Periodical—APA

Give year, month, and day for a periodical published every week or every two weeks. Don't use the abbreviation *p.* (or *pp.*) for magazines or journals.

Brink, S. (2005, March 28). Eat this now! *U.S. News & World Report*, 56–58.

26. Signed Article in a Monthly or Bimonthly Periodical—APA

Give the year and month(s) for a periodical published every month or every other month. Insert the volume number, italicized with the periodical title. Put the issue number in parentheses; don't italicize it, and don't put a space before it.

Fallows, J. (2008, January/February). The $1.4 trillion question. *The Atlantic,
301*(1), 36–48.

27. Unsigned Article in a Weekly or Monthly Periodical—APA

The price is wrong. (2003, August 2). *The Economist, 368*, 58–59.

28. Signed Article in a Daily Newspaper—APA

Use the abbreviation *p.* (or *pp.* for more than one page) for items from newspapers.

Green, P. (2008, January 31). The slow life picks up speed. *The New York Times*,
p. D1.

29. Unsigned Article in a Daily Newspaper—APA

Oscars ready plans to deal with strike. (2008, January 31). *The Denver Post*, p. B3.

30. Editorial, Letter to the Editor, or Review—APA

Primary considerations. (2008, January 27) [Editorial]. *The Washington Post*, p. D6.

Finanger, E. (2008, February). [Letter to the editor]. *Outside*, 14.

Shenk, D. (2003, Spring). Toolmaker, brain builder. [Review of the book *Beyond
Big Blue: Building the computer that defeated the world chess champion*].
The American Scholar, 72, 150–152.

31. Article in a Looseleaf Collection of Reprinted Articles—APA

Hayden, T. (2002). The age of robots. In E. Goldstein (Ed.), *Applied Science 2002. SIRS 2002*, Article 66. (Reprinted from *U.S. News & World Report*, pp. 44–50, 2001, April 23).

OTHER PRINT REFERENCES

32. Published and Unpublished Letters—APA

In the APA system, unpublished letters are considered personal communication inaccessible to general readers, so they don't appear in the References list. Personal communications are cited only in the body of the paper (see also item 66).

Williams, W. C. (1935). Letter to his son. In L. Grunwald & S. J. Adler (Eds.), *Letters of the century: America 1900–1999* (pp. 225–226). New York: Dial Press.

33. Map or Chart—APA

Colorado Front Range Mountain Bike Topo Map [Map]. (2001). Nederland, CO: Latitude 40.

34. Report or Pamphlet—APA

National Commission on Writing in America's Schools and Colleges. (2003). *The neglected "R": The need for a writing revolution* [Report]. New York: College Board.

Student Environmental Coalition. (2005). *Reduce, reuse, recycle* [Brochure]. Normal, IL: Author.

35. Legal Source—APA

Include the name of the case, the citation (usually a volume number, publication title, and page) or a record number, the name of the court deciding the case (if other than the US Supreme Court), and the year of the decision. The following example shows the citation for a published case. See Appendix D of the APA *Publication Manual* for other types of legal citations.

Brown v. Board of Educ., 347 U.S. 483 (1954).

ELECTRONIC AND ONLINE SOURCES

In general, APA recommends giving the same information, in the same order, as you would for a print source: author name(s), date of publication, title, and publication information (title, volume, issue, pages). Then you add as much retrieval information as others will need to locate the source. This retrieval information may include a DOI number (see example 39) or it may consist of a "Retrieved from" statement along with a URL. In certain cases, you may also need to include the date you retrieved the information.

- DOI (Direct Object Identifier): These numerical codes are sometimes assigned to online journal articles and are typically located on the first page of the online article or included in the database. The DOI for an article will be the same even if the article appears on many different Web sites. As a result, you don't use a URL or a "retrieved from" statement if a source contains a DOI. Include the number after the publication information. Note: This is a change from earlier APA formats.

- URL: You should include the full URL for most works accessed online, including any articles that don't have a DOI. If the material is only available by search or subscription, include the URL of the home page up to the first slash. If a URL must be divided on two or more lines, only break the address before slashes or punctuation marks (except within "http://"). Don't use a hyphen, underlining, italics, angle brackets, or an end period.

- Databases: A retrieval line is not needed for materials located on widely available databases like library subscription services. If, however, the source is difficult to locate, include the name of the database in the retrieval line.

- Retrieval date: Include the date you retrieved the information only if the item does not have a publication date, is from an online reference book, or is likely to be changed in the future (such as a prepublication version of an article, a Web page, or a Wiki). Note: This is a change from the previous APA style. APA recommends citing the "archival" or permanent version of a source whenever possible. Usually, an archival version is one that either has appeared in print, has a volume and issue number, or has a specific publication date. APA has determined that retrieval dates are unnecessary for archival versions.

Treat information from an online source that your readers can't readily retrieve for themselves—for example, an e-mail message—as a personal communication. Never include it in your References list; instead, cite it in the text with a parenthetical notation saying it's a personal communication. (Also see example 66.) If you have a scholarly reason to cite a message from a newsgroup, forum, or electronic mailing list that is available in an electronic archive, then see examples 52 or 53.

ELECTRONIC BOOKS

36. Entire Electronic Book—APA

Provide information about the print version, if available. The retrieval statement gives the specific URL of the work.

Adams, H. (1918). *The education of Henry Adams*. New York: Houghton Mifflin.
 Retrieved from http://www.columbia.edu/acis/bartleby/159/index/html

37. Chapter from Electronic Book—APA

Gembris, H. (2006). The development of musical abilities. In R. Colwell (Ed).
MENC handbook of musical cognition and development. New York:
Oxford University Press (pp.124–164). Retrieved from Ebrary database
at http://site.ebrary.com.bianca.penlib.du.edu/

In this example, the name of the database (Ebrary) is given, along with the initial part of the URL where the book was specifically found.

38. Thesis or Dissertation—APA

Stuart, G. A. (2006). *Exploring the Harry Potter book series: A study of
adolescent reading motivation*. Retrieved from ProQuest Digital
Dissertations. (AAT 3246355)

The number in parentheses at the end is the accession number.

ELECTRONIC JOURNALS

39. Article with DOI Assigned—APA

Gurung, R., & Vespia, K. (2007). Looking good, teaching well? Linking liking,
looks, and learning. *Teaching of Psychology, 34*(1), 5-10. doi:
10.1207/s15328023top3401_2

40. Article with No DOI Assigned—APA

Pollard, R. (2002). Evidence of a reduced home field advantage when a team
moves to a new stadium. *Journal of Sports Sciences 20*(12), 969–974.
Retrieved from http://0-find.galegroup.com.bianca.penlib.du.edu:
80/itx/start.do?prodId=AONE

No retrieval date is included because the final version of the article is being referenced.

41. In-press Article—APA

In-press means that an article has been accepted for publication but has not yet been published in its final form. Therefore, there is no publication date, and the retrieved from statement includes a date.

George, S. (In press). How accurately should we estimate the anatomical
source of exhaled nitric oxide? *Journal of Applied Physiology*.
doi:10.1152/japplphysiol.00111.2008. Retrieved February, 2008 from
http://jap.physiology.org/papbyrecent.shtml

OTHER ELECTRONIC PERIODICALS

42. Newspaper Article—APA

Wilson, J. (2005, March 5). EPA fights waste site near river. *Los Angeles Times.*
Retrieved from http://www.latimes.com/news/science/environment
/la-me-moab05.html

43. Online Magazine Content Not Found in Print Version—APA

Shulman, M. (2008, January 23). 12 diseases that altered history. [Online
exclusive]. *U.S. News and World Report.* Retrieved January 28, 2007,
from http://health.usnews.com/articles/health/2008/01/03/12-diseases-
that-altered-history.html

44. Web Page or Article on Web Site—APA

Think again: Men and women share cognitive skills. (2006). *American
Psychological Association.* Retrieved January 18, 2006, from
http://www.psychologymatters.org/thinkagain.html

ELECTRONIC REFERENCE MATERIALS

45. Online Encyclopedia—APA

Turing test. (2008). In *Encyclopædia Britannica.* Retrieved February 9, 2008,
from http://www.britannica.com/bps/topic/609757/Turing-test

Because the reference is to a work that may change, a retrieval date is included.

46. Online Dictionary—APA

Asparagus. (n.d.). *Merriam-Webster's online dictionary.* Retrieved February 9,
2008, from http://dictionary.reference.com/browse/asparagus

47. Online Handbook—APA

Gembris, H. (2006). The development of musical abilities. In R. Colwell (Ed).
MENC handbook of musical cognition and development. New York:
Oxford University Press. 124–164. Retrieved October 8, 2007, from
http://0-site.ebrary.com.bianca.penlib.du.edu/lib/udenver
/Doc?id=10160594

48. Wiki—APA

Machine learning. (n.d.). Retrieved January 5, 2008, from Artificial Intelligence
Wiki: http://www.ifi.unizh.ch/ailab/aiwiki/aiw.cgi

Note that (n.d.) means "no date."

ELECTRONIC ABSTRACTS

49. Abstract from Secondary Source—APA

Walther, J.B., Van Der Heide, B., Kim, S., Westerman, D., & Tong, S. (2008). The role of friends' appearance and behavior on evaluations of individuals on Facebook: Are we known by the company we keep? *Human Communication Research 34*(1), 28–49. Abstract retrieved April 20, 2008 from PsycINFO database.

50. Abstract Submitted for Meeting or Poster Session—APA

Wang, H. (2007). Dust storms originating in the northern hemisphere of Mars. AGU 2007 Fall Meeting. Abstract retrieved from http://www.agu.org /meetings/fm07/?content=program

OTHER ELECTRONIC REFERENCES

51. Personal or Professional Web Site—APA

Hesse, Doug. (2008, November). Home page. Retrieved November 21, 2008, from http://http://portfolio.du.edu/dhesse

Association for the Advancement of Artificial Intelligence. (2008, March). Retrieved March 17, 2008, from http://www.aaai.org

Because material on a Web site may change, use a retrieved from date.

52. Message on a Newsgroup, Online Forum, or Discussion Group—APA

Boyle, F. (2002, October 11). Psyche: Cemi field theory: The hard problem made easy [Msg 1]. Message posted to news://sci.psychology.consciousness

53. Message on an Electronic Mailing List (Listserv)—APA

Haswell, R. (2005, October 17). A new graphic/text interface. Message posted to Writing Program Administrators electronic mailing list, archived at http://lists.asu.edu/archives/wpa-l.html

APA advises using *electronic mailing list*, as Listserv is the name of a specific software.

54. Course Home Page—APA

St. Germain, S. (2003, Summer). Myths and fairytales: From *Inanna* to *Edward Scissorhands*. Retrieved February 20, 2005, from http://www.public.iastate. edu/~sgermain/531.homepage.html

55. Blog (Web Log) Post—APA

McLemee, S. (2008, January 1). To whom it may concern. Message posted to
    http://www.artsjournal.com/quickstudy/

56. Video Web Log Post—APA

APA treats every video posted online as a Video Web log, which suggests a regular series of postings. In fact, many videos are not produced in Web log format. Still, we present the APA format. Also see 59, for online television programs or movies.

Tobias, R. (2008, February 7). *Ranching the new West.* [Video file]. Video posted
    to http://www.lifeonterra.com/

Wesch, M. (2007, January 31). *Web 2.0 ... the machine is us/ing us.* [Video file].
    Video posted to http://www.youtube.com/watch?v=6gmP4nk0EOE

57. Online Digital Recording—APA

Komunyakaa, Y. (2005). My father's love letters. Retrieved March 7, 2005, from
    the Academy of American Poets Web site: http://www.poets.org
    /poems/poems.cfm?prmID=2065

58. Audio Podcast—APA

Business marketing with podcast: What marketing professionals should know
    (2005, October 13). *Podblaze.* Podcast retrieved http://business.podblaze.com/

59. Online Television Program—APA

If producers or directors can be identified, list them in the author position. Include the episode title, if any, and the title of the series. If it is a one-time program, list only the title.

Bender, J. (Director/Producer). (2008, January 30). The beginning of the end. *Lost.*
    Video retrieved February 1, 2008, from http://dynamic.abc.go.com
    /streaming/landing

60. Online Advertisement—APA

Samsung. (2005, November). [Advertisement]. Retrieved from
    http://rollingstone.com

61. Computer Software or Video Game—APA

Provide an author name, if available. Standard software (Microsoft Word) and program languages (C++) don't need to be given in the References list.

Guitar hero III: Legends of rock. (2007). [Video game]. Santa Monica: Activision.

62. Brochure—APA

US Department of Agriculture. (2007). *Organic foods and labels.* [Brochure]. Retrieved December 8, 2008, from http://www.ams.usda.gov/nop /Consumers/brochure.html

63. Policy Brief—APA

Haskins, R., Haskins, R., Paxson, C., & Donahue, E. (2006). *Fighting obesity in the public schools.* Retrieved from http://www.brookings.edu/~/media /Files/rc/papers/2006/spring_childrenfamilies_haskins/20060314foc.pdf

64. Presentation Slides—APA

Alaska Conservation Solutions. (2006). *Montana Global Warming* [PowerPoint slides]. Retrieved from http://www.alaskaconservationsolutions.com/acs /presentations.html

65. Graphs, Maps, Other Images—APA

New York Times Online. (2005, September 24). *Hurricane Rita.* [Interactive map]. Retrieved from http://www.nytimes.com/packages/html/national /20050923_RITA_GRAPHIC/index.html

OTHER NONPRINT REFERENCES
66. Interview—APA

In APA style, a personal interview is considered personal communication and is not included in the References list. Cite the interview in the text with a parenthetical notation saying that it's a personal communication.

Randi Friedman (personal communication, June 30, 2007) endorses this view.

Because a published interview is recoverable by readers, treat it as you would a journal or magazine article, depending on its place of publication.

Zoglin, R. (2003, December 15). Ten questions for Oprah Winfrey. *Time*, 8.

67. Lecture, Speech, or Address—APA

Kennedy, J. F. (1960, September 12). Speech to the Greater Houston Ministerial Association, Rice Hotel, Houston, TX.

68. Motion Picture—APA

Capra, F. (Director/Producer). (1934). *It happened one night* [Motion picture]. United States: Columbia Pictures.

Capra, F. (Director/Producer). (1999). *It happened one night* [Videocassette]. (Original motion picture released 1934)

Madden, J. (Director), Parfitt, D., Gigliotti, D., Weinstein, H., Zwick, E., &
Norman, M. (Producers). (2003). *Shakespeare in love* [DVD]. (Original
motion picture released 1998)

69. Music Recording—APA

Smetana, B. (1975). *My country* [Recorded by the Czech Philharmonic Orchestra
with K. Anserl conducting]. [Record]. London: Vanguard Records. (1975)

Springsteen, B. (2002). Lonesome day. On *The rising* [CD]. New York: Columbia
Records.

Radiohead. (2007). Jigsaw falling into place. On *Rainbows* [MP3]. Radiohead.

70. Live Performance—APA

Miller, A. (Author), & McLean, C. (Director). (2005, September 27). *All my sons*
[Theatrical performance]. Center for the Performing Arts, Normal, IL.

71. Work of Art, Photograph, or Musical Composition—APA

Cassatt, M. (1891). *La toilette* [Artwork]. Chicago: Art Institute of Chicago.

Mydans, C. (1999, October 21–November 28). *General Douglas MacArthur landing
at Luzon, 1945* [Photograph]. New York: Soho Triad Fine Art Gallery.

Schubert, F. (1822). *Unfinished symphony* [Musical composition].

72. Radio or Television Broadcast—APA

Burns, K. (Writer/Producer), & Barnes, P. (Producer). (1999, November 8). *Not for
ourselves alone: The story of Elizabeth Cady Stanton and Susan B.
Anthony* [Television broadcast]. New York and Washington, DC: Public
Broadcasting Service.

If you're citing a television series produced by and seen on only one station, cite
its call letters.

73. Information Services—APA

Chiang, L. H. (1993). *Beyond the language: Native Americans' nonverbal
communication.* (ERIC Document Reproduction Service No. ED368540)

74. Advertisement—APA

Swim at home. (2005). [Advertisement]. *The American Scholar 74(2)*, 2.

75. Images—APA

If you're reproducing an image in your paper, follow the guidelines for graphics in item 16 in 37c. Include the citation in the body of your paper. If you're
only referring to an image, cite the photographer or illustrator (if known), the
title (or a brief description of the image), and source information.

Arthur Miller in 1961. (2005). [Photograph]. *The American Scholar 74(2)*, 123.

APA

37g What are APA format guidelines for research papers?

Ask whether your instructor has instructions for preparing a final draft. If not, you can use the APA guidelines here. For an illustration of these guidelines, see the student paper in 37h.2.

GENERAL INSTRUCTIONS—APA

Use 8 1/2-by-11-inch white paper. The APA *Publication Manual* recommends double-spacing for a final manuscript of a student research paper. Set at least a one-inch margin on the left (slightly more if you submit your paper in a binder) and leave no less than one inch on the right and at the bottom.

Leave one-half inch from the top edge of the paper to the title-and-page-number line (*header*). Leave another one-half inch (or one inch from the top edge of the paper) before the next line on the page, whether that's a heading (such as "Abstract" or "Notes") or a line of your paper.

🚫 **Alert:** Most word-processing programs set the top and bottom margins at one inch as their default. Also, they generally set the "header" function at a default of one-half inch. Therefore, formatting the margins for your paper is probably less troublesome than it might seem. You simply need to check the default settings. ●

Use indents of one-half inch for the first line of all paragraphs, except in an abstract, the first line of which isn't indented. Don't justify the right margin. Indent footnotes one-half inch.

ORDER OF PARTS—APA

Number all pages consecutively. Use this order for the parts of your paper:

1. Title page
2. Abstract (if required)
3. Body of the paper
4. References
5. Appendixes, if any
6. Footnotes, if any
7. Attachments, if any (questionnaires, data sheets, or other material your instructor asks you to include)

TITLE-AND-PAGE-NUMBER LINE FOR ALL PAGES—APA

Use a title-and-page-number line on all pages of your paper. Leaving a margin of one-half inch from the top edge of the paper, type the title (use a shortened version if necessary), leave a five-character space, and then type the page number. End the title-and-page-number line one inch from the right edge of the paper. Ask whether your instructor wants you to include your last name in this title-and-page-number line. The "header" feature on a word-processing program will help you create the title-and-page-number line easily.

TITLE PAGE—APA

Use a separate title page. On it, begin with the title-and-page-number line described above, using the numeral *1* for this first page. Then, center the complete title vertically and horizontally on the page. Use two or more double-spaced lines if the title is long. Don't italicize or underline the title or enclose it in quotation marks. On the next line, center your name, and below that center the course title and section, your professor's name, and the date.

Alerts: (1) Use the following guidelines for capitalizing the title of your own paper and for capitalizing titles you mention in the body of your paper. (For capitalization of titles in the References list, see Quick Reference 37.1.)

(2) Use a capital letter for the first word of your title and for the first word of a subtitle, if any. Start every noun, pronoun, verb, adverb, and adjective with a capital letter. Capitalize each main word in a hyphenated compound word (two or more words used together to express one idea): *Father-in-Law, Self-Consciousness.*

(3) Don't capitalize articles (*a, an, the*) unless one of the other capitalization rules applies. Don't capitalize prepositions and conjunctions unless they are four or more letters long. Don't capitalize the word *to* used in an infinitive. ●

ABSTRACT—APA

See 37d for advice about what to include in an abstract of your paper. Type the abstract on a separate page, using the numeral *2* in the title-and-page-number line. Center the word *Abstract* one inch from the top of the paper. Don't italicize or underline it or enclose it in quotation marks. Double-space below this title, and then start your abstract, double-spacing it. Don't indent the first line.

SET-OFF QUOTATIONS—APA

Set off (display in BLOCK-STYLE form) quotations of forty words or more. Double-space to start a new line for the quoted words, indenting each line of the (double-spaced) quotation one-half inch or five spaces from the left margin. Don't enclose the quoted words in quotation marks.

If you're quoting part of a paragraph or one complete paragraph, don't indent the first line more than one-half inch. But if you quote two or more paragraphs, indent the first line of the second and subsequent paragraphs one inch from the text margin.

When the quotation is finished, leave one space after the sentence-ending punctuation, and then give the parenthetical citation. Begin a new line to resume your own words.

REFERENCES LIST—APA

Start a new page for your References list immediately after the end of the body of your paper. Use a title-and-page-number line. Drop down one inch from the top of the paper and center the word *References*. Don't italicize, underline, or put it in quotation marks. Double-space below it. Start the first line of each entry at the left margin, and indent any subsequent lines one-half inch from the left margin. Use this "hanging indent" style unless your instructor prefers a different one. Double-space within each entry and between entries.

NOTES—APA

Whenever you use a content note in your paper (37e), try to arrange your sentence so that the note number falls at the end. The ideal place for a note number is after the sentence-ending punctuation. Use a numeral raised slightly above the line of words and immediately after the final punctuation mark.

Put any notes on a separate page after the last page of your References list. Use a title-and-page-number line. Then, center the word *Footnotes* one inch from the top of the paper. Don't italicize or underline it or put it in quotation marks.

On the next line, indent one-half inch and begin the note. Raise the note number slightly (you can use the superscript feature in your word-processing program), and then start the words of your note leaving no space. If the note is more than one typed line, don't indent any line after the first. Double-space throughout.

37h A student's APA-style research paper

The final section of this chapter presents a student research paper prepared to conform to APA style. We discuss the researching, planning, drafting, and revising processes of the student, Shawn Hickson, and show the final draft of the paper, including its abstract.

Case Study

Shawn Hickson was given this assignment for a research paper in a general psychology class: Write a research paper of 1,250 to 1,700 words about an aspect of contemporary life that interests you and which psychologists have studied. For guidance, refer to the *Simon & Schuster Handbook for Writers,* Chapters 32 through 34. Use the documentation style of the American Psychological Association (APA) explained in Chapter 37. Your topic and working bibliography are due in two weeks. An early draft of your paper is due two weeks later. (Try to get that early draft close to what you hope will be your final draft, so that comments from me and from your peers can concretely help you write an excellent final draft.) Your final draft is due one week after I've returned your early draft (with comments) to you.

37h.1   Researching and writing the paper

When Shawn Hickson read her assignment, she was both pleased and intimidated by the amount of choice she had. She started PLANNING by listing several broad topics, finding that she was most interested in current technologies: cell phones, pagers, video games, computers, and MP3 players. She added to her list by thinking how each of these influenced several areas of life: school, work, entertainment, social life, communication. She recalled a lecture from a sociology course about how people today communicated more extensively than at any other point in history, yet they were spending less time together in person. This led to an early research question, "How do face-to-face interactions compare with cell phone or online interactions?" While she personally thought online dating services were strange, she was intrigued that they seemed to be popular among many people. She wondered, then, what role physical appearances played.

Shawn checked to see whether she could find enough sources useful for research on this topic. From her home computer, she went to her college's library home page. She searched the catalog with several keywords, including "physical appearance," "relationships," "dating," "physical attraction," and "Internet dating." She also used combinations of these terms in a Boolean search and generated a list of books, including several that hadn't been checked out. Next, she turned to online databases, which generated citations for dozens of journal, magazine, and newspaper articles. Some of them had full-text versions online, and she printed those that looked promising. Then, she went to her college library to check out several books and to review some other materials that were available only in the library.

Shawn also used the Google search engine to browse her keywords. However, she tended to turn up dating sites and bulletin boards. She thought some were entertaining and might be interesting as examples, but she ultimately decided they didn't have enough substance to use for this particular paper.

From all the sources she identified, Shawn compiled a WORKING BIBLIOGRAPHY, typing sources into a file on her computer. The working bibliography that she submitted consisted of twenty-nine SOURCES, though she had reviewed and rejected about ten others, including several she eliminated because they were of poor quality or seemed too technical for her to grasp easily. Shawn didn't intend to use all twenty-nine sources, but she wasn't yet sure where her drafting would go. Not surprisingly, her instructor urged her to reduce the list once DRAFTING began; otherwise, Shawn would risk writing too little about too much. Her instructor also recommended a colleague in the psychology department who had a scholarly interest in what attracted people to each other. Shawn arranged a brief interview with the psychology instructor, who directed her to some classic studies on the topic.

After spending several hours reading her sources and taking some content notes, Shawn began to weed out material. She narrowed her list to sixteen sources, took detailed notes on each, and began to group her material into emerging subtopics. Eventually, she dropped five of the sources.

Shawn realized that she'd still need to narrow the TOPIC sufficiently to shape a THESIS STATEMENT. The narrowing process worried her because she had been told in other college courses that her topics for research papers were too broad. She was determined this time to avoid that same problem.

To start drafting her paper, Shawn spread her note cards around for easy reference, but she felt somewhat overwhelmed by the amount of information at hand, and she wrote only a few sentences. To break through, she decided to type a DISCOVERY DRAFT to see what she had absorbed from her reading and notetaking. That very rough draft became her vehicle for many things, including creating an effective thesis statement, inserting source information according to APA documentation style, and checking the logical arrangement of her material.

Revising for Shawn started with her thesis statement, a process that helped her further narrow her focus. She started with "Physical appearances affect people's responses to each other," which her research supported but which was extremely broad and bland. Her next version served her well: "When people meet face to face, they form opinions based on physical char-

APA

acteristics including age, attractiveness, ethnicity, and appearance of wealth, but when they meet online they have to form opinions using other criteria." This thesis proved useful in revising the discovery draft into a true first draft, but the process made it clear to Shawn that she was covering too much for a 1,250- to 1,750-word research paper, and she dropped some material. She decided first to inform readers about the affect of appearances (or their absence) on first meetings and then to explore why people responded as they did. For her final draft, Shawn used this more focused thesis statement: "The presence or absence of physical characteristics during first meetings can influence how people respond to each other."

Using the *Simon & Schuster Handbook for Writers* as a guide, Shawn had to attend very closely to the details of correct parenthetical IN-TEXT CITATIONS (sections 37b and 37c) within her paper and a correct REFERENCES list (sections 37f and 37g) at the end. Because she'd used MLA DOCUMENTATION STYLE in other courses, she made sure not to confuse the two styles. For example, she saw that APA-style parenthetical citations include the year of publication (whereas MLA-style citations don't). For format and style details of the References list at the end of her paper, she found Quick Reference 37.1 especially helpful.

As Shawn checked the logical arrangement of her material, she dropped some aspects of physical appearance when she finally narrowed her topic sufficiently. A couple of hours at the computer led her to develop examples beyond attractions in dating, including how teachers and parents treat children whom they judge to be cute, and how gender and ethnicity influence people's expectations. Shawn learned from her research experiences the difference between researching a topic too broadly (and therefore gathering too many sources for the assignment) and researching a few aspects of a topic in depth by focusing on selected sources. Her final draft, which appears on the following pages, draws on eleven sources, a number that is down considerably from the twenty-nine with which she started.

37h.2 Analyzing the research paper

Shawn's paper, including her title page and abstract page, is shown here. For guidelines on writing an abstract, see 37d and 37g.

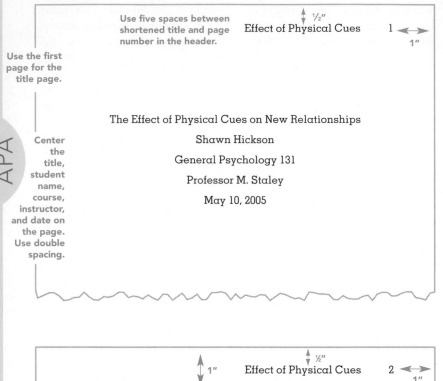

Use five spaces between shortened title and page number in the header.

Use the first page for the title page.

The Effect of Physical Cues on New Relationships

Shawn Hickson

General Psychology 131

Professor M. Staley

May 10, 2005

Center the title, student name, course, instructor, and date on the page. Use double spacing.

Abstract

Communication via the Internet has allowed people to form friendships and relationships in new ways. Research shows that individuals respond to new acquaintances at least partly according to how attractive they perceive the new friends to be. The absence of physical cues in Internet chat rooms or e-mail discussions means that people form impressions that are less affected by superficial factors. As the Internet changes, however, these differences may diminish.

Place abstract, if required, on the second page.

Double-space

continued >>

Effect of Physical Cues 3

The Effect of Physical Cues on New Relationships

Over the past 20 years, the Internet has enabled people to meet others from around the world with a few simple keystrokes. Occasionally, these interactions extend beyond the confines of chat rooms and e-mail discussions, so that individuals arrange to meet in person. Of course, people have learned to be cautious because others online can easily misrepresent themselves and their intentions. Nonetheless, lasting friendships, romances, and even marriages have resulted from first interactions that have happened online. Surprisingly, research shows that compared with people who meet face to face, those who meet on the Internet develop a greater liking for each other (McKenna, Green, & Gleason, 2003). This result is an example of a larger phenomenon: The presence or absence of physical characteristics during first meetings can influence how people respond to each other.

Judging People by Appearances

It can be troubling to know that something as shallow as someone's physical attractiveness can affect how people treat that person. However, the truth is that even if people do not mean to judge others based on their appearance, they tend to do so. Dion, Berscheid, and Walster (1972) showed research participants pictures of stereotypically attractive and unattractive individuals and then asked them to judge the people in the photographs according to several personality traits. The researchers found that the more attractive a person was judged to be, the more desirable traits that person was judged to have. For example, people might believe that

APA STYLE:
1-inch margins; double-space throughout

INTRODUCTION

APA-STYLE IN-TEXT CITATION: Doesn't require page numbers for a paraphrase or summary; check whether your instructor prefers that you include them

THESIS STATEMENT: Gives paper's focus

FIRST HEADING

PARAGRAPH 2: Provides background information

APA-STYLE INTEGRATED CITATION: Author name cited in text; date cited in parentheses

continued >>

(Proportions shown in this paper are adjusted to fit space limitations of this book. Follow actual dimensions discussed in this book and your instructor's directions.)

beautiful women are smarter or that handsome men are more clever. Several studies found that individuals assume that attractive people will agree with them more often than those who are unattractive; they assume that the attractive person will be more like them (Miyake & Zuckerman, 1993).

PARAGRAPH 3: Provides further examples of thesis

Even when people are young, appearance colors how others perceive them. Studies of preschoolers show that both peers and teachers treat children differently on the basis of their physical appearances. Both expect attractive children to be more active socially, and teachers believe that attractive children have more academic potential (Kachel, 1996). Perhaps more astounding, some controversial research shows that children's physical appearances may affect how their very own parents treat them (Bakalar, 2005).

PARAGRAPH 4: Provides information and bridges to next paragraph

Attractiveness has a different importance for men and women. While both sexes value physical attractiveness in brief relationships, men tend to view it as vital in long-term relationships. In contrast, women tend to regard other qualities more highly, especially financial stability and high social status (Singh, 2004).

PARAGRAPH 5: Summarizes research findings

However, for men and women alike, physical cues at the first meeting can shape not only impressions but also behaviors. Snyder, Tanke, and Berscheid (1977) showed male participants a picture of either an attractive or an unattractive female and then asked the men to rate her personality traits. Results of this initial rating were very similar with those obtained by Dion et al. (1972). Snyder's group next took the study one step further. Each male participant then had a phone conversation with a female participant who he thought was

continued >>

Effect of Physical Cues   5

the female from the picture. In these conversations, men treated their phone partners as if the women possessed the characteristics they believed went along with the photograph. However, the men really knew nothing about the women; they had assigned the women traits simply on the basis of a photograph. Even more interesting, women responded in a manner that was consistent with the images that were being projected onto them. Attractive women who were treated as if they were unattractive actually behaved as if they were, and vice versa. What happened was a clear example of a self-fulfilling prophecy (Snyder et al., 1977). Judgments based on appearance clouded other realities.

Meeting on the Internet

Meeting people online, especially through e-mail or in a chat room, obviously differs from meeting them face to face because there are no physical cues, only other people's words. Do people meeting in that environment engage one another differently? A study conducted by McKenna et al. (2003) suggests that they do. McKenna and colleagues divided participants into two groups: an experimental group and a control group. All participants had two separate conversations, one in person and the other online. Both conversations took place with the same person. Those in the control group knew this, but those in the experimental group believed they were talking with two different people. Participants in both groups then rated the quality of the interactions on three factors: (a) the quality of the conversations, (b) the degree to which they felt they had gotten to know the other person, and (c) how well they liked the other person in general. For the control groups,

Replaces names with *et al.* because this is second reference to same work with multiple authors

SECOND HEADING

PARAGRAPH 6: Explains research found on the Internet

Creates clarity by using letters in parentheses to identify factors

continued >>

Effect of Physical Cues   6

the ratings were similar in all categories, for both in-person and online conversations. However, differences emerged with the participants who thought they had been interacting with two different people, not the same person: They consistently rated the Internet partner higher in all three categories.

PARA-
GRAPH
7:
Inter-
prets
findings
summarized
in previous
paragraph

One probable explanation for this occurrence is that Internet interactions do away with traditional physical judgments. Attractiveness, extreme shyness, speech impediments, and many other superficial factors can hinder people from expressing their true selves and accepting others who are deficient in one area or another (McKenna et al., 2003). Because early judgments determine how two people will interact, a physical meeting makes it harder for some individuals to become comfortable and disclose themselves at the same level as they would in a situation where physical cues don't matter.

PARAGRAPH
8:
Explains
interests of
people
meeting
online

By the time people engage in online romantic relationships, according to researcher Malin Sveningsson (2002), they have already established a written relationship based on common interests. They know each other on a basis other than that of physical characteristics. Most people who enter chat rooms do so with the hope of making "contact with people, getting into a rewarding discussion, or just small-

APA-STYLE
IN-TEXT
CITATION:
Requires
page
number for
direct
quotation;
uses *p.* not
page

talking and having a good time in general" (p. 49). Those who meet on Internet chat sites or electronic mailing lists nearly always come together over a shared interest. A chat room frequenter named Richard explained his reasons for taking part in online conversations: "When you enter a place like that, you just want somebody to talk to . . . so you actively [look] for

continued >>

Effect of Physical Cues   7

people who [have] something to say. And all the time you [make] comments just to find someone who [has] something to tell" (p. 50). Women and men are nearly equal in their use of the Internet for purposes of community. The Cyber Dialogue group found that about 27% of women and 31% of men first went to the Internet to "join an online community" and that 85% of women and 82% of men came to believe that "the Internet community is an important part" of their lives (Hawfield & Lyons, 1998). It appears, then, that the primary motivation for both men and women is not physical but rather communicative.

Attractiveness is hardly the only physical quality by which men and women judge others. Broad features of identity such as race, gender, and ethnicity can also trigger uninformed responses. Researcher Lisa Nakamura (2002) found that when a person's race is revealed on the Internet, he or she can be just as subject to prejudicial assumptions as if the reality had been revealed face to face. Because of this, some people online deliberately try to mask their race or sex. They want others to judge them by what they say and think rather than by how they look, especially in a first encounter.

Whether Internet communication will continue to support first meetings that occur purely in writing is uncertain. With the increased use of digital images and audio, the Internet has begun to provide more and more physical cues. Participants in chat rooms tend to request images earlier as a sign of interest. People can post false photographs or videos, of course, but deception complicates any desired face-to-face meeting later on. Further, the sound of a person's voice shapes others'

> Shawn uses brackets in quotation to show that she (not the speaker) has altered wording to improve clarity
>
> Uses statistics to illustrate example

> PARAGRAPH 9: Gives other factors that influence relationships

> PARAGRAPH 10: Explains how increased use of images and sounds changes nature of online meetings

continued >>

APA

APA-STYLE
IN-TEXT
CITATION:
Includes
paragraph or
screen
number for
direct
quota-
tion
from
online
source
without
numbered
pages

perceptions. When voice communication over the Internet becomes more prevalent, it is likely that our stereotypical notions will return. Dr. Clifford Nass of Stanford University has predicted that when voice becomes a part of online interaction, people will "apply gender stereotypes" (Eisenberg, 2000, para. 6). Nass says that people tend to interpret the female voice as being "less accurate," with deeper male voices projecting authority. Some voices are perceived as more attractive than others, too.

CONCLU-
SIONS:
Final segment
summarizes
main points
and looks to
the future

Conclusions

Research on Internet relationships suggests that communication without visual cues can increase people's acceptance of one another. In face-to-face meetings, people form impressions based solely on physical appearance, impressions that influence both the way they treat others and the way those people respond. People who are treated well, for example, tend to take on positive characteristics. Because Internet conversations rely more heavily on the quality of communication than on superficial factors, meeting online allows people to suspend judgments based on appearance. This advantage may disappear as images and sounds increasingly accompany online meetings. Perhaps society would be healthier if people judged others not by their looks but by their character as expressed in words and ideas; however, the current tendency to treat stereotypically attractive and unattractive people differently shows the remoteness of that ideal.

continued >>

Effect of Physical Cues   9

References

Bakalar, N. (2005, May 3). Ugly children may get parental short
    shrift. *The New York Times*, p. F7.

Dion, K., Berscheid, E., & Walster, E. (1972). What is beautiful is
    good. *Journal of Personality and Social Psychology, 24*(3),
    285–290.

Eisenberg, A. (2000, October 12). Mars and Venus on the Net:
    Gender stereotypes prevail. *New York Times*. Retrieved
    from http://www.nytimes.com/2000/10/12/technology
    /12VOIC.html

Hawfield, K., & Lyons, E. (1998). Conventional wisdom about
    women and Internet use. Refuting traditional
    perceptions. Retrieved March 25, 2005, from
    http://elab.vanderbilt.edu/research/papers/html
    /studentprojects/women/conventional_wisdom.html

Kachel, J. (1996, March). Good looks count during childhood.
    Brown University Child and Adolescent Newsletter, 12(3).
    Retrieved April 7, 2005, from Academic Search Elite
    database.

McKenna, K. Y., Green, A. S., & Gleason, M. E. (2003).
    Relationship formation on the Internet: What's the big
    attraction? *Journal of Social Issues, 58*(1), 9–31.

Miyake, K., & Zuckerman, M. (1993). Beyond personality
    impressions. *Journal of Personality, 61*(3), 411–436.
    doi: 10.1111/1467-6494.ep9402021314

Nakamura, L. (2002). *Cybertypes: Race, ethnicity, and identity
    on the Internet.* New York: Routledge.

Begins
References
on new
page

Double-
spaces
through-
out

APA

Lists
Refer-
ences in
alphabetical
order by
author

Provides a
source that
appears only
on the Web

continued >>

Effect of Physical Cues   10

Singh, D. (2004). Mating strategies of young women: Role of

physical attractiveness. *Journal of Sex Research, 41*(1),

43–54.

Snyder, M., Tanke, E. D., & Berscheid, E. (1977). Social

perception and interpersonal behavior: On the self-

fulfilling nature of social stereotypes. *Journal of

Personality and Social Psychology, 35,* 656–666.

Sveningsson, M. (2002). Cyberlove: Creating romantic

relationships on the Net. In J. Fornäs, K. Klein, M.

Ladendorf, J. Sundén, & M. Sveningsson (Eds.), *Digital

borderlands: Cultural studies of identity and interactivity

on the Internet* (pp. 48–78). New York: Lang.

APA

Provides
source
information
for chapter in
a book

38

Chicago Manual (CM) and Council of Science Editors (CSE) Documentation

This chapter presents two more systems of documentation (in addition to MLA STYLE in Chapter 36 and APA STYLE in Chapter 37). They are the styles of the University of Chicago Press (CM) and the Council of Science Editors (CSE). The following directory provides a list of the CM-style entries you'll find in this chapter. For the CSE directory, turn to page 714.

CM-STYLE DIRECTORY

CM-STYLE DOCUMENTATION

38a   What is CM-style documentation?

The Chicago Manual of Style (CM) endorses two styles of documentation. One CM style is an author-date style, similar to the APA style of IN-TEXT CITATIONS (Chapter 37), that includes a list of sources usually titled "Works Cited" or "References." The other CM style uses a **bibliographic note system**. This system gives information about each source in two places: (1) in a footnote (at the bottom of a page) or an endnote (on a separate page following your paper) and, (2) if required, in a BIBLIOGRAPHY that begins on a separate page. We present the bibliographic note system here because it's often used in courses in such humanities subjects as art, music, history, philosophy, and sometimes English. Within the bibliographic note system, there are two substyles: "full" and "abbreviated."

38a.1   The full bibliographic note system in CM style

The CM full bibliographic note system requires you to give complete information, in a footnote or an endnote, the first time you cite a source. Because you're giving full information, you don't need to include a bibliography page.

If you cite a source a second time, you provide shortened information that includes the last name(s) of the author(s) and the key words in the work's title. The following example uses the full bibliographic note system.

TEXT

Ulrich points out that both Europeans and Native Americans told war stories, but with different details and different emphases.[3]

FULL FOOTNOTE (SAME PAGE) OR ENDNOTE (SEPARATE PAGE FOLLOWING TEXT)

3. Laurel Thatcher Ulrich, *Age of Homespun: Objects and Stories in the Creation of an American Myth* (New York: Knopf, 2001), 269.

SECOND CITATION OF THIS SOURCE

6. Ulrich, *Age of Homespun*, 285.

38a.2 The abbreviated bibliographic note system, plus bibliography, in CM style

In the abbreviated bibliographic note system, even your first endnote or footnote provides only brief information about the source. You provide complete information in a bibliography, which appears as a separate page at the end of the paper. Following is an example using the abbreviated bibliographic note system.

TEXT

Ulrich points out that both Europeans and Native Americans told war stories, but with different details and different emphases.[3]

ABBREVIATED FOOTNOTE (SAME PAGE) OR ENDNOTE (SEPARATE PAGE FOLLOWING TEXT)

3. Ulrich, *Age of Homespun*, 269.

BIBLIOGRAPHY (SEPARATE PAGE AT END OF THE PAPER)

Ulrich, Laurel Thatcher. *Age of Homespun: Objects and Stories in the Creation of an American Myth.* New York: Knopf, 2001.

Alert: Use either the full or the abbreviated bibliographic note style, but don't mix them. Ask your instructor which style he or she prefers. Remember that CM style requires a separate bibliography only if you use the abbreviated notes style.

Quick Reference 38.1 provides guidelines for compiling CM-style bibliographic notes.

CM

Quick Reference 38.1

■ ■ ■ ■ ■ ■ ■

Guidelines for compiling CM-style bibliographic notes

TITLE AND PLACEMENT OF NOTES

If you're using endnotes, place them all on a separate page, before your bibliography. Center the heading "Notes," without using italics, underlining, or quotation marks, an inch from the top of the page. If you're using footnotes, place them at the bottom of the page on which the source needs to be credited. Never use a title above any note(s) at the foot of the page. CM generally uses blank space (not a line) to divide the footnote(s) from the body text.

TITLE AND PLACEMENT OF BIBLIOGRAPHY

The abbreviated notes style requires a bibliography, which begins on a separate page at the end of the paper, following the endnotes page. An inch from the top of the page, center the heading "Bibliography" or "Works Cited" (either is acceptable in CM style). Don't underline the heading or put it in quotation marks.

FORMAT FOR ENDNOTES AND FOOTNOTES

Include an endnote or a footnote every time you use a source. Number notes sequentially throughout your paper whether you're using endnotes or footnotes. Use superscript (raised) arabic numerals for the footnote or endnote numbers in your paper. Position note numbers after any punctuation mark except the dash. The number comes best at the end of a sentence, unless that position would be so far from the source material that the citation would be confusing. Don't use raised numbers in the endnote or footnote itself. Place the number followed by a period, on the same line as the content of the note. Single-space both within each note and between notes. Indent each note's first line about three-tenths of an inch (0.3-inch tab), which equals about three characters, but place subsequent lines flush left at the margin.

SPACING AFTER PUNCTUATION

A single space follows all punctuation, including the period.

AUTHORS' NAMES

In endnotes and footnotes, give the name in standard (first-name-first) order, with names and initials as given in the original source. Use the word *and* before the last author's name if your source has two or three authors. For more than three authors, list only the first followed by *and others*. In the bibliography, invert the name: last name, first name. If a work has two or more authors, invert only the first author's name. If your source has up to ten authors, give all the authors' names. If your source has eleven or more authors, list only the first seven and use *et al.* for the rest.

continued >>

Quick Reference 38.1 (continued)

CM

CAPITALIZATION OF SOURCE TITLES
Capitalize the first and last words and all major words.

SPECIAL TREATMENT OF TITLES
Use italics for titles of long works, and use quotation marks around the titles of shorter works. Omit *A, An,* and *The* from the titles of newspapers and periodicals. For an unfamiliar newspaper title, list the city (and state, in parentheses, if the city isn't well known): *Newark (NJ) Star-Ledger,* for example. Use postal abbreviations for states.

PUBLICATION INFORMATION
Enclose publication information in parentheses. Use a colon and one space after the city of publication. Give complete publishers' names or abbreviate them according to standard abbreviations in *Books in Print.* Omit *The* before and *Co., Inc.,* and so on after a name. Spell out *University* or abbreviate to *Univ.* Never use *U* alone. Also spell out *Press.* Never use *P* alone. Don't abbreviate publication months.

PAGE NUMBERS
For inclusive page numbers, give the full second number for 2 through 99. For 100 and beyond, give the full second number only if a shortened version would be ambiguous: 243–47, 202–6, 300–404. List all discontinuous page numbers. (See "First Endnote or Footnote: Book" toward the end of this box.) Use a comma to separate parenthetical publication information from the page numbers that follow it. Use the abbreviations *p.* and *pp.* with page numbers only for material from newspapers, for material from journals that do not use volume numbers, and to avoid ambiguity.

CONTENT NOTES
Try to avoid using CONTENT NOTES. If you must use them, use footnotes, not endnotes, with symbols rather than numbers: an asterisk (*) for the first note on that page and a dagger (†) for a second note on that page.

FIRST ENDNOTE OR FOOTNOTE: BOOK
For books, include the author, title, publication information, and page numbers when applicable.

    1. Eudora Welty, *One Writer's Beginnings* (Cambridge, MA: Harvard University Press, 1984), 25–26, 30, 43–51, 208.

continued >>

FIRST ENDNOTE OR FOOTNOTE: ARTICLE

For articles, include the author, article title, journal title, volume number, year, and page numbers.

1. D. D. Cochran, W. Daniel Hale, and Christine P. Hissam, "Personal Space Requirements in Indoor versus Outdoor Locations," *Journal of Psychology* 117 (1984): 132–33.

SECOND MENTION IN ENDNOTES OR FOOTNOTES

Second (or later) citations of the same source can be brief. See 38b for an explanation.

38a.3 Citing graphics in CM style

Place the credit line for a table or illustration from another source next to or directly below the reproduced material. (If you intend to publish your paper, you must obtain permission to reprint copyrighted material from its source.) Spell out the terms *map*, *plate*, and *table*, but abbreviate *figure* as *fig.*

Reprinted by permission from Dennis Remington, A. Garth Fisher, and Edward Parent, *How to Lower Your Fat Thermostat: The No-Diet Reprogramming Plan for Lifelong Weight Control* (Provo, UT: Vitality House International, 1983), 74, fig. A2–1.

38b What are CM guidelines for bibliographic notes?

The CM directory that appears at the beginning of this chapter corresponds to the sample bibliographic note forms that follow. In a few cases, we give sample bibliography forms as well. If you need a model that isn't here, consult *The Chicago Manual of Style,* Fifteenth Edition (Chicago: University of Chicago Press, 2003), which gives footnote, endnote, and bibliography forms for a multitude of sources.

BOOKS AND PARTS OF BOOKS—PRINT

1. Book by One Author—CM

Footnote or Endnote

1. Becky Bradway, *Pink Houses and Family Taverns* (Bloomington, IN: Indiana University Press, 2001).

Bibliography

Bradway, Becky. *Pink Houses and Family Taverns.* Bloomington, IN: Indiana University Press, 2001.

The format for the bibliography is the reverse of the format for the note, in which first lines indent. In bibliographic form, the first line is placed flush left to the margin and the second and other lines are indented three-tenths to one half inch (0.3-inch–0.5-inch tab). Notice also where periods replace commas and where parentheses are omitted.

2. Book by Two or Three Authors—CM

Footnote or Endnote

1. Edward E. Gordon and Elaine H. Gordon, *Literacy in America: Historic Journey and Contemporary Solutions* (Westport, CT: Praeger, 2003).

2. John K. Lynam, Cyrus G. Ndiritu, and Adiel N. Mbabu, *Transformation of Agricultural Research Systems in Africa: Lessons from Kenya* (East Lansing: Michigan State University Press, 2004), 41.

Bibliography

Gordon, Edward E. and Elaine H. Gordon. *Literacy in America: Historic Journey and Contemporary Solutions.* Westport, CT: Praeger, 2003.

Lynam, John K., Cyrus G. Ndiritu, and Adiel N. Mbabu. *Transformation of Agricultural Research Systems in Africa: Lessons from Kenya.* East Lansing: Michigan State University Press, 2004.

In a bibliography entry, invert only the name of the first author listed.

3. Book by More Than Three Authors—CM

1. Wendy Saul and others, *Beyond the Science Fair: Creating a Kids' Inquiry Conference* (Portsmouth, NH: Heinemann, 2005), 72.

4. Multiple Citations of a Single Source—CM

For subsequent references to a work you've already named, use a shortened citation. Give the last name of the author, the title of the work, and the page number, all separated by commas. Shorten the title if it's longer than four words. This example shows the form for a subsequent reference to the work fully described in item 1.

1. Bradway, *Pink Houses*, 25.

If there are more than three authors for a source, use only the name of the first author, followed by *and others* or *et al.* The following example shows the shortened citation for the work in item 3.

2. Saul et al., *Beyond the Science Fair*, 72.

If you cite two or more authors with the same last name, include first names or initials in each note.

3. Eudora Welty, *One Writer's Beginnings*, 25.

4. Paul Welty, *Human Expression*, 129.

If you cite the same source as the source immediately preceding, you may use *ibid.* (capitalized at the beginning of a note), followed by a comma and the page number, instead of repeating the author's name and the title.

5. Ibid., 152.

5. Book by a Group or Corporate Author—CM

1. American Psychological Association, *Publication Manual of the American Psychological Association*, 5th ed. (Washington, DC: American Psychological Association, 2001).

2. Boston Women's Health Collective, *Our Bodies, Ourselves for the New Century* (New York: Simon & Schuster, 1998).

If a work issued by an organization has no author listed on the title page, give the name of the organization as the author of the work. The organization may also be the publisher of the work.

6. Book with No Author Named—CM

1. *The Chicago Manual of Style*, 15th ed. (Chicago: University of Chicago Press, 2003).

Begin the citation with the name of the book.

7. Book with an Author and an Editor—CM

1. Emily Brontë, *Wuthering Heights*, ed. Richard J. Dunn (New York: Norton, 2002).

In this position, the abbreviation *ed.* stands for "edited by," not "editor." Therefore, *ed.* is correct whether a work has one or more than one editor. (Also see items 10 and 16.)

8. Translation—CM

1. Milan Kundera, *The Unbearable Lightness of Being*, trans. Michael Henry Heim (New York: HarperPerennial Library, 1999).

The abbreviation *trans.* stands for "translated by," not "translator."

9. Work in Several Volumes or Parts—CM

The following notes show ways to give bibliographic information for a specific place in one volume of a multivolume work. Use whichever you prefer, staying consistent throughout a paper.

1. Ernest Jones, *The Last Phase*, vol. 3 of *The Life and Work of Sigmund Freud* (New York: Basic Books, 1957), 97.

1. Ernest Jones, *The Life and Work of Sigmund Freud*, vol. 3, *The Last Phase* (New York: Basic Books, 1957), 97.

If you're citing an entire work in two or more volumes, use the form shown below.

2. Ronald Chrisley, ed., *Artificial Intelligence: Critical Concepts*, 4 vols. (London: Routledge, 2000).

10. One Selection from an Anthology or an Edited Book—CM

1. Laura Trujillo, "Balancing Act," in *Border-Line Personalities: A New Generation of Latinas Dish on Sex, Sass, and Cultural Shifting*, ed. Robyn Moreno and Michelle Herrera Mulligan. (New York: Harper, 2004), 61–72.

11. More Than One Selection from an Anthology or an Edited Book—CM

If you cite more than one selection from the same anthology or edited book, give complete bibliographical information in each citation.

12. Signed Article in a Reference Book—CM

1. John C. Burnbam, "Freud, Sigmund," in *The Encyclopedia of Psychiatry, Psychology, and Psychoanalysis*, ed. Benjamin B. Wolman (New York: Henry Holt, 1996), 220.

13. Unsigned Article in a Reference Book—CM

1. *Encyclopaedia Britannica*, 15th ed., s.v. "Ireland."

The abbreviation *s.v.* stands for *sub verbo*, meaning "under the word." Capitalize the heading of the entry only if it's a proper noun. Omit publication information except for the edition number.

14. Second or Later Edition—CM

1. Anthony F. Janson, *History of Art*, 6th ed. (New York: Abrams, 2001).

Here the abbreviation *ed.* stands for "edition." Give the copyright date for the edition you're citing.

15. Anthology or Edited Book—CM

1. Eduardo del Rio, ed., *The Prentice Hall Anthology of Latino Literature* (Upper Saddle River, NJ: Prentice Hall, 2002).

Here the abbreviation *ed.* stands for "editor." For a source with two or more editors, use the plural *eds.*

16. Introduction, Preface, Foreword, or Afterword—CM

1. Elizabeth Fox-Genovese, foreword to *Southern Mothers*, ed. Nagueyalti Warren and Sally Wolff (Baton Rouge: Louisiana State University Press, 1999).

If the author of the book is different from the author of the cited part, give the name of the book's author or editor after the title of the book, preceded by the word *by* or *ed.* (for "edited by").

17. Unpublished Dissertation or Essay—CM

1. Gina Anne Stuart, "Exploring the Harry Potter Book Series: A Study of Adolescent Reading Motivation" (PhD diss., Utah State University, 2006), 21.

List the author's name first, then the title in quotation marks (not italicized), a descriptive label (such as *PhD diss.* or *master's thesis*), the degree-granting institution, the date, and finally the page numbers you're citing.

18. Reprint of an Older Book—CM

1. Marian Anderson, *My Lord, What a Morning* (1956; repr., Urbana: University of Illinois Press, 2002).

Republishing information is located on the copyright page. List the original date of publication first, followed by the publication information for the reprint.

19. Book in a Series—CM

1. Dorothy J. Goldman, *Women Writers and World War I*, Literature and Society Series (New York: Macmillan, 1995).

If the series numbers its volumes and the volume number isn't part of the title, you would include the volume number after the series title. Separate the volume number from the series title with a comma.

20. Book with a Title Within a Title—CM

1. Aljean Harmetz, *The Making of "The Wizard of Oz"* (New York: Hyperion, 1998).

If the name of a work that's usually italicized appears in an italicized title, put quotation marks around it. If the name of a work that's usually in quotation marks appears in an italicized title, keep it in quotation marks.

21. Government Publication—CM

1. House Committee on Resources, *Coastal Heritage Trail Route in New Jersey*, 106th Cong., 1st sess., 1999, H. Rep. 16.

If a government department, bureau, agency, or committee produces a document, cite that group as the author. In a bibliography entry, the author is often identified as *U.S. Congress,* followed by either *House* or *Senate* and the committee or subcommittee, if any, before the title of the document.

22. Published Proceedings of a Conference—CM

1. Anne Dobyns, "Civil Disobedience and the Ethical Appeal of Self-Representation," in *Rhetorical Democracy: Discursive Practices of Civic Engagement,* ed. Gerald A. Hauser and Amy Grim (Mahwah, NJ: Erlbaum, 2003), 131–36.

Treat published conference proceedings as you would a chapter in a book.

23. Secondary Source from a Book—CM

When you quote one person's words, having found them in another person's work, give information as fully as you can about both sources. CM style recommends, however, that original sources be consulted and cited whenever practical.

1. Mary Wollstonecraft, *A Vindication of the Rights of Woman* (1792), 90, quoted in Caroline Shrodes, Harry Finestone, and Michael Shugrue, *The Conscious Reader,* 4th ed. (New York: Macmillan, 1988), 282.

2. Caroline Shrodes, Harry Finestone, and Michael Shugrue, *The Conscious Reader,* 4th ed. (New York: Macmillan, 1988), 282, quoting Mary Wollstonecraft, *A Vindication of the Rights of Woman* (1792), 90.

PERIODICALS—PRINT

24. Signed Article in a Daily Newspaper—CM

1. Penelope Green, "The Slow Life Picks Up Speed," *New York Times,* sec. D, January 31, 2008, national edition.

Many newspapers print more than one edition a day and reposition the same articles on different pages. CM style recommends that, when applicable, you identify the specific edition (such as *Southeastern edition* or *final edition*); make this the last information in the entry, preceded by a comma. For a paper that specifies sections, use *sec.* before the section's letter or number or use *section* for a section's name (such as *Weekend section*). If a paper gives column titles, you may use the title (not italicized or in quotation marks) in addition to or in place of the article title. Separate all items with commas.

25. Editorial, Letter to the Editor, or Review—CM

1. "Primary Considerations," editorial, *Washington Post,* sec. B, January 27, 2008.

2. Emily Finanger, letter to the editor, *Outside*, February 2008, 14.

3. David Shenk, "Toolmaker, Brain Builder," review of *Beyond Big Blue: Building the Computer That Defeated the World Chess Champion*, by Feng-Hsiung Hsu, *American Scholar* 72 (Spring 2003): 150–52.

Before page numbers, use a comma for popular magazines and a colon for journals.

26. Unsigned Article in a Daily Newspaper—CM

1. "Oscars Ready Plans to Deal with Strike," *Denver Post*, sec. B, January 31, 2008.

27. Signed Article in a Weekly or Biweekly Magazine or Newspaper—CM

1. Christine Gorman, "How to Age Gracefully," *Time*, June 6, 2005, 73–74.

For general-readership weekly and biweekly magazines and newspapers, give the month, day, and year of publication. Separate page numbers from the year with a comma.

28. Signed Article in a Monthly or Bimonthly Periodical—CM

1. James Fallows, "The $1.4 Trillion Question," *The Atlantic*, January/February 2008, 36–48.

For general-readership monthly and bimonthly magazines, give the month and year of publication. Separate page numbers from the year with a comma.

29. Unsigned Article in a Weekly or Monthly Periodical—CM

1. "The Price Is Wrong," *Economist*, August 2, 2003, 58–59.

30. Article in a Collection of Reprinted Articles—CM

1. Thomas Hayden, "The Age of Robots," in *Applied Science*, Social Issues Resources Series (Boca Raton, FL: Social Issues Resources, 2002).

Cite only the publication actually consulted, not the original source. If you use a bibliography, cite its location in both the reprinted publication you consulted and the publication where the article first appeared.

31. Article in a Journal with Continuous Pagination—CM

1. Phyllis Tyson, "The Psychology of Women Continued," *Journal of the American Psychoanalytic Association* 46, no. 2 (1998): 361–64.

32. Article in a Journal That Pages Each Issue Separately—CM

1. Linda Adler-Kassner and Heidi Estrem, "Rethinking Research Writing: Public Literacy in the Composition Classroom," *WPA: Writing Program Administration* 26, no. 3 (2003): 119–31.

The issue number of a journal is required if each issue of the journal starts with page 1. In this example, the volume number is 26 and the issue number, abbreviated *no.*, is 3.

INTERNET SOURCES

If there is a print version of the source (as in item 35), provide information about that source. Also include information about how to find the electronic version. Unlike some other documentation styles (such as MLA), CM style doesn't generally recommend including access dates, nor does it use angle brackets around URLs. Following are examples in CM style of a few common types of electronic sources. For additional types, consult *The Chicago Manual of Style*.

33. Online Book—CM

Include the author's name, the title, and access information—in this case, the name of the organization that sponsors the site, and the URL.

1. Kate Chopin, *The Awakening* (Washington, DC: PBS, 1998), http://www.pbs.org/katechopin/library/awakening.

34. Article from a Periodical Available Only Online—CM

Include the author, title of the article, title of the publication, volume and issue number (if given), publication date, and URL.

1. Jody Shipka, "This Was (NOT!!) an Easy Assignment," *Computers and Composition Online*, fall 2007, http://www.bgsu.edu/cconline/not_easy/.

35. Article Accessed Through a Database—CM

Include the author, title of the article, title of the publication, volume and issue numbers (if given) of the original publication, the original publication date, and the URL of the database through which you accessed the article. CM style recommends that you include an access date when citing information retrieved through a database. Insert the access date in parentheses after the URL, followed by a period.

1. Gail Dutton, "Greener Pigs," *Popular Science* 255, no. 5 (November 1999): 38–39, http://proquest.umi.com (accessed September 2, 2007).

36. Source from an Internet Site—CM

Provide the author's name, the title of the Web page, the title or owner of the site, and the URL. When no specific author is listed, you may use the owner of the site as the author, as in the following example. Include an access date if your source is likely to be updated frequently, as is often the case with Internet sites.

1. Association for the Advancement of Artificial Intelligence, "AI Overview," Association for the Advancement of Artificial Intelligence, http://www.aaai.org/AITopics/html/overview.html (accessed January 22, 2008).

37. Electronic Mailing List—CM

1. T. Caruso, e-mail to Calls for Papers mailing list, June 30, 2002, http://www.cfp.english.upenn.edu/archive/2002-09/0041.html.

38. E-Mail Message—CM

1. Eliana Pessin, e-mail message to Georgia Dobyns, November 11, 2007.

39. Web Log Entry—CM

1. Scott McLemee, "To Whom It May Concern," Web log posting to *Quick Study*, January 1, 2008, http://www.artsjournal.com/quickstudy/ (accessed May 14, 2008).

40. Online Video or Podcast—CM

1. Michael Wesch, *Web 2.0 . . . The Machine is Us/ing Us*, video posted January 31, 2007 (accessed July 7, 2007).

Wesch is the director and producer of this video.

OTHER SOURCES

41. Speech or Conference Presentation—CM

1. Peter Leslie Mortensen, "Meet the Press: Reading News Coverage of Research on Writing" (paper presented at the annual meeting of the Modern Language Association, Washington, DC, December 29, 2005).

To cite a paper read at a meeting, give the name of the meeting in parentheses, along with the location and the date.

42. Personal Interview—CM

1. Randi Friedman, interview by author, August 30, 2008, Austin, Texas.

For an unpublished interview, give the name of the interviewee and the interviewer, the date of the interview, and the location of the interview. CM style recommends that you incorporate this information into the text, rather than place it in a note.

43. Published and Unpublished Letters—CM

1. William Carlos Williams to his son, 13 March 1935, in *Letters of the Century: America 1900–1999*, ed. Lisa Grunwald and Stephen J. Adler (New York: Dial, 1999), 225–26.

2. Theodore Brown, letter to author, December 7, 2005.

For an unpublished letter, give the name of the writer, the name of the recipient, and the date the letter was written.

44. Film, Videotape, or DVD—CM

1. Marc Norman and Tom Stoppard, *Shakespeare in Love*, DVD (1998; New York: Miramax Films/Universal Pictures, 2003).

2. Robert Riskin, *It Happened One Night*, VHS (1934; Hollywood: Columbia Pictures, 1999).

In note 1, the first information gives the authors of the screenplay. If the point of the note was about the director or the producers, then the title would appear first and *directed by* or *produced by* would follow a comma after the title along with the relevant names.

45. Sound Recording—CM

1. Bedrich Smetana, *My Country*, Czech Philharmonic, Karel Anserl, Vanguard SV-9/10.

Bedrich Smetana is the composer, and Karel Anserl is the conductor.

2. Bruce Springsteen, "Lonesome Day," on *The Rising*, Sony CD B000069 IIKII.

46. Computer Software—CM

1. *Guitar Hero III: Legends of Rock*, 2007. Activision, Santa Monica.

2. *Dreamweaver*, Ver. MX, Macromedia, San Francisco, CA.

Place the date or version (or release) number, abbreviated *Ver.* or *Rel.*, directly after the name of the software. Then, list the company that owns the rights to the software, followed by that company's location.

CSE-STYLE DOCUMENTATION

38c What is CSE-style documentation?

The Council of Science Editors, or CSE, produces a manual to guide publications in the mathematics, the life sciences, and the physical sciences. The information in 38c and 38d adheres to the style guidelines in the seventh edition of that manual, *Scientific Style and Format* (2006). For up-to-date

information about any changes, go to the organization's Web site at http://www
.councilscienceeditors.org.

Scientific journals and publishers are notoriously independent in how they
handle documentation, and scholars submitting work to specific journals always
check which documentation rules apply. Similarly, students in science courses
should ask their instructors about the specific guidelines they're to follow. Still,
the CSE documentation style provides useful guidelines.

Like the MLA (36) and APA (37) styles, CSE has two components: (1) citations within the text (called "**in-text references**") tied to (2) a bibliography
(called "**end references**") at the end of the text. However, CSE offers three different options for in-text references: the "Citation-Sequence" system, the
"Name-Year" system, and the "Citation-Name" system. We explain each, below.
CSE finds all three systems acceptable, each with its advantages and disadvantages. However, it most strongly endorses the Citation-Name system. Therefore, if you have a choice, we advise to you follow the Citation-Name system.
In any case, be consistent; don't mix systems.

38c.1   The CSE citation-sequence system

The Citation-Sequence system uses numbers in the text to refer to a numeri-
cally arranged END REFERENCES list. Here's how it works.

1. The first time you cite each source in your paper, assign it an arabic
   number in sequence, starting with 1.

2. Mark each subsequent reference to that source with the assigned number.

3. Use superscript (raised) numbers for source citations in your sentences,
   although numbers in parentheses are also acceptable.

4. Don't use footnotes or endnotes to credit your sources. Use only a References list, and number the entries in the order of their appearance in
   your paper. Start with the number 1, followed by a period, and then the
   content of the citation. Never list sources alphabetically. Never underline or use italics for titles of works.

Here's an example of a sentence that includes in-text citations and the corresponding cited references.

IN-TEXT REFERENCE

Sybesma[1] insists that this behavior occurs periodically, but Crowder[2]
claims never to have observed it.

END REFERENCES

1. Sybesma C. An introduction to biophysics. New York: Academic; 1977.
   648 p.

2. Crowder W. Seashore life between the tides. New York: Dodd, Mead; 1931. New York: Dover Reprint; 1975. 372 p.

Thereafter, throughout your paper, follow each citation of Sybesma's *Introduction to Biophysics* by a superscript [1] and each citation of Crowder's *Seashore Life* by a superscript [2].

When you're citing more than one reference—for example, a new source and three previous sources as well as a source from your first page—list each source number, followed by a comma with no space. Use a hyphen to show the range of numbers in a continuous sequence, and put all in superscript: [2,5–7,9]

Quick Reference 38.2 gives guidelines for compiling a References list for the Citation-Sequence system. Especially pay attention to the Arrangement of Entries in a Citation-Sequence system.

Quick Reference 38.2

Guidelines for a References list (CSE-style)

TITLE
Use "References" or "Cited References" as the title (no underlining, no italics, no quotations marks). (CSE also permits "Bibliography" or "Literature Cited" as acceptable titles.)

PLACEMENT OF LIST
Begin the list on a separate page at the end of the research paper. Number the page sequentially with the rest of the paper.

CONTENT AND FORMAT OF CITED REFERENCES
Include all sources that you quote, paraphrase, or summarize in your paper. Center the title one inch from the top of the page. Start each entry on a new line. If an entry takes more than one line, indent the second and all other lines under the first word, not the number. Single-space each entry and double-space between entries.

SPACING AFTER PUNCTUATION
CSE style specifies no space after date, issue number, or volume number of a periodical, as shown in the models in 38d.

ARRANGEMENT OF ENTRIES—CITATION-SEQUENCE SYSTEM
Sequence and number the entries in the precise order in which you first used them in the body of your paper. Put the number, followed by a period and a space, at the regular left margin.

continued >>

Quick Reference 38.2	(continued)

ARRANGEMENT OF ENTRIES—NAME-YEAR SYSTEM
Sequence the entries in alphabetical order by author, then title, etc. Do not number the entries.

ARRANGEMENT OF ENTRIES—CITATION-NAME SYSTEM
Sequence the entries in alphabetical order by author, then title, etc. Number the entries. Put the number, followed by a period and a space, at the regular left margin.

AUTHORS' NAMES
Reverse the order of each author's name, giving the last name first. For book citations, you can give first names or use only the initials of first and (when available) middle names; for journal citations, use only initials; however, CSE style recommends you use only initials. Don't use a period or a space between first and middle initials. Use a comma to separate the names of multiple authors identified by initials; however, if you use full first names, use a semicolon. Don't use *and* or *&* with authors' names. Place a period after the last author's name.

TREATMENT OF TITLES
Never underline titles or enclose them in quotation marks. Capitalize a title's first word and any proper nouns. Don't capitalize the first word of a subtitle unless it's a proper noun. Capitalize the titles of academic journals. If the title of a periodical is one word, give it in full; otherwise, abbreviate the title according to recommendations established by the *American National Standard for Abbreviations of Titles of Periodicals*. Capitalize a newspaper title's major words, giving the full title but omitting *A, An,* or *The* at the beginning.

PLACE OF PUBLICATION
Use a colon after the city of publication. If the city name could be unfamiliar to readers, add in parentheses the postal abbreviation for the US state or Canadian province. If the location of a foreign city will be unfamiliar to readers, add in parentheses the country name, abbreviating it according to International Organization for Standardization (ISO) standards. Find ISO abbreviations at http://un.org/Depts/cartographic/english/geoinfo/geoname.pdf.

PUBLISHER
Give the name of the publisher, without periods after initials, and use a semicolon after the publisher's name. Omit *The* at the beginning or *Co., Inc., Ltd.,* or *Press* at the end. However, for a university press, abbreviate *University* and *Press* as *Univ* and *Pr,* respectively, without periods.

continued >>

> ## Quick Reference 38.2 (continued)
>
> ### PUBLICATION MONTH
> Abbreviate all month names longer than three letters to their first three letters, but do not add a period.
>
> ### INCLUSIVE PAGE NUMBERS
> Shorten the second number as much as possible, making sure that the number isn't ambiguous. For example, use 233–4 for 233 to 234; 233–44 for 233 to 244; but 233–304 (not 233–04) for 233 to 304.
>
> ### DISCONTINUOUS PAGE NUMBERS
> Give the numbers of all discontinuous pages, separating successive numbers or ranges with a comma: 54–7, 60–6.
>
> ### TOTAL PAGE NUMBERS
> In the citation for an entire book, the last information unit gives the total number of book pages, followed by the abbreviation *p* and a period.
>
> ### FORMAT FOR REFERENCES ENTRIES: BOOKS
> The basic format for the **Citation-Sequence** and **Citation-Name Systems** is
>
> Author(s). Title. Edition [if other than first]. Place of publication: Publisher; Date. Pages.
>
> For "Pages," list total pages when citing an entire work or inclusive pages when citing part of a book. Note that the Author, Title, and Edition sections end with a period. Place of publication is followed by a colon, and Publisher by a semicolon. Date and Pages end with a period.
>
> 1. Primrose SB, Twyman RM, Old RW. Principles of gene manipulation. London: Blackwell; 2002. 390 p.
>
> The basic format for the **Name-Date System** is
>
> Author(s). Date. Title. Edition [if other than first]. Place of publication: Publisher. Pages.
>
> Primrose SB, Twyman RM, Old RW. 2002. Principles of gene manipulation. London: Blackwell. 390 p.
>
> ### FORMAT FOR CITED REFERENCES ENTRIES: ARTICLES
> The basic format for the **Citation-Sequence** and **Citation-Name Systems** is
>
> Author(s). Article title. Journal title. Date;Volume(Issue):Pages.
>
> Each section ends with a period. Notice there is no space after the semicolon, before the parentheses, or after the colon. Abbreviate a journal's name only if it's
>
> continued >>

standard in your scientific discipline. For example, *Exp Neurol* is the abbreviated form for *Experimental Neurology.* In the following example, the volume number is 184, and the issue number, in parentheses, is 1.

1. Ginis I, Rao MS. Toward cell replacement therapy: promises and caveats. Exp Neurol. 2003;184(1):61–77.

The basic format for the **Name-Year System** is

Author(s). Date. Article title. Journal title. Volume(Issue):Pages.

Ginis I, Rao MS. 2003. Toward cell replacement therapy: promises and caveats. Exp Neurol. 184(1):61–77.

38c.2 The CSE name-year system

In the Name-Year system, in-text references include the last name of the author or authors, along with the year of publication, placed in parentheses. The end references in this system are organized in alphabetical order by author. (This system resembles APA style.)

IN-TEXT REFERENCE

This behavior occurs periodically (Sybesma 1977), although some claim never to have observed it (Crowder 1931).

or

Sybesma (1977) insists that this behavior occurs periodically, but Crowder (1931) claims never to have observed it.

END REFERENCE

1. Crowder W. Seashore life between the tides. New York: Dodd, Mead; 1931. New York: Dover Reprint; 1975. 372 p.

2. Sybesma C. An introduction to biophysics. New York: Academic; 1977. 648 p.

If there are two authors, give both names in the in-text reference, separated by *and.* If there are more than two authors, give only the first author's name, then include *et al.* and the publication year. If no author is given, include the first word or first few words of the title, followed by an ELLIPSIS and the date.

IN-TEXT REFERENCE

Various therapies have proven effective (Treatment . . . 2007).

Quick Reference 38.2 gives guidelines for compiling a References list. Especially pay attention to the Arrangement of Entries in a Name-Year system.

38c.3 The CSE citation-name system

In the Citation-Name system, the in-text references use numbers to refer to end references that are arranged alphabetically. In other words, first complete the list of end references, arranging them alphabetically by author. Then, number each reference; for example, if you were documenting references by Schmidt, Gonzalez, Adams, and Zurowski, in your end references, they would be arranged:

1. Adams . . .

2. Gonzalez . . .

3. Schmidt . . .

4. Zurowski.

Finally, your in-text references should use a superscript number corresponding to the name in your end references. The system resembles the Citation-Sequence system, except that the alphabetical order of the end references determines the number rather than the order of appearance in the text.

IN-TEXT REFERENCES—CITATION-NAME

Sybesma[2] insists that this behavior occurs periodically, but Crowder[1] claims never to have observed it.

END REFERENCES—CITATION-NAME

1. Crowder W. Seashore life between the tides. New York: Dodd, Mead; 1931. New York: Dover Reprint; 1975. 372 p.

2. Sybesma C. An introduction to biophysics. New York: Academic; 1977. 648 p.

Quick Reference 38.2 gives guidelines for compiling a References list. Especially pay attention to the arrangement of entries in a Citation-Name system.

38d What are CSE guidelines for sources on a list of references?

The CSE directory on page 714 corresponds to the sample references that follow. If you need a model not included in this book, consult the seventh edition of *Scientific Style and Format*. The examples that follow are for the Citation-Sequence and Citation-Name Systems; the Name-Date system differs by the placement of the date and by not numbering the entries. See Quick Reference 38.2 for illustrations of the differences.

BOOKS AND PARTS OF BOOKS

1. Book by One Author—CSE

1. Hawking SW. Black holes and baby universes and other essays. New York: Bantam; 1993. 320 p.

Use one space but no punctuation between an author's last name and the initial of the first name. Don't put punctuation or a space between first and middle initials (*Hawking SW*). Do, however, use the hyphen in a hyphenated first and middle name (for example, *Gille J-C* represents *Jean-Claude Gille* in the next item).

2. Book by More Than One Author—CSE

1. Wegzyn S, Gille J-C, Vidal P. Developmental systems: at the crossroads of system theory, computer science, and genetic engineering. New York: Springer-Verlag; 1990. 595 p.

3. Book by a Group or Corporate Author—CSE

1. Chemical Rubber Company. Handbook of laboratory safety. 3rd ed. Boca Raton (FL): CRC; 1990. 1352 p.

4. Anthology or Edited Book—CSE

1. Herrman B, Hummel S, editors. Ancient DNA: recovery and analysis of genetic material from paleontological, archeological, museum, medical, and forensic specimens. New York: Springer-Verlag; 1994. 1020 p.

5. One Selection or Chapter from an Anthology or Edited Book—CSE

1. Basov NG, Feoktistov LP, Senatsky YV. Laser driver for inertial confinement fusion. In: Bureckner KA, editor. Research trends in physics: inertial confinement fusion. New York: American Institute of Physics; 1992. p. 24–37.

6. Translation—CSE

1. Magris C. A different sea. Spurr MS, translator. London: Harvill; 1993. 194 p. Translation of: Un mare differente.

7. Reprint of an Older Book—CSE

1. Carson R. The sea around us. New York: Oxford Univ Pr; 1951. New York: Oxford Univ Pr; 1991. 230 p.

8. All Volumes of a Multivolume Work—CSE

1. Crane FL, Moore DJ, Low HE, editors. Oxidoreduction at the plasma membrane: relation to growth and transport. Boca Raton (FL): CRC; 1991. 2 vol.

9. Unpublished Dissertation or Thesis—CSE

1. Baykul MC. Using ballistic electron emission microscopy to investigate the metal-vacuum interface [dissertation]. Orem (UT): Polytechnic Univ Pr; 1993. 111 p. Available from: UMI Dissertation Express, http://tls.il.proquest.com/ hp/Products/DisExpress.html, Document 9332714.

10. Published Article from Conference Proceedings—CSE

1. Tsang CP, Bellgard MI. Sequence generation using a network of Boltzmann machines. In: Tsang CP, editor. Proceedings of the 4th Australian Joint Conference on Artificial Intelligence; 1990 Nov 8–11; Perth, AUS. Singapore: World Scientific; 1990. p 224–33.

PRINT ARTICLES FROM JOURNALS AND PERIODICALS

11. Article in a Journal—CSE

1. Ginis I, Rao MS. Toward cell replacement therapy: promises and caveats. Exp Neurol 2003;184(1):61–77.

Give both the volume number and the issue number (here, *184* is the volume number and *1* is the issue number). There is no space between the year and the volume, the volume and the issue, or the issue and the pages.

12. Journal Article on Discontinuous Pages—CSE

1. Richards FM. The protein folding problem. Sci Am 1991;246(1):54–7, 60–6.

13. Article with No Identifiable Author—CSE

1. Cruelty to animals linked to murders of humans. AWIQ 1993 Aug;42(3):16.

14. Article with Author Affiliation—CSE

1. DeMoll E, Auffenberg T (Department of Microbiology, University of Kentucky). Purine metabolism in *Methanococcus vannielii*. J Bacteriol 1993;175:5754–61.

15. Entire Issue of a Journal—CSE

1. Whales in a modern world: a symposium held in London, November 1988. Mamm Rev 1990 Jan;20(9).

The date of the symposium, November 1988, is part of the title of this issue.

16. Signed Newspaper Article—CSE

1. Kilborn PT. A health threat baffling for its lack of a pattern. New York Times 2003 Jun 22;Sect A:14.

Sect stands for *section.* Note that there is no space between the date and the section.

17. Unsigned Newspaper Article—CSE

1. Supercomputing center to lead security effort. Pantagraph (Bloomington, IL) 2003 Jul 4;Sect A:7.

18. Editorial or Review—CSE

CSE allows "notes" after the page number(s) that will help readers understand the nature of the reference.

1. Leshner AI. "Glocal" science advocacy. Science 2008;319(5865):877. Editorial.

2. Myer A. Genomes evolve, but how? Nature 2008;451(7180):771. Review of Lynch M, The Origins of Genome Architecture.

ELECTRONIC SOURCES ON THE INTERNET

In general, CSE style requires you cite electronic sources by including the author's name, if available; the work's title; the type of medium, in brackets, such as [*Internet*] or [*electronic mail on the Internet*]; the title of the publication if there's a print version or, if not, the place of publication and the publishing organization; the date the original was published or placed on the Internet; the date you accessed the publication, preceded by the word *cited* enclosed in brackets; and the address of the source, if from the Internet or a database. Omit end punctuation after an Internet address.

19. Books on the Internet—CSE

1. Colwell R, editor. MENC handbook of musical cognition and development [Internet]. New York (NY): Oxford Univ Pr; c2006 [cited 2008 Feb 4]. Available from: http://site.ebrary.com.bianca.penlib.du.edu/

20. Articles with Print Versions on the Internet—CSE

1. Pollard R. Evidence of a reduced home field advantage when a team moves to a new stadium. Journal of Sports Sciences [Internet]. 2002. [cited 2007 Nov 5]; 20(12):969–974. Available from: http://0-find.galegroup.com.bianca.penlib .du.edu:80/itx/start.do?prodId=AONE

21. Articles Available Only on the Internet—CSE

1. Overbye D. Remembrance of things future: the mystery of time. The New York Times on the Web [Internet]. 2005 Jun 28 [cited 2005 Dec 11]. Available from: http://www.nytimes.com/2005/06/28/science/28time.html

22. Web pages—CSE

Begin with author, if available; otherwise, begin with title.

1. Think again: men and women share cognitive skills [Internet]. Washington, DC: American Psychological Association; 2006 [cited 2007 Jan 17]. Available from: http://www.psychologymatters.org/thinkagain.html

2. Welcome to AAAI [Internet]. Menlo Park (CA): Association for the Advancement of Artificial Intelligence. c2008 [cited 2008 Mar 17]. Available from: http://www.aaai.org

23. Videos or Podcasts—CSE

1. Wesch M. Web 2.0 . . . the machine is us/ing us [video on the Internet]. 2007 Jan 31 [cited 2007 Dec 14]. Available from: http://www.youtube.com/watch?v=6gmP4nk0EOE

OTHER SOURCES

Include the type of medium in brackets after the title. Examples include [*map*], [*CD*], [*DVD*], [*poster*], and so on.

24. Map—CSE

1. Russia and post-Soviet republics [political map]. Moscow: Mapping Production Association; 1992. Conical equidistant projection; 40 × 48 in.; color, scale 1:8,000,000.

25. Unpublished Letter—CSE

1. Darwin C. [Letter to Mr. Clerke, 1861]. Located at: University of Iowa Library, Iowa City.

26. Video Recording—CSE

1. Nova—The elegant universe [DVD]. Boston: WGBH; 2004. 2 DVDs: 180 min, sound, color.

27. Slide Set—CSE

1. Human parasitology [slides]. Chicago: American Society of Clinical Pathologists; 1990. Color. Accompanied by: 1 guide.

28. Presentation Slides—CSE

1. Beaudoin E. Fruit fly larvae [PowerPoint slides]. Denver, CO: University of Denver; 2007 Oct 17. 49 slides.

PART

6

Writing Across the Curriculum— and Beyond

39

Comparing the Disciplines

39a What is writing across the curriculum?

Writing across the curriculum refers to the writing you do in college courses beyond first-year composition. Good writing in various subject areas, such as history, biology, or psychology, has many common features. However, there are also important differences. This section will help you adapt general principles of writing so you'll be successful in writing across the curriculum.

People commonly group academic disciplines into three broad categories: the humanities, the social sciences, and the natural sciences. Each has its own knowledge, vocabulary, and perspectives on the world; its own specialized assignments and purposes; its own common types of SOURCES* (3b); and its own expected documentation styles (Chapters 36–38).

No matter what differences exist among the academic disciplines, writing processes and strategies interconnect and overlap across the curriculum. It's always important to consider the WRITING SITUATION, including your TOPIC, PURPOSE, AUDIENCE, ROLE, CONTEXT, and SPECIAL REQUIREMENTS (1b). Every paper benefits from attention to the WRITING PROCESS, including PLANNING, SHAPING, DRAFTING, REVISING, EDITING, and PROOFREADING (Chapter 2), and certain types of writing, such as reports, SUMMARIES, ANALYSES, and SYNTHESES, are common in disciplines across the curriculum. Chapter 3 provides extensive discussion of specific types of papers common in many academic situations. Quick Reference 39.1 compares elements of the academic disciplines.

To understand some of the differences among the disciplines, consider these three quite different paragraphs about a mountain.

HUMANITIES

The mountain stands serene but troubled above the surrounding plains, like a peaceful leader threatened by a noisy crowd. Giant timber—part of a collage of evergreen and deciduous trees—conceals the expansive mountain's slope. At its base, a cool stream flows over flat and jagged rocks, gray, orange, and steel blue. Next to the outer bank of the stream stands a shingled farmhouse, desolate, yet suggesting its active past. Unfortunately, billboards, chairlifts, and trinket shops litter the scene, landmarks of unrelenting commercial life that

---

*Words printed in SMALL CAPITAL LETTERS are discussed elsewhere in the text and are defined in the Terms Glossary at the back of this book.

Quick Reference 39.1

Comparing the disciplines

Discipline	Types of assignments	Primary sources	Secondary sources	Usual documentation styles
HUMANITIES e.g., history, languages, literature, philosophy, art, music, theater	essays, response statements, reviews, analyses, original works such as stories, poems, memoirs	literary works, manuscripts, paintings and sculptures, historical documents, films, plays, photographs, artifacts from popular culture, personal experiences	reviews, journal articles, research papers, books	MLA, CMS
SOCIAL SCIENCES e.g., psychology, sociology, anthropology, education	research reports, case studies, reviews of the literature, analyses, ethnographies	surveys, interviews, observations, tests and measures	journal articles, scholarly books, literature reviews	APA
NATURAL SCIENCES e.g., biology, chemistry, physics, mathematics	research or lab reports, reports of data, research proposals, science reviews	experiments, field notes and direct observations, measurements	journal articles, research papers, books	often CSE but varies by discipline

have no patience with mere nature. Thoreau would hardly have chosen this place to escape his crowded society.

SOCIAL SCIENCES

Among the favorite pastimes of North American city dwellers is the "return to nature." Many people plan trips to mountains even though they hardly want a purely natural experience. They know they have arrived at the mountain that they have traveled hundreds of miles to see because huge billboards are directing them to its base. As they look up the mountain, dozens of people are riding over the treetops in a chairlift, littering the slope with paper cups and food wrappers. At the base of the mountain stands the inevitable refreshment or souvenir stand, found at virtually all American tourist attractions. People seem to want things "natural" but not too natural. Just as chain restaurants provide travelers with comfortably familiar surroundings, so do commercial enterprises keep mountain visitors within their comfort zones.

NATURAL SCIENCES

The mountain rises approximately 9,600 feet above sea level. The underlying rock is igneous, of volcanic origin, composed primarily of granites and feldspars. Three distinct biological communities are present on the mountain. The community at the top of the mountain is alpine, dominated by very short grasses and forbs. At middle altitudes, the community is a typical northern boreal coniferous forest community, and at the base and lower altitudes, deciduous forest is the dominant community. This community has, however, been highly affected by agricultural development along the river at its base and by recreational development.

These examples illustrate that each discipline has its own perspective and emphasis. The paragraph written for the humanities describes and interprets the mountain from the writer's personal perspective. The paragraph written for the social sciences focuses on the behavior of people as a group. The paragraph written for the natural sciences is an objective observation of natural phenomena. Of course, the lines between disciplines can blur.

39b What are primary research and secondary research in the disciplines?

As we discussed in section 7b, different source materials lead to different kinds of writing. In the humanities, primary sources are original creative works, including novels, stories, poems, autobiographies, plays, films, musical compositions, and works of art (Chapter 40). In the social and natural sciences, primary sources may include your own research, generated by conducting experiments, surveys, or careful observations. Or they may include books and articles in which researchers report findings from their research studies for the first time (Chapter 41).

SECONDARY SOURCES are scholarly writings that SUMMARIZE, ANALYZE, or SYNTHESIZE primary sources. In the humanities, secondary sources offer analysis and interpretation of primary works. In the social and natural sciences, secondary sources summarize, then synthesize findings, and draw parallels that offer new insights. You might review Quick Reference 4.4 on page 114 to understand the distinctions between primary and secondary sources.

39c What can help me write assignments in various disciplines?

A useful strategy for writing assignments in different disciplines is to analyze successful writings that match the requirements of your assignment. Instructors sometimes provide models for such papers or point you to similar published works. Following are some types of questions that will help you analyze model writings.

1. Are papers divided by subheadings or not?
2. Are specific parts required? Is there a specified format?
3. Does the paper require sources? If so, do writers tend to place most of their sources in one place (for example, near the beginning), or do they place sources throughout?
4. What kinds of sources appear in the writing? Are they primary or secondary? Which kinds of books, periodicals, or other sources does the writer tend to use?
5. Is the tone informal or very formal? Do writers use first person or third person?
6. Is the writing characterized by explanations and discussions that are full and expansive or concise and terse?
7. To what extent are writers expected to include their opinions or personal experiences, and to what extent are they expected to rely on objective analyses or source materials?
8. What is the mix of summary and analysis or interpretation?
9. What are typical introduction and conclusion strategies in model sources?
10. What documentation style does the writer use?

39d How do I use documentation in the disciplines?

Writers use DOCUMENTATION to credit the sources they've used and to help their readers learn more. A writer who neglects to credit a source is guilty of PLAGIARISM (35b).

DOCUMENTATION STYLES differ among the disciplines. In the humanities, most fields use the documentation style of the Modern Language Association (MLA), as explained and illustrated in Chapter 36. Occasionally, the humanities use CM (Chicago Manual) style, as explained and illustrated in Chapter

38. In the social sciences, most fields use the documentation style of the American Psychological Association (APA), as explained and illustrated in Chapter 37. In the natural sciences, documentation styles vary widely, although the Council of Science Editors (CSE) style is frequently used (see Chapter 38). Ask each of your science and technology instructors about the particular documentation style required for his or her assignments.

For more help with your writing, grammar, and research, go to **www.mycomplab.com**

40

Writing About the Humanities and Literature

40a What are the humanities?

The humanities consist of a set of disciplines that seek to represent and understand human experience, creativity, thought, and values. These disciplines include literature, languages, philosophy, and history, although some colleges group history with the social sciences. Also, many colleges consider the fine arts (music, art, dance, theater, and creative writing) part of the humanities, while other colleges group them separately.

40b What types of sources do I use in the humanities?

In the humanities, existing documents or artifacts are PRIMARY SOURCES, and the writer's task generally is to analyze and interpret them. Some humanities papers will require SECONDARY SOURCES. These are articles and books that someone has written to explain or interpret a primary source. For example, suppose you're writing about a movie you saw. The movie is a primary source. If you consult a review of that movie, the review would be a secondary source.

40c What types of papers do I write in the humanities?

Because the humanities cover an impressively broad range of knowledge, writing in the humanities covers many types and purposes.

SUMMARIES

Occasionally your instructor will request an objective summary of a text; you might need to tell the plot of a novel or present the main points of an article. Generally, however, a summary is a means to a larger end. For example, writing an interpretation often requires you to summarize parts of the source so that your points about it are clear. See section 7f.1.

SYNTHESES

SYNTHESIS relates several texts, ideas, or pieces of information to one another (4c). For example, you might read several accounts of the events leading up to the Civil War and then write a synthesis that explains what caused that war. See section 7f.4.

RESPONSES

In a response, you give your personal reaction to a work, supported by explanations of your reasoning. Even though a response is a personal reaction, think of it as writing to inform or, even, to argue; provide reasons for your response so your readers understand clearly why you believe as you do and so that they're convinced your response is reasonable. Some instructors want you to justify your response with references to a text, while other instructors do not. Clarify what your instructor wants before you begin. See section 7f.2.

NARRATIVES

When you write a NARRATIVE, you construct a coherent story out of separate facts or events. You might do the kind of work that a biographer does, gathering information about isolated events in people's lives, conducting interviews with those people or with others who knew them, or researching letters or other writings and related SOURCES—all to form a coherent story of their lives.

INTERPRETATIONS

An interpretation explains the meaning or significance of a particular text, event, or work of art. You present your point of view and explain your reasoning, and the quality of your reasoning determines how successfully you've conveyed your point. See section 7f.3.

CRITIQUES

In a critique (also called a CRITICAL RESPONSE or a review), you present judgments about a particular work, supported by your underlying reasoning.

Critical responses and reviews may focus on the literary form, or genre, of a work. Responses or reviews may focus on a work's accuracy, logic, or conclusions. Finally, responses or reviews may analyze a work's relations to other works or a work's similarities to and differences from the "real" world.

ANALYSES

When you engage in analysis, you explain texts, events, objects, or documents by identifying and discussing important elements in them. These elements can include matters of form (how the work is put together) or of ideas (what the work means). The humanities use a number of **analytic frameworks**, or systematic ways of investigating a work. Quick Reference 40.1 summarizes some common analytic frameworks used most notably in literary analysis.

Quick Reference 40.1 ■ ■ ■ ■ ■ ■ ■

Selected analytic frameworks used in the humanities

RHETORICAL
Examines how and why people use LOGIC, EMOTION, and ETHOS to create desired effects on specific audiences, in specific situations (see Chapter 4).

FEMINIST
Focuses on how women are presented and treated, concentrating especially on power relations between men and women.

CULTURAL/NEW HISTORICAL
Explores how social, economic, and other cultural forces influence the development of ideas, texts, art, laws, customs, and so on. Also explores how individual texts or events provide broader understandings of the past or present.

DECONSTRUCTIONIST
Assumes that the meaning of any given text is not stable or "in" the work. Rather, meaning always depends on contexts and the interests of those in power. The goal of deconstruction is to produce multiple possible meanings of a work, usually to undermine traditional interpretations.

FORMALIST
Centers on matters of structure, form, and traditional literary devices (plot, rhythm, images, symbolism, DICTION).

MARXIST
Assumes that the most important forces in human experience are economic and material ones. Focuses on power differences between economic classes of people and the effects of those differences.

continued >>

> **Quick Reference 40.1**   (continued)
>
> ---
>
> **READER-RESPONSE**
> Emphasizes how the individual reader determines meaning. The reader's personal history, values, experiences, relationships, and previous reading all contribute to how he or she interprets a particular work or event.

40d Which documentation style do I use to write about the humanities?

Most fields in the humanities use the documentation style of the Modern Language Association (MLA), as explained and illustrated in Chapter 36. Some disciplines in the humanities use Chicago Manual (CM) style, as explained in Chapter 38. Writers use documentation to give credit to the sources they've used. A writer who neglects to credit a source is guilty of PLAGIARISM.

EXERCISE 40-1   Consider how you could use some of the frameworks in Quick Reference 40.1 to analyze the photograph in Figure 40.1.

Figure 40.1 Use analytic frameworks to view this photograph.

40e What is literature and why write about it?

Literature includes fiction (novels and short stories); drama (plays, scripts, and some films); poetry (poems and lyrics); as well as nonfiction with artistic qualities (memoirs, personal essays, and the like).

Writing about literature generates insights about your reading. It helps you understand other people, ideas, times, and places. It shows you how authors use language to stir the imaginations, emotions, and intellects of their readers. Finally, writing is a way to share your own reading experiences and insights with other readers.

40f What general strategies can help me write about literature?

When you write about literature, you want to read the work closely as well as actively (Chapter 4). Such reading involves asking what the work means, why the author made a particular choice, and why readers react to the work as they do. Quick References 40.2, 40.3, and 40.4 list several questions or elements that encourage active reading.

Sometimes instructors ask students to answer questions that deal with material on a literal level, that is, to tell exactly what is said on the page. If a question asks what happens in the plot or what a passage is saying, you need to answer with a SUMMARY or PARAPHRASE of the work. If a question asks about the historical context of a work, or asks for biographical or situational information about the author, you probably need to do some research and then report exactly what you find.

More often, assignments call for making INFERENCES. Making inferences means reading "between the lines" to figure out what is implied but not stated. This reading skill is especially crucial for reading literature because it tends to "show" rather than to "tell." Inferential thinking is necessary when your instructor asks you to discuss why a character does something for which the author provides no explicit reason. It's necessary when your instructor asks you to explain the effect of images in a poem, to discuss how a work implies the author's stance on a social issue, or to analyze how the author depicts the role of women, men, or specific ethnic groups.

Writing effective papers about literature involves more than summarizing the plot. It involves CRITICAL THINKING and SYNTHESIS. In such papers, you state a CLAIM (an observation or a position about the work of literature) and convince your readers that the thesis is reasonable. To be effective, your papers must be thorough and well supported. For support, you make direct references to the work, by SUMMARIZING, PARAPHRASING, and QUOTING specific passages

(35h–35j) and by explaining precisely *why* and *how* the selected passages support your interpretation.

40g How do I write different types of papers about literature?

When you read, look for details or passages that relate to your thesis. Mark up the text as you read by selectively underlining passages or by writing notes, comments, or questions in the margin. Alternatively, take notes separately.

WRITING A PERSONAL RESPONSE

In a personal response paper, you explain your reaction to a literary work or some aspect of it. You might write about why you did or did not enjoy reading a particular work; discuss whether situations in the work are similar to your personal experiences; explain whether you agree or disagree with the author's point of view and why; or answer a question or explore a problem that the work raised for you.

WRITING AN INTERPRETATION

An interpretation explains the message or viewpoint that you think the work conveys. Most works of literature are open to more than one interpretation. Your task, then, is not to discover the single right answer. Instead, your task is to determine a possible interpretation and provide an argument that supports it. The questions in Quick Reference 40.2 can help you write an effective interpretation paper.

Quick Reference 40.2　　　　　　■ ■ ■ ■ ■ ■ ■

Questions for an interpretation paper

1. What is a central theme of the work?
2. How do particular parts of the work relate to the theme?
3. If patterns exist in the work, what might they mean? Patterns include repeated images, situations, words, and so on.
4. What meaning does the author create through the elements listed in Quick Reference 40.3?
5. Why might the work end as it does?

WRITING A FORMAL ANALYSIS

A formal analysis explains how elements of a literary work function to create meaning or effect. Quick Reference 40.3 describes some of the major literary elements that you might expect to use in formal analyses.

Quick Reference 40.3

Major elements of formal analysis in literary works

PLOT	Events and their sequence
THEME	Central idea or message
STRUCTURE	Organization and relationship of parts to each other and to the whole
CHARACTERIZATION	Traits, thoughts, and actions of the people in the plot
SETTING	Time and place of the action
POINT OF VIEW	Perspective or position from which the material is presented—by a narrator, a main character, or another person either in the plot or observing the plot
STYLE	How words and sentence structures present the material
IMAGERY	Descriptive language that creates mental pictures for the reader
TONE	Author's attitude toward the subject of the work—and sometimes toward the reader—expressed through choice of words, imagery, and point of view (Chapter 1)
FIGURE OF SPEECH	Unusual use or combination of words, as in metaphor and simile, for enhanced vividness or effect
SYMBOLISM	Meaning beneath the surface of the words and images
RHYTHM	Beat, meter
RHYME	Repetition of similar sounds for their auditory effect

To prepare to write a formal analysis, read the work thoroughly, looking for patterns and repetitions. Write notes as you read to help you form insights about these patterns and repetitions.

WRITING A CULTURAL ANALYSIS

A cultural analysis relates the literary work to broader historical, social, cultural, and political situations. Instructors might ask you to explain how events or prevailing attitudes influence the writing of a work or the way readers understand it. Quick Reference 40.4 lists some common focuses for cultural analysis.

Quick Reference 40.4

Major topics for cultural analysis

GENDER	How does a work portray women or men and define—or challenge—their respective roles in society?
CLASS	How does a work portray relationships among the upper, middle, and lower economic classes? How do characters' actions or perspectives result from their wealth and power—or the lack thereof?
RACE AND ETHNICITY	How does a work portray the influences of race and ethnicity on the characters' actions, status, and values?
HISTORY	How does a work reflect—or challenge—past events and values in a society?
AUTOBIOGRAPHY	How might the writer's experiences have influenced this particular work? Similarly, how might the times in which the writer lives or lived have affected his or her work?
GENRE	How is the work similar to or different from other works of its type (plays, sonnets, mysteries, comic novels, memoirs, and so on)?

40h What special rules apply to writing about literature?

When you write about literature, certain special elements come into play.

40h.1 Using present and past tense correctly

Always use the PRESENT TENSE when you describe or discuss a literary work or any of its elements: *George Henderson* [a character] ***takes*** *control of the action and* ***tells*** *the other characters when they may speak.* The present tense is also correct for discussing what the author has done in a specific work: *Because Susan Glaspell* [the author] ***excludes*** *Minnie and John Wright from the stage as speaking characters, she* ***forces*** *her audience to learn about them through the words of others.*

Use a PAST-TENSE VERB to discuss historical events or biographical information: *Susan Glaspell* ***was*** *a social activist who* ***was*** *strongly* ***influenced*** *by the chaotic events of the early twentieth century.*

40h.2 Using your own ideas and secondary sources

Some assignments call for only your own ideas about the literary work that is the subject of your essay. Other assignments require you additionally to use

SECONDARY SOURCES, books and articles in which experts discuss some aspect of the literary text or other material related to your topic.

You might use secondary sources to support your own ideas, perhaps by drawing on the ideas of a scholar who agrees with you or debating the ideas of a scholar who disagrees with you. Or, if you think that you have a new or different interpretation, you might summarize, analyze, or critique what others have written, to provide a framework for your own analysis. You can locate secondary sources by using the process discussed in Chapter 34. A particularly important resource for research about literature is the *MLA International Bibliography,* which is the most comprehensive index to literary scholarship.

As with all source-based writing, you need to DOCUMENT primary sources and secondary sources because you want to ensure that readers never mistake someone else's ideas as yours. Otherwise, you're PLAGIARIZING (see Chapter 35). Most literature instructors require students to use the DOCUMENTATION STYLE of the Modern Language Association (MLA) that we described in Chapter 36. However, check with your instructor.

40i Sample student essay

The student essay that follows is a literary analysis of two poems by Claude McKay that draws on SECONDARY SOURCES.

Born in 1889 on the Caribbean island of Jamaica, Claude McKay moved to the United States in 1910 and became a highly respected poet. Paule Cheek, a student in a class devoted to writing about literature, chose to write about Claude McKay's nontraditional use of a very traditional poetic form, the sonnet. A sonnet has fourteen lines in a patterned rhyme and develops one idea. In secondary sources, Cheek found information about McKay's life that she felt gave her further insights into both the structure and the meaning of McKay's sonnets "In Bondage" and "The White City." For your reference, both poems appear below.

IN BONDAGE
I would be wandering in distant fields
Where man, and bird, and beast, lives leisurely,
And the old earth is kind, and ever yields
Her goodly gifts to all her children free;
Where life is fairer, lighter, less demanding,   5

And boys and girls have time and space for play
Before they come to years of understanding—
Somewhere I would be singing, far away.
For life is greater than the thousand wars
Men wage for it in their insatiate lust,   10
And will remain like the eternal stars,
When all that shines to-day is drift and dust.
But I am bound with you in your mean graves,
O black men, simple slaves of ruthless slaves.

THE WHITE CITY

I will not toy with it nor bend an inch.
Deep in the secret chambers of my heart
I muse my life-long hate, and without flinch
I bear it nobly as I live my part.
My being would be skeleton, a shell,   5
If this dark Passion that fills my every mood,
And makes my heaven in the white world's hell,
Did not forever feed me vital blood.
I see the mighty city through a mist—
The strident trains that speed the goaded mass,   10
The poles and spires and towers vapor-kissed,
The fortressed port through which the great ships pass,
The tides, the wharves, the dens I contemplate,
Are sweet like wanton loves because I hate.

Cheek 1

Paule Cheek

Professor Bartlestone

English 112, Section 03

14 March 2008

Words in Bondage: Claude McKay's

Use of the Sonnet Form in Two Poems

The sonnet has remained one of the central poetic forms of the Western tradition for centuries. This fourteen-line form is easy for poets to learn but difficult to master. With its fixed rhyme schemes, number of lines, and meter, the sonnet form forces writers to be doubly creative while working within it. Many poets over the years have modified or varied the sonnet form, playing upon its conventions to keep it vibrant and original. One such writer was Jamaican-born Claude McKay (1889-1948).

The Jamaica of McKay's childhood was very different from turn-of-the-century America. Slavery had ended there in the 1830s, and McKay was able to grow up "in a society whose population was overwhelmingly black and largely free of the overt white oppression which constricted the lives of black Americans in the United States during this same period" (Cooper, *Passion* 5-6). This background could not have prepared McKay for what he encountered when he moved to America in his twenties. Lynchings, still common at that time, were on the rise, and during the Red Scare of 1919 there were dozens of racially motivated riots in major cities throughout

continued >>

(Proportions shown in this paper are adjusted to fit space limitations of this book. Follow actual dimensions given in this book and in your instructor's directions.)

the country. Thousands of homes were destroyed in these riots, and several black men were tortured and burned at the stake (Cooper, *Claude McKay* 97). McKay responded to these atrocities by raising an outraged cry of protest in his poems. In two of his sonnets from this period, "The White City" and "In Bondage," we can see McKay's mastery of the form and his skillful use of irony in the call for social change.

McKay's choice of the sonnet form as the vehicle for his protest poetry at first seems strange. Since his message was a radical one, we might expect that the form of his poetry would be revolutionary. Instead, McKay gives us connote a poetic form that dates back to the early sixteenth century and was originally intended to be used exclusively for love poems. The critic James R. Giles notes that this choice

> is not really surprising, since McKay's Jamaican education and reading had been based firmly upon the major British poets. From the point quite early in his life when he began to think of himself as a poet, his models were such major English writers as William Shakespeare, John Milton, William Wordsworth. He thus was committed from the beginning to the poetry which he had initially been taught to admire. (44)

McKay published both "The White City" and "In Bondage" in 1922, and they are similar in many ways. Like most sonnets, each has fourteen lines and is in iambic pentameter. The diction is extremely elevated. For example, this quatrain from "In Bondage" is almost Elizabethan in its word choice and order:

continued >>

Cheek 3

For life is greater than the thousand wars

Men wage for it in their insatiate lust,

And will remain like the eternal stars,

When all that shines to-day is drift and dust.

(lines 9-12)

If this level of diction is reminiscent of Shakespeare, it is no accident. Both poems employ the English sonnet rhyme scheme (a b a b c d c d e f e f g g) and division into three quatrains and a closing couplet. McKay introduces a touch of his own, however. Although the English sonnet form calls for the "thematic turn" to fall at the closing couplet, McKay defies convention. He incorporates two turns into each sonnet instead of one. This allows him to use the first "mini-turn" to further develop the initial theme set forth in the first eight lines while dramatically bringing the poem to a conclusion with a forcefully ironic turn in the closing couplet. Specifically, in "The White City," McKay uses the additional turn to interrupt his description of his "Passion" with a vision of "the mighty city through a mist" (9). In "In Bondage," he uses the additional turn to justify his desire to escape the violent existence that society has imposed on his people.

McKay also demonstrates his poetic ability through his choice of words within his customized sonnets. Consider the opening of "In Bondage":

I would be wandering in distant fields

Where man, and bird, and beast, lives leisurely,

And the old earth is kind, and ever yields

Her goodly gifts to all her children free;

Where life is fairer, lighter, less demanding,

continued >>

> And boys and girls have time and space for play
> Before they come to years of understanding--
> Somewhere I would be singing, far away. (1-8)

The conditional power of *would* in the first line, coupled with the alliterative *wandering*, subtly charms us into a relaxed, almost dreamlike state in which the poet can lead us gently through the rest of the poem. The commas in the second line force us to check our progress to a "leisurely" crawl, mirroring the people and animals that the line describes. By the time we reach the eighth line, we are probably ready to join the poet in this land of "somewhere . . . far away."

Then this optimistic bubble is violently burst by the closing couplet:

> But I am bound with you in your mean graves,
> O black men, simple slaves of ruthless slaves.
> (13-14)

In "The White City" McKay again surprises us. This time, he does so by turning the traditional love sonnet upside down; instead of depicting a life made endurable through an overpowering love, McKay shows us a life made bearable through a sustaining hate:

> I will not toy with it nor bend an inch.
> Deep in the secret chambers of my heart
> I muse my life-long hate, and without flinch
> I bear it nobly as I live my part.
> My being would be a skeleton, a shell,
> If this dark Passion that fills my every mood,
> And makes my heaven in the white world's hell,
> Did not forever feed me vital blood. (1-8)

continued >>

Cheek 5

If it were not for the presence of "life-long hate" in the third line, this opening would easily pass as part of a conventional love sonnet. However, as the critic William Maxwell notes in "On 'The White City'," the first quatrain is "designed to ambush those anticipating another rehearsal of love's powers." The emotion comes from "deep in the secret chambers" of the speaker's heart (2), it allows him to transcend "the white world's hell" (7), and it is a defining "Passion." Once again, however, McKay uses the couplet to defy our expectations by making it plain that he has used the form of the love sonnet only for ironic effect: "The tides, the wharves, the dens I contemplate, / Are sweet like wanton loves because I hate" (13-14).

McKay's impressive poetic ability made him a master of the sonnet form. His language could at times rival even Shakespeare's, and his creativity allowed him to adapt the sonnet to his own ends. His ironic genius is revealed in his use of one of Western society's most elevated poetic forms to critique that same society. He held that critique so strongly that shortly after publishing these poems, McKay spent six months in the Soviet Union, where he met with Communist leaders (Hathaway 282). McKay once described himself as "a man who was bitter because he loved, who was both right and wrong because he hated the things that destroyed love, who tried to give back to others a little of what he had got from them . . ." (qtd. in Barksdale and Kinnamon 491). As these two sonnets show, McKay gave back very much indeed.

continued >>

Cheek 6

Works Cited

Barksdale, Richard, and Kenneth Kinnamon, eds. *Black Writers of America: A Comprehensive Anthology.* New York: Macmillan, 1972. Print.

Cooper, Wayne F. *Claude McKay: Rebel Sojourner in the Harlem Renaissance.* Baton Rouge: Louisiana State UP, 1987. Print.

---, ed. *The Passion of Claude McKay.* New York: Schocken, 1973. Print.

Giles, James R. *Claude McKay.* Boston: Twayne, 1976. Print.

Hathaway, Heather. "Claude McKay." *The Concise Oxford Companion to African American Literature.* Ed. William L. Andrews, Frances Smith Foster, and Trudier Harris. New York: Oxford UP, 2001. 282-83. Print.

Maxwell, William. "On 'The White City.'" *New Negro, Old Left: African American Writing and Communism Between the Wars.* New York: Columbia UP, 1999. *Modern American Poetry.* Web. 5 Mar. 2008 <http://www.english.uiuc.edu/maps/poets/m_r/mckay/whitecity.htm>.

McKay, Claude. "In Bondage." *Literature: An Introduction to Reading and Writing.* 8th ed. Ed. Edgar V. Roberts and Henry E. Jacobs. Englewood Cliffs: Prentice, 2007. 949-50. Print.

---. "The White City." *Literature: An Introduction to Reading and Writing.* 8th ed. Ed. Edgar V. Roberts and Henry E. Jacobs. Englewood Cliffs: Prentice, 2007. 1212. Print.

41

Writing in the Social Sciences and Natural Sciences

SOCIAL SCIENCES

41a What are the social sciences?

The social sciences focus on the behavior of people as individuals and in groups. The field includes disciplines such as economics, education, political science, psychology, sociology, and certain courses in geography. At some colleges, history is included in the social sciences; at others, it's part of the humanities.

41b What kinds of sources do I use in the social sciences?

Some methods used in the social sciences lead to **quantitative research**, which seeks to count things or translate information into numerical data to analyze statistically. Other methods lead to **qualitative research**, which relies on careful descriptions and thorough written interpretations.

In the social sciences, PRIMARY SOURCES include surveys and questionnaires, observations, interviews, and experiments. When writing about information you gather, you analyze and explain what the sources mean or why they're significant.

SURVEYS AND QUESTIONNAIRES

Surveys and questionnaires systematically gather information from a representative number of individuals. To prepare a questionnaire, use the guidelines in Quick Reference 32.1 on page 519.

OBSERVATIONS

Some writing in the social sciences requires direct observations of people's behaviors. In reporting your observations, tell what tools you used, because they might have influenced what you saw. For example, it would be important to state whether a photo was posed or candid because human subjects behave differently when they know they are being photographed.

INTERVIEWS

You might interview people to gather opinions and impressions. Remember that interviews aren't always reliable because people's memories are imprecise, and their first impulse is to present themselves in the best light. Try to interview as many people as possible so that you can cross-check information.

EXPERIMENTS

The social sciences sometimes use data from experiments as a source. For example, if you want to learn how people react in a particular situation, you can set up that situation artificially and bring individuals (known as "subjects") into it to observe their behavior.

With all methods of inquiry in the social sciences, you need to be ethical. Professional social scientists must seek explicit written permission from their subjects, and colleges have official panels to review research proposals to make sure the studies are ethical. Check with your instructor to see whether you need to have your study approved.

41c What are writing purposes and practices in the social sciences?

The purpose of much writing in the social sciences is explanatory. Writers try to explain both what a behavior is and why it happens. SUMMARY and SYNTHESIS (7f.1, and 7f.4) are important fundamental strategies for explanatory writing in the social sciences. INTERPRETATIONS and ANALYSES (7f.3) are common when social scientists write about problems and their solutions.

Other kinds of writing that are common in the social sciences include REPORTS OF OBSERVATIONS (7d), CASE STUDIES (7d.4), and ETHNOGRAPHIES (7d.5). Social scientists also write REPORTS AND ANALYSES OF DATA (7e.1; 7e.2), ESSAYS OF APPLICATION (7f.5), PROPOSALS (7g.2), and, of course, RESEARCH PAPERS (7g.4).

Social scientists are particularly careful to define their KEY TERMS when they write, especially when they discuss complex social issues. For example, if you're writing a paper on substance abuse in the medical profession, you must first define what you mean by the terms *substance abuse* and *medical profession.* Without defining such terms, you confuse readers or lead them to wrong conclusions.

In college courses in the social sciences, your goal is usually to be a neutral observer, so most of the time you need to use the THIRD PERSON (*he, she, it, one, they*). Using the FIRST PERSON (*I, we, our*) is acceptable only when you write about your own reactions and experiences. Some writing in the social sciences overuses the PASSIVE VOICE (15o and 15p). Style manuals for the social sciences, however, recommend using the ACTIVE VOICE whenever possible.

41d What are different types of papers in the social sciences?

Instructors will sometimes assign the same kinds of writing in the social sciences we explained for the humanities in section 40c. Four additional types of papers are case studies, research reports, research papers (or reviews of the literature), and ethnographies.

CASE STUDIES

A case study is an intensive study of one group or individual. We discussed them in some detail in section 7d.4, but here are some additional perspectives. If you write a case study, describe situations as a neutral observer. Refrain from interpreting them unless your assignment says that you can add your interpretation to your report. Also, always differentiate between fact and opinion (4d.1).

A case study is usually presented in a relatively fixed format, but the specific parts and their order vary. Most case studies contain the following components: (1) basic identifying information about the individual or group; (2) a history of the individual or group; (3) observations of the individual's or group's behavior; and (4) conclusions as well as possible recommendations that resulted from the observations.

RESEARCH REPORTS

Research reports explain your own original research based on PRIMARY SOURCES. These may result from interviews, questionnaires, observations, or experiments. Research reports in the social sciences often follow a prescribed format: (1) statement of the problem; (2) background, sometimes including a review of the literature; (3) methodology; (4) results; and (5) discussion of findings.

RESEARCH PAPERS (OR REVIEWS OF THE LITERATURE)

More often for students, social science research requires you to summarize, analyze, and synthesize SECONDARY SOURCES. To prepare a **review of literature**, comprehensively gather and analyze the sources that have been published on a specific topic. Sometimes a review of the literature is a part of a longer paper, usually the "background" section of a research report. Other times the entire paper might be an extensive review of the literature.

ETHNOGRAPHIES

Ethnographies are comprehensive studies of people interacting in a particular situation. Section 7d.5 provides advice on writing them.

41e What documentation style should I use in the social sciences?

If you use sources when writing about the social sciences, you must credit them using documentation. The American Psychological Association (APA) is the most commonly used documentation style in the social sciences. APA style uses PARENTHETICAL REFERENCES in the body of a paper and a list of REFERENCES at the end. We describe APA documentation style in detail in Chapter 37, providing a sample student research paper using APA style in section 37h.

Chicago Manual (CM) documentation style is sometimes used in the social sciences. The CM BIBLIOGRAPHIC NOTE style is described in detail in Chapter 38.

NATURAL SCIENCES

41f What are the natural sciences?

The natural sciences include disciplines such as astronomy, biology, chemistry, geology, and physics. The sciences focus on natural phenomena. Scientists form and test hypotheses, which are assumptions made to prove their logical soundness and consequences in the real world. They do this to explain CAUSE AND EFFECT (4d.3) as systematically and objectively as possible.

The scientific method, commonly used in the sciences to make discoveries, is a procedure for gathering information related to a specific hypothesis. The scientific method is the cornerstone of all inquiry in the sciences. Quick Reference 41.1 gives guidelines for using the scientific method.

41g What are writing purposes and practices in the natural sciences?

Because scientists usually write to inform their AUDIENCE about factual information, SUMMARY and SYNTHESIS are important fundamental writing techniques. Exactness is extremely important in scientific writing. Readers expect precise descriptions of procedures and findings, free of personal bias. Scientists expect to be able to *replicate*—repeat step by step—the experiment or process the researcher carried out and obtain the same outcome.

Completeness is as important as exactness in scientific writing. Without complete information, a reader can misunderstand the writer's message and reach a wrong conclusion.

> ### Quick Reference 41.1   ■ ■ ■ ■ ■ ■ ■
>
> #### Guidelines for using the scientific method
>
> 1. Formulate a tentative explanation—known as a *hypothesis*—for a scientific phenomenon. Be as specific as possible.
> 2. Read and summarize previously published information related to your hypothesis.
> 3. Plan and outline a method of investigation to uncover the information needed to test your hypothesis.
> 4. Experiment, following exactly the investigative procedures you've outlined.
> 5. Observe closely the results of the experiment, and write notes carefully.
> 6. Analyze the results. If they prove the hypothesis to be false, rework the investigation and begin again. If the results confirm the hypothesis, say so.
> 7. Write a report of your research. At the end, you can suggest additional hypotheses that might be investigated.

Because science writing depends largely on objective observation rather than subjective comments, scientists generally avoid using the FIRST PERSON (*I, we, our*) in their writing.

When writing for the sciences, you're often expected to follow fixed formats, which are designed to summarize a project and present its results efficiently. Writers in the sciences sometimes use charts, graphs, tables, diagrams, and other illustrations to present material. In fact, illustrations, in many cases, can explain complex material more clearly than words can, as in Figure 41.1.

41h What documentation style should I use in the natural sciences?

If you use secondary sources when you write about the sciences, you are required to credit your sources by using documentation. Documentation styles in the various sciences differ somewhat from discipline to discipline and, even, from publication to publication. Ask your instructor which style to use.

The Council of Science Editors (CSE) has compiled style and documentation guidelines for the life sciences, the physical sciences, and mathematics. CSE documentation guidelines are described in sections 38c and 38d.

COMMON DISEASES AND INFECTIONS WITH THEIR MICROBIAL CAUSES

	Bacteria	Fungus	Protozoa	Virus
Athlete's foot		▲		
Chickenpox				▲
Common cold				▲
Diarrheal disease	▲		▲	▲
Flu				▲
Genital herpes				▲
Malaria			▲	
Meningitis	▲			▲
Pneumonia	▲	▲		▲
Sinusitis	▲	▲		
Skin diseases	▲	▲	▲	▲
Strep throat	▲			
Tuberculosis	▲			
Urinary tract infection	▲			
Vaginal infections	▲	▲		
Viral hepatitis				▲

Figure 41.1 A table conveying data

41i How do I write different types of papers in the natural sciences?

Kinds of writing that are common in the natural sciences include REPORTS AND ANALYSES OF DATA (7e.1; 7e.2), LAB REPORTS AND EMPIRICAL STUDIES (7e.3), and RESEARCH PAPERS (7g, 4).

Two additional major types of papers in the sciences are *reports* and *reviews*.

41i.1 Science reports

Science reports tell about observations and experiments. When they describe laboratory experiments, as is often the case in academic settings, they're usually called laboratory reports. Formal reports feature the eight elements identified in Quick Reference 41.2. Less formal reports, which are sometimes assigned in introductory college courses, might not include an abstract or a review of the literature. Ask your instructor which sections to include in your report.

Quick Reference 41.2 ■ ■ ■ ■ ■ ■ ■

Parts of a science report

1. **Title.** Precisely describes your report's topic. Your instructor may require a title page that lists the title, your name, the course name and section, your instructor's name, and the date. If so, there is no

continued >>

Quick Reference 41.2 (continued)

recommended format in CSE style; generally, students use APA format (37g) or their instructor's.

2. **Abstract.** Provides a short overview of the report to help readers decide whether your research interests them.

3. **Introduction.** States the purpose behind your research and presents the hypothesis. Any needed background information and a review of the literature appear here.

4. **Methods and Materials.** Describes the equipment, material, and procedures used.

5. **Results.** Provides the information obtained from your efforts. Charts, graphs, and photographs help present the data in a way that is easy for readers to grasp.

6. **Discussion.** Presents your interpretation and evaluation of the results. Did your efforts support your hypothesis? If not, can you suggest why not? Use concrete evidence in discussing your results.

7. **Conclusion.** Lists conclusions about the hypothesis and the outcomes of your efforts, paying particular attention to any implications that can be drawn from your work. Be specific in suggesting further research.

8. **References.** Presents references cited in the review of the literature, if any. Its format conforms to the requirements of the documentation style preferred by your instructor.

SAMPLE STUDENT SCIENCE REPORT

The sample science report presented on the following pages was written by a student in an intermediate course in biology. Like the sample report, yours would likely follow APA format for margins, page numbering, and title page. The text and references would follow CSE-style recommendations.

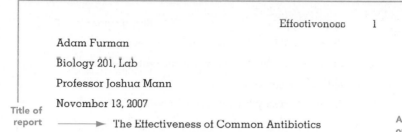

Effectiveness   1

Adam Furman

Biology 201, Lab

Professor Joshua Mann

November 13, 2007

Title of report ———→ The Effectiveness of Common Antibiotics

Title of subsection ———→ Introduction

Abstract omitted on this sample

The purpose of this experiment was to test the effectiveness of antibiotics against two common bacteria.

Antibiotics are substances that inhibit life processes of bacteria. There are two types of antibiotics. One interferes with cell wall synthesis, causing death. The other disrupts protein synthesis, thus preventing replication.

Escherichia coli is a gram-negative bacterium. It is found in the colon of many mammals, including humans. Commonly, it contaminates beef and chicken products. *Staphylococcus epidermidis* is a gram-positive bacterium found naturally on the skin. This bacterium is often the cause of infected burns and cuts. Both bacteria were used in this experiment.

It is hypothesized that five chemical antibiotics will be effective against both bacteria. Also hypothesized is that two natural antimicrobials, echinacea and garlic, would not work very well.

Methods and Materials

Using aseptic techniques, two petri dishes were inoculated. *Staphylococcus epidermidis* was used on one dish and *Escherichia coli* on a second dish. A sterile paper disc was saturated with Streptomycin. The disc was placed on one of the dishes. The process was repeated for the other dish. Both

continued >>

Effectiveness   2

dishes were marked with identification and location of the paper discs. Each of the following was also saturated on paper discs and placed into its own zone on both dishes: sterile water (control), ampicillin, erythromycin, chloramphenicol, tetracycline, gentamycin, echinacea, and garlic.

The dishes were incubated overnight at room temperature. The zone of inhibition of growth in centimeters was measured and recorded.

Results

Streptomycin, a protein synthesis disrupter, worked effectively to prevent growth of the *S. epidermidis* and the *E. coli*. Tetracycline inhibited the reproduction of the *S. epidermidis* and the *E. coli*. Ampicillin, a common bactericide, worked better on the *S. epidermidis* than the *E. coli*, because the *S. epidermidis* is gram positive and the *E. coli* is gram negative. Gentamycin effectively prevented the growth of *E. coli*. Erythromycin and chloramphenicol behaved similarly to the ampicillin.

The antibiotics behaved as expected in regard to effectiveness against gram-positive and gram-negative bacteria. As hypothesized, the echinacea inhibited growth only slightly, indicating that it probably would not function as an antibiotic. The garlic had a zone of inhibition greater than expected for a non-antibiotic. Zero centimeters of inhibition from the sterile water control demonstrates that there was no contamination of the experiment.

Discussion section omitted in this sample

continued >>

Effectiveness   3

Conclusion

The results imply that the ampicillin would be an effective treatment against *S. epidermidis* infection and gentamycin would prove effective in treating an infection of *E. coli*.

As with any experiment, it would be wise to repeat the tests again to check for accuracy. Other antibiotics could be tested against a larger range of bacteria for broader results.

No Cited References needed in this type of science report

41i.2   Science reviews

A science review is a paper discussing published information on a scientific topic or issue. The purpose of the review is SUMMARY: to assemble for readers all the current knowledge about the topic or issue. Sometimes, the purpose of a science review is SYNTHESIS: to suggest a new interpretation of the old material. In such reviews, the writer must present evidence to persuade readers that the new interpretation is valid.

If you're required to write a science review, you want to (1) choose a very limited scientific issue currently being researched; (2) use information that is current—the more recently published the articles, books, and journals you consult, the better; (3) accurately PARAPHRASE (35i) and SUMMARIZE (35j) material; and (4) DOCUMENT your sources (Chapters 36–38). If your review runs longer than two or three pages, you might want to use headings to help your reader understand the organization and idea progression of your paper. See Chapters 32–34 for advice on finding and using sources.

42

Making Presentations and Using Multimedia

42a What are presentations?

Presentations, which are speeches often supported with multimedia tools, are common not only in academic disciplines across the curriculum, but also in work and public settings. Preparing a presentation and drafting a paper involve similar processes, and the information in Chapters 1 and 2 will help you. The rest of this chapter will provide additional information for preparing presentations and using multimedia tools.

42b How does my situation focus my presentation?

Just as you need to adjust your writing according to each SITUATION, so you need to adjust presentations to fit PURPOSES, AUDIENCES, ROLES, and any SPECIAL CONSIDERATIONS. Consider three different situations.

- You want to address a group of students to inform them about a film club you're starting.
- You need to persuade a management group at work to adopt a new set of procedures for making purchasing decisions.
- You plan to give a toast at a friend's wedding to express your feelings and to entertain the wedding guests.

Different approaches will be successful in each instance because your purpose and audience are different.

The three main purposes for presentations are to entertain, to INFORM and to PERSUADE (1b). In academic and work situations, the last two are most important. For an oral presentation, determine your purpose, and keep it in mind as you draft and revise your speech. Common INFINITIVE PHRASES for an informative presentation include: *to explain why, to clarify, to show how, to report, to define, to describe,* and *to classify.* Common phrases for a persuasive presentation include: *to convince, to argue, to agree with, to disagree with, to win over, to defend,* and *to influence.*

42c How do I adapt my message to my audience?

Adapting your presentation to your listening audience means holding their interest and being responsive to their viewpoints. Consult the general strategies for analyzing audiences in Quick Reference 2.1. Especially consider your listeners' prior knowledge of your topic, their desire to learn more, and whether they agree with your point of view. You'll find that your audience falls into one of three categories: *uninformed, informed,* or *mixed.*

UNINFORMED AUDIENCE	Start with the basics, and then move to a few new ideas. Define new terms and concepts, and avoid unnecessary technical terms. Use visual aids and give examples. Repeat key ideas—but not too often.
INFORMED AUDIENCE	Don't waste your audience members' time with the basics. From the beginning, reassure them that you'll be covering new ground. Devote most of your time to new ideas and concepts.
MIXED AUDIENCE	In your introduction, acknowledge the more informed audience members who are present. Explain that you're going to review the basic concepts briefly so that everyone can build from the same knowledge base. Move as soon as possible toward more complex concepts.

Adapting your presentation to the general needs and expectations of your audience doesn't mean saying only what they might want to hear. It means rather that you need to consider their knowledge of your topic and their interest in it. You can then make your message understandable and relevant by using appropriate language and examples.

42d How do I organize my presentation?

As with essays, an oral presentation has three parts: INTRODUCTION, BODY, and CONCLUSION. Within the body, you present your major points, with support for each point. Drafting a SENTENCE OUTLINE gets you close to your final form and forces you to sharpen your thinking. Quick Reference 42.1 shows you a sample outline for an oral presentation.

Quick Reference 42.1 ∎ ∎ ∎ ∎ ∎ ∎ ∎

Organizational outline for an oral presentation

Title: _____

Topic: _____

Specific purpose: _____

Thesis statement: _____

  I. Introduction (followed by a clear transition to point 1 in the body)

 II. Body
    A. Major point 1 and specific supporting examples (followed by a clear transition from point 1 to point 2, perhaps with a brief reference to the introduction)
    B. Major point 2 and specific supporting examples (followed by a clear transition from point 2 to point 3, perhaps with a brief reference to point 1 and the introduction)
    C. Major point 3 and specific supporting examples (perhaps with a brief reference to points 1 and 2)

III. Conclusion (Refer to your introduction but do not repeat it verbatim or your audience will lose interest.)

INTRODUCING YOURSELF AND YOUR TOPIC

Your ETHOS is perhaps even more important in speaking than in writing. Your audiences needs to trust you and, even, like you. All audience members want to know three things about a speaker: Who are you? What are you going to talk about? Why should I listen? To respond effectively to these unasked questions, try these suggestions.

- Grab your audience's attention with an interesting question, quotation, or statistic; a bit of background information; a compliment; or an anecdote. If necessary to establish your credibility—even if someone has introduced you—briefly and humbly mention your qualifications as a speaker about your topic.

- Give your audience a road map of your talk: Tell where you're starting, where you're going, and how you intend to get there. Your listeners need to know that you won't waste their time.

FOLLOWING YOUR ROAD MAP

Although much advice for writing applies to oral presentations, listening to a presentation is very different from reading an essay. When you're reading an article and lose sight of the main point, you can reread a few paragraphs. But when you're listing to a speech, you can't go back. As a result, audiences generally need help following the speaker's line of reasoning. Here are some strategies to keep your listeners' minds from wandering and to help them follow your points.

- Signal clearly where you are on your road map by using cue word transitions such as *first, second,* and *third;* or *subsequently, therefore,* and *furthermore;* or *before, then,* and *next.*
- Define unfamiliar terms and concepts, and follow up with strong, memorable examples.
- Occasionally tell the audience what you consider significant, memorable, or especially relevant, and why. Do so sparingly, at key points.
- Provide occasional summaries at points of transition. At each interval, recap what you've covered and say how it relates to what's coming next.

WRAPPING UP YOUR PRESENTATION

Demonstrate that you haven't let key points simply float away. Try ending with these suggestions.

- Never let your voice volume fall or your clarity of pronunciation falter because the end is in sight.
- Don't introduce new ideas at the last minute.
- Signal that you're wrapping up your presentation using verbal cues, such as "In conclusion" and "Finally." When you say "finally," mean it!
- Make a dramatic, decisive statement; cite a memorable quotation; or issue a challenge. Allow a few seconds of silence, and then say "thank you." Use body language, such as stepping slightly back from the podium, and then sit down.

42e How do I research and write a presentation?

Doing research for an oral presentation requires the same kind of planning as doing research for written documents. To keep yourself calm and focused, divide the preparation into manageable tasks according to a realistic time line. Set small goals and stick to them to give yourself enough time to research, organize, and practice your presentation. Review Chapters 33–35 for help on finding and evaluating sources, taking notes, planning a research strategy, and documenting sources. An oral presentation won't have a WORKS CITED or REFERENCES list to be read out, but your listeners might appreciate a handout in which you list your sources. In academic situations, your instructor might ask you to turn in your Works Cited or References.

Most of the preparation involved in an oral presentation is written work. Writing helps you take four important steps in your preparation: (1) to organize your thoughts; (2) to distance yourself from the ideas and remain objective; (3) to pay attention to words and language; and (4) to polish for clarity and impact.

When drafting your speech, it may help you to review Chapter 8 on style and tone. In particular, see sections 8d and 8e for a discussion of a medium LEVEL OF FORMALITY in language, which is an appropriate level for most public speaking. Careful DICTION (12d) will make your speech both easy to listen to and memorable.

An oral presentation calls for the same careful language selection that you employ in your writing. Here are some tips on using language in oral presentations.

- Recognize the power of words. For example, read this statement by Winston Churchill, made after World War II: "Never in the field of human conflict was so much owed by so many to so few." Now try substituting the word *history* for "the field of human conflict." Note that while the single word *history* is more direct, using it destroys the powerful impact of the original words. Also consider this version: "Never in the field of human conflict did so many people benefit from the contributions of a relatively few others." This sentence is much less effective because it loses the PARALLELISM of the original (Chapter 10).

- Never alienate your audience by using words, phrases, or examples that could offend your listeners or people connected with them.

- Use GENDER-NEUTRAL LANGUAGE by avoiding sexist terms and inappropriate words and expressions (12f).

- Present yourself with dignity in body language, tone of voice, and dress.

42f How do I incorporate multimedia into my presentation?

Multimedia elements such as visual aids, sound, and video can reinforce key ideas in your speech by providing illustrations or concrete images for the audience. If done well, they can make long explanations unnecessary and add to your credibility. Still, they can never take the place of a well-prepared presentation.

42f.1 Using traditional visual aids

Here are various types of visual aids and their uses. For each of them, always make text and graphics large enough for others to read and grasp at a distance.

- **Posters** can dramatize a point, often with color or images. Because you need to make sure posters are large enough for everyone in your audience to see them, they tend to work best with smaller audiences of thirty or fewer.

- **Dry-erase boards** are preferable to chalkboards because you can use various colors that are visually appealing on them. Use them to roughly sketch an illustration or to emphasize a technical word. Doing this adds a dynamic element to your presentation, but take care not to turn your back on the audience for more than a few seconds.

- **Handouts** are useful when the topic calls for a longer text or when you want to give your audience something to refer to later. Short, simple handouts work best during a presentation, but longer, more detailed ones are more effective at the end; remember that listeners can pay more attention to what's on the page than to you, and you don't want to compete with yourself! Always include DOCUMENTATION information for any SOURCES on the handout. A strategic handout can be a useful backup just in case other technologies are missing or broken; remember to wait until everyone has one before you begin speaking about it.

- **Transparencies** require an overhead projector. You can prepare them in advance, either by hand or by using a computer and printer, which helps clarity and also allows you to incorporate visual materials. For emphasis during a presentation, you can write on transparencies with a marker.

42f.2 Using electronic media

Computers offer a range of possibilities for enhancing oral presentations, and they are by far the most common means of including images and sounds. The trick is to make sure that they add to your presentation rather than distract your audience. You need to balance the time you spend developing multimedia materials with the time you spend writing and practicing your presentation.

POWERPOINT PRESENTATIONS

Microsoft PowerPoint® is the most widely used presentation software that creates digital slides. Another program, called "Impress" is available for free from www.openoffice.org. These slides can contain words, images, or combinations of both; they can even include sound or movie clips. To project your slides during a presentation, you need an LCD projector connected to your computer and a screen.

To design PowerPoint slides, follow the principles of unity, variety, balance, and emphasis discussed in Chapter 45. Never present so much information on each slide that your audience pays more attention to reading it than to listening to you. Also, never simply read large amounts of text from your slides; your audience will quickly—and rightfully—become bored. Remember the power of photographs, illustrations, or other visual materials for conveying information or making points (4j, 4k, 4m, and Chapter 45).

Figure 42.1 A sample PowerPoint slide

Figure 42.1 is an example of an effective PowerPoint slide prepared for a presentation about a community service project. The slide is clearly titled, well balanced, and has an image to capture attention. It presents the points concisely and clearly.

SOUND AND VIDEO CLIPS

A brief sound file (for example, a sentence or two from a speech) or a video clip (perhaps 20 to 30 seconds of footage from an event) can occasionally help you illustrate a point. These clips can be excerpts from a CD or DVD, or MP3, WAV, QuickTime, FLV, or other files on a computer. Always keep them brief and be absolutely sure that your audience will recognize immediately that they enhance your message and aren't just for show. You can also embed video clips into a PowerPoint presentation using excerpts from MPG, QuickTime, or Windows Media files.

42g How do I plan for multimedia in my presentation?

Few things can frustrate you more than technology troubles. Always have a backup plan. Computers and projectors have a tendency to act up just at the times you're most nervous or the situation is most important, and few things annoy audience members more than watching people fiddle with technology. If you or a technician can't solve the problem in a minute or two, shift to your plan B, which might consist of selected transparencies, a strategic short hand-out, or even no multimedia at all. Plan and practice for all situations.

If you're making a PowerPoint presentation, you need to operate in advance the computer system you'll be using. If you intend to hook up your laptop computer to an LCD projector, make sure you bring with you—and practice installing—all of the connecting cables and cords. Arrive early to double-check that any technology you're planning to use is available and working, even if you've practiced with it beforehand. Learn how to turn on computers, video players, and projectors. Learn how to raise or lower the screen, if you're using one, and how to dim the lights.

42h What presentation styles can I use?

Presentation style is the way you deliver what you have to say. You may mem-orize it, read it, map it, or speak without notes. In general, avoid the last style until you have considerable experience giving speeches, unless otherwise in-structed by your professor or someone in your workplace.

MEMORIZING YOUR PRESENTATION

Memorized talks often sound unnatural. Unless you've mastered material well enough to recite it in a relaxed way, choose another presentation style. After all, no safety net exists if you forget a word or sentence. Fortunately, instructors rarely require you to memorize long presentations.

READING YOUR PRESENTATION

You can bore your audience when you read your entire presentation aloud. Burying your nose in sheets of paper creates an uncomfortable barrier between you and your audience because you appear painfully shy, unprepared, or insin-cere. If you have no choice but to read, avoid a monotone voice. Vary your pitch and style so that people can listen more easily. In addition, try these tips.

- Become familiar with your words as much as possible so that you can look up from the pages to make frequent eye contact with your audience.
- Place the sheets of paper on a podium instead of holding them.
- Keep your hands out of your pockets. Use them to gesture instead.
- Turn your body—not just your head—to your right, left, and straight ahead so that you can look at everyone in your audience.

MAPPING YOUR PRESENTATION

Mapping means creating a brief outline of the presentation's main points and examples and then using that outline to cue yourself as you talk. Quick Refer-ence 42.2 contains additional suggestions for mapping your presentation.

> **Quick Reference 42.2** ■ ■ ■ ■ ■ ■ ■
>
> **Preparing materials for delivering a mapped presentation**
>
> - Type your key words in a large font for easier reading.
> - Highlight the most important point(s) you want to make.
> - Use only one side of a page or card to avoid losing your place.
> - Number your pages or cards in large type in case you drop them.
> - Clearly distinguish your introduction, body, and conclusion so that your audience can follow along easily.
> - Mark cues to yourself on your pages for pauses, emphasis, and use of visuals.
> - Include information on your sources so that you can briefly mention them (and offer to give more details after your speech).

42i How do I use my voice effectively?

Your voice is the focus of any oral presentation. If you're unsure whether you can be heard in a particular setting, speak briefly and then ask your listeners whether they can hear you. When you use a microphone, speak into it without raising your voice.

Speak naturally but clearly. Articulate your words by pronouncing the end of each word. Swallowing word endings leads to poor speech delivery. Speak slowly and deliberately—but make sure that your words have rhythm and pace so that your listeners will stay engaged. Vary your tone of voice for emphasis and clarity. Pause every now and then to let your points sink in.

42j How do I use nonverbal communication?

Your body language can either add to or detract from your message. Eye contact is your most important nonverbal communication tool because it communicates confidence and shows respect for your listeners. If you have to walk up to the front of a room or a podium, don't begin speaking before you get there and are looking directly at the audience. Smile or nod at your listeners as you begin. To do this smoothly, you need to memorize your first few sentences.

Use appropriate facial expressions to mirror the emotions in your message. Gestures, if not overdone, contribute to your message by adding emphasis; they are best when they appear to be natural rather than forced or timed. If you use a podium, stand squarely behind it. When gestures aren't needed, rest your hands on the podium—don't scratch your head, dust your clothing, or fidget. You may step slightly forward or backward from a microphone to indicate transitions in your message, but never sway from side to side. And, of course, dress appropriately for your audience and the type of event.

42k What can I do to practice for my oral presentation?

Good delivery requires practice. In preparing to speak, figure in enough time for at least four complete run-throughs of your entire presentation, using visuals if you have them. When you practice, keep the following in mind:

- Practice conveying ideas rather than particular words so that your TONE doesn't become stilted.
- Time yourself and cut or expand material accordingly.
- Practice in front of a mirror or videotape yourself. As you watch yourself, notice your gestures. Do you look natural? Do you make nervous movements that you weren't aware of as you spoke?
- Practice in front of a friend. Ask for constructive feedback by posing these questions: What was my main point? Did the points flow? Did any information seem to come from out of nowhere or not fit in with the information around it? Did I sound natural? Did I look natural? How did the visuals add to my message?

42l How can I overcome stage fright?

If you suffer from stage fright, remember that the more prepared and rehearsed you are, the less frightened you'll be. Your aim is to communicate, not to perform. If you worry that your audience will see that you're nervous, Quick Reference 42.3 suggests ways to overcome physical signs of anxiety.

42m How do I make a collaborative presentation?

A common practice in many academic settings—and in business and public situations—is to present an oral report as part of a group. All members of the group are required to contribute in some way to the collaborative enterprise. The advice in section 6a will help you work together productively. Here are some additional guidelines for effective collaborative presentations:

- Make sure, when choosing a topic or a position about an issue, that most members of the group are familiar with the subject.

- Lay out clearly each member's responsibilities for preparing the presentation. Try to define roles that complement one another; otherwise, you may end up with overlap in one area and no coverage in another.

- Agree on firm time limits for each person, if all members of the group are expected to speak for an equal amount of time. If there is no such requirement, people who enjoy public speaking can take more responsibility for delivery, while others can do more of the preparatory work or contribute in other ways.

- Allow enough time for practice. Good delivery requires practice. Plan at least four complete run-throughs of your presentation, using any visuals you have. Although each member can practice on his or her own part alone, schedule practice sessions for the entire presentation as a group. This will help you (a) work on transitions, (b) make sure the order of presenters is effective, (c) clock the length of the presentation, and (d) cut or expand material accordingly.

- As you practice your presentation, have different group members watch in order to make suggestions, or videotape the practices. Notice your gestures. Do you look natural? Do you speak clearly and at an effective pace?

Quick Reference 42.3   ■ ■ ■ ■ ■ ■ ■

Overcoming anxiety during an oral presentation

- **Pounding heart.** Don't worry: No one else can hear it!

- **Trembling hands.** Rest them on the podium, or put your hands behind your back or hold your outline or notes until the shaking stops. It will.

- **Shaky knees.** Stand behind the desk or podium. If neither is available, step forward to emphasize a point. Walking slowly from one place to another can also help you get rid of nervous energy.

- **Dry throat and mouth.** Place water at the podium, but use a glass rather than a bottle, which is more distracting. Never hesitate to take an occasional sip, especially at a transition point.

- **Quavering voice.** Speaking louder can help until this problem disappears on its own, which it always does. The sooner you ignore the quaver, the faster it will stop.

- **Flushed face.** Although you might feel as if you're burning up, audiences don't notice. The heat always fades as you continue speaking.

For more help with your writing, grammar, and research, go to **www.mycomplab.com**

43

■ ■ ■ ■ ■ **43** ■

Business and Professional Writing

43a Who writes in the workplace?

If you plan to have a job or already have one, chances are that writing is or will be a large part of your life. Writing infuses most job situations, from corporate offices, not-for-profit agencies, schools, and health care facilities to farms and factories. People write to co-workers inside organizations; they write to customers or service providers outside them. Even people who work independently (consultants, therapists, artists, craftspeople, and so on) keep records, apply for grants, correspond with customers, and advertise their services.

All workplace writing benefits from moving its way through the WRITING PROCESS as it seeks to INFORM or to PERSUADE. Indeed, never before in your writing have the acts of revising, editing, and proofreading carried as much weight as they do in business writing. The slightest error reflects negatively on the writer personally and on the larger world of the company that employs the writer.

There are five main categories of business writing: (1) correspondence and e-mails (43d), consisting of MEMOS (43e), LETTERS (43f), and other messages (43g–h); (2) reports and manuals (43i); (3) proposals (43j); (4) presentations (Chapter 42); and (5) advertising or other marketing materials. Except for this last category, which is often playful and informal in order to win public interest, work-related writing needs to be professional in TONE, concise, and well informed. It can't contain slang, abbreviations, or informal words or expressions. Recipients expect it to use standard EDITED AMERICAN ENGLISH grammar, spelling, and punctuation. Perhaps nowhere is this more important than in your RESUME (43k) and JOB APPLICATION LETTER (43l).

⊕ ESOL Tip: In some cultures, work-related correspondence is often sprinkled with elaborate language, many descriptive details, and even metaphors. Most US businesses, however, expect correspondence that gets to the point quickly, is highly concise, and is written in clear language. ●

43b What are typical policies concerning business writing?

Most workplaces have policies that strictly govern their employees' use of the organization's e-mail system and stationery. As soon as you start with a new employer, speak to your supervisor about policies. Also ask for the employee manual and take time to read it carefully. If no one seems to know the official policy, always assume that the policies are strict until you're told differently. See Quick Reference 43.1 for a list of typical business writing policies for employees.

Quick Reference 43.1

■ ■ ■ ■ ■ ■ ■

Typical business writing policies for employees

- Companies reserve e-mail systems and any uses of company letterhead stationery for their operations only.

- Companies own all correspondence written, sent, or received via e-mail or other means, including courier or regular mail. Furthermore, their administrators and supervisors at all levels have complete access to view and save all of this correspondence.

- Companies prohibit employees from writing, sending, or receiving correspondence (by any means) with content that is potentially harmful to the company. This includes, but is not limited to, content that makes libelous comments, enters into preliminaries to contractual agreements or into contracts themselves, contains chain letters, mentions material that degrades someone, circulates confidential or embarrassing information, or reveals other offensive material.

- Companies have the right to monitor your Internet use. If you spend time shopping online or viewing sites not related to work, you might be subject to discipline.

- Companies own the writing (and other products) you produce in their employment.

43c What are legal considerations concerning business writing?

Legal considerations involving business writing involve two entities at least: you as an employee and the company for which you work.

43c.1 Legal considerations involving you as an employee

Because employers have complete access to your business e-mail, business letters, and business memos, they can use such documents as evidence of your job performance. You might not be aware during the normal course of your workday that your supervisors have access to your written conduct of business, but they do legally. Judge your writing, therefore, as if it were being read in a formal assessment of your work.

43c.2 Legal considerations involving your company

For legal purposes, your business e-mail as well as your business letters and business memos written on company letterhead stationery may be used as evidence in legal disputes, in court, and by the government, regarding you or the company you work for. In some situations, e-mails sent to customers or other parties within and outside the company may be construed as legally binding on the company; therefore, they're your responsibility.

43d What are special considerations concerning business e-mail?

E-mail is the primary form of written business communication today. Therefore, use it with special care, even though you might use it quite informally in your personal life. Here are some overriding guidelines for business use.

- Find out whether personal e-mail is tolerated. (You can usually find e-mail policies in an employee manual.) Even if personal e-mail is permitted, realize that monitoring systems in most workplaces can quickly identify such e-mails. Therefore, you might want to avoid sending or receiving personal e-mails on your workplace computer.

- Ask your supervisor whether there are restrictions regarding the size of attachments that you can send or receive. (Large attachments can overload the computer system at work.) If there are restrictions, use NETIQUETTE and alert your recipients about the size of any large attachments before you send them. In turn, ask senders to alert you before sending large ones to you.

- Protect the ID numbers and passwords you're assigned or have created to access your organization's electronic systems. As an employee, you're accountable for all activity conducted on password-protected accounts.

Some businesses automatically insert or require employees to insert a DISCLAIMER—a statement appended to the top or bottom of e-mails designed to protect the company from legal liability. The value of disclaimers is limited. Only a court of law can determine the effectiveness of such statements, but they might prove effective in limiting a company's liability in some cases.

43d.1 Following guidelines for content of work-related e-mail

The subject line in an e-mail tells your recipients how to sort, file, and prioritize a message. Be very specific in stating your subject so that you don't show disrespect for your recipient's time. You might have to write the same people more than one e-mail about different subjects in the same day, but at least your recipients will be able to keep their records straight.

NO (VAGUE)	YES (SPECIFIC)
Travel Approval	Approval Request for Chicago Trip
E-mail Policy	New E-mail Retention Policy
Meeting	Meeting on Annual Report Schedule
Schedule Change	Cancellation of Chicago Trip

In the "Cc" or "Copies" space, insert the e-mail addresses of people who need to see your message, even when they aren't expected to respond. Never send copies to people who don't really need the information; it can backfire and simply annoy someone who already has too many messages in his or her Inbox. If you use the "Bcc" (Blind Copy) space, you're sending a copy to people without your primary recipients knowing about it. Generally, people consider blind copying rude because it's akin to talking behind someone's back. However, certain rare, delicate situations might call for it. For example, in a mass mail-out, it would be good netiquette to blind copy dozens of customers because you would be protecting their privacy by not disclosing their e-mail addresses to everyone else.

For the message of your e-mail, single-space the text, and double-space between paragraphs and before your complimentary closing. Start paragraphs flush left at the margin. When you need to include a separate document of more than a paragraph or two with your e-mail, such as a report, compose it as a separate document in your word-processing program, and attach it to your e-mail using the "Attachments" function of your e-mail service. Attached documents, rather than copied and pasted documents, look better because they maintain the original formatting (margins, spacing, italics). As you compose your message, follow the principles in Quick Reference 43.2.

Figure 43.1 is an example of a professional e-mail.

43d.2 Using e-mail netiquette

Netiquette, a word coined from *net* and *etiquette*, refers to good e-mail manners. For example, unless your business recipients give you permission to loosen

---

To: sherrel.ampadu@jpltech.com
From: Chris Malinowitz <cmalinowitz@chateauby.com>
Subject: Confirming Meeting Arrangements
Cc: dmclusky@chateauby.com
Bcc:
Attached: C:\Documents and Settings\Desktop\Chateau Menus.doc

---

Dear Ms. Ampadu:

I am writing to confirm the final arrangements for your business meeting on June 17, 2009, at our conference center.

As you directed, we will set the room in ten round tables, each seating six. We will provide a podium and microphone, an LCD projector and screen, and a white board with markers. I understand that you will be bringing your own laptop. Our technician can help you set up.

You indicated that you would like to provide lunch and refreshments at two breaks. Attached please find our menus. You will need to make your lunch selections at least 48 hours in advance.

If you have any questions or wish to make any changes, I would be pleased to accommodate your needs. Thank you for choosing The Chateau at Brickyard.

Sincerely,

Chris Malinowitz
Catering Director, The Chateau at Brickyard

Figure 43.1 A professional e-mail

your level of formality, always address them by their full names and titles, especially when your recipients are people you've never met or corresponded with before. As important, always use GENDER-NEUTRAL LANGUAGE. Finally, try to reply to e-mail messages within one or two days after receiving them. When you can't respond quickly, always acknowledge that you've received a message. Say when you'll reply, and don't forget to follow up.

Quick Reference 43.2   ■ ■ ■ ■ ■ ■

Content of a business e-mail

- Keep the message of your business e-mail brief and your paragraphs short. Reading a screen is harder on the eyes than reading a print document.

- Restrict each business e-mail to one topic, even if you have to write the recipients about more than one topic in the same day.

continued >>

Quick Reference 43.2 (continued)

- Start your business e-mail with a sentence that tells what your message is about.

- Put the details of your business e-mail message in the second paragraph. Supply any background information that your recipients aren't already aware of or might have forgotten.

- Conclude your e-mail in a short, final paragraph by asking for explicit information or specific action, if needed; or by restating your reason for writing (for example, keeping someone apprised of a situation or reporting on a meeting).

- If your e-mail runs longer than three to four paragraphs, add topic headings to help your readers speed through the material.

- Never write in all capital letters (WE NEED TO TAKE ACTION NOW) or all lowercase letters (i think we need to check with the denver office). Not only are they annoying to read, but all capital letters are considered the written equivalent of rudely shouting. All-lowercase letters suggest laziness and a lack of respect.

- At the end of your message, before your full name and position, use a commonly accepted complimentary closing, such as *Sincerely, Cordially,* or *Regards.*

- Be cautious about what you say in a business e-mail. After all, the recipient can forward any e-mail, including ones received as blind copies, to others without your permission, even though this practice is considered unethical and rude.

- Forward an e-mail message only if you've asked the original sender for permission.

43e How do I format and write memos?

Memos are usually exchanged internally (within an organization or business). Today e-mail takes the place of most memos, unless the correspondence requires a paper record or signature. The guidelines for writing e-mail (43d.1) also pertain to memos. The appropriate form of communication—paper memos or e-mail—depends on what's customary in your work environment.

The standard format of a memo includes two major parts: the headings and the body.

To:	[Name your audience—a specific person or group.]
From:	[Give your name and your title, if any.]
Date:	[Give the date on which you write the memo.]
Re:	[State your subject as specifically as possible in the "Subject" or "Re" line.]

The content calls for a beginning, middle, and end, with all parts holding closely to your topic. Don't ramble. If you need more than one or, at most, two pages, change your format into that of a brief report. Here are some guidelines for preparing a memo.

- **Introduction:** Briefly state your purpose for writing and why your memo is worth your readers' attention. Mention whether the recipient needs to take action, making it clear either here or at the conclusion.
- **Body:** Present the essential information on your topic, including facts the recipient needs to know. If you write more than three or four paragraphs, use headings to divide the information into subtopics so that the memo can be scanned quickly.
- **Conclusion:** End with a one- to two-sentence summary, a specific recommendation, or what action is needed and by when. Finish with a "thank you" sentence.

43f   How do I write business letters?

Business letters are more formal and official than business e-mails or business memos. Choose to write a business letter, rather than a business e-mail, to add appropriate weight and respect to your message, for ceremonial occasions, and to ensure that your message is placed on the record and thereby becomes part of a "paper trail." Business letters generally fall into two official categories based on their purposes.

- **Regular business letters** are business-to-business communications. These letters make up the majority of business correspondence. Always use company letterhead stationery, and follow any special guidelines for style or format that your company uses.
- **Social business letters** are letters to business colleagues on matters that serve a business-related social function, such as congratulations on an achievement, condolences in a time of loss, thank you letters, invitations to social events, and the like. Given that these letters are written in a business context, social business letters may be written on company letterhead stationery.

774 43f BUSINESS AND PROFESSIONAL WRITING

There are some general guidelines for addressing recipients in business letters. The old-fashioned "To Whom It May Concern" rarely reaches the right person in an organization. Use the full name of your recipient whenever possible. If you can't locate a name, either through a phone call to a central switchboard or on the Internet, use a specific category—for example, "Dear Billing Department," placing the keyword "Billing" first (not "Department of Billing"). Always use gender-neutral language. Figure 43.2 is an example of a business letter from a not-for-profit group.

Here are guidelines for the format and content of your business letters.

- **Paper:** Use 8½ × 11-inch paper. The most suitable colors are white, off-white, and light beige. Fold your business letters horizontally into thirds to fit into a standard number 10 business envelope (9½ × 4 inches). Never fold a business letterhead stationery page in half and then into thirds.

- **Letterhead stationery:** Use the official letterhead stationery (name, address, and logo, if any) of the business where you're employed. If no letterhead stationery exists, imitate the format that others have used. If no such tradition exists, center the company's full name, address, and phone number at the top of the page, and use a larger and different font than for the content of your letter.

- **Format:** Without indents, use single spacing within paragraphs and double spacing between paragraphs. All lines start flush left, which means at the left margin. This is called **block style**. An equally acceptable alternative form is called **modified block style** in which the lines for the inside address and the body begin flush left but the heading, closing, and signature begin about halfway across the page. Quick Reference 43.3 (on page 776) lists the features of block style and modified block style letter formats.

Use block or modified block formats for business correspondence of a personal nature, such as job application letters, letters of complaint concerning personal matters, or letters asking for information for you personally. Use plain white paper, and if you have personal stationery, use it.

ArtsFlamenco

3B-243 West 21st Street
New York, NY 10011
artsflamenco@msn.com
www.artsflamenco.org

January 11, 2009

Mr. Antonio Alducin
Advisor, Latino Heritage Club
George Washington High School
324 Mapleview Road
Englewood, New Jersey 07631

Dear Mr. Alducin,

We enjoyed speaking with you earlier this week regarding *ArtsFlamenco*'s arts-in-education programs. We can certainly work with you to develop an after-school workshop that ties in elements of Spanish language, culture, music, and dance.

We are enclosing three program plans and their estimated costs. For your further interest, we are also including a DVD showing clips from two of our recent arts-in-education programs. After you have reviewed these materials, please contact us to discuss any questions you might have.

We very much look forward to speaking with you again.

All the best,

Jorge Navarro

Jorge Navarro
President and Artistic Director

Encl: 3

A Section 501(c)(3) New York Not-for-Profit Corporation

Figure 43.2 A business letter in block style

Quick Reference 43.3 ▪ ▪ ▪ ▪ ▪ ▪ ▪

Features of block and modified block styles

BLOCK-STYLE FORMAT

- Begin the dateline two inches below the top of the page or three lines below the last line of the letterhead, depending on the depth of the letterhead copy.
- Begin all elements at the left margin.
- Allow one inch for left, right, and bottom margins.
- Leave three blank lines between the dateline and the inside address.
- Leave one blank line between the inside address and the salutation.
- Leave one blank line between the salutation and the body.
- Type the body single-spaced and leave one blank line between paragraphs.
- Leave one blank line between the body and complimentary closing.
- Leave three blank lines between the complimentary closing and the signature block.

MODIFIED BLOCK STYLE FORMAT

- Begin the dateline two inches below the top of the page or three lines below the last line of the letterhead, depending on the depth of the letterhead copy.
- Center:
  - Dateline
  - Complimentary closing
  - Signature block
- Allow one inch for left, right, and bottom margins.
- Leave three blank lines between the dateline and the inside address.
- Leave one blank line between the inside address and the salutation.
- Leave one blank line between the salutation and the body.
- Type the body single-spaced and leave one blank line between paragraphs.
- Leave one blank line between the body and complimentary closing.
- Leave three blank lines between the complimentary closing and the signature block.

43g How do I prepare a meeting agenda?

An agenda is a plan for a meeting. It lets everyone who is attending know the purpose of the meeting and the topics it will cover. The specific forms of an agenda can vary from company to company, so if you're asked to prepare one, the best way to begin is to study the agendas and minutes of prior meetings of the same group.

Agendas sent before the meeting can help everyone prepare for it, especially if some individuals are to give reports or review materials ahead of time. (In fact, preparing an agenda in advance might let you know a meeting is unnecessary, that information can be shared through an e-mail, or a decision can be made without getting everyone together; no one likes meetings that waste time.) Agendas generally provide the following information:

1. The time, date, and place of the meeting (and perhaps a list of who will attend).

2. The topics of the meeting, in the order in which the group will take them up (perhaps with the approximate amount of time to be devoted to each), and with a note about who (if anyone) is in charge of that particular topic.

3. The purpose of each topic on the agenda. For example, is the purpose simply to share or discuss information? Is the purpose, rather, to make decisions or judgments? People attending the meeting need to know what they're expected to accomplish.

4. A list of what material needs to be reviewed ahead of time or what will be available at the meeting.

Figure 43.3 shows you the agenda for an informal meeting.

43h How do I write meeting minutes?

Minutes are the record of a meeting. Generally, minutes cover all important topics that were discussed, both those on the agenda and not. Exactly what is defined as "important" is hard to know when you're new to a company, so your best route is to write down just about everything that comes up. Pay special attention to any decisions the group made, any votes, and any assignments of tasks to individuals or groups. After the meeting you can ask at least two colleagues who were there to advise you about what to leave out when you write up the minutes.

On rare occasions, minutes are very detailed, recording all the points and nuances raised, in an approach that seems something like a transcript. Most times, however, the minutes are much shorter, briefly summarizing the

FORMAT OF HEADING
Name and title centered, single-spaced
Double space to date and time on one line and location on one line
"Agenda" two lines below

Human Resources Department
Planning Meeting for Open Enrollment Communication

Friday, July 18, 2008, 3–4 p.m.
Michigan Avenue Conference Room

Agenda

Attendees
Margaret Alexander, HR
Joanna Bergstrom, HR Director-Organizer
Rebecca Greenfield, Freelance HR Writer/Editor
Larry Jordan, HR Services
Bob LeGorce, Finance
Bernard Moore, HR Services
Chris Papparello, Finance

Topics	**Discussion leader (time)**
• Introductions/Roles and Responsibilities	Joanna (5 minutes)
• Tentative enrollment dates	Joanna and Bob (5 minutes)
• Possible benefits plan changes	Bob (10 minutes)
• Goals/strategies for communication	Bob and Chris (10 minutes)
• Communication elements	Joanna and Beth (25 minutes)
• Next steps/assignments	Joanna (5 minutes)

REQUIRED IN INFORMAL AGENDA
Organization or department name
List of attendees
Topics to be discussed

OPTIONAL IN INFORMAL AGENDA
Statement of purpose after title of meeting
Bullets for names
Name of chair or organizer
Time allotments

Figure 43.3 Agenda for a meeting

highlights and focusing on conclusions and decisions that were reached rather than on all details. Such minutes summarize outcomes, not entire discussions. Minutes generally have several elements:

1. Date, time, and place of the meeting, including when it began and ended.

2. Who was present (and perhaps who was absent).

3. Summaries of topics, decisions, and responsibilities.

Using headings or lists can help organize the minutes.

Sometimes who takes the minutes is assigned spontaneously at the beginning of a meeting, often to new employees. Therefore, always go to meetings prepared with a laptop or a notebook, pens or pencils—and a smile. Once they're written, minutes can be distributed in paper copies or, more frequently, as e-mail attachments, or on a protected company Intranet site or blog. You'll need to follow the method your company or supervisor prefers. It goes without saying that you want to edit and proofread the minutes very carefully.

The sample set of minutes shown in Figure 43.4 is being communicated by e-mail because the minutes-taker found out this is the traditional way the minutes of this particular group are circulated.

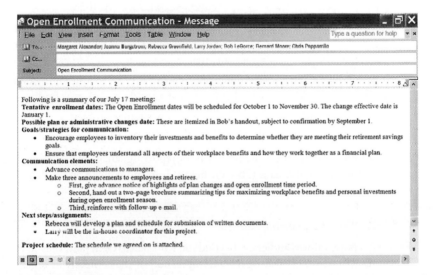

Figure 43.4 Meeting minutes

43i How do I write business reports and manuals?

Reports and manuals are documents that exist for the purpose of informing others inside or outside the workplace. Some manuals explain procedures or processes to help employees do their work consistently and effectively: how to handle specific situations (filing claims, dealing with customer concerns, processing orders, and so on). Customers often see "how-to" manuals when they buy a new product. Other manuals document policies. Among the most important of these are employee or personnel manuals, which explain things like workplace dress and behavior, benefits, use of technology, and so on.

If you're in charge of writing a manual, clarity and completeness are your most important considerations. Readers need to be able to find information easily and be able to use it accurately. As a writer, you need to anticipate the questions people will have and write the manual accordingly. Analyzing your audience is crucial. Document design is important as you lay out the information in the most effective way.

43i.1 Writing internal reports

Internal reports are designed to convey information to others in your workplace. They can be various lengths and serve various purposes. Consider four examples:

- You attend a professional meeting and provide a report on what you learned there for your supervisor and for colleagues who weren't there.
- You're working on a lengthy project. You report on your progress so that others can understand what you have completed, what remains, and what problems or delays you anticipate, if any.
- You conduct extensive consumer research through telephone interviews with potential customers, and you summarize and analyze your findings.
- You identify all the available solutions to a particular problem and write a report that discusses the strengths and weaknesses of each.

In each of these cases, follow the principals of reporting, analyzing, and interpreting information and data (7b–7c). Being clear and concise are especially vital.

43i.2 Writing external reports

External reports inform audiences beyond the workplace. Generally, they have a secondary function of creating a good impression of the company or organization. Probably the most common examples are annual reports, in which companies summarize for investors their accomplishments during the previous

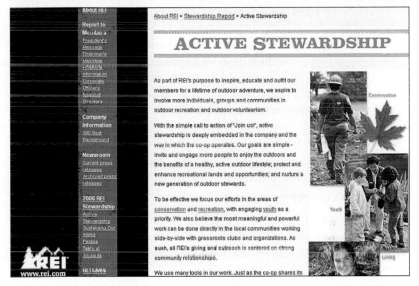

Figure 43.5 A company's external report

years, especially their profits and losses. However, other kinds of external reports are also common. For example, a school principal may write a report to parents that explains students' results on a statewide achievement test. Figure 43.5 shows a section of one company's report.

Because external reports are written for more general audiences, they require explaining many terms and concepts that would be clear to your co-workers. Document design, whether in print or on the computer screen, is also important (Chapter 45). Notice how the report in Figure 43.5 uses images and color.

43j   How do I write business proposals?

Proposals persuade readers to follow a plan, choose a product or service, or implement an idea. A marketing specialist might propose a new product line. A teacher might propose a change in the curriculum. A leader in a not-for-profit organization might propose a way to raise funding. Proposals generally describe a project, the steps for starting and completing the project, and how much it will cost.

Readers evaluate proposals based on how well the writers have anticipated and answered their questions. If some readers have a high level of knowledge about the subject of the proposal, and others have little, then you need to explain the basic information and offer a glossary of terms. Here are some guidelines for preparing a proposal.

INTRODUCTION   Explain the purpose and scope of the project. Describe the problem that the project seeks to solve. Lay out the solution your project will provide. Include dates for beginning and completing the work. Project the outcomes and the costs. Be accurate and precise.

BODY   What is the product or service? What resources are needed? What are the phases of the project? What is the detailed budget? Precisely how is each phase to be completed? By what date is each phase to be completed? How will the project be evaluated?

CONCLUSION   Summarize briefly the benefits of this proposal. Thank readers for their time. Offer to provide further information.

43k   How do I write a resumé?

A **resumé** details your accomplishments and employment history. Its PURPOSE is to help a potential employer (the AUDIENCE) determine whether you'll be a suitable candidate for employment. To make a favorable impression, follow the guidelines for writing a resume in Quick Reference 43.4.

Quick Reference 43.4   ■ ■ ■ ■ ■ ■ ■

Guidelines for writing a resumé

- Place your name, address, e-mail address, and telephone number at the top. If you have a professional Web site or online PORTFOLIO (Chapter 47), include the URL.

- Make sure you have a professional e-mail address. No employer will be impressed by beermaster@gmail.com or daddyslittlegirl@hotmail.com.

- Make it easy to read. Label the sections clearly, and target the resumé to the position you want. Help employers see your most significant attributes as quickly and as easily as possible.

- Adjust your resumé to fit your PURPOSE. For example, if you're applying for a job as a computer programmer, you'll want to emphasize different facts than you would if you're applying for a job selling computers in an electronics store.

- Use headings to separate blocks of information. Include the following headings, as appropriate: Position Desired or Career Objective;

continued >>

Quick Reference 43.4 (continued)

Education; Experience; Licenses and Certifications; Related Experience; Honors or Awards; Publications or Presentations; Activities and Interests; and Special Abilities, Skills, and Knowledge.

- When you list your work experience, place your most recent job first; when listing education, place your most recent degrees, certificates, or enrollments first.

- Write telegraphically. Start with verb phrases, not with the word *I,* and omit *a, an,* and *the.* For example, write "Created new computer program to organize company's spreadsheets" instead of "*I* created *a* new computer program to organize *the* company's spreadsheets."

- Include only relevant information.

- Tell the truth. Even if you get the job, an employer who discovers you lied will probably fire you.

- Include references, or state that you can provide them on request. (Be sure to have them at hand so that you can respond speedily to such a request.) Before you start the job application process, ask people who can comment on your professional qualifications if you may list them as references.

- Fit all of the information on one page. If you need a second page, make sure the most important information is on the first page.

- Use high-quality paper that is white or off-white.

- Prepare your resumé in three different formats: traditional print, digitally scannable, and plain text.

- Proofread carefully; even one spelling error or one formatting error can eliminate you from consideration.

Your resumé can take many formats, and an employer may specifically require one of them.

Traditional print resumés can take advantage of the full range of document design, including columns, different fonts, graphics, and so on. Still, you want the overall effect to be clean and clear. Figure 43.6 shows an example of a traditional print resumé.

Scannable resumés are designed to be scanned by machines that digitize their content. Sophisticated software then searches the database to match key terms to position requirements. As a result, these resumés need to be simpler: don't use columns, different fonts, lines or other graphics, bold or italics fonts, and so on. Choose a clean sans serif font such as Arial or Geneva in a 10–12

MONICA A. SCHICKEL

1817 Drevin Avenue
Denver, CO 80208
Cell phone: (303) 555-7722
E-mail: mnsschl@wordnet.com
Professional portfolio: www.schickelgraphics.net

OBJECTIVE: Entry level position as a graphic designer or publications assistant

EXPERIENCE

9/08 – present   **Publications Intern** (half-time; paid), *Westword* (Denver, CO)
- Design advertisements
- Prepare photographs for publications
- Lay out the "Tempo" section
- Fact-check, edit, and proofread articles

6/06 - 8/08   **Customer Service Representative,** Wells Fargo Bank (Aurora CO).
- Sold accounts to customers; made all sales goals
- Created promotional posters

4/03 - 8/05   Evening Assistant Manager, McDonalds Restaurant (Longmont, CO).
- Supervised 7 cooks and counter workers
- Assured food and service quality

EDUCATION

8/07 – present   Bachelor of Arts, The University of Denver, expected June 2009
Major: Graphic Arts; Minor: Digital Media Studies

8/05 – 5/07   AA General Education, Front Range Community College, May 2007

SKILLS AND SELECTED EXPERIENCES

- Expert in complete Adobe Creative Suite
- Expert in complete Microsoft Office Suite
- Excellent Spanish language skills
- Illustrator and photographer; have completed several commissions (see portfolio, above)
- Vice President, Student Residence Halls Association
- Cartoonist and Designer, *The DU Clarion* (campus newspaper)
- Excellent customer service skills

REFERENCES: Available on request

Figure 43.6 A traditional print resumé

point size. Include keywords that the computer can match to the job. Figure 43.7 on page 786 shows a scannable version of the resumé in 43.6.

Plain text resumés are simpler yet. They can be pasted directly into e-mails (for companies that won't open attachments for fear of viruses) or into application databases. If you have time to prepare only one type of resumé, we suggest you create one that's scannable.

431 How do I write a job application letter?

A **job application letter** (sometimes called a *cover letter*) always needs to accompany your resumé. Avoid repeating what's already on the resumé. Instead, connect the company's expectations to your experience by emphasizing how your background has prepared you for the position. Your job application letter, more than your resumé, reflects your energy and personality. However, there are limits; this is not the place to be too cute or clever.

Each job application letter needs to be tailored to each job. While you can use basic information in multiple letters, one generic letter will not represent you effectively. Among other things, a very general letters tells prospective employers that you didn't care enough to address the specific circumstances of their organizations. Here are guidelines for writing a job application letter.

- Use one page only.
- Overall, think of your letter as a polite sales pitch about yourself and what benefits you can bring to the company. Don't be shy, but don't exaggerate.
- Use the same name, content, and format guidelines as for a business letter (43f).
- Address the letter to a specific person. If you can't discover a name, use a gender-neutral title such as *Dear Personnel Director.* Below we explain how to write gender-neutral salutations.
- Open your letter by identifying the position for which you're applying.
- Mention your qualifications, and explain how your background will meet the job requirements.
- Make clear that you're familiar with the company or organization; your research will impress the employer.
- End by being specific about what you can do for the company. If the job will be your first, give your key attributes—but make sure they're relevant. For instance, you might state that you're punctual, self-disciplined, eager to learn, and hardworking.
- State when you're available for an interview and how the potential employer can reach you.

Monica A. Schickel
1817 Drevin Avenue
Denver, CO 80208
Cell phone: (303) 555-7722
E-mail: mnsschl@wordnet.com
Professional portfolio: www.schickelgraphics.net

KEYWORDS

Publications experience, graphic design, editing, photography, supervisor, editing,
customer service, digital media, excellent Spanish, Adobe creative suite,
Photoshop, InDesign, Quark, CSS, Dreamweaver, Web design, illustrator, proofread,
Excel, Access, Publisher, newspaper, layout, sales, willing to relocate

OBJECTIVE

Entry level position as a graphic designer or editorial assistant

EXPERIENCE

Publications Intern (half-time; paid), Westword (Denver, CO). September 2008 to
present
—Design advertisements
—Prepare photographs for publications
—Lay out the "Tempo" section
—Fact-check, edit, and proofread articles

Customer Service Representative, Wells Fargo Bank (Aurora CO). April 2006-
August 2008
—Sold accounts to customers; made all sales goals
—Created promotional posters

Evening Assistant Manager, McDonalds (Longmont, CO). June 2003-August 2005
—Supervised 7 cooks and counter workers
—Assured food and service quality

EDUCATION

Bachelor of Arts in Graphic Design, Minor in Digital Media Studies
The University of Denver, expected June 2009

Associate of Art in General Education, Front Range Community College, May 2007

SKILLS AND SELECTED EXPERIENCES

Expert in complete Adobe Creative Suite
Expert in complete Microsoft Office Suite
Excellent Spanish language skills
Illustrator and photographer; have completed several commissions (see portfolio, above)
Vice President, Student Residence Halls Association
Cartoonist and Designer, Clarion (newspaper)
Excellent customer service skills

REFERENCES AVAILABLE ON REQUEST

Figure 43.7 A scannable resumé

- Edit and proofread the letter carefully. If you have to hand-correct even one error, print the letter again.

For an example of a job application letter, see Figure 43.8.

Monica A. Schickel
1817 Drevin Avenue
Denver, CO 80208

Cell phone: (303) 555-7722
E-mail: mnsschl@wordnet.com
Professional portfolio: www.schickelgraphics.net

May 5, 2009

Jaime Cisneros
Publications Director
R.L. Smith Consulting
2000 Wabash Avenue
Chicago, IL 60601

Dear Mr. Cisneros:

Please consider my application for the graphic designer position currently being advertised on your company's Web site. I believe that my professional experiences, education, and skills prepare me well for this opportunity.

I am currently completing a paid internship at Westword, a weekly features and entertainment magazine in Denver, CO, where I have worked as an effective member of a creative team. My responsibilities have included designing advertisements, laying out sections, and editing photographs. Other related experience includes commissions as an illustrator and photographer. My professional portfolio demonstrates the range and quality of my work. As the enclosed resumé notes, I have additional experience in business environments.

Next month I will earn a BA in graphic design from The University of Denver, where my course of study has included extensive work in graphic design, photography, drawing, and illustration. Simultaneously, I will complete a minor in digital media studies that has included courses in Web design, video editing, and sound editing. I have expertise in all the standard software applications that would be relevant to your position.

I would be pleased to provide further information and to interview at your convenience. The opportunities at R.L. Smith closely match my background and goals, and the prospect of joining your team in Chicago is exciting. I look forward to discussing how I can contribute to your publications department.

Sincerely,

Monica A. Schickel

Monica A. Schickel

Figure 43.8 A job application letter

ESOL Tip: In some cultures, job applications may include personal information, such as an applicant's age, marital status, number of children, religion, or political beliefs. In North America, however, this is not standard practice. Such personal information does not help an employer determine how well you can perform a particular job, so avoid including it in your application. ●

Thinking, speaking, and writing with gender-neutral language (12f) is very important in the workplace, particularly when addressing recipients in memos, job application letters, and so on. Following are some guidelines for writing a gender-neutral salutation:

1. Telephone or send an e-mail to the company to which you're sending the letter. State your reason for contacting them, and ask for the name of the person you want to receive your letter.

2. Address men as Mr., and address women as Ms., unless you're specifically told to use Miss or Mrs. If your recipient goes by another title such as Dr. or Professor, use it.

3. If you can't identify a proper name and need to use a title alone, keep the title generic and gender-neutral.

> **NO** Dear Sir: [sexist]
> Dear Sir or Madam: [sexist for both genders]
>
> **YES** Dear Human Resources Officer:
> Dear Apple Sales Manager:

For more help with your
writing, grammar, and research,
go to **www.mycomplab.com**

44

Writing for the Public

44a What is public writing?

Public writing is intended for people who are reading for reasons other than work, school, or professional obligations. Instead, they read it out of interest or a desire to keep informed. Some public writing is also known as CIVIC

WRITING because you're writing to affect knowledge, actions, or beliefs among other citizens in a democratic society.

Examples of writing for the public include a letter or e-mail to refute a newspaper editorial, a program for a play or concert, a brochure to draw new members into a service organization, a proposal to build a town park, a fund-raising letter for a worthy cause, a script for a radio announcement, a Web site for a hobby or social cause that interests you, a blog on current events or a specific issue, or an e-mail urging your representative to vote for a certain bill.

44b How can I understand public writing situations?

As the examples in section 44a indicate, public writing takes a wide range of forms, depending on the situation. The familiar categories of TOPIC, PURPOSE, AUDIENCE, ROLE, and CONTEXT/SPECIAL REQUIREMENTS are especially important for understanding your options and requirements (1b).

Much public writing has the purpose of INFORMING or PERSUADING, and our earlier advice applies. One thing to keep in mind is that, unlike an instructor or someone in a work setting, public audiences aren't obligated to read your work, for the most part. This means that you have to take particular care as you write for them, especially when you're writing for an AUDIENCE that you don't know personally. Among other things, this means analyzing your readers and establishing your credibility for them.

"Establishing credibility" means convincing your readers that they need or want to listen to you. Create a strong ETHOS by being accurate and honest and by explaining your connection with the readers. What do you have in common with them?

For example, if you're writing a letter to the editor of your local newspaper, you'll gain credibility if you begin, "As a resident of Green County for twelve years," and then state your position. By establishing yourself first as a member of your audience's community, you convey that you have a sincere and long-standing interest in the welfare of that community.

Establishing credibility in public writing can also come through your style and ingenuity. After all, another common purpose of this writing is to entertain. Newspapers and magazines are full of feature stories that inform, certainly, but that are also enjoyable to read.

People also write for the public for the pleasure of expressing themselves. They share opinions on plays or on presidents; they talk about music or about moods. Social networking sites and software like Facebook or MySpace (46h) are prime examples of this purpose, as are certain blogs and the online comment sections maintained by many newspapers. However, expressing yourself doesn't give you license to be insulting, irresponsible, or inflammatory—at least if gatorbait wrote on Mar 24, 2008 9:15 PM:

i say if you don't feel like tipping the delivery guy, then you should get off your fat lazy butts and go pick it up yourself. but alas, you people are too busy sitting in front of the tv while you scratch yourself and wonder how you'll ever lose that tire that magically appeared around your midsection. ...that is until you drip ice cream all over the front of your shirt and you realize that you'd better polish off the whole container before it melts. cheap, lazy townies.

Figure 44.1 A poor example of an online comment

you expect anyone to pay attention to you. (And what's the point of publishing your writing if you don't want readers?) The writer in Figure 44.1 posted this comment in an online discussion about how much to tip pizza deliverers: Maybe the writer enjoyed insulting his or her readers, but the tone and approach (not to mention the capitalization and punctuation) did little for the writer's position.

44c How do I write reports for the public?

Reports for the public vary in length, format, and content. An *action brief* from a political organization might consist of a few pages detailing recent developments on an issue of concern, such as a proposed law. Often these are published on Web sites or distributed through e-mail messages.

Write your material in an evenhanded TONE so that your credibility is supported by your fairness. If you want to criticize something, be sure your argument is well reasoned and supported—and that it lacks BIAS or malice toward any person(s) or specific idea(s). This doesn't mean that your writing needs to be limp. Indeed, you can choose writing that's spirited, enthusiastic, and even stirring.

44c.1 Public reports

Figure 44.2 (page 792) shows the executive summary of a report on climate changes in the American West. An executive summary is a brief overview sometimes included before a lengthy report. The report was produced by The National Resources Defense Council. The entire work was published online and as a 64-page booklet. Figure 44.3 (page 793) shows a "fact sheet," a four-page version of the longer report.

To write a public report, follow the guidelines in Quick Reference 44.1.

Quick Reference 44.1 ▪ ▪ ▪ ▪ ▪ ▪ ▪

Writing a public report

- Decide your purpose. Will you only inform, or will you also analyze the information you present? Or—going one step further—will you make a recommendation based on the information and your analysis?

- State your findings objectively. Though you may later bring in your opinion by recommending a course of action, your credibility depends on your first reporting accurately.

- Organize a formal report using the following sections. Depending on the purpose of your report, however, you might combine or expand any of the sections.

  - **Executive summary:** Provides a very brief summary of the entire report, including conclusions or recommendations.

  - **Introduction:** Explains the purpose of the report, describes the problem studied, and often describes or outlines the organization of the entire report.

  - **Methods or sources:** Describes the data or information that were collected for the report and how they were gathered.

  - **Results:** Presents the findings of the report.

  - **Discussion:** States the meanings and implications of your findings.

  - **Conclusion:** Makes recommendations or simply summarizes the findings.

44c.2 Policy briefs

A policy brief is a kind of public report in which experts put technical information into a form that nonexperts and decision makers can understand. These days, most of them are published on the Internet. "To brief" someone is to inform them in a concise way. The usual purpose of policy briefs is to persuade people with facts and analysis that support a specific decision. Your readers need to perceive you as objective and careful, basing your position on logic and evidence. On the other hand, if you want to use a policy brief in a research paper, carefully analyze the quality of the source (34m). Figure 44.4 (page 794) shows the opening of a policy brief.

EXERCISE 44-1   Using your Internet browser, enter "policy brief" (in quotation marks so that you search for this specific phrase), and the following other terms (one at a time): food, health, energy, crime, or other terms that interest you. List the policy briefs you find for each, and evaluate their quality.

Executive Summary

H uman activities are already changing the climate of the American West. This report by the Rocky Mountain Climate Organization (RMCO) and the Natural Resources Defense Council (NRDC), drawn from 50 scientific studies, 125 other government and scientific sources, and our own new analyses, documents that the West is being affected more by a changed climate than any other part of the United States outside of Alaska. When compared to the 20th century average, the West has experienced an increase in average temperature during the last five years that is 70 percent greater than the world as a whole. Responding quickly at all levels of government by embracing the solutions that are available is critical to minimizing further disruption of this region's climate and economy.

The West Is Getting Hotter

The planetary warming that scientists predict will result from human emissions of heat-trapping gases is already underway. In February 2007, the Intergovernmental Panel on Climate Change (IPCC) declared, "Warming of the climate system is unequivocal," and it is "very likely" that most of the warming since the middle of the 20th century is the result of human pollutants.

The American West has heated up even more than the world as a whole. For the last five years (2003 through 2007), the global climate has averaged 1.0 degrees Fahrenheit warmer than its 20th century average. For this report, RMCO found that during the 2003 through 2007 period, the 11 western states averaged 1.7 degrees Fahrenheit warmer than the region's 20th century average. That is 0.7 degrees, or 70 percent, more warming that for the world as a whole. And scientists have confirmed that most of the recent warming in the West has been caused by human emissions of heat-trapping gasses.

Understanding the Conclusions of the IPCC

The Intergovernmental Panel on Climate Change (IPCC) recently released *Climate Change 2007*, an assessment of the current scientific understanding of climate change and its effects, prepared by hundreds of scientists and approved by the governments of countries in the United Nations. Key terms used by the IPCC (and often quoted in this report) were defined as follows:

- "Very likely" means greater than 90 percent probability of occurring.
- "Likely" means about an 80 percent probability of occurring.
- "Very high confidence" means at least 9 out of 10 chances of being correct.
- "High confidence" means about 8 out of 10 chances of being correct.
- "Medium confidence" means 5 out of 10 chances of being correct.

iv

Figure 44.2 Executive summary of a public report

44d How do I write arguments for my community or decision makers?

Writers can influence public opinions or actions by decision makers by writing persuasive arguments. Perhaps you want to endorse a new public project or react to a proposal or endorse a law under consideration.

Climate Facts

White "bathtub rings" show the pre-drought water level of Lake Powell in Arizona

Hotter and Drier: The West's Changed Climate

Human activities are already changing the climate of the American West. A new report by the Rocky Mountain Climate Organization (RMCO) and the Natural Resources Defense Council (NRDC), drawn from 50 scientific studies, 125 other government and scientific sources, and our own new analyses, documents that the West is being affected more by a changed climate than any other part of the United States outside of Alaska. When compared to the 20th century average, the West has experienced an increase in average temperature during the last five years that is 70 percent greater than the world as a whole. Responding quickly at all levels of government by embracing available solutions is critical to minimizing further disruption of this region's climate and economy.

To read the full report on the impacts of global warming in the West, visit www.nrdc.org/policy.

For more information, please contact:
Theo Spencer at NRDC
(212) 727-2700

Stephen Saunders at RMCO
(303) 880-4598

www.nrdc.org/policy

March 2008
© Natural Resources Defense Council

The West Is Getting Hotter

The planetary warming that scientists predict will result from human emissions of heat-trapping gases is already underway. In February 2007, the Intergovernmental Panel on Climate Change (IPCC) declared, "Warming of the climate system is unequivocal," and it is "very likely" that most of the warming since the middle of the 20th century is the result of human pollutants.

The American West has heated up even more than the world as a whole. For the last five years (2003 through 2007), the global climate has averaged 1.0 degree Fahrenheit warmer than its 20th century average. RMCO found that during the 2003 through 2007 period, the 11 western states averaged 1.7 degrees Fahrenheit warmer than the region's 20th century average—which represents 70 percent more warming than for the world as a whole. The West has also experienced more frequent and severe **heat waves**, with the number of extremely hot days increasing by up to four days per decade since 1950.

More Rapid Warming in the West	
2003 to 2007 5-Year Average Temperatures Compared to 20th Century Averages	
Planet	+1.0°F
Western United States	+1.7°F
Colorado River Basin	+2.2°F
Arizona	+2.2°F
California	+1.1°F
Colorado	+1.9°F
Idaho	+1.8°F
Montana	+2.1°F
Nevada	+1.7°F
New Mexico	+1.3°F
Oregon	+1.4°F
Utah	+2.1°F
Washington	+1.4°F
Wyoming	+2.0°F

Figure 44.3 A fact sheet based on a report

44d.1 Letters to the editor

When you respond to a previous piece of writing in a publication, always begin by referring precisely to the source, using title, section, and date, if possible.

Many letters to the editor (most often sent as e-mails) propose solutions to a community problem. These letters aim to persuade other readers that a

**The Future
of Children**
PRINCETON-BROOKINGS

POLICY BRIEF   SPRING 2006

Fighting Obesity in the Public Schools

Ron Haskins, Christina Paxson, and Elisabeth Donahue

> Childhood obesity is a growing national problem. Federal, state, and local
> policymakers and practitioners recognize the need to take strong action.
> Public schools are playing a central role in fighting childhood obesity
> despite both political and financial constraints. But schools should do
> even more to reduce the availability of junk food, make school meals more
> nutritious, and increase students' daily exercise.

Figure 44.4 Opening of a policy brief

problem exists and that a particular solution isn't only feasible but also the
most advantageous of all the possible alternatives. Follow the general guidelines for writing ARGUMENTS (see Chapter 5). Use the format for a business
letter or e-mail, and keep the following guidelines in mind when writing to
propose a solution:

- Explain briefly the specific problem you're attempting to solve.
- Tell how your solution will solve all elements of the problem.
- Address briefly the possible objections or alternatives to your proposed
  solution.
- State why your solution offers the most advantages of all the alter-
  natives.

In the letter in Figure 44.5, a citizen argues for preserving a city park in
its present form.

44d.2 Editorials, op-ed pieces, and reviews

Editorials are fairly short arguments that appear in newspapers and magazines.
So are *"Op-Ed"* pieces (short for "opposite editorial," in reference to where they
were usually published in newspapers—on the right-hand page, "opposite" the
newspaper's editorials). They are also called "commentaries" or "opinion pieces."
Reviews discuss movies, books, plays, music and so on, explaining and summarizing them for readers and commenting on their quality. All are common
forms of public writing.

To the Editor:

Re "Parking Plan Threatens Green Space" (news article, May 14):

For well over a century, Lincoln Park has provided a welcome oasis in downtown Springfield. In this park, office workers eat lunches, schoolchildren play on the way home, and evening concerts and other events unite the community.

It is very shortsighted, then, that the City Council now considers converting a third of the park into additional parking.

I acknowledge that parking downtown has gotten difficult. As the manager of a small shop, I know that our customers sometimes have trouble finding a parking place. However, the park itself is one of the reasons our downtown has become more popular in the past decade.

Ironically, destroying the park's attractive green space will reduce the need for more parking, which will hurt business.

A better solution is for the city to purchase the vacant property at the corner of Main and Jefferson and build a multistory garage. No doubt this option is more expensive than using the park. However, the land would be available cheaply, a multistory garage would actually provide more parking than the park land, and a preserved park would bolster business, thereby increasing tax revenues. I'm sure most citizens would prefer to leave future generations a legacy of trees, grass, and inviting beaches rather than a debt of sterile concrete.

Joel C. Bradway
Springfield, May 17, 2009

Figure 44.5 A letter printed from a community newspaper

44e What other types of public writing exist?

Many people write simply to express themselves or to entertain others. The most obvious examples are fiction, poetry, plays, film scripts, journals, and scrapbooks. In addition, many people produce newsletters, brochures, or similar documents, using not only words, but also graphic designs and images (Chapter 45).

COLUMNS

Columns are a series of pieces written by one author, usually appearing on a regular basis. Columnists tend to focus on a particular topic: sports, relationships, politics, food, and so on.

WEB SITES

Writing for the Internet is perhaps the broadest form of public writing, in the sense that anything you post there is available to any reader with online access. On the Internet, you might post book reviews on a bookseller's Web site or a message about an upcoming concert to a newsgroup. You might create a Web site about your talents, interests, or accomplishments, or a Web site for an organization, a social cause, or a special interest group. Chapter 46 discusses writing for the Web in detail.

BLOGS

One form of public writing is the Web log (BLOG), an online journal that a writer updates on a fairly regular basis. Some writers focus their blogs on a single topic or a narrow range of topics. Others record the events of their lives, as in a diary open for the world to read. We explain how to write blogs in 46e.

For more help with your writing, grammar, and research, go to **www.mycomplab.com**

45

Document and Visual Design

45a What is visual design?

Visual design refers to the appearance of a document (how it looks), as opposed to its content (what it says). We're using the term *document* to refer broadly to all kinds of texts, including papers, reports, letters, brochures, flyers, posters, PowerPoint slides, and Web pages. Designing documents includes everything from choosing typefaces, heading styles, and colors, to selecting and placing photographs, illustrations, or other graphics.

Chapter 4 explained how to analyze visual images, and the advice there can help you choose images for your own documents. However, visual design involves the relationship between words and images. A well-designed document shows that you respect your readers and have spent time formatting your work

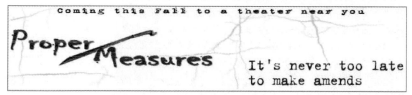

Figure 45.1 Two Internet banner advertisements

so that it's attractive and helps achieve your PURPOSE. For example, imagine two movie Internet banner advertisements, both movies with the same name. Figure 45.1 shows these two movie titles designed in very different ways. What can the design tell you about the movie before you even see a preview for either one?

On larger documents, many smaller elements work together to emphasize certain points by focusing a reader's attention, portraying a complex message in an efficient manner. Note how all of the elements in the poster in Figure 45.2 work together.

Some documents follow formats that are fairly standardized, such as letters, memos, and e-mail messages (Chapter 46). Papers you write in academic settings usually follow guidelines established by the Modern Language Association (Chapter 36); the American Psychological Association (Chapter 37); the Chicago Manual of Style; or the Council of Science Editors (both in Chapter 38). Check with your instructor about which style to use. Some instructors encourage—or even require—design elements such as photos, illustrations, and diagrams. However, before spending time and effort incorporating extensive design elements into academic work, ask your instructor whether he or she appreciates design elements.

Other document types—flyers, brochures, annual reports, reports on special projects, programs for concerts or plays, and so on—invite more design creativity and originality. Consider, once again, the public service announcement in Figure 45.2. Overall, the best design is always the one appropriate to the PURPOSE and writing situation at hand.

You don't have to be a graphic artist to produce well-designed documents. Even if you only have a few tools and a little knowledge, you can still produce

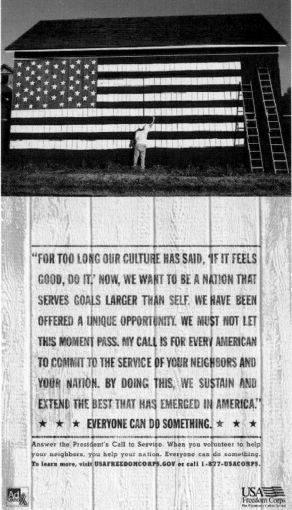

Figure 45.2 A poster showing various design elements

visually effective documents. Word processing programs such as Microsoft Word, Corel WordPerfect, and the freely available OpenOffice are sufficient for designing most basic documents. Graphic design software such as Adobe Photoshop or freely available GIMP allows you to edit photos, create other complex images, and format them to place into your word-processed document.

45b What are basic principles of design?

The basic principles of design—whether for a chair, a car, a painting, a written document, or a Web page—are unity, variety, balance, and emphasis. **Unity** results from repetition and consistency of like elements. **Variety** comes from an appropriate break from unity that adds interest or sets elements apart. **Balance** refers to a sense of harmony or equilibrium. **Emphasis** directs the reader of the design to what is most important. Quick Reference 45.1 describes how to check for these principles.

Quick Reference 45.1 ■ ■ ■ ■ ■ ■ ■

Checklist for document design

- **Unity:** Do all elements in my document work together visually, such as a consistent font for consistent content? Is there a consistent use of bitmap or vector images?

- **Variety:** Have I introduced elements, where appropriate, that break up monotony, such as headings in a different font from that used in my content? Do these elements add clarity? Do my images add to content?

- **Balance:** Are the elements of my document in proportion to each other, such as equally placed text elements countering or mirroring equally placed images?

- **Emphasis:** Does my document design draw attention to key information, such as framing important text, or placing important elements in the middle or at the top?

The flyer that a student produced for The Nature Club in Figure 45.3 reflects the four basic design principles. UNITY results from similar parts of the flyer sharing the same features. All of the headings in this example (except the title) use the same font and color, a color that matches colors in the photographs, and all of the body text uses the same font. In addition, dates for the speakers and events are displayed in a matching indented format. VARIETY in the flyer comes from the use of photographs to complement the text. Headings, colors, and font sizes are different from the main text. Variety is also one way to create EMPHASIS. For example, the title of the organization is the largest text on the page and is in a different font. Headings signal different types of information, and the ample use of white space allows information to stand out clearly. The contact information is emphasized through the use of a frame and white background that sets the information apart.

Finally, the page demonstrates BALANCE in many ways. The center or focal point of the flyer is split into quadrants, each side with two evenly spaced text and picture elements.

The Nature Club

Please join us!

The Nature Club is open to all members of the campus community. Our purpose is to share our common enjoyment of nature and to address environmental concerns. We meet the first Wednesday of each month, 7:00 p.m., at 114 Mercer Hall

Spring Speakers

James Franklin
Biology
"Prairie Wildlife"
January 15

Sarah Minkowski
Political Science
"Alaskan Refuges and Energy Policy"
February 12

Cesar Sanchez
The Nature Conservancy
"The Last Best Places"
March 12

Sherita Jones
State Representative
"Pending Environmental Legislation"
April 9

Upcoming Special Events

- Fundraising Dance for The Nature Conservancy
  February 19

- Salt River Canoeing
  April 18

- Camping and Hiking in Grand Teton National Park
  June 3-10

> *For more information, contact*
> Jesse Longland, President
> The Nature Club
> jklong@tnc.gkztg.edu

Figure 45.3 A flyer for The Nature Club

EXERCISE 45-1 Figures 45.4 and 45.5 (see pages 801 and 802) are two alternative versions of the flyer for The Nature Club. Each of the two has problems with unity, variety, balance, or emphasis—or a combination of all four. Work alone or in groups to identify the problems in each design.

THE NATURE CLUB

Spring Speakers

James Franklin
Biology
"Prairie Wildlife"
January 15

Sarah Minkowski
Political Science
"Alaskan Refuges
and Energy Policy"
February 12

Please join us!

The Nature Club is open to all members of the campus community. Our purpose is to share our common enjoyment of nature and to address environmental concerns. We meet the first Wednesday of each month, 7:00 p.m., at 114 Mercer Hall

Cesar Sanchez
The Nature Conservancy
"The Last Best Places"
March 12

Upcoming Special Events

Fundraising Dance for The Nature Conservancy
February 19
Salt River Canoeing
April 18
Camping and Hiking in Grand Teton National Park
June 3-10

Sherita Jones
State Representative
"Pending Environmental Legislation"
April 9

For more information, contact Jesse Longland, President, The Nature Club
jklong@tnc.gkztg.edu

Figure 45.4 A poorly designed flyer

45c How do I design with text?

Text consists of letters and words. To format text, you need to decide which typeface—such as Times or Arial Schoolbook—that you'll use. Also called *fonts,* they come in two major categories. **Serif** fonts have little "feet" or finishing lines at the top and bottom of each letter; **sans serif** (*sans* is a French term

THE NATURE CLUB

Please join us!

The Nature Club is open to all members of the campus community. Our purpose is to share our common enjoyment of nature and to address environmental concerns. We meet the first Wednesday of each month, 7:00 p.m., at 114 Mercer Hall

Spring Speakers

James Franklin, Biology, "Prairie Wildlife", January 15
Sarah Minkowski, Political Science, "Alaskan Refuges and Energy Policy", February 12
Cesar Sanchez, The Nature Conservancy , "The Last Best Places", March 12
Sherita Jones, State Representative, "Pending Environmental Legislation", April 9

Upcoming Special Events

Fundraising Dance for The Nature Conservancy February 19
Salt River Canoeing April 18
Camping and Hiking in Grand Teton National Park June 3-10

For more information

Jesse Longland
President
The Nature Club
jklong@tnc.gkztg.edu

Figure 45.5 Another example of a poorly designed flyer

meaning *without*) don't. Times New Roman is serif; Arial is sans serif. When considering font use, there are two qualities to keep in mind. The first quality, *readability*, refers to the ease of reading a particular block of text. Some studies have suggested that the serifs at the bottom of each letter help guide readers' eyes through lines of text; therefore, when you're writing longer segments of text, use serif fonts. The second quality, *legibility*, refers specifically to the design of fonts and whether they are visible or not to a reader, making them easy to see.

Sans serif fonts are highly legible and are good for short, isolated lines such as headings and captions.

Remember that a font can set a tone, so avoid using a playful font (**Comic Sans MS)** or a simulated handwriting font (*Kaufmann*) in academic and business writing. Fonts come in different sizes (heights) that are measured in "points" (units smaller than .02 inch). For body text in longer documents, use 10- to 12-point serif typefaces.

8 point   12 point   16 point   24 point

45c.1   Highlighting text

Highlighting draws attention to key words or elements of a document. You can highlight in various ways, but in all cases, use moderation.

BOLDFACE, ITALICS, AND UNDERLINING

Italics and underlining—they serve the same purpose—have special functions in writing (for example, to indicate titles of certain works, as we discuss in 30f and Chapters 36–38), but they're also useful for emphasis and for headings. **Boldface** is reserved for heavy emphasis.

BULLETED AND NUMBERED LISTS

You can use bulleted and numbered lists when you discuss a series of items or steps in a complex process, or summarize key points or guidelines. A bulleted list identifies items with small dots, squares, or other shapes and symbols. Lists provide your reader with a way to think of the whole idea you're communicating. For this reason, they work particularly well as summaries.

COLOR

Adding color to a document can change it dramatically. In addition to including colorful visuals or BORDERS (45e), you can also change the font color or use a colored background for certain words or sections. Take time, however, to think about your reasons for adding color to your text. How does color suit the type of document? How will it help you accomplish your purpose? Use color sparingly for variety and emphasis.

JUSTIFYING

When you make your text lines even in relation to the left or right margin, you're **justifying** them. There are four kinds of justification, or ways to line up text lines on margins: left, right, centered, and full.

Most academic and business documents are left justified, which means that the right ends of the lines are unjustified, or *ragged*. Center, right, and full justification are useful for designing shorter documents (flyers, posters, and so on) because they can attract attention.

Left justified text (text aligns on the left)

Right justified text (text aligns on the right)

Center justified text (text aligns in the center)

Full justified text (both left and right justified to full length, or measure, of the line of type)

INDENTATION

When you move text toward the right margin, you are **indenting**. Using the ruler line in your word-processing program to control indentations makes it easier to make global changes in your indentation. The top arrow of the bar sets the paragraph indentation, while the bottom arrow sets the indentation for everything else in the paragraph. MLA-style Works Cited pages and APA References pages use *hanging indentations* in which the first line of an entry aligns at the left margin and every following line is indented. Indent bulleted and numbered lists to make them stand out, as in the list in 45d.

SETTING MARGINS

Margins are the boundaries of a page, which means the white space or blank areas at the top, bottom, and sides of a paper or screen. College essays, research papers, and most BUSINESS WRITING call for one inch of space on all sides.

Narrow margins allow you to fit more information on a page but also decrease the amount of white space available. This can make a page appear cluttered, dense, and difficult to read. Wide margins let you fit less information on a page. For ACADEMIC WRITING, margins greater than one inch make your document look thin because there's less content on a page.

45d How do I use headings?

Headings clarify how you've organized your material and tell your readers what to expect in each section. Longer documents, including handbooks (like ours), reports, brochures, and Web pages, use headings to break content into chunks that are easier to digest and understand. In academic writing, APA style favors headings, whereas MLA tends to discourage them. Following are some guidelines for writing and formatting headings.

- **Create headings in a slightly larger type than the type size in the body of your text.** You can use the same or a contrasting typeface, as long as it coordinates visually and is easy to read.
- **Keep headings brief and informative.** Your readers can use them as cues.
- **Change the format for headings of different levels.** Think of levels in headings the way you think of items in an outline (see 2e). Level one headings show the main divisions of a document. Level two headings divide material that appears under level one headings, and so on. Changing the format for different levels of headings creates a clear outline for the reader. You can do this in various ways: centering heads or left justifying them; using a different font or type size; highlighting using **boldface,** *italics,* or underlining; or using various combinations of capitals and lowercase letters. Always be consistent in the style you use within each document.
- **Use parallel structure.** All headings at the same level should be similar in kind. For example, you might make all first-level heads questions and all second-level heads noun phrases. Quick Reference 45.2 presents common types of headings, with examples showing parallel structure.

Quick Reference 45.2 ■ ■ ■ ■ ■ ■ ■

Style choices for headings

- **NOUN PHRASES can cover a variety of topics.**
  Executive Branch of Government
  Judicial Branch of Government
- **Questions can evoke reader interest.**
  When and How Does the President Use the Veto Power?
  How Does the Supreme Court Decide Whether to Consider a Case?
- **GERUNDS and *-ing* phrases can explain instructions or solve problems.**
  Submitting the Congressional Budget
  Approving the Congressional Budget
- **Imperative sentences can give advice or directions.**
  Identify a Problem
  Draft the Bill

45e How do I use borders?

Borders are lines used to set apart sections of text. They can take a number of forms, from single lines of varying thickness to patterns. A single rule (a simple straight line, horizontal or vertical) can emphasize breaks between major sections of a long report. Borders around text serve to set off information, as in a table or chart.

45f How should I incorporate graphics?

Graphics, also called *images* or *visuals,* can enhance document design when used appropriately. A visual can condense, compare, and display information more effectively than words, but only if its content is suitable. A graph showing how sales increased over a period of time, for example, makes the point more quickly and clearly than an explanation.

CHARTS, GRAPHS, AND TABLES

Business and scientific reports rely heavily on charts and graphs, as do some research papers. They're compact ways to present large amounts of information. The next four figures illustrate bar graphs (45.6), line graphs (45.7), pie charts (45.8), and tables (45.9).

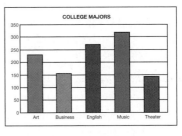

Figure 45.6 Bar graphs compare values, such as the number of different majors at a college, as shown in this graph.

Figure 45.7 Line graphs indicate changes over time. For example, advertising revenue is shown over an eight-month period in this chart.

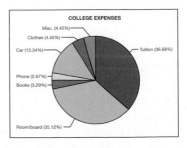

Figure 45.8 Pie charts show the relationship of each part to a whole, such as a typical budget for a college student, as shown in the chart.

TABLE 45.1 TOTAL NUMBER OF STUDENTS IN SERVICE PROJECTS

Semester	Students	Percentage (%) of Student Population
Spring 2008	1,321	25.8
Summer 2008	394	6.6
Fall 2008	2,425	38.1

Figure 45.9 Tables present data in list form, as shown here, allowing readers to grasp much of the information at a glance.

In academic or business documents, especially lengthy ones, number figures and tables, if more than one, and number them sequentially. If possible, choose only one term in a relatively short piece of writing: *Table 1, Table 2;* or *Figure 1, Figure 2,* and so forth.

CLIP ART

Clip art refers to pictures, sketches, and other graphics available on some word-processing programs. It can also be downloaded from the Internet, sometimes from free sites, and sometimes for a small fee. Although clip art is rarely, if ever, appropriate in academic writing and business writing, it can add interest to flyers, posters, newsletters, and brochures designed for certain audiences.

PHOTOGRAPHS

In an age of digital cameras, not to mention an age when cell phones have the capacity to take pictures and send them around the world, **photographs** are everywhere. Because you can fairly easily download photographs from a digital camera, you can place them easily into documents. You can also scan photographs from printed photos or from books and articles. The Internet is another source of images; several Web sites (including many at libraries) offer thousands of photographs for free. Most images online, however, are copyrighted, and thus you need to gain permission to use images for any type of publication. Quick Reference 45.3 contains terms and special considerations when using images found on the Web.

Quick Reference 45.3

■ ■ ■ ■ ■ ■ ■

Considerations when using visuals from the Web

Always observe copyrights. Images, just like text, are copyrighted as soon as they are fixed in any medium. In other words, most images online are owned by somebody. Searching for images using Google or Yahoo might provide

continued >>

access to images useful for a project, but such results can hide the legal rights of the author of the image from you. Although the copyright law is fairly generous in allowing students to use found images for projects done strictly for courses, you should document the source of the image. If you're using an image in a project for a wider audience, including any Web-based project, you need to get permission from the photographer or whomever owns the rights. Here are some important terms to understand.

- Rights-Managed—when an image is rights-managed, it means that the owner of the image charges you, the user, based on how you will use the image. Many stock-photo Web sites such as http://www.images .com offer pricing options for use of photos.

- Royalty-free—this does not mean the image is free. Instead, the author of the image is selling a one-time use of the photo for a flat fee and doesn't expect royalties from your use of the image. Web sites such as http://www .istockphoto.com offer many royalty-free photos.

- Creative Commons—creative commons is a copyright alternative that allows authors to control how others may or may not use their works without the added issue of asking permissions. There are many creative commons options available at http://creativecommons.org/. A number of photos at Flickr, see http://www.flickr.com/creativecommons/, have a creative commons license.

- Public Domain—Works in the public domain are free to use in whatever fashion a user wants without gaining permission first. Government publications and images are, by law, in the public domain. Web sites such as the National Archives, http://www.archives.gov offer many public domain images that you may use.

Once a photograph is in your computer, you can place it in your document, usually with an "Insert" or "Import" command. A modest software program, such as the pictures toolbar within Microsoft Word, can help you adjust a photograph by cropping it (trimming the top, bottom, or sides), rotating it, or making it larger or smaller. A powerful program like Adobe Photoshop lets you modify colors or create special effects.

For additional help in using visuals in your documents, follow the guidelines in Quick Reference 45.4.

45g   What is page layout?

Layout is the arrangement of text, visuals, color, and space on a page. You'll want to arrange these elements so that you follow the basic principles of design (45b).

Guidelines for using visuals

- **Design all visuals to be simple and uncluttered.**

- **Use the highest resolution and best images possible.** Small images stretched to fit an area will not look professional and can disrupt a document's design. It's always best to use large pictures and then reduce the size later. Reducing the size of a picture will not harm the resolution, while stretching a picture to make it bigger will.

- **Include a heading or title for each visual.** Doing so helps readers quickly understand what they're seeing.

- **Never use unnecessary visuals.** Make sure all visuals clearly contribute to your PURPOSE. Putting cute clip art on the pages of your writing won't make your reader think your work is well done. However, including a chart that summarizes your findings might.

- **Consider your audience and their sensibilities.** You don't want to offend your readers, nor do you want them to be confused.

- **Credit your source if a visual isn't your own.** Always avoid plagiarism by crediting your source using DOCUMENTATION. If you're using a visual (including a photograph) for a public purpose other than for a class project, you need written permission to use it in your work.

Experiment with ideas for layout by creating a variety of mock-up pages on a computer or by sketching possibilities by hand.

You might also see if any suitable **templates** are available. A template is a professionally designed form that shows you where to place visuals in relation to text; a template has predefined typefaces, heading styles, margins, and so on. Page layout software and most word-processing software have a variety of templates for brochures, flyers, newsletters, and many other types of documents; and several Web sites offer them, too.

Quick Reference 45.5 explains how to position texts and visuals.

You have many options for placing images in relation to text. Figure 45.10 shows one standard kind of placement, the image centered above the words. In contrast, Figure 45.11 shows the text wrapped around the picture, which creates a better sense of connection between the two. Finally, Figure 45.12 illustrates that words can also wrap elements other than photographs, in this case a list enclosed in borders forming a box.

Quick Reference 45.5

■ ■ ■ ■ ■ ■ ■

Guidelines for positioning text and visuals

- Consider the size of visuals in placing them so that they don't cluster at the top or the bottom of a page. That is, avoid creating a page that's top-heavy or bottom-heavy.

- To create balance in a document, imagine it as divided into halves, quarters, or eighths. As you position texts or images in the spaces, see which look full, which look empty, and whether the effect seems visually balanced.

- Use the "Table" feature of your word-processing program to position text and visuals exactly where you want them. Turn off the grid lines when you're done so that the printed copy shows only the text and visuals.

- Avoid splitting a chart or table between one page and the next. If possible, the entire chart or table needs to fit on a single page. If it runs slightly more than a page, look for ways to adjust spacing or reduce words. If you have no choice but to continue a chart or table, then on the second page, repeat the title and add the word *continued* at the top.

- Use the "Print Preview" feature to see what each printed version will look like, which will help you revise before completing your final document.

- Print copies of your various layouts and look at them from different distances. Ask others to look at your layouts and tell you what they like best and least about each.

USING WHITE SPACE

White space, the part of your document that has neither text nor visuals, allows readers to read your document more easily and to absorb information in chunks rather than in one big block. White space indicates breaks between ideas and thereby focuses attention on the key features of your document.

Flyers, brochures, posters, reports, Web pages, and similar documents tend to make extensive and varied use of white space because they rely heavily on graphics. Styles change over time, but most current professional designers prefer an uncluttered look with lots of white space.

However, our research shows that students who are involved in a volunteer project actually achieve better grades than those who are not. One possible reason is that having too much free time actually encourages people to waste it; being busier forces them to be more organized.

Figure 45.10 An image centered above text

However, our research shows that students who are involved in a volunteer project actually achieve better grades than those who are not. One possible reason is that having too much free time actually encourages people to waste it; being busier forces them to be more organized. A more interesting reason is that volunteering for a meaningful project gives people a sense of purpose that carries over into other phases of their lives. Students who  are concerned about the state of the environment, for example, draw energy from working with others who share their passion.

Figure 45.11 Text wrapped around the image

However, our research shows that students who are involved in a volunteer project actually achieve better grades than those who are not. One possible reason is that having too much free time actually encourages people to waste it; being busier forces them to be more organized. A more interesting reason is that volunteering for a meaningful project gives people a sense of purpose that carries over into other phases of their lives.

Successful volunteers:
-Follow their passions
-Budget their time
-Have positive outlooks
-Seek likeminded others

Figure 45.12 Text wrapped around a box

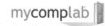

Multimodal Texts and Writing for the Web

46a What are multimodal texts?

Multimodal texts communicate through multiple (MULTI-) means, materials, and modes (-MODAL). They combine words with images or even sound and video. As a result, while some multimodal texts are meant for print, others exist only in digital forms. Examples include posters and flyers, PowerPoint presentations, Web sites, movies, videogames, and podcasts. Chapter 45 explained how a document's design contributes to its meaning, but the mode of a text also influences its meaning. Because new technologies give writers many options concerning the look and delivery of their communications, understanding how to design in multiple modes can make you a more sophisticated writer and communicator, both in college and beyond.

In academic settings, an instructor may assign a specific kind of text: a traditional paper, a poster, a Web site (46d), a blog (46e), a wiki (46f), a podcast (46g), or so on. We explain each below. On other occasions, however, the choice of a mode may be up to you.

Keep in mind that your writing situation must guide that choice. Sometimes a visual or audio presentation doesn't work as well as text alone. Also recognize that as you increase the complexity of your message by adding various media, you also increase the chance that your readers can get distracted or confused. In other words, multimodal writing often requires more attention and work than you may have planned.

EXERCISE 46-1 The cuneiform clay tablet in Figure 46.1 was written over 4,000 years ago. Compare this form of communication to more contemporary modes such as books, Web sites, and MP3 files. Create a list of the advantages and disadvantages of each mode.

46b What do I need to know about creating multimodal projects?

All elements within a multimodal text should effectively engage an AUDIENCE and clearly contribute to the overall PURPOSE of the piece. Also, consider that

Figure 46.1 Cuneiform tablet, circa 2400 BCE, Library of Congress

a visual or audio presentation must also have unity, development, and coherence. When people read, hear, or watch an example of each mode, they expect it to follow certain conventions. Just as with traditional writing, the best way to learn these conventions is to read, listen, or watch many of them, analyzing to see how they work. As you compose multimodal projects, the strategies of generating, planning, and organizing all apply.

46c What is writing for the Web?

Writing for the Web means producing documents that are designed specifically to be read online. The World Wide Web consists of millions of sites (one or many connected pages) and billions of pages (a document within a site). Of course, many documents that appear on the Web were actually written for print publication. This includes articles in databases (34c), online versions of newspapers and magazines, and even papers placed on the Web as Word documents and PDF (Portable Document Format) files.

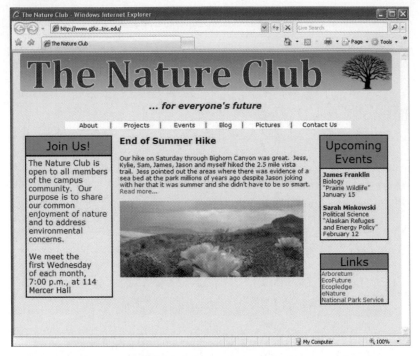

Figure 46.2 The Nature Club's home page

As you know, Web pages are common in academic, business, and public settings. They inform, entertain, and persuade through text, images, animation, sound, and video. Because Web sites allow readers to jump from page to page to find information within a site and beyond, they provide exceptional flexibility. When you design a Web site you need to consider not only how a page looks but also how it relates to others, both ones you've created and ones already online. Writing for the Web means you can freely and easily change the content of your pages.

Figure 46.2 shows the home page of The Nature Club's Web site (the club whose flyer we discussed in Chapter 45). Some of the information is similar to the information on the flyer shown there. However, the Web page allows more personal and up-to-date news about the organization, and the addition of links helps organize the Web site into various sections, including picture albums. Visitors to this page can tell in a glance what kinds of information the site contains and go directly to the pages that interest them.

EXERCISE 46-2 Discuss how the Web site in Figure 46.2 differs from the flyer in Figure 45.2. How do the purposes of those two modes shape those differences?

46d How do I create a Web site?

The **Web writing process** has five parts: (1) writing the content, (2) creating the structure of the content, (3) designing the layout of the material on the computer screen, (4) checking whether the Web material is usable, and (5) loading the Web site on a **server**, a computer that is always online and available to Internet users. This process has many similarities with the general processes for doing any type of writing; planning, revising, and editing are crucial, for example (Chapter 2).

46d.1 How do I plan content for my Web site?

The Web differs from other media in distinct ways that affect your writing.

- Web writing calls for smaller blocks of text than print writing. Web readers prefer not to scroll down long sections of information.
- Web writing highlights the connections or links between related Web sites.
- Web writing emphasizes visual elements such as color and pictures.

As you plan your writing ask yourself these questions:

- What purpose will my site fulfill? Is it to inform, to persuade, to entertain?
- Who will my readers be? What knowledge and expectations will they have? How will they need to navigate—that is, move—within my site?
- What is the size of my Web writing project? How many pages will I want and how much content will I include in each?
- Should I include links to other Web sites? Which sites will support my purpose, perhaps with an illustration, an explanation, a reference, or so on?

46d.2 How do I create a structure for my Web site?

Web structure is the organization of the content and documents that site creators include in a Web project. Almost all Web sites have a **home page** that introduces the site and provides links to the other pages that the site contains. The home page functions like a table of contents in print or, perhaps, the entryway to a building. It should be appealing and give visitors to the home page clear directions for how they can navigate your site, or move from page to page. Here are some guidelines for creating a site's structure.

- Determine all of the pages your site might contain and whether these pages should be grouped into **categories** (groups of pages all on the same topic).
- Generate a list of categories. You might use the planning techniques of BRAINSTORMING, FREEWRITING, and CLUSTERING discussed in Chapter 2.

- Plan a Web structure by drawing a map of all of your separate documents and the best way they connect to one other. Figure 46.3 shows two possible structures.

- Plan **hyperlinks**, which are direct electronic connections between two pages. Combinations of hyperlinks are the glue that holds Web writings together.

46d.3 How do I design Web pages?

Once you've drafted a map of your Web site, you begin designing and creating your individual Web pages. Generally, all the pages within a site need to have the same basic design and similar navigation features to ensure that the site is unified and that users have an easy, pleasant experience. Most guidelines and principles that contribute to good design in printed documents apply equally to Web design. Use the basic design principles of unity, variety, balance, and emphasis discussed in Chapter 45.

Begin by planning a Web page's general appearance. Make decisions about the placement of texts and graphics, the use of color and white space, and what you want to emphasize. Early in your planning process, you might look at some Web sites that seem similar to what you have in mind. Figures 46.4 and 46.5 show two popular designs. In these figures, A is a *banner* or title of the Web site or organization, B is an onsite menu of links to the various pages of the site, C is the main section for content, and D is for offsite or additional links.

Figure 46.6 (page 819) is the home page of the National Science Foundation. Notice how the menu for onsite categories (B) appears under the heading (A) with the center section filled with the home page content (C). Figure 46.7

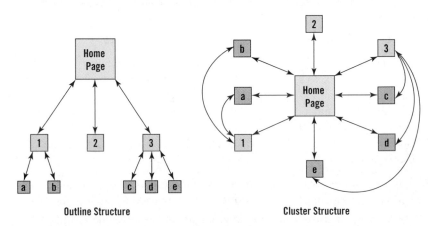

Outline Structure   Cluster Structure

Figure 46.3 Two possible Web site structures

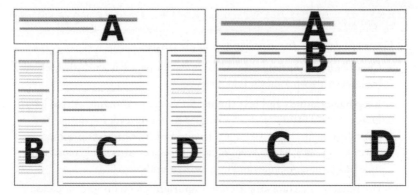

Figure 46.4 Popular Web design 1   **Figure 46.5** Popular Web design 2

(page 820) is the home page of the National Archives, which has the menu for onsite categories (B) on the left side. In both examples, readers can tell at a glance what kinds of information the Web site contains, and then go directly to the pages that interest them. Quick Reference 46.1 contains some general advice about designing Web pages.

46d.4   How do I use Web writing software?

Web pages are written in a computer program language called **HTML,** for **H**yper**T**ext **M**arkup **L**anguage. Although it's possible to create Web pages directly using HTML, it's easier to use a WYSIWYG (**W**hat **Y**ou **S**ee **I**s **W**hat **Y**ou **G**et) HTML editor—a program that generates tags, or codes, in much the same way that word-processing programs generate boldface type or other formatting.

USING STYLE SHEETS AND TABLES

Most contemporary Web designs use CSS (**C**ascading **S**tyle **S**heets). What CSS allows you to do is define what particular elements, such as headings, links, and block text will look like, and then all you have to do is define each element and apply the style sheet. For example, by applying a different style sheet to The Nature Club Web site (Figure 46.2), we changed the entire look of the site (Figure 46.8, page 821), and all we did was change one brief code.

Tables allow you to use HTML editors to place text and images accurately. The word *table* here differs from the display visual shown in section 45f. Unlike designing with pen and paper or with computer drawing software, HTML editors don't allow you to position materials immediately at different points on the screen. First, you have to define specific areas, and the easiest

---

Quick Reference 46.1 ■ ■ ■ ■ ■ ■ ■

General advice for designing Web pages

- **Choose an appropriate title.** Make sure your page has a title that tells readers exactly what they'll find there.

- **Keep backgrounds and text simple.** Strive for a clean, uncluttered look. Dark text on a plain light background is easiest to read. In contrast to print documents, SANS SERIF fonts tend to be easier to read on computer screens than SERIF fonts. Avoid multiple typefaces, sizes, and colors, multiple images and graphics, and busy backgrounds.

- **Use images to attract attention to important elements and to please the reader.** Readers will tend to look first at pictures and graphics on a page, so choose and then position them to reinforce your page's content.

- **Unify the pages in your site.** Keep the overall appearance of pages within one site consistent in terms of typefaces, graphics, and color. Make sure pages share some features, perhaps the same basic layout, font, color scheme, and header or **navigation bar** (the set of links on every Web page that allows users to get back to the site's home page and to major parts of the site). This can be easily accomplished using the **style sheet** in your HTML editor (see 46d.4).

- **Provide identifying information.** Generally, the bottom of a page includes the date the page is updated, or added to, along with contact information for the site's creator or administrator.

---

way to do this is with tables. A table divides the screen into a grid of spaces. You can then change the size of different rows, columns, or cells in the table to place blocks of text, images, links, and so on exactly where you want them. Tables allow you to fix images in the same place in relation to the text regardless of different browsers viewers may have. Figure 46.9 (page 822) shows the basic table design underlying The Nature Club home page.

46d.5 How do I incorporate images into Web pages?

Web pages can include many different kinds of graphics. For example, bullets can mark off a list of items, as they do in print documents. Borders or rule lines can divide the page. You can also use photographs imported from a digital camera, scanned from print, or downloaded from the Internet, along with clip art and other graphics. Quick Reference 46.2 covers ways to use graphics most effectively.

Be careful and respectful using any images that you haven't created yourself, especially when copying images from the Internet. E-mail the site's creator to ask permission before using any image you have saved from another source.

Figure 46.6 The home page of the National Science Foundation

Quick Reference 46.2 ■ ■ ■ ■ ■ ■ ■

Using graphics effectively on the Web

- **Only use images that enhance your message or design.** Most images require lots of digital storage space and loading time. Therefore, use only the images that enhance your page.

- **Resize or crop the image using graphic design software.** Although you should use the largest, highest resolution digital images possible, you should size the image and set the resolution at 72 ppi (pixels per inch) before you insert it into your design.

- **Save the image in a compressed format.** The two most popular formats for images on the Web are Graphic Interchange Format (GIF) and Joint

continued >>

> ### Quick Reference 46.2 (continued)
>
> Photographic Experts Group (JPEG). If you have a button, small piece of clip art, or a black and white picture, GIF is an ideal format since these types of graphics only use a few colors. JPEG uses 16.7 million colors and compresses the file size of the picture by getting rid of empty space and blending like colors together. In a detailed photograph, you would never notice such a change. However, this process of blending and squeezing can leave little imperfections in solid color images. Also, each time you save a JPG image, it recompresses it so that even a good photo can turn into mud if repeatedly worked on and saved in this format.

Figure 46.7 The home page of the National Archives

Quick Reference 45.4 explained some terms and considerations when using images in document design, and they also apply to images for Web sites. As with any source that you did not create yourself, you should document where any

Figure 46.8 The Nature Club's home page with a different CSS

images you use came from. For the correct DOCUMENTATION format for your graphic sources, see Chapter 36 (MLA), Chapter 37 (APA), or Chapter 38 (CMS and CSE). Also see the copyright considerations in Chapter 45.

EXERCISE 46-3   Working alone or in a group, further analyze the use of images on the Web page in Figure 46.6. For help, consult the discussions of images in Chapter 4 and visual design in Chapter 45. Optional: Choose one or more current Web sites on the Internet for your analysis.

46d.6   How do I edit my page and test usability?

Before you publish your Web page (that is, before you upload it to a server), edit and proofread it as carefully as you would a print document. The key difference between editing a Web page and a print document is that you also need to check that all of the interactive parts of your Web page are working properly. Before you finalize your Web page, use the following checklist:

- **Are any images broken?** Broken images show up as small icons instead of the pictures you want. The usual cause of broken images is mistyping the file name or failing to upload the image.

- **Do all the links work?** For each link to a page on your own site, be sure a file with that exact name exists on the server. Mistyped or mislabeled files can cause broken links.

- **Is the Web site user-friendly?** Ask your friends, classmates, or colleagues to report any sections in which information is unclear or difficult to find. They can also provide feedback about your content.

46d.7 How do I display my Web page?

After you've created and tested a Web page, you're ready to display it on the Web. To do this, you need two things: First, you need space on a WEB SERVER, a centralized computer always online and primarily dedicated to storing and making Web pages available. Second, you need the ability to load all of your files to that server, including the page(s) you've made and any associated graphics that you've included.

FINDING SPACE ON THE WEB

If you have a commercial Internet Service Provider (ISP), you may be able to use it to post your Web site. Your college may offer Web space to its students,

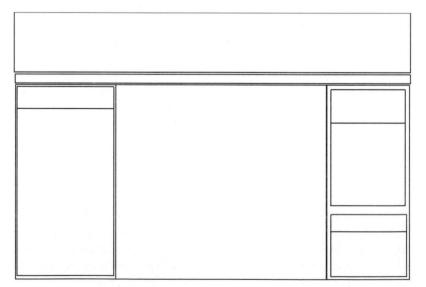

Figure 46.9 Tables used to create The Nature Club home page

so check with your computing service office. Some services on the Internet offer free Web space as well as help in building Web pages. Try searching for "free Web hosting." Note that if you use "free" Web space, the provider may insert advertising on your page.

You'll also need some kind of File Transfer Protocol (FTP) program to upload the HTML files to your Web server. The host of your space should be able to advise you on the best way to upload files and which FTP program to use.

PUBLISHING YOUR PAGE

Posting a Web page is a form of publishing. Like all original writings, your Web site is automatically copyrighted. If you want to make this clear to users (to discourage PLAGIARISM, for example) include a copyright notice by typing the word *copyright,* the copyright symbol ©, the year of publication, and your name. If you want feedback, include your e-mail address. If you use material from SOURCES, credit them completely by using DOCUMENTATION; you might include a link titled "Works Cited," "References," or "Sources" that takes your readers to a separate page. Always ask for permission to use someone else's work on your Web site. Plagiarism is plagiarism (35b), whether the medium is print or electronic.

46e How do I write in a blog?

A Web log, or blog, is a type of Web site that displays a series of posts, or items, usually diary-like entries or observations, but also images, videos, audio files, and links. There are thousands of blogs on the Internet, with most focused on a particular topic.

Some instructors have students keep blogs as a course requirement. This follows the tradition of having students keep journals as a regular way of writing about course content. The twist is that others can easily read and comment on each person's postings. If you're assigned to produce a course blog, your instructor will provide specific directions. Figure 46.10 shows a typical blog design.

If you'd like to create your own blog, decide on a type and purpose. Some blogs collect links and ask others to comment on those links. For example, Digg (http://digg.com/) and Fark (http://www.fark.com/), two popular news blogs, collect news story links and users' brief comments on them. Other blogs, such as Reuters (http://blogs.reuters.com/us/) invite much longer response posts about current news stories or happenings around the Web. Still other blogs provide original material or refer to happenings in somebody's life (an example is Figure 1.2, on page 7). Decide, then, whether you want a blog that collects, responds, reports, or is more like a journal.

Figure 46.10 A typical blog design

Next, you'll want to figure out how much control you want over your blog's appearance. Some software allows you to easily start blogging almost immediately with little worry or knowledge. However, if you would like to have more control, you may need to buy server space and set up the software yourself. CMS (**C**ontent **M**anagement **S**oftware) such as Movable Type and Drupal are powerful programs to design, write, and maintain your own blog.

You need to find an AUDIENCE that cares about your perspective. You might participate in blogs and network with others, eventually gaining people who are interested in what you have to say. Most important, have something interesting to say. Not all blogs have to be public, but if you want to take advantage of the technology of sharing your ideas and experiences with others, you should make these ideas and experiences entertaining, persuasive, and enlightening. Quick Reference 46.3 contains some guidelines.

46f How do I write in a wiki?

A wiki is a technology that allows anybody to change the content of a Web page without using special Web writing or uploading software. Wiki is a Hawaiian word meaning "fast," and the name refers to how quickly people using this technology can collaborate and revise information. One of the more popular wiki applications is the online encyclopedia, Wikipedia. (See Figure 1.7 on page 20.)

Guidelines for writing in a blog

- **Pick a unique title for your blog.** People and Internet search engines will recognize your blog if it has a good title.

- **Decide whether to use your own name or a made-up username.** You can protect your privacy to some degree if you have a *pseudonym* (literally, a "false name") or *username*. Especially if you're writing about controversial topics or taking controversial positions, you might not want employers, instructors, or even relatives to know your identity. Of course, an anonymous username doesn't give you license to be irresponsible or unethical. On the other hand, the advantage of your real name is that you get credit (and, we suppose, blame) for your writings. Think carefully about this decision.

- **Observe netiquette.** NETIQUETTE refers to etiquette in online environments like the Web. Remember, the Internet is available around the world to many people in many cultures and of many ages. What might seem normal in your life isn't necessarily normal to someone else online. So be respectful in your posts, avoid vulgar language or SHOUTING (typing in all capital letters), and if you disagree with somebody, try to find common ground or evidence to the contrary rather than resorting to *ad hominem* (4j) attacks.

- **Link, show, and share.** Use the Web and its multimodality in your posts. Include links in your posts to other, similar posts or items from the Web. Post images, videos, or audio files, but do respect copyrights. And share your posts and blog with others through the use of a blogroll or by participating on other blogs. Blogging is about sharing your ideas and experiences with others so that they might share their ideas and experiences with you.

The technology behind wikis is similar to that in blogs; both use software that runs in the background and organizes the content. However, wikis and blogs serve different purposes. Wikis are designed to allow collaborative writing and presentation rather than individual commentary and response. A wiki entry, or node, is updated and presented immediately as the content of a Web site. Whatever was written at a particular node before it was edited is deleted, and the new content replaces it. In some ways, a wiki is more temporary than any other type of multimodal writing because many people can change it.

Wikis can be useful tools for collaborative writing projects because they keep a draft in front of all group members all the time. Individuals can easily make contributions and changes. However, as you can imagine, this can also lead to complications. If you're using a wiki for a college project, you'll want to review strategies in Chapter 6 for writing with others.

There is usually no need to create a wiki if one already exists to serve a particular purpose. Contributing to the existing wiki is usually time better spent. However, if you want to create a wiki for an unmet need, such as providing information for an upcoming election, creating a collaborative space for a business, or designing a study aid for a course, setting one up is fairly easy. Simple software like Pbwiki (http://pbwiki.com/education.wiki) will allow you quickly to start creating your own wiki without worrying about server space. However, if you need more control, you will have to install specialized software such as TikiWiki, MediaWiki, or SnipSnap on a dedicated Web server. In either case, you should observe the guidelines in Quick Reference 46.4 for writing or revising a wiki node.

Quick Reference 46.4　　　　　■ ■ ■ ■ ■ ■ ■

Guidelines for writing in a wiki

- **Revise with respect for others.** When revising a node, always consider ways to preserve what was originally written before deleting what another person has written. The strength of a wiki is in its ability to allow people to collaborate their expertise, so try to maintain what others have said. In some cases, you might post on a wiki and find you totally disagree with what is written. Instead of deleting what's there, you might add qualifications, for example, adding words like, "possibly" or phrases such as "in some cases" or "some have argued." However, you might also add another section to the node entitled "opposing arguments" (see 5l) and then add an alternative viewpoint to the node.

- **Cite your sources whenever possible.** Much of the controversy concerning Wikipedia in recent years has to do with the fact that some entries do not have cited references. Whenever possible, if updating or adding to a wiki, you should cite your sources, and in some cases, find corroborating sources. Any addition to a wiki node that contains reference to reputable sources is less likely to be deleted or revised later.

- **Remember a wiki is multimodal.** Just as with a blog, use the Web and its multimodality in your node edits. Include links and references from other sources on the Web. Post images, videos, or audio files, respecting copyrights in every case. The Web is suited to multimodal presentation, so take advantage of this capability when revising or writing in a wiki.

EXERCISE 46-4　　Considering what you know about blogs, wikis, and multimodal writing, what are the benefits of using Wikipedia? What are the drawbacks?

46g How do I create podcasts or videos?

Podcasts are short audio or video files (for example, as on YouTube) that are distributed via the Internet. People can view or listen to them directly online (called "streaming") or as downloads to their computers or a digital player such as an Apple iPod. (Not every podcast can be downloaded.) Audio podcasts are oral presentations, and serious ones need to be carefully planned and written so that listeners can easily follow them, just as they would a speech. Video podcasts often imitate formats that appear on television, although the production is usually not as elaborate. A podcast might be a useful source for a paper. Take care to evaluate and cite it as you would any source, and follow the appropriate documentation styles (Chapters 36–38).

Although you can create advanced Web designs or flyers with affordable computer software and hardware, creating a professional audio or video presentation or podcast can require more specialized and expensive equipment. However, you should still be able to produce effective podcasts if you observe the guidelines in Quick Reference 46.5. Plan, draft, revise, and edit a podcast just as you would any other writing project.

Quick Reference 46.5　　　■ ■ ■ ■ ■ ■ ■

Guidelines for producing a podcast

- **Consider the benefits of the mode.** Besides thinking about your AUDIENCE and PURPOSE, you need to also consider whether an audio or video is an effective mode for your situation. Producing audio or video requires far more time than any other type of multimodal writing, which becomes a factor when deciding whether to take on such a project. Additionally, audio and video are both linear in nature, which is to say that a good podcast has a beginning, a middle, and an end, and listeners or viewers can't easily skip around.

- **Create and practice a script.** You should write out a script that contains not only what you intend to say but also list how you will say particular passages, what might be appearing on the camera during a particular section, as well as cues for music or sound effects. Once the script is written, you should practice the script often by reading it aloud, just as you would if you were practicing a musical instrument or a part in a play.

- **Create a storyboard for video projects.** A storyboard is a series of rough sketches (you can use "stick" people, for example) that show the major scenes or elements in your video. It helps you plan the sequence and keep track of what shots you need to make.

continued >>

> ### Quick Reference 46.5 (continued)
>
> - **Find an appropriate place to record.** When recording audio or video, you should always be aware that microphones and cameras record more than you might have intended. Background sounds such as your neighbor's television, the wind, or the fan in your computer might go unnoticed in your day to day life, but as soon as you record your podcast, everybody will be able to hear them. Many universities have practice rooms in the music departments that are specifically designed to dampen noise, but at least look for a quiet place with good acoustics to record any audio.
>
> - **Use the best equipment available to you.** Although many digital cameras have record-to-video functions, you will get better footage from a dedicated video camera. Similarly, although a laptop might have a built-in microphone, a dedicated microphone will produce the best results. Some music departments have recording rooms with professional equipment that you can rent for less than a professional studio would cost. However, you might not have access to such equipment at your university. Ask faculty, friends, and neighbors if they have access to any equipment that you might borrow.

46h What do I need to know about writing in social networking sites?

Social networking Web sites like MySpace and Facebook allow you to share your experiences, interests, and writing with other people of similar interests. Designing in these sites is limited by the software that each company uses, but you can still make your Web site interesting and effective. Most of the visual design elements that have been discussed in this chapter are applicable to setting up your space on a social networking Web site. For example, many MySpace and Facebook pages suffer from complicated and dark backgrounds with dark text, making them difficult to read. Consider Quick References 46.1 and 46.3 when designing and writing on a social networking Web site.

There are some additional considerations when using any social networking Web site. Remember that even if you have made your page private, a friend of a friend or even a future employer could easily end up viewing material that you meant only close friends to see. People have lost jobs and job opportunities because of what employers have seen on their pages. Always assume that anything you post is public and permanent. Only post images, text, or music that you are confident are appropriate and that represent you well.

Figure 46.11 Example of a social networking site

On the other hand, because of the powerful social networking capability, an effectively designed page might attract potential employers or professional contacts more easily than a traditional resumé or Web site. Make sure, then, to represent yourself well for multiple audiences. Because viewers can often link to your friends' pages as well, make sure you accept friends who also reflect well on you. Additionally, although you might think that private information such as your address or phone number is safe from others if you are listed as private, this information still can be leaked. You're not as anonymous as you might think. These concerns shouldn't scare you from creating a presence on a social networking site that you and others can enjoy. Just be cautious and only post personal information when absolutely necessary.

For more help with your writing, grammar, and research,
go to **www.mycomplab.com**

mycomplab

47

■ ■ ■ ■ ■ ■ ■ **47** ■

Creating a Writing Portfolio

47a What is a writing portfolio?

A portfolio is a collection of your writings that you present to others in order to achieve some purpose. You might be familiar with artists or graphic artists who make portfolios of their work in order to show gallery owners or prospective employers. Writing portfolios are similar collections of best works. Students frequently need to submit them at the end of a course, as part or all of their final grades. Some students are required to submit a portfolio of work at the end of their major or program to demonstrate what they've accomplished in the previous two or four years. Portfolios can even be part of the hiring process for some jobs, as candidates show their skills and experiences in a sample of their best work. Figure 47.1 shows one student's online career portfolio.

As we explain in this chapter, portfolios can exist in physical, paper formats, or they can exist electronically, in digital versions. There are four key steps in making a successful portfolio: collecting all of your writings; selecting the works to include in a given portfolio; writing an introduction to, or analysis of, those works; and designing the presentation format. We explain each step below.

47b What do I need to collect for a portfolio?

To put it simply: Save everything you write. Save every paper and project, every exam or lab report, even every draft. You can't put together a good portfolio if you don't have plenty of works to choose from, including plenty of works to ignore. Because computer storage is so cheap and plentiful, it's easy to keep electronic copies of everything. It's a good idea to keep paper copies, too, especially when they have instructor's comments or grades; some portfolios, such as those submitted for awards or graduate school admissions, often require instructors' comments.

47c How do I choose works to include in a portfolio?

Selection is crucial to an effective portfolio. Rather than including everything you've written, you need to choose your best pieces that satisfy the requirements of the portfolio. One obvious thing you need to do is to meet any

Figure 47.1 A student's career portfolio

requirements for the number of works or pages to include. If you're asked to select three pieces, don't include two or four. If you're asked to submit a total of 20–25 pages, don't turn in 17 or 29. Beyond those specific requirements, you need to pay attention to specific things requested in a particular situation.

47c.1 Portfolios that demonstrate your general writing ability

Consider this kind of assignment: "Present three works that best display your strengths as a writer." Clearly, you're going to choose your best writing, which sounds simple. However, you might additionally judge whether you can choose pieces that show a range of your abilities. For example, if you're choosing from six papers, and three of them are all the same kind of writing, you might not want to include all of them. Instead, you might choose at least one different kind of paper that allows you to show how versatile you are. (Of course, if the other papers are considerably weaker than the three similar ones, go with your strengths.)

47c.2 Portfolios that demonstrate a particular quality or set of qualities

Consider another kind of situation: "One goal in this course was to improve your ability to write for different situations. Create a portfolio of three works that demonstrate how you're able to write for different audiences and purposes and in different roles." In this case, you need to choose works that reflect different writing situations. Choosing becomes a little more like putting together a puzzle, as you look for the right combination of writings that allows you to meet the requirement. Occasionally, this means that a strong work gets omitted because it doesn't fit all the purposes. Often, you need to choose works that satisfy multiple requirements. For example, you might choose papers A and B to illustrate different audiences, papers A and C to show different purposes, and B and C to show different roles.

47c.3 Portfolios that demonstrate improvement

Consider a third kind of portfolio: "Select four examples of your writing from this semester that demonstrate how your writing has developed." In this case, your instructor wants to see your improvement. One way to do this is to choose writings from the beginning, middle, and end of the course. Another way is to choose both early and late, revised drafts from the same paper. In this kind of portfolio, as well as the others, an introductory or analytic statement will be valuable.

47d How do I write a portfolio introduction, reflection, or analysis?

A statement or essay in which you introduce or explain the works you're presenting is an important part of most portfolios. This writing, which may range from a few paragraphs to several pages, depending on the situation and requirements, can go by several names: introduction, reflection, analysis, reflective introduction, reflective analysis, and so on. While there are subtle differences in each of these names, the basic elements are the same: You want to introduce yourself as a writer; you want to introduce the works that follow (perhaps with a one- or two-sentence summary of each of them); and you want to make some points about them, especially how they satisfy your purpose.

Whatever the purpose, it's helpful to think of the reflective introduction as a kind of argument. You're making claims about your work, and you're providing support for those claims. For example, if you say, "These pieces show my ability to adjust my writing for academic and popular audiences," then you need to "prove" your assertion. In this case, your evidence is one or more of the papers in the portfolio, and you'll want to summarize, paraphrase, or quote the appropriate passage. You'll need to explain how the evidence fits your claim. A helpful basic structure is the following:

1. Claim about your writing.

2. Summaries, paraphrases, or quotations from papers in the portfolio that support the claim.

3. Discussion of how the summary, paraphrase, or quotations support your claim.

Repeat this pattern for as many claims as you have about your portfolio. The following example illustrates weak and strong sections from reflective introductions.

EXAMPLE

Weak and Strong Sections from a Reflective Introduction [The following paragraph is common to all three examples that follow.]

During the 2008 spring semester, I completed five papers in English 101, revising each of them several times with response from my peers and feedback from my instructor. At times the process was frustrating; I came into the course feeling confident about my writing, but I learned that there's always room for improvement. As I reflect back on my experiences, I'm especially satisfied with new strategies I learned for making effective arguments and with the skills I acquired about different kinds of academic papers. This portfolio includes three papers I've chosen to represent my current strengths as a writer.

Weak [Same introduction as above]

One quality apparent in these papers is my ability to adjust writings for different audiences, both academic and general. For example, "Analyzing the Merits of Organic Produce" addresses an academic readership. In contrast, "Is that Organic Apple Really Worth It?" is aimed at a more general audience.

Better [Same introduction as above]

One quality apparent in these papers is my ability to adjust writings for different audiences, both academic and general. For example, "Analyzing the Merits of Organic Produce" addresses an academic readership. This can be seen in my consistent use of APA citation style and a scholarly tone suitable for experts, as in my opening sentence, "Research on the health values of organic produce over nonorganic reveals that this issue remains unresolved" (Johnson, 2006; Akule, 2007).

In contrast, my paper "Is that Organic Apple Really Worth It?" is aimed at a more general audience. That paper uses scenes and examples designed to engage readers with a friendly tone. This is clear in my opening sentence, "As sticker shock in the grocery checkout line continues to worsen, consumers have to judge whether everything in their carts belongs there."

Strong [Same introduction as above]

One quality apparent in these papers is my ability to adjust writings for different audiences, both academic and general. For example, "Analyzing the Merits of Organic Produce" addresses an academic readership, specifically members of the scientific community looking for a review of the literature. This can be seen in my consistent use of APA citation style and a scholarly tone suitable for experts. One example is my opening sentence, "Research on the health values of organic produce over nonorganic reveals that this issue remains unresolved" (Johnson, 2006; Akule, 2007). The paper begins bluntly and directly because I decided scholars would require little orientation and would value my getting right to the point. Stressing that "research . . . reveals," emphasizes my ethos as a careful scholar, a quality reinforced by my including two citations. Academic readers will value this ethos more than they would an opinionated or informal one. The objective and cautious tone of "remains unresolved" differs from a more casual phrase like "is messy."

In contrast, my paper "Is that Organic Apple Really Worth It?" is aimed at a more general audience, such as readers of a weekly news magazine. That paper uses scenes and examples designed to engage readers with a friendly tone. On pages seven and eight, for example, I include an interview with organic grower Jane Treadway in which I narrate the setting. The way I reach out to general readers is clear even in my opening sentence, "As sticker shock at the grocery check out continues to get scarier, all of us have to judge whether everything in our carts belongs there." I've chosen a common experience and referred inclusively to "all of us," trying to show readers that I'm one of them. The phrase "sticker shock" and the reference to prices getting "scarier" both inject common touches.

The first (weak) example simply makes a claim and points readers generally to a couple of examples. The second (better) example goes into more detail, referring to specific parts of the papers to illustrate the claim. However, that example lacks the discussion of the final (strong) example. Notice how that last one comments on the elements that are quoted or paraphrased, so that readers can see just how they're connected to the claim.

47e How do I present a paper portfolio?

Paper portfolios can come in several formats, from a set of papers stapled or clipped together, to items included in a folder or a binder. Obviously, it's important that you follow any specific directions from your instructor. You should also clarify whether you're to revise and reprint your writings or whether the portfolio should contain only the original works, perhaps with your instructor's comments. It's useful to number all the pages in the portfolio, as a whole.

Generally, your portfolio will contain the elements identified in Quick Reference 47.1.

Quick Reference 47.1 ■ ■ ■ ■ ■ ■ ■

Items to include in a portfolio

Cover page Include a title, your name and contact information, the course, and the date. The cover page may include some images or other graphical elements, if appropriate.

Contents List all of the pieces included in the portfolio, beginning with the reflective introduction, along with their page numbers.

Reflective introduction See section 47d.

Writing 1. [Optional, if required, draft for Writing 1]

Writing 2. [Optional, if required, draft for Writing 2]

And so on, for as many writings in the portfolio.

47f How do I create a digital portfolio?

Digital portfolios have the same elements as paper ones, with the important difference that they're made to be viewed on a computer, often online. As a result, digital portfolios offer versatility that paper portfolios can't. Digital portfolios can include sound files and videos as well as papers. They can allow different kinds of MULTIMODAL texts. They have the advantage of being portable and easily revised, and you can export works from a digital portfolio into other settings—for example, from a course portfolio into one you might compile for your major. Once again, you need to follow your instructor's specific directions. He or she may require either a paper or a digital portfolio; produce the type assigned. Also, follow any specific directions regarding format or design.

Digital portfolios can take several forms. In the simplest ones, you just upload your work into an online course management program, such as Black-Board. Another simple digital portfolio requires you only to place your work into an online template. Don't worry; your instructor will provide specific directions for these kinds of portfolios.

More sophisticated digital portfolios take advantage of the computer's powerful ability to create links between files. You can do this with a word-processing program, such as Microsoft Word. Take a look at this section from the example on page 833.

One quality apparent in these papers is my ability to adjust writings for different audiences, both academic and general. For example, "Analyzing the Merits of Organic Produce" addresses an academic readership. This

Figure 47.2 A student's digital portfolio

> can be seen in my consistent use of APA citation style and a scholarly tone suitable for . . .

The blue underlined text is a link that readers can click to take them directly to the paper. The most highly developed digital portfolios have an opening page that allows readers to understand all of the elements in the portfolio. From these pages, which combine the functions performed by the cover and contents pages of a paper portfolio, readers can link to any of the components in the portfolio. In digital portfolios, all the elements of visual design are important. Figure 47.2 shows one example.

For more help with your writing, grammar, and research, go to **www.mycomplab.com**

PART

7

■ ■ ■ ■ ■ ■

Writing When English
Is Not Your First Language

A Message to Multilingual Writers

If you ever worry about your English writing, you have much in common with us and many US college students. Still, we recognize that multilingual writers face special challenges. Depending on how, when, and where you began learning English, you might feel very comfortable with spoken English but not academic, written English. Or you might understand English grammar quite well, but you might struggle with idioms and slang. Multilingual writers' different backgrounds in English will affect the kinds of writing challenges they face. For example, you might be an international student just learning the expectations of academic English, or you might be a bilingual student who went to high school in the United States. You might be an adult returning to school encountering academic language for the first time, or you might be a student who received an advanced degree in another country but must now master academic writing in English. To become a skilled writer in English, though, you will likely need to concentrate on almost every word, phrase, sentence, and paragraph in ways native speakers of English do not.

Many multilingual writers get very upset about the errors that they make in written English. We encourage you not to get frustrated about errors, but to learn from them. The good news is that errors demonstrate that you're moving normally through the stages of second-language development. As with your progress in speaking, listening, and reading in a new language, developing writing skills takes time. The process of learning to write English is like learning to play a musical instrument. Few people can play fluently without first making many errors.

What can help you advance as quickly as possible from one writing stage to another? If you attended school elsewhere before coming to the United States, we recommend that you start by thinking about school writing in your first language. Recall how you were taught to present ideas in your written native language, especially when explaining information, giving specific details, and arguing logically about a topic. Then compare it to how writing American English works. Making yourself aware of the similarities and differences will help you learn English strategies more easily.

Most college essays and research papers in the United States are direct in tone and straightforward in structure. Typically, the THESIS STATEMENT (the central message of the piece of writing) is at the end of the first paragraph or, in a longer piece of writing, in the second paragraph. Each paragraph that follows relates in content directly to the essay's thesis statement. Also, each paragraph after the thesis statement needs to begin with a TOPIC SENTENCE that contains the main point of the paragraph, and the rest of the paragraph supports the point made in the topic sentence. The final paragraph brings the content to a logical conclusion that grows out of what has come before.

As you continue writing in English, you might look for interesting ways to blend the traditions and structures of writing in your first language with the conventions of academic writing in the United States. It's important to honor your culture's writing traditions and structures; they reflect the richness of your heritage. At the same time, you can adapt to and practice the writing styles typical in the United States. The *American Heritage English as a Second Language Dictionary,* which is available in paperback and hardcover, can ease your way with English words and expressions. If your college library doesn't own a copy, ask your professor to request that the reference librarian purchase a few copies for students to consult.

The *Simon & Schuster Handbook* offers three special features that we've designed specifically for you as a multilingual learner. Chapters 8 through 31 focus on the most challenging grammar issues that you face as you learn to write English. In other chapters throughout the book, ESOL Tips offer you more helpful hints about possible cultural references and grammar issues. Finally, in Chapter 49, we've provided an "English Errors Transferred from Other Languages" chart. In this chart, you'll find information about trouble spots that commonly occur when speakers of certain first languages (Spanish, Russian, and so on) speak, read, or write in English.

Distinctive variations in school writing styles among people of different cultures and language groups have interested researchers for the past thirty years. If you have written academically in languages other than American English, you might notice similarities and differences between the writing you have done in school prior to now and the writing you are asked to do in English. As individuals, we greatly enjoy discovering the rich variations in the writing traditions of our students from many cultures of the world. As American writing teachers, however, our responsibilities call for us to explain what you need to do as writers in the United States. If you were in one of our classes, we would say "Welcome!" and ask you to teach us about writing in your native language. You bring a richness of experience in communicating in more than one language that most US students have never had, and you should be proud of that experience. Using the knowledge of writing in your first language, we could then help you learn how to approach writing effectively in the United States so that you will succeed as a writer and learner in a US college.

Lynn Quitman Troyka

Doug Hesse

48 ■ ■ ■ ■ ■ ■

Multilingual Students Writing in US Colleges and Universities

48a How is writing taught in US colleges?

Multilingual students who went to high school outside the United States may find that teachers and students in this country behave differently from teachers and students in their home countries. If you're one of these students, you might be surprised by the seemingly informal interaction between teachers and students in the United States. No matter how you interpret what you might see, rest assured that the casual teacher-student relationship is based on respect. Instructors still expect students to pay attention, obey class rules, and meet all assignment deadlines.

In the United States, teachers usually expect students to participate in class discussions. This can be very challenging for multilingual students if they aren't used to this style of classroom interaction, especially if they don't feel confident about speaking English. If this is the case for you, do your best to make as many contributions to class discussion as you possibly can. The more you try, the easier it will become.

When your instructors assign work, they may show you model papers. It can be very helpful to examine the parts of these sample papers to see how the authors have organized information, presented main points, and supported those main points. This is especially true if the assignment is a new type of writing for you. When you look at examples, be sure you know which aspects of the papers your teacher thinks are strong, and which aspects he or she thinks need improvement. Of course, when you analyze sample papers, you're doing so only to learn which writing techniques work well. Remember: Don't copy phrases, ideas, content, or images from them. In the United States, copying someone else's work is called PLAGIARISM*, and it's ethically and legally wrong. For a detailed discussion about plagiarism, see Chapter 35.

If your instructor asks you to analyze a sample paper, pay close attention to the features of that type of paper. For example, the characteristics that make a lab report effective are not always the same characteristics that make a

---

*Words printed in SMALL CAPITAL LETTERS are discussed elsewhere in the text and are defined in the Terms Glossary at the back of this book.

narrative essay effective. Chapter 7 explains some types of academic writing that are common in the United States.

Just as classroom expectations and writing assignments differ from culture to culture, the way that writing is taught also varies. In writing classes in US colleges, many instructors teach a process approach to writing. This approach emphasizes the steps that writers go through as they compose assignments for themselves and for college and work. The basic steps are planning, drafting, revising, editing, and proofreading. For more specific details about the writing process, see Chapter 2 of this handbook.

Sometimes multilingual students become so concerned about making grammar mistakes that they neglect taking enough time to think about the ideas in their paper. Always remember that writing is about communicating ideas. To ensure you're conveying your own ideas and fulfilling the requirements of your assignments, spend as much time thinking about the content of your paper as you do working on your grammar. You might find it helpful to work on content and grammar separately as you draft. For help in working on thinking of ideas and expressing them, review sections 2b–2f, which describe activities to help you come up with interesting material for your writing.

48b How does my past writing experience affect my writing in English?

Thinking about your own writing experiences and learning about others' can help you set goals for improving your writing. Exercise 48-1 can help you do both.

EXERCISE 48-1   Think about the following sentences. For each sentence, write "True," "False," or "I'm not sure." If invited, share your answers with your instructor so he or she can learn more about your previous writing experiences. Next, write your thoughts about all or some of the statements, which can give you insight into yourself as a writer in English. Outside of class, you might also discuss your answers with one or more of your multilingual classmates or friends.

1. I am better at writing in another language than I am at writing in English.
2. I have more experience writing in another language than I do in English.
3. I feel confident about writing in English.
4. I received all of my secondary (high school) education outside the United States.
5. When I write in English, I have trouble finding the appropriate vocabulary.
6. When I write in English, I use a dictionary that translates words between English and my first language.
7. When I write in English, I use an English-English dictionary.
8. When I write in English, I use a computer spell-check program.

9. When I write in English, I use a computer grammar-check program.

10. In the past, I have written many different kinds of papers in English.

11. When I write in English, I can write fairly quickly.

12. I think I will need to write a lot for my major.

13. I think I will need to write a lot in English for my future career.

14. When I write in English, I sometimes have trouble generating ideas.

15. A serious problem I have with writing in English is writing correct sentences.

48c How can I know what my instructor expects in my writing?

Your past writing experiences influence the way you approach writing assignments. In the next passage, a bilingual student illustrates how her past experiences influenced her interpretation of writing assignments in the United States. (Note: The original draft has been edited to improve readability.)

> When I studied here, I felt puzzled with different types of writing assignments. When I wrote my first term paper, I really did not know what my professor did expect from me and how to construct my paper. My previous training in my first and second language writing taught me little about how to handle writing assignments by using composing strategies. Since language teaching in my country is exam-oriented, I learned to write in Chinese and in English basically in the same way. Under the guidance of my professor, I read a sample paper, analyzed its content and structure, and tried to apply its strengths to my own writing. Writing was not a creative process to express myself but something that was to be copied for the purpose of taking exams. As a result, when I don't have a sample for my assignments, I really don't know how to start.

Like this student, you may have difficulty understanding what your instructor expects you to do when completing a specific writing assignment. Your instructor may expect you to take a clear position on your topic. He or she may want you to use examples from your personal experience to support your ideas, quotations and specific ideas from an assigned reading, outside sources, or all three. Do not hesitate to ask your instructor questions about the assignment to make sure you understand exactly what he or she expects.

EXERCISE 48-2   Have you ever had trouble figuring out what an instructor expected from you when he or she assigned a writing exercise? Have you ever written a paper and later found out that what you wrote was not at all what your instructor expected? Write a paragraph or two describing your experiences.

When your instructor gives you a writing assignment, you may not know how to start because you don't know much about the topic. This might be especially true if the topic that your instructor asks students to write about relates to aspects of American culture that you're not very familiar with. If you feel this is the case, you might need to talk to your instructor about the situation and try to find more information about the topic in newspapers or magazines or by discussing the topic with other students. Similarly, if you're writing about your own culture, keep in mind that your instructor and classmates may not know very much about it. This means you may need to explain information for them in more detail than you would if you were writing a paper for people who share your cultural background.

EXERCISE 48-3 Have you ever written or read something that didn't make sense because it didn't include the necessary cultural background information? Write a paragraph or two describing your experiences and explaining the source of miscommunication. Before you begin, read the following passage by a student who describes the importance of providing background information in writing. (Note: This excerpt has been edited for readability.)

> If I were writing in Chinese to Chinese readers and wanted to quote a story in Chinese history as evidence, I would simply have to mention the name of the people involved in the historic event or briefly introduce the story. However, when I am writing in English to tell the readers the same story, I have to tell the whole story in detail, even though I might only want to use a small part of it in my essay. Otherwise, the readers will surely get lost.

48d How do I organize my writing?

As part of the writing process, many instructors ask students to write an OUTLINE and a THESIS STATEMENT for their papers (2d–2e). Some writers from other countries have observed that American readers expect papers to have a standardized organization and communicate their purpose in a clear, obvious way. In some cases, this rigid structure poses challenges. For example, one bilingual student wrote that when he writes in his first language, he can use a "flexible organization" and can place his thesis "at the beginning, middle, or end of the essay" or "simply leave the thesis out and then let the reader draw the conclusion to show respect for the reader's intelligence." He explains that he finds it challenging writing in English because he must follow a "restricted organization" that presents a thesis in the first paragraph and then supporting subtopics and detailed examples. Keep in mind, though, that you need to follow the conventions of the type of writing you're assigned (Chapter 7).

EXERCISE 48-4 Are there differences between how you were taught to organize your writing in the past and how your instructors expect you to organize it now? Describe the differences in a paragraph or two, and, if you can, draw a picture that illustrates the differences. Before you begin, think back to the paragraph in Exercise 48-3 and what the student wrote about the differences organizing his papers in Chinese and English. Also, consider the following descriptions of organization in writing. (Note: Both of these examples have been edited for readability.)

EXAMPLE 1   Russian composition is not about composing supportive arguments around your own personal opinion, but instead is about composing a hierarchy of others' opinions on a certain topic. The process is very much like making a chain: You pick a citation and link it to another citation and so on.

EXAMPLE 2   From my TOEFL [Test of English as a Foreign Language] preparation class, I learned the basic framework for English writing: introduction plus body paragraphs plus conclusion, with topic sentences in the body paragraphs. I was impressed by the great difference between writing in my first language and English writing. For example, in a persuasive essay, writers from my country usually prefer to explain the problem first and then come up with their opinion. But for English writing, writers may be more likely to express the opinion at the very beginning and then give reasons to support the idea.

48e   How can I use other writers' work to improve my writing?

If you are writing a paper based on other texts that you have read, such as a reading your teacher has given you or sources you have found for a research project, it is important to understand how directly your teacher wants you to draw on the text(s). For example, he or she may want you to read the text and simply use it as a springboard for your own ideas; however, your instructor may also expect you to read and analyze the text closely and refer to specific ideas and sentences in the source text when you write your paper. It can be especially difficult for multilingual students to analyze a text closely and write about it without relying too heavily on the author's wording and sentence structure. In US colleges and universities, however, using another author's words, sentence structure, or even ideas without giving the author credit is considered to be a serious offense called PLAGIARISM, or stealing something that belongs to someone else (Chapter 35). In contrast, in some cultures, reliance on the author's wording is not a problem, and may even be seen as a way of complimenting the author. As one bilingual student said, "When you are writing in my first language, you can always feel free to copy good sentences from other articles or writing pieces. But in the United States, it is a violation of copyright. When you are writing in English, you cannot use someone else's work without citing it."

Chapter 35 of this handbook provides detailed information about how to document sources and avoid plagiarism. Documenting sources in your writing is very important in US academic writing because it helps to develop your credibility as a writer, or what we often call your ETHOS (5g.2). Giving credit to the original authors shows that you have done the necessary background work to find out what other people have said on a topic. Documenting sources, especially those written by experts, can help develop your credibility because your sources are reliable. Chapters 36–38 provide examples of four different documentation styles that you might use in your academic writing in the United States. Always ask your instructor if you're uncertain which style to follow.

48f   What kind of dictionary do I use?

Although it can be helpful to use a dictionary that translates words from your native language into English, sometimes such dictionaries are not adequate. One ESOL student, who has problems with word choice, says that dictionaries "don't always work" because some terms are "translated literally." She goes on to explain that when she uses dictionaries, she doesn't accept just any definition. The student learns how to use a word in a "real English way" and whether it is "appropriate to use in a certain context."

If you realize that you need a dictionary that does more than translating words between your native language and English, you might try an English-English dictionary (also called a "Learner's Dictionary"), especially one that was written for nonnative learners of English. Using an English-English dictionary can also help you increase your vocabulary in English as you learn different ways to express the same idea.

48g   What should I do with my classmates' and instructor's comments?

As part of the writing process, you and your classmates may participate in peer response, sometimes called peer review or peer editing. (See Chapter 6.) You might exchange papers or sit together and read your paper to the students in your group. The purpose of peer response is to offer and receive advice about how to improve your writing from your classmates. This type of group work may be uncomfortable for you if teachers in your home country did not assign group work or expect students to critique each other's work, or if you prefer working individually. Here are some strategies to help make peer response successful for you and your classmates.

- Let your group members know you really do want them to give you advice on your paper so that you can improve its quality before you turn it in for a grade.
- Ask your group members specific questions about your writing.
- Provide other group members with specific, considerate advice about their writing. Two strategies in written English can make suggestions more tactful:

  Ask questions about your other group members' essays. For example, asking "How does this reason relate back to your claim?" sounds more polite than stating "This reason doesn't relate to your claim." Your question also helps the author to revise and make his or her writing better.

  Use modals to "hedge" your suggestions. In English, modal verbs are often used to "soften" a command. For example, if you write, "This reason does not seem to relate to your claim," the word "seem" makes the observation more polite than if you write, "This reason does not relate to your claim."

- Talk to your instructor if you don't know whether you need to follow a specific piece of advice from a classmate.
- See Chapter 6 for more information about peer response.

In addition to receiving feedback from your classmates, try to get feedback from your instructor before he or she gives your paper a grade. Instructors expect to see significant changes based on their comments. If you have questions about how to revise your writing in response to what your teacher has told you, you need to talk to your instructor or a tutor.

48h Where can I find strategies for editing my work?

When you are satisfied with the content, organization, and development of the ideas in your paper, you need to focus on language-related concerns in your writing. Chapter 49 outlines strategies for proofreading your papers.

48i How can I set long-term goals for my writing?

Improving your writing can take a long time, whether you are writing in your first language or in a second, third, or fourth language. Some students find it helpful to set long-term goals for writing to help them focus on what to improve. You may want to talk to a professor in your major (or in a subject you are thinking about majoring in) so that you can ask him or her what kinds of writing you might be expected to do later, both in your college courses and in the workplace (if you plan to work in an English-speaking environment or in a context where English is used to communicate with other nonnative English speakers).

EXERCISE 48-5 Interview a professor in your major (or in a subject you are thinking about majoring in). Ask him or her the following questions, and write a report about the answers you receive. Compare your report with that of a classmate.

1. What kinds of writing do you assign to students in your classes?
2. How do students learn how to write these assignments?
3. (Choose one or two types of writing assignments that the professor mentions.) What are the important parts of this assignment? What steps do students go through to complete this kind of assignment?
4. When you grade student writing, what aspects are most important to you?
5. What kinds of writing do graduates in this major usually do in the workplace?
6. Can you show me some examples of student writing from your courses?

For more help with your writing, grammar, and research,
go to **www.mycomplab.com**

Handling Sentence-Level Issues in English

49a How can I improve the grammar and vocabulary in my writing?

The best way to improve your English-language writing, including your grammar and vocabulary, is by writing. Many students also find it helpful to read as much as they can in English to see how other authors organize their writing, use vocabulary, and structure their sentences. Improving your writing in a second language—or a first language, for that matter—takes time. You will probably find that your ability to communicate with readers improves dramatically if you work on the ideas outlined in the previous chapter, including understanding the writing assignment and improving the organization and ideas in your writing. Sometimes, though, readers may find it hard to understand your ideas because of grammar or word choice problems in your sentences. In other cases, readers may become distracted from your ideas because you have a great many technical errors. We have designed this chapter to help you improve in these areas.

49b How can I improve my sentence structure?

Sometimes students write sentences that are hard to understand because of problems with overall sentence structure or length. For example, one student wrote the following sentence, which contains sentence-level errors.

> When the school started, my first English class was English 1020 as a grammar class, I started learning the basics of grammar, and at the same time the basic of writing, I worked hard in that class, taking by the teacher advice, try to memorize a lot of grammar rules and at the same time memorize some words I could use them to make an essay point.

To correct the structural and length errors, the student needs to do several things to improve the sentence. She needs to break it into several shorter sentences (Chapter 20). Also, she needs to revise her sentences so that they clearly connect to each other. Additionally, she needs to work on her verb tenses in certain phrases, such as "to make an essay point." This means she needs to ask for extra help at the writing center or from her instructor. After patient study and work, her revision might look like this:

> When school started, my first English class, English 1020, was a grammar class, where I started learning the basics of grammar. At the same time, I learned the basics of writing. I worked hard in that class, taking the teacher's advice and memorizing a lot of grammar rules. In addition, I memorized some words I could use in my essays to make my points.

EXERCISE 49-1 Many different revisions of the previous example of a student's uncorrected paragraph are possible. Write a different revision of that student's paragraph.

EXERCISE 49-2 A student wrote the following passage in a paper he wrote about his experiences learning English. Rewrite the passage, improving the student's sentence structure and punctuation. In your revision of this passage, correct any errors that you see in grammar or spelling. Afterward, compare your revision with a classmate's. Then examine a piece of your own writing to see if you need to revise any of your sentences because of problems with sentence structure. (While you are doing this, if you have any questions about correct word order in English, see Chapter 52.)

> I went to school in my country since I was three years old, I was in Arabic and French school, and that's was my dad choice because his second language is French. So my second language at that time was French. In my elementary school I started to learn how to make an essay in French and Arabic. I learned the rules and it is too deferent from English. But later on when I was in my high school I had two choices between English class and science class so I choose the science because that's was my major. After I graduate I went to American university and I start studying English and my first class was remedial English for people doesn't know anything about this language. I went to this class about two months and then I have moved to a new place and I start from the beginning as an ESL student.

49c How can I improve my word choice (vocabulary)?

An important aspect of writing in a second language is having enough vocabulary to express your ideas. Many students enjoy learning more and more words to be able to communicate precise meanings. For example, one multilingual student explains that she has improved her writing and made it more "desirable" by using "words as tools." She also says that by using "different words every time" she "refreshes" her writing and "eliminates the routine" from it. You, too, can experiment in your writing with new words that you hear and read in other contexts. To help make sure you're using a new word in the right way, we recommend the *American Heritage English as a Second Language Dictionary*, which is available in paperback and hardback. It can ease your way with English words and expressions because it's intended specifically for multilingual learners of English.

49d How can I find and correct errors in my own writing?

Some multilingual writers find it easiest to find and correct their grammar errors by reading their writing aloud and listening for mistakes. This method is often preferred by students who feel their spoken English is better than their written English. Other writers like to ask a friend who is a native speaker of English to check their writing for grammatical mistakes. Still other multilingual writers prefer to circle each place where they think they've made an error and then use their handbook to check themselves.

Many multilingual writers like to keep a list of the types of grammar errors they make so that they can become especially sensitive to errors when proofreading their papers. The best system is to make a master list of the errors in categories so that the checking can be as efficient as possible. Section 49j provides an example of how to track your errors in English.

49e How can I correct verb form (tense) errors in my writing?

Many multilingual writers consider verb-form errors the most difficult to correct. They want to be sure that their verb forms express the appropriate time frame for the event or situation they're describing. For a detailed discussion of verb forms, see 15b–15f.

EXERCISE 49-3   Read the following passage in which a student describes her experience learning to write in English. The student's instructor has underlined errors related to time frames expressed by the verbs. Correct the underlined verbs, changing them to the correct time frames.

> I must have started writing when I was nine years old. I remember my father used to give us papers and watercolors and let us draw as much as we want. At the end, he made sure that we write comments about why we have sketched the way we did. The only written thing that I find dating to that period was a kind of comment about a picture which I have sketched of a village enveloped in water.
> I don't remember much about the kind of writing assignments we have at school, whether in my native language Arabic, or in my second languages, at that time, English and French. That period is a little bit hazy in my mind. However, I remember that whenever we had the chance to go to school, we made sure that we fill the playgrounds with creative farewell sentences indicating that we have been there. It is our little game against the witchcraft of war and against the will of the principal, who forgive us easily once we have recited the multiplication table or sing the national anthem.

If you struggle with errors in verb tense in your writing, try reading through your draft once and circling all of the verbs. Then check each one in isolation.

49f How can I correct my errors in subject-verb agreement?

Subject-verb agreement means that a subject (a noun or a pronoun) and its verb must agree in number and in person. In the following two sentences, notice the difference in the way the subjects and the verbs that describe their actions agree: *Carolina runs charity marathons. They give her a sense of accomplishment.*

For more information about subject-verb agreement, review Chapter 17. To help you put subject-verb agreement rules into practice, try the next exercise.

EXERCISE 49-4   Examine the following student's description of his experiences learning English. The student's instructor has underlined verbs that do not agree with their subjects. Correct the underlined verb forms, changing them to agree with their subjects.

I describe the way I learned English as a natural way, where one first learn how to speak and communicate with others, before learning the grammar rules that supports a language. When I arrived in the United States, I works hard to improve my communications skills in English, trying to speak even when the people does not understand me. Also, making friends with native speakers help a person learn the language. One can learn from them every single minute that one spend with them.

Do you have similar problems with subject-verb agreement in your own writing? Examine something you've written recently to check whether your subjects and verbs agree. Try underlining the subject and verb in each sentence to isolate the words in the sentence that need to agree.

49g   How can I correct my singular/plural errors?

In English, if you're referring to more than one noun that is a count noun, you must make that noun plural, often by adding an -s ending. If you would like more information on this topic, see Chapter 50. To help you recognize when necessary plural forms are missing, try the next exercise.

EXERCISE 49-5   In the following passage, a student comments on the differences between writing in English and in Chinese. The student's instructor has underlined only the first two nouns that need to be plural. Read the passage, correct the two underlined nouns, and then find and correct the other nouns in the passage that need to be plural.

English and Chinese have many similarity. They both have paragraph, sentence, and punctuation mark, like comma, full stops, and question marks. The biggest difference is that English has an alphabet with letter, while Chinese uses symbol for writing. My mother told me that about two thousand year ago, people in China used picture to draw what they wanted to say on turtle shells. Day after day, the pictures changed and turned into the Chinese character.

Examine a piece of your own writing and make sure that you have used plural words correctly.

49h   How can I correct my preposition errors?

Prepositions are words such as *in, on, for, over,* and *about,* which usually show where, how, or when. For example, in the sentence *She received flowers from her friend for her birthday,* the prepositions are *from* and *for.* Unlike some other languages, English has many prepositions, and knowing which one to use can be very difficult. You can find information about using prepositions in section 14h and in Chapter 53. To practice finding and correcting preposition errors in your own writing, complete the next exercise.

● **EXERCISE 49-6**   In the following passage about one student's learning
● experiences as a second-language learner, the student's instructor has underlined
● problems with preposition use. Try to correct the preposition errors. In some
cases, more than one answer may be correct. If you can't find the information you
need from Chapter 53 or in a dictionary, you might ask a native English speaker
for help.

> I've always wanted to learn languages other than my native language.
> I started taking English and French lessons of school and I liked the idea
> of becoming fluent for at least one language. I thought English would
> help me a lot to the future because it could help me communicate to
> people from all over the world.

If prepositions are something you struggle with in your own writing, ask
an instructor or a native speaker of English to underline the errors in preposition usage in a piece of writing that you have done. Then go through your
writing and correct the errors that have been underlined.

49i What other kinds of errors might I make?

Depending on your language background and your prior experience with writing in English, you may make errors related to the use of articles (*a, an, the*),
word order (where to place adjectives and adverbs in sentences), and various verb
forms and noun forms (for example, problems with noncount nouns and helping verbs). For example, the next sentence has a problem with one article and
the order of an adjective: *The New York City is a place exciting.* The corrected
sentence is *New York City is an exciting place.*

Chapters 50 through 55 address grammar errors that are often made by
multilingual writers. Try to keep track of your most common errors and refer
to the relevant sections of this handbook for help.

49j How can I keep track of my most common errors?

One way of becoming more aware of the types of errors you make is to keep
track of the errors you often make in the papers you write. You can ask your
instructor or a tutor to help you identify such errors, and you can make a list
of them that you update regularly. Remember the passage from Exercise
49-3 about a student's experiences learning to write? After the student examined the teacher's comments on her paper, she made a list of her errors and included a correction and a note about the error type for each. After making this
list of her errors, the student writer realized that many of her errors related to
verb form.

Specific Error	Correction	Type of Error
as much as we want	wanted	verb form
that we write comments	wrote	verb form
about why we have sketched	had	verb form
which I have sketched	had	verb form
we fill the playground	filled	verb form
that we have been there	had	verb form
once we have recited	had	verb form

EXERCISE 49-7   Using one or more pieces of your writing, make an error list similar to the previous one. (You could make this list on a sheet of paper or in an electronic file.) Examine the list. What are the most common types of errors that you make? Once you have identified your common error types, refer to the relevant proofreading exercises in the previous sections of this chapter and to the relevant ones in Chapters 50 through 55. Also, remember to keep your common errors in mind when you proofread your future writing assignments. You might even keep a master checklist that you can return to when you proofread your writing.

49k   How can I improve my proofreading skills?

The most effective way to improve your proofreading skills is to practice frequently. Proofread your own writing and, after you have done so, ask your instructor, a tutor, or a friend who is a native English speaker to point out the location of errors that you did not see on your own. If you know you often make a particular kind of error, such as errors with subject-verb agreement (Chapter 11), ask the person helping you to check for these problems specifically. When you know which errors you've made, try to correct the errors without help. Finally, have your instructor or tutor check your corrections.

Another effective way to improve your proofreading skills is to exchange your writing with a partner. You can check for errors in his or her writing and he or she can check for errors in yours. You might find that, at first, it is easier to find errors if you look for one kind of error at a time. Try Exercises 49-8 and 49-9 for more proofreading practice.

EXERCISE 49-8   The following passage was written by a bilingual student about her experiences learning to write in English. After you read it, rewrite it, correcting the linguistic errors you find.

I've always faced some problem in writing in English as it took me some time to get used to it. Facing these complexities encourage me to developed my skills in English writing. My first class in English was about grammar, spelling, and writing. I realize later that grammar is hard to learn, so I knew I have to put in a lot of effort to understand it perfectly and use it properly. I also had some difficulties for vocabulary, as it was hard to understand the meaning of some word.

Another thing that helped me with my English was when my mother enroll me in an English learning center that specialize in teach writing skills. After a month of taking classes, my teacher saw some improvement in my grammar and vocabulary. To test me, she asked me to write an essay on how to be successful. I was really excite of it and started write it immediately. After I finish my essay and my teacher check it, my teacher suggested that I take a few more classes for her. She taught me how to organized my ideas. After finishing these classes I realize that my writing was getting much better with time.

EXERCISE 49-9 In the following paragraph, a student describes the study of English at private schools in Japan. After you read the paragraph, rewrite it, correcting the errors that you find.

Recently, the number of private language schools are increased in Japan. These schools put special emphasize on oral communication skills. In them, student takes not only grammars and reading classes, which help them pass school examinations, but also speaking, listening classes. They can also study English for six year, which is same period as in public schools. Some of the teacher in these school are native speaker of English. Since these teachers do not use Japanese in the class, the students have to use the English to participate it. They have the opportunity to use the English in their class more than public school students. It is said that the students who took English in private schools can speak English better than those student who go to public schools.

The following chart contains information about errors that may be caused by a difference between your native language and English. The chart does not include all languages or all possible errors. Instead, it focuses on languages commonly spoken by ESOL students in the United States, and it includes errors that often cause significant difficulties for students.

ENGLISH ERRORS TRANSFERRED FROM OTHER LANGUAGES

Languages	Error Topic	Sample Errors	Corrected Errors
Singulars and Plurals (Ch. 50)			
Chinese, Japanese, Korean, Thai	no (or optional) plural forms of nouns, including numbers	NO: She wrote many good **essay.** NO: She typed two **paper.**	YES: She wrote many good **essays.** YES: She typed two **papers.**

continued >>

Languages	Error Topic	Sample Errors	Corrected Errors
Hebrew, Italian, Japanese, Spanish	use of plural with embedded plurals	NO: We cared for five **childrens.**	YES: We cared for five **children.**
Italian, Spanish	adjectives carry plural	NO: They are **Americans** students.	YES: They are **American** students.

Articles (Ch. 51)

Chinese, Japanese, Hindi, Korean, Russian, Swahili, Thai, Turkish, Urdu	no article (*a, an, the*) but can depend on whether article is definite/ indefinite	NO: He ate sandwich.	YES: He ate **a** sandwich.

Word Order (Ch. 52)

Arabic, Hebrew, Russian, Spanish, Tagalog	verb before subject	NO: **Questioned Avi** the teenagers.	YES: **Avi questioned** the teenagers.
Chinese, Japanese, Hindi, Thai	inverted word order confused in questions	NO: **The book was it** heavy?	YES: **Was the book** heavy?
Chinese, Japanese, Russian, Thai	sentence adverb misplaced	NO: We will go home **possibly** now.	YES: **Possibly,** we will go home now.

Gerunds, Infinitives, and Participles (Ch. 54)

French, German, Greek, Hindi, Russian, Urdu	no progressive forms or overuse of progressive forms with infinitive	NO: They **talk** while she **talk.**	YES: They **are talking** while she **is talking.**
		NO: They **are wanting** to talk now.	YES: They **want** to talk now.
Arabic, Chinese, Farsi, Russian	omit forms of *be*	NO: She happy.	YES: She **is** happy.
Chinese, Japanese, Korean, Russian, Thai	no verb ending changes for person & number	NO: She **talk** loudly.	YES: She **talks** loudly.
Arabic, Chinese, Farsi, French, Thai, Vietnamese	no or nonstandard verb-tense markers	NO: He **laugh** yesterday.	YES: He **laughed** yesterday.
		NO: They **has arrived** yesterday.	YES: They **arrived** yesterday.
Japanese, Korean, Russian, Thai, Vietnamese	nonstandard passives	NO: A car accident **was happened.**	YES: A car accident **was caused by the icy roads.**

50

Singulars and Plurals

50a What are count and noncount nouns?

Count nouns name items that can be counted: *a radio* or *radios, a street* or *streets, an idea* or *ideas, a fingernail* or *fingernails.* Count nouns can be SINGULAR or PLURAL.

Noncount nouns name things that are thought of as a whole and not split into separate, countable parts: *rice, knowledge, traffic.* There are two important rules to remember about noncount nouns: (1) They're never preceded by *a* or *an,* and (2) they are never plural.

Here are several categories of noncount nouns, with examples in each category:

GROUPS OF SIMILAR ITEMS	clothing, equipment, furniture, jewelry, junk, luggage, mail, money, stuff, traffic, vocabulary
ABSTRACTIONS	advice, equality, fun, health, ignorance, information, knowledge, news, peace, pollution, respect
LIQUIDS	blood, coffee, gasoline, water
GASES	air, helium, oxygen, smog, smoke, steam
MATERIALS	aluminum, cloth, cotton, ice, wood
FOOD	beef, bread, butter, macaroni, meat, pork
PARTICLES OR GRAINS	dirt, dust, hair, rice, salt, wheat
SPORTS, GAMES, ACTIVITIES	chess, homework, housework, reading, sailing, soccer
LANGUAGES	Arabic, Chinese, Japanese, Spanish
FIELDS OF STUDY	biology, computer science, history, literature, math
EVENTS IN NATURE	electricity, heat, humidity, moonlight, rain, snow, sunshine, thunder, weather

Some nouns can be countable or uncountable, depending on their meaning in a sentence. Most of these nouns name things that can be meant either individually or as "wholes" made up of individual parts.

COUNT	You have **a hair** on your sleeve. [In this sentence, *hair* is meant as an individual, countable item.]
NONCOUNT	Kioko has black **hair**. [In this sentence, all the strands of *hair* are referred to as a whole.]
COUNT	**The rains** were late last year. [In this sentence, *rains* is meant as individual, countable occurrences of rain.]
NONCOUNT	**The rain** is soaking the garden. [In this sentence, all the particles of *rain* are referred to as a whole.]

When you are editing your writing (see Chapter 2), be sure that you have not added a plural -*s* to any noncount nouns, for they are always singular in form.

Alert: Be sure to use a singular verb with any noncount noun that functions as a SUBJECT in a CLAUSE. ●

To check whether a noun is count or noncount, look it up in a dictionary such as the *Dictionary of American English* (Heinle and Heinle). In this dictionary, count nouns are indicated by [C], and noncount nouns are indicated by [U] (for "uncountable"). Nouns that have both count and noncount meanings are marked [C;U].

50b How do I use determiners with singular and plural nouns?

Determiners, also called *expressions of quantity,* are used to tell how much or how many with reference to NOUNS. Other names for determiners include *limiting adjectives, noun markers,* and ARTICLES. (For information about articles—the words *a, an,* and *the*—see Chapter 51.)

Choosing the right determiner with a noun can depend on whether the noun is NONCOUNT or COUNT (see 50a). For count nouns, you must also decide whether the noun is singular or plural. Quick Reference 50.1 lists many determiners and the kinds of nouns that they can accompany.

Alert: The phrases *a few* and *a little* convey the meaning "some": *I have* **a few** *rare books* means "I have *some* rare books." *They are worth* **a little** *money* means "They are worth *some* money."

Without the word *a,* the words *few* and *little* convey the meaning "almost none": *I have* **few** [or *very few*] *books* means "I have *almost no* books." *They are worth* **little** *money* means "They are worth *almost no* money." ●

Quick Reference 50.1

■ ■ ■ ■ ■ ■ ■

Determiners to use with count and noncount nouns

GROUP 1: DETERMINERS FOR SINGULAR COUNT NOUNS

With every **singular count noun,** always use one of the determiners listed in Group 1.

a, an, the	a house	an egg	the car
one, any, some, every, each, either, neither, another, the other	any house	each egg	another car
my, our, your, his, her, its, their, nouns with *'s* or *s',*	your house	its egg	Connie's car
this, that	this house	that egg	this car
one, no, the first the second, etc.	one house	no egg	the fifth car

GROUP 2: DETERMINERS FOR PLURAL COUNT NOUNS

All the determiners listed in Group 2 can be used with **plural count nouns.** Plural count nouns can also be used without determiners, as discussed in section 50b.

the	the bicycles	the rooms	the idea
some, any, both, many, more, most, few, fewer, the fewest, a lot of, a number of, other, several, all, all the	some bicycles	many rooms	all ideas
my, our, your, his, her, its, their, nouns with *'s* or *s'*	our bicycles	her rooms	student's ideas
these, those	these bicycles	those rooms	these ideas
no, two, three, etc.; *the first, the second, the third,* etc.	no bicycles	four rooms	the first ideas

continued >>

Quick Reference 50.1 (continued)

GROUP 3: DETERMINERS FOR NONCOUNT NOUNS

All the determiners listed in Group 3 can be used with noncount nouns (always singular). Noncount nouns can also be used without determiners, as discussed in section 47b.

the	the rice	the rain	the pride
some, any, much, more, most, other, the other, little, less, the least, enough, all, all the, a lot of	enough rice	a lot of rain	more pride
my, our, your, his, her, its, their, nouns with 's or s'	their rice	India's rain	your pride
this, that	this rice	that rain	this pride
no, the first, the second, the third, etc.	no rice	the first rain	no pride

50c How do I use *one of,* nouns as adjectives, and *states* in names or titles?

ONE OF CONSTRUCTIONS

One of constructions include *one of the* and a NOUN or *one of* followed by a DETERMINER-noun combination (*one of my hats, one of those ideas*). Always use a plural noun as the OBJECT when you use *one of the* with a noun or *one of* with an adjective-noun combination.

NO   *One of the* **reason** to live here is the beach.

YES *One of the* **reasons** to live here is the beach.

NO   *One of her best* **friend** has moved away.

YES *One of her best* **friends** has moved away.

The VERB in these constructions is always singular because it agrees with the singular *one,* not with the plural noun: **One** *of the most important inventions of the twentieth century* **is** [not *are*] *television.*

For advice about verb forms that go with *one of the . . . who* constructions, see 17l.

NOUNS USED AS ADJECTIVES

ADJECTIVES in English do not have plural forms. When you use an adjective with a PLURAL NOUN, make the noun plural but not the adjective: *the* **green** [not *greens*] *leaves.* Be especially careful when you use a word as a MODIFIER that can also function as a noun.

> The bird's wingspan is ten inches. [*Inches* is functioning as a noun.]
>
> The bird has a ten-inch wingspan. [*Inch* is functioning as a modifier.]

Do not add *-s* (or *-es*) to the adjective even when it is modifying a plural noun or pronoun.

> **NO** Many **Americans** students are basketball fans.
>
> **YES** Many **American** students are basketball fans.

NAMES OR TITLES THAT INCLUDE THE WORD *STATES*

States is a plural word. However, names such as *United States* or *Organization of American States* refer to singular things—one country and one organization, even though made up of many states. When *states* is part of a name or title referring to one thing, the name is a SINGULAR NOUN and therefore requires a SINGULAR VERB.

> **NO** The **United States have** a large entertainment industry.
>
> **NO** The **United State has** a large entertainment industry.
>
> **YES** The **United States has** a large entertainment industry.

50d How do I use nouns with irregular plurals?

Some English nouns have irregularly spelled plurals. In addition to those discussed in section 31c, here are others that often cause difficulties.

PLURALS OF FOREIGN NOUNS AND OTHER IRREGULAR NOUNS

Whenever you are unsure whether a noun is plural, look it up in a dictionary. If no plural is given for a singular noun, add *-s* to form the plural.

Many nouns from other languages that are used unchanged in English have only one plural. If two plurals are listed in the dictionary, look carefully for differences in meaning. Some words, for example, keep the plural form from the original language for scientific usage and have another, English-form plural for nonscientific contexts: *formula, formulae, formulas; appendix, appendices, appendixes; index, indices, indexes; medium, media, mediums; cactus, cacti, cactuses; fungus, fungi, funguses.*

Words from Latin that end in *-is* in their singular form become plural by substituting *-es: parenthesis, parentheses; thesis, theses; oasis, oases.*

OTHER WORDS

Medical terms for diseases involving an inflammation end in *-itis: tonsillitis, appendicitis.* They are always singular.

The word *news,* although it ends in *s,* is always singular: *The* **news is** *encouraging.* The words *people, police,* and *clergy* are always plural even though they do not end in *s: The* **police are** *prepared.*

EXERCISE 50-1 Consulting all sections of this chapter, select the correct choice from the words in parentheses and write it in the blank.

EXAMPLE At the beginning of every school year, all (student, students) students can expect (homework, homeworks) homework that teaches them about the toll-free No Bully hot line.

1. One of the main (reason, reasons) _____ for such a hot line is the change in tempers and violent capacities of (American, Americans) _____ students.

2. Because students are often bullied by a fellow classmate when outside the classroom, it is important that they receive (information, informations) _____ about how to react when confronted by such a threat.

3. Many a child in the (United State, United States) _____ is in danger not only of being teased and taunted by others but also of being the victim of a crime in which (blood, bloods) _____ is spilled, such as from assault or robbery.

4. Because (many, much) _____ classrooms are unsupervised after school, this (time, times) _____ becomes especially dangerous.

5. In a moment of danger, (ignorance, ignorances) _____ can be deadly, so the No Bully hot line was set up to give students (advice, advices) _____ on how to handle bullying and other threatening situations.

51

Articles

51a How do I use *a*, *an*, or *the* with singular count nouns?

The words *a* and *an* are called **indefinite articles**. The word *the* is called the DEFINITE ARTICLE. Articles are one type of DETERMINER. (For more on determiners, see 14f; for other determiners, see Quick Reference 50.1 in 50b.) Articles signal that a NOUN will follow and that any MODIFIERS between the article and the noun refer to that noun.

a chair	the computer
a brown chair	the teacher's computer
a cold, metal chair	the lightning-fast computer

Every time you use a singular count noun, a COMMON NOUN that names one countable item, the noun requires some kind of determiner; see Group 1 in Quick Reference 50.1 (in 50b) for a list. To choose between *a* or *an* and *the,* you need to determine whether the noun is **specific** or **nonspecific**. A noun is considered *specific* when anyone who reads your writing can understand exactly and specifically to what item the noun is referring. If the noun refers to any of a number of identical items, it is *nonspecific.*

For nonspecific singular count nouns, use *a* (or *an*). When the singular noun is specific, use *the* or some other determiner. Quick Reference 51.1 can help you decide when a singular count noun is specific and therefore requires *the.*

! **Alert:** Use *an* before words that begin with a vowel sound. Use *a* before words that begin with a consonant sound. Go by the sound, not the spelling. For example, words that begin with *h* or *u* can have either a vowel or a consonant sound. Make the choice based on the sound of the first word after the article, even if that word is not the noun.

an idea	a good idea
an umbrella	a useless umbrella
an honor	a history book ●

Quick Reference 51.1 ■ ■ ■ ■ ■ ■ ■

When a singular count noun is specific and requires *the*

- **Rule 1: A noun is specific and requires *the* when it names something unique or generally and unambiguously known.**

  The sun has risen above the horizon. [Because there is only one *sun* and only one *horizon*, these nouns are specific in the context of this sentence.]

- **Rule 2: A noun is specific and requires *the* when it names something used in a representative or abstract sense.**

  Benjamin Franklin favored the turkey as the national bird of the United States. [Because *turkey* and *national bird* are representative references rather than references to a particular turkey or bird, they are specific nouns in the context of this sentence.]

- **Rule 3: A noun is specific and requires *the* when it names something defined elsewhere in the same sentence or in an earlier sentence.**

  The ship *Savannah* was the first steam vessel to cross the Atlantic Ocean. [*Savannah* names a specific ship.]

  The carpet in my bedroom is new. [*In my bedroom* defines exactly which carpet is meant, so *carpet* is a specific noun in this context.]

  I have a computer in my office. The computer is often broken. [*Computer* is not specific in the first sentence, so it uses *a*. In the second sentence, *computer* has been made specific by the first sentence, so it uses *the*.]

- **Rule 4: A noun is specific and requires *the* when it names something that can be inferred from the context.**

  Monday, I had to call the technician to fix my computer again. [A *technician* would be any of a number of individuals; *the technician* implies the same person has been called before, and so it is specific in this context.]

One common exception affects Rule 3 in Quick Reference 51.1. A noun may still require *a* (or *an*) after the first use if more information is added between the article and the noun: *I bought a sweater today. It was a* (not *the*) *red sweater.* (Your audience has been introduced to *a sweater* but not *a red sweater*, so *red sweater* is not yet specific in this context and cannot take *the*.) Other information may make the noun specific so that *the* is correct. For example, *It was the red sweater that I saw in the store yesterday* uses *the* because the *that* CLAUSE makes specific which red sweater the writer means.

51b How do I use articles with plural nouns and with noncount nouns?

With plural nouns and NONCOUNT NOUNS, you must decide whether to use *the* or to use no article at all. (For guidelines about using DETERMINERS other than articles with nouns, see Quick Reference 50.1 in 50b.) What you learned in 51a about NONSPECIFIC and SPECIFIC NOUNS can help you choose between using *the* or using no article. Quick Reference 51.1 in 51a explains when a singular count noun's meaning is specific and calls for *the*. Plural nouns and noncount nouns with specific meanings usually use *the* in the same circumstances. However, a plural noun or a noncount noun with a general or nonspecific meaning usually does not use *the*.

> Geraldo grows **flowers** but not **vegetables** in his garden. He is thinking about planting **corn** sometime. [three nonspecific nouns]

PLURAL NOUNS

A plural noun's meaning may be specific because it is widely known.

> **The oceans** are being damaged by pollution. [Because there is only one possible meaning for *oceans*—the oceans on the earth—it is correct to use *the*. This example is related to Rule 1 in Quick Reference 51.1.]

A plural noun's meaning may also be made specific by a word, PHRASE, or CLAUSE in the same sentence.

> Geraldo sold **the daisies from last year's garden** to the florist. [Because the phrase *from last year's garden* makes *daisies* specific, *the* is correct. This example is related to Rule 3 in Quick Reference 51.1.]

A plural noun's meaning usually becomes specific by its use in an earlier sentence.

> Geraldo planted **tulips** this year. **The tulips** will bloom in April. [*Tulips* is used in a general sense in the first sentence, without *the*. Because the first sentence makes *tulips* specific, *the tulips* is correct in the second sentence. This example is related to Rule 3 in Quick Reference 51.1.]

A plural noun's meaning may be made specific by the context.

> Geraldo fertilized **the bulbs** when he planted them last October. [In the context of the sentences about tulips, *bulbs* is understood as a synonym for *tulips*, which makes it specific and calls for *the*. This example is related to Rule 4 in Quick Reference 51.1.]

NONCOUNT NOUNS

Noncount nouns are always singular in form (see 50a). Like plural nouns, non-count nouns use either *the* or no article. When a noncount noun's meaning is specific, use *the* before it. If its meaning is general or nonspecific, do not use *the*.

> Kalinda served us **rice.** She flavored **the rice** with curry. [*Rice* is a noncount noun. By the second sentence, *rice* has become specific, so *the* is used. This example is related to Rule 3 in Quick Reference 51.1.]

> Kalinda served us **the rice that she had flavored with curry.** [*Rice* is a non-count noun. *Rice* is made specific by the clause *that she had flavored with curry*, so *the* is used. This example is related to Rule 3 in Quick Reference 51.1.]

GENERALIZATIONS WITH PLURAL OR NONCOUNT NOUNS

Rule 2 in Quick Reference 51.1 tells you to use *the* with singular count nouns that carry general meaning. With GENERALIZATIONS using plural or noncount nouns, omit *the*.

> **NO**   The tulips are the flowers that grow from the bulbs.

> **YES** Tulips are flowers that grow from bulbs.

> **NO**   The dogs require more care than the cats do.

> **YES** Dogs require more care than cats do.

51c   How do I use *the* with proper nouns and with gerunds?

PROPER NOUNS

PROPER NOUNS name specific people, places, or things (see 14b). Most proper nouns do not require ARTICLES: *We visited **Lake Mead** with **Asha** and **Larry**.* As shown in Quick Reference 51.2, however, certain types of proper nouns do require *the*.

GERUNDS

GERUNDS are PRESENT PARTICIPLES (the *-ing* form of VERBS) used as nouns: ***Skating** is challenging.* Gerunds are usually not preceded by *the*.

> **NO**   The constructing new bridges is necessary to improve traffic flow.

> **YES** Constructing new bridges is necessary to improve traffic flow.

Use *the* before a gerund when two conditions are met: (1) The gerund is used in a specific sense (see 51a), and (2) the gerund does not have a DIRECT OBJECT.

Quick Reference 51.2　　■ ■ ■ ■ ■ ■ ■

Proper nouns that use *the*

- **Nouns with the pattern *the . . . of . . .***
  - **the** United States **of** America
  - **the** Republic **of** Mexico
  - **the** Fourth **of** July
  - **the** University **of** Paris
- **Plural proper nouns**
  - **the** United Arab Emirates
  - **the** Johnsons
  - **the** Rocky Mountains [*but* Mount Fuji]
  - **the** Chicago Bulls
  - **the** Falkland Islands [*but* Long Island]
  - **the** Great Lakes [*but* Lake Superior]
- **Collective proper nouns (nouns that name a group)**
  - **the** Modern Language Association
  - **the** Society of Friends
- **Some (but not all) geographical features**
  - **the** Amazon　　　**the** Gobi Desert　　　**the** Indian Ocean
- **Three countries**
  - **the** Congo　　　**the** Sudan　　　**the** Netherlands

NO　　**The designing fabric** is a fine art. [*Fabric* is a direct object of *designing*, so *the* should not be used.]

YES　　**Designing fabric** is a fine art. [*Designing* is a gerund, so *the* is not used.]

YES　　**The designing of fabric** is a fine art. [*The* is used because *fabric* is the object of the preposition *of* and *designing* is meant in a specific sense.]

EXERCISE 51-1　　Consulting all sections of this chapter, decide which of the words in parentheses is correct and write it in the blank. If no article is needed, leave the blank empty.

EXAMPLE　　For (a, an, the) _____ years, people have worked under (a, an, the) the assumption that (a, an, the) the best remedy for (a, an, the) a burn is butter.

1. This kind of treatment seems to be (a, an, the) _____ good idea because butter looks and feels like ointment, but butter doesn't contain (a, an, the) _____ antibacterial property like ointment does.

2. In using butter to treat (a, an, the) _____ burns, you are coating (a, an, the) _____ skin with debris that must be removed later to keep it from interfering with (a, an, the) _____ healing process.

3. In actuality, cold water without ice will not only ease (a, an, the) _____ pain but also prevent scarring and further damage.

4. In fact, (a, an, the) _____ person who keeps the finger submerged for at least several minutes and as long as half an hour will have (a, an, the) _____ least painful or scarred burn, according to doctors.

5. However, if (a, an, the) _____ burn is serious, (a, an, the) _____ first person to be consulted should be a doctor.

For more help with your writing, grammar, and research, go to **www.mycomplab.com**

■ ■ ■ ■ ■ ■ **52**

Word Order

52a How do I understand standard and inverted word order in sentences?

In **standard word order**, the most common pattern for DECLARATIVE SEN-TENCES in English, the SUBJECT comes before the VERB. (To understand these concepts more fully, review 14l through 14p.)

SUBJECT   VERB

That book   was heavy.

With **inverted word order**, the MAIN VERB or an AUXILIARY VERB comes before the subject. The most common use of inverted word order in English is in forming DIRECT QUESTIONS. Questions that can be answered with a yes or no begin with a form of *be* used as a main verb, with an auxiliary verb (*be, do, have*), or with a MODAL AUXILIARY (*can, should, will,* and others; see Chapter 55).

QUESTIONS THAT CAN BE ANSWERED WITH A YES OR NO

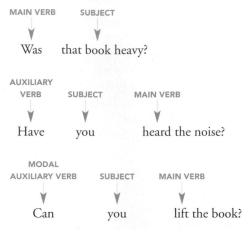

MAIN VERB	SUBJECT
Was	that book heavy?

AUXILIARY VERB	SUBJECT	MAIN VERB
Have	you	heard the noise?

MODAL AUXILIARY VERB	SUBJECT	MAIN VERB
Can	you	lift the book?

To form a yes-or-no question with a verb other than *be* as the main verb and when there is no auxiliary or modal as part of a VERB PHRASE, use the appropriate form of the auxiliary verb *do.*

AUXILIARY VERB	SUBJECT	MAIN VERB
Do	you	want me to put the book away?

A question that begins with a question-forming word such as *why, when, where,* or *how* cannot be answered with a yes or no: **Why** *did the book fall?* Some kind of information must be provided to answer such a question; the answer cannot be simply yes or no because the question is not "*Did* the book fall?" Information on *why* it fell is needed: for example, *It was too heavy for me.*

INFORMATION QUESTIONS: INVERTED ORDER

Most information questions follow the same rules of inverted word order as yes-or-no questions.

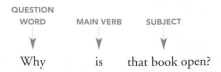

QUESTION WORD	MAIN VERB	SUBJECT
Why	is	that book open?

QUESTION WORD	AUXILIARY VERB	SUBJECT	MAIN VERB
What	does	the book	discuss?

QUESTION WORD	MODAL AUXILIARY	SUBJECT	MAIN VERB
When	can	I	read the book?

INFORMATION QUESTIONS: STANDARD ORDER

When *who* or *what* functions as the subject in a question, use standard word order.

QUESTION WORD: SUBJECT	MAIN VERB
Who	dropped the book?

QUESTION WORD: SUBJECT	MAIN VERB
What	was the problem?

 **Alert:** When a question has more than one auxiliary verb, put the subject after the first auxiliary verb. ●

FIRST AUXILIARY	SUBJECT	SECOND AUXILIARY	MAIN VERB
Would	you	have	replaced the book?

The same rules apply to emphatic exclamations: ***Was** that book heavy!* ***Did** she enjoy that book!*

NEGATIVES

When you use negatives such as *never, hardly ever, seldom, rarely, not only,* or *nor* to start a CLAUSE, use inverted order. These sentence pairs show the differences, first in standard order and then in inverted order.

I have never seen a more exciting movie. [standard order]

Never have I seen a more exciting movie. [inverted order]

She is not only a talented artist **but also** an excellent musician.

Not only is she a talented artist, **but she is also** an excellent musician.

I didn't like the book, and **my husband didn't either.**

I didn't like the book, and **neither did my husband.**

Alerts: (1) With INDIRECT QUESTIONS, use standard word order.

NO   She asked **how did I drop** the book.

YES   She asked **how I dropped** the book.

(2) Word order deliberately inverted can be effective, when used sparingly, to create emphasis in a sentence that is neither a question nor an exclamation (also see 9e). ●

52b   How can I understand the placement of adjectives?

ADJECTIVES modify—describe or limit—NOUNS, PRONOUNS, and word groups that function as nouns (see 14f). In English, an adjective comes directly before the noun it describes. However, when more than one adjective describes the same noun, several sequences may be possible. Quick Reference 52.1 shows the most common order for positioning several adjectives.

Quick Reference 52.1   ■ ■ ■ ■ ■ ■ ■

Word order: cumulative adjectives

1. **Determiners, if any:** *a, an, the, my, your, this, that, these, those,* and so on
2. **Expressions of order, including ordinal numbers, if any:** *first, second, third, next, last, final,* and so on
3. **Expressions of quantity, including cardinal (counting) numbers, if any:** *one, two, few, each, every, some,* and so on
4. **Adjectives of judgment or opinion, if any:** *pretty, happy, ugly, sad, interesting, boring,* and so on
5. **Adjectives of size or shape, if any:** *big, small, short, round, square,* and so on
6. **Adjectives of age or condition, if any:** *new, young, broken, dirty, shiny,* and so on
7. **Adjectives of color, if any:** *red, green, blue,* and so on
8. **Adjectives that can also be used as nouns, if any:** *French, Protestant, metal, cotton,* and so on

continued >>

9. **The noun**

1	2	3	4	5	6	7	8	9
a		few		tiny		red		ants
the	last	six					Thai	carvings
my			fine		old		oak	table

52c How can I understand the placement of adverbs?

ADVERBS modify—describe or limit—VERBS, ADJECTIVES, other adverbs, or entire sentences (see 14g). Adverbs may be positioned first, in the middle, or last
in CLAUSES. Quick Reference 52.2 summarizes adverb types, what they tell
about the words they modify, and where each type can be placed.

Quick Reference 52.2   ■ ■ ■ ■ ■ ■ ■ ■

Word order: positioning adverbs

ADVERBS OF MANNER	• describe *how* something is done	Nick **carefully** groomed the dog
	• are usually in middle or last position	Nick groomed the dog **carefully.**
ADVERBS OF TIME	• describe *when* or *how long* about an event	**First,** he shampooed the dog.
	• are usually in first or last position	He shampooed the dog **first.**
	• include *just, still, already,* and similar adverbs, which are usually in middle position	He had **already** brushed the dog's coat.
ADVERBS OF FREQUENCY	• describe *how often* an event takes place	Nick has **never** been bitten by a dog.
	• are usually in middle position	
	• are in first position when they modify an entire sentence (see "Sentence Adverbs" below)	**Occasionally,** he is scratched while shampooing a cat.

continued >>

Quick Reference 52.2 (continued)

ADVERBS OF DEGREE OR EMPHASIS	• describe *how much* or *to what extent* about other modifiers • are directly before the word they modify • include *only*, which is easy to misplace (see 21a)	Nick is **extremely** calm around animals. [*Extremely* modifies *calm*.]
SENTENCE ADVERBS	• modify the entire sentence rather than just one word or a few words • include transitional words and expressions (see 7g.1), as well as such expressions as *maybe, probably, possibly, fortunately, unfortunately,* and *incredibly* • are in first position	**Incredibly,** he was once asked to groom a rat.

⊗ Alert: Do not let an adverb separate a verb from its DIRECT OBJECT or INDIRECT OBJECT. ●

EXERCISE 52-1 Consulting all sections of this chapter, find and correct any errors in word order.

1. A beautiful few flowers began to bloom in my garden this week.

2. A neighbor asked me, "You did grow all these yourself?"

3. "Yes," I replied, "the roses are my favorite husband's, but the tulips are my favorite."

4. My neighbor, who extremely was impressed with my gardening efforts, decided to grow some flowers of her own.

5. Weeks later, as I strolled by her house, I saw her planting happily seeds from her favorite type of plant—petunias.

53

■ ■ ■ ■ ■ ■

Prepositions

Prepositions function with other words in PREPOSITIONAL PHRASES (14o). Prepositional phrases usually indicate *where* (direction or location), *how* (by what means or in what way), or *when* (at what time or how long) about the words they modify.

This chapter can help you with several uses of prepositions, which function in combination with other words in ways that are often idiomatic—that is, peculiar to the language. The meaning of an IDIOM differs from the literal meaning of each individual word. For example, the word *break* usually refers to shattering, but the sentence *Yao-Ming broke into a smile* means that a smile appeared on Yao-Ming's face. Knowing which preposition to use in a specific context takes much experience in reading, listening to, and speaking the language. A dictionary like the *Dictionary of American English* (Heinle and Heinle) can be especially helpful when you need to find the correct preposition to use in cases not covered by this chapter.

53a How can I recognize prepositions?

Quick Reference 53.1 lists many common prepositions.

Quick Reference 53.1				■ ■ ■ ■ ■ ■ ■
Common prepositions				
about	around	beside	down	inside
above	as	between	during	instead of
across	at	beyond	except	into
after	because of	but	for	like
against	before	by	from	near
along	behind	concerning	in	next
among	below	despite	in front of	of

continued >>

Quick Reference 53.1 (continued)

off	outside	since	under	within
on	over	through	underneath	without
onto	past	throughout	unlike	
on top of	plus	till	until	
opposite	regarding	to	up	
out	round	toward	with	

53b How do I use prepositions with expressions of time and place?

Quick Reference 53.2 shows how to use the prepositions *in, at,* and *on* to deliver some common kinds of information about time and place. Quick Reference 53.2, however, does not cover every preposition that indicates time or place, nor does it cover all uses of *in, at,* and *on*. Also, the Quick Reference does not include expressions that operate outside the general rules. (Both these sentences are correct: *You ride **in** the car* and *You ride **on** the bus*.)

Quick Reference 53.2 ■ ■ ■ ■ ■ ■ ■

Using *in*, *at*, and *on* to show time and place

TIME

- *in* **a year or a month** (*during* is also correct but less common)

  in 1995   **in** May

- *in* **a period of time**

  in a few months (seconds, days, years)

- *in* **a period of the day**

  in the morning (afternoon, evening)

  in the daytime (morning, evening) *but* **at** night

- *at* **a specific time or period of time**

  at noon   **at** 2:00   **at** dawn   **at** nightfall

  at takeoff (the time a plane leaves)

  at breakfast (the time a specific meal takes place)

- *on* **a specific day**

  on Friday   **on** my birthday

continued >>

Quick Reference 53.2	(continued)

PLACE

- *in* a location surrounded by something else

  in the province of Alberta   in the kitchen

  in Utah   in the apartment

  in downtown Bombay   in the bathtub

- *at* a specific location

  at your house   at the bank

  at the corner of Third Avenue and Main Street

- *on* a surface

  on page 20

  on the second floor *but* in the attic *or* in the basement

  on Washington Street

  on the mezzanine

  on the highway

53c   How do I use prepositions in phrasal verbs?

Phrasal verbs, also called *two-word verbs* and *three-word verbs,* are VERBS that combine with PREPOSITIONS to deliver their meaning. In some phrasal verbs, the verb and the preposition should not be separated by other words: *Look at the moon* [not *Look the moon at*]. In **separable phrasal verbs,** other words in the sentence can separate the verb and the preposition without interfering with meaning: *I threw away my homework* is as correct as *I threw my homework away.*

Here is a list of some common phrasal verbs. The ones that cannot be separated are marked with an asterisk (*).

SELECTED PHRASAL VERBS

ask out	get along with*	look into
break down	get back	look out for*
bring about	get off	look over
call back	go over*	make up
drop off	hand in	run across*
figure out	keep up with*	speak to*
fill out	leave out	speak with*
fill up	look after*	throw away
find out	look around	throw out

Position a PRONOUN OBJECT between the words of a separable phrasal verb: *I threw it away.* Also, you can position an object PHRASE of several words between the parts of a separable phrasal verb: *I threw **my research paper** away.* However, when the object is a CLAUSE, do not let it separate the parts of the phrasal verb: *I threw away **all the papers that I wrote last year.***

Many phrasal verbs are informal and are used more in speaking than in writing. For ACADEMIC WRITING, a more formal verb is usually more appropriate than a phrasal verb. In a research paper, for example, *propose* or *suggest* might be a better choice than *come up with.* For academic writing, acceptable phrasal verbs include *believe in, benefit from, concentrate on, consist of, depend on, dream of* (or *dream about*), *insist on, participate in, prepare for,* and *stare at.* None of these phrasal verbs can be separated.

EXERCISE 53-1 Consulting the preceding sections of this chapter and using the list of phrasal verbs in 53c, write a one- or two-paragraph description of a typical day at work or school in which you use at least five phrasal verbs. After checking a dictionary, revise your writing, substituting for the phrasal verbs any more formal verbs that might be more appropriate for academic writing.

53d How do I use prepositions with past participles?

PAST PARTICIPLES are verb forms that function as ADJECTIVES (54f). Past participles end in either *-ed* or *-d,* or in an equivalent irregular form (15d). When past participles follow the LINKING VERB *be,* it is easy to confuse them with PASSIVE verbs (15n), which have the same endings. Passive verbs describe actions. Past participles, because they act as adjectives, modify NOUNS and PRONOUNS and often describe situations and conditions. Passive verbs follow the pattern *be* + past participle + *by: The child **was frightened by** a snake.* An expression containing a past participle, however, can use either *be* or another linking verb, and it can be followed by either *by* or a different preposition.

- The child **seemed frightened by** snakes.
- The child **is frightened of** all snakes.

Here is a list of expressions containing past participles and the prepositions that often follow them. Look in a dictionary for others. (See 54b on using GERUNDS after some of these expressions.)

SELECTED PAST PARTICIPLE PHRASES + PREPOSITIONS

be accustomed to	be disappointed with (*or* in someone)
be acquainted with	be discriminated against
be composed of	be divorced from
be concerned/worried about	be excited about

be finished/done with   be married to
be interested in   be pleased/satisfied with
be known for   be prepared for
be located in   be tired of (*or* from)
be made of (*or* from)

53e   How do I use prepositions in expressions?

In many common expressions, different PREPOSITIONS convey great differences in meaning. For example, four prepositions can be used with the verb *agree* to create five different meanings.

agree to means "to give consent": *I cannot agree to my buying you a new car.*

agree about means "to arrive at a satisfactory understanding": *We certainly agree about your needing a car.*

agree on means "to concur": *You and the seller must agree on a price for the car.*

agree with means "to have the same opinion": *I agree with you that you need a car.*

agree with also means "to be suitable or healthful": *The idea of having such a major expense does not agree with me.*

You can find entire books filled with English expressions that include prepositions. The following list shows a few that you're likely to use often.

SELECTED EXPRESSIONS WITH PREPOSITIONS

ability in	different from	involved with *someone*
access to	faith in	knowledge of
accustomed to	familiar with	made of
afraid of	famous for	married to
angry with *or* at	frightened by	opposed to
authority on	happy with	patient with
aware of	in charge of	proud of
based on	independent of	reason for
capable of	in favor of	related to
certain of	influence on *or* over	suspicious of
confidence in	interested in	time for
dependent on	involved in [*something*]	tired of

54

Gerunds, Infinitives, and Participles

PARTICIPLES are verb forms (see 15b). A verb's *-ing* form is its PRESENT PARTICIPLE. The *-ed* form of a regular verb is its PAST PARTICIPLE; IRREGULAR VERBS form their past participles in various ways (for example, *bend, bent; eat, eaten; think, thought*—for a complete list, see Quick Reference 15.4 in 15d). Participles can function as ADJECTIVES (*a smiling face, a closed book*).

A verb's *-ing* form can also function as a NOUN (***Sneezing** spreads colds*), which is called a GERUND. Another verb form, the INFINITIVE, can also function as a noun. An infinitive is a verb's SIMPLE or base FORM, usually preceded by the word *to* (*We want everyone **to smile***). Verb forms—participles, gerunds, and infinitives—functioning as nouns or MODIFIERS are called VERBALS, as explained in 14e. This chapter can help you make the right choices among verbals.

54a How can I use gerunds and infinitives as subjects?

Gerunds are used more commonly than infinitives as subjects. Sometimes, however, either is acceptable.

> **Choosing** the right health club is important.

> **To choose** the right health club is important.

🛇 **Alert:** When a gerund or an infinitive is used alone as a subject, it is SINGULAR and requires a singular verb. When two or more gerunds or infinitives create a COMPOUND SUBJECT, they require a plural verb. (See 14l and 17e.) ●

54b When do I use a gerund, not an infinitive, as an object?

Some VERBS must be followed by GERUNDS used as DIRECT OBJECTS. Other verbs must be followed by INFINITIVES. Still other verbs can be followed by either a gerund or an infinitive. (A few verbs can change meaning depending on whether they are followed by a gerund or an infinitive; see 54d.) Quick Reference 54.1 lists common verbs that must be followed by gerunds, not infinitives.

Yuri **considered** *calling* [not *to call*] the mayor.

He was having trouble *getting* [not *to get*] a work permit.

Yuri's boss **recommended** *taking* [not *to take*] an interpreter to the permit agency.

Quick Reference 54.1   ■ ■ ■ ■ ■ ■ ■

Verbs and expressions that must be followed by gerunds

admit	dislike	object to
anticipate	enjoy	postpone
appreciate	escape	practice
avoid	finish	put off
consider	give up	quit
consist of	imagine	recall
contemplate	include	resist
delay	mention	risk
deny	mind	suggest
discuss	miss	tolerate

GERUND AFTER *GO*

The word *go* is usually followed by an infinitive: *We can **go to see*** [not *go seeing*] *a movie tonight.* Sometimes, however, *go* is followed by a gerund in phrases such as *go swimming, go fishing, go shopping,* and *go driving: I will **go shopping*** [not *go to shop*] *after work.*

GERUND AFTER *BE* + COMPLEMENT + PREPOSITION

Many common expressions use a form of the verb *be* plus a COMPLEMENT plus a PREPOSITION. In such expressions, use a gerund, not an infinitive, after the preposition. Here is a list of some of the most frequently used expressions in this pattern.

SELECTED EXPRESSIONS USING *BE* + COMPLEMENT + PREPOSITION

be (get) accustomed to	be interested in
be angry about	be prepared for
be bored with	be responsible for
be capable of	be tired of
be committed to	be (get) used to
be excited about	be worried about

We **are excited about** *voting* [not *to vote*] in the next presidential election.
Who **will be responsible for** *locating* [not *to locate*] our polling place?

⬤**Alert:** Always use a gerund, not an infinitive, as the object of a preposition. Be especially careful when the word *to* is functioning as a preposition in a PHRASAL VERB (see 53c): *We are committed to changing* [not *to change*] *the rules.* ⬤

54c   When do I use an infinitive, not a gerund, as an object?

Quick Reference 54.2 lists selected common verbs and expressions that must be followed by INFINITIVES, not GERUNDS, as OBJECTS.

She **wanted** *to go* [not *wanted going*] to the lecture.

Only three people **decided** *to question* [not *decided questioning*] the speaker.

Quick Reference 54.2   ■ ■ ■ ■ ■ ■ ■

Verbs and expressions that must be followed by infinitives

agree	decline	like	promise
arrange	demand	manage	refuse
ask	deserve	mean	wait
attempt	expect	need	want
beg	hesitate	offer	
claim	hope	plan	
decide	learn	pretend	

INFINITIVE AFTER *BE* + COMPLEMENT

Gerunds are common in constructions that use a form of the verb *be* plus a COMPLEMENT and a PREPOSITION (see 54b). However, use an infinitive, not a gerund, when *be* plus a complement is not followed by a preposition.

We **are eager** *to go* [not *going*] camping.

I **am ready** *to sleep* [not *sleeping*] in a tent.

INFINITIVE TO INDICATE PURPOSE

Use an infinitive in expressions that indicate purpose: *I read a book **to learn** more about Mayan culture.* This sentence means "I read a book for the purpose of learning more about Mayan culture." *To learn* delivers the idea of purpose more concisely (see Chapter 11) than expressions such as *so that I can* or *in order to*.

INFINITIVE WITH THE FIRST, THE LAST, THE ONE

Use an infinitive after the expressions *the first, the last,* and *the one: Nina is the first **to arrive*** [not *arriving*] *and the last **to leave*** [not *leaving*] *every day. She's always the one **to do** the most.*

UNMARKED INFINITIVES

Infinitives used without the word *to* are called **unmarked infinitives,** or sometimes *bare infinitives.* An unmarked infinitive may be hard to recognize because it is not preceded by *to.* Some common verbs followed by unmarked infinitives are *feel, have, hear, let, listen to, look at, make* (meaning "compel"), *notice, see,* and *watch.*

> Please let me **take** [not *to take*] you to lunch. [unmarked infinitive]
>
> I want **to take** you to lunch. [marked infinitive]
>
> I can have Kara **drive** [not *to drive*] us. [unmarked infinitive]
>
> I will ask Kara **to drive** us. [marked infinitive]

The verb *help* can be followed by a marked or an unmarked infinitive. Either is correct: *Help me **put*** [or *to put*] *this box in the car.*

🕐 **Alert:** Be careful to use parallel structure (see Chapter 10) correctly when you use two or more gerunds or infinitives after verbs. If two or more verbal objects follow one verb, put the verbals into the same form.

> **NO** We went **sailing** and **to scuba dive.**
>
> **YES** We went **sailing** and **scuba diving.**
>
> **NO** We heard the wind **blow** and the waves **crashing.**
>
> **YES** We heard the wind **blow** and the waves **crash.**
>
> **YES** We heard the wind **blowing** and the waves **crashing.**

Conversely, if you are using verbal objects with COMPOUND PREDICATES, be sure to use the kind of verbal that each verb requires.

> **NO** We enjoyed **scuba diving** but do not plan **sailing** again.
> [*Enjoyed* requires a gerund object, and *plan* requires an infinitive object; see Quick References 54.1 and 54.2 in this chapter.]
>
> **YES** We enjoyed **scuba diving** but do not plan **to sail** again. ●

54d How does meaning change when certain verbs are followed by a gerund or an infinitive?

WITH *STOP*

The VERB *stop* followed by a GERUND means "finish, quit." *Stop* followed by an INFINITIVE means "interrupt one activity to begin another."

> We **stopped** *eating.* [We finished our meal.]
>
> We **stopped** *to eat.* [We stopped another activity, such as driving, to eat.]

WITH *REMEMBER* AND *FORGET*

The verb *remember* followed by an infinitive means "not to forget to do something": *I must remember to talk with Isa. Remember* followed by a gerund means "recall a memory": *I remember talking in my sleep last night.*

The verb *forget* followed by an infinitive means "fail to do something": *If you forget to put a stamp on that letter, it will be returned. Forget* followed by a gerund means "do something and not recall it": *I forget having put the stamps in the refrigerator.*

WITH *TRY*

The verb *try* followed by an infinitive means "make an effort": *I tried to find your jacket.* Followed by a gerund, *try* means "experiment with": *I tried jogging but found it too difficult.*

54e Why is the meaning unchanged whether a gerund or an infinitive follows sense verbs?

Sense VERBS include words such as *see, notice, hear, observe, watch, feel, listen to,* and *look at.* The meaning of these verbs is usually not affected by whether a GERUND or an INFINITIVE follows as the OBJECT. *I saw the water rise* and *I saw the water rising* both have the same meaning in American English.

EXERCISE 54-1 Write the correct form of the verbal object (either a gerund or an infinitive) for each verb in parentheses. For help, consult 54b through 54e.

EXAMPLE People like (think) to think that they have a good memory, but everybody shows signs of forgetfulness from time to time.

1. Think about (ride) _____ the railroad to work on a rainy Monday morning.

2. The comfortable reclining seats let passengers (take) _____ a relaxing nap on the way to work.

3. Because of the rain, commuters are forced (bring) _____ an umbrella and a raincoat, along with their usual traveling items.

4. Once they reach their destination, passengers forget that they need their umbrellas and raincoats (walk) _____ the few blocks to work.

5. (Step) _____ out into the rain makes the passengers suddenly realize that they've left their umbrellas and raincoats on the train, which has already left the station.

54f How do I choose between -*ing* and -*ed* forms for adjectives?

Deciding whether to use the -*ing* form (PRESENT PARTICIPLE) or the -*ed* form (PAST PARTICIPLE of a regular VERB) as an ADJECTIVE in a specific sentence can be difficult. For example, *I am amused* and *I am amusing* are both correct in English, but their meanings are very different. To make the right choice, decide whether the modified NOUN or PRONOUN is causing or experiencing what the participle describes.

Use a present participle (-*ing*) to modify a noun or pronoun that is the agent or the cause of the action.

Micah described your **interesting** plan. [The noun *plan* causes what its modifier describes—interest; so *interesting* is correct.]

I find your plan **exciting**. [The noun *plan* causes what its modifier describes—excitement; so *exciting* is correct.]

Use a past participle (-*ed* in regular verbs) to modify a noun or pronoun that experiences or receives whatever the modifier describes.

An **interested** committee wants to hear your plan. [The noun *committee* experiences what its modifier describes—interest; so *interested* is correct.]

Excited by your plan, they called a board meeting. [The pronoun *they* experiences what its modifier describes—excitement; so *excited* is correct.]

Here are frequently used participles that convey very different meanings, depending on whether the -*ed* or the -*ing* form is used.

amused, amusing	depressed, depressing
annoyed, annoying	disgusted, disgusting
appalled, appalling	fascinated, fascinating
bored, boring	frightened, frightening
confused, confusing	insulted, insulting

offended, offending   reassured, reassuring

overwhelmed, overwhelming   satisfied, satisfying

pleased, pleasing   shocked, shocking

EXERCISE 54-2 Choose the correct participle from each pair in parentheses. For help, consult 54f.

EXAMPLE It can be a (satisfied, satisfying) <u>satisfying</u> experience to learn about the lives of artists.

1. The artist Frida Kahlo led an (interested, interesting) _____ life.

2. When Kahlo was eighteen, (horrified, horrifying) _____ observers saw her (injured, injuring) _____ in a streetcar accident.

3. A (disappointed, disappointing) _____ Kahlo had to abandon her plan to study medicine.

4. Instead, she began to create paintings filled with (disturbed, disturbing) _____ images.

5. Some art critics consider Kahlo's paintings to be (fascinated, fascinating) _____ works of art, though many people find them (overwhelmed, overwhelming) _____.

For more help with your writing, grammar, and research, go to **www.mycomplab.com**

Modal Auxiliary Verbs

AUXILIARY VERBS are known as *helping verbs* because adding an auxiliary verb to a MAIN VERB helps the main verb convey additional information (see 15e). For example, the auxiliary verb *do* is important in turning sentences into questions. *You have to sleep* becomes a question when *do* is added: *Do you have to sleep?* The most common auxiliary verbs are forms of *be, have,* and *do.* Quick References 15.6 and 15.7 in section 15e list the forms of these three verbs.

MODAL AUXILIARY VERBS are one type of auxiliary verb. They include *can, could, may, might, should, had better, must, will, would,* and others discussed in this chapter. Modals differ from *be, have,* and *do* used as auxiliary verbs in the specific ways discussed in Quick Reference 55.1. This chapter can help you use modals to convey shades of meaning.

Quick Reference 55.1 ■ ■ ■ ■ ■ ■ ■

Modals versus other auxiliary verbs

- Modals in the present future are always followed by the SIMPLE FORM of a main verb: *I **might go** tomorrow.*

- One-word modals have no *-s* ending in the THIRD-PERSON SINGULAR: *She **could** go with me; he **could** go with me; they **could** go with me.* (The two-word modal *have to* changes form to agree with its subject: *I **have to** leave, she **has to** leave.*) Auxiliary verbs other than modals usually change form for third-person singular: *I **do** want to go; he **does** want to go.*

- Some modals change form in the past. Others (*should, would, must,* which convey probability, and *ought to*) use *have* + a PAST PARTICIPLE. *I **can do** it* becomes *I **could do** it* in PAST-TENSE CLAUSES about ability. *I **could do** it* becomes *I **could have done** it* in clauses about possibility.

- Modals convey meaning about ability, necessity, advisability, possibility, and other conditions: For example, *I **can go*** means "I am able to go." Modals do not describe actual occurrences.

55a How do I convey ability, necessity, advisability, possibility, and probability with modals?

CONVEYING ABILITY

The modal *can* conveys ability now (in the present), and *could* conveys ability before (in the past). These words deliver the meaning "able to." For the future, use *will be able to.*

> We **can** work late tonight. [*Can* conveys present ability.]
>
> I **could** work late last night, too. [*Could* conveys past ability.]
>
> I **will be able to** work late next Monday. [*Will be able* is the future tense; *will* here is not a modal.]

Adding *not* between a modal and the MAIN VERB makes the CLAUSE negative: *We **cannot** work late tonight; I **could not** work late last night; I **will not be able to** work late next Monday.*

⚠️ **Alert:** You will often see negative forms of modals turned into CONTRACTIONS: *can't, couldn't, won't, wouldn't,* and others. Because contractions are considered informal usage by some instructors, you will never be wrong if you avoid them in ACADEMIC WRITING, except when you are reproducing spoken words. ●

CONVEYING NECESSITY

The modals *must* and *have to* convey a need to do something. Both *must* and *have to* are followed by the simple form of the main verb. In the present tense, *have to* changes form to agree with its subject.

> You **must** leave before midnight.
>
> She **has to** leave when I leave.

In the past tense, *must* is never used to express necessity. Instead, use *had to.*

> **PRESENT TENSE**   We **must** study today. We **have to** study today.
>
> **PAST TENSE**   We **had to** [not must] take a test yesterday.

The negative forms of *must* and *have to* also have different meanings. *Must not* conveys that something is forbidden; *do not have to* conveys that something is not necessary.

> You **must not** sit there. [Sitting there is forbidden.]
>
> You **do not have to** sit there. [Sitting there is not necessary.]

CONVEYING ADVISABILITY OR THE NOTION OF A GOOD IDEA

The modals *should* and *ought to* express the idea that doing the action of the main verb is advisable or is a good idea.

> You **should** go to class tomorrow morning.

In the past tense, *should* and *ought to* convey regret or knowing something through hindsight. They mean that good advice was not taken.

> You **should have** gone to class yesterday.
>
> I **ought to have** called my sister yesterday.

The modal *had better* delivers the meaning of good advice or warning or threat. It does not change form for tense.

> You **had better** see the doctor before your cough gets worse.

Need to is often used to express strong advice, too. Its past-tense form is *needed to.*

> You **need to** take better care of yourself. You **needed to** listen.

CONVEYING POSSIBILITY

The modals *may, might,* and *could* can be used to convey an idea of possibility or likelihood.

> We **may** become hungry before long.

> We **could** eat lunch at the diner next door.

For the past-tense form, use *may, might,* and *could,* followed by *have* and the past participle of the main verb.

> I **could have studied** French in high school, but I studied Spanish instead.

CONVEYING PROBABILITY

In addition to conveying the idea of necessity, the modal *must* can also convey probability or likelihood. It means that a well-informed guess is being made.

> Marisa **must** be a talented actress. She has been chosen to play the lead role in the school play.

When *must* conveys probability, the past tense is *must have* plus the past participle of the main verb.

> I did not see Boris at the party; he **must have left** early.

EXERCISE 55-1   Fill in each blank with the past-tense modal auxiliary that expresses the meaning given in parentheses. For help, consult 55a.

EXAMPLE   I (advisability) <u>should have</u> gone straight to the doctor the instant I felt a cold coming on.

1. Since I (necessity, no choice) _____ work late this past Monday, I could not get to the doctor's office before it closed.

2. I (advisability) _____ fallen asleep after dinner, but I stayed awake for a while instead.

3. Even after I finally got into bed, I (ability) _____ not relax.

4. I (making a guess) _____ not _____ heard the alarm the next morning, because I overslept nearly two hours.

5. When I finally arrived at work, my boss came into my office and said, "Julie, you (necessity) _____ stayed home and rested if you are sick."

55b   How do I convey preferences, plans, and past habits with modals?

CONVEYING PREFERENCES

The modal *would rather* expresses a preference. *Would rather,* the PRESENT TENSE, is used with the SIMPLE FORM of the MAIN VERB, and *would rather have,* the PAST TENSE, is used with the PAST PARTICIPLE of the main verb.

We **would rather see** a comedy than a mystery.

Carlos **would rather have stayed** home last night.

CONVEYING PLAN OR OBLIGATION

A form of *be* followed by *supposed to* and the simple form of a main verb delivers a meaning of something planned or of an obligation.

I **was supposed to meet** them at the bus stop.

CONVEYING PAST HABIT

The modals *used to* and *would* express the idea that something happened repeatedly in the past.

I **used to** hate going to the dentist.

I **would** dread every single visit.

! **Alert:** Both *used to* and *would* can be used to express repeated actions in the past, but *would* cannot be used for a situation that lasted for a period of time in the past.

> NO   I **would** live in Arizona.
>
> YES   I **used to** live in Arizona. ●

55c How can I recognize modals in the passive voice?

Modals use the ACTIVE VOICE, as shown in sections sections 55a and 55b. In the active voice, the subject does the action expressed in the MAIN VERB (see 15n and 15o).

Modals can also use the PASSIVE VOICE (15p). In the passive voice, the doer of the main verb's action is either unexpressed or is expressed as an OBJECT in a PREPOSITIONAL PHRASE starting with the word *by*.

> PASSIVE   The waterfront **can be seen** from my window.
>
> ACTIVE   I **can see** the waterfront from my window.

> PASSIVE   The tax form **must be signed** by the person who fills it out.
>
> ACTIVE   The person who fills out the tax form **must sign** it.

EXERCISE 55-2   Select the correct choice from the words in parentheses and write it in the blank. For help, consult 55a through 55c.

EXAMPLE   When I was younger, I (would, used to) <u>used to</u> love to go bicycle riding.

1. You (ought to have, ought have) _____ called yesterday as you had promised you would.

2. Judging by the size of the puddles in the street outside, it (must be rained, must have rained) _____ all night long

3. Ingrid (must not have, might not have been) _____ as early for the interview as she claims she was.

4. After all the studying he did, Pedro (should have, should have been) _____ less frightened by the exam.

5. I have to go home early today, although I really (cannot, should not) _____ leave before the end of the day because of all the work I have to do.

EXERCISE 55-3   Select the correct choice from the words in parentheses and write it in the blank. For help, consult 55a through 55c.

EXAMPLE   We (must have, must) must study this afternoon.

1. Unfortunately, I (should not, cannot) _____ go to the movies with you because I have to take care of my brother tonight.

2. Juan (would have, would have been) _____ nominated class valedictorian if he had not moved to another city.

3. You (ought not have, ought not to have) _____ arrived while the meeting was still in progress.

4. Louise (must be, must have been) _____ sick to miss the party last week.

5. Had you not called in advance, you (may not have, may not have been) _____ aware of the traffic on the expressway.

For more help with your writing, grammar, and research,
go to **www.mycomplab.com**

TERMS GLOSSARY

This glossary defines important terms used in this handbook, including the ones that are printed in small capital letters. Many of these glossary entries end with parenthetical references to the handbook section(s) or chapter(s) where the specific term is fully discussed.

absolute phrase A phrase containing a subject and a participle that modifies an entire sentence. (14n) *The semester [subject] being [present participle of be] over, the campus looks deserted.*

abstract A very short summary that presents all the important ideas of a longer piece of writing. Sometimes appears before the main writing, as in APA style.

abstract noun A noun that names something not knowable through the five senses: *idea, respect.* (14b)

academic writing Writing you do for college classes, usually intended to inform or to persuade. (1d)

action verbs Strong verbs that increase the impact of your language and reduce wordiness. *Weak verbs,* such as *be* or *have,* increase wordiness. (11c)

active reading Reading for critical understanding, using such strategies as making interpretations; looking for bias or omissions; assessing evidence, reasoning processes, claims of cause and effect; applying the reading to other contexts; and so on.

active voice An attribute of verbs showing that the action or condition expressed in the verb is done by the subject, in contrast with the *passive voice,* which conveys that the action or condition of the verb is done to the subject. (15n, 15o)

adjective A word that describes or limits (modifies) a noun, a pronoun, or a word group functioning as a noun: *silly, three.* (14f, Chapter 18)

adjective clause A dependent clause, also known as a *relative clause.* An adjective clause modifies a preceding noun or pronoun and begins with a relative word (such as *who, which, that,* or *where*) that relates the clause to the noun or pronoun it modifies. Also see *clause.* (14p)

adverb A word that describes or limits (modifies) verbs, adjectives, other adverbs, phrases, or clauses: *loudly, very, nevertheless, there.* (14g, Chapter 18)

adverb clause A dependent clause beginning with a subordinating conjunction that establishes the relationship in meaning between the adverb clause and its independent clause. An adverb clause modifies the independent clause's verb or the entire independent clause. Also see *clause, conjunction.* (14p)

agreement The required match of number and person between a subject and verb or a pronoun and antecedent. A pronoun that expresses gender must match its antecedent in gender also. (Chapter 17)

analogy An explanation of the unfamiliar in terms of the familiar. Like a simile, an analogy compares things not normally associated with each other; but unlike a simile, an analogy does not use *like* or *as* in making the comparison. Analogy is also a rhetorical strategy for developing paragraphs. (3i, 21d, 41b)

analysis A process of critical thinking that divides a whole into its component parts in order to understand how the parts interrelate. Sometimes called *division,* analysis is also a rhetorical strategy for developing paragraphs. (3i, 4b, 40h, 41f)

analytic frameworks Systematic ways of investigating a work. (40c)

antecedent The noun or pronoun to which a pronoun refers. (16l–16s, 7o–7t)

APA style See *documentation style.*

appeals to reason Tools a writer uses to convince the reader that the reasoning in an argument is sound and effective; there are three types—logical, emotional, and ethical appeals. (5j)

apply In writing, to examine how a particular theory, interpretation, or perspective explains or fits—or doesn't—a specific situation or reading.

appositive A word or group of words that renames a preceding noun or noun phrase: *my favorite month,* **October**. (14n)

argument A rhetorical attempt to convince others to agree with a position about a topic open to debate. (1c, Chapter 5)

argument to the person (also known as "ad hominum") A logical fallacy that involves finding fault with an individual rather than more properly with the argument he or she has made. Example: *Don't believe Smith's views on the environment because he dresses so strangely.*

articles Also called *determiners* or *noun markers,* articles are the words *a, an,* and *the. A* and *an* are indefinite articles, and *the* is a definite article; also see *determiner.* (14f, Chapter 51)

assertion A statement. In a thesis statement, an assertion expresses a point of view about a topic; in an argument, an assertion states the position you want to argue. (2d, 5d)

assessing reasoning processes Judging whether the claims made in a piece of writing are justified by the evidence, reasons, explanations, and thinking presented. Often involves asking whether certain facts or statements actually lead to certain conclusions.

audience The readers to whom a piece of writing is directed; the three types include *general audience, peer audience,* and *specialist audience.* (1d)

auxiliary verb Also known as a *helping verb,* an auxiliary verb is a form of *be, do, have, can, may, will,* or certain other verbs, that combines with a main verb to help it express tense, mood, and voice. Also see *modal auxiliary verb.* (15e)

balanced sentence A sentence composed of two parallel structures, usually two independent clauses, that present contrasting content. (10b)

base form See *simple form.*

bias In writing, a distortion or inaccuracy caused by a dislike or hatred of individuals, groups of people, or ideas. (4c.2)

bibliographic notes In a note system of documentation, a *footnote* or *endnote* gives the bibliographic information the first time a source is cited. (35f, 36d.2, Chapter 38)

bibliography A list of sources used or consulted for research writing. (Chapters 36, 37, and 38)

block style Style used in writing business letters. Block style uses no indents, single spacing within paragraphs and double spacing between paragraphs. All lines start flush left, which means at the left margin. (43f)

blog Shortened form of "**Web log**," a kind of online journal. (46e)

body paragraphs Paragraphs that provide the substance of your message in a sequence that makes sense. (3d)

Boolean expressions In a search engine, symbols or words such as And, Or, Not, and Near that let you create keyword combinations that narrow and refine your search. (34l)

borders Lines used to set apart sections of text. (45e)

brainstorming Listing all ideas that come to mind on a topic and then grouping the ideas by patterns that emerge.

bureaucratic language Sometimes called *bureaucratese;* language that is overblown or overly complex. (12l)

business writing Writing designed for business, including letters, memos, resumes, job application letters, and e-mail messages. (1d, 3a, Chapter 43)

case The form of a noun or pronoun in a specific context that shows whether it is functioning as a subject, an object, or a possessive. In modern English, nouns change form in the possessive case only (city = form for subjective and objective cases; city's = possessive-case form). Also see *pronoun case.* (16a–16k)

cause and effect The relationship between outcomes (effects) and the reasons for them (causes). Cause-and-effect analysis is a rhetorical strategy for developing paragraphs. (3i, 4h, 4i)

chronological order Also called *time order,* an arrangement of information according to time sequence; an organizing strategy for sentences, paragraphs, and longer pieces of writing. (3h)

citation Information that identifies a source quoted, paraphrased, summarized, or referred to in a piece of writing, *in-text citations* appear within sentences or as *parenthetical references*. Also see *documentation*. (Chapters 34 and 35)

civic writing Writing done to influence public opinion or to advance causes for the public good. (44d)

claim States an issue and then takes a position on a debatable topic related to the issue. A claim is supported with evidence and reasons, moving from broad reasons to specific data and details. (5d)

classical argument An argument with a six-part structure consisting of introduction, thesis statement, background, evidence and reasoning, response to opposing views, and conclusion. (5e)

classification A rhetorical strategy for paragraph development that organizes information by grouping items according to underlying shared characteristics. (3i)

clause A group of words containing a subject and a predicate. A clause that delivers full meaning is called an *independent* (or *main*) *clause*. A clause that lacks full meaning by itself is called a *dependent* (or *subordinate*) *clause*. Also see *adjective clause, adverb clause, nonrestrictive element, noun clause, restrictive element*. (14p)

cliché An overused, worn-out phrase that has lost its capacity to communicate effectively: *flat as Kansas, ripe old age*. (12i)

climactic order Sometimes called *emphatic order*, an arrangement of ideas or other kinds of information from least important to most important. (3h, 5e)

clip art Refers to pictures, sketches, and other graphics available on some word processing programs. (45f)

clustering See *mapping*.

coherence The clear progression from one idea to another using transitional expressions, pronouns, selective repetition, or parallelism to make connections between ideas. (3g)

collaborative writing Students working together to write a paper. (Chapter 6)

collective noun A noun that names a group of people or things: *family, committee*. Also see *noncount noun*. (14b, 17j, 17t)

colloquial language Casual or conversational language. Also see *slang*. (12h)

comma fault See *comma splice*.

comma splice The error that occurs when only a comma connects two independent clauses; also called a *comma fault*. (Chapter 20)

common noun A noun that names a general group, place, person, or thing: *dog, house*. (14b)

comparative form The form of a descriptive adjective or adverb that shows a different degree of intensity between two things: *bluer, less blue; more easily, less easily*. Also see *positive form, superlative form*. (18e)

comparison and contrast A rhetorical strategy for organizing and developing paragraphs by discussing similarities (*comparison*) and differences (*contrast*). It has two patterns: *point-by-point* and *block organization*. (3i)

complement An element after a verb that completes the predicate, such as a direct object after an action verb or a noun or adjective after a linking verb. Also see *object complement, predicate adjective, predicate nominative, subject complement*. (14n)

complete predicate See *predicate*.

complete subject See *subject*.

complex sentence See *sentence types*.

compound-complex sentence See *sentence types*.

compound construction A group of nouns or pronouns connected with a coordinating conjunction. (16d)

compound noun See *subject*.

compound predicate See *predicate*.

compound sentence See *coordinate sentence, sentence types*.

compound subject See *subject*. (14l, 17e)

compound word Two or more words placed together to express one concept. (31g)

conciseness An attribute of writing that is direct and to the point. (Chapter 11)

concrete noun A noun naming something that can be seen, touched, heard, smelled, or tasted: *smoke, sidewalk*. (14b)

conjunction A word that connects or otherwise establishes a relationship between two or more words, phrases, or clauses. Also see *coordinating conjunction, correlative conjunction, subordinating conjunction.* (14i)

conjunctive adverb An adverb, such as *therefore* or *meanwhile,* that communicates a logical connection in meaning. (14g)

connotation An idea implied by a word, involving associations and emotional overtones that go beyond the word's dictionary definition. (12d)

contraction A word where an apostrophe takes the place of one or more omitted letters. (27d)

coordinate adjectives Two or more adjectives of equal weight that modify a noun. (24e)

coordinate sentence Two or more independent clauses joined by either a semicolon or a comma with coordinating conjunction showing their relationship; also called a *compound sentence.* Also see *coordination.* (9d)

coordinating conjunction A conjunction that joins two or more grammatically equivalent structures: *and, or, for, nor, but, so, yet.* (14i, 20b)

coordination The use of grammatically equivalent forms to show a balance or sequence of ideas. (9d, 9e)

correlative conjunction A pair of words that joins equivalent grammatical structures, including *both . . . and, either . . . or, neither . . . nor, not only . . . but* (or *but also*). (14i)

count noun A noun that names an item or items that can be counted: *radio, streets, idea, fingernails.* (14b, 50a)

critical reading A parallel process to critical thinking where you think about what you're reading while you're reading it. (4d)

critical response Formally, an essay summarizing a source's central point or main idea. It includes a *transitional statement* that bridges this summary and the writer's synthesized reactions in response. (4f)

critical thinking A form of thinking where you take control of your conscious thought processes. (4a, 4b, 40g)

cumulative adjectives Adjectives that build meaning from word to word: *distinctive musical style.* (24e)

cumulative sentence The most common structure for a sentence, with the subject and verb first, followed by modifiers adding details; also called a *loose sentence.* (9q)

dangling modifier A modifier that attaches its meaning illogically, either because it is closer to another noun or pronoun than to its true subject or because its true subject is not expressed in the sentence. (21d)

declarative sentence A sentence that makes a statement: *Sky diving is exciting.* Also see *exclamatory sentence, imperative sentence, interrogative sentence.* (14k)

deduction, deductive reasoning The process of reasoning from general claims to a specific instance. (4i)

definite article See *articles.*

definition A rhetorical strategy in which you define or give the meaning of words or ideas. Includes *extended definition.* (3i)

demonstrative pronoun A pronoun that points out the antecedent: *this, these; that, those.* (14c, 14f)

denotation The dictionary definition of a word. (12e.1)

dependent clause A clause that cannot stand alone as an independent grammatical unit. Also see *adjective clause, adverb clause, noun clause.* (14p, 19b)

description A rhetorical strategy that appeals to a reader's senses—sight, sound, smell, taste, and touch. (3i)

descriptive adjective An adjective that names the condition or properties of the noun it modifies and (except for a very few, such as *dead* and *unique*) has comparative and superlative forms: *flat, flatter, flattest.*

descriptive adverb An adverb that names the condition or properties of whatever it modifies and that has comparative and superlative forms: *happily, more happily, most happily.* (14g)

determiner A word or word group, traditionally identified as an adjective, that limits a noun by telling how much or how many about it. Also called *expression of quantity, limiting adjective,* or *noun marker.* (14f, 50b, Chapter 51)

diction Word choice. (12d)

digital portfolio A collection of several texts in electronic format that you've chosen to represent the range of your skills and abilities. (1f)

direct address Words naming a person or group being spoken to. Written words of direct address are set off by commas. (24g) *The answer, **my friends**, lies with you. Go with them, **Gene.***

direct discourse In writing, words that repeat speech or conversation exactly and so are enclosed in quotation marks. (22e, 24g, 28b)

direct object A noun or pronoun or group of words functioning as a noun that receives the action (completes the meaning) of a transitive verb. (14m)

direct question A sentence that asks a question and ends with a question mark: *Are you going?* (23a, 23c)

direct quotation See *quotation.*

direct title A title that tells exactly what the essay will be about. (2i)

discovery draft A first draft developed from focused freewriting. (2g)

disclaimer A statement appended to the top or bottom of e-mails designed to protect the company from legal liability. (43d)

documentation The acknowledgment of someone else's words and ideas used in any piece of writing by giving full and accurate information about the person whose words were used and where those words were found. For example, for a print source, documentation usually includes names of all authors, title of the source, place and date of publication, and related information. (35a–35k, Chapters 36–38)

documentation style A system for providing information about the source of words, information, and ideas quoted, paraphrased, or summarized from some source other than the writer. Documentation styles discussed in this handbook are MLA, APA, CM, CSE, and COS. (33h, Chapters 36–38)

document design A term for the placement of tables, graphs, and other illustrations on printed and online material. (Chapter 45)

double negative A nonstandard negation using two negative modifiers rather than one. (18c)

drafting A part of the writing process in which writers compose ideas in sentences

and paragraphs. *Drafts* are versions—*first* or *rough, revised,* and *final*—of one piece of writing. (2g)

edited American English English language usage that conforms to established rules of grammar, sentence structure, punctuation, and spelling; also called *standard American English.* (12b)

editing A part of the writing process in which writers check the technical correctness of grammar, spelling, punctuation, and mechanics. (2j)

ellipses Punctuation consisting of three periods that shows material has been omitted. Example: *(1) That person playing the loud music should leave. (2) That person . . . should leave.*

elliptical construction The deliberate omission of one or more words in order to achieve conciseness in a sentence. (14p, 22h, 11d.3)

emotional appeal Rhetorical strategy which employs the use of descriptive language and concrete details or examples to create a mental picture for readers, leading them to feel or understand the importance of a claim. Greek name is *pathos.* (5g)

essential element See *restrictive element.*

ethical appeal Rhetorical strategy intended to reassure readers that the writer is authoritative, honest, fair, likable, and so on. Greek name is ethos. (5g)

ethnography A research method that involves careful observation of a group of people or a setting, often over a period of time. Ethnography also refers to the written work that results from this research.

euphemism Language that attempts to blunt certain realities by speaking of them in "nice" or "tactful" words. (12k)

evaluate A step in the critical thinking process where you judge the quality of the material you are assessing. (4b, 4c.3, 4g)

evidence Facts, data, examples, and opinions of others used to support assertions and conclusions. Also see *sources.* (4g)

exclamatory sentence A sentence beginning with *What* or *How* that expresses strong feeling: *What a ridiculous statement!* (14k)

expletive The phrase *there is (are), there was (were), it is,* or *it was* at the beginning of a clause, changing structure and postponing the subject: *It is* Mars *that we hope to reach.* [Compare: *We hope to reach Mars*]. (11c)

expository writing See *informative writing.*

expressive writing Writing that reflects your personal thoughts and feelings. (1b)

faulty parallelism Grammatically incorrect writing that results from nonmatching grammatical forms linked with coordinating conjunctions. (10e)

faulty predication A grammatically illogical combination of subject and predicate. (22g)

field research Primary research that involves going into real-life situations to observe, survey, interview, or be part of some activity. (32c)

figurative language Words that make connections and comparisons and draw on one image to explain another and enhance meaning. (12c)

finite verb A verb form that shows tense, mood, voice, person, and number while expressing an action, occurrence, or state of being.

first person See *person.*

focused freewriting A technique that may start with a set topic or may build on one sentence taken from earlier freewriting. (2g)

formal outline An outline that lays out the topic levels of generalities or hierarchies that marks them with Roman numerals, letters, numbers indented in a carefully prescribed fashion. (2f)

frames A part of a Web page that functions independently of the other parts of the page. (Chapter 46)

freewriting Writing nonstop for a period of time to generate ideas by free association of thoughts. Also see *discovery draft.* (2g)

fused sentence See *run-on sentence.*

future perfect progressive tense The form of the future perfect tense that describes an action or condition ongoing until some specific future time: *I will have been talking.* (15j)

future perfect tense The tense indicating that an action will have been completed or a condition will have ended by a specified point in the future: *I will have talked.* (15i)

future progressive tense The form of the future tense showing that a future action will continue for some time: *I will be talking.* (15j)

future tense The form of a verb, made with the simple form and either *shall* or *will,* expressing an action yet to be taken or a condition not yet experienced: *I will talk.* (15g)

gender The classification of words as masculine, feminine, or neutral. (17s, 12f)

gender-free language See *gender-neutral language.*

gender-neutral language Also called *gender-free language* or *nonsexist language,* it uses terms that do not unnecessarily say whether a person is male or female, as with *police officer* instead of *policeman.* (17s, 12f)

generalization A broad statement without details. (1c)

gerund A present participle functioning as a noun: *Walking is good exercise.* Also see *verbal.* (14e, 51c, Chapter 54)

helping verb See *auxiliary verb.*

homonyms Words spelled differently that sound alike: *to, too, two.* (31f)

home page The opening main page of a Web site that provides access to other pages on the site categories. (46d)

HTML (Hyper Text Markup Language) A computer program language used for Web pages. (46c)

hyperbole See *overstatement.*

hyperlink Connection from one digital document to another online. (46d)

idiom A word, phrase, or other construction that has a different meaning from its literal meaning: *He lost his head. She hit the ceiling.* (Chapter 53)

illogical predication See *faulty predication.*

imperative mood The mood that expresses commands and direct requests, using the simple form of the verb and often implying but not expressing the subject, you: *Go.* (15l)

imperative sentence A sentence that gives a command: *Go to the corner to buy me a newspaper.* (14k, 19b.3)

incubation The prewriting technique of giving ideas time to develop and clarify.

indefinite article See *articles, determiner.*

indefinite pronoun A pronoun, such as *all, anyone, each,* and *others,* that refers to a non-specific person or thing. (14c, 14f, 17i)

independent clause A clause that can stand alone as an independent grammatical unit. (14p)

indicative mood The mood of verbs used for statements about real things or highly likely ones: *I think Grace is arriving today.* (15l, 22d)

indirect discourse Reported speech or conversation that does not use the exact structure of the original and so is not enclosed in quotation marks. (22e, 24h)

indirect title Hints at an essay's topic; tries to catch the reader's interest by presenting a puzzle that can be solved by reading the essay. (2i)

indirect object A noun or pronoun or group of words functioning as a noun that tells to whom or for whom the action expressed by a transitive verb was done. (14m)

indirect question A sentence that reports a question and ends with a period: *I asked if you are leaving.* (23a, 23c, 48a)

indirect quotation See *quotation.*

induction The reasoning process of arriving at general principles from particular facts or instances. (4h)

inductive reasoning A form of reasoning that moves from particular facts or instances to general principles. (4h)

inference What a reader or listener understands to be implied but not stated. (4d)

infinitive A verbal made of the simple form of a verb and usually, but not always, *to* that functions as a noun, adjective, or adverb. Infinitives without the word *to* are called *unmarked* (or *bare*) *infinitives.* (14e, 15k, Chapter 54)

infinitive phrase An infinitive, with its modifiers and object, that functions as a noun, adjective, or adverb. Also see *verbal phrase.* (14e)

informal language Word choice that creates a tone appropriate for casual writing or speaking. (1d, 12g)

informal outline Non-traditional outline that doesn't follow the rules of a *formal outline.* (2f)

informative writing Writing that gives information and, when necessary, explains it; also known as *expository writing.* (1b)

intensive pronoun A pronoun that ends in *self* and that emphasizes its antecedent. Also called *reflexive pronoun. Vida **himself** argued against it.* (14c)

interjection An emotion-conveying word that is treated as a sentence, starting with a capital letter and ending with an exclamation point or a period: *Oh! Ouch!* (14j, 24j)

interrogative pronoun A pronoun, such as *whose* or *what,* that implies a question: ***Who** called?* (14c, 19b)

interrogative sentence A sentence that asks a direct question: *Did you see that?* (14k)

in-text citation Source information placed in parentheses within the body of a research paper. Also see *citation, parenthetical reference.* (36h, 37h)

intransitive verb A verb that does not take a direct object. (15f)

invention techniques Ways of gathering ideas for writing. Also see *planning.*

inverted word order In contrast to standard order, the main verb or an auxiliary verb comes before the subject in inverted word order. Most questions and some exclamations use inverted word order. (17h, 9r, Chapter 51)

irony Words used to imply the opposite of their usual meaning. (12c)

irregular verb A verb that forms the past tense and past participle in some way other than by adding *-ed* or *-d.* (15d)

jargon A particular field's or group's specialized vocabulary that a general reader is unlikely to understand. (12k)

journalist's questions Who? What? When? Where? Why? How? Traditionally, every news story should answer these questions.

justify When used as a design term, it refers to aligning text evenly along both the left and right margins. (45c)

key terms In an essay, the words central to its topic and its message. (5d)

keywords The main words in a source's title or the words that the author or editor has identified as central to that source. Use keywords in searching for sources online or in library databases. (34c)

layout The arrangement of text, visuals, color, and space on a page. (45g)

levels of formality Word choices and sentence structures reflecting various degrees of formality of language. A formal level is used for ceremonial and other occasions when stylistic flourishes are appropriate. A medium level, neither too formal nor too casual, is acceptable for most academic writing. (12b)

levels of generality Degrees of generality used to group or organize information or ideas as you write, as when moving from the most general to the most specific. Conversely, *levels of specificity* move from the most specific to the most general.

levels of specificity Degrees of specificity used to group or organize information or ideas as you write, as when moving from the most specific to the most general. Conversely, *levels of generality* move from the most general to the most specific.

limiting adjective See *determiner*.

linking verb A main verb that links a subject with a subject complement that renames or describes the subject. Linking verbs, sometimes called *copulative verbs,* convey a state of being, relate to the senses, or indicate a condition. (15a, 15c)

logical appeal Rhetorical strategy that intended to show readers that the reasoning depends on formal reasoning, including providing evidence and drawing conclusions from premises. Greek name is *logos.* (5g)

logical fallacies Flaws in reasoning that lead to illogical statements. (4i)

main clause See *independent clause*.

main verb A verb that expresses action, occurrence, or state of being and that shows mood, tense, voice, number, and person. (14d, 15b)

mapping An invention technique based on thinking about a topic and its increasingly specific subdivisions; also known as *clustering* or *webbing.*

margins The boundaries of a page, which means the white space or blank areas at the top, bottom, and sides of a paper or screen. (45c)

mechanics Conventions governing matters such as the use of capital letters, italics, abbreviations, and numbers. (Chapter 30)

memo or memorandum A brief form of business correspondence with a format that is headed with lines for "To," "From," and "Subject" and uses the rest of its space for its message. (43e)

metaphor A comparison implying similarity between two things. A metaphor does not use words such as *like* or *as,* which are used in a simile and which make a comparison explicit: *a mop of hair* (compare the simile *hair like a mop*). (12d)

misplaced modifier Describing or limiting words that are wrongly positioned in a sentence so that their message is either illogical or relates to the wrong word or words. Also see *squinting modifier.* (21a)

mixed construction A sentence that unintentionally changes from one grammatical structure to another, incompatible one, so that the meaning is garbled. (22f)

mixed metaphors Incongruously combined images. (12c)

MLA style See *documentation style, parenthetical reference.*

modal auxiliary verb One of a group of nine auxiliary verbs that add information such as a sense of needing, wanting, or having to do something or a sense of possibility, likelihood, obligation, permission, or ability. (15e, Chapter 55)

modified block style An alternative to block style, in modified block style the lines for the inside address and the body begin flush left but the heading, closing, and signature begin about halfway across the page. (43f)

modifier, modify A word or group of words functioning as an adjective or adverb to describe or limit another word or word group. Also see *misplaced modifier.* (14n, Chapter 18, 9d)

mood The attribute of verbs showing a speaker's or writer's attitude toward the action by the way verbs are used. English has three moods: imperative, indicative, and subjunctive. Also see *imperative mood, indicative mood, subjunctive mood.* (15l, 15m)

multimodal The use of a combination of words and images. (4l)

narrative A rhetorical strategy that tells a story; a narrative deals with what is or what has happened. (3i)

navigation bar The set of links on every Web page that allows users to get back to the site's home page and to major parts of the site. (46c)

netiquette Coined from the word etiquette, netiquette is good manners when using e-mail, the Internet, and online sites such as bulletin boards, chatrooms, etc. (43d)

noncount noun A noun that names a thing that cannot be counted: *water, time.* Also see *collective noun.* (14b, Chapters 50 and 51)

nonessential element See *nonrestrictive element.*

nonrestrictive clause See *nonrestrictive element.*

nonrestrictive element A descriptive word, phrase, or dependent clause that provides information not essential to understanding the basic message of the element it modifies and so is *set off* by commas. Also see *restrictive element.* (24f)

nonsexist language See *gender-neutral language.*

nonspecific noun A noun that refers to any of a number of identical items; it takes the indefinite article *a, an.* (51a)

nonstandard English Language usage other than what is called *edited American English.* (12b)

noun A word that names a person, place, thing, or idea. Nouns function as subjects, objects, or complements. (14b)

noun clause A dependent clause that functions as a subject, object, or complement. (14p)

noun complement See *complement.*

noun determiner See *determiner.*

noun phrase A noun and its modifiers functioning as a subject, object, or complement. (14o)

number The attribute of some words indicating whether they refer to one (*singular*) or more than one (*plural*). (15a, 17b, 22b, Chapter 49)

object A noun, pronoun, or group of words functioning as a noun or pronoun that receives the action of a verb (*direct object*); tells to whom or for whom something is done (*indirect object*); or completes the meaning of a preposition (*object of a preposition*). (14m)

object complement A noun or adjective renaming or describing a direct object after verbs such as *call, consider, name, elect,* and *think: I call the most obsessive joggers fanatics.* (14n)

objective case The case of a noun or pronoun functioning as a direct or indirect object or the object of a preposition or of a verbal. A few pronouns change form to show case (*him, her, whom*). Also see *case.* (Chapter 16)

outline Technique for laying out ideas for writing. An outline can be formal or informal. (2f)

overstatement Deliberate exaggeration for emphasis; also called *hyperbole.* (12c)

paragraph A group of sentences that work together to develop a unit of thought. They are the structured elements of an essay, which is composed of an *introductory paragraph, body paragraphs,* and a *concluding paragraph.* Also see *shaping.* (Chapter 3)

paragraph arrangement Ordering sentences by specific techniques to communicate a paragraph's message. (3h)

paragraph development Using specific, concrete details (RENNS) to support a generalization in a paragraph; rhetorical strategies or patterns for organizing ideas in paragraphs. (3f, 3i)

parallelism The use of equivalent grammatical forms or matching sentence structures to express equivalent ideas and develop coherence. (Chapter 10)

paraphrase A restatement of someone else's ideas in language and sentence structure different from those of the original. (35i)

parenthetical reference Information enclosed in parentheses following quoted, paraphrased, or summarized material from a source to alert readers to the use of material from a specific source. Parenthetical references, also called *in-text citations,* function together with a list of bibliographic information about each source used in a paper to document the writer's use of sources. Also see *citation.* (36b)

participial phrase A phrase that contains a present participle or a past participle and any modifiers and that functions as an adjective. Also see *verbal phrase.* (14o)

passive construction See *passive voice.*

passive voice The form of a verb in which the subject is acted on; if the subject is mentioned in the sentence, it usually appears as the object of the preposition *by*: *I was frightened by the thunder.* [Compare the active voice: *The thunder frightened me.*] The passive voice emphasizes the action, in contrast to the *active voice,* which emphasizes the doer of the action. (15n)

past participle The third principal part of a verb, formed in regular verbs, like the past tense, by adding *-d* or *-ed* to the simple form. In irregular verbs, it often differs from the simple form and the past tense: *break, broke, broken.* (14e, 15b, 54f)

past perfect progressive tense The past perfect tense form that describes an ongoing condition in the past that has been ended by something stated in the sentence: *I had been talking.* (15j)

past perfect tense The tense that describes a condition or action that started in the past, continued for a while, and then ended in the past: *I had talked.* (15g, 15i)

past progressive tense The tense that shows the continuing nature of a past action: *I was talking.* (15j)

past subjunctive The simple past tense in the subjunctive mood. (15m)

past tense The tense that tells of an action completed or a condition ended. (15g)

past-tense form The second principal part of a verb, in regular verbs formed by adding *-d* or *-ed* to the simple form. In irregular verbs, the past tense may change in several ways from the simple form. (15b, 15d)

peer-response group A group of students formed to give each other feedback on writing. (Chapter 6)

perfect infinitive Also called *present perfect participle,* a tense used to describe an action that occurs before the action in the main verb. (15k)

perfect tenses The three tenses—the present perfect (*I have talked*), the past perfect (*I had talked*), and the future perfect (*I will have talked*)—that help show complex time relationships between two clauses. (15g, 15i)

periodic sentence A sentence that begins with modifiers and ends with the independent clause, thus postponing the main idea—

and the emphasis—for the end; also called a *climactic sentence.* (9q)

periodical A publication such as a newspaper, magazine, or journal that is published at a regular interval, that is "periodically."

person The attribute of nouns and pronouns showing who or what acts or experiences an action. *First person* is the one speaking (*I, we*); *second person* is the one being spoken to (*you, you*); and *third person* is the person or thing being spoken about (*he, she, it, they*). All nouns are third person. (15a, 17b)

personal pronoun A pronoun that refers to people or things, such as *I, you, them, it.* (14c, 16n)

personality The sense of the writer that comes through his or her writing; for example, friendly, bossy, shy, assertive, concerned, angry, and so on.

persuasive appeal Rhetorical strategies which appeal to the emotions, logic, or ethics of readers. (5g)

persuasive writing Writing that seeks to convince the reader about a matter of opinion. It is also known as *argumentative writing.* (Chapter 5)

phrasal verb A verb that combines with one or more prepositions to deliver its meaning: *ask out, look into.* (53c)

phrase A group of related words that does not contain both a subject and a predicate and thus cannot stand alone as an independent grammatical unit. A phrase functions as a noun, verb, or modifier. (14o)

plagiarism A writer's presenting another person's words or ideas without giving credit to that person. Documentation systems allow writers to give proper credit to sources in ways recognized by scholarly communities. Plagiarism is a serious offense, a form of intellectual dishonesty that can lead to course failure or expulsion. (Chapter 35)

planning An early part of the writing process in which writers gather ideas. Along with shaping, planning is sometimes called *prewriting.* (Chapter 2)

plural See *number.*

podcasts Brief sound files that are shared over the Internet, somewhat like online radio broadcasts. (46g)

positive form The form of an adjective or adverb when no comparison is being expressed: *blue, easily.* Also see *comparative form, superlative form.* (18e)

possessive case The case of a noun or pronoun that shows ownership or possession: *my, your, their,* and so on. Also see *case, pronoun case.* (Chapter 16, 27a–27c)

predicate The part of a sentence that contains the verb and tells what the subject is doing or experiencing or what is being done to the subject. A *simple predicate* contains only the main verb and any auxiliary verbs. A *complete predicate* contains the verb, its modifiers, objects, and other related words. A *compound predicate* contains two or more verbs and their objects and modifiers, if any. (14l)

predicate adjective An adjective used as a subject complement. *That tree is leafy.* (14n)

predicate nominative A noun or pronoun used as a subject complement: *That tree is a maple.* (14n)

prediction A major activity of the *reading process,* in which the reader guesses what comes next. (4c)

premises In a deductive argument expressed as a syllogism, statements presenting the conditions of the argument from which the conclusion must follow. (4h)

preposition A word that conveys a relationship, often of space or time, between the noun or pronoun following it and other words in the sentence. The noun or pronoun following a preposition is called its *object.* (14h, Chapter 53)

prepositional phrase A preposition and the word it modifies. Also see *phrase, preposition.* (14h, 14o)

presentation style The way you deliver what you have to say. Memorization, reading, mapping and speaking with notes are different types of presentation styles. (42h)

present infinitive Names or describes an activity or occurrence coming together either at the same time or after the time expressed in the main verb. (15k)

present participle A verb's *-ing* form. Used with auxiliary verbs, present participles function as main verbs. Used without auxiliary verbs, present participles function as nouns or adjectives. (14e, 15b, 55f)

present perfect participle See *perfect infinitive.*

present perfect progressive tense The present perfect tense form that describes something ongoing in the past that is likely to continue into the future: *I have been talking.* (15j)

present perfect tense The tense indicating that an action or its effects, begun or perhaps completed in the past, continue into the present: *I had talked.* (15g, 15i)

present progressive tense The present-tense form of the verb that indicates something taking place at the time it is written or spoken about: *I am talking.* (15j)

present subjunctive The simple form of the verb for all persons and numbers in the subjunctive mood. (15m)

present tense The tense that describes what is happening, what is true at the moment, and what is consistently true. It uses the simple form (*I talk*) and the *-s* form in the third-person singular (*he, she, it talks*). (15g, 15h)

prewriting All activities in the writing process before drafting. Also see *planning, shaping.*

primary sources Firsthand work: write-ups of experiments and observations by the researchers who conducted them; taped accounts, interviews, and newspaper accounts by direct observers; autobiographies, diaries, and journals; expressive works (poems, plays, fiction, essays). Also known as *primary evidence.* Also see *secondary source.* (32a, 32d)

process A rhetorical strategy in writing that reports a sequence of actions by which something is done or made. (3i)

progressive forms Verb forms made in all tenses with the present participle and forms of the verb *be* as an auxiliary. Progressive forms show that an action, occurrence, or state of being is ongoing. (15g, 15j)

project proposal A piece of writing intended to persuade readers that a future project is worth doing and that the writer has the ability and resources to complete the project successfully.

pronoun A word that takes the place of a noun and functions in the same ways that nouns do. Types of pronouns are *demonstrative, indefinite, intensive, interrogative, personal, reciprocal, reflexive,* and *relative.* The word (or words) a pronoun replaces is called its *antecedent.* (14c, Chapter 16)

pronoun-antecedent agreement The match in expressing number and person—and for personal pronouns, gender as well—required between a pronoun and its antecedent. (17o–17t)

pronoun case The way a pronoun changes form to reflect its use as the agent of action (*subjective case*), the thing being acted upon (*objective case*), or the thing showing ownership (*possessive case*). (16a–16k)

pronoun reference The relationship between a pronoun and its antecedent. (16l–16s)

proofread The act of reading a final draft to find and correct any spelling or mechanics mistakes, typing errors, or handwriting illegibility; the final step of the writing process. (2k)

proper adjective An adjective formed from a proper noun: *Victorian, American.* (30e)

proper noun A noun that names specific people, places, or things and is always capitalized: *Dave Matthews, Buick.* (14b, 30e, 51c)

proposal of solution A piece of writing intended to persuade readers that a particular problem is best solved by the solution explained in that writing.

public writing Writing intended for readers outside of academic and work settings. (Chapter 44)

purpose The goal or aim of a piece of writing: to express oneself, to provide information, to persuade, or to create a literary work. (1b)

quotation Repeating or reporting another person's words. *Direct quotation* repeats another's words exactly and encloses them in quotation marks. *Indirect quotation* reports another's words without quotation marks except around any words repeated exactly from the source. Both *direct* and *indirect quotation* require *documentation* of the *source* to avoid *plagiarism.* Also see *direct discourse, indirect discourse.* (Chapter 28, 35h)

readers Readers are the audiences for writing; readers process material they read on the literal, inferential, and evaluative levels. (4c)

reading process Critical reading that requires the reader to read for *literal meaning,* to draw *inferences,* and to *evaluate.* (4c)

reasons Statements or ideas presented in order to provide support for a claim.

reciprocal pronoun The pronouns *each other* and *one another* referring to individual parts of a plural antecedent: *We respect **each other.*** (14c)

References In many documentation styles, including APA, the title of a list of sources cited in a research paper or other written work. (33h, 33i, 34c, 35f)

reflexive pronoun A pronoun that ends in *-self* and that refers back to its antecedent: *They claim to support **themselves.*** (14c)

regular verb A verb that forms its past tense and past participle by adding *-ed* or *-d* to the simple form. Most English verbs are regular. (15b, 15d)

relative adverb An adverb that introduces an adjective clause: *The lot **where** I usually park my car was full.* (14g)

relative clause See *adjective clause.*

relative pronoun A pronoun, such as *who, which, that, whom,* or *whoever,* that introduces an adjective clause or sometimes a noun clause. (14c)

RENNS Test See *paragraph development.* (3f)

research question The controlling question that drives research. (33c)

research writing Also called *source-based writing,* a process in three steps: conducting research, understanding and evaluating the results of the research, and writing the research paper with accurate documentation. (Chapter 33)

respond In writing, to provide your reaction to a reading or idea, with reasons and explanations for your response.

restrictive clause See *restrictive element.*

restrictive element A word, phrase, or dependent clause that contains information that is essential for a sentence to deliver its message. Do not set off with commas. (24f)

revising, revision A part of the writing process in which writers evaluate their rough drafts and, based on their assessments, rewrite by adding, cutting, replacing, moving, and often totally recasting material. (2i)

rhetoric The area of discourse that focuses on the arrangement of ideas and choice of words as a reflection of both the writer's purpose and the writer's sense of audience. (Chapter 1)

rhetorical strategies In writing, various techniques for presenting ideas to deliver a writer's intended message with clarity and impact. Reflecting typical patterns of human thought, rhetorical strategies include arrangements such as chronological and climactic order; stylistic techniques such as parallelism and planned repetition; and patterns for organizing and developing writing such as description and definition. (3i)

Rogerian argument An argument technique adapted from the principles of communication developed by the psychologist Carl Rogers. (5j)

role The position the writer is emphasizing for a given task; for example, student, client, taxpayer, parent, supervisor, helper, critic, or so on.

run-on sentence The error of running independent clauses into each other without the required punctuation that marks them as complete units; also called a *fused sentence* or *run-together sentence*. (Chapter 20)

sans serif Font types that do not have little "feet" or finishing lines at the top and bottom of each letter. (45c)

search engine An Internet-specific software program that can look through all files at Internet sites. (34l)

secondary source A source that reports, analyzes, discusses, reviews, or otherwise deals with the work of someone else, as opposed to a primary source, which is someone's original work or firsthand report. A reliable secondary source should be the work of a person with appropriate credentials, should appear in a respected publication or other medium, should be current, and should be well reasoned. (34a, 34i)

second person See *person*.

sentence See *sentence types*.

sentence fragment A portion of a sentence that is punctuated as though it were a complete sentence. (Chapter 19)

sentence outline Type of outline in which each element is a sentence. (2f)

sentence types A grammatical classification of sentences by the kinds of clauses they contain. A *simple sentence* consists of one independent clause. A *complex sentence* contains one independent clause and one or more dependent clauses. A *compound-complex sentence* contains at least two independent clauses and one or more dependent clauses. A *compound* or *coordinate sentence* contains two or more independent clauses joined by a coordinating conjunction. Sentences are also classified by their grammatical function; see *declarative sentence, exclamatory sentence, imperative sentence, interrogative sentence*. (14k, 14q, 9f)

sentence variety Writing sentences of various lengths and structures; see *coordinate sentence, cumulative sentence, periodic sentence, sentence types*. (9a)

serif Font types that are characterized by little "feet" or finishing lines at the top and bottom of each letter. (45c)

server A computer that is always online and available to Internet users. (46b)

sexist language Language that unnecessarily communicates that a person is male or female. For example, *fireman* is a sexist term that says only males fight fires, while *fire fighter* includes males and females. (17s, 12f)

shaping An early part of the writing process in which writers consider ways to organize their material. Along with planning, shaping is sometimes called *prewriting*.

shift Within a sentence, an unnecessary abrupt change in *person, number, subject, voice, tense, mood*, or *direct* or *indirect discourse*. (22a–22c)

simile A comparison, using *like* or *as*, of otherwise dissimilar things. (12c)

simple form The form of the verb that shows action, occurrence, or state of being taking place in the present. It is used in the singular for first and second person and in the plural for first, second, and third person. It is also the first principal part of a verb. The simple form is also known as the *dictionary form* or *base form*. (15b)

simple predicate See *predicate*.

simple sentence See *sentence types*.

simple subject See *subject.*

simple tenses The present, past, and future tenses, which divide time into present, past, and future. (15g, 15h)

singular See *number.*

slang A kind of colloquial language, it is coined words and new meanings for existing words, which quickly pass in and out of use; not appropriate for most academic writing. (12a)

slanted language Language that tries to manipulate the reader with distorted facts. (12g)

source-based writing See *research writing.*

sources Books, articles, print or Internet documents, other works, and persons providing credible information. In *research writing*, often called *outside sources*. (Chapters 34 and 35)

spatial order An arrangement of information according to location in space; an organizing strategy for sentences, paragraphs, and longer pieces of writing. (3h)

specific noun A noun understood to be exactly and specifically referred to; uses the definite article *the.* (51a)

split infinitive One or more words coming between the two words of an infinitive. (14b)

squinting modifier A modifier that is considered misplaced because it is not clear whether it describes the word that comes before it or the word that follows it. (21a)

standard American English See *edited American English.*

standard word order The most common order for words in English sentences: The subject comes before the predicate. Also see *inverted word order.* (9r, Chapter 52)

stereotype A kind of hasty generalization (a *logical fallacy*) in which a sweeping claim is made about all members of a particular ethnic, racial, religious, gender, age, or political group. (4i)

subject The word or group of words in a sentence that acts, is acted upon, or is described by the verb. A *simple subject* includes only the noun or pronoun. A *complete subject* includes the noun or pronoun and all its modifiers. A *compound subject* includes two or more nouns or pronouns and their modifiers. (14l)

subject complement A noun or adjective that follows a linking verb, renaming or describing the subject of the sentence; also called a *predicate nominative.* (14n)

subjective case The case of the noun or pronoun functioning as a subject. Also see *case, pronoun case.* (Chapter 16)

subject tree Shows you visually whether you have sufficient content, at varying levels of generality or specificity, to start a first draft of your writing. A subject tree also visually demonstrates whether you have a good balance of general ideas and specific details.

subject-verb agreement The required match between a subject and a verb in expressing number and person. (17b–17n)

subjunctive mood A verb mood that expresses wishes, recommendations, indirect requests, speculations, and conditional statements. *I wish you were here.* (15l, 15m)

subordinate clause See *dependent clause.*

subordinating conjunction A conjunction that introduces an adverb clause and expresses a relationship between the idea in it and the idea in the independent clause. (14i, 20c.4, Chapter 9)

subordination The use of grammatical structures to reflect the relative importance of ideas. A sentence with logically subordinated information expresses the most important information in the independent clause and less important information in dependent clauses or phrases. (Chapter 9)

summary A brief version of the main message or central point of a passage or other discourse; a critical thinking activity preceding synthesis. (35j)

superlative form The form of an adjective or adverb that expresses comparison among three or more things: *bluest, least blue; most easily, least easily.* (18e)

syllogism The structure of a deductive argument expressed in two *premises* and a *conclusion.* The first premise is a generalized assumption or statement of fact. The second premise is a different assumption or statement of fact based on evidence. The conclusion is also a specific instance that follows logically from the premises. (4h)

synonym A word that is very close in meaning to another word: *cold* and *icy.* (12d)

synthesis A component of critical thinking in which material that has been summarized, analyzed, and interpreted is connected to what is already known (one's prior knowledge) or to what has been learned from other authorities. (4b, 4f)

tag question An inverted verb-pronoun combination added to the end of a sentence, creating a question that asks the audience to agree with the assertion in the first part of the sentence. A tag question is set off from the rest of the sentence with a comma: *You know what a tag question is, don't you?* (24g)

tense The time at which the action of the verb occurs: the present, the past, or the future. Also see *perfect tenses, simple tenses.* (15g–15k)

tense sequence In sentences that have more than one clause, the accurate matching of verbs to reflect logical time relationships. (15k)

thesis statement A statement of an essay's central theme that makes clear the main idea, the writer's purpose, the focus of the topic, and perhaps the organizational pattern. (2d)

third person See *person.*

title The part of an essay that clarifies the overall point of the piece of writing. It can be *direct* or *indirect.* (2i)

tone The writer's attitude toward his or her material and reader, especially as reflected by word choice. (1d, Chapter 8)

topic The subject of discourse. (1b)

topic sentence The sentence that expresses the main idea of a paragraph. A topic sentence may be implied, not stated. (3e)

Toulmin model A model that defines the essential parts of an argument as the *claim* (or *main point*), the *support* (or *evidence*), and the *warrants* (or *assumptions behind the main point*). (5h)

transition The connection of one idea to another in discourse. Useful strategies within a paragraph for creating transitions include transitional expressions, parallelism, and the planned repetition of key terms and phrases. In a long piece of writing, a *transitional paragraph* is the bridge between discussion of two separate topics. Also see *critical response.* (3g.1, 3j)

transitional expressions Words and phrases that signal connections among ideas and create coherence. (3g.1)

transitive verb A verb that must be followed by a direct object. (15f)

understatement Figurative language in which the writer uses deliberate restraint for emphasis. (12e)

unity The clear and logical relationship between the main idea of a paragraph and the evidence supporting the main idea. (3d, 3e)

unstated assumptions Premises that are implied but not stated. (4h)

usage A customary way of using language. (Chapter 13)

valid Correctly and rationally derived; applied to a deductive argument whose conclusion follows logically from the premises. Validity applies to the structure of an argument, not its truth. (4i)

variety In writing, the presence of different types or lengths of sentences, a diverse vocabulary, kinds of examples or evidence, and so on.

verb Any word that shows action or occurrence or describes a state of being. Verbs change form to convey time (*tense*), attitude (*mood*), and role of the subject (*voice,* either *active* or *passive*). Verbs occur in the predicate of a clause and can be in verb phrases, which may consist of a main verb, auxiliary verbs, and modifiers. Verbs can be described as *transitive* or *intransitive,* depending on whether they take a direct object. Also see *voice.* (Chapter 15)

verbal A verb part functioning as a noun, adjective, or adverb. Verbals include *infinitives, present participles* (functioning as adjectives), *gerunds* (present participles functioning as nouns), and *past participles.* (15c, Chapter 54)

verbal phrase A group of words that contains a verbal (an infinitive, participle, or gerund) and its modifiers. (14o)

verb phrase A main verb, any auxiliary verbs, and any modifiers. (14o)

verb tense Verbs show tense (time) by changing form. English has six verb tenses. (15g)

visual design Refers to the appearance of a document (how it looks), as opposed to its content (what it says). (45a)

voice An attribute of verbs showing whether the subject acts (*active voice*) or is acted on (*passive voice*). Verbs are sometimes referred to as *strong* or *action verbs* or *weak verbs*. (15n–15p)

warrants One of three key terms in the *Toulmin model* for argument; refers to implied or inferred assumptions. They are based on *authority, substance,* and *motivation.* (5h)

Web See *World Wide Web.*

webbing See *mapping.*

Web page On the Internet, a file of information. Such a file is not related in length to a printed page, as it may be a paragraph or many screens long. (46c)

Web site One page or a home page that provides links to a collection of documents or files related to the home page. (46c)

Web structure The organization of the content and documents that site creators include in a Web project. (46d)

white space The part of a document that has neither text nor visuals. (45g)

wiki A Web site that allows multiple readers to change its content. (46f)

wordiness An attribute of writing that is full of empty words and phrases that do not contribute to meaning. The opposite of *conciseness.* (11a)

World Wide Web The *Web,* a user-friendly computer network allowing access to information in the form of text, graphics, and sound on the Internet. (Chapter 46)

working bibliography A preliminary list of useful sources in research writing. (33i)

Works Cited In MLA documentation style, the title of a list of all sources cited in a research paper or other written work. (36a)

writer's block The desire to start writing, but not doing so. (2h)

writing process Stages of writing in which a writer gathers and shapes ideas, organizes material, expresses those ideas in a rough draft, evaluates the draft and revises it, edits the writing for technical errors, and proofreads it for typographical accuracy and legibility. The stages often overlap; see *planning, shaping, drafting, revising, editing, proofreading.* (Chapters 1 and 2)

writing situation The beginning of the writing process for each writing assignment as defined by four elements: topic, purpose, audience, special requirements. (1b)

CREDITS

ArticleFirst Advanced Search search engine, copyright © OCLC Online Computer Library Center, Inc. Reprinted by permission. FirstSearch and WorldCat are registered trademarks of OCLC Online Computer Library Center, Inc (page 547).

University of Denver Penrose Library, catalog title and author search, reprinted with permission of the University of Denver (page 553).

PsychINFO search, reprinted with permission of the American Psychological Association, publisher of the PsycINFO ® Database. Copyright © 2005, APA, all rights reserved. For more information, contact PscyINFO©apa.org (page 555).

Results page, reprinted with permission of the American Psychological Association, publisher of the PsycINFO ® Database. Copyright © 2005, APA, all rights reserved. For more information, contact PscyINFO©apa.org (page 556).

Google subject directory for "Organic Food," courtesy of Google (page 563).

From *The Creation of the Media,* by Paul Starr. Copyright © 2004 by Paul Starr. Reprinted by permission of Basic Books, a member of Perseus Book Group (page 605).

"Business, Pleasure and the Personal Essay," Harriet Malinowitz, *College English*, Copyright 2003 by the National Council of Teachers of English. Reprinted and used with permission (page 611).

EBSCO Research search engine, copyright © 2005 by EBSCO Publishing, Inc. All rights reserved (page 615).

Maine Organic Farmers & Gardeners Association Web page, courtesy of the Maine Organic Farmers & Gardeners Association (page 620).

YouTube Web page, reprinted by permission of Mike Wesch & YouTube (page 622).

REI external report, reprinted with permission of REI (page 781).

From *The Future of Children,* a collaboration of The Woodrow Wilson School of Public and International Affairs at Princeton University and The Brookings Institution (page 794).

USA Freedom Corps ad, courtesy of the Ad Council (page 798).

Ecology Action Center logo, reprinted with permission of the Ecology Action Center (page 811).

The Crooked Timber website, crookedtimber.org, reprinted by permission of David Krewinghaus (page 824).

PHOTOS

Rob Crandall/Stock Boston (page 106).

Peter Vadnai (page 131).

Scott Cunningham/Merrill Education (page 133).

Getty Images—Stockbyte (page 134).

The Ad Council and U.S. Department of Education, Education Excellence Partnership (page 136).

Paul Conklin/Getty Images, Inc.—Taxi (page 135).

Douglas Hesse (page 158).

Douglas Hesse (page 160).

Bob Mahoney/The Image Works (page 165).

AP Wide World Photos (page 733).

USA Freedom Corps/Ad Council (page 798).

Christie's Images/Corbis/Bettmann (page 813).

INDEX

NOTES

NOTES

NOTES

ABOUT THE AUTHORS

Lynn Quitman Troyka, Adjunct Professor in the Graduate Program in Language and Literature at the City College (CCNY) of the City University of New York (CUNY), has also taught at Queensborough Community College. Former editor of the *Journal of Basic Writing,* she has had her writing and research published in major journals and various scholarly collections. She also conducts workshops in the teaching of writing. Dr. Troyka is coauthor of *Quick Access Reference for Writers,* Sixth Edition, Pearson Prentice Hall; *QA Compact,* Second Edition, Pearson Prentice Hall; the Canadian editions of her *Simon & Schuster Handbook for Writers* and *Quick Access Reference for Writers; Structured Reading,* Seventh Edition, Prentice Hall; and *Steps in Composition,* Eighth Edition, Prentice Hall.

Dr. Troyka is a past chair of the Conference on College Composition and Communication (CCCC); the Two-Year College Association (TYCA) of the National Council of Teachers (NCTE); the College Section of NCTE; and the Writing Division of the Modern Language Association (MLA). She received the 2001 CCCC Exemplar Award, the highest CCCC award for scholarship, teaching, and service; the Rhetorician of the Year Award; and the TYCA Pickett Award for Service.

"This information," says Dr. Troyka, "tells what I've done, not who I am. I am a teacher. Teaching is my life's work, and I love it."

Doug Hesse, Professor of English and Director of Writing at the University of Denver, previously held several positions at Illinois State University, including Director of the Honors and Writing Programs and also Director of the Center for the Advancement of Teaching. Dr. Hesse earned his PhD from the University of Iowa. He has also taught at the University of Findlay, Miami University (as Wiepking Distinguished Visiting Professor), and Michigan Tech.

Dr. Hesse is a past chair of the Conference on College Composition and Communication (CCCC), the nation's largest professional association of college writing instructors. A past president, as well, of the Council of Writing Program Administrators (WPA), Dr. Hesse edited that organization's journal, *Writing Program Administration.* He has been a member of the executive committee of the National Council of Teachers of English (NCTE) and chaired the Modern Language Association (MLA) Division on Teaching as a Profession.

He is the author of over fifty articles and book chapters in such journals as *College Composition and Communication, College English, JAC, Rhetoric Review,* and the *Journal of Teaching Writing* and in such books as *Essays on the Essay; Writing Theory and Critical Theory; The Writing Program Administrator's Sourcebook; Literary Nonfiction; The Private, the Public, and the Published;* and *Passions, Pedagogies, and 21st Century Technologies.* He is also coauthor with Lynn Quitman Troyka of *Quick Access Reference for Writers,* Sixth Edition, Pearson Prentice Hall and *QA Compact,* Second Edition, Pearson Prentice Hall. He has consulted at over forty colleges and universities.

The writing program he directs at the University of Denver is only one of twenty-five internationally to receive the CCCC Certificate of Excellence. "Of all these accomplishments," says Dr. Hesse, "the one that matters most to me was being named Distinguished Humanities Teacher. That one came from my students and suggests that, in however small a way, I've mattered in their education and lives."

Lynn Quitman Troyka   Doug Hesse